SHADOWS AND THE LIGHT

A COMPANION TO THE BIBLE

— EYE-WITNESS ACCOUNTS —

Enlightenment

Lucille L. Turfrey

Library of Congress Control Number:		2020922499
ISBN:	Hardcover	978-1-6641-0039-8
	Softcover	978-1-6641-0040-4
	eBook	978-1-6641-0038-1

All scripture in *Shadows and the Light* is a personal paraphrase written in poetic form by the author.

Print information available on the last page.

Rev. date: 01/07/2021

To order additional copies of this book, contact:
Xlibris
AU TFN: 1 800 844 927 (Toll Free inside Australia)
AU Local: 0283 108 187 (+61 2 8310 8187 from outside Australia)
www.Xlibris.com.au
Orders@Xlibris.com.au
817520

CONTENTS

Shadows and the Light

— THE BIBLE —
ITS PEOPLE AND THEIR STORIES

THE WITNESSES
The Personal Accounts of Bible Characters
in the Rhythms of Scripture

BOOK ONE

THE PEOPLE AND THEIR PLANS

HEBREW POETRY
THE RHYTHMS OF SCRIPTURE

The author has selected Hebraic styles of poetry in this book rather than the more familiar rhyming patterns (though rhythm has been generally retained) because the poems are closely aligned with the Bible. These styles include progression, agreement, antithesis, Q&A, acrostic, repetition, and paraphrase. Each will be in evidence. The rhythmic blank verse encountered most often is of iambic metre though modified because of space constraints on the page.

Where the actual text of Scripture is written in poetic form and when psalms appear, rhyme is also incorporated in **Shadows** *and THE LIGHT*.

Many poems are set to known hymn tunes–ready for worship.

This separate font will indicate biblical poetry and hymns. The text will be set accordingly though somewhat compromised by revised spacing.

Italics indicate God's speech, flush right, indicating *LIGHT*. Where evil **shadows** appear in a testimony, the words are set **flush left in bold.**

1 Peter 2:9 (paraphrased) gives emphasis to the reasons for God's interaction with Israel:

You are a chosen people, a royal priesthood, a holy nation, a people belonging to God, that you may declare the praises of Him who called you out of darkness into His wonderful LIGHT.

•••••••••

All poetry and art–including the cover painting (detail from a larger work titled *The Faith We Hold*), are by the author and are subject to copyright restrictions. I am deeply indebted to Mavis Smith, the proof-reader; Lynette Green has also given valued assistance in this regard. The weaving of my design titled *Enlightenment* (see page 1) was worked by Dawn Kop, life-long friend and ministry colleague.

Between the 'book-ends' of the Bible will be found the history of the ages. Where there is history, there are people. Here is the story of humankind, the written record of the soul's search for meaning, its journey to Home as viewed from a biblical perspective.

In the pages of Scripture, the great questions concerning existence find their consummate answers in God, the *YHVH*-LORD* who is pleased to disclose His Person, His Nature, His Purposes, His Redemptive Plan, His Justice, His Mercy, Grace and, yes, Love— through His people!

In this volume the rhythms of the universe find a harmony with human experience and the testimonies of God's people become the poetry of thought—at times, the soaring of inspiration, the meditations of prayer, the courage of commitment, but also the intrusion of the vindictive, the evil, for here we are confronted with the human condition and its need of redemption. We will observe how the LORD stepped in to break down the man-built barriers, providing His answer to the human circumstance.

Certainly not a translation, though at times hovering near a paraphrase, the poems travel reasonably close to biblical truth throughout and provide a means of understanding the deeper nuances of Scripture that may perhaps otherwise pass us by. More precisely, the book may be termed a '*Companion to the Bible*'.

I was on assignment to Russia where my responsibilities had begun to take shape. One night, I was resting in bed when the Lord broke into my pensive thoughts. His words held a clarity not found in the static of Earth. "Get up, take pencil and paper, and begin to write!" What then was set on the page that night was not actually dictated to me, but I felt inspired and began:

Deep darkness shrouds the face of deep, upon a formless void...

I had discovered, suddenly, a freedom in poetic fluency—the rhythms of Genesis had begun: The Bible released its testimonies!

---

*YHVH: Hebrew—the 'holy tetragram' from which 'Jehovah' is ultimately derived. 'LORD' is the English translation, scripted traditionally in upper case.

THE TRANSLUCENT 'DAYS'

"Let there be LIGHT"

THE CREATION

Deep darkness shrouds
the face of deep, upon
a formless void;
non-entity, a black expanse.
Appalling night, infinity
of dark where light can find
no path to liberate its way.
The dark of night
o'er spreads a waste
of nothingness:
an emptiness enfolded in
deep ebony, the sombre
shade of dearth,
a lifeless, sterile space.

Grim darkness manifest,
existence nullified
where light ne'er dwelt.
No mass, no shape, no orb
nor sphere to grant
the light a place to shine,
nowhere to radiate its beam
within this comprehensive
night.

No sun, no shining star,
and neither moon!
Deep darkness, void
of form–a universal
emptiness.

Yet, here is space for God
to act, The *YHVH Elohim*–
Eternal, all-pervasive
LORD.
He takes the nothingness,
creates, solidifies a shape
to mould the heavens and
the earth; from thence, to set
in order time and space.
He speaks:

Let there be LIGHT.

And there was *LIGHT*!

He liberates the *LIGHT*
to strike the form, illumine
shape and, with the *LIGHT*,
releases hope of life
to come.
In separating dark from
LIGHT, He speaks
His Lordship of
the day and night.
God sees that this is good
and gives His blessing to
each passing phase
of day and night.

Eternal Spirit moves upon
the restless tides of seas,
the ocean's wind-swept
waves, to brood, and
nurture elementary life.
Then, by His awesome
power, a great rock mass

appears to pierce
the water's face.
Damp surfaced is the land
which yields the green life
forms of grass and moss.
God sees that this is good
and gives His blessing to
the land and seas.

And then, at God's own
word, the trees are born—
such glorious canopies!
Giant masters of the
undulating hills,
now reaching up in
strength, aspiring to
the LORD who grants
them birth.

He strews profusely the
bright painted flowers at
their feet; a glorious spring
had now appeared
to liven all the scenes
and grants the trees their
fruit to procreate in earth.
God sees that this is good
and gives His blessing to
the burgeoning plants.

Now God allows the mists,
which blanketed the
incubating nursery of life,
to fold away, draw back
their clouded veil

and show the earth the
splendour of the heavenly
lights; long days and nights
of brilliant lights to rule
the azured skies above.
God sees that this is good
and gives His blessing to
the spacious universe.

God speaks again:

*So let the waters bound
with multitudes of fish
of curious form, surprising
shapes, in variegated,
iridescent hues. And let
the skies abound with birds
to fly this great expanse
of sky. I give to them
a voice, a song to cheer
the days and nights.*

God sees that this is good
and gives His blessing to
marine and airborne life.

Again, the speech of God:

*Now, let the earth bring
forth the creatures of
the land and each according
to its kind: the creeping
things, the prancing things,
the leaping and the trudging
things, the slithering things,
the fleet of foot to dance.*

Exquisite workmanship–
each creature of His care.
God sees that this is good
and gives His blessing to
the creatures of the land.

Before the back of time,
before the bringing of
the Earth to being, before
His radiant beams of light
were seen, God thought
of humankind! He knew
Redemption's Plan and set
in course the way for man
to rise to the Abode of God.
He built a glorious universe
as home for humankind,
then said:

*The time is right to mould
the triune human form
in likeness to Ourselves:
form, mind, and spirit-soul,
to have dominion, rule the
Earth and tend My garden
here. They'll learn the ways
of Earth and care for every
creature's store for good
of man and beast. I'll share
My love with humankind,
reveal My glory unto them!*

Out from the reddened
earth he comes, God's
adam-man, perfect and pure,
and wholly innocent.

God breathes within
the man and brings to birth
a living soul and places
woman at his side–
a partnership sublime.
God sees that this is good,
and gives His blessing to
this trinity of flesh,
of mind, and soul.

A Sabbath rest the LORD
bequeaths for them,
upon creation's finished
work, where–in the worship
raised to Him–He can
rejoice with humankind
in wondrous fellowship
where soul is kin to Soul!

O Eden joy where *LIGHT*,
and *LIFE*,
and *LOVE* dance in
the harmonies
of God and man:
communion eloquent,
a partnership of grace
and love.

....

HUMANKIND
Genesis 1

The Crucial Analysis

Say, what am I?
A cosmic accident?
Atomic particles,
conveniently aligned,
and harmonised with Earth?
A watery womb, by
'*Intricate Design*',
took DNA, via genes
and chromosomes,
to helix frames, the key to life.
A game of chance?
A Masterpiece
that birthed this child,
uniquely me!

So, who am I?
Mere animated mud?
A body taking sustenance
from sand, composed
of dust made moist within
a pregnant womb?
'*Intelligent Design*'
has gifted wisdom to
a matrixed form!
Does this analysis prove soil,
or soul? I'm Fathered by
A Master-Mind,
An Architect Supreme
created me!

Soul, why am I?
A peerless plan?
What does it mean,
to be connected to
all life yet move a mind
beyond The womb of apes?
'*Inspired Design*'
has breathed discerning
faculties in me: I know, and
know I know! I've found
the purpose schemed!
The Master Plan?
To lend Eternity
to 'soil', to me!

ADAM–A GARDENER
Genesis 2

How beautiful, this Eden
land! Here is a garden
where I walk in step with
Him, the *YHVH*-LORD
who granted me this
perfect home.

He comes to me, He talks
with me, He shares with me
the wonders of this precious
place. He speaks to me
of all the mysteries the
universe displays;
a grandeur wrought by
His creative power.

GENESIS 2:

The LORD has taught
me many things; I hear
His Voice: He calls to me,
He whispers too; I hear Him
audibly and in my heart!

This is my home! And yet
I know it is God's land.
He's gifted me with ground
to till, to nurture and
to coax the tender plants
to bear with seasons as
the sun ascends to warm
the soil, give colour to
the blossom, bud and
every fruit that's grown.

I am the gardener;
I tend this pristine land
and also guide the animals
to placid streams. I have
responsibilities: there is
a purpose in my life.
As evening nears I rest
from tasks set for the day.

I wait to hear the footfall of
His tread within this vale
where tree and flower
lend perfume to the wafted
air. The LORD will tarry
with me here to teach life
values   what it means
to love, to trust, to walk
in grace. I'm learning what

faith means: I see Him not
but know His smiling face!
There's much to learn: I am
as yet so innocent;
I hold His hand today.

And now,
the *YHVH*-LORD
is near: He brings to me
a bride, my Eve!
What greater gift than this
could He bestow?
Eve is the other half
of me; I am complete
for Eve is bone of bone
and flesh of flesh
of me: we'll love always
as 'one' in every way.
I'll live to please
my Eve and care for her
as God requires…
He speaks His will:

*All things within this garden
are My gift; but one,
forbidden, 'fruit'. You are
the highest form of all
created life. I've gifted you
with power to know
the right from wrong;
please learn My discipline!
I've breathed in you
the Breath of Life.
You are a triune being and*

so like the Triune Elohim.
Discern the consequence
of choice and prove
your body, mind, and soul
are whole. There is a way
for humankind to rise
to the Eternal Home of God!

I'll need to start today
remembering the truth that
YHVH-LORD has taught!

EVE
Genesis 3

He silent slid, so sleek and
serpent-like, this Satan
one who sought a kingdom
meant for holy things.
His goal was Earth from
which the Adam-man
was formed within God's
hands in Eden's dawn.

And, lying there in wait,
just near the 'Testing
Tree', he planned
the awful crime to stain
life's innocence and bring
the pain that claimed
creation's prize for he
would win the world
by 'serpent' wiles
and hence, the heights

of Heaven, the light
of Lucifer reclaim!

Within the morning light,
my man and I, his bride,
came dancing in the dawn.
We knew the warmth
of sun upon our flesh,
unclothed, before Him,
Spirit-Light within our
hearts, with God
illumining the mind:

Taste all these lovely things,
these foods, these fruits,
prepared to satisfy and
nourish you. Take each
of these, though, not this
'fruit': please, learn the
discipline of God!
The day you take of this
—whatever form it takes—
down from the 'Testing
Tree', your LIGHT will dim
and death will surely come
as night does follow day!
For, by this choice, and by
this 'fruit', the strength of
innocence is lost.

There lay that 'serpent'
shadow on the path, deep
hidden from the dawn,
to coil about unwary feet—

imprison in his charm,
as I, and then my Adam,
came to view again the
'Testing Tree', observe
its luscious fruit.

Could leaf, or branch,
or fruit of this sufficient
testing offer us to know
the discipline of God
and find what strength
obedience brings?

The striking 'serpent'
hissed relentlessly
his captivating speech:
Yes! Claim your dawn:
this 'fruit' shall now bring
light to you! Yes! Grasp
your fate: Take, eat, and
you will live! WHO says
this brings the Night?
He would not dare strike
or extinguish it who gave
you such delightful Light!

I saw the shimmering one
and I was drawn into the
shadows where to test,
with him, my appetite.
At first intrigued, I sensed
a rising tide of lust for
fruit not meant for mc.
Draw back, the inner
voice Creator-LORD

had placed in me did urge
of peril now so near.

I pondered, too, the ethic
rule that He had shared
with us. The 'serpent' saw
me pause, about to turn
from him. The Satan wiles
intensified—my eyes
were drawn by dark,
hypnotic gaze. I yearned,
delighting in the myriad
hues reflected in his
glorious form.

I was beguiled by
passion's thirst;
his piercing eyes,
like fangs, held mine.
He coiled intimidating
challenges about my mind.
Here was consuming,
base desire revealed.
I yielded to the tempting
'fruit'. Then, clinging to
the 'Testing Tree',
I longed to taste,
once more, this one
forbidden 'fruit'.

My Adam came into
the path to search for
my companioning:
My Adam, come to me,
excite with me in tasting,

knowing, luscious 'fruit'…
And, from his shadowed
lair, the 'serpent' slyly
smiled. Thus tempted, I,
then Adam chose to listen
to the plausible. We taste
the offering then. Our eyes
had seen and nought
would stem our hunger
for forbidden 'fruit'…

What taste is this, so fair
upon the tongue, yet bitter
gall in swallowing?
The 'Testing Tree' had
sealed our fate. Take, eat,
and find your strength,
the Satan-'serpent' said.
Why now this weakness in
the heart? Our hands
have taken to our soul
this 'fruit', we had
betrayed the trust of God,
the LORD of *LIGHT*.

The knowledge gained
when he, the dark,
insidious one, inserted in
our questing minds
the thirst for faith's
alternatives—to live as
heavenly beings, all
knowing, too, like as the
LORD—was knowledge
gained at our expense.

The death of innocence,
gave knowledge of just
what a single sin can do!
We felt bereft, bereaved.
Our hands performed this
dreaded deed, our lips
consumed the fruit
detested now; ours was
obedience lost in lusted
flesh! Yes! Claim the dawn
that 'snake' beguiled.
What now? The coming
Night—he lied, and cosmic
chasms opened wide.

ADAM
Genesis 3

I hide me from the *YHVH*-
LORD; this tree should
keep me from His
penetrating gaze, these
leaves conceal my shame,
these shadows ease my
pain of light …

That 'snake' was right!
I know my fate, but fate
of deepest night, and not
the days God gave to me!
In Spirit-truth, I died
today–he lied, that 'snake'!
I walk within the deeply
shadowed lanes of sin
with slithering, sliding,

'serpent' tracks upon my
dusty track. He stole my
Light and turned it dark.
LORD, curse his measly
mound of earth!

The *YHVH* comes to
search for me in shade
though nought of night
resides in Him. He walks
on evening dew; I hear His
footfall through the gloom
of deepening evening mist.
He comes again to me
within this garden now
bereaved of peace—
He still would keep our
trysting place? He halts
by me…
Such fear! He plans
to take accounting of the
day: He speaks my name,
my red-earth 'Adam'
name, confirming what
is done this blackest day:

*Your Paradise is lost,
O Adam, child of Earth,
yet all is not despair:
The One, in time fulfilled,
who comes, Who is of
LIGHT, will bring returning
dawn and cripple Satan's
head to halt his deadly
march. My LIGHT is not*

*extinguished by the darkest
night though Satan schemes
to hold you in his night.*

With this, the Vale of
Eden closed. This outer
darkness is so cold,
I am bereft of peace.
The Eden of the past can
be no more our ideal
home, the place where
God companioned us, and
counselled us in ways
of worship and of deed—
such knowledge now so
rare! We'd sensed a power
within to hold us to the
narrow path He'd set.

With every passing day,
that strength increased.
We'd found a knowledge
linked with Godly ways—
a knowledge deeper than
the mind. It guided us,
encouraged us—Creator
LORD was pleased.

But then, he came, the
'serpent' one who
promised knowledge
avalanched. Oh yes, the
knowledge came—
an avalanche to drown
us there, for then we
found the strength

of blatant sin in us,
the power of evil ways
and weakness of the good.
'twas knowledge of the
night that closed about
our fragile flesh, and
shrouded knowledge we
had gained in Eden's
morning light.

We learned discrimination
of the good but, from the
mound of sin! We'd lost
the ground of good
whereon, before our very
gaze, the face of sin would
be revealed, the truth
indicting falsity! But, lust
in us compelled to sin, we
flirted with the Satan one
who dragged us to the dust
with him. Here was our
fall, our Fall from Grace.

In Eden, strength was love
but, now, the strength
is sin, the weakness love.
We've lost a life in that
disgrace! My soul is now
imprisoned in the shroud
of night, and Paradise
is lost... But now, I hold
to glimmering hope—His
LIGHT still shines on me.

..... oOo .....

THE TRANSGRESSING YEARS
Formation—*LIGHT* and Shade
ABEL
Genesis 4:1-4

Behold, the babe of ewe
and ram, the firstling of
the flock. This precious
lamb, it frolics in the sun;
no blemish is disclosed in
him, this choicest, lamb.

I need an offering—
could this atonement make,
this lamb, for offering,
this lamb now 'speak'
my yearning after Him
who gave me all?

I take him in my arms,
he nought suspects of me;
his trusting gaze, such as
is of the gambolling lambs,
would search me as I raise
the knife then light the
flickering flames.

Oh, *YHVH, Elohim*,
receive this gift, this
choicest gift, receive me
also to Your side...

What is this *LIGHT*,
so brighter far than flame,
now kindled in my soul?

CAIN
Genesis 4:5-16

**Supposing sacrifice
The LORD requires
to hold me in His grace,
I take these sheaves, the
harvest grains of wheat,
as Abel did his lamb.
This wheat would make
 my bread! One sheaf
I will not miss…
I light the flame,
it smoulders on the rock.
Why? This is such a
cloying smoke and bleeds
my eyes with tears; my
breath is suffering…
The *Elohim*
is not appeased!**

**He chose the lamb above
my sheath and Abel over
me! I like it not!
My conscience—heart
voice—warns me deep
within: Beware of sin,
it lies here—at your door!
What sin? I dare to ask.
No! None shall master
Cain… I've done the thing**

**I did not think to do,
but did—his blood is on
my hands! I can't erase
this stain though frantic
threshed within the sand.
I'll hide this blood, my
brother's blood…**

**What? LORD? I do
not hold my brother's
hand, I keep, I guard him
not… His blood, it weeps
now in the sand? My sin,
my dreadful deed, my sin
is more than I can bear.
What will become of me?
I go into a darkened place
where death would stalk
me, haunt me on my path.
How dark this night…**

How great the grace of God!
This wondrous sign upon
my brow, I feel it now.
And, east, I face the rising
sun—a light upon my way,
A *LIGHT* to guide
my life, my only hope!

JUBAL
Genesis 4:21

*Take reed of rush that
swings within the wind—*

the whispering wind—
and breathe upon it now.

I take,
I blow upon the reed:
its sound is true
and pleasant to the ear.
I think to make a melody…
Such voice: the sound of
Heaven! My fingers dance
upon the reed, upon
these opened vents.

I see
the sunlight prancing on
my melodic reed—along
its slender surface, thus
evoking untried sounds.

Create the rhythmic tune:
its ebb and flow, also
its high and low, its grace,
its rhythm and its sound.

I hear!
It's in my throbbing heart.
It's written on my mind
and there is music in my
soul. A *LIGHT* of joy
burns deep within.

I find
imprisoned eloquence
of music grand breaks free
like sunlight from
the nimbus cloud of night.

I know
This is the dawn of all
who seek to play the music
of the heart and speak,
in song, the praise
of *Elohim.*

SETH
Genesis 4:25-26

Oh, *YHVH*-LORD,
I call upon Your Name.
You are as what You are,
as what You were, as what
You'll be: eternally the
same. I speak Your Name,
I plead my cause: I know
Your Presence now,
within this place.

I speak the NAME—
the Name revered
and lisped when on
my mother's lap
or dandled on
my father's knee.

The winter nights
were long; we huddled by
the burning log which
sentinelled our home.
We needed light and
warmth to pass

the evening hours.
The glowing embers there
caressed the faces loved.

I there have traced the lines
of grief on mother's wistful
face, my father's furrowed
brow where sweat had lain.
Their speech had sombre
sounds in echoing the sagas
past. They mourned the
heritage they'd lost, of
Eden's home, and Light
of Heaven's Face.

They spoke of You, and
how You walked and talked
with them in Eden's
bowers–a glory not regained
though yearned they long.
They lived these memories
in every waking hour.

My parents set
the yearning in my heart
which longs for God.
LORD, come to fill this
emptiness. My brother,
Abel's blood is in the
ground; I know not where
my brother Cain!

My brother Cain:
perhaps he's sons–
his very own to people

Earth, and find a road
to Paradise again. I stay me
here: I stand on holy
ground, I know You near:
I bring You now my son,
my first-born son:
my Enosh, son of Seth!

I lift him to Your *LIGHT*—
LORD, bless my son,
that he would learn
to speak The NAME!

ENOCH
Genesis 5:18-24

Long years ago, those many
years, I took those steps—
the first at mother's hand.
I faltered, tottered, then I
fell; I skinned my knees!

I stood right up and courage
took to walk, then run
and leap the rocks and
brooks. I chased the
butterflies, the deer
so fleet of foot.

I came to adult years
with steadied, ordered
tread—it is the way of men
to be sedate, steadfast.

I went my way in peace,
more measured in my gait
for fear the work would
wane. I have not walked
alone these many years;
I am a man of prayer!
I've found the truth of this:
he walks with God who
speaks to Him in prayer.
And, listens, too, within
the meditation's calm.

I hear Him now approach!
He calls my name, I heed
His Voice, His guiding, and
His guarding too. I feel
that He's my Friend!

My LORD has shared
the things of Heaven,
of Paradise regained.
I see Him now! I come to
Him. My footprints are
no more! I walk with Him
in *LIGHT*—Eternal *LIGHT*!

METHUSELAH
Genesis 5:21-17

The notches on this rod
are numbered in the
hundreds now. The first
of these marked well
my birth, so many seasons

past. I took this rod
when but a child; so firm
it stood me up. I wished
to walk as father had—
a man who walked
with *YHVH*–LORD .
I walked on in
my father's steps:
He taught me how to pray.
He nurtured me in ways
sublime but, one day past
in time, I found his steps
no more. I know, within
the heart of me,
he lives with God!

I take this rod, this tested
rod, to make my pathway
sure, to bear the burden of
the miles I've trudged
with calf and cow.
And, as the seasons came
and went, I marked their
passing with a stone.
See, here, these marks,
these many notches on
my rod: my able years,
my stable years,
the seasons of my joys,
and those of fears for child,
for wife, for aging years.

I mark this rod! The snows
that grace these mountain
peaks are also in my hair!

And though my back bears
all the weight of labour and
of burdens borne these
many years, it bends
of sorrows, and of woes.
My rod still holds me
firm…

This aging rod is gnarled,
just as my wrinkled hands,
with lines of years far past
nine hundred—more!
My years of time are spent;
I tire, I place my rod down
at my side. My eyes are
dim, I seek the *LIGHT*
of Heaven…

(There lies a wooden rod
upon the ground, an aged,
a notched and lonely thing
yet strangely beautiful:
it speaks of times and man
long passed).

NOAH

Genesis, 6 – 9

See now this ark: how sure,
secure, its rugged frame.
The cubits and the shape
are right—the finished
work, a style of form
beyond men's dreams!

One thing:
How did He know that I'd

obey? He tested faith,
it seems!

See now these beasts:
from east and west they
come in pairs for sheltering
within this wooden frame.
See how they hasten here!

One thing:
How will I tend this stock?
By patient calm,
it seems!

See now this mist,
this nimbus cloud, enlarge
to veil the peerless blue
and shadow all the land
this fateful day: The
heavens weep today!

One thing:
How did He shut us in?
It is by grace,
it seems!

Where is the night,
and, where the day? Who
knows? Ah! Nature knows
her times by crowing cock
and milk of lowing beast!

One thing:
How will we know
the opening day?
It is by trust
it seems!

See how this dove,
this pleasant dove, brings
peace. I see her o'er
the waste—the seething, the
tempestuous, raging sea;
(the raven's lost).

One thing:
Who knows the way
to land? He steers us on,
it seems!

See now, I wait…
At evening hour, my dove,
how does she fare, out
there? Will she return?
Oh, yes, my dove!
"Peace" brings
an olive leaf!

One thing:
When will we find
the sun again?
In His own time,
it seems!

The dawn has come,
the mountain height is dry!
This ark of grace is open
wide and stock, redeemed,
emerge to face the day.
One thing—Oh, LORD:
what awesome sight is this
where splendid colours lie?
It is Your Promise Bow…
I see!

THE FOREMAN
Genesis 11

**Bricks!
More bricks, now,
over here! We'll build
this awesome tower,
the latest evidence
of our ascendancy.
I'm proud of this,
the great, the grand
strategic project of our
time. We purposed in
our hearts to build a
stairway to the gods…**

**This special recipe of
reddest, moistened clay
I've moulded in my hands
when taking rest from
making bricks—these
solid bricks—It's in the
form of man. I'll breathe
within its nostrils yet. My
breath! Perhaps I'll give
it birth, who knows,
this shape created just like
me. I am a clever man,
I AM!**

**Bricks!
More bricks, lift them
high, We mean to reach
the stars this season,
very soon–perhaps today!**

The scheme is grand, the
mastery of measurement
and means. I'm proud
of this great pile of rocks
that reaches, even higher,
up. One day, I'll stand
upon its top-most brick,
proclaim achievement of
the present age of time.
I so do long for this!
We've come so far, these
recent years, we've
answers found for many
puzzling things. Our
yearning for the dazzling
things has stretched our
latent powers, our will,
our ingenuity, our wildest
dreams. And now, behold
this tower! We'll celebrate
our own success and dance
upon the stairs: I am,
today, a merry man,
I AM!

Bricks!
More bricks to craft this
day. This edifice would
claim to cleave the very
skies. We are the clan of
man that will be gods
for nought can thwart our
plans. I'm proud of this,
the very peak, the height
of man's perfection and

his mastery of bleating
beasts whose powers of
thought are nought. They
cower at our commands!
We have the power of
abstract thought you see;
we know the how and
why: we are enlightened
man! And well this tower
will testify to all mankind
of this, our powers, our
genius—this scheme of
grandeur fit for kings
and priests. But no, what
need have we for prattling
priests? There is no place
for them, our destiny is in
our hands! Now I will be
both king and priest:
the worshipper the
worshipped—even me!
I am a 'holy' man,
I AM!

Bricks!
More bricks, we reach
the clouds. The height of
bricks now disappears, the
mists of night roll in. It's
early yet! Perhaps this is
a cloud of storm to halt
us for the day. I'm proud
of this, our grandest feat—
this amazing edifice— …
What now? A flashing,

jagged light of storm?
The lightning is so fierce,
the thunder, boding ill.
I trust it threatens not the
stair from which to view
the earth from heaven—
Oh save our precious plan!
This rumbling grows, it
roars—*CRASH*! Bricks
lie shattered in the sand!
Oh! What's this burning
fire upon my blathering
tongue, this hammering
within my brain? I speak
but none can comprehend,
nor can I them. A bleak
confusion reigns:
I am a lonely man,
I am m...

Oh Look, the bricks
have fallen down!
What's that you say?
I do not understand.

..... oOo .....

THE
'TRANSITIVE'
YEARS
The Patriarchs—
Vocation, Volition

ABRAM
Genesis 12

I think I've always known
it so, a guiding Hand upon
my life, a powerful, urge
within the secret place
where Godward thoughts
lie buried deep, until they
rise in me. I've known
such thoughts as these,
I KNOW!

I've known the greatest
height of Ur. That pile
of rock cast high to call
upon the liking, and the
striking, of the gods has left
an empty shrine within
my inmost soul; I know
not why it's thus:
HOW SO?

I've heard, within my
father's house —Yes,
Terah, man of Ur,
Chaldees—
of One Supreme, the God
of all! I knew Him not—
His Face was not disclosed
to me. I searched in vain
for hint of Him, I hope
to call on Him.
WHERE GO?

I've heard the Voice

of Heaven, a *Flame*,
not words, the urgent call
that stirs my inmost mind,
entreats to open audience
with Him. He is the One
made known to me,
in dreams—or visions—
clear as *LIGHT*!
I BOW!

I know You now, the
YHVH-LORD, who claims
my dreams, my hope!
You plant the living seeds
of Heaven within my heart.
I'll follow for those dreams
unto a future till, today,
I have not known.
But I will trust:
I'LL GO!

THE TREK
Genesis 13

Migrating families
fear much in arid country
lands where scarcity of
water, food, and sustenance
had grieved. We all but
settled down in Haran but,
far westward we must go.
And then, my father died:
SUCH WOE!

The LORD then called
to me:

*Now, leave all that you
know and go into a country
I will show to you—I'll bless
you there with sons
and so much more. And, you
will be a blessing too;
I'll care for you!
FROM NOW!*

We came to Canaan's
verdant land; we trekked
until I heard His Voice:

*This is the land
I'll give to you!*

We settled in this lovely
place made holy by
the grace of God.
We came to it with
grateful hearts.
JUST SO!

The Egypt trek was not
a plan that I would
advocate. It went from bad
to worse—I all but lost
my wife of many years.
The king repented of
his greed for God is good…
I have forgiveness now.
I'LL GROW.

My nephew, Lot, and I
must part. We'd grown
so very rich with herds
and flocks and treasure too.
We had to separate.
Lot chose the best, the
fertile land—I hope he will
be safe from wiles and
wickedness:
STAY TRUE!

ABRAHAM
Genesis 17 – 18

Now, let me introduce
myself once more:
now Abraham! You see,
I'm going to be a dad! Yes!
I'm to father sons, at last!
And, many more so far
from kith and kin. My sons,
and daughters too of course,
will be as even numberless
as shifting sand upon
the shore of seas beyond
horizons of this land.
My Sarah laughed!

He greeted me, the
EL SHADDAI;
He challenged me to walk
within the Light of His own
Face! He asked of me

a perfect life of true
integrity… He came to me
when I was all of 99!
He said that He would make
with me a covenant.
It would take two
to make these promises;
He'd keep His own and
asked that I hold faith.
My Sarah laughed!

I questioned Him,
the *YHVH*-LORD:
How can my Sarah, wife,
and I now bring to birth one
child, not asking how could
we then rear the millions
more, the countless ones.
Let Ishmael be my heir!

*You'll call his name Isaac
and he and his descendants
will give heed to all My will.*

My Sarah laughed!

I sit within my tent to muse
beneath the favoured
terebinth–the tree that
sentinels the plains from far
beyond. I call this home!
So, let me see, the men were
three; my proffered
hospitality received,
they sat at ease. They

questioned me, they surely
challenged me.
My Sarah laughed!

The One of three—that sat
to speak with us that day—
His eyes reminded me…
My LORD! I knew that
gaze within my heart; that
light-filled Face is known
to me today, indeed!
It warmed my heart to see
it now. His eyes held mine,
I thought again of promises
and covenant. He spoke
my new-known name!
My Sarah laughed!

A multitude, like as the
sands, the shore-line sands,
much more! And I? The
doubt was strong, yet I
recalled the promises
of *YHVH*–LORD.

And so the sands,
the countless stars:
my sons, of sons, to be?
A child, for childless us?
The gifts of God are
limitless: I know it's so!
My Sarah laughed!

THE INTERCESSOR
Genesis 18 – 19

I know it, LORD.
I would agree, I see the sin
of Sodom is a blight upon
the Earth, a stench within
the nose! Gomorrah's
devious deeds are grievous
deeds as like the pitch
that seethes beneath its
mouldering, dank mound,
a tainted ground—
a dangerous ground tonight.

But, LORD, my kin resides
within the gates. I wish it
were not so but Lot lives
there. He's not succumbed
to deadly sins—he is
a righteous man, and pure!

And, LORD, there'd be
more righteous, too, I'm
sure, within those wasted,
white-washed walls. I pray
for those, the righteous men,
this very night.

My LORD, I stand before
You now to plead their
cause, the souls of those
who've sin opposed—
their hands are clean.

O LORD, don't sweep away
the righteous with
the evil men, as though

the saint and sinner are
the same. I plead for fifty
righteous souls this
grief-filled night. O LORD,
I'd be so bold, I am but dust
and ash, it seems, Yet once
again I'd speak:
LORD what of forty-five,
or forty, thirty-five,
just men, I plead!

I can't abide a thought
You'd find the righteous
and the wicked just the
same and swept away
within a tide of judgement
flames this night. O LORD!

Oh, would You hear
my prayer for twenty souls?
I'd state the case for ten, the
righteous souls? You'd stay
Your hand for ten?

You've heard my prayer
for ten! I praise Your will
and turn again unto my
Mamre tent to contemplate
the ways of *YHVH*-LORD,
the God of Grace.

O LORD, my frame
a shadow casts upon the
ground before my feet,
a lurid light behind
with stench of sulphur in

the air. I dread not even ten
just men my LORD could
find within that place.
I wonder, what of Lot?
Is everyone consumed?
This putrid pall extends.
I'll trust the LORD for Lot!

THE WORSHIPPER
Genesis 22

I've seen the sacrifice of
sons—It turns my stomach
gall! What misplaced awe
of gods! How could those
blocks of altar stones
receive the stain of blood—
the blood of innocence,
the livid flames of sullied
sacrifice, the death
of sons?

You ask of me this thing?
My Isaac for the stone and
fire? This dreadful thing
You ask of me? You tempt
my faith, O LORD!
This is far past Your just
demands; I search the Mind
of God to find the answer
for a sacrifice—my dear,
loved son?...

Come, Isaac lad,
we go to worship and

to pay our dues with God.
We'll take this bundled
wood for sacrifice upon
the mound of rock we'll
build due north of here—
yes, on a march of miles.
I need your company
today, upon the way,
my son!

How dear, O LORD, how
dear this boy, this promised
one of age. My Sarah, could
she not be spared the grief
for one who's gone before
his timely years?
My grief, as well, burns
deep. What's that, my son?
You ask, no lamb
for sacrifice? The LORD
provides the sacrifice,
my son!

The pyre is built; I take the
knife, it trembles, flashes in
the Light—my son
outstretched, appalled,
upon the pile of wood.

What's that I hear?
A sound of bleating in
the thorns? You've come,
You've answered prayer.
You tried my faith but
this I say with thanks:

LORD, You gave me back
my son!

(O LORD, Your grace is
here… What's that You say
to me right here?
This gifted lamb—atoning
lamb—is like YOUR Son?!
How can it be? I understand
it not but: I will trust Your
word! You'd give
Your son?)

THE BEREAVED
Genesis 23

Light of my life, my love,
I mourn your last of days.
My bride of carefree, eager
youth, beloved always—
the mother of my son,
the matriarch from whom
the issue of my loins did
come in *YHVH's* grace.

Through all our wanderings
by impulse of the LORD,
you faithful, graceful, ever
were; you kept the pace!
I grieve your breathless
form! The furrows of
the years are featured there,
though stilled,
upon your lifeless face.

I trace those well-loved
lines forlorn of comfort
now; I fear the joyless,
loveless nights, the lonely
days. I lay you now to rest
within this Mamre cave
that could have been
a gift, a salve,
to Heaven's praise.

But no, this precious plot
must lose me much, for
you! I've weighed
accounted cost within
my hands, my gaze.
I know this land, at least, is
ours when flesh returns to
formless dust, fulfilling then
the *YHVH's* ways.

THE SERVANT
Genesis 24

Yes sir!
I've been in service now
these fifty years, or more.
The master, Abraham,
once Abram, that's for sure,
has given to my serving
hands the charge of son and
heir. The man and son are
close: I've seen them leave
for sacrifice;

was glad of their return!
The lad had gathered stature
then. Yes, overnight it
seemed: There was a
measure in his tread
I had not seen before.
The lad's become a man.
This worship surely blesses
sons, I said… How bright
the noble stars do shine
above young Isaac's tent!

Yes sir!
I find it such an honour, sir,
to serve a man like as of
him—my master, Abraham.
He trusts his greatest wealth
to me and, now,
his precious son.
I have been charged,
you see, to seek a bride
for master's son;
I spoke my solemn oath
on that! He laid it on
the line for me—he knew
full well his own intent.

Yes, sir:
Young Isaac's bride would
come from master's kith
and kin, he says,
and not from Canaan's
pagan brides. He loves
the lad, this child of his

advancing years, as one
above the countless stars
that shine on Isaac's
home-based Mamre tent!

No, sir!
I have not trekked this way
before. I take this journey
far for master Abraham.
The land ahead is sparse of
life—it is an arid desert
land; I fear the drifting
sands. My charge weighs
heavy now! And, when the
journey's done, what then?

Oh, SIR:
How will I fare, I say, and
how select the choice I'm
bound to make for master,
and for his loved son?
I'll choose a bride for Isaac?
This thing's a burden on my
heart—a choice for love,
and life. This is a heavy
charge. I search for guiding
stars above my pilgrim tent.

Yes, SIR!
That's what I'll do.
The plan is good by which
I'll seal the choice for
master Abraham… I thirst!
I'll stay right by this well;
the chosen one will come

this day. I'm charged, upon
my sacred oath, to seek
the one most suited now.
How mark the character
beyond the beauty and
her grace of form?
I'll search for kindness…

Yes SIR!
First, the quenching
of my thirst and then my
camels to be slaked of
thirst… Here is the one
to gladden Isaac's heart. I'm
offered respite now,
from desert heat, the
burning sands, the blazing,
seething, sun. The evening
star has led me on to father
Bethuel and his tent!

Yes, sir!
I gather Laban is your
name; I thank you for your
welcome here. My master,
Abraham, speaks well
of you, his nearest kin. It's
true, my mission is
immense, I say. Let me
explain the charge he gave
to me: He set for me a
master plan. Rebekah met
the test, she met my quest.

Yes!, sir …

I'd pondered with the
LORD who led me on these
many miles. I knew as when
she offered me the cooling
draught, and then my
camels, too, she'd please
young Isaac well. I ask
you now, can you allow
this sister's absence from
her family's home, and kin?
She gladly comes? I praise
the LORD! The eastern
stars forever shine upon
Rebekah's empty tent!

Yes, sir!
The deed is done. I rest now
from the task. This journey
had the blessing of the
LORD, I know. Yes, Master
Abraham, the choice is
made. It gladdens me
to speak the news–the bride
arrives. My charge
has been fulfilled.

Yes, sir,
Your Isaac saw her in the
western sun. The shadows
weren't so long, as if, I say,
to dim her beauty and
her lovely grace. I saw the
joy, I say, with which he
sped to welcome her
and speak of how the

journey must have tired
her on the way. She met
his tender gaze, a smile
was in her eyes, I say.
The days of her betrothal
will soon pass. She'll be
his bride... The morning star
so brightly shines on
Isaac's marriage tent!

ESAU
Genesis 25:19 – 34

**He grabbed my heel the
day that I was born—first
born: you mark them well,
my angry words—I am
first-born from the womb!
I had to struggle free from
him. He clutched my foot
to be, ahead of me, the
first! But I, not he, before
the end will claim the
blessings meant for both
of us, the matchless twins!**

**He simpers at our
mother's knee of things
I've done, or failed to do
to such as he, the measly
wimp. And, spoiled for all
the things he seeks
of her, he pesters me
and brings me wrath.**

I fight, then scamper to
my father's side!

He took the love my
mother would have
showered on me but for
his scheming ways. He
stays fast by her homely
tent, he clutches at
her skirts for aid. He claims
her love. I have it not! He
seeks attention every day.

He cares not that I fret
for her to mother me
and share, with her,
my boyish pride
in things I've done and,
sometimes, what I failed to
do. I'd seek her tender
comfort, and forgiveness,
too, if not for Jacob at her
welcome side. It seems her
home is his, not mine.
He is a 'jacob'; he's a cheat!
I tell my father this and
hide. I ate his wretched
stew! A mass of pottage
but it tasted fine. Its tang
was in my nostrils as
I came in sight of home
tents. The hunt was long,
I tired; no game was to

be seen though I had tried
the hunt. I turned for
home. My spear was clean,
my shoulder short of hard-
won game for night's
repast. I needed meat!
Now, give him due,
that Jacob knows sweet
recipes of stews and,
though I like him not,
I'd give my hand, at times,
for taste of Jacob's stew.

He tempted me that night
with herbs sublime;
I was so famished from the
hunt. The victuals fumed.
 I ate them at my father's
own right side. He stole
my right! The birthright
was my very own, though
he had tried to steal it from
the first by gripping me
within the womb to
struggle free before I faced
the light. Yes, it was me,
not him; yes, I was first
from mother's pains. But
now, I've lost the right
of birth. That mess
of pottage was his wile
to steal from me what
first was mine. I thought

what help has birthright
now for me when I, so
famished, fell to the
bended knee to ask for
stew? I savoured meat
and gave to him on oath,
that scheming Jacob, all
my rights. And now, when
lost, I mourn for them as
not before. I wept, that
night, for father's pride.

JACOB
Genesis 27 – 28

How dark the night!
The very vault of Heaven is
closed away from *LIGHT*.
Where is the God
of Abraham and of his Isaac
now, I ask? My father
promised me—he said, in
childhood's days, the
YHVH-LORD Eternal IS,
eternal stands Supreme,
above all other gods
of lands we've trekked
in summer days and
moonlit nights of peace.
I find Him not! I am
alone in this dread place
and home I've not though
I had taken to myself the
birthright and the blessing,

too, away from Esau. He's
my twin; I am estranged
from him! The one who
roamed throughout
our youth, he now is home;
he claims my place as well
as his at father's stool and
mother's arms. I am
bereaved of parent love!
How dark the night!

How deep the night!
My desolation pierces me;
the day was sharp with
grief. I'd seen the suffering
etched on my mother's
brow when, in the firmest
verdict of my deed,
transgressing Esau's rights,
it seemed I must escape
for life. I fled from him,
and those who love me best.

I laid right down to sleep
upon my pillow—this great
flat stone which nought
of comfort brings.
The evening dews have
chilled my bones; I shudder
in the breeze. My sleepless
eyes now scan the shapeless
night for faintest gleam
of pascal moon, perhaps
a guiding star!

This fearing wanderer
would falter on the first
of alien nights. What is my
fate? I fear for all my future
years—I think I shall
not see, again, the face of
family to comfort me; no
Isaac or Rebekah, beloved
mother, ever more:
How deep the night!

How bright this *LIGHT*!
What is it that I dream?
Far brighter, different than
the day, this beam
that drives me to my knees
for, now ascending and
descending on those rays
like as of stairs, I see the
angels of the holy
YHVH-LORD!

He comes to me. Oh, surely,
God is in this place!
I knew it not, for I had seen
but darkest, deepest night,
my grieving heart, and
empty, wasted years of
youth. He means to comfort
me, to give me hope to live
again. Renewed in faith,
relieved that, by His grace,
my grief is not the more
than I could bear of sin's

eventual consequence.
I bring the matter of
my guilt in prayer to Him
and seek that He would
guard and guide through all
my length of days.
A pilgrimage begins this
night. I name, for Him, this
place as Bethel—*House
of God*… How bright
is Heaven's *LIGHT*!

JACOB
Genesis 29 – 31

**These many years of
sojourn in this alien land,
undoubted, have now
mellowed me. I trust
though, if I'm honest once,
I still can see the very
'jacob', wily ways in me.
My uncle, Laban, must
have found it so though,
at the first, he trusted me
to keep his many flocks
of pesky goats and such.
I saw the means to make
my glowing pile of gold
grow great with streaky
goats with stripes and
spots on all of uncle's
flocks—I fleeced him so!**

He'd played his tricks on
me, it's true. He cheated
on the cheat! You see,
I fell in love! His daughter
Rachel was so fair but
Leah, dear, her eyes were
crossed! They all but put
me off the elder girl
whose hand I should
have sought, I surely
found. I chose, instead,
my Rachel love.
Then, Laban played
his hand when I was
drunk with love. And, in
the morning's brazen
light with all revealed,
I met my woe!

My sister wives have
shown their equal share
of wiles, intrigues and
simple vice, manipulating
me, in turn, to father sons.
I'd served for seven years
for one. And, when
the Laban trick was then
exposed, I served for seven
more, just for my love.
This seemed as twice of
seven nights—perhaps it
was! But, fourteen years
I fully served for both.
My wives had brought
me many worthy sons

though Rachel gave me two
I love her so!

'Now! Name your utmost
wage!' their father said.
He planned to hold me to
this foreign land that
harboured me from
Esau's vicious wrath.
It's time to go!

The Laban clan suspect
the means by which I'd
gathered wealth. I know
not why. I've only taken
what's my own—
though granted, streaks
and stripes and spots on
flocks have multiplied
beyond day dreams. I
gloat. The stock I count
add up to more than
Laban's measly flocks:
I'll have to go!

My wages changed ten
times, or more. I've told
my wives of this, to their
dismay: 'Your father's
attitude has changed;
you'll see it, too, with
opened eyes,' I sagely said.
I told them, also, God had
caused the blots and spots
and blemishes that spoiled

His cherished flocks.
('twas just a little lie,
the paler kind). I told, in
truth, of vows I'd made,
of promises the LORD
had made. It's time to find
if Esau's wrath has waxed
or waned. I had to know:
My friend, or foe? I'll go
to him, this twin of mine
who's been the bane of life
since I was birthed. I see
the dust of his approach…
He hates me so!

Four hundred men, you
say? Four hundred
strong? Esau would send
a host against his twin?
I'm past youth's wiles but,
for this crisis in my life,
I'll dredge me up a plan,
or maybe, two! I'll sit
upon this rugged rock
and wait. Up yonder there,
divided by the gifted
flocks; both wives and
sons will mellow his
intent; I know he won't
see them as foe!

JACOB–ISRAEL
Genesis 32

I've been redeemed!

from all that's past—
the old man, yes; the 'jacob'
that was me. You see:

I've been reclaimed!
I had no pride in what was
me but shackles held me
fast in what was me.
My 'jacob' ways had
wounded many people
through the years—my
wives and sons as well,
I fear. Released at last
at no great cost—except
my pride—I'm free. You
see, no more the 'jacob'
man within; though none
might tell but for this smile,
this warmth in me:
I feel the *LIGHT* of God
upon my face!

I've been renewed!
The struggle of the night
was long! I wrestled with
this One who came, on eve,
to challenge me, though
what the looming challenge
was, I scarce can tell. He
met His match, He did!
Though in the victory there,
I felt as in the Home of
God, the Man more agile
and of awesome power
much more than I

who fought Him all
the night! I chose
to struggle on until
He blessed me whole! This
ground is 'Peniel'! I've seen
'The Face of God' and yet
I live to tell of it! I'd
looked with awe
into those searching eyes
and knew! He's righted all
my grievous wrongs
upon the day!

I've been reborn!
I'm 'Israel'—*a prince with
God*! Could any slip again
into the mother's womb,
to be reborn, receive just
one more chance to live
again without the pains
of what is past of sins and
all those misdemeanours,
deeds, of selfish gain?
This is indeed a miracle
upon my soul!

I know, within the heart
of me, a birth again, a life
that's new, from this
encounter with the LORD!
Yet, who could tell, but for
my limp—the 'wonder
wound', of *Elohim*,
upon my hip!

JOSEPH
Genesis 37:1 – 23

O Father, dear,
come quick to me. I've
much to tell; you'll hear
it well, I'm sure. You see,
my dream last night
revealed to me how special
now I am. I tell it all, my
wonder dream: My sheaf
of wheat was taller, far,
than all the rest we'd
harvested. My brothers'
sheaves were measly, poor,
just strewn upon
the ground, in fact.

But mine, dear Dad,
stood tall and true as if
the rest had bowed their
heads to worship me as
best of all the nearest clan!
Just like my precious coat,
my coloured coat, the
vivid coat you've woven
me, declaring that I am
your favoured son.

O Father, dear,
come quick to me. I've
much to tell of dreams
I viewed before the dawn
had come. My star shone

brightest and my star
was high, so high above
the rest. It glowed and
shone upon the flickering
ones, the dipping ones: my
brothers and your sons,
just so! The stars could
not outshine my one true
glow. The sun and moon
then bowed before my
star—that's you, my Dad
and Mother, too!

The family bows down
to Joseph's star! Just like
my coat, my coloured coat,
the jewelled coat, the
rainbow coat you've sewn
for me, discloses how I am
your favourite son…

O Father, dear,
come quick to me.
I need to tell, this is no
dream! I fear my life!
I need your help to pull
me up and stand me firm
and safe on higher
ground! This pit is foul!
I'm thrown here now
because your sons, the
other ones, have cast their
spite on me who hurt them
not. I came with food

to succour them when in
the task of shepherding.
Your wandering sheep.
O, please, redeem my life
out from this miry clay
in which I sink. O, not
my coat, my lovely coat,
my splendid coat! The
rainbow coat is bloodied
now to sham a death—
your desperate son!

JOSEPH, THE SLAVE
Genesis 39

I'm sold—into a foreign
land! It's come to this,
the jealousies, the anger for
those dreams that turned my
head. All pride—it goes
before a fall, you know,
and I am proof of that.
It took that deed, that
blatant deed of hate
deep rooted in my brothers'
hearts—so wretched were
their aims to hide from
father my true fate.
I'm sold—into a slavery!

This Egypt is so very grand:
It's civilisation at its peak,
I am convinced of that.

And where am I?
I had found grace within my
master's eyes; he favoured
me—I can't tell why,
except to say, he saw,
my master Potiphar, that I
was true to *YHVH*-LORD.
He gave to me the oversight
of all he owned.

I'm sold—into a servitude
once more, and this dark
deed by subterfuge.
The wily wife of Potiphar
made sure I would not win.
Integrity it seemed, would
ruin me. But then, again,
I found a friend: My jailer
gave to me the oversight of
other prisoners like me!
I see to it that each are kept
in best of health;
I care for all.

THE DREAMERS
Genesis 40

The Butler
I tell you, friend,
I fear my dream! How can
I now explain to you,
the Hebrew man,
what fate my dream
revealed?

I fear it is my own this day!
A vine, I saw, entwined
as three of branches fair.
These budded, then they
blossomed on the vine.

The branch grew heavy with
its ripening fruit. I came to
take for harvesting,
and then bring wine before
the lord, my Pharaoh King.
I placed the glass within
his hands to please.
My dream then dimmed.

The Baker
I tell you, man,
I fear my dream! How can
I tell with clarity to you,
the Hebrew man,
whose frightening fate
I fear? I fear it is my own
today! I saw my baskets
placed upon my head.
All three contained
the bread I'd baked and
tasty morsels: scones and
cakes my lord the Pharaoh
King's sweet tooth
desires—such dainty,
tasty breads he likes!

But, as I sped to take my

baking to my lord,
my Pharaoh King,
the ravens swooped
and then they pecked
those dainty breads.
My dream then dimmed.

Joseph
I'll tell the one:
within three days, his
fortunes are restored—he'd
take the wine unto the king.
I'll tell the other that,
within three days, his last
of days is spent—the
Pharaoh takes his head,
also, his life. I tell the one:

It is a joy to share with you
such news as this. Yes, all
your days, you'll serve the
king. I tell the other:
It is a grief to bring this
news; You've been a friend
the many days we've served
the king.

THE PHARAOH
Genesis 41

Call the guards!
Go! Bring at once the seers
to me—all those who read
the stars; the men of

matchless wisdom in
describing scenes of visions
rare; all those untangling
mysteries and able in
explaining dreams.

I've dreamed two dreams
this night–though what their
aim, I cannot tell,
I feel their potency the
while and know, at least,
they must be told.
The fate of Egypt rests on
this; I speak as Pharaoh
now! Be up, and go
to bring these men
before the dawn!

Here are the dreams that
pain my mind: the one of
cattle and, the other, corn:
of seven years–of fat
then thin. And then the poor
consumed the prime.

What can it mean? What is
this puzzle plaguing to the
mind and disengaging
sleep? What are the
mysteries contained within?
Give me the answer to my
dreams; you are
well trained in wisdom's
ways—you're skilled
in knowledge of

the stars, all the mysterious.
It's mine to dream, and
yours to tell the dream.
I bid you: Think!
Go, search your minds,
reveal the reason for my
grief or, by the stars,
I'll see you gone!

Slave, pour some wine,
I wait the quest. You give
me news as well as wine?
There is a youth who knows
just how to tell of dreams?

Go, bring the Hebrew lad
to me. Perhaps he knows
what seers have failed to see
and so, to speak...

You stand before the
Pharaoh and you say you
cannot tell, but God—your
God—can bring the matter
to your gaze? Speak on, my
lad for I declare: the truth
should hold no fear!

Pharaoh complies!
There's merit in your words.
So! Seven years
of plenty, seven of drought:
I like your explanation and
also all your plans to meet
the crisis when it comes.
I find my mind at peace.

You speak the truth. When
famine strikes, the Pharaoh
and his Egypt will be saved
as planned. The saviour
with the wisest scheme:
it's you, young Joseph. Yes!
The Spirit of the LORD,
your God, empowers your
mind; I raise you now to
stand from now
at Pharaoh's side!

JOSEPH
Genesis 42 – 48

My God!
What's this? Do startled
eyes deceive? These men
who bow before me now
within the precincts of my
power; these men do bear
familiar ways! These
Hebrew men, these
shepherds: Yes! I've
known them since my
youngest days. How could I
once forget these men—
my brothers Reuben,
Simeon, and Dan! There's
present each of... ten? But,
where's the youngest,
Benjamin? My closest kin,
my mother's youngest son;
I love him much

for we are two of one,
our father's choicest wife—
perhaps these men will feel
regret when seeing me?

My God!
The stars! The stars of
which I'd dreamed when in
my youthful days and spoke
of them in uninvited ways.
My brothers have fulfilled
the dream! They bow in
supplication here within
my own ascendant light!

Oh God!
Also, the sheaves of corn!
The dreams of youth
do haunt me now for,
in this day, I feel the joy
of finding them. Then,
sorrow wraps me round
its shroud for father, does
he live? And, Benjamin–
what's news of him? I need
to test my brothers now;
perhaps, today, they know
and feel a genuine remorse.

My God!
How could such brothers
ever change their hearts'
desires, their wicked ways,
their inclinations and, their
will concerning such as

would disturb their ease?
Have they forgotten past
misdeeds, their murderous
intent or do they mourn for
one who thoughtless was
but meant no harm? How
may I bide in silence for
their earnest love?

O LORD!
It's not thought to be wise
to speak until I know,
beyond the doubt,
the hearts of men like these.
Do they retain, each one,
the same vindictive ways,
or not? Perhaps this day,
I'll gain the right response!

O, LORD!
They met the test, my
brothers all—they passed
the hurdles set for them.
And, to their honour, they
did falter not within the
snare I set for them. Yes,
there were moments where I
felt unsure of them and their
intent. But when my wrath
was feigned to frighten
them far past an act
of servitude, to anger and
to traits of utter shame to
search their truest colours
yet, they fought

the while to save the one,
yet, not themselves! I find
the clearest sign of noble
selflessness: I surely find
their characters reformed!

O, LORD!
My heart did weep for them
though eyes were dried
when, in their presence,
there that morn. I longed for
the embrace which will
resolve the conflicts of the
years and bring to peace our
warring ways. I heard
a mellowed tone of tongue,
a gentleness whene'er they
spoke of father and of
Benjamin. I saw the shock
of unbelief as cups and
coins from brother's sacks
confronted with a blatant
crime! They knew it not
to be themselves—a sign
of true integrity; I find
but righteous lives
all now renewed.

O, LORD!
I worship at Your feet as
they did bow to me in
gratitude. I aim to serve
You all my days, my words
and deeds to speak Your
praise! For every crisis,

every care of life, You
meant it unto good for me
and those who once had
meant me harm. My heart
rejoices in the scene: my kin
combined as one. And now
I celebrate, once more, the
light I saw on father's
wrinkled face. My brothers,
too, they found forgiving
grace themselves. I joy in
brothers reconciled; I find
the family now restored!

JACOB–ISRAEL
Genesis 49 – 50

My family, come, my heart
does hold the blessing and
the bane. For each, my
sons, I speak the *LIGHT*;
I speak the **Shade**–
of blessing or, a curse–
appropriate and just,
to guide through life,
to know the right from wrong
and live for *YHVH*–LORD.

Reuben:
Excelling well in power,
in honour, and, in strength
but now, a man defiled

and turbulent as ceaseless
streams that empty in
the ceaseless sea: Your
blessing will be empty, too,
and swept away as with
the tide.

Simeon and **Levi**, too:
your violent ways, your hate
and cruelty annul the
blessings meant for you.
Dispersed, where you
reside.

Judah:
O, praise the LORD! Your
strength is as the lion.
And, as a lion, you'll rule,
your sceptre hold its sway
until the coming One.
The 'Judah Lion'
will take the sceptre,
none deride.

Zebulun:
Your eyes shall scan the
ocean tides–your lands
shall skirt the middle sea.
Your shores will be a
peaceful place
For all such men that sail
worldwide.

Issachar:
Beware the 'donkey' deed!
You seek the rest and
idleness of pleasant lands—
you'll find the stress and
strain of labours that in grief
you'd hide.

Dan:
You'll be a ruler and a judge
with wisdom as an asp—as
cunning too, prepared to halt
the enemy that's at
your side.

Gad:
Much peril lies within your
path though, at the end,
you'll find that you will
triumph o'er what will
betide!

Asher:
The produce of your land
will succour all until replete.
Yes, there'll be food till
satisfied.

Naphtali:
The dancing doe describes
Your trails, so delicate
And dancing like the prancing

deer! With such as these,
such agile steps, you'll make
your way, you will
abide.

Benjamin:
The prowling wolf, rapine
and ravenous, you'll plunder
by the day. Then, sit at night
with appetite, dividing,
gorging; and no foe
in sight.

Ephraim and Manasseh,
The older shall the lesser
be, the first born not as great
as he. But both these sons
of Joseph shall increase the
nation's strength and give
the double rights unto
Rachel, the one for whom
I sighed.

Joseph:
My son, so dearly loved,
I see you fruitful as a vine
where branches spread
beyond the borders of the
land—they spread in safety,
too, of *El Shaddai*. He is
your Shepherd and your
Rock! The God of Israel

will bless you: blessings of
the heavens and all the
earth are yours;
the blessings of the depths
and breadth—how blessed
of home, and blessed of
sons: far greater blessings
than the timeless hills,
the mountains' lofty heights.
These blessings for the
prince of men and, of his
brothers, still
their pride.

These words of blessing are
complete; I rest now for the
grave…
And Joseph wept
that night!

..... oOo .....

THE
TRANSLOCATING
YEARS
Captive: Body and Soul
AMRAM
Exodus 1:1 – 2:4 (6:18 –20)

The shadows of the night
are cast and oil is burning
low; our earthen lamp will
bear its flame not more
than but an hour.

The night will snuff it out
and, soon. This light is as
my faith, I fear; what little's
left is, as the oil, about
to be consumed in 'night'.
And yet, as flame, it lingers
on—perhaps the *LIGHT* is
stronger than this clouded
night. I little know.

But I would speak my faith
into the night and long for
oil to feed its flickering
flame. I pray the prayer of
night: O God, the Great
Unknown, yet surely
known, I'd speak
the holy NAME but it
is lost from lips
and heart. The servitude
of years has claimed
the knowledge once we had.
I search my mind
and of the Clan but none
can speak of what Your
NAME would be but, just,
You ARE! I hold to that!

Yes, this I know.
But there is nought of hope
in me. How may I find the
oil that kindles hope again?
So often we have heard the
sagas, secrets, of the clans;
the ventures of the past

are whispered round about
and held in heartfelt trust
This is our heritage of
faith—of this I surely know!
My faith is as the flame—
when all seems lost,
it flickers on! And could
I dare to hope, to pray
a Saviour born to set our
people free? This is the way
for *LIGHT*
to conquer all the night so
we may find deliverance
and, soon… This baby on
my knee, my son, could he
find liberty? I pray You,
Great Unknown, yet known:
Please, save this child;
perhaps for him, the sparing
of the bricks,
that he would truly know
an Exodus.

JOCHEBED
Exodus 2:1 – 10 (6:18 – 20)

God of our fathers,
Great Unknown, yet known,
we bring to You the sadness
of the night. My little one,
our child will face the Nile
before the dawn. Oh, may
the night draw on,
the sun refuse its light!

Our clan has carried many
griefs these years.
How long, O God,
how long, this servitude
of tears? Our men who
stagger with the weight
of work, the welt of
whips—they age before
their years. They slave
beyond the day though tire
before the noon. I pray
for them, and for my child,
my little one–before
the dawn, I'll see his face
no more… I pray for you,
my son, and for the mighty
Nile to bear you up within
this reeded ark of pitch
to take you to an Exodus.

MIRIAM
Exodus 2:1 – 10

I've nursed my baby brother
here within my arms on
many precious days
while mother stirred
the fuming pot
of gruel, the food prepared
for father dear when he
returns to home and takes
his nightly rest.
I've swept this floor and

tidied up when mother
needed to recline to feed
my baby brother here.
My mother, and my father,
too, do grieve this night, and
so do I. We mourn this baby
boy who brought such joy
where joy was not.
We'd bide our grief in
shadows of the gloom.
But, hide it not we can
this night for we must float
him on the tide before
the rising sun. Then I will
go to watch his way along
the Nile. But father must
return to bare his back
before the rod. This slavery
appears to sap his strength,
his will to live. O Great
Unknown, but known, I
pray You, spare our days
that we may see a new dawn
when I'll dance and play my
tambourine to celebrate with
all the Hebrew faithful
clans, an Exodus!

AARON
Exodus 4:14

O God, the Great Unknown,
but known, I want

my brother back! I need
him now. He is the boy
I asked of You when mother
was 'with child'. I asked
for him that he would be
the one to play with me
beyond the kilns, to hunt
with me at sphinx and dunes
and see with me
the pyramids my father
built—I think—with his
own laboured hands.

With him not here,
I'll be alone and soon, I'm
old enough to work with
father at the kilns.

This slavery brings much to
fear. It is too much for us to
work the mud without the
straw! What kind of bricks
are these that soon will
crumble to the dust? They'll
have our heads for those!
If I am grown into a man,
I'd be a priest to lead my
people back to You—
the Great Unknown,
but known. I'd fill my Levi
patriarch with pride
if he were still alive, and he
would see a priest in me
when I am grown. I need
my brother here; we'd find

a way to break the bonds to
one day force, with might,
an Exodus!

THE 'NURSE'
Exodus 2:5 – 10

How strange the ways
of The Unknown but
known! He hears our
prayers—we are not left
alone to fate. Confusing,
that we are enchained
yet blessings come
in startling ways! My
'Moses' boy is in my
arms—a miracle of grace!
When child is gone, and
hope is lost, a beacon shines
within the night, My boy
returns to me!
And, I am given charge of
him. The princess asks for
me to nurse this Hebrew
child. They little know,
the royalty, he is my own!
Now I may cradle him
within my arms to hush
him into sleep.

Now hush, my babe,
To take your rest,
Your mother's near
Your sleeping nest.
Now wings my prayer,

Let none annoy
But keep you safe,
My 'Moses' boy.

The lullaby has pacified;
I lay him down to sleep.
Oh, what a great advantage
has my child. Perhaps he is
the one to rescue us—or do
I hold the empty aspiration
of a doting Mother here?…

The Palace classroom
fascinates! The tutors at
whose feet you sit to learn
the rules of math, impart
intriguing mysteries as well:
the ancient arts, the curious
arts, the gathered wisdom of
the sage and seer.

My boy, you've learned
your lessons very well.
There's nothing on the
tablets in this library's vast
expanse you do not know!
I stand here by the
colonnade in shadow of
the pyramids and palms
but not to so intrude as call
attention to my caring
presence here—your 'nurse
and ever-present aide'.
My boy, remain immune
from things, the magic

things, intriguing things,
but damaging to what
you've learned from me, so
integral to all you know of
faith. I'd teach you much
as well of knowledge that
has never been engraved
on any stone or scroll.

I share with you the
language and the heritage of
these, your kin, to keep and
ponder in your heart—
a 'prince' of Egypt may not
let his halting tongue to be
defiled by speaking in the
Hebrew vein. But, let it flow
within your mind, engrave it
on your tender heart.

Now, take this rhyme and
keep it silent in your brain,
but active in your soul.
Rehearse its lines,
vernacular, its very truth—
it speaks of home, and God!

I've been beyond
These palace walls
Where work is grim,
And grief appals.
The Clans won't come
Within this gate,
They look to Heaven;
For 'Saviour' wait.

Conundrums for my son,
the learned one—the
'prince'—young Moses,
close to Pharaoh's side:
we've lost THE NAME, the
Holy Name! Of all we need,
beside redemption to be
wooed and won, we seek
The Holy Name!
Go! Search THE NAME,
fulfil, within your skills,
a mother's dream!

MOSES–THE
SHEPHERD
Exodus 2:11 – 3:1

That morning dawned
the same as any dawn I've
known here, in this barren
waste of trackless land.
The dew still clung to
graceful fronds
and bladed grass; the rising
sun made each a jewelled
branch. My flocks were
placid in the dawn and
cropping at the scrub
and tufted spinifex. Among
them all was not a vagrant
one, disturbing to my muse;
they seemed content to
graze upon the moistened
grass. I cherished their
serenity. This pastoral scene

was healing for my wounds
of loved ones lost, although
I'd had my fill of Egypt's
halls and palaces. Enough,
it's true, of Hebrews too—
my thoughtless, thankless,
kin so prone to moan.
I'd only meant to champion
them! How could I know
the scorn they held, their
dark mistrust of me,
the extricated 'Moses'
prince. I thought of mother,
Jochebed: It's only now,
in retrospect, of time
elapsed, I feel the full
import of all she said,
and did, for me, her son.

Though worn and calloused
were her hands, so gentle
were those hands to me;
they taught the tender
mother-love I'd never lost,
I'd never felt in Egypt's
hallowed halls of power
and fame. I know that what
she shared of One
Unknown, but known, was
crucial to my soul's release:
Go! Search THE NAME,
she said. It was as though
the world hung on
her words, its fate within
the worthy balances.

And, search I did!
The scrolls, the parchments,
and the stones—the tablet
stones—all these were blank
of One Unknown, yet,
somehow, known!
My quest remained elusive
till, within this arid place,
bereft of slabs with
wisdom's careful words,
my utmost joy: I came to
know of HIM right here!

MOSES–THE AMAZED
Exodus 3:2 – 6

The brambled branches
held, as yet, the jewelled
drapes of dew. The dawn
was rising higher; the sun
was hastening, once more,
to claim the peerless blue.
The rutted earth responded
with its shadows and
its shafts of light; the scene
was soothing to my sad
belaboured soul.

I settled to my work
of shepherding the flock
contented, bleating scarce
and keeping undisturbed
the peace of dawn's pure
hour. It seemed that I had

touched Eternity, and time
stood still upon the fertile
land. I gazed as one
transfixed—how well
the dew glows in the light,
I thought, and then I
realised my shadow lay
behind the shrub for here,
I saw a blaze was kindled.
Then it was I heard—
or thought I heard—
a crackling of the shrub
in yielding to the flames
though it was not, I found,
consumed in any way.

Do eyes deceive? Those
leaves now look more
verdant than before the
fiercest flame.
The magic arts of Egypt's
seers had never once
beguiled my gaze with such
phenomena! I took a closer
look, intrigued. How burns
this fire? What feeds
the flame when leaves and
branches aren't consumed?
I knew not how!

And then, a greater wonder
challenged me:
a Voice within, a Voice
beyond all thought—
the ear, or even heart.

This was enthralling sound!
And I, becalmed, had
neither power nor will to
run from it, no strength
to speak, to ask my question,
seek the unimagined Source
of Flame and Voice. And
yet I thought to bow before
the *LIGHT*!

You stand on holy ground!

The tone of the Unseen,
Unknown, required my
reverence; my feet to sense
the scene of holy ground.

My flocks content,
Their bleating scarce and,
in this place, this holy
ground, I knew a Presence
and a Power profound that
deigned to Call me near:
I AM! He said! My soul
then leaped! It is
THE NAME! The One
Unknown, now known!

*I AM the God of Abraham,
Of Isaac, of Jacob–Israel!*

I've found my quest! This
Presence is The One who
knows, The One who's
known! *I AM* is known!

MOSES–THE CALLED
Exodus 3:4 – 17

Moses! Moses!

Here am I! Who speaks?

*Remove your sandals,
stand upon this holy
ground. I call you hence,
to come apart, to enter in
My Presence for I AM,
the One you've searched
for all your years, the One
you've heard and known
from mother's knee.*

*Although THE NAME was
lost, yet I AM: He who
guided you and drew you to
this holy hill, to Horeb:
Mount of God the One who
knows your inner will,
your purposing to search
for God, to find The Name.
Moses! Moses!*

Yes! Here am I–You call
my name, my Moses name?

*I AM the God of Abraham,
of Isaac, of Jacob–Israel!*

I hide my face; I fear to
gaze upon the features of
my God for none can look
on God and live! I bow deep

to this holy ground!
I wait expectantly.

*Indeed, I've seen My people
at the kilns, the clay and
sands. I've seen all Egypt's
fierce brutality. I've heard
their cry, their bitter plea—
they always trusted Me but
hope was vanquished, dead.*

> *Moses! Moses!*

You ARE—You are the
YHVH-LORD!

*I grieve the suffering of My
sons. I've come to rescue
them, to bring them to a
Land of Promise, to a land
where milk and honey flow.
Now go! Your time to act
has come—your waiting
years are done! I challenge
you! Return to them and
bring My people out. Go!
Break the chains, release
the bonds, remove their
yokes, those slavish yokes;
My people need An Exodus!*

> *Moses! Moses!*

LORD! Who am I that I
should go? I've turned my
hand to shepherding!

*Now, I will shepherd you,
and lead you to this Holy
Hill and you, and all My
people, here, will worship
Me. Upon this Mount I will
be known of them and you.
I'll guide you here.*

But Who? O LORD, just
who, what NAME to give
to those who doubt my word
and ask, "What is
THE NAME?"

*The one who found
THE NAME now asks?
I AM the One who IS! I AM
the past, the present and the
One to come. Go forth!
I AM WHO I WILL BE!*

**MOSES–THE
MESSENGER**
Exodus 4:18 – 6:1

*Moses! Moses! Go, now:
Proclaim this news to all:
Israel is My first-born son!
Return him now to Me!*

LORD, that should shake
the Pharaoh's heart! A
stroke will come at very
least! The Hebrews are as
dust to him. How, then,
would he release the men

out from their wretched
kilns and bricks?

Moses! Moses!
Go say: Let My son go
that he may worship the
I AM at My holy mount!

Of all the things I'd say
to him, this surely hardens
Pharaoh's heart!
What 'Holy Hill' could be,
he'd scorn, beyond the
dunes of Egypt's dawn?

Moses! Moses!
Then, say: Now! Let My
people go that they may
dance the festival of their
release among the desert's
rolling dunes of sand.

I speak the words O LORD,
but how will Pharaoh
recompense my quest?
How could he smile on this?
He'll laugh our quest for life
to desert dust for this!

Moses! Moses!
I say: Now, you will see
what I will do to Pharaoh's
vile and vicious schemes!

Make haste, O *YHVH–*
LORD.
The troubles all intensify

they lay the blame at
Aaron's feet and, at my
own. Make haste to help!

THE PHARAOH
Exodus 6:2 – 10:29

The look of him! He dares
to come in camel coat, and
reeking of the camel, too,
no doubt. He raves about
some desert 'god' as
though some alien deity
would veil the radiance of
the sun and glowing moon
above! What awesome
power has he beyond
our gods? A creeping,
crawling rod—a viper,
snake? It scares me not!
By all the gods of Egypt,
now: I will not let slave
labour go from us!

The nerve of him! What
blasted nerve! Oh yes, I
well remember him from
early days. We played as
one, we did, in childish
ways and he, the first-born
one who claimed my
father's heart! I envied
him, though he, as one
of Hebrew birth, could

never rise to Pharaoh's
side and kingship of my
fatherland. He pleads in
vain. By all the gods of
Egypt, now: I will not let
those vagrants go!
The gall of him! What
gall...
The stench of blood is in
the air, and croaking
frogs, and stinging gnats;
these beastly flies, they soil
my bread! The creatures
of the field all die.

And now, this plague:
Erupting boils! The
heavens cloud with deadly
hail; the locusts swoop and
darkness dulls the dunes
and homes. My heart is
stone! By all the gods of
Egypt, now: I will not let
this people go!

THE LORD!
Exodus 11:1 – 12:30

*Your home is covered by the
blood, reclaiming blood, the
blood of an unblemished
lamb, besprinkled on
the door. The lintels of each
door receive, also, this sign
of grace: wherever blood is*

*found, the Messenger
of Death shall pass on, over
you. All those now sheltered
by the signature of blood
shall know My solemn news
is for the homes of Egypt's
men and families this night.
They'll know the grief, the
loss, bereavement brings
before the dawning light
betrays the scene of death in
home and field. The time
has come for your release.*

*I AM the LORD who
shelters you and bids you
come to eat in haste and in
the sharing of this meal
Recall: I set you free.*

*Your hurt is covered by the
blood—renewing blood! It
brings you life. The past
is dead, the dawn ahead;
the pascal moon shines on
the spring of your
deliverance. This meal
recalls your epic suffering.
These were the 'marah'
years for you–the taste
of bitter herbs, and gall; the
'haroseth' of mortar-bricks,
the gruel of slavery. But,
with it too, the free-will*

offering of thanks in
gratitude for life's release.
This cress reminds each that
in midst of pain, the spring
returns to comfort you!

I AM the LORD who
rescues you: Take up the
matzoth loaf and break it so
and, as you share
unleavened bread,
remember Me:
I broke your yokes!

Your heart is covered by the
blood—redeeming blood.
The pascal lamb is offered
for your soul's release.
From far before the dawn of
time, I've planned for every
soul's release; from far
before the dawn of time,
I've planned a Lamb for
sacrifice—the choicest
Lamb, the Father's Pet with
neither blemish nor of spot
will be the price for the
redeemed. The cost of 'life
for life' is given—an
offering of a sacrifice.

Your sin is covered by the
shedding of the guiltless
blood to cleanse the past of
sin's foul deeds and break

the bonds of slavery, your
servitude to sin is past!

I AM the LORD; your life is
in atoning, saving blood!
And as you share the cup:
Recall: the Lamb is Mine!

….. oOo …..

THE TRANSITIONAL YEARS
Liberty—Redemption's Plan
AARON
Exodus 12:31 – 14:22

It's there he stands with
shepherd staff in hand.
Alone he stands,
his vantage point, the height
from which his silhouette is
hallowed in
the dawn. Though, is he
shepherd or the mighty
'prince' of Israel—
the 'general'? He's leader of
this thronging crowd, this
rag-tag band of men, their
boys, and women with their
drapes and tents, their pots
and pans; their booty, too!
How strange that, when the
dawn of our release has

come, I partner him. The
very thing for which I'd
longed when but a little boy
and he, the babe. We never
chanced to play the games
I'd planned—I lost him to
the courts of Pharaoh and
to the princely things. We
hardly knew each other
then—a gulf had lain
between. But now, when we
are all but past our prime of
years long gone,
I find I stand with him!

The family prayers have
come to mind. The *YHVH*-
LORD—we've found THE
NAME—has heard our
plaintive cries and seen
our woe. He called me,
Aaron, out to follow, too.
And following, to share the
load with him—the
'shepherd prince' of Israel.
This hassled host will take
some shepherding for here's
the barrier: the reedy sea
impedes the path
of our advance. What now?
A mighty hurricane!

These waves are whipped
up by the wind; the
atmosphere is charged with
fear and apprehension,
for— behind—yet just a
mile or two away, the
rumble and the rising dust
from chariots. The Pharaoh
means to have us yet; he
need not haste! We're cut
off by the tide! So, he
will slash us down and rid
himself at last of us or, drag
us back to bake those
blasted bricks—I'd rather
die, released to sands!

Do eyes deceive? Is this a
mirage here, a trick of light?
The wind has lifted back the
waves for us and, there,
now Moses leads transfixed
in stance but with his
shepherd staff yet pointing
to the way by which
to find deliverance at last!
The slaves, now free, need
no encouragement to test
the sand beneath the sea—
they find it dry!
This nation comes to birth
in Exodus!

**MOSES, THE LEADER–
WITH ISRAEL**
Exodus 14:10 – 31

All Israel waits!
And, fear is in their rant:
Oh, Moses, did you find no
graves among the kilns that
you should bring us here
and leave us all to die?
What have you done?
We wanted to be left alone.

Did we not tell you, then,
far better for Israel to be as
slaves of Egypt, there, than
die upon the dunes
out here?

No need for fear!
The test is in the trust:
I plead, take courage here
and you will surely see
deliverance. The LORD will
act for you today. Be still
within your soul to see, for
Pharaoh's men will be no
more. The worst that they
could do is done, forever
gone! Believe, now trust
the LORD and you
will see!

The Angel of The LORD
strides on, ahead. I've seen
Him there. I just obey, that
we would know the way of
access to the Holy Hill

of God—beyond.
Wherever *YHVH* moves:
For them, the foe, it is the
Night. For us, the Day for
our escape! This strange
phenomenon, this beacon of
the darkest night:
our *LIGHT*!

Why cry to Me?

The LORD inquires!
I raise my staff and trust!
See how the waters part,
they now divide!
There is a path ahead:
it's dry! The wind abates,
the water now returns to its
appointed place and spreads
its mantle o'er
the sand. For Pharaoh's
men, a quagmire, then:
the grave!

**MOSES–
CHOIRMASTER**
Exodus 15:1 – 18
(Tune: *Europe–Ode to Joy*)

Holy, holy, is Your Name,
LORD,
The *Jehovah—El-Shaddai*.
You're our strength:
our song we raise

For our soul's salvation.
From the heart we bring
You praise,
We exalt Your holy Name:
You will reign in power and
grace, LORD:
The *Jehovah–El Shaddai.*

Holy, holy, is Your Arm,
LORD,
You have shattered Satan's
power;
You have claimed the
victory:
LORD, You rule in majesty!
You will lead us through the
valley,
There's a path through
sorrow's sea,
There's a way to liberty!
LORD: *Jehovah—El
Shaddai.*

Holy, holy, is Your Hand,
LORD,
Now outstretched in
blessing.
Who is like You, strong to
save us?
Lifted up by Your Right
Hand,

LORD, we worship You in
praise,
Awesome in Your majesty,
Glorious is Your holiness,
LORD: *Jehovah—El
Shaddai.*

Holy, holy, is Your Love,
LORD,
Precious and unfailing.
The redeemed receive
assurance
As we trek through desert
lands.
There is grace for every
weakness
As Your children seek Your
aid;
There is strength for our
endurance:
LORD: *Jehovah—El
Shaddai.*

Holy, holy, is Your mountain;
We aspire, LORD, to
ascend.
Grant us peace for our
abiding;
Let the columned cloud and
fire
Bring us to Your holy

dwelling,
There, within the sanctuary;
Know Your Presence in
adoring
LORD: *Jehovah—El
Shaddai!*

A CLANSMAN
Exodus 15:22 – 27

We'd travelled on with
spirits high beyond the
dunes due east of there—
The Exodus—where opened
waters of the sea stood back
upon a heap on either side.
Yes, heap! I'd never seen
the like of it before!
We marched from there
with songs of joy and
jubilant a full half day
or so. The sun bleached
down upon the clans and
soon the wonder of new
hope was lost e'er noon;
(though, not my own).

Our spirits plunged, as did
the sun behind us in the
afternoon near eve.
We passed the night—that
first of nights beyond The
Exodus—in mounting

agony all the day and night,
we'd marched without
a quenching of our thirst
that raged and threatened to
consume us all.
We'd been a day and night
without respite and then the
morning came once more.
The sands were still
as dry as dust with not
a single blade of grass.
And, some of us began
to think that a return,
maybe, to Egypt would now
cheer us more than this;
(though, not myself).

Another day wore on, much
thirstier than did the first.
The spinifex, it seemed,
began to wilt. And, so
did many of the clans.
I pitied them, the elderly,
the very young, the maids,
the maimed. When yet the
third dread day came with
such intense and deadly heat
more dire and drastic than
the first, the children wailed
the elderly complained
of this and that at length;
(though, not myself).

But, when the third day

ceded to the night, I must
admit, I joined the rest in
wailing and complaining of
    our plight to Moses,
    'shepherd prince'.

(We spoke of him as that,
    though, if one could be a
prince, it should be me for I
am Judah, son of Judah, but
I mind it not. Our Moses is
    the chosen one of *YHVH*
    (and I know it well.)

It was the 'shepherd-prince'
who now has led us to this
barren waste. We'd reached
    the direst, fiercest stage
of questioning his reasoning
power, his brain! Was this
    the actual route the LORD
had meant for us to take?
The clans might march right
        back to Egypt now;
        (though, not myself)!

Now here, beyond the third
of parching days, there was
no choice remaining for the
    either one of ways to go.
Return? Or, wander on? Our
strength had sapped, had
        failed–we'd waste
upon these desert dunes.

Just then, a stronger man
than most, who'd braved
the land ahead, had news
    for us of water close
at hand—just there, beyond
the nearest dune, in fact!
    (I heard him yell).

Our sore, and miraged eyes
refused, at first, to focus on
the swaying palms against
the blatant sun for it had
tricked like that a day or
two ago. A wonder, but our
strength revived, sufficient
    to be clutching at the sand
and crawling on to drown
our thirst within the
welcome lake! We sank into
    the cooling water there;
    (I plunged as well)!

What trick is this of fate,
or God, to drag us to this
direst plight then leave us
    here as desert waste?
    The water taken to the
mouth betrayed our fate—
the waters were but *marah*,
bitter and so putrid, rank,
for each of us, a bitterness
    upon the tongue with
    stomach retching up
its bile. There wasn't any

hope to slake our thirst:
we'd die upon the dunes and
mourned by none!
(Yes, me as well)!

There Moses stood before
the Clans. He heard our
grievous cries: As mute
as palm branch held,
he stepped right down
towards the *marah* waters;
stood, then flung the branch
into the muddy pool.
It bobbed and floated there
then stilled. The murky
waters cleared at once.
Then one young man
moved down once more
to test the waters there.
(Could I believe)?

A shout for joy! The waters
were made sweet, so right
for us to drink. I was the
first, I think, to thrash
the waves in ecstasy. We
drank! We drank our fill
(and more, I think)!

Then, Moses spoke to us—
already we are finding that
He knows the ways of God,
he trusts the LORD!
(I do, myself).

Moses said that *YHVH*
made the waters sweet;
'twas not the branch of
palm, nor weakest wailing
of the faintest heart!
The LORD is in this place,
he said. Now, harken to the
LORD, obey His Voice and
Will. Then, see His hand
at work for us. He means
to care for us, to succour us,
and bring good health
as well. We had a doubt
concerning this;
(though, not myself)!

I knew it would come right
before the end though, just
perhaps, allow me please,
the little doubt—just once
when I had all but died upon
these cruellest desert
sands… What's this? We
move again? To what?
To where, we'll go
(and me as well)?

LORD, help me not
to doubt Your plans
for us again, I prayed.
Perhaps it would not be
so long, or far, I hope—
this latest movement
of the Clans. I'm sure that

some would want to tarry
here at *Marah* now;
(though, not myself)!

I sensed still better blessings
than the first where *marah*
turned, by miracle so grand,
from mire to nectar—Oh, so
rare! What further blessing
had the LORD in store
for us whose battered feet
were blistered on the burning
sands?... So! Here's what
comes to those who trust
in His great Name, the ever-
present *YHVH Elohim*
for *Elim* Waters wait for all
who dare to leave yon
Marah's transient pool!
(and me as well).

Here, see the gracious Hand
of God—the many pools in
this oasis place are twelve!
Enough for each of us—
the clans are twelve! And
date palms live beside each
pool—as thirst is quenched,
our healthy appetite as well!
Ah, what a camping ground
we have—this is the gift of
God unto His own: a place
to rest, a place to gather all
our strength again. Our God
is surely *YHVH*-LORD!

His healing touch is all
we need. And, we are now
renewed in Him, and ready
for the next long pilgrimage
to 'Home' each time the
fiery, cloudy pillar moves—
this is our guiding beacon
for the day and night–we
dance to celebrate
this *Elim* camping ground;
(though, not myself—
I bathe my blistered feet)!

A CLAN MEMBER
Exodus 16

Come, quickly, Hannah
dear! There lies a frost
of purest white upon the
ground out here. I knew
not that the night was then
so cold that it would make a
frost. But there it lies! This
mystery feels not so cold
within this morning's light,
transforming for us all
the desert land to Heaven's
Land! The sun, it shimmers
on the dew; what beauty in
the early dawn today!

I'll melt this ice within
my hands and sip its water
to refresh my lips for there

is nought to eat this dew-
blessed morn, for us.
But, what is this?
This taste upon my tongue?
Why am I now so blessed?

Come, quickly, Hannah
dear! Now, tell to me,
please do, what manner of
a frost is this that tastes
of all that's best in food—
the sweet, the pure, and
succulent; so tasty too!

What *manna* of a frost
is this that brings to us
a breakfast and a lasting
lunch? We've all we need
throughout the day, today!

Come, quickly, Hannah
dear! It's Moses, telling us
that *YHVH*, yes, The LORD
provides for us today
and every day, except
the Sabbath Rest!

A WORSHIPPER
Exodus 16:23 – 36

It is the Sabbath Rest
from eve to eve, upon
the Seventh Day. I come

with quiet, untrammelled
tread, un-sandalled feet,
as would become the one
who enters in to God.
He would the worshipper
to know the ground
whereon he stands is holy
ground, as is this day
devoted unto holiness,
and worshipping, in prayer.

I silent come, responding to
His call, draw near the One
who welcomes into prayer,
delighting me to share in
Heaven's richest fare. And,
in His grace, I find my life
revived in joy!

It is the sweetest rest
from eve to eve, upon
the Seventh Day. I come
with folded hands and,
blessed! The LORD decrees
this day should bring
respite from toil.

The daily labour stayed,
demands of work set down,
and burdens lost in His
serenity, I enter in
His precious rest.

I'm prone to haste, to seek

His aid, reclaim my strength
and labour on but find
no time for inner calm.

Suffice this day to worship
Him, to find my soul's
release, and in this tranquil,
holy, desert place, my life
restored in grace.

It is a wholesome rest
from eve to eve, upon
the Seventh Day. I come
with free, unfettered mind,
the cares of yesterday
resigned, for He receives
the weighty load to lay
unburdened at His feet;
I lay it down most happily.

He shoulders it, my load;
the strain of toil is gone and
I am bless'd to know His
loving care. With longing
I would come upon
this Sabbath Rest to find
my shelter in the calm of
God. My mind, it calls
to Mind; it seeks His will
and ways. I find my soul
renewed in love.

It is the choicest rest
from eve to eve, upon
the Seventh Day. I come
with waiting heart; this is
the hour for trysting with
the LORD. The pilgrim soul
returns to 'Home' within
the place of prayer. He
waits to bless, embrace His
child, and I am held there in
His care. I come adoring,
speaking now the language
of the heart where lips are
stilled. The voice of prayer
requires no aural path
where awe transcends my
need. And, in His *LIGHT*,
He 'lightens' me:
I am replete.

MOSES,
MOUNTAINEER
Exodus 19

It reaches up
to pierce the heaven's
height, this mountain
solitary within the
wilderness. Alone it stands,
a sombre monolith of
granite rifts, a rock of ages
past, impervious to desert
storms and driven sands.
The air is still, the arid
wastes becalmed. There is
an awesome quiet and yet,

the calm is all but audible.
This is a fearsome place,
As though the mount be
habitat of One whose
holiness forestalls the
entrance of a pilgrim or,
a priest of sacredness.
It stands alone, apart.

It beckons me,
it bids me to the heights,
this massive awesomeness
within the wilderness.
Oh, yes, I know it well for I
was shepherd to the flocks
of Jethro near those
rugged peaks and here
I found THE NAME!

"I AM"
has led me to His Mount
again. He wills that I
would follow Him into the
heights, to scale these peaks
that I would know once
more His audience
profound! This is, indeed,
a holy place! Alone,
I come apart from them,
those milling, mulling,
Israelites.

I'll tread this upper ground,
in these heights. But, will
He deign to visit me,

and, what would be His
purposing? It yields its
place to One who treads the
heights—this holy Horeb
Mount within the
wilderness. The mountain
trembles as the mists
enshroud, a cloud to veil the
Face of God. I hear
His footfall near: He comes
to me. I bow, deep to the
ground, afraid to look on
Him—Eternity drawn near.
He speaks and Light is all
about, the rocks irradiate.
This is a sacred place!
And sacred is His Word to
me—I hear Him now:

I carried you on eagle's
wings, I brought you to
Myself. I will possess you as
My people here—a priestly
kingdom, holy, pure.
I've seen all that does need
to be addressed within
Israel: It's time to be
'discipled' in the Law!

..... oOo .....

TRANSFORMING YEARS:

Desert Discipline
Exodus 20:1 – 17

```
     //              \\
    //    I AM        \\
   //   YHWH-LORD      \\
  //                    \\
 //        1.            \\
```

I AM THE ONE TRUE GOD
NOW WORSHIP ONLY ME
(I'll lead to wholeness and
to holiness.)

2.
BEFORE NO IDOL BEND THE
KNEE TO WORSHIP IT
(Know Me and trust in My
unfailing love.)

3.
GIVE HONOUR TO MY NAME,
RESPECT ME FOR I AM THE
LORD
(Know there is a consequence for
one dishonouring the LORD.)

4.
THE SABBATH DAY IS HOLY:
BE AT REST AND DO NO WORK
(I, YHWH-LORD, have blessed
this day: let worship be your
quest.)

5.
GIVE HONOUR TO YOUR
PARENTS THROUGHOUT LIFE
(Love and care for parents:
they have nurtured you.)

```
     //              \\
    //    I AM        \\
   //   YHWH-LORD      \\
  //                    \\
 //        6.            \\
```

REFRAIN FROM
KILLING ANYONE
(Life is My gift to you:
(Cherish every living being.)

7.
MARRIAGE IS SACRED:
DO NOT DISHONOUR SPOUSE
(Remain true and respect
your marriage vows.)

8.
KNOW YOUR WORTH, DON'T
STEAL ANOTHER'S WEALTH
(By falsely claiming property
you'll reap a harsh reward.)

9.
SPEAK THE TRUTH ALWAYS:
ABHOR FALSE TESTIMONY
(Slander, lies, will jeopardise
the wholly innocent.)

10.
DO NOT COVET, IT BETRAYS:
ENVY NO ONE, CARE FOR ALL
(The assets of another soul
do not belong to you.)

MOSES, MAN OF LAW
Exodus 20 – 31

He calls me up to meet
Him here, upon the
heights of Horeb–Sinai,
within the wilderness:

Come up to Me upon this
Mount, Abide with Me these
days and nights
Within the covering cloud.

The Glory of the LORD
comes down to me; He
shares with me such
heavenly things within
the cloud. His glory glows
as does a fire: This is 'The
Writing Place'! He burns
a text with *LIGHT* upon
these slabs of stone.

His Finger etches out Ten
Laws, Decrees, by which
His people will discern
the ethics of the LORD
and live within His
holy disciplines.

I tarry here,
upon the highest peak
and Horeb glows as fire
within the wilderness. I am
immersed in cloud yet
LIGHT is here, of Him

the all-pervasive LORD!
His Spirit breathes, inspires
my soul with visions rare—
designs and shapes of holy
things—a tabernacled
holiness; He wills for us to
come apart and worship
none but Him.

This is 'The Pattern Place',
the way of entry, via the
blood; the offerings, the
inner lights; the garments
for His priests; the altars,
and the oils—the perfumed
incense to prepare for
prayer within this place.
I worship Him!

MOSES, THE LEADER
Exodus 32

O God!
What have they done?
This scene below, it reeks!
What horror greets me
here? This people of the
Covenant, how soon they
come to this! The western
sun has caught, exposed,
in light, the subtle glint
of burnished gold. They
bow to it: a golden calf!
An idol of the past, this

golden calf—so alien to
what we know—reveals
a truly wretched alien,
monstrous thing and,
lewd! The people fling
themselves about,
debauched and decadent!
I am appalled!

O God!
I came from them, that
day, to You, at Your
behest. I left them there
upon that barren waste of
land but in good, Aaron,
hands, I thought. I'd lost
the track of time up there,
upon the mountain peaks
of Horeb, scene of sanctity
so pure. It seemed like all
Eternity was in my grasp,
abiding in Your view
where sense of time
grew dim, not clear.
But, there was time
enough for them to be
forgetful of their promises.
And now, it comes to this!

O God!
I'm sick and tired of them!
Forever in their mulish
mood they are most surely
lacking in their gratitude.

They all complain their
woefulness but are
forgetful of the wondrous,
myriad ways in which You
comfort them in grace
each day. I wash my hands
of them, contempt is what
I feel for them! These
slabs of Decalogue
I cast upon the ground
of Sinai, these precious,
Holy Laws I cast upon
their lawlessness!
No more the written
Holy Law of God—
It splinters in the dust!

O God!
But what is Law? What is
its worth? Its use? The
Law can do no other than
reveal the face of sin! You
said, up there, that man
should have no other gods,
serve only You; that we
should make no idols,
graven shapes of any
living thing at which
to bow the bended knee,
our heads and hearts. The
Laws You gave were just
and true. And, in Your
Law, there is indictment
of the wrongs of vagrant,

sinful Israel, Your slabs
of Holy law: I grieve—
they're broken now!

O God!
The slabs are smashed!
They pointed to our many
sins and seemed to give
no remedies. Yet, for these
broken slabs of rock, I feel
bereft for they outlined
Your will, and ways, for us
each to obey. Thank God!
 I now do realise You
grant the Second Laws
upon the face of these new
slabs, another chance to
store Your Law upon
this ancient, rugged face
of sundered rock and yes,
O LORD, Your Word
within our hearts! We
hear Your Word, we trust
that You will lead us now!

AARON, THE HIGH
PRIEST
Exodus 25 – 40

This Holy Place
which stands supreme
within the centre of our
camp, was fashioned in

the Mind of *YHVH Elohim*.
It is a tabernacle that's so
aptly draped in woven
cloth with rich fine thread.
It stands, you see, a 'trinity':
The Outer Court–
the common ground of
worshippers–for us a shield
(as flesh to soul), in
guarding all the sacred
ground that is within
the Sanctuary:

The Holy Place,
the first of Sanctuaries,
(this curtained room),
is entered from the Outer
Court by way of the great
Brazen Altar for the daily
sacrifice of lambs and, see
the Cleansing Laver there,
before the doorway
opening, for none may enter
in with grimy hands and
feet. Then we may enter in
to God, we priests, to serve
the LORD within
the sacred Sanctuary.
This Holy Place,
illumined, as it is,
with the *Menorah* Lamp,
the sevenfold 'tree' of light
which never wanes but
burns throughout both day

and night, becomes the
inner place of prayer.
So, this is central to the
'triune' tent. We bring the
bread of every clan and lay
it on the Table, there, before
the presence of the LORD.
And, at the Golden Altar,
here, our prayers ascend
to *YHVH–LORD* within
this Sanctuary.

The Holiest Place,
beyond The Veil, that is,
the secret Sanctuary: this is
the heart of 'trinity'. Here
stands the Ark of Covenant.
Within the Ark is placed the
slabs of Law and also there
is *manna* sweet. Its golden
sentinels, two pensive
Cherubim, enshrine the
Mercy Seat stained in
atoning blood. Here dwells
the *YHWH*-LORD:
The Holiest One, whose
radiant *LIGHT* glows in
this Sanctuary.

The Holiest Place,
so simple is its frame yet
all surpassing in its pure,
majestic form! Here beats
the Heart of God who

deigns, designs, our joyous
worshipping. He bids us
come to Him, the LORD,
for He will bless us here, in
prayer. Would that the Veil
would rend that I may stand
within His great *Shekinah
LIGHT* before the Mercy
Seat, atoned, and find
my Sanctuary!

This Holy Place—
it harbours secrets hidden in
the Mind of God for those
to know who worship Him.
It hints at 'Trinity',
but He is One! And, where
is flesh of God that we
should see him, there, upon
the common ground of
Earth? And, should we
come to *YHVH* here via
sacrifice? But whose? Oh,
yes! There's something
more He has in mind
for us to know. So, could
this Veil be just as 'flesh'
to hold in perfect trust,
His Sanctuary?

MOSES, THE RADIANT
Exodus 33 – 34

He called me to His *LIGHT*,
The *YHVH*-LORD. I came

to Him, ascending on
the rugged Horeb slopes.
The mountain glowed like
as of fire upon the summit
peaks. The winds which
coursed along the gullies
there were sudden stilled.

They paused, to wait the
calm of His own Presence
there. I was enthralled in
utmost awe of Him, The
LORD, Eternal *Elohim*.
I hid by massive rocks
yet I would trust. I listened
for the Voice of calm, the
Voice that, not from great
earthquakes, but for the
inner soul is meant.

I heard Him, gentle, soft—
with silence all about—
speak peace within my
conscious thought. I saw
the LORD pass by—a sight
not meant for earthly eyes
but for the sight of soul.

I saw Him there! My eyes
then saw, within a golden
glow, the frame of Him,
when He had passed me,
right on by, majestically!
I felt the heat of *LIGHT*,

a light that burned within
yet singed me not upon the
skin—a *LIGHT* too bright
for human eyes.

Should I avert my gaze?
I thought. Could eyes
contain the sights
of earth, of skies, of holy
things within the Tabernacle
Tent, if once–this once–
I ventured one scant gaze
within this pure, *Shekinah*
Glow, to search His Frame,
His Face, His Personage?
The *LIGHT* was warm and
welcoming. His voice
invited tenderly with
grace divine:

Lift up your eyes to LIGHT!
My Glory shall now pass
this place before your face!

I long had yearned that He
would show to me the glory
of His being, the *YHVH*-
LORD, confirm for me
continuing care.

The burdens of the task He
gave to me would scarce
seem weighted ever more
in this perspective of His
grace to me. He called

me 'friend', *Shekinah* glory
glowed and, all around,
celestial *LIGHT* by grace
illumined me.

I walk within this *LIGHT*–
an aftermath of ecstasy for,
on the mountain height,
I met the *YHVH*-LORD
and stood within *Shekinah*
LIGHT. I heard Him say,
with my own ears:

My Presence shall be with
you and, you'll find your
rest, your joy, in Me!

He placed me in a cleft of
rock and covered me with
his own hand to shield my
earthly gaze from His most
Heavenly Countenance until
He'd passed by me.

And, then, I saw His frame:
Oh, glorious sight!
Oh, LORD, You've
favoured me", I said; "Go
with me down all future
years. Forgive our foolish
ways, our sins, our
wickedness. Receive us
as Your very own!

He signed, that day,

a Covenant with me upon
this face of rock, His
covenanting rule for life!
You tell me now, my face,
it shines? I'll veil *Shekinah*
LIGHT from all: This sight
is for The Tent and
Presence of the LORD.

BEZALEL,
THE ARTIST
Exodus 35 – 36

Yes, come into my studio!
I'll stay my hand the while,
it needs its rest. The touch
must be precise, the turn of
gold just right. It needs
deft handling of the tensile
tools and concentration of
the mind, to bring about the
craftsmanship for which
I, Bezalel, am known.
I am the Tabernacle artist
and I cherish all my tasks!

Do come and sit awhile;
the resting time is vital to
the artistry. This gentle light
evokes the shapes, designs,
imaginings sublime which
draw me to my very special
task: to seek, most urgently,
the capturing in gold and

precious stones of what was
first in dreams (I think),
implanted in my fertile
mind to bring about the art!

Come, see amazing crafts
my hands have formed.
But not my patterning,
you understand. It is the
LORD directing me...
His Spirit broods in me,
inspiring with these shapes,
unspeakable in beauteous
grace and matchless
elegance; exquisite in their
symmetry; and here, you
see, each dazzling in its
opulence for God Himself.

Come, share my wonder at
the moulding of these
crafts! He blesses me in
thought and touch, the
YHVH-LORD. My sensing
fingers feel the unformed
substances and look, the
shape appears that was
designed in the Abode of
Heaven, yet standing here,
supreme, those finished
articles standing within
my humble artist's studio.

Come, see the gifts they

bring, the worshippers, who
would their offerings give
joy to Him who is the
YHVH–LORD!

Materials of gold, of red,
and purple—each superb,
and fit for offerings. Each
gift is meant for God's own
Hand; each sanctified
so we may worship Him,
the *YHVH*-LORD,
for whom we build this
wondrous, tabernacled
Dwelling Place!

A CLANSMAN
Exodus 40:34 – 38

I love to sit
here, at the entrance
to my tent, as evening
shadows fall. I watch each
day—about this twilight
hour, according to the sun—
this wondrous miracle
of light. Observe it now
with me as all the peaks
of Horeb rise as sentinels
against the setting sun!
See how the shadows fall
across the Tabernacle Tent?
Near now, you'll see the
great light shine.

Behold it now:
that Columned Cloud above
the Tent: the evening marks
its change from softest
cloud to *LIGHT*.

This is a strange
phenomenon; the glow
comes from within and born
not of the sun. Deep
shadows of the eventide
are creeping fast across
the burning desert sands;
they reach our tents—
the day is now no more.
And, here it is! The
breathless holy hour:
the Columned *LIGHT*
is here for all to see!

How still it is…
The LORD is pleased to
dwell without the need
to hurry on. We'll 'bide
right here. But, when
the Cloud is fused with
urgent energy, we'll lift our
pegs and fold our tents for
pilgrimage. It is the *LIGHT*
of God's own Presence,
YHVH-LORD, within our
camp. His dwelling is
within the Tent. See how
the *LIGHT* now shines:

God's Guiding *LIGHT* is
here!

A CELEBRATING FATHER
Exodus 40

Come, Sarah child; now
place the garland of the
desert rose upon your raven
hair; it is the day of days!
We'll go with all the
families of Clans to stand in
our appointed place before
the Tabernacle Tent. You
see, embroidered is the very
last of Veils for hanging in
the Holiest Place. We'll
dance before the afternoon
arrives today in celebration
of this Holy Place, rejoicing
in the finished work.

Here, Sarah child; stay close
by us! With all the families
of Clans to throng and claim
a space in which to view the
scene where Moses is,
you will be sure to lose
your place! Come up, upon
my shoulders, dear: This is
the day for memories to
carry through the years.

This is the New Year's Day,
the New Beginning Day!
Now, have you chosen well
your resolution for the year,
my child? Remember it
tomorrow, too!

See, Sarah child: the
spectacle begins; the Priests
are dressed in all their
finery! They march towards
the holy Tent. There's
Bezalel, my teacher, he who
taught me how to work with
artistry so far beyond my
skill; he is so wise
in artist's ways.

He taught me very well in
purposing the finest work
and fit for worshipping the
YHVH-LORD. I worked
upon the Ark, you know. It
passed the searching gaze
Of him, the artist, Bezalel.

Oh, Sarah child: the great
Procession's underway.
They take the golden things
from Bezalel—in
sacred ritual. Oh, see the
sun's bright flashing light
shine on the gold and
jewellery. Spectacular,

the great *Menorah* Lamp
is carried in. Just hear the
gasps all round, in awe of
what is seen. All eyes are
fastened on the sight of
crafted, wondrous
crafted workmanship.
The Veils are all in place,
and Moses waits.

Look, Sarah child: see how
the entourage of Aaron with
his sons proceeds towards
the Tabernacle now. Moses
waits for them. They march
with measured tread. It is a
solemn thing that they will
undertake. They bow.

Anointing Oil is poured
and they are 'holy now
unto the LORD' and
separated unto *YHVH's*
holy, sovereign will.
Their priesthood will
remain: for this and all the
generations yet to be,
they'll serve within
the Holy Place!

Now, Sarah child: The Ark,
it comes. The *manna* sweet,
such as you gather in the
dawn, is placed within the
Golden Box together with

the holy Written Word
of Covenant—the Slabs of
Law! The Cover for the
Ark, with Cherubim I've
wrought with my own
offered hands, is set
in place. They've gone with
it beyond the Veil; the
Column Cloud emits such
LIGHT that glory fills
the Holiest Place.

AARON, THE HIGH PRIEST
Leviticus 1 – 7

My task is an atoning task!
I stand between The Altar
and the worshipper. He
brings his lamb for sacrifice,
and I present the offering
unto the *YHVH*-LORD,
the *El Shaddai*. The lamb
is pure, and innocent; no
blemish or of spot I find in
it, the eyes so doleful in
the last of setting suns.
Those eyes, they scan
my face as if to find
a sparing glance.

I place my hand upon its
head, expressing thus my
sentiment. I know its fate.

So trustingly its gaze rests
on my face. I turn
from it and take my knife.
I gash the lamb, deny it life;
I feel its heart, its vibrancy
no more, its life has ebbed
away. There nought
remains of it but flesh
and blood for sacrifice.

The Altar fire is burning
there—eternal flame—it
never fades, it flairs now as
the sacrifice ascends in
smoke: aroma choice,
unto the *YHVH*-LORD.

The worshipper has sinned;
he pleads his cause—
the LORD is pleased!
Forgiveness is His own
response to sacrifice:
unfaithfulness in humankind
is more than matched
by utmost grace!

The blood has flowed;
it seeps on down the Altar,
there. A life has gone
to God who gave it birth—
the blood, a life, propitiates
the wrath of God—He loves
us so! (Some raindrops
fall—could these be tears
of *YHVH*-LORD?)

This is a lesson for our
need: It costs a life to be
atoned, to be then
reconciled to God!

WHAT COULD THIS SAY
TO US?

THE PRIEST,
ORDAINED
Leviticus 8 – 9

The one ordained by God
must come for cleansing,
whole: without, within.
The washing of the hands
and feet, anointing of
the head with oil and,
flowing as it does all down
the coursing of my beard,
I'm cleansed today and
sanctified to *YHVH*–LORD!

This linen tunic folds about
my flesh, the purest cloth;
the sash is cast about my
waist. The robe is donned,
the ephod, sacred garb, is
placed upon the robe
to clothe the priest.
The jewelled breastplate
forms a shield of precious
stones to bear with *U-rim*,
Thummim, decide their lot
in mysteries of God.

The sign of golden
"Holiness" surmounts
the turban on my head—
the priest most high is
sanctified to stand within
the Holiest Place:
just once a year—on the
Atonement Day.

My sons stand, reverent
at my side and robed in
priestly garments, too.
They bow for their
anointing now with oil.

The blood of sacrifice
is poured for consecrating
priests. A touch of blood
upon our flesh and on our
garments too, the blood.

We stand, atoned by blood,
belonging to the LORD
for life is in the blood!
He grants us life to serve
within the Holy Place for
we are set apart for prayer—
our prayers! The ritual now
complete, we stay within
for seven days for dread
of death if once we stray out
from the peace of *YHVH's*
Sanctuary. And then, upon
the seventh day, we are
released from

thralling mysteries! We
come before the Altar here
and bow before the
awesome Presence of the
YHVH–LORD:
His glory shines within the
Tent: our consecration is
complete: whole and holy.
Now *YHVH* smiles on us!

AARON: THE
ATONEMENT DAY
Leviticus 16

The day I dread is here! It
may demand my life as yet
for I must bring the blood of
sacrifice unto the Holy Ark
and sprinkle it across the
Caphah Lid—the Mercy
Seat—within the very room
of Him, the *YHVH*-LORD!

My sons are dead for
treating it with less than a
true holiness. They trod
distrustfully and moved
within the Holy Place in
mortal pride and artifice,
corrupt. I mourn for them,
my sons; on this Atonement
Day with all their sins
laid bare. How may they
stand on His great

Judgement Day? How may
I enter in beyond that Veil,
to stand before the all-
consuming Majesty and ask
these eyes of mine to look
upon the Cherubim, to view
the Mercy Seat, behold the
Caphah— Cover—there,
of gold most pure atop the
Ark: the site of His Abode.

His Holiness is there the
most acutely known. How
may I stand there with
the sacred things of God
Most High? There's nought
to shield me from
His wrath if I should,
careless, tread into His
searching sight though it
be all but momentarily.

I do believe I have the
special right to come.
My sacred course
is set, here is the sacrifice,
the kids of goat made ready
now and held there, at the
Gate, in readiness.

Divest me of the priestly
garb, The finery described
within the Book of Rules.
The precious things—

unique, the rich, ornate
embroideries: I cast them
down and take the clothes,
the whitest linen clothes—
so plain and primitive in
style but purely white.
These give to me the mode
by which I may approach
the Utmost Holiness—
the *YHVH*-LORD.

I have, in dreams, observed
of One, the Highest Priest of
all. Perhaps it's to be
centuries before He steps
upon the common soil to
don, one day, the linen
garb—a breathless moment
in Eternity. I dream of One
who has the right, the One
to answer sin! And, He
would rend the Veil in
entering the Holiest Place
for our release, atone for
sin—the Sinless One,
the once, for all!

I understand it not, my
dream. It is a ghastly
scene—unique! A
nightmare gruesome in
extreme. I shun, I fear,
that 'Lamb' of Sacrifice
where Priest becomes
the choicest Offering!

Unthinkable, that God
would, sorrowed, look upon
that sacrifice for sin, receive
it through rent Veil;
this death, vicariously, for
sin atone! And yet, I can't
erase this dream out from
my contemplative mind.
(I think there's something
more for me to learn!)

My reverie, though, takes
me from my solemn task
this day! I take the stones—
the *U-rim* and the
Thummim—to decide the
fate of each of these two
goats: the one, a scape—
the other, slain today:
atoning sacrifice.

The blood is drawn, it sits
rich red within the Bowl.
The utter climax of the
sacrifice now comes. I am
beyond the Veil, with
hyssop branch to sprinkle
drops of blood upon
the Ark. Does this atone for
me and for all Israelites:
the sins—the mighty
and the small?

I feel a peace enfolding me.
This awesome room

is feared no more! I sense
a smile of *LIGHT* upon my
face. A wholesomeness
envelops all of me. It is as
though, this day, the LORD
receives me to Himself
and grants me life renewed.
I stand atoned, revived:

I AM AT PEACE—
AT ONE WITH GOD.

MOSES: THE
FESTIVALS
Leviticus 23

Now, hear, O Israel!
These are the Feasts you
will observe—the Seven
Festivals according to the
spoken word of *YHVH
Elohim.* I, Moses, speak
His sacred ordinance. I
would that you could
hearken now!

These Festivals,
these seasons of your
fervent joy, reveal
allegiance to your God.
You will acknowledge that
your sweet provisions are
His mercy on unworthiness,

He means to mortify your
sin in consequence of the
Atoning Sacrifice. You will
discover His forgiveness
and His reconciling acts
of grace and be restored
to Him and know His inner
peace, The *YHVH Elohim.*

Hear, now, O Israel,
His sacred ordinance for
celebrating all the Feasts
and fasts—the Festive Days
and Weeks. This is the
tabulation of God's
guidance given for all
rituals: the rules and rites.

The SABBATH rite must
stand as basic to the annual
festivals. This day was first
ordained within the dawning
years of time that's known,
the Day of Rest when
Elohim had brought
to being: for six of seven
days, the tasks of labour
will suffice but, on the last,
the seventh day, do take
your rest, enshrine this
lasting ordinance to
celebrate—in all the
generations yet to come—
assembling to regard

His sacredness.

Hear, now, O Israel:
On the most sacred date,
recall the past upon the
evening of Nissan—
the fourteenth day—and
mark this sacred 'PESAH'
time for, as this special
night will come,
remember well
The Exodus and thence,
the Feast of PASSOVER,
(of life escaped from death).
This brings your utmost joy!
The yearly Feast begins
upon the morning of
the fifteenth day.

No yeast shall 'work' your
bread and, every day within
this week, the Festival
requires that bread
unleavened shall be made.
This is a lasting ordinance
to celebrate—in all the
generations yet to come—
assembling to recall our
great deliverance from
Egypt's sullied soil!

Hear, now, O Israel:
In Sivan, mark you well the
harvest—days of HAG
HABIKKURIM—

the reaping time of wheat.
With First Fruit Festivals,
bring in the sheaves, the
first of grain, the first
of days, unto the priests for
waving in the Presence of
the *YHVH Elohim.*
Do come, the first
of seven days,
when Sabbath is complete.
(This will be a day of days)!

The *YHVH*–LORD
accepts the wave, together
with the sacrifice—a lamb
without defect. And, with
the wine of offering and
grain ascending in the
flames, so pleasant, come:
celebrate as 'one' in joy
this lasting Ordinance
in generations yet to come
when all assemble to record
the LORD's own wondrous
faithfulness.

Hear, now, O Israel:
In following the First Fruit
Feast, you'll count full
seven weeks, continuing the
HAG SHABBUOT
for fifty days from first
Sabbath for, on this final
day, the new grain offering

will be presented to
the LORD: two loaves of
finest flour and baked with
yeast—together with the
sacrifice of rams, of bull,
of goat, of lamb without
a blemish—this, the best
aroma, pleasing to the
YHVH-LORD.

Do know, by these, the
peace, the joy, of God.
This is a lasting ordinance
to celebrate in gratitude,
in generations yet to come,
assembling to recall His
Providence.

Hear, now, O Israel:
The special month of Tishri
will commence with ROSH
HASHANAH—the Feast
announced with trumpet
blasts. It is a day of rest:
Attempt no work but come,
in worship, to the altar fires
of sacrifice this day.

Return your thanks for
blessings of *YHVH's*
gracious, guardian care.
This is a lasting ordinance
to celebrate in thank-
fulness—in generations yet

to come— assembling to
recount the Lord's own
loving-kindness to us all.

Hear, now, O Israel:
the tenth of Tishri Day
denotes the date of YOM
KIPPUR–the Reconciling
Day. Deny yourselves
by fasting and present
yourselves before he LORD
by fasting and present
yourselves before the
LORD in humble penitence.

It is the day when sacrificial
blood atones for sin of priest
and people, both, the all as
one—the priest enters the
Holiest Place but once each
year, beyond the Veil for
all, presenting self in ritual
where blood is spilt upon
the Mercy Seat for here,
the LORD receives the
intercession of the blood,
for all, yes: all!

And, this Atonement Day
shall be a lasting ordinance
to celebrate—in generations
yet to come—assembling to
recount for all, The LORD's
own righteousness.

Hear, now, O Israel:
In Tishri, too, shall be the
feast of Booths–HAG
HASSUKKOT.
Your tabernacles shall be
made from branches, and
the boughs of trees. Make
your abode within the
booths for seven days.

This Feast shall bring
a true remembrance of
the families that, once upon
a time, their only shelter
was a booth when *YHVH*-
LORD did bring you out
from slavery to this, the
desert place, where you
were formed into a nation
sacred to His Name.

Within this Feast, select
the choicest fruit from trees
and palms. Rejoice before
the LORD in each of seven
days, plus one! And, this
shall be a lasting
ordinance—in generations
yet to come—assembling
to respond unto
YHVH's Sovereignty.

Hear, now, O Israel:
These are the *YHVH*-
LORD's great Feasts.

They are appointed for
a holy convocation—where
each one of them includes
the sacrifice where joy and
sorrow for our sins become
entwined: The sorrow for
the sins each one of us have
perpetrated in the year just
gone; the joy expressing
what we know of how
the *YHVH*-LORD receives
our sacrifice throughout
each thankful year.

Our prayers, our
thankfulness, for all His
care for us, His guarding
and His guiding through the
year, for all His providential
care, ascend. He then
forgives us for each sin.

We celebrate in this—
and in the generations yet
to come—assembling to
reflect upon God's
perfect Holiness.

THE LIGHT BEARER
Leviticus 24

Menorah sheds its light
within the Holy Place. It
shines in praise of *YHVH*-

LORD. The pure, the clear,
the oil of olive flows. It fills
the bowl in each *Menorah*
branch as was constructed
in the lamp. It feeds the
seven stems of light that
never wanes; the night
escapes its rays. Such night
can never douse or conquer
the *Menorah's* burning
light. The night's right place
is outside, in deep darkness
of the arid desert sands.
God, the Eternal *LIGHT*,
has conquered all the night
by His creative power.

Menorah casts its light:
My silhouette is seen upon
the folds of curtained walls.
If there would be a shadow
cast upon my earthly path,
grant that it be indicative
of You—the LORD of
LIGHT— who stands by me.

Oh, *YHVH*-LORD, so let it
be that all my life shall be a
silhouette cast in the mould
of worship, and of prayer
each day. O LORD, I pray
that the *Menorah* light so
shines as to illumine all my
days and ways and be a
beacon that attests Your

Presence with me now.
Menorah grants its light
as token of Eternal Day!
This light which often I've
discerned in worshipping,
reflects the *LIGHT*—
Eternal Flame: The *LIGHT*
of God, the very Source of
LIGHT, that they may see,
the Israelites, a sign of God
in me. As light does carry
nought of night, of shadow,
or of stain, but shows it up:
so may my light be carried
worthily with nought of
shadow on my soul to mar
before the people of the
LORD, the Holy *LIGHT*
of *YHVH*–LORD in me.

THE TABERNACLE BAKER
Leviticus 24

I'm represented in the bread
that stands upon the table in
the Holy Place—the bread
of Clans—for every Tribe,
a loaf of bread,
and representative of
Jacob's sons. My tribal loaf
is placed together with the
Presentation Bread, as

'shown' before the very
Presence of the LORD.
I'm represented here;
LORD, could my bread,
when consecrated to
Your Holy Name, be broken
ritually to feed the hungry,
nourish them? How stands
my brokenness for them
—how nourishing, my life,
as broken 'bread' for them?
Oh, break my bread this day
for them, the poor,
Dear LORD.

A PRIEST AT PRAYER
Leviticus 24

The sweetest scent of
prayer; the tone, the heart-
felt sigh, arises in the
fragrant style of purest
incense, here, ascending to
the *YHVH*-LORD.

Aroma, scented deep and,
oh, so pungent, takes the
urgency of faith, though
weak, as incense lifts its
'breath', like prayer
ascending to the
YHVH-LORD.

Receive these prayers, O
LORD, these intercessions,

for the needs of those who
cannot find a prayer within
themselves to lift,
ascending to the
YHVH-LORD.

My prayer of thanks, as
incense flows, is lifted now
within this worship
stream of honest gratitude.
Receive this earnest prayer
for grace ascending to the
YHVH-LORD.

My prayers adore, esteem,
the LORD; I bow in *LIGHT*.
A heart-felt word, it is
sincere, serene, as faith
aspires like holy incense
from the bowl this prayer,
ascending to the
YHVH-LORD.

THE JUBILANT PRIEST
Leviticus 25

My times are in Your hands,
O LORD,
my times are Yours for to
control, decree, the length
of days, the seasons and the
years. Two score and nine,
the seven years of seven:
these years have

been fulfilled today.
Since I was birthed,
You've nurtured me.
With this in mind,
I come to Jubilee!

Rejoice awhile, my soul,
Before the LORD, for all
before the LORD, for all the
ways His loving-kindness
reached into my life to add
this priceless joy! Through
days of doubt I knew the
shadowed stress of fears
and misted tears.

These sorrows also come,
awhile, to summon me to
grief. I've lingered in the
pain of them those many
days and nights, until You
came to comfort me,
O *YHVH*–LORD,
with gentle hands to lift me
from a dark despond and
give me back today
my vibrant life!

The springs have followed
on from winter's chill; the
summers followed spring,
and You have brought me to
my autumn days full
mellowed, ripe of skill
in wisdom's years:

Bring in the Jubilee!

I give You thanks,
O *YHVH*–LORD,
for every year an added
grace, it seems, has
followed on along the path
that You did plainly set
for me. I bow in humble
gratitude: I recognise
the good that flows
upon these sands!

I consecrate the coming
year unto Your providence.
A mercy You dispense,
the liberty of man and
land and beast—a Sabbath
Rest of years—the seven of
the seven are past and duly
given is our ordinance.

In years to come, this day
will be the reconciling time
for friends and families,
a time for the return
of those transgressed of
years. Your ethics, LORD,
would set the sacred tune
and tone to celebrate the
national Jubilee!

All that I have is Yours,
O LORD: the land, the fruit,

the flocks; Your people are
but sojourners to tend
the Promised Land
beyond these desert sands
and usher in Your great
Redemption Plan.
…
O LORD, redeem my soul,
in this, my Jubilee!

……….

THE CENSUS TAKER
Numbers 1 – 4

There is a place for
everyone of righteous form
and faith who lives in God's
community! The national
heritage should now
be known by tribe and
family. And every man is
known by name! But first,
select the man whose godly
character denotes the leader
traits of faith and fealty.

All know these men!
They bear distinctive marks
of true nobility. By these,
each represents his Clan.
The whole community, in
rank on rank of men, will
come according to their
ancestry. The strength of
Israel, God's people here,

is represented now within
the lists of first-born men in
every tribe and home.
The strength of each will be
assessed: the census
numbers those assigned
to take up arms. And then,
aside, the Levite men,
whose strength is otherwise
engaged, their task
is now to serve the LORD!

Their task is set, secure; it is
their joy to serve the LORD
within the glow of the
Menorah, shining in the
Tabernacle Tent. Each Clan,
its place, each man his task:
Israel is organised!

AARON'S BLESSING
Numbers 6:22-27

*SHALOM (Peace):
The blessing of the *YHVH*-
LORD be yours in heart,
in home, in hand.

SHALOM:
The blessing of His keeping
power be yours to guard
each day.

SHALOM:

The blessing of His Shining
Face be yours to grant
you lasting joy.

SHALOM:
The blessing of His
countenance be yours,
enlightening your life.

SHALOM:
The blessing of His gracious
hand be yours to comfort
and to guide.

SHALOM:
The blessing of His
Presence now be yours to
calm your soul in peace.

SHALOM:
The blessing of His Holy
Name be yours: He IS
your ALL in all:
SHALOM.

THE WORSHIPPEER
Numbers 7

What offering may I bring
to place in worship now
before the priest? I have but
empty hands, I have no
hoarded wealth.

I've known a leanness
through the years of slavery;
the precious gold
was sparse when baking
bricks—the wage?
a measly stew of grain!
What could I offer
YHVH-LORD?

What offering can I give
to grace the Holy Place?
I have but trinkets handed
down in heritage. I've kept
them carefully through
years of slavery. There are
no hoardings, large or small;
what gold there is within
these rings could be
of little worth to
YHVH-LORD.

This offering I can bring
to place before the LORD:
the gift of hands—I offer
Him my strength of days,
to serve Him well;
also, devotion's mind
to meditate upon His ways
and open heart to thank Him
for deliverance, my
YHVH-LORD!

....

MOSES, AT TABERAH
Numbers 11

Just look at all of them!
They huddle at the flaps of
tents; they whisper, groan,
bemoan their wretched
fate, and rouse their
neighbours, there, into
a state of ire of me who'd
been so very bold to rescue
them from their most
grievous state of slavery!

Observe the stance on
each of them! The rabble,
how they raise the dust
with stamping feet,
disgusted with their
boring daily fare: the
manna and the springs
that quench their thirst
at oases so clear and wide,
enough to succour and
to save that thankless,
snivelling lot of them!

They cry for onions, and
the leeks of Egypt yet.
So, let them cry, I say!
And, once they'd peeled
these fine vegetables,
they'd cry again and
that's for certain, sure!
They would go back—I'd

let them too, so glad to see
their stubborn backs,
that moaning, mumbling
mob! We long for leeks!
they moan; they crave
each day for change,
for Egypt's vegetables and
fruit. They cry, so fast
forgetting all the pain they
knew at Egypt's kilns.
They're bored with
similarity! Their moaning
pays a price: They've
angered *YHVH*-LORD!

Are they my children
now, this motley hoard?
O LORD do You expect
that I should carry them
as babes within my laden
arms? Do You require
that I should ever be
their caring, codling
nurse, accept their sins?
Why nurture them at all,
I ask, these simpering
Israelites?

They moan again for
meat—it's unavailable!
They wail the while until
my ears are full of their
unjust complaints! Where
do I get the meat for such

as these? I cannot carry
thus, this people anymore,
myself! The burden's
great and more than I
from now can really bear
of every one of them!

If this is how it is to be,
then, take my weary life—
this very moment. Now!
If I have found some
favour in Your gracious
sight, then grant me rest—
Yes, give me peace! The
insolence that's thrown
at me each day is always
undeserved. This deep
disgrace I can no longer
bear... You'd come right
down to us?

You'd bless the Elders,
too? You'd grant Your
Spirit now, to them, the
Holy Spirit that You
granted me when first
You called me on into
Your *LIGHT*?

You'd give them all
the strength they'd need
each day? For Israel?
You'd act for all today?
You ask, *Israel, into the
Tent* for consecration

and for grace? That, when
the morn shall rise, the
meat will be supplied?
There'll be so much they
will not dare to ask for
more again? They'll be
surprised, amazed?
They'll cry, This food
is now enough!?

But, LORD, the meat?
You say, More than
 enough for all?
 How could there ever
be enough for such
as they? Do You expect
I'd feed them all? How
could there ever be
enough if all the herds
were slaughtered whole,
and all the seas were
harvested—enough, for all?

I've said more than
enough, it's true!
When will I learn to hold
my mouth? I should
have known! The Arm
of *YHVH*-LORD is
never short. He sent
the quail in from the sea
upon prevailing winds.
The Spirit Wind has also
come and we rejoice
in Him: He IS, our LORD!

MIRIAM, THE PREJUDICED
Numbers 12

And so, it comes to this
at last! a banishment from
Israel and all I hold most
dear is gone! I've found
abandonment of rank
and all responsibilities
as well, cast out from tent,
my family, and friends,
as tumbleweed on desert
sand; I'm scattered on the
restless winds. I've taken
seriously my many tasks:
I held strategic claims to
leadership. It's only what
was due to me as sister of
'Moshe'–Moses, of course.
One couldn't leave it to
the likes of Zipporah! It
really wouldn't do to have
Zipporah brought to
prominence and take a
civic stance in camp!

As prophetess, yes, I was
sought to soothe, cajole,
and speak of all the
oracles which came to me
upon the winds, or so it
seemed to me. But speak
I did, and much on his
behalf, my harassed kin,

in camp where everyone,
from child to chief would
would claim his precious
time, his patience, too.
I only sought to stand
by him, to share the load,
to take just some of the
burdens from his mind.
Aaron too, we spoke of it,
the load that Moses bore.
We sought to take our own
right place for we're the
older two. We'd shielded
Moses from his birth.

I'd raced, for him, beside
the Nile to care for him
then gave him up to
mother's care—in palace,
I in hut. Those were such
sorrowed years. But then he
came to us when as a man
and most mature, refined,
he sought to stage the
Exodus. He needed our
support, our guidance
and our coaxing ways
with every tribe—
so loathe they were to
leave the past. But finally,
they came with us. The
Exodus was underway!
I've held strategic
prominence with songs

and also tambourine.
They looked to me for
everything. And Aaron—
statesman that he is—
and oldest of the Clan,
deserves as high a place,
or higher yet, than
younger brother Moses,
who'd tend always
to stand alone, not seek
our help, our seasoned
guidance there, our
wisdom and our aid.

Our age holds precedence,
you see, and Moses ought
to know us well enough
that we would never
undermine his lead. But he
is handicapped. He needed
Aaron from the start, his
speech so halting, so
constrained! He really
ought have given us our
rightful place beside him
there, in charge of all.

I've been concerned since
when he came to introduce
us to his bride. Imagine, if
you will, my own dismay
when, on that day, she
turned to face me in the
brightest light. So! This
is Zipporah, his wife?!

Yes, devastating in the
least, my shock, my
startled gaze. He had not
told, or warned us, of the
fact his Cushite bride was
dark! Yes, *DARK!*
How could I deal with
that? An alien? And *dark*?

How could he do this thing
to all his loving family who
had thought the sun and
moon shone out of him!
The rightful need for a
just acknowledgement
has caused us all so many
tensions in a suffering
Clan where no one cared.

I've said my piece! I've let
him know she would not
do to take the place
of prophetess within the
camp. He really does not
see the point! They say
that truest love is blind!

I've tried, with brother
Aaron too, to steer the
Clans away from her.
And that is when I really
overstepped the mark,
it seems. I grieve the day!
The Cloud, it moved. The
LORD, He came to make

His own displeasure plain.
But, sorrow for myself,
I found His righteous
judgement fell on me!
I felt the first hint of
abandonment of hope for
then the Holy Presence
Cloud removed from me.
I'm bereft of life and love.

O God! I think I see the
LIGHT, the point of it,
my own disgrace! I've
come to understand
a little more, the years
of wilderness, the years
of loneliness, my sister,
Zipporah, has had to bear
of hate and prejudice and
blinded pride. I've found
it's not the skin that takes
the colour of the soul.

My skin is whitest white
yet I am shunned. I am
as scum of all the Earth.
My hands, my face, you
see, are leper-white! I'm
banished to the wilderness.
I've learned, at last, the lot
of those whose colour cuts
them off, adrift from those
who set superior sails
and, slander penury!
I see: It's fellow-feeling

that does make us
wondrous kind–
and 'wise', of course!
I've heard it said, and I
agree. I am alone as she,
Zipporah's been, alone
through all the years!
O LORD that I could
now return to welcome
her, the sister that I never
had but always yearned.

O LORD, I plead. I know
that *YHVH*-LORD does
care for us, His people,
even in this arid, desert
place. And, He has never,
and He won't abandon
me. I know this now for,
in my deep need, I sought
His aid. I prayed that He
would hearken to my cry.
I've learned that true
humility will bring to me
His care; one day, I'll see
my family again!

CALEB and JOSHUA
Numbers 13 – 14

It's Caleb, Sir, reporting in!
I've taken time to greet my
wife then came straight on,
forthwith, to you. The dust
of desert sand remains—

forgive my unkempt mode
of dress! The views, our
news, are much too grand to
leave it yet another hour!
See, Joshua is at
my side; he'll share
with me in this report.
We've quite a tale to tell!
It was a fascinating brief
you gave that day to us.
We've walked a 'thousand
miles', or more, we think.
And, every mile held
challenges each day!

A wondrous journey, Sir!
The land ahead is more
than we had hoped that it
could be! My strength
renews in retrospect
of every aspect of that land.
Ah! Now I see the other
Ten—the team is
congregating, too.
I'm sure that our reports are
all you'll need to judge
logistics, take your
cognisance of each to plan
the course we'll take to
forge ahead and claim the
Promised Land.

O Moses, Sir, the Promised
Land! We've never seen the
like of it! I fear we cannot

fully detail all its beauties,
panoramas, or abundance of
its choicest, wondrous store!
I think it more than all
the rest of Earth could
surely offer us to feed
and nurture Israel.

You will be thrilled
with our complete report!
Now, Sir, I here present the
whole report. You'll find
that I've combined my
comprehensive coverage
with Joshua's own 'Three-
Point-Plan' which he'll
elaborate, in turn. I bring,
therefore, the survey's
scope and he, the martial
strategy by which to take
the land ahead of us
in conquering, forthwith,
the wondrous whole!

So, first: 'The Panoramic
View': We stood together,
he and I; our eyes beheld in
morning light, the Salty Sea,
of which we've heard
in heritage folk-lore, from
birth. Towards the north,
there flows a stream of
living water—Jordan's tide.
It flows a gentle stream of

water through the LORD's
own wondrous Promised
Land. Now, Joshua:

My greetings, Sir!
It's good to see and speak
with you once more. Good
health to you: *Shalom*!
The river is strategic to
our plans. It's clear to me,
we must assess the season
e'er we cross the stream.

At times, it will be
treacherous. And then, when
floods abate, a simple task
for such as us. The site to
cross is chosen now—
I've marked it well! So,
Caleb, tell:

A fortress stands not far
from Jordan's western
shore—in native parlance,
Jericho. Its walls are
massive yet, we know in
YHVH's strength, it's ready
for the conquering!

We stand assured:
All Israel's children will
survive! Please, Joshua,
announce just now the
'Three-Point-Plan' that
you'd engage to take this

fort, and on, forthwith, into
the Promised Land:

The plan is set according to
this basic stance:

1. *YHVH* stands at battle's
head. We will not move
ahead of Him—we'll seek
to know His strategy.

2. Take COURAGE for
the fearful, weak and
wavering can have no place
within our entourage. The
need to meet opposing arms
will call for strength of an
unwavering faith.

3. True DISCIPLINE!
I cannot stress enough this
vital aspect of the task.
We've much to learn in
this regard. We'll have to
hone our fighting force
to conquer all the land.
The Plan, therefore, shall
be expressed in this great
battle-cry:

FAITH, FORTITUDE,
AND FORWARD *GO!*

I, Caleb, will now set the
scene ahead: the route we
took from there forthwith,

then plunged us deep,
surprisingly, into some
canyons there. On every
side, majestic hills
unfolded, one on one,
like as the rolling waves
of seas engaged with winds
and flowing tides. The steep
terrain, however, does not
present us with an obstacle
too stark for us—we train
for such as every day we
march through all the
blistering heat and harsh
abodes of desert sands.

But then, the view:
stupendous, marvellous!
We stood, silent, to savour
it! We stood awhile on
mountain heights to wait the
rising sun. A stream of light
flashed from the distant east
to show Moriah's height
where Israel's patriarch,
Abraham, once almost gave
his son for sacrifice.

He found that *YHVH* held
the lad quite safe. There
stands the city—Salem, oh,
so fair! Just right to raise
a holy Temple there for,
one great future day,
a new Joshua will come,

to bring to liberty and light
all those who dwell
in shadowed vales.

Rise up, O Clans, to claim
your heritage—the
Promised Land—where
milk and honey flow like
mountain streams

We turned due north,
forthwith, from there along
the length of land. There is
a central spine of rugged
hills and vales. And, from
a vantage point, we saw
the sea and all the land of
coastal plains and northern
strand—a rich and verdant
pastoral land where flocks
are grazing peacefully.

And, oh, the fruit and
vegetables, such as the like
there never was! We ate to
our content from many olive
groves, fruit-laden trees.

Let's waste no time. Yes! in
the morn let's galvanise
invasion plans for we
are ready for the march
ahead where *YHVH* means
that we should go:
On, to the land supreme

The Promised Land He
offers us!

I, Moses, now will speak!
You see these spies, the ten
who came into the camp
before you both returned,
their prior reports have
previously swayed the
Clans to nameless fears.

Advance can never, at
this time, take place—not
while this generation lasts!
The LORD has made His
judgement on the spies
and Clans!

So slow to anger is the
YHVH-LORD: His love
abounds, forgiveness lows,
yet He decrees justice,
and punishment for guilt.
The men who saw His
glory in the Exodus and
Horeb-Sinai, rebel
and fail in faith of Him.
They'll never see the
Promised Land;
they'll die in dust of all
these arid desert sands:
Our youth will take
The Promised Land!
It is the youth who will
go home and be at peace.

THE CHOIR
Numbers 21:12-20
Tune: *Quam Dilecta*

Spring up, O Well divine,
To quench my thirsting soul;
Restore this life of mine;
O LORD, renew the whole.

Flow deep, O Well sublime,
Refresh my fainting heart;
To me Your waves incline,
And flow through every part.

Flow out, O Well pristine,
A crystal, flowing tide;
Come, purify, refine,
For cleansing, I abide.

Flow wide, O Well, combine
The dancing sunlight and
The rippling waves so shine
To draw me to your strand.

Flow on, O Well sanguine,
Each desert place redeem.
The joy of life is mine
Within Your healing stream.

....

A SMITTEN CLANSMAN
Numbers 21

He led us to this pit of
snakes, this Moses—man
or beast is he to lead us to
this ghastly place? These
snakes will surely mean
our death!

I'm bitten now! I feel a
sharp, excruciating pain,
so staggering my death
will come e'er long, before
the sun declines beyond
the dunes!

We plead for aid; the
rising tide of pain, and
fear of death, has made
the valley ring with cries
of abject suffering.
O God, do quench this
grievous pain.

The poison pangs are
reaching to the hearts of
those of us who writhe
in agony among afflicted
kin whose terror knows
no bounds.

While life ekes out, we
plead in hope that *YHVH*-
LORD relents an ire of sin
that drove us to this pit.
O LORD, redeem us or
we die!

I see that Moses lifts his
staff and on it is a snake
of bronze! The sun strikes
flashing light upon the
burnished snake: I hope
in it!

The pain abates! I feel,
anew, a cleansing of the
blood. I am redeemed! In
looking to the staff raised
high, we are now saved
by faith!

BALAAM, AND HIS ASS
Numbers 22 – 24

Did this, my braying ass,
just speak? Or, am I
dreaming wasted dreams?
A talking ass? I am the ass
for thinking donkeys bray
in words! And yet I heard,
distinct, a voice!

The ass I heard? Or,
someone else? The whole
affair has gotten out of
hand! I search the sense
of it! A talking ass? Indeed!

And yet, the strange events
just past would make me
wonder if I heard my
stubborn ass speak truth
at last! They wanted me
to preach a curse upon
the Desert Clans just now
approaching from the arid
south—the Moabites are
fussed with fear!

My client, Balak—he is
the king of Moab—pleaded
for a curse! I know full
better far than that—
to speak a curse on *YHVH's*
troops! Refusal none would
take. I found myself, at their
command and now about
to be cajoled to curse.
I spoke of my own
reticence. They growled!

I swear I heard that ass of
mine say something plainly
unto me. In acting queer,
it would not budge.
I took my strap and slapped
its flank. The wretched
beast lay in the mud!
I kicked it in the shins;
it brayed. It said, as clear
as my own wife, it seems!
What have I done, deserving
this catastrophe,

deserving this challenge?
And then I saw the reason
why! The angel of the
LORD drew near. He surely
put me in my place.
The braying ass it seems,
no wonder went to Earth!

I've sinned again. I spoke
the word of my regret and
patted happy beast. We
went upon our way with
clear instructions from the
LORD! In Balak's presence,
I did speak the oracle of
God on them. The blessing
of the LORD I gave, no
curse! I'd be as they! What
have you done? the king of
Moab then inquired in ire.

I speak but what the LORD
requires, I said. He fills my
mind and heart with truth
which I would speak or,
dread a consequence.
I spoke the second time.
Again, a blessing on the
Clans of God. The LORD
will speak, I said, then He
will act. He blesses us!

Now, hear another oracle:
the oracle of one who sees
and hears the visions and

the words of God:
How beautiful is Israel!
How beautiful your tents,
the place of your abode.
The valleys bloom as
gardens there, and river-
lands will fill your store
at harvest time.

No use to vent your anger
now on Balaam for you all
were warned I'd speak
but from the LORD. I warn
you now: your future's
grim! I see Him, though not
nigh, behold Him from
afar—a Star of Dawn,
arising as a Mighty Prince,
with sceptre and a crown.

He is the conquering King
who comes into this
world, advancing through
the years, the future years
of time ahead. All Israel's
wondrous strength is drawn
from Him—He is the
Everlasting LORD whose
reign will know no end.
He reigns!

MOSES, AND HIS
MEMOIRS
Deuteronomy 1 – 31

Bring now the writing slabs
to me, the stones, and
carving things; The time
has come to set it down,
the record of the passing
years. We carry, bound,
within our stocks, the slabs
of Law and history that
YHVH-LORD required
to be set down
for future heritage.

Now, take your tool! We
start today to write the text
I mean to use in my address
to all the clans on *YHVH*-
LORD's appointed day, as
planned! The Introduction
sets the scene, begins the
saga as God speaks:

*You've stayed enough on
Horeb's plain. Break camp,
advance today! Advance
towards your utmost aim:
your entrance to the
Promised Land.
I've given you this land:
Proceed! Possess your
cherished heritage!*

The early days were tense
with all the varied aspects of
the tasks the *YHVH*-
LORD required of us.
Those griefs did not, at first,

Memoirs cont.

assuage our fears.

The elders of the tribes were
then selected for their
wisdom and their strength
of character, to share
the heavy load on my
behalf.

Then, as the LORD
commanded us, twelve spies
were sent to view the land
to bring back news of how
we'd fare. Your courage
failed; you failed!
What grief!

You thought of giants, of
city walls, and fearsome
fighting men, when all you
had to do was trust the
LORD! You would
conquer, never fail!

You've seen how God did
carry you as fathers carry
sons who tire before the
noontide's due; He went
ahead, prepared the way
for faltering Israel!

I have to say, as well, it was
because of you my feet shall

fail to stand upon the land
I'd longed to view
all through these
forty years.

It's Joshua who'll lead
the way across the Jordan to
the land. Your children will
inherit it, and they will
march to conquer
every fear.

You've sinned, repented,
sinned, throughout the years
of pilgrimage, but never
truly learned the ways of
YHVH-LORD; you angered
Him, the LORD!

It was upon your sins our
route in circles went—not
truly on, and never truly
back, those years; such
wasted years as faith
grew dim!

You'd learn respect for
Jacob's land, you shall
desire that special strand;
but how you fared is
wondrous still in *YHVH's*
generous care.

The days of battle were both
fierce and sparse; your

Memoirs cont.

enemies were fought with
YHVH-LORD: delivering
all for faith!

You've nothing lacked; He
led you all the days,
companioned you within
the cloud, instructed then,
rebuked for failings,
and for sins.

To all the youth who will
proceed: The Promised
Land of God has been
prepared for you from Sea
to Kinnereth.

I pleaded with the LORD,
Do let me go to tread the
Beulah Land and there,
to worship You. He said,
in language clear and plain
to me:

*Enough! You'll go to
Pisgah's height.
But Joshua, the champion:
commission him,
encourage him;
he does not share your
mortal plight.*

Now hear, O Israel, the
Laws by which I govern
you—I teach but what's
directed by the LORD:
turn not: His ways
applaud.

Observe these Laws of God.
Your wisdom, then, will be
as *LIGHT* to nations round
about; they'll test your
ways respecting
YHVH–LORD!

Let not your hands forget,
nor let your memory dim,
of all you've seen and heard
these many years of Him:
Remember still the
YHVH-LORD!

Those Horeb days, they
brought to birth this nation
under God; the mountain
blazed with fire; GOD
wrote the Decalogue!

He gave the pattern for your
life; do worship Him—no
shapes of stone, or carving,
take to worship them
on pain of death
for sin!

Memoirs cont.

Become corrupt, then, as the
night does follow day, the
judgement of the LORD
will flow, consuming you;
He'll scatter you on
alien winds.

But, if you seek the LORD,
you'll find Him when you
search for Him with all your
heart; He will be found of
you. Be true to
Covenant!

Consider now the former
days—all creation's plan:
where are such schemes as
these, the LORD's design?
This nation, *YHVH*-LORD
has planned.

These works were wrought
that you would know the
LORD is God—beside Him
is no other god. You've
seen His deeds and heard
His words.

Acknowledge that
the *YHVH*–LORD
is God. Now take it to your
heart this day; keep His
decrees, commands,

I give to you this day,
as planned.

I've set before you, in this
screed, the record of these
forty years; we've traced
together good and ill, the
light of joy, shadows
of pain.

Now, take the tool once
more to write: a second saga
is to be, as quoted, written
down. Observe, Israel,
the scope with which
we write.

The Covenant has been
confirmed as is—No, not
the Covenant of Abraham,
but *YHVH's* word to us
when He did speak as face
to Face!

The Voice of *YHVH* echoed
on the Mount, out from the
Cloud—through flames of
fire, He spoke: He showed
His Majesty.

And, on that day, you did
agree whate'er the LORD
commands, you'd keep,
you'd listen and obey.

Memoirs cont.

The LORD is pleased
with fealty!

Now, show you care to
follow in the ways of God—
walk in the path He sets,
prepares, for future years
for you'll prosper, live
for Him.

Now hear, O Israel,
the LORD our God is ONE!
Love God with all your
heart, soul, and your
strength; write this upon
your heart!

Impress these Laws upon
your young, converse with
them at home, and in
community; enshrine the
Law on hand and head,
for memory's sake.

When you shall come to
cross the stream and take
your heritage in towns and
farms, be careful to remain
as faithful in the time ahead.

And, make no treaties with

the men of alien lands; do
not entwine their families
with yours for they will
draw you to a
wicked way.

The LORD, your God,
selected you from all the
people of the Earth; you are
the people of His choice,
you are His treasured,
chosen race.

He chose you to possess
the land; He'd promised
Abraham just that. With
mighty hand you were
redeemed! Yes! He is the
faithful God!

God keeps His Covenant
of Love with those who
keep their word. And so,
you'll live in health and
wealth, and blessed
by God!

Remember how the LORD
your God has led you on to
humble you, to test your
hearts and if you would
obey His word, His ways
applaud.

Memoirs cont.

He nurtured you and
succoured you, sustained
you through the years; He's
bringing you into a land
of living waters and on
verdant ground.

You've found that bread
alone does not suffice, it's
by the word of God. Let not
your all-sufficiency, lead
you to pride. He gives
you all.

It's not by might of any
righteousness you've
gathered to yourselves: you
enter in the Promised Land
by His own choice, not what
you earn.

I've prayed for you and
yearned for you, I pleaded
with the LORD for you;
your sins would lead to
death but for the boundless
grace of God.

Forgiving you, the LORD
decreed His holy Laws by
which you'd live; and,
written by the hand of God,

these Laws reside in
offered blood.

And now, O Israel,
what does the LORD, your
God, now ask of you? Do
trust His word, resolve to
love and serve the LORD
always.

Observe the LORD's
commands—observe not
with the sight alone but in
the heart of you: they're for
your good, by God's own
matchless grace.

Now, cherish all the words
of God—embody them
symbolically; yes, hold
them, bind them, keep them
for the peoples yet
to come.

Remember well all your
relationships—you are a
people treasured, choice,
as holy to the LORD; of all
the people of the Earth
you're His!

As thankful people, come
before the Presence of the

Memoirs cont.

LORD, to bring your tithes
into His store, and there
rejoice in praise of Him,
your LORD.

Be liberal with your open
hands, supply the poor and
overborne; do give as freely
as you're given, not
grudgingly, but running
over all!

The blessing of the LORD
be yours: In coming in, and
going out, you're blessed; in
home and health, in fruit
and flock, and family:
all blessed!

I've set before you in this
screed, the record of the
Covenant. We've traced
together good and ill,
the **shadows** and
the *LIGHT*.

Now, take your tool once
more to write the final saga
of my words: we've viewed
the terms of Covenant, the
Covenant renewed!
Through all these

forty years, the LORD has
led; your clothes retained
their warp and weft; no
sandals were re-heeled
throughout!

You ate no bread and drank
no wine; your daily fare was
from God's hand, that you'd
know He is the LORD: His
love for you has known
no end.

You stand before the LORD
this day: do know He comes
to you, confirms and seals
the Covenant so you would
be, forever His alone all
your days.

The secret things of the
Most High are mysteries
to mortal men; but those
revealed are as the *LIGHT*
that we may follow in
His Way.

The Covenant is in your
hands; none needs to reach
to Heaven to bring it down;
nor far away, o'er sea.
His word is near,
today!

Memoirs cont.

No need to swim that
farthest sea to reach the will
of God; His word is in your
mind, it's in the heart. Obey
His living word
today.

The LORD now sets before
you here, a prosperous life,
or tragic death; it's in your
hands to make the choice
—obey, or disobey:
your choice!

Be strong, courageous in
your heart. Be not afraid,
nor terrified; the LORD
is with you all the unknown
way. He'll never leave, will
not forsake.

This Law, as writ, shall be
reread in every seven years.
When debts are cancelled,
time is set! Make ready now
your sacred vows
to make.

Here, **shadows** and His
glorious *LIGHT* are cast on
sacred slabs of Law; there's
LIGHT enough for grace!

In *LIGHT* the **shadows** are
dispelled!

THE CHOIR
Deuteronomy 32:11, 12.
Tune: Crimond, C.M.

'The Eagle Song'

LORD, lift us up on eagle
wings,
Above Earth's binding care;
You carry us, encourage us,
In the abode of prayer.

You stir the soul, entreat
us now,
Far greater heights to dare;
You challenge us to trust Your
grace
Within the realm of prayer.

Released to soar, on wings of
joy,
Into the heights so rare;
Your Spirit-Breath will bear
us up,
Up to the Light in prayer.

Transcending earthly sight
and sound,
Of hallowed peace aware,
Our highest aim: to seek
Your Face,

Commune with You
in prayer.

Descending from the heights
sublime,
The daily task to bear,
We claim the strength
imparted in
This sacred hour of prayer.

THE CHOIR
Deuteronomy 32
Tunes: Spohr, 8.6.8.6.8.6.

'The Song of Praise'

O sing in praise of God
with us,
His matchless love proclaim!
Descending as the showers
on Earth
His tender mercies came.
Abundant streams of grace
now flow:
O, glorify His Name.

O share in praise of God
with us,
His wondrous works forthtell!
He is the rock, the Righteous
One
Who has done all
things well;
His faithfulness endures

through time:
His perfect ways extol!

O praise Creator LORD
with us:
He formed, and made
us His;
He claimed us for His own,
He called
Us from the wilderness
To find new life in Him;
He stoops
To comfort our distress.

O sing of all His saving grace:
Through all the desert lands
He brought us near to guard
and guide
us with His powerful hands;
He lifts the soul on
eagle wings
to soar in light's expanse.

O praise the LORD, His
mercies stand
Though oft we fail Him so;
His loving-kindness leads
us where
The oil and honey flow.
Sustained and nourished by
His grace,
We would be faithful too.

Rejoice, O people of

the LORD,
Extol His righteous ways:
The LORD is all-compassion
with such loving grace!
O praise His steadfastness,
this Mighty Rock,
Through all our length
of days.

MOSES:
THE BLESSINGS
Deuteronomy 33

The LORD has shone, as
LIGHT, upon the Tribes
of Israel. He rides upon
the wind as glorious,
all-conquering King. His
Heavenly Hosts accompany
Him. And, when all Israel
comes, assembling and
worshipping, these are
my Blessing Prayers:

:::

May **Reuben** live in
prominence, preserve
his soul from death;
may all his tribe increase.

The cry of **Judah**, hear,

O LORD, and bring him to his
people there, defending them
with strength of hand and arm.
O may You bring him victory
against his many foes.

May *U-rim* and
the *Thummim*, too,
remains in **Levi's** hand.
You've surely tested
him and he has kept
Your sacred word.

He's guarded all the covenant:
He offers incense prayers
and sacrifice upon the Brazen
Altar, there. Oh bless his gifts,
increase his skills, eradicate
his many foes.

O **Benjamin**, beloved of God,
now rest secure in Him: the
LORD becomes your Shield
and carries you aloft
as father does, his son.

Let **Joseph** yet be blessed:
May precious dew from heaven
fall and mingle with the flowing
depths of streams throughout
your watered land. The
choicest gifts of rugged
mountain heights,

the fruitfulness of endless hills,
the Earth and all its fullness
and the favour of the *YHVH-*
LORD for ever fall upon the
prince of all—majestic prince
he is, with strength of oxen that
will trample all his foes.

Now, **Ephraim**, and
Manasseh, too,
their Clans combine
a mighty host.

Rejoice, O **Zebulun**. Rejoice
Issachar, your going out, your
coming in, is blessed.
Joy in abundance of
the rolling seas,
and treasures of the sands
are yours—O may your
worship righteous be.

And, blessed is he who
strengthened **Gad's** domain,
he rules there as
a Lion—the choicest land
is his; in leadership, may Gad
command.

The precious Clan of **Dan**
is playful as a cub of lions.
The lion will spring—
he rules his land.
Abounding in the favour

of the LORD is **Naphtali**
enriched—in choicest
blessings rare, he'll own
strategic land.

Most blessed of sons are
Asher's sons for he finds
favour with his kin; with
fragrant oil his cleansing
streams. And strong will be
your gates: as iron and brass,
secure; and, as your days,
so shall your strength
forever be.

The God of **Jeshurun**–all
Tribes of Israel–is He who
reigns in Heavenly Majesty.
Eternal God is He who is
your refuge and your strength.
And, underneath,
supporting you, the Everlasting
Arms!

:::

How blessed you are, O **Israel**,
where is the like
of you? A people saved,
secure, in God. Your shield
and weapon is the LORD.
In Him you dwell secure!

....

MOSES:
HIS
BENEDICTION
Deuteronomy 34

My times are at an end;
I've penned the final slab—
the Log of Law, the Civil
Codes, the Ordinance
of God, are all consigned
beneath the tool,
it seems, as written by
the hand of God—
although He gave
to me the tool. I turn from
texts of Law and such:
A stirring's in the air.

E'er long, the Cloud will
move and Israel will all be
gone from here. They stand
upon the verge, these many
hosts of Tribes; they wait
the sign which calls them
forth to stand within the
Promised Land.

But as for me, my heart
is home! I've known a
harmony with *YHVH*-
LORD that eased the pain
of my regress when I, in
anger, smote the barren
rock, transgressed the
holiness of God

and I, who always
challenged sin, did sin. His
judgement stands!

I've lost my hope to cross
the Jordan's tide. Now He's
forgiven me—He calls
me 'friend', He speaks with
me as face to Face—
Shekinah Glory yet still
glows within my heart.

And now, the end does
hasten on. I now have
appointment with
my LORD
to keep and one more
journey yet to make before
the end of it—the life
I gave to Him when in my
prime: to take this people
out, achieve The Exodus!

The deed is done. It is
fulfilled, the calling that He
gave to me. I see Israel now
folding up their tents and I
must fold my own—then,
walk towards The Dawn!

The day I've longed for is
now here! This Nebo is so
very steep, though there is
strength in me as yet!
I climb… My gaze is on

the Face of God; I see with
clarity the scene He means
for me to view before
the day is done...

And now, on Pisgah's lofty
height, I see, it seems, the
whole wide Earth spread out
before my weary feet.
This Jordan strand, this
lovely land; these fields,
these flocks, these folds—
I see the whole of it and I
rejoice in what He promises
to those who covenant with
YHVH-LORD.

And more, I see! My gaze
was fixed on Canaan's
shore—it was our hope,
the aim of pilgrimage, to
take God's gift for Jacob's
brood in processing the
cherished Covenant.

But, what's Beyond—when
flesh decays? We did not
see beyond the limits of
a land so very fair as this.
But Oh, the view today!
Beyond this strand,
I view my Promised Land!
My body will return
to dust. What care?

I need no more this veil
of flesh, I dwell in
Beulah Lan...

..... oOo .....

THE
TRANSPORTING
YEARS

SETTLEMENT
The Promised Land

JOSHUA, THE
CHALLENGE
Joshua 1

I miss him so! His towering
strength, the wisdom of
successive years, his solid
and his unquenched faith
in God set him apart,
enabled him to hold our
trust to follow him
to mountain and to arid
wilderness. But all the while
we marked his gaze—
it faltered not from Face
of God. He was the friend
of *YHVH*-LORD!

The Challenge

And I, the captain of the
fighting force, was pleased
to call him friend. I served
him many years in outcome
of the Call of God. He laid
His hand on me; somehow,
I knew the ordination of
the *YHVH*–LORD!

I felt the Holy Wind breathe
deep within my soul and
I was fortified that day,
made whole, and equal to
the task. Without experience
as this, the flesh would fail
for fright of every
consequence in all the hasty
judgements, all the rash
displays of novice
leadership which I would
convey. Perhaps, I'll fail the
LORD… The *YHVH*-LORD
has come to me—His words
were so encouraging:

*I'm with you, Joshua! Just
as I was with Moses, just the
same! I'll never leave, I'll
not forsake. You know he
was My friend. In just that
way, I'll be with you!
Be strong, therefore, take
courage. And take care to
nurture all the Law that's
found within your heart.
Let not this Law depart but
meditate upon its words
both in the light and when
the shades of night are dim.
Do not be terrified! I AM
The LORD: I walk with you!*

I have my first address to
make—My officers will
take the words of my
commands to Israel.
I must convey to them
my confidence in God
lest they should falter for
their grief of him who left
us near to Pisgah's height
those days ago. My courage
does not fail—I sense
the Fire of God within my
soul. The message that I'll
give to galvanise the Clans
to cross the Jordan now,
is that of *YHVH*-LORD.

RAHAB, AND THE SCARLET CORD
Joshua 2

A scarlet cord upon a
window frame—so vivid in
the light—That's all I have
to seal my fate. I have the
word of men who came

to spy the land, take stock of
all we have, and what they
mean to have when they
invade.

A scarlet cord—a 'line' of
blood—such colour in the
sun— the signal of a saving
grace! And, grace it be for
such as I if only I could trust
the words of them, I'd know
I'm free when
they invade.

This scarlet cord—I take
the sign as a lifeline of hope
this day! I'll trust this line
that marks my home:
The God of them, I trust.
He never fails in all His
strategies: I will walk free
from fear when
they invade!

JOSHUA, IN COMMAND
Joshua 3 – 5:12

I've had this strategy to
hand for nigh on forty
years, it's true! And, Caleb,
you'll remember it so very
well; we spoke of it when,

from our first foray, as
spies, we came to Moses
with the plan that
complemented all we said
when putting forth our
own report in face of ten
who disagreed with us.

WE CAME, WE SAW,
WE MEANT TO
GO!

But, here today we are as
one—we mean to follow
God's command to pass on
through the Jordan stream
and reach the western shore
dry shod! The strategy is
this: We trust!

The *YHVH*-LORD is in
command. Take boundless
courage: all for all. Then,
on we march to conquer
now: The catch-cry of
this mighty host:

FAITH, FORTITUDE,
AND FORWARD:
GO!

Ahead of us, a thousand
yards, the priests will take
the Ark of God to guide—
we'll see the way ahead.

This night we consecrate
ourselves; in light of dawn,
the march begins: Prepare to
see amazing things!
The LORD will show that
He's with you and me, and
all Israel. Draw nigh
and listen to His words:

> *I AM WITH YOU SO:*
> *NOW FORWARD*
> *GO!*

Choose twelve just men
from all the Clans and, as
the Ark proceeds ahead to
enter into Jordan's flood—
behold, the wondrous power
of God: You see?
The water flows back on
itself to stand erect, a 'wall'
to guard us as we pass
on through the path it
makes. The priests now
stand on driest ground:

THE TIME HAS COME
TO FORWARD
GO!

The twelve just men,
selected now—Each man
of you must choose a rock
out from the river-bed
where priests now stand,

the Ark aloft. Go, take
them over to the western
shore. Each will be placed
to serve as sign for a
memorial. These stones
will call to mind, in future
days, this act of *YHVH-*
LORD to save us all!

GET INTO STEP AND
FORWARD
GO!

We knew The Exodus and
how the waters of the sea
rolled back but covered
Egypt's men. We now have
seen, this day, repeated
miracles! The waters of the
Jordan flood rolled back for
the invasion. Now we stand
on holy ground! The Ark,
the stones, are in Gilgal—
Tonight, we celebrate
the sacred Covenant!

WE STAND AT EASE,
WE FORWARD
GO!

JOSHUA: THE
ENCOUNTER
Joshua 5:13 – 15

I stood by Jericho

to muse on what the day
would hold. I claimed a
message from the LORD
in prayer. But then, in
looking up, I saw him there,
right on my path—a mighty
man of valour, all supreme.
He drew his sword yet, it
was strange, I knew no fear.

I stood my ground and
asked what was the man's
intent—against, or for us
was this man who stood at
arms? He smiled at me,
magnificent in stance and
speech. At once, I was
'disarmed'! It's neither,
for I stand now in command
of all the armies of
the *YHVH*-LORD!

I came for your awareness,
that the *YHVH*-LORD sees
right prevail today!
I fell to ground in awe of
him, in true amazement that
the LORD would so reveal
intent of Heaven. I asked,
What is the message of
the *YHVH*–LORD?

*Already it is given: the
ground on which you stand
is holy ground!*

This was the Angel of the
LORD!

RAHAB, IN JERICHO
Joshua 6

The eastern road from
Jordan's flow is empty yet
for none do go from here
and none do come. There is
an air of waiting all abroad.
We lack a freshening
breeze, the birds have
ceased their song. The
children cease their play.

They whimper and the men
of war are huddled in a
crumbling heap for fear of
what is heard around our
ancient town concerning all
the Israelites. The gates are
shut and barred. The guards
upon the tower, attending to
the scene, are still, alert, but
anxious, quiet: they wait for
all those hoards to come:
the Israelites.

I've found my vantage point
and peer across the 'scape,
out from my window for a
sign of them today.
But, nothing stirs, not e'en
the scarlet cord I've hung

strategically, down from the
window frame. There's
deadly calm, the palms
hang drooped, the sycamore
is still. A breathless hush
occurs—so very calm.

We fear for they
will surely come upon
us soon: those Israelites.
The city holds a fear of
doom as though a darkened
cloud descends, a deepening
pall of utter gloom.
Yes, they will come:
the conquering Israelites!

I see a distant stream: the
hordes of Israel become
a milling, moving mass.
I hear a wail upon the wall!
My scarlet cord is small,
a flimsy thing in face of
what I see. How will it serve
to bring the recompense
of what I've done for
Israelites? Yet, I will trust
this fragile scarlet cord.

Somehow, I know they'll
keep the promise that
they gave; they swore it by
the God of Israel! I've
bargained for my family,
too. They hope the scarlet

cord will hold for them,
releasing them to live.
The conquering force now
comes as rank on rank
of marshalled hosts—
a never-ending stream
of them, the Israelites!

The battle looms—they're
here! And, what a sight.
I have no words to speak of
it. This is a vast procession.
See their trumpeters and
fighting men and, priests
beyond the fighting men.

Look there: a golden box
with folded wings of
cherubim atop—a glorious
thing. See how the sun now
seems to choose this centre
piece on which to focus all
its searching beam.

The *LIGHT* reflected is
much fiercer than the sun!
What can it be, this box?
Revered it is and processed
slowly and with due respect,
so solemnly ahead of
them: The Israelites.

And, then, towards the rear,
more fighting men. But,
what is this? The fight is not

engaged? They march on
past and round the wall they
go. A curious thing
and no mistake. And, not a
sound they make! No priest,
nor armed, nor parent, nor
the children there, do
sound—except that
awesome, rhythmic pound
of marching feet, though
nothing else for us to fear.

An eerie calm, more quiet
than when before they came
but for those tramping
feet—the tread of
them, the Israelites…

Now, what is this? They
speak a preachment to our
king and all the men of
Jericho! A preachment of
the Majesty of God Most
High! A standard to behold,
and keep, of reverence and
holy fear of all that is
defiled? This speaks to me
of sins that must
be cast aside.

There is a need to vouch
that, if we chose to follow
wholesome ways, receive
the hosts of Israel as friends
and, welcome Israel's God

as well, we'd all be saved
and, always free! They do
example Godly ways,
these Israelites…

It's been six days of solemn
tramping of those feet and
silent trumpeters! The daily
march is on its way once
more and, seven days
it has now been! It almost is
a comic thing to see them
come so silently and go so
mute but, regal too,
this spectacle at Jericho.

The march is almost done.
But, no! they come again…
And then, again…
the fourth… the fifth…
the sixth… the seventh time
they march, we've been
encircled seven times.
:
The trumpets sound,
the people shout; the
thunderous noise of it!
An awesome force
we feel…

The walls! The walls,
have fallen down!
The bricks are crumbling as
I speak and screaming chaos
fills the air.

They come for us…
My family's safe.
We'll stand close by
the cord. The fire begins,
the city's razed.
But I am one with them,
the Israelites!

ACHAN
Joshua 7

Yes! Yes! I know the ban;
I've heard the terms He
set—the LORD! I think
it's mean for does He
really mean that there's
to be not one thing for
myself, not one?
Just look at these! I've
never seen the like—this
Shinar shawl, the shekels,
silver, and the gold!
And, here I am, alone with
all this sumptuous gain.
They'll never know.
My cloak is very large—
voluminous, you see!
The cloak will hide this
pretty horde and I'll
return to camp and stash
the precious loot from
prying eyes! There's men
who've died today and we
were on the run.

That men from Israel
should die so soon
beyond the day of
triumph–Jericho–oh, no!

The LORD has failed
to come to help us here
at Ai. He said He would
so, why should we know
an ultimate defeat?
Oh, no! they say it is
the *YHVH* Ban! The Ban
has been defiled. I stand
condemned in my own
soul. I coveted, and so
I took, concealed the loot
within the shadows of
my tent. These hands,
my greed, have sealed the
fate of all the fighting men
who died. So I, myself,
must pay the price.

Yes! Achan, son
of Carmi, me! I've sinned!
I brought the spoil into
the camp and doing that,
I brought the sin that
claims my sorry life.
My final gain is nought!
My name means *trouble*
and I found it so
tonigh...

……….

JOSHUA: VINICATED!
Joshua 8

A sorrow is upon us here,
we grieve the passing of
our fighting men. And
Achan too who brought us
to this plight where all seem
punished for the sin of one.
A punishment?
Ah, no! This was a
consequence, I know,
but we are grieved; we find
a shadow on the sun where
God is sorrowed for the sin
of humankind—of Israel!

I've been to dust and ash for
this; my clothes are rent.
But, God has raised me up
again with hope renewed—
instilled in me that, in the
cleansing from the sin that
took away our right to be
aligned with *YHVH*-LORD,
we are allowed an access to
His holy strategies who
promises this land and, too,
our victory over all the
pagan people here. It's
'Faith, and Fortitude, and
Forward, Go!'
Now, in my faith that's
fortified, I find a strategy of

God by which to conquer
Ai. These people will
not stand to scorn the God
of Israel! Our valiant faith
has stood the test once more
for God, the *YHVH*-LORD
had planned a strategy
unique by which the men
of Ai were deceived. They
took our bait, forsook their
fort and rallied for the total
vanquishment of Israel.
They little thought that
forts, unguarded, will most
surely fall! It did! The
whole is gone! And we are
vindicated! All!

JOSHUA, AT GIBEON
Joshua 9

We've been deceived by
Gibeon! We knew not
whence they came,
these men of tattered clothes
of threadbare thongs, and
crumbling bread. They
acted as subservient to us
all—that's true. They came
upon us unannounced as we
were resting in the Gilgal
Camp. They said they'd
journeyed far—a trek
to make a covenant

with us. We questioned
them, of course, but all
the signs were of the truth.
It surely seemed that they
had travelled many days.
We'd make no covenant
with Canaan's men! They
emphasised their knowledge
of the LORD—how none
can conquer Him—that's
true! Their elders gave them
counsel for to come, to meet
with us and make a covenant
of—wait for it—of …
servitude?!

Their bread was warm when
they set out, their wineskins
full and firm but now they
each were torn, in tatters, as
the bags upon their donkeys'
backs. We took their word;
we did not ask the counsel
of the LORD—we let them
live. We swore an oath
of life with them.

Somehow, I sensed as
though a veil was cast upon
the sun, a shadow fell across
the place where we reclined
to choose our want of them
before the noon. And then,
we found, just three days

hence, that they had bested
us! We could not strike the
town of Gibeon for there
they were, in league with us
by covenant! A crafty plot
indeed. The host of Israel
now rued the day when we
had been misled!

Our fighting men would
conquer them right then
and there. But, No!
God's wrath would rest on
us if what we swore could
be annulled in conflict on
a battlefield of spite.
So, why did they deceive?

They knew the outcome
would be servitude;
they seemed as not to mind,
accepting that their lot
would be to fill the pails
and chop the wood.

They chose to cast their lot
with us, evading certain
death. But, I recall, we are
at fault—we sought no
counsel of the LORD. And
yet I think that He is not
disastrously displeased..
What's more, the men of
Gibeon have choicest and

select of roles—to wait
upon the altar of the LORD!
They'll earn their keep, I'm
told: The wood is scarce,
the water must be drawn
from wells. It seems they
have incentive for the task.
But, I recall, we sought not
counsel from the LORD!

THE CHRONICLER
Joshua 10 – 12

The pace of this invasion
has not waned. There hardly
seems an hour but that the
fighting men have gone
or come with their reports
of all the battles fought
and won through trust.

The chronicles recording
each have lengthened every
day, it seems. It is my aim
to highlight all strategic
days of conquering.

I make my notes:
Our servants, men of
Gibeon, have found already
that the LORD does watch
His own! And they are one
with us as from the time

of covenant. They sent for
us. Their peril was indeed
profound—confederate
kings from near at hand
converged on them to rout
them all for their deflection
to our mighty Clans.

They knew their need of
help, they've learned to trust
in *YHVH*-LORD. They
knew we would not fail
to come soon to their aid.
We knew, right from the
start, the victory was ours
for God had said,

I give them to your hands!

The men of Gibeon have
found that, to identify with
us—the LORD of us—
obtains the gain of trust,
the fruit of faith; we fought
for righteousness and, yes,
for worthy aims.

It was as though the *LIGHT*
in us has once more proved
ascendancy o'er all
the dark, the dingy ploys
and deviant powers of evil
men who daily sought
our sudden end.

Chronicles cont.

I make my notes:
The storm of hail that on
that day accompanied the
routing of the allied troops
was deadly in extreme.
We sheltered from the blast
but they had nowhere else
to run from us and from
the fiercest hail we'd seen.
It signed the end of all
resistance of these men.
I sign the chronicle.

I make my notes:
The sun stood still! It
lengthened all the day.
The lesser light, the moon,
refused to wax or wane that
day! The God who made
the heavens and all the
countless stars confirmed
continued mastery of all
the skies could hold; yes, all
the stellar stars above—
they work for God,
not God for them!

I make my notes:
The day extended thus was,
yes, enough to rout the
whole confederacy intent
on our eventual demise.

The forces of resistance
waned, the strength
of Israel waxed at once!
Resistance spelled the doom
of all the kings who ranged
their forces up against
Israel. Belligerent, those
men took life into their
hands in setting out to quell
Israel and the LORD!

I make my notes:
I chronicle the kings, the
towns, the forces ranged
against us there, all through
the south. This is a purge of
sin from off the land. It is
a land defiled throughout
where all the fierce
abominations, flagrant and
profane, have brought a ruin
on themselves—
the people of the land.
There's no repenting of
sin's stains; an odious
stench is found all round!

I make my notes:
We herald now a cleansing
time for long, in mercy, God
had stayed His hand. These
people knew the price of
sin, for Sodom and also
Gomorrah was a case in

Chronicles cont.

point. Of Sihon, Og, they
knew. Oh, yes, they knew
the price of sin, but seemed
to little care until it was too
late. They should have seen
what mercy does for those
who seek salvation from the
LORD of Hosts—as Gibeon
and Rahab had.

I make my notes:
It does appear that those
who dwell in shadowed
night would there prefer
to be for fear the *LIGHT*
would penetrate their dark,
depraved, designs, would
show them up, confront
them with their blatant
crimes. But see, our
presence here is as
a beacon light that shows
the sin for what it is—
a crime against the LORD!

I make my notes:
The nations to the north
and west: Hazor, Philistia,
Sharon, combined
to test our strength. They
found the strength of
YHVH-LORD instead. He
calmed our fears. We tamed

the horses there and sprang
upon our enemies whom
God delivered to
our hands. From Goshen
to the Lebanon we've
marched and won the battles
there. The kings who ranged
against our force from east
to west
of Jordan Vale, they too
have come to their demise.
I've listed thirty-one in all
who did resist us and
the *YHVH*-LORD!
I here conclude my notes.

JOSHUA:
ALLOTMENTS
Joshua 13 – 21

There's been a change of
plans for me! I've been a
fighting man through all my
life, it seems. But I am old;
the years have taken toll
of me–my fortitude has
waned. And, *YHVH*-LORD
has seen my pain. His
mercy is forever sure. He
came to me in grace as I lay
down to rest. He said to me:

*It is enough, what you have
done; what's left is for the*

Allotments cont.

years ahead. The clans will
now complete the task I
gave to conquer all the land
The time is right to change
your role. Look to the plans
for settlement: Divide for
them, the whole.

I so divide:

Manasseh, **Reuben**, **Gad**.
First, to the east of Jordan's
flow: There is a balm in
Gilead—this land will suit
them all, I know!

The **Levi** clan's inheritance
is with them all—they own,
themselves, no actual land:
their wealth is God!

Now, **Caleb**, friend of many
years, my true cohort and
him not Jacob bred like I:
A choicest gift for him, no
less! The land he's stood
upon, that's his—this
Edomite so truly God's,
he's one of us and is so
blessed. He's wise, and
faithful to the last. He is so
strong but time it is for his
request to be fulfilled:
"Give me this mount," he

asked. And so, the mount is
his—this Hebron land!
He goes with God's own
promises; in faith, he takes
the LORD's own word—he
walks in *LIGHT* each day!

Now, **Judah's** land: This is
the largest, premier clan.
One day, I'm sure, they'll
march through Salem's
gates and take command.
The Jebusites will be a thorn
in all their sides, but Judah
will prevail and win the land
and, **Simeon's** noble clan
within.

The double clans of
Joseph's sons are blessed
with much of what is
choicest land for Shechem
and the Sharon Rose will
beautify the grant. The rest,
all seven Clans, will still
have need to claim
inheritance.

I've sought, through spies'
intelligence, just what their
several lands will hold.
Now, all the facts are
known, assessed. I therefore
say to Israel today:
it's **Benjamin** whose lot

Allotments cont.

is cast: To him, the mounts
at Judah's north. Such holy
sites included are, for
Benjamin, the land well
known of Jacob's dream.
Then, Ramah, Mizpah,
Gibeon, Jerusalem, to
border with the Judah clan.

The warrior clan of
Zebulun, so brave and so
devout, receive a northern
land of beauty rare and
fertile for their keep.

For **Issachar**, the fertile
land so beautiful,
of Jezreel is apportioned
next. He'll need a strength
of purpose, with an arm as
strong, to keep this great
thoroughfare of land intact.

To **Asher** now: the richest
soil. It's hoped his wealth
and, also, neighbourhood
will fail to tempt him from
his highest aims.

And, **Naphtali**—what
beauteous land is his for
there, the Galilee, the
shining sea, this jewel is
for Naphtali. May he reflect
the *LIGHT* of God as does
the sun on Galilee.

Now, **Dan**, the clan that last
receives its land: He'll fight
for it to claim a lovely tract
where Jordan's flow will
rise to water all the land
for his supply.

I said, the last: not quite,
for now that all are settled
in allotments granted them,
I feel that now I will receive
my plot: Timnath-Heres,
within the hillside of
Ephraim,
my own allotted land.

The Shiloh scene was all
serene—Few Clans had
made a grouch that they had
been short-changed.
They know, the Clans, that I
have worked with *YHVH*-
LORD to sort all the
allotted boundaries.

It is of God that all receive
the suited lot that fell to
them. We've made our
plans for refugees as well.
These many cities are
as named within the record

Allotments cont.

chart. The guilty and the
innocent will have their turn
to speak in self-defence as
to these allotted towns
they go. May all retreat
from sin and take the chance
to reach the area allotted to
their clan.

We've found, again, that
YHVH-LORD is faithful to
all things He planned and
scoped for us. There has not
failed of one good thing in
all that He has said to us.
The record stands!

JOSHUA 22: FINAL REPORT
Joshua 22

The eastern Clans who
chose their land before we'd
crossed the Jordan's tide,
have each fulfilled
the terms of their own
promises to Israel. They'd
done their share, ensuring
all were safe within their
own prescribed inheritance
before they rested from the
fight. It's time they went.

I have released them now
with words of sound advice.
They've learned to pray
within the battle's fray, they
each have placed their trust
in *YHVH*-LORD. But what
will be their way when all
of fear has gone? Will faith
then wane and falter, too?
I speak to all: now hear
instructive words
of sound advice:

Take care, as you return
unto your homes, to go with
God! Take, in your hearts,
the Law of Him you learned
to serve right from the
Mount of Holiness—
when we were camped
at Horeb, Sinai. Yes, love
the LORD and walk within
His ways, obey His will,
hold fast to Him, and serve
Him all your days, with all
your heart, and all your soul.
I send you 'home' with all
the blessings yours and, too,
my helpful words
of sound advice…

We've had some word of
them—disquieting news at
that! So soon they go their
way, not only to the homes

but to some deviant ways.
They've built an altar very
near to Jordan's banks.
They choose to differ in
their ways of worship
there; their mode is not
as set for Israel's Clans—
they've heard but heeded
not, it seems, my words
of sound advice.

The gathered Clans of Israel
at Shiloh meet to strategize
their fate. The troops at
arms set off to strongly
challenge bold recalcitrance
and what the meaning
is of this first, flagrant
choice of theirs to treat
the faith of all the Clans
so very carelessly.

How could they break
their faith in *YHVH*-LORD
like this, to build a pile,
rebelling, too. They've
scorned without
a thought, my words
of sound advice.

The news is good! We've
heard the reasons for the
plans they had by what
they'd built—that pile of
rock for worshipping.

Emissaries had called
attention to the pile and
said, If what you find is all
to our distaste, come back to
us, to where the Tabernacle
stands and share our land
with us. They saw the point
of our concern and right
away believed our words.

They said, The Mighty One,
the LORD, He knows, and
you should know the nature
of our plans: We took
your sound advice!

We have not turned away
from worship of the LORD.
Know, by this altar here,
we mean to mark our faith
instead! Let all who see
these rocks today, and in the
years to come, take stock of
us, we serve the *YHVH*-
LORD! This is the witness,
here, that we will worship,
wholly and in faith, within
the LORD's appointed
place—Shiloh, or, where the
LORD designs, we'll go!
Far be it from each one
of us to ever turn,
rebellious, from the LORD
with stubborn dark design!
Behold: this witness that's

between us shows the
YHVH-LORD is God and
Him we serve! They've
heeded sound advice!

JOSHUA: THE
FAREWELL
Joshua 23 – 24

I reminisce –
A solemn muse for, as I've
said, the years have taken
all their toll, I'm tired, my
time is at its ebb; my life is
stretched out to its span
of years. and what a life it's
been—so full, adventurous.

I ascertain
that I have wholly served
the *YHVH*-LORD. He's
been my life, my all,
my impetus, I owe
Him all, my life!

I reminisce –
I will address the Clans:
I've called   them here
to Shechem for Farewell.
The Elders, here, the leaders
and officials, all present
themselves as ONE!
Now, where do I begin?
Ah, yes, the years, the times

that passed before our gaze
we look to them.

I reminisce –
The LORD has said,
and I repeat:

*Your forefathers had lived
beyond the flow—the River
Grand. I took from them
your father, Abraham.
I led him, gave him Isaac
and the Jacob lad as well.
But he went down to Egypt's
land. I brought you out and
spread a darkness then
between the land and you.*

*I brought you to the
Promised Land. You
crossed the flood of
Jordan's tide and came to
Jericho. Then, all the land
I gave into your ready,
willing hands. You drove
men out as hornets do—they
ran from you. You did not
once accomplish all these
feats with your own sword
for I, the YHVH-LORD
did give it unto you, the land
for which you did not toil,
the towns you did not build,
but live there now. You eat
the fruit of grapes and figs,*

and olives too; the vineyard
and the orchards there you
did not plant. The milk and
honey flow to you always.

I reminisce –
Remember, fear the LORD
and serve Him with all
faithfulness and joy.
Though, if your own desires
are not to His design: now,
choose yourselves,
this day, whom you will
serve–the gods beyond the
River Grand, or even gods
within your land. But, as for
me, and my house: know
that we will serve the
YHVH-LORD as we
have done always!

I'd reminisce –
but must go on. What do
you say? Oh, let it far
remove from us a
thought that we'd forsake
the LORD! It was the
LORD, Himself, who
brought us here—out from
the slave domain of yore.
Our LORD performed great
signs before our eyes,
protected us through all
the years. He drove our
enemies from us! We too

will serve the *YHVH*-
LORD! He is our God:
We mean to follow on!

To reminisce –
You have not proved ability
to wholly serve the LORD!
A Holy God, and jealous of
His own, He won't forgive
rebellious ways. If you
forsake, He'll turn from
you, the Clans of Israel.
He'll make an end of you!

But, No! We'll serve the
LORD—we make this
Covenant! you say.
You've witnessed this
against yourselves; you've
pledged your lives to Him,
to serve the LORD always?
Yes, we are witnesses!

You'll reminisce—
in days to come—for here
we make this Covenant with
God. Record it on the slabs
of Law! This rock, this oak,
will mark the promising.
He's placed, you see,
a *LIGHT* upon your path
that you may step, and
never stumble there: His
Law is *LIGHT*. You've
heard His words; you'll

walk His ways? This rock is
raised in faith this day.
Now, walk each day
by faith!

To reminisce –
It is my will to leave you
now: A life-time comes to
dreams…

I bid farewell to you…

….. oOo …..

THE TRANSIENT YEARS

Justice—The Rule of Law

THE JUDGES' CHRONICLER

Judges 1 – 8

I am the Judges'
chronicler.
The text is now so
carefully engraved upon
the surface of the slab.
The Chronicles are now
reserved for all our
history's page and
purposes. I've tabulated
for the book events which,
sequenced, came and went

as history always does—
sometimes the Shadows,
then *The LIGHT*, are cast
upon our history's open
page. I've scripted what
it was that caused retreat,
defeat, the fall from grace.
I write that saga in
remorse!

Through all the years
of Joshua, our nation lived
in Covenant—
they wholly served
the *YHVH*-LORD.

But they forgot the very
thing that kept them pure,
immune from all the
sullied influence of sin
surrounding peoples plied
into our many varied
neighbourhoods.
You see, it was, for all
their worship,
congregating at Shiloh,
all Israel's Clans set out
to praise the LORD in all
their chants and songs but
not, it seems, within their
homes. The Holy Name
was not involved, the
LORD was never known
from mother's knee nor

father's tomes, neglect
of heritage condoned.
Then, as the young grew
up to adulthood these
children could not look to
God, not knowing how to
speak to Him. I'll trace
for you the paths of
all the darkest Shadows
and *The LIGHT*—
the Shadows came as
creeping low, as mostly
imperceptible. They came
so sudden, though, they've
cast a pall. A gloom has
crept across the page
of the abundant life which
once had been so bright.

I tally, too, what brought
The LIGHT of *YHVH*–LORD
once more to scurry
Shadows cast. I'll show for
you the structure of this
tabulation of the times;
it tells the whole of it for,
look at this: the sin, the
grace—the answer now:
The Clans did sin!
The lengthening shadows
then were cast. The
YHVH-**LORD** revealed
His wrath as shadows
deepened into night.

Israel recalled the NAME:
and so was found relieving
LIGHT. Then, leaders came
from *YHVH*-LORD:
They were as *LIGHT* unto
our path: The battle fought,
the battle won! and we were
bathed in glorious *LIGHT*.

**But then, again all Israel
sinned. Deep shadows
came once more.**

Now, if we'd find some
comfort here upon the sorry
saga of our times, do please
observe the chosen ones
who came, from *YHVH*, to
be judge. Apostasy would
hold its sway if not for such
as they. So, here is *LIGHT,*
again, upon the Holy Land.

You'll see how, first,
I have recalled some past
events so that I find the
true transition of this tome
from all the slabs of
God's man: Yes, Joshua.

The Clan of Judah, with his
close confederates, the Clan
of Simeon, did act in
deference to the LORD,
securing their own land.

But then, they did not
finalise the work
appointed them to do. The
conquered king, although,
did find that what he'd
sown, that did he reap.
Jerusalem, that hardy
fort, remained elusive
yet for Benjamin is weak
and can't exert a strength
to win the day. But Bethel
fell into our hands–
a traitor there disclosed
a way, a secret and
secluded path,
by which we forced
the victory.

The angel of the LORD
came down, exposing the
discountenance of God
upon the Clans for their
deliberate, malcontent
at Laws which governed
"Holiness unto the
LORD". Reminding of
the ways of God in Exodus
and in the Covenant,
he then proclaimed:

Therefore, because of this,
your malcontent, you'll
find
but thorns within your
sides and ruination in your

thirst for Canaan's lewd
and dark idolatry. This is
a blatant sin!
The people wept at this
but did not change their
bold intent to stray.

And then, within the cycle
of the sin and sun, the sin,
the sun, the Judges came—
as raised by God to lead,
inspire and govern all His
people everywhere
according to the plan
of *YHVH*-LORD. The kin
of Caleb (Othniel), was first
to free the land. There was
charisma in his rule and all
were pleased with him.

A plague of evil followed
on from Othniel's just rule
of Law. The hordes of
Moab seized the land.
Our people fell to bondage
there. They cried for pity
in their plight. Then Ehud
came to them from
YHVH-LORD! And, by
his own left hand, he won
the day and rallied Israel.
That valiant man, the
Judge Shamgar, the son
of Anath, was the next.
He came to do his part.

**His exploit with
the goad so gallantly
against the Philistines
shall be remembered
long in oral history.**

**When Ehud went the way
of aged flesh, Israel was
sold. Yes, sold to sin—
into a time of slavery, no
less! And Canaan's king,
Jabin, with his own aide,
the General Sisera,
established mastery and,
in a harsh regime, with
iron fists and chariots,
retained supremacy. They
were exceeding cruel and
crushed the latent hopes of
Israel, the vagrant sons of
God. The times were such
that, in despair, they cried,
remembered, prayed to
the *YHVH*-LORD for aid.**

The prophet, Deborah,
the wife of Lappidoth,
whose court was held
by Ramah and Bethel within
the shade of tranquil palms,
had earned respect in wise
considering of all the many
quandaries of the Clans.
I've heard it said—perhaps
it's true—that other lands
and other times may not
abide a woman's rule. We
have no fears with Deborah
in control! We see that
man's authority, in truth,
comes not because of
gender, nor the strength of
arm, nor even strength of
voice! Such clues are not
for leadership.

What is the need? Integrity,
sincerity, and strength of
aim and purpose for
the task. Yes! Strength of
aim, not arm! And if the
man, as Barak did, forsakes
the challenge of the task,
why place him in the lead,
to take control? I say, today,
just find the very one
whose strength of purpose,
sense of right, would all the
qualities of leadership
provide for those in need
of strength and right!

So, Deborah is the choice of
YHVH-LORD, a 'Mother in
Israel'! The strategy in
place, the troops engage the
foe and, by the end of just
one day, a vanquishment is
made and Sisera is foiled—
in fitful sleep.

In satisfaction of a task
another wife, his foe!
Well done, I give to you
the "Victory Song":

DEBORAH
VICTORY SONG

Tune: "Mozart",8.8.8.8.8.8.
Iambic. (See Judges 5).

I'll sing in praise of
YHVH-LORD;
The music of my soul is joy!
My song is of Your matchless
grace
For those renouncing
sin's alloy;
This worship offering of
my praise
Resigns my will to
Your employ.

O LORD, in glorious strength
You come,
All nature bows at Your
command;
The clouds release their
burdened rains,
The earth receives its
nourishment,
And mountain heights rejoice
to see
The powerful force of Your
right hand.

You have not left us
comfortless
For, when we chose
a winding way
With little strength to call
our own,
Your boundless mercy in
our day
Now reaches us to bear
us up
And in Your paths our feet
to stay.

O LORD, You lead Your
people on
To victory in the march
of life.
In days of woe, in deep
distress,
You grant us courage for
the strife.
Then, in Your wondrous
righteousness,
We find our Rock to anchor life.

I waken to the new born day
And lift my voice to sing Your
praise.
All earthly kingdoms wax and
wane,
Their kings do reign a span
of days.
Then, in the stream of time, are
lost

But *YHVH*-LORD eternal is.

LORD, grant the Sun of
Righteousness
To dawn upon our lives
this day;
Arise in splendour, Heavenly
LIGHT
To shine within our hearts
always
That, seeing You, we may
reflect
The glorious *LIGHT* of Love's
pure rays.

....

GIDEON
Judges 6 – 8

The locusts swarmed yet
once again; the crops were
set, 'twas harvest and the
hordes have come again.
When will there be an end
to it? The land was raped
and we despaired.

We'd taken to ourselves
the ways, the worship, and
the forms of gods
the peoples of this land
do use to satisfy their native
urge to bow before the

powers that be and we
forgot the *YHVH*-LORD.
We did not listen to
LORD! He'd warned of
this; He said to Israel:

*If you forsake, then
I'll forsake!*

It is as if His word is done.
We turned from Him: we
did forsake—we were bereft
of *YHVH*-LORD!

We cried to Him: O LORD,
Your aid we've ruined in
the dust of hopes despoiled
and trampled in the ground.
Do come to us; by Your
strong arm now right the
wrongs they do to us. We
look to You: Turn not!

He sat there by the Oprah
Oaks, this lordly Man,
observing me as wheat was
threshed, where wine is
pressed to trick the hordes
of Midian. He drew me
then into converse, with
respite from my toil.

I came to him, the Stranger,
there; I greeted with the
peace: *Shalom.*
He said, The LORD is with

you now, O mighty warrior;
He hears your plea! But, sir,
I said, If God still cares,
why is it that we still
do weep?

LORD, why has all this
trouble come, where are the
wonders of the LORD? Our
fathers spoke of many deeds
the *YHVH*-LORD
has wrought for us.

I ask You here, then why
not now; how long will He
delay to act? I looked at
him, his countenance—
it shone, as light of sun,
This man is the Man of
God! I waited, awed,
upon His word:

Go in the strength you have
to save all Israel from
Midian's grasp.

The strength I have? But
Lord, I have no strength!
My Clan is weak, the
weakest of Manasseh, yet,
and I am least within
my home—my father's
youngest son—I fear that I
can't go to rescue them!

And then He said,
the LORD, to me:

I will be with you as
you strike all Midian
and they will fall.

If I have found some favour
in Your eyes, I said, Give
me a sign by which I'll
know that You are HE!

I need to know if You're the
LORD whom I have loved
the while —but secretly
for fear of fault
or ridicule. Oh, please,
remain until I bring an
offering to Your hands.

I went, and came: He did
remain. He took the food
of offering, consumed
it as a sacrifice of fire
on stone and then
He left.

Ah! Sovereign LORD! I've
seen the LORD! We stood
together there as face to
Shining Face! And then
the LORD did speak again.
He said, *Shalom* to me!

He came in peace—I live,
I know no fear of Him!
I have discovered: God
is Peace! I built an altar
there and named it:

'*YHVH*-LORD IS PEACE
TO ME'

He called me to a bold
venture: I'd strike the Baal
and all its stately avenue—
the idol and the grove.
My father's wrath
would be engaged but
YHVH-LORD would
conquer Baal.

They searched, and found
the source of it, my boldest
deed for Him, the LORD.
So, when the villagers
did seek my life for sacrifice
I found my father stood
by me. He challenged all
the might of Baal.

The 'locusts' came again
and poised
for onslaught by Jezreel.
I found a new and mighty
spirit deep within.
I blew the trumpet, called
the Clans to arms then

waited lone until they
congregated there.

I sought encouragement—
a sign that what I had to do
would be the plan of God,
not mine. See, LORD,
I place this fleece upon
the floor. LORD, send
Your dew to dampen all
the fleece but spare
the floor.

Upon the morn the fleece
was damp, although the
floor was dusty yet.
I must be sure! I tried again:
O LORD, please spare Your
anger but let fleece be dry,
the floor be wet; I pray
in faith. Next morning, it
was so.

The stage was set. I counted
all—we totalled over thirty
thousand men. Surprising
me, the LORD declared
these were too many for the
fight for in their strength
alone they'd boast, forget
their Saviour was
the LORD.

Hark now:

I said to them: All those
who fear to follow Gideon,
turn back. They did! All
twenty-two of thirty-two.
We had ten thousand still.
But then, again, the LORD
did intervene, declaring that
another test was due
to them.

The water test revealed
them best: the men alert
to enemies and also those
who cared not how their
backs were turned. But
LORD, of thousands, thirty-
two, we've dwindled down
to just three hundred
fighting men.

'It is enough!
Take heed:
you fight with
YHVH-LORD!

Enough—with God—for we
would look to Him for aid.
He then instructed me to spy
the Midian camp
to gather what intelligence
I could. I quaked, but
YHVH–LORD had spoken:
I'd obey!

And then:

their troops were 'locusts',
but, in searching out
the Midian camp, I
overheard a dream that they
recalled one night:
These men of Midian
were scared!

They're scared of me!
And, of the LORD! I'd be
a 'tumbling barley loaf'
to them, I'd strike the heart
of them. My 'bread' would
see them dead.

I worshipped *YHVH*-LORD
for this. He'd given all of
Midian into our hands that
very night. We went in
haste to rally Israel—
that is, at least my small
but faithful band of men.
We readied then our
weaponry.

We took a trumpet each and
then an earthen jar. Three
companies in place,
we made our move. The
trumpets blared, the jars
were broken then revealing
a bright light that pierced
the night. It was a
terror scene.

There was a slaughter there
as all the foe fell on each
other's necks. They routed
them, themselves! We had
no need to do the deed.
Yes! all were vanquished
there for all our inner,
utmost peace.

JOTHAM'S PARABLE
Judges 9

The trees within the forest
sway, they bend into the
forceful wind; they move
with it whichever way
the wind will wind its
wheezy way. Trees sway—
there is no inner force
they have to counteract
its blast. It is with man,
the same! They bend
the way prevailing winds
would wind.

No inner force they show, to
stand immune from forces
beating on their fragile
purposes, there is
no strength to master
influence that leans a tree,
to earth. The trees within
the forest say they need

a forest giant that they
might follow him—to beat
against the wind, control the
forces that would take their
branches, sap their strength;
a tree that would example
be to them…

No doubt does man, his
search the same, seek for
that 'tree' which, lordly
giant, would shelter him and
offer him the shade for
which he craves before the
heat of strife would sap
one's strength—a 'tree'
that would example him
from birth.

The trees within the forest
stay to congregate their
choice for bough or brush
of him, the 'lord' of trees,
that they might offer him
the 'throne' of trees—a
crown upon the canopy.
Who'd take the crown?...

And man will have his way,
at that, of congregating
to decide the choice
of lord—just as the trees!
A throne for him, a crown
for him. Who'd take the
force of wind and throw

Who'd take the force of
wind and throw it back
with mirth?

The trees, as is the forest's
way, approached the
swaying olive with the
crown; they bowed but he
would rather spend his days
in making oils—receive
his honour in that way.
So then, the lot befell
the fig.

He fobbed the offer off for
he preferred to harvest
choicest fruit. The trees
besought the vine. It had a
sturdy stem but fruit was all
delight to everyone, they'd
stay their hand; the vine
could not despoil the wine
and cause an untimely
demise!

The trees within the forest
may have felt, at this,
despair of hope for neither
olive, fig, nor vine would
take the crown, the throne.
Each had excuse, his selfish
aim. While good trees wept,
they preened, in peace,
their fronds.

In just this way, the man
most apt to lead would turn
to selfish gain and leave in
lurch all those who need
example to aspire. While
good men weep, they turn
their 'fronds' to gainful
ends, no care to find
on Earth.

The trees within the forest
fray then turned to greet the
bramble bush which
drooped its leafless limbs
so near the earth. Could it
be king? At least, it seized
its chance and then,
the promises:

"Come, stand within the
shade I have for you—
a refuge here you'll find.
But here I'll snare
you with my spikes
and thorns…

It is, with men, the same!
The men most worthy to be
king will sit in ease while
measly men would take the
lead and rule the Earth!
What will it take today for
wise men with integrity

to reign; a mighty king
of worth?

The forest giants are gone
today; the one who claimed
the crown and throne—the
leafless, creeping, vicious
thorn—has taken to the axe.
He's cut my brethren down
for fear that one, more
straight of character, would
take, in victory,
his place.

Beware, Abimelek, you
noxious 'weed', a forest fire
will flare your cruel thorns
then blaze you into ash!
And you, the 'forest' that
did crown his head: beware,
O Shechem, for the flames
will soon reveal you have
no worth.

CAMEOS FROM THE CHRONICLER
Judges 10 – 12

Now I, the Judges'
chronicler, will take my
scripting tools again.
I here outline the final group
of seven men

who, in their turn, led Israel
for *YHVH*-LORD. For most,
these are but cameos of
minor men, almost—
not quite.

A cameo of **Tola**, Judge of
Israel—of Issachar, he came
to save the land again.
There is no scope of brave
exploit; he quietly did his
work and brought a gentle
ray of hope. He knew the
strength of God and ruled
the Clans for twenty years
or more. He is recalled as
a beloved and warm.

A cameo of **Jair** the Judge
from Gilead: He brought
with him a healing balm to
troubled Israel (and what a
'donkey-train' of sons
he had.) He was a man of
wisdom in his years. It was
observed of him, by name,
'enlightened' of the LORD.

A cameo of **Jephthah**,
Judge: a mighty warrior of
Gilead—a castaway from
family shame, but then
old Jephthah's fortunes
changed (his people pleaded

Chronicles cont.

his return to save
them from the Ammonites).
The man was brave, and
rash! Misplaced, his vow to
God, it caused him darkest
grief—an agony of deep
remorse. He knew the
nation's history well, but
not the God he sought to
make a vow in gratitude
for how far short of
YHVH's ways, his foolish
sentiment. Although,
according to his name,
God opened up
the way ahead for him.

A cameo of **Ibzan**, Judge.
He was a sturdy man of
consequence. The nation
found its peace through him
and, too, God's providence
did smile upon this
prosperous judge who lived
in Bethlehem, the very
House of bread. It could be
said of him, the service that
he gave was just as splendid
as his name.

A cameo of **Abdon**, Judge:
the son of old Hillel, he
came from Ephraim.

If donkeys prove the wealth
of men, this Abdon was
immensely rich. He was the
last, but one to judge Israel.
His name suggests he
served them well. I turn
from him and give you now
the man whose strength
is legendary.

SAMSON:
THE WEAK, STRONG
MAN
Judges 13 – 16

I stand as blind, deprived
of eyes. I may no longer see
the light of day but not of
savages who stole my gaze
and strength—that of the
Nazarite—of body and
of soul.

I stand between two pillars
here—these are my lone
support within the temple of
Dagon, the stronghold of the
enemy: imprisoned in Gaza.

I rue the day Delilah
schemed on me. This is the
day of consequence of
all that's past of **Samson**,

me! Before the end of it,
this day, I take my muse to
cite the days, and many, oh
so many ways, I played
the fool!

My birth was in the plan of
God; my parents knew that
He did visit them, prepare
them for their child's own
nurturing—as Nazarite,
I must fulfil commands
of *YHVH*-LORD.

My strength it was of
YHVH-LORD. In wisdom's
ways I followed all the rules
for wholesome, holy life.
My hair, as Nazarite, was
never cut and discipline
completely ruled
my ways.

Each day, a deed of strength
decreed that all the
Philistines were in a state of
sore distress by me. With
jawbone of an ass, I made a
host of 'donkeys' out of all
those Philistines who
loathed and hated us.

And then, my eyes espied
Delilah and I swooned!

A Philistine, it's true, but
she was pleasing to the eye
and was my heart's desire.
My gaze did plunge me
into lusting want
of her.

Delilah was the object of
my love, my passioned,
selfish will. She loved
me not—I know it now.
She chanced my love
to gain the clue
to sourcing out
my strength.

I knew it all my days that
I was set apart for God
as wholly pure yet, I
had played the fool! I let
Him down and told the clue:
my length of hair!
Delilah cut my hair as I
yet slept!

I was undone! My strength
did ebb; the mighty Samson
gouged of eyes and all my
strength —I rued again my
foolish act of love and
vowed to take my own
revenge by asking God to
break my chains, give back
my ailing strength.

That's why I stand between
these columned poles.
O LORD, my God,
remember me, now
strengthen me. The
vengeance shall be of the
LORD; His enemies shall
plunge beneath...

MICAH–
HIS IDOLATRY
Judges 17 – 21

The silver ephod and the
idol cast became my rich
inheritance. I worshipped
them and had the aid
of my young Levi priest
who stayed at my own
home. He was my safest
guarantee that *YHVH*-
LORD would smile on me
and grant me all desires!
 I have no king—I do
what's right, you see,
in my own eyes!

Some Danite troops who
spied my wealth—the
ephod and the idols cast—
returned to grasp my
cherished, choicest things.
They stole my priest as

well, those men who
tempted him to higher
power and dignity. I wept
the while and sorrowed
then. We have no king; all
Israelites behave as they
believe is always right
in their own eyes!

I'm Levite from
Ephraim's heights;
men sought to steal
my concubine.
Her father snared my
presence far beyond
a useful time but then
we left. In Gibeah a rage
took place the like of
which would terrify. I took
a great revenge. I had no
king who stood for justice
there, no leadership, no
sensible foray for peace—
the slyest deeds I chose
were right, you see,
in my own eyes.

The evidence of sacrifice
of human flesh brought
Israel, at once, to Mizpah
where a judgement would
be made on this foul deed.
I told them of the blackest
night. Israel did mobilise.

The slaughter of the clans
was great and, in the end,
all Benjamin was cast aside
and all but lost. We have
no king. Though it is wrong,
all Israel do what is right
in our own eyes.

ELIMELECH OF BETHLEHEM
Ruth 1:1 – 5

This famine haunts the
village homes; the bin of
flour, the vase of oil is
spent. The young are
famished, listless, wan.
I scan the sun-path of the
sky in search of haze or
dew, if not a hopeful cloud
to burst upon our thirsty
land. But there is none—
the sky is bare! The former
and the latter rains have
failed and sowing grain is
lost as winnowed for a meal
of bread. The poor bend to
the earth in search of
gleaning from the
harvest past.

The barren soil neglects to
give a produce for their
doubtful sustenance.
O Bethlehem,
The House of Bread,
you fail your kin, all those
who now would call you
'home'. Your arid hills
present no hope for
harvesting. My darling,
Naomi, has grief enough
for our two sons remain
in hapless health.

The elder one, our Mahlon,
is a sickly youth and weak.
And then, our Chilion is
failing now. We need
to aid and nourish them lest
they should die. And I,
Elimelech (*My God
is King*), will bring a joy to
Naomi, my *pleasant* one,
my lovely wife delightful to
my heart. We are about
to take a journey out from
this most pleasant clime.

O Bethlehem,
The House of Bread;
we search for bread. Your
wasted hills no longer yield
the grain which would
sustain. We go to alien
lands in search of food.
LORD, guide us now.

NAOMI, THE BEREAVED
Ruth 1:6 – 15

My grief is more than I can
bear; I've been to sack and
ash for them, my weakling
one, my failing one—
my Mahlon and my Chilion,
Elimelech, my husband:
dead! I grieve for them.
My sad despair has closed
the light of hope from me.
Where is the *God,*
my King today? Elimelech,
I fail the trust he had of
Him, the *YHVH*-LORD,
for now I am bereaved;
I dare not look to Him
through nights of grief.

O Bethlehem,
The House of Bread,
I long to see your hills and
village kin once more. O
lead me, saddest hope, unto
my home again.
My grief is borne as is this
load; I carry both the grief
and spoil of years, sparse
spoil, indeed. It's little fare,
but all I have of him, and
them who died before their
time, Now, I'm bereft of
them… My daughters,

wives of sons, please go:
Your homes await
you now. Return to Moab
in your grief of this, your
widowhood, as yet
so young in years. Farewell,
my Orpah fresh with charm.
Soon may the shadows of
your grief dispel as love
returns to nurture you.

O Bethlehem,
The House of Bread,
your hills are far. So, Ruth,
true *friend* to me, please go,
return with Orpah; then I
can depart accompanied by
my abject grief
of all I've lost.

RUTH, THE DEVOTED
Ruth 1:16 – 18

Entreat me not to leave
you now to stray from on
your homeward way, nor to
return this day to Moab, no
longer following the path
you tread. Where you would
go, there I will go and
where you lodge, there I
would lodge. And all your
people—all your kin—
they'll also be as kin to me.
Your LORD, the God

Almighty, He shall be my
El Shaddai; I'll worship
Him. And, where you die
my Naomi, I shall—
as your familial friend—
I'll also die.

O Bethlehem,
The House of Bread,
I'll go into your hills. May
God so do to me, and more
also, if anything but death
will cause to separate.
I'll go with you, I'll find my
life again with you. So
young, I grieve your son
who is no more but, yet,
I see his smile in you.
He had your eyes, your
lovely, kindly eyes—so
deep, a well without a depth
to mete or measure yet. He
had your winsome ways.
With you, my husband's
memory remains deep in
my heart. So, I will stay
with you. Together, let us
find our strength, our
fortitude sustained.

O Bethlehem,
The House of Bread,
You draw us to your
beauteous, homing hills;
receive myself, with

Naomi, unto your pleasant
hills and fields.

NAOMI, RETURNING PILGRIM
Ruth 1:19–22

Refrain from naming me,
as once you did, as Naomi!
You'll find no longer is the
pleasantness you knew,
with me. I deeply grieve;
stark bitterness enshrouds
my soul. Yes! Call me
Marah—*bitterness*!
Elimelech and our two sons
with me did leave our
sheltered home in
Bethlehem for Moab's alien
fields. We went out full,
replete—though all that
famine sent us out. And
now, quite empty I return
with nought! No resource
yet remains of them.

O Bethlehem,
The House of Bread,
the *YHVH*-LORD has stolen
all my joy. If full I am, it is
with grief; your hills do
bring Naomi no joy. Now,
Ruth, we each must gather
grain while yet

the harvest lasts. We've
come just on the barley-
gathering days and each of
us, today, may glean the
fields to earn our bread
for winter months.

Take my advice to glean not
near a field where other
workers may appear as
jealous of your alien grace.
Be sensitive to care for
those who smile with
kindness, so allowing you
the grain that's felled within
your chosen path for
there are those who'll
welcome you.

O Bethlehem,
The House of Bread,
encourage now my Ruth to
find her home within your
open hills. Place plenteous
gleanings in her path.

RUTH, THE GLEANER
Ruth 2:1 – 19

O Naomi, I've gleaned
today throughout the sunlit
hours and found such
weight of grain my basket
breaks! Come, see this
golden grain I've gleaned,
this precious grain! The
master of the fields I've
gleaned has smiled on me.
I'm sure the gleaning's
greater than I've known
before. It is as though the
master's men encourage me
to glean too near
the harvesting and yet no
word of caution comes from
them. I glean immune from
any daily care!

O Bethlehem,
The House of Bread,
I comprehend your name.
Your grain will make the
choicest bread—these hills
have yielded all our gain.
O, let me tell you, Naomi,
how Boaz: The powerful
master of the fields, did
come to me in grace. He
said of me, Who is this
lass? And I, requesting
courteously, did ask for his
permission for my gleaning
there. He told me then to
stay with his own servant
girls to glean and slake my
thirst with them. I asked
him, why he did this thing.
He said that he had heard of
my great kindness unto

you!—It was my joy. Yes,
he has spoken thus.

O Bethlehem,
The House of Bread,
I sense a new, exciting thing
upon your hills for Boaz
prayed that *YHVH*-LORD
will shelter me.

NAOMI,
THE ROMANCER
Ruth 2 – 3

My daughter fair, my Ruth,
my *friend*, this Boaz is a
rich and kindly man with
care for living and the dead.
He is our relative, and close
to us—a kinsman who
redeems! It will be good
for you to stay, as he
requests, close by his girls
through harvest time, until
the very last of grain is
gathered in this year.
Remain each day near
him—in other fields you
may be harmed. You'll live
awhile with me throughout
these harvest days. I'll see
to all necessities of food
and shelter here, at home.

O Bethlehem,
The House of Bread,
the shadows of the past
seem gone, the nights of
grief have lessened now.
These hills of home
are truly ours!

Now, Ruth, I age in years
and have but little time
to settle you. This night
Boaz will winnow wheat.
So, go to him and, as he
sleeps, your mantle you
should cast to cover him.
Then at his feet do humbly
lie—he is a man of honour;
as he wakes, invite him to
enfold you in his mantle
there. He'll know of your
desire to marry him. As I
know Boaz well, you'll be
betrothed. He'll not
mishandle you at any time.

Our Bethlehem,
The House of Bread,
will shelter you and all will
welcome you, the alien
widow, 'home'. Our hills
will surely take you to
their heart, as one!

We'll pray as one!

BOAZ, THE KINSMAN REDEEMER
Ruth 4

Please, gather round, all you
within the city gate. There is
a case we must decide. I call
my kin—the one who's
closest kinsman to the dead
Elimelech.
　Take heed, my friend:
you've opportunity to take
your place as kinsman for
his wife. You see, she's due
to sell some land. You have
the chance to offer her the
true redemption price. You
do accept? You have the
right, of course, and I will
honour it, your duty done
in grace.

O Bethlehem,
The House of Bread,
if kinsman, the redeemer,
acts to take this tract of hill,
I know I also lose my Ruth,
to me betrothed.

A very worthy deed you do
it's true, my kinsman, and
you know of course that, on
the day you buy the land,
You gain as well, the widow
of the son: the sonless

Moabite!...You seem
perplexed. You fear you
may endanger your estate?
You'd much prefer that I
redeem the whole? I do
accept! I lift my shoe; I give
to you, as is our due to
formalise the contract of
a 'kin-redeemer', so!

O Bethlehem,
The House of Bread,
You nourish me–I've won
my bride! I bring her to my
hills, and heart, I feel as
though I'm kin to kings!

….. oOo …..

THE TRANSPARENT YEARS
Authentic, Able Leadership

HANNAH, THE CHILDLESS
1 Samuel 1

My lips would speak my
thoughts but silent is my
speech; inaudible, the
sounds of deep and poignant
agony. I inward weep,

My tear-stained prayer
ascends as with the
hint of incense there,
beyond the Veil. I stand,
a solemn soul, before the
Holy Place, beseech the
YHVH-LORD of this, my
grievous heart complaint
for, in my choicest hours
with him, Elkanah, flesh of
flesh, as one, I cannot yield
to him a son out from our
dearest love. And she, the
rival of my love, does taunt,
belittle me within his eyes.
He loves me yet, I know,
but I would gladden him,
delight to bring to him the
issue of his loins—and I,
a mother too.

Am I but drunk? As if the
wine had clouded all my
need for prayer? But no, the
sharpest pangs of grief
would bear as mute a word
of testimony as to the
depth of sorrow that I know
for my own sterile, lifeless
womb. Yes! Here I stand.
My hope of Him, the
YHVH-LORD, the light of
kindness shining on my life,
that He would mercy me

and bring to us, the husband
of my humble life,
and me, a 'promise child'.
LORD grant a gift.

Here, shadows that would
pall the highest hopes would
seem to shift, to dissipate
in purest light of dawn:
The priest now prays with
me and brings security of
hope. I find I take God at
His given word.

My time will be fulfilled in
birth! There'll be a son for
Elkanah and me. And I now
give my word unto the
YHVH-LORD: The child,
when weaned, I dedicate
to Him to serve within
the Holy Place, a sacred
priest before the LORD.
What He will give of joy
I take in faith, by faith repay
this promised, precious gift
to me. I dedicate this
choicest gift of grace: I give
my heart's delight to Him!

HANNAH–A HYMN OF PRAISE
1 Samuel 2:1 – 11

Tune: *Colne, Martyrdom,* C.M.

My heart rejoices in
the LORD,
You are my strength of days;
My lips shall sound Your
worthiness,
Delighting in Your praise.

I worship in Your holiness,
None other is my goal;
I would aspire to seek
Your strength,
The 'Rock' that guards
the soul.

You know my anxious
thoughts, O LORD,
You all my hopes perceive,
You weigh each deed,
my fears relieve,
Your grace I now receive.

O LORD, you are the
Fount of Life,
You raise us from the dust;
Our wealth in You is
measureless,
Your ways are true and just.

You set us, LORD, upon
the 'Rock';
You are our Hiding Place!
Your paths are sure, You
guard our steps
And grant Your perfect peace.

Now, through Your strength,
we shall prevail;
Our every hope is You!
Anoint us to Your service,
LORD,
As we our vows renew.

ELI: REPORT ON WICKEDNESS
1 Samuel 2:12 – 36

**The fond regard of youth
is gone! My sons defile,
appal, with blatant crimes
against the LORD, and
those who come to offer
sacrifice, upon the brazen
altar, lambs for offering
as would the Law demand
of all. They steal the very
flesh before the moment
of the gifting comes, with
brash and brutal force.
Contempt and scorn they
place upon the sacred
sacrifice we offer now.**

And Samuel, all the while
this child example is to us—
to them and me. His
winsome ways enhance his
ministry within the Holy
Place. This child, he grows

Eli's Report cont.

within the smile and
Presence of the LORD!

**I hear disquieting news of
them, the sons I loved and
lost. I now despair and live
in fear for them. Each day
their crimes increase—
my Hophni and my
Phinehas. But, why these
ravenous, lustful crimes
within the portals of the
House of God? That they
should take as whores
the women who reside
just near the precincts
of the Holy Place?**

**It is a wickedness
they do and who can
intercede a crime that's
done against the LORD?
There is no one at all
who saves them this
disgrace: Their souls
will be required of them.**

And Samuel, all the while,
example gives to one and
all. Observe his stature, and
his grace. The linen ephod
that he wears prepares
him for his future days

when he must take our
sullied, sin-stained place.

SAMUEL:
HIS CALLING
1 Samuel 3

Samuel! Samuel!

I think I heard my name.
Someone has called to me.
How can it be, before the
dawn? I know not if my ears
are yet awake! Was I
asleep? And, did he call,
Eli? Ah, yes, that's who I
heard. I'll go to Master-
Priest. He called to me.

Yes? Here I am—you called
my name just now. I heard;
I do obey. You called me
not? But yet, I heard my
name. It was distinct to me.
You must have called, then
slept once more. But here
I am to do the thing for
which you called. You did
not speak my name? How
strange, I heard my name.

Samuel! Samuel!

Ah! Now, It's clear. My
name! It was Eli who called

my name. I'll go to him for he did speak my name once more to me. You called me not? How come I heard my name again within the shadow of the early dawn? O Master, did you not speak out my name? I've come to you for you most surely did just call my name. I'm ready now for what it is you want of me to do. You called me not? How strange.

Samuel! Samuel!

I'm hardly in my bed when, once again, I'm called. I'll go to him—Perhaps he tests obedience. O Master, here I am for, yes, you surely called my name! You did not call? And now you know the source of it—the voice that called? It is the LORD? He calls my name?

Oh, why would He so speak with me? I am afraid to know. Oh, please, what can I say to Him if once He calls me by my name again. I greatly fear to hear! Just say, Speak, LORD, for I, Your servant hears.

Samuel! Samuel!

A silent sound yet heard so loud! It is the LORD, and I have heard! Speak, LORD, for I, Your servant hears You call my name!

Samuel, Samuel!

O LORD, You called my name! My ears were sound asleep though, all the while, I heard You in my heart it seems—an inner Voice much closer than my breathing is to me for sure. And now You come to stand by me, a little boy, but here You stand. LORD, You have called and I will hold the solemn news You speak within my heart, then tell of it, proclaim the judgements of the LORD, but not before You will it to be heard. O yes, LORD, I will train to be Your prophet, priest, and judge. When I'm a man, I'll never let Your holy words drop idle on the ground as waste. I'll be Your voice today! I hear, and I will do Your will today and every future day as well, I vow.

THE ELDERS: OUR DEFEAT
1 Samuel 4

These ravening wolves up
from the coast do pester us
and rankle us. They're all
inclined to snatch from us
our very lands, our homes.
They think to master us
and subjugate our hope to
their all-powerful threats.
We won't oblige!

These Philistines intend to
master us and snatch our
liberty, enchain us in
their snares, attack us
with their spears and iron
bars. They think to
pillage, take the spoils
to live in ease.
We can't oblige!

This vicious army from
the coastal plains would
take the heights of Israel
as well. They'd slaughter
us with half the chance.
But see! The Ark of
Covenant will thwart
the powerful enemy.
Our 'Mascot' won't oblige
just what we ask of it!
Defeat: the blackest night!

How could the Ark
have let us down?
We've lost the fight.
And now, the Ark has
gone to them. Those
Philistines have made
a sacrifice: they stole
our choicest heritage.
We've lost the Ark!
Our precious Ark.
We must oblige!

ELI'S DAUGHTER-IN-LAW
1 Samuel 4:19-22

My son is 'Ichabod':
the glory gone! The LORD
forsook, departed, He has
fled from us–We are
alone! The gathered gloom
is spread through all our
homes; the shining Face
of God is turned from us.
We fled from Him at first;
we stood our ground,
alone and blind, forsook
the *YHVH*–LORD!

O 'Ichabod', my son,
Where is the *glory* now?
That holy thing, the Ark
of Covenant, no longer

stands its holiest ground;
The cherubim do hide
from us. We are forsaken!
We're bereft and they,
the Philistines, do take the
glory glow and we know
gloom of darkness now.

Yes, son, my 'Ichabod',
is there no way for us to
know the smile, the
shining Face of God, the
YHVH-LORD once more?
This is a land of deep
despair where hope is lost.
The foe, they subjugate
the *LIGHT* we knew to
their own glory now.
LORD, come to us anew,
we are in need of You!

A PHILISTINE PRIEST
1 Samuel 5 – 6

These maddening boils
and blains are painful far
beyond all reasoning. I'm
loathe to say, just how
embarrassing it is, for all
concerned. We cannot sit
or lie or walk or stand for
them—especially, sit! We
kneel for ease and, also,
for a plea before the lord,

Dagon. We'll plead
a wholesome remedy.

Oh, ease these sores!
The soothsayers would
rant and wave their oils,
their painful potions, all
about. They bring no ease.
We cannot kneel through-
out our days! But, how to
get the heat and poison
out of us? Who tries?
We're pleading for a balm
to soothe our woe. Dagon,
oh please, a salve!

I've heard it said, it's true,
no doubt: the reason for
these boils and blains is
that gold box we stole in
war from Israel. As far
as I'm concerned, why
don't we send it back?
It's been but trouble from
the start and if this plague
is all because that box is
here, we're sick of it!
Dagon, please soothe
these festering sores.

As priest of Dagon, I'm
appalled! I've itched my
way towards the temple
gate where Dagon stood
before this dawn. He's

gone, our god! The mighty
Dagon, god, is gone! He
fell upon his face; he lays
now shattered in the dust
there before that box—
the Ark of Covenant!
No use, to seek his aid—
our dusty god Dagon,
who cannot save!

It is that wretched box,
that golden, glory box!
It has now crumbled, it's
without a head or hands.
Do hush it up. Those
Israelites would fling their
scorn at us if they but
knew our plight of pain
with none to heal and
mend our loathsome
agonies. We've proved
this painful point: Dagon
can't soothe our sores!

We took Israel's box of
gold to Ashdod: What a
plague! So! Send it down
to Gath, we said. The
plague increased. So, on it
went to Echron. Then, the
cry, Enough! went up.
Please send the artefact
back whence it came.
We've had enough of it,
and of the boils it's given

to us each itchy day—
Dagon, he can't oblige!

We've planned a final test
of it, that wretched box!
Let Israel take it back.
But we will send it on its
way; as cows will need
their new-born calves:
the calves that cart the
golden box will rush right
back as lowering calves
will do—unless the LORD
of Israel controls the
Ark... He does! Dagon,
we've failed!

SAMUEL: THE
EBENEZAR STONE
1 Samuel 7

It now is time to set an
obelisk for remembrance—
a marker for re-call to show
from whence we've come,
also, to where we go upon
our every guided pilgrim
journeying. Through all the
time that's past, the *YHVH*-
LORD has been our help,
our hope, through all the
years. Sometimes we knew
it not; we trudged along the
human way as if alone—

our footprints in the sands
of time had marked a lonely
way it seemed; but God
was there! He came to us,
encouraged us, and
urged us on to reach the
utmost heights, to seek the
LIGHT, the **shadows** shun.

The space upon this rock,
this obelisk, would fail to
give account of deeds,
exploits, events, and dreams
significant within our march
of endless years in time.
But, none-the-less,
a brief Outline:

Remember Abraham,
the man of Covenant. And
then, the stately lad, Isaac,
and son of Isaac: Israel, his
kin, the brothers twelve—
all patriarchs to us and, in
the train of Abraham. Recall
the great Moses, that giant
of men who led us out
from Egypt, right up to
the Promised Land.

Remember all the ways the
LORD has led. Remember,
too, the given Law of God.
Remember also the Atoning
Plan as blood is spilt upon

its lid, the Mercy Seat,
the Ark of Covenant.

So many sins have marred
our march. No wonder if the
LORD did then forsake us
to ourselves, our wilful
ways. He drew us back
into His fold as sheep upon
His choice pastures. He
nurtured us, and led us on,
down through eventful
years. And now, we set this
special marker stone:
We raise this obelisk—
our *Ebenezer* to the LORD,
the rock that bears this sign
for us: Yes! 'HITHERTO':
The Past is Grace!
Yes! Hitherto, the LORD
has been our Help. He does
not leave us 'lone' and
never will. O *Ebenezer,*
Praise the *YHVH*–LORD!

… oOo …..

THE TRANSPIRING YEARS

The Kingdom—Dynasty Builders

SAMUEL: HIS
QUANDARY
1 Samuel 8

A king?
For Israel?
But You have always been
our Sovereign, *YHVH*–
LORD!

We bow
to You, O LORD;
to Your Theocracy–
there is no other LORD!

How come
they plead a king,
would serve a king and turn
from You to slavery?

You say
the sons have not
the character to lead
all Israel; they sin!

I know,
I see that they
walk not the ways of God;
they serve dishonestly.

They sin,
they stray from truth,
perverting justice in
the office of the Judge.

And now,
the Elders ask
me to appoint a king
for I am aged and grey.

But, LORD,
how can it be?
It would be You that they
reject; not me, Samuel!

But then,
all history shows,
from Egypt until now,
forsaking is their wont.

You ask
that I should warn
them of their doom when
they would serve a king?

I'll tell
them, LORD, the truth
of it–the chains that wrap
about one's self and kings!

They'll know,
but listen they will not!
They'll march headlong
into their own demise.

They want
to be like nations
all about! But, what is it
they know of *LIGHT*?

Agreed?
You grant their plea?
And, what of me, O LORD–
Must I agree the plea?

Your will,
O LORD, be done;
I'm listening and would
Your will obey: A king!

SAUL: KING OF ISRAEL
1 Samuel 9 – 10

I wonder, if the donkeys had
not strayed, would I be king
tonight? What thoughts are
these? I dreamed the thing!
I am no king, or son of
kings; I strain to find the
sense of it. Can you?

The donkeys strayed, I'm
sure of that! My father said
he needed me to find the
beasts. The donkeys strayed,
and I'm a king! There is no
sense in that. I traced the
straying hooves
for days until we came to
Zuph. Near here, we gained
instructions from some
maids, so ready to give help.
You ought to find

the seer, they said, just
straight ahead of here.
It is the day of sacrifice; all
wait for him to come before
the celebrations will begin.
We went in haste and found
the man then coming
through the gates to us just
as we entered in the town.

The seer caught sight of me.
He seemed surprised, he
paused, as though he heard
a voice though no one stood
by him. I heard it not
but something did arrest
him in his tracks. I spoke; I
asked directions of the seer.
I am the seer, he said.

Go on ahead of me until you
reach the place of sacrifice.
You'll eat with me today.
Then, in the morn, I'll set
your mind at ease.
I'll tell you what is in your
heart: the steeds for which
you search are found. He
knew before I told my
quest! Indeed, he was a seer.
Within his eyes I seemed
to see a special destiny
to which I'd be involved.

He spoke again; he hinted at

some special thing in me
that, through my family,
would all desires of Israel
be found. What could he
mean? I spoke, reminding
him that I am from the
smallest Clan—of
Benjamin—How could he
make such claims of me?
But Samuel, that was his
name, walked on and
brought my aide and me
into the festive hall and
seated us right at the
honoured place with him.
We stared in disbelief.

But yes, that was our place!
The best of roasted cuts was
offered us. We ate that day
with Samuel—the most
revered and honoured man
throughout the whole of
Israel. And in the evening
hours when we'd returned
into the town, we both
conversed, the seer and I,
until the early hours of
dawn on the next day.

The dawn had all but come
in gorgeous robes of light
when Samuel called me to
the roof. He hosted us most
plenteously; he even walked

with us along the way.
And then, he asked
my aide to go on up ahead.
He spoke with me alone.
He shared with me some
mysteries. How he had
known before the time,
I could not tell but, as he
said, the day unfolded as
the plan he gave to it.

I was amazed—I knew of it
before events took place,
according to the seer's own
prior remarks: There were
two men by Rachel's Tomb.
The news they gave? The
donkeys have returned, men
search for me instead! My
father is distraught with
fear! At Tabor's Tree, I'd
find three men with gifts
of bread. And, then, the
Prophets' March—the
harps, the lyres and
tambourines, ecstatic
speech—these all occurred
just as he'd said.

The Holy Spirit, Power of
God, descended, breathed
on me, infused me with
great strength. And then,
I found a new and lovely
thing in me—I felt renewed!

A special grace
was birthed in me which
was as God designed.
Oh, no! It must have been
a dream! The sun
became too hot; a stroke
I took. But what was this?
Pure oil upon my brow!
A pungent, aromatic oil,
as holy oil is pungent in the
vial. I do recall the touch,
the speech, and then the
pouring of the purest oil,
anointing me before the
YHVH-LORD! I'm Saul,
the King of Israel!

SAMUEL,
THE MONARCH
1 Samuel 10

The chieftains of the Clans
arrive with all their
delegates, to stand
before the great watch-
tower, attend this
convocation at Mizpah.
I feel a reticence today, so
personal to me though I
fulfil the ordinance
of *YHVH*-LORD whose will
I would obey. They ask
a king to reign. The LORD,

in grace, does grant their
whim. I will announce,
today, that He has even now
made choice of him,
a king for Israel. It's time!
I will the speech begin:

Hear now, O Israel, I speak
the words of *YHVH*-LORD
upon this Convocation Day.
You sought a king; you
asked for him. You rush
headlong as though it is
your dearest wish to be
servile! You'd bow the knee
before your king,
a monarch of the Earth
and not the One I AM!

Hear now, O Israel, today!
You've had a Monarch all
the years. He brought you
up from Egypt's toil and He
delivered you from their
great power and saved you
from the wretched fate
of all the souls so long
oppressed. You've wished
to crown the head of one
among yourselves, refusing
to receive the LORD, your
rightful King! What comes
of those who do rely on
kingly whims and all

His strategies? You're bound to him! He'll drain your powers, your stocks, your lands; you'll pay his way, delete your way. He'll bind your will to craven aims. He'll set himself above the Law, increase the rules by which you'll be subservient to him!

Now hear, O Israel, I speak: You seek the dawning of an age, a glorious, golden age of brilliant *LIGHT*? Beware the gathering clouds of storm, with lengthening **shadows** bringing night!

You ask a king? You'll have your king! Present yourselves: the choice is made! Yes, one by one, each Clan, present yourselves. Now march on by. We come to Benjamin– the least of Clans. I call the family of Matri…

But, where is he, the one who stands full head and shoulders over all? He can't be missed! He hasn't come? O LORD, where is the 'chosen one'? You say he's come, he's hiding much afraid, among the baggage there, adjacent to the crowding clans? "Go! fetch the son of Kish to me!" Ah, here he comes to us. What reticence!

Now hear, O Israel: Behold, your king! He comes to you. Here's the anointed one. Now, take the crown: Saul is the king!

LONG LIVE THE KING!

SAUL: FIRST KING OF ISRAEL
1 Samuel 11 – 13

I wonder how a king should lead? They've crowned me king and here I am, behind my oxen in the fields to plough the straightest furrow and that's what I would do to be the best a king can really be in Israel. But, how to rule? Where is my guide for that? How do I rule with all the straightest furrows in the land? I'd be example to Israel but who have I to teach my rule, a mentor true, to guide the

king? I wonder how a king
should act? These men of
Jabesh-Gilead have told a
sorry tale. They weep:
compatriots! The spirit stirs!
My anger boils as caldrons
do from deep within my
trembling soul.

I'll send this flesh to Israel:
A sign for you, all Israel–
your oxen are as flesh of
these, my own, if you
refuse enlistment with
Israel, refuse to follow
Samuel, and Saul, the king
of Israel you've crowned!

I wonder how a king should
goad the troops of Israel to
lead, enthuse my men and
take them on to victory that
counts with God? It seems
the ire I feel is transferred to
my men! They stand, they
fight with me this day.
The spirit or the LORD
inspires, empowers us now.

We do prevail, we've won
our way! The enemy we
rout! No, never be it 'we',
it is the LORD who leads us
both—the prophet-priest
and me, all Israel's king!

I wonder how a king should
reign? As Samuel leads to
Gilgal's halls, so I must go;
I am the king and this new
reign will Samuel affirm for
me. There have been those
so slow to move, to bow
before the king. The people
seek their heads.

But no! Not so!
We recognise the LORD's
command—It's He who
really rescued Israel!
I've been confirmed as king
today. We celebrate before
the LORD. This is a
massive, God-blessed
enterprise.

I wonder how a king should
hear? This partnership with
Samuel is strong, but he is
old and grey. The great
responsibility is now with
me. I stand with him today.

He bids farewell to all Israel
today. He testifies to
faithfulness; the people all
agree, applaud. His
testimony praises God;
He tells the saga of the
years, the wandering and
conquering of Samuel and

me, King Saul of Israel.

I wonder how a king should
fear? This thing that Samuel
does before the eyes of king
and Israel: he speaks
of evil now. It was an evil
thing to seek a king.
And I am he!

This is an utter fear to me!
Look, see, he says: the
wheat does sway within the
wind—it's harvest time, but
lightning strikes the land,
and thunder rolls—
an awesome storm before
the LORD. We stand in awe
of *YHVH*–LORD this day.

I wonder how a king should
work now Samuel has
calmed our fears? He
prayed for Israel and the
king. He called us all to
faithfulness. My task is
clear: The Philistines!

The trumpet sounds—the
King commands! We wait
for Samuel. He fails to
come! I'll take the task
of prophet-priest to plead…
He comes, does Samuel. He

groans. It seems I lacked
the faith required of kings—
a judgement looms!

A REPORTER
1 Samuel 14

He stands so tall, so manly
tall, this youth, the son of
Saul. His graceful ways, his
charm, his kindly deeds, are
those we've come to know
of Jonathan, the son of Saul,
the king. His bravery is told,
admired, by all—
his kin, the king, the priests,
the army, and his many
friends. And servants too,
they tell of how he lives,
and loves, and laughs,
and longs; they tell.

Prince Jonathan
courageously commands
his fighting men. They are
a fearless troop—they'd die
for him! He shows initiative
in waging war upon those
pilfering and plundering
those alien Philistines.

Take yesterday, exampling
this: He went alone, with

one—his faithful aide—the
armour-bearer of Prince
Jonathan. Amazingly, they
stood their ground to fight
the Philistines and won!

The enemy were many men
but ran from them, the two
of them, whose strength was
of the *YHVH*–LORD.
The men of Israel were all
enthralled to see the prince
and aide demoralise their
many foes.

The fight enlarged as Israel
joined in the fray. They
waged a glorious battle.
An earthquake spawned
more fear as the tumult
increased—a panic sent by
YHVH-LORD. They fled!

But there arose a great
distress in Israel's camp:
King Saul decreed that none
should eat before the night.
They fought with hunger
and with thirst for none
defied the edict of the king.
But Jonathan was ignorant
of his father's ban.

How could he know of this?

His appetite was raised
with honey from an oozing
comb. He'd tasted it before
his men could warn the
consequence of it, his
sipping of the honey-comb.

Prince Jonathan could see
no sense in the command
of Saul, his father-king.
He told of how the honey
nourished him—his strength
had been revived.
He thus excused himself.

And Israel's men had then
quite hurriedly prepared
some meat and gorged
themselves. It was not
faithfully prepared. The
hungry men forgot
themselves and gorged
upon untreated meat.

The king, at least, did then
endeavour to obey the
ordinance of *YHVH*-LORD.
He sought to cancel out
the sin of gorging bloodied,
unblessed food. A sacrifice
was made to ease the wrath
this feast had caused.

The king was vexed—he'd

made a foolish curse! Prince
Jonathan, his son and heir,
had sinned against the vow
and curse; such deeds were
dire for they'd, in abject
consequence, incur the
direst punishment.

The priest had strongly
warned a silence from the
YHVH-LORD. The dice
informed King Saul of
Jonathan—the sin was his!
Such sins demanded death.
Saul was appalled but
altered not his word!

Now, Israel abhorred the
thought that Jonathan
the prince should die.
They spoke for him and
pleaded with the king for
him. The prince, their
'shining light' was then
redeemed as champion.

SAMUEL: THE
CONDEMNATION
1 Samuel 15

**King Saul: You stand
condemned!
You heard the ban**

**invoked by God. The
wickedness of the warrior
Amalekites has grieved the
LORD. Their poisonous
malignancy must be
excised; they were to be
erased. The ban included
all they touched, the
whole, destroyed by fire.**

**King Saul, you stand
condemned!
You failed your test today.
The LORD is sorrowed
for your deeds. Potential is
not realised in your own
immaturity. You say the
ban has been fulfilled,
the land was cleansed?**

**Then, what is this I hear—
this bleating and this
lowing in my ears? You've
sorrowed me for sin
committed here; I grieve
your faithlessness.**

**King Saul, you stand
condemned!
The winsomeness of youth
has been displaced and
pride has intervened;
usurped your earlier good
character. Oh, why did**

you resort to blatant,
sinful disobedience? And
now, you lie! You had not
meant to judge the king,
Agag, and punish him
forthwith, it seems.

King Saul! You stand
condemned!
And from the very speech
of you, yourself, you speak
the blatant lie! You think
you will appease the
LORD with changes of
the mind concerning
sacrifice? The LORD
prefers the listening ear
and the obedient heart; He
bids you be attentive, too,
unto His will and ways.

King Saul! You stand
condemned!
You now agree your
depth of sin but don't
accompany it with a
regret, repentance or
desire to worship God
in truth. Rejection of the
YHVH–LORD has caused
Him to reject also the king
of Israel... Rent garments
are a sign of grief and,
schism too, it seems!

SAMUEL: THE CHOICE
1 Samuel 16

I now record what *YHVH*-
LORD commanded me:

*Come Samuel, cast off
your care and fill the royal
vial with oil. Now, go to
Bethlehem, 'The House of
Bread', that fairest village
in the hills where the good
shepherds tend their sheep
on peaceful pasture lands.
Though, in your age, you
know some fear? You think
of Saul, the now rejected
king—that he will do
some mischief to yourself
if once he knows the oil
you carry in the vial is for
anointing purposes? I know!*

*You will replace King Saul
with royalty of My design.
Your solemn task is to
discern a worthy man. Take
with you a calf for sacrifice.
Invite the grandson of
Boaz–make sure of Jesse,
and his strapping sons!
When you arrive, you'll find
the town astir about your
coming there. They'll be*

afraid. They wish no harm.
You'll greet them with the
peace: 'Shalom'.
Encourage, consecrate,
partake the lawful sacrifice.

You enter now the gate:
Observe the man, Jesse.
His sons include the youth
to be anointed king. The
eldest? Surely he? But, no!
View not the height nor
features fair—I look not
there but on the heart.

The second comes, the third,
the fourth. Not these; nor is
the fifth to seventh—the
chosen one's not here!
You'll ask for him, the
absent one. He tends his
father's flocks upon the
placid hills of Bethlehem.

Now, here he comes.
Observe his tread, his
his stance, his steady gaze,
his countenance. A whole-
some youth! Arise and take
the vial prepared. Now,
break the seal and pour
the oil on Israel's king!

Young David bows to take
the oil; his family's dazed—

that Samuel should choose
the lad. They are amazed at
this anointing of their kin.
My Spirit rests on him; his
strength will find its Source
in YHVH: King of kings!

DAVID, THE
SHEPHERD BOY
1 Samuel 16

The oil has flowed upon
my brow, anointing me,
the chosen of the LORD,
to be messiah-king.

But I'm a shepherd boy!
My heart is in these hills,
these peaceful hills where
sheep may safely graze.

My home is in these hills—
here is my joy! My sheep
will feed in pleasant fields
and placid streams.
I rescue them from death
and fear no evil there.
The goodness of the LORD
will follow me always.

I sing today of it!
Some verses came to me
just now; I place each line

of them within my mind.
Oh, stay with me while
I put pen to words:

DAVID'S SHEPHERD
SONG
Psalm 23
Tune: *Crimond,* C.M.

How wonderful it is to know
The LORD now shepherds me;
He leads me in a pleasant field,
I rest within the lea.

By quiet streams
refreshment comes
Where purest waters flow;
My soul is now refreshed
in grace,
His faithfulness I know.

He shepherds me,
He leads me on
In paths of righteousness;
I praise His precious Name,
my LORD,
He guards and guides always.

Sometimes in shadowed
paths I tread,
In valleys of deep grief;
My Shepherd's there,
He comforts me;
He grants my soul relief.

He cares for me in
danger's day,
Anointing me with oil;
The cleansing, flowing
oil of joy:
His choicest balm for toil.

His goodness never-failing,
sure,
His mercies when I roam;
These blessings flow
throughout my days:
My Shepherd leads me
"Home"!

…..

DAVID–
THE GIANT KILLER
1 Samuel 17

I've faced my giants at
times, and mastered them,
as every man has faced a
foe—sometimes without,
sometimes, within! My
giants were **shadows**
looming in the night.

I've found there's many
ways to face a test of
whether courage acts within
one's self. I've had my early
tests and I have won the
battles faced upon a day!

The challenges of youth
do strike more fiercely
now. The foes I've faced
in recent times are more
substantial, well-defined.
I've stood my ground
with giants like that.

I've looked them in the eyes
and challenged them to do
their worst. I've found a
strength in me to win the
day from them. A giant is
now no stronger than
the given ground!

I've found stray sheep
within the vale of death,
emerged more strong
than when I entered in the
vale. I've faced the fear and
found its strength was less
than courage gained.

I've faced a bear, the height
of it immense—it fell before
the strength I found for it,
as did the lion! It's great,
to face a giant and not
with fear retreat from it.

I saw Goliath there, with
scornful taunts that did
immobilize all Israel.

The army had no heart to
challenge him. This giant
would fall upon his pride,
it was so consummate!

I offered then to stand and
fight the giant. King Saul
did fear for me, his armour
gave to me. It was, of
course, too large for me—
I'd fail the fight with it.

I used agility and guile to
take my chance with him.
He thought I'd fled to hide
behind a boulder at the
brook; I took five stones.
And then my faithful
sling I did employ:

A sudden jerk, my sling
released its shot. The giant
was struck. He fell down
dead. So simple was the
rout, but Israel rejoiced;
they hailed my simple shot
a miracle of *YHVH*–LORD!

King Saul was much
relieved; he called to me.
How gratified I was that he,
the king, would think me so,
and ask that I should come,

take up a special task,
companioning himself!

King Saul, the king of
Israel!
I silent, thought of him—old
Samuel, the prophet-priest,
anointing oil, and God!
Have I once more, a giant
to face and fight? I'm but
a shepherd lad at heart.

DAVID–THE MINSTREL

1 Samuel 16, 18; Psalm 8

How saddening, to see
the mentally deranged in
epic struggles to survive in
able sanity today. The lucid
moments are the more a
sorrow for the laden cares
and thoughts of what the
tortured mind so smitten
might have been. Saul's
sadness was so keen.

When such a malady
should strike a national
giant, the illness must be
dealt with carefully to hide
the true complaint lest he
should be distained and
deplored, disowned; the

king's authority usurped.

I have some several
thoughts from what the
seers do say as to the cause
of it. The practically
inclined declare it is
a dark adversity where
all the brain contains
disease no potions could
resolve and this controls
his fevered mind.

But others say, instead,
the sufferer at times will
be confronted by a struggle
grim within the soul of him,
the soul is stressed by some
foul thought or deed that is
retained within the mind
and it is cankered there
without release to heal
the sin-sick soul.

I know not why King Saul
does struggle, thus, within
himself. It seems he
wars between his best
and worst. At times, his
eyes are murderous; It's
then I stay alert for there,
his anger twists on me. So
suddenly he takes his spear
and aims it at my heart!
I watch him, there.

His restless countenance
conveys betraying inner
storms for Saul has entered
in the soul's bleak night.
How oft an evil sprite does
strike him down, my king,
in melancholic moods
that may his sanity forsake.

My life's at risk
and when I see his
countenance does alter
on a whim, I must evade his
spear, retreat until the storm
abates and blessed peace
will settle him once more
and he is of a lucid, tranquil
mood at last. I yearn for him
on these such painful days.

How music charms,
and calms, the restless soul
My harp's cadence of joy,
its lilting lays, its
companying psalms,
express the depth of heart
emotions—witnessing the
soul's tranquillity restored
by nature's balm. I long
to see the king serene!

My fingers pluck
the strings to free their
melodies; caressingly they
coax elusive tunes, the harp

responds; pure music flows:
Such gentle harmonies and
such rhythmic, soothing
sounds. And then I know
the king finds peace.

I play the zephyr breeze
on fleecy clouds in from the
sea; I play the sun upon the
dappled dales, the swiftly
flowing stream, the flowers
in waving grass, the birds
and wind on leaves in
the majestic trees.

I sing the stars
that gleam at night.
I meet my tunes with words
in psalms to God Most
High–I sing in praise.
I'd have the king to think,
remembering well each day
the *YHVH*-LORD when
every dark and drastic muse
might seep into his soul; I'd
lift my joyful heart to praise
the Holy Name—I will sing
an ode to God!

A PSALM OF PRAISE
Psalm 8
Tune: *Chalvey*, D.S.M.

"O LORD, Your precious Name
Is praised in all the Earth!
Your matchless glory
shines above
The heavens in radiant light.
The children chant Your praise
And foes do flee from Truth.
I contemplate the skies:
the sun,
The moon and stars so bright.

So! What is man that You
Should be so mindful of
His many needs, and care
for him?
You crown Your chosen heir
With glory, honour, near
To angels, and You've planned
For him to guard throughout
the Earth,
The creatures of Your care.

O LORD, our LORD,
Your Name
Is praised in all the Earth;
You rule in glorious majesty.
Your glory shines above
The heavens, the moon,
the stars
You've set in place, and yet
You care for us each one
beyond
All else, O LORD of Love!"

. . . .

I love this man,
the king; he is the father
of my dearest friend, the
prince. I'd die for him, the
king, and yet, sometimes,
he'd take my life! I'll care
for him, create these tunes,
placate his grief, restore his
peace, and stand by him
through all my days.

DAVID–FRIENDSHIP
1 Samuel 19, 20

There is a choicest kin that's
not of blood; more close
than family ties, it is
entwined with purposes as
one. The bonds we share
are blessed bonds, inspiring
mutual joy. Though oh,
so wrenched apart at times,
the unity remains, for both,
intact. Our friendship
unimpaired, our spirits
meet; one knows another's
need and cares for it.

Such are the bonds I know
with Jonathan, the princely
son of Saul. He has a
strength in him that's
metered not in strength

of arm but strength of
character. The light within
his eyes is such that's found
in kindliness and also
thoughtfulness, just as a
friend should be. But, father
Saul would have my life.
This is my grief. The prince
goes in to Saul to plead for
me. He marks my
innocence, my loyalty.
He pleads it right!

I would not care to be
unpatriotic of King Saul,
a fugitive in hiding from
the troubled king.
And yet it seems, it comes
to this, as does the prince
perceive, for Jonathan
brings news of audience:

This news he brings is grief
to me! The king revealed his
hate of me. We make
a pact, as friends are wont
to do, when separation
looms. So! We must bid
farewell for distant climes.
Prince Jonathan then sends
his guidance via an arrow's
path. It falls beyond my
'bode. The news?

The danger grows: Depart!

So, I must go as does
the arrow go—
beyond my sheltered home.
We part in grief, we weep,
then leave in peace that is
of *YHVH*-LORD.

DAVID–THE FUGITIVE
1 Samuel 21 – 30

I have, within my memory,
the phases of my flight from
Saul. They fresh remain,
those desperate days. I trace
again the many ways
the LORD has led me on.
It is amazing that my life is
spared from each and every
passing phase of fear. But,
there are those who aided
me–without such helping
hands, I would have
perished in these barren
lands. Deserted and
forlorn of hope, I'll tell
of them, my true cohorts:

Ahimelech – Nob.
My first respite from Saul
was in the priestly town
of Nob, quite near
Jerusalem. Ahimelech, the
priest, great-grandson of the

famed Eli, presided there.
I had to utilise some guile.
Ahimelech did question me,
concerned about the fact
I was alone. He heard,
then chose to meet my need
for bread that day.
But from the Holy Place
he took the hallowed loaves
and blessed them to
my thankful use.
(I hope this has no evil
consequence).

Achish – Gath

My flight progressed; I fled
to Gath. A most enthralling
thing occurred for there,
the servants of the king
(Achish, the king of Gath,
that is), proceeded to refer
to me as king. Yes! Israel's
king, no less! It really was
absurd for here was I,
a fugitive! They saw me as
a king–with reason, too.
This raised my fears.
To save my life, I feigned
insanity. The king relented,
(though he scorned
my pose).

Family – Mizpah

My journey took a torturous
route—I fled away
to Adullun. My friends
and family came to me,
a cave became our hiding
place. I feared the worst
for them so took them to
Mizpah, the watch-tower
of Moab so far away.
(O LORD do watch for us)!
The king became disposed
to grant them sanctuary.
My friends, who formed
a troop to fight and guard
my way and I returned
at once to Judah's hills,
(as Gad the prophet
counselled me).

Abiathar

There came into our forest
camp a priest of Nob–
Ahimelech's own son,
Abiathar, alive! I found
that Saul had learned of
my own visit to the priestly
town, the succour of the
sacred bread, also,
possession of Goliath's
sword. The penalty was
death—a reek of mad
revenge upon the priests.
My heart was wrenched,
I'd taken loaves and scant
obeyed the terms.

(Was this a rightful
punishment)?

Jonathan – Ziph

He came to me, did
Jonathan, right to the secret
caves at yonder Ziph.
His soul is truly knit with
mine—he helped me find
new strength in God.
He gave such very strong
encouragement to me that
day. He pointed me to faith
in God, to know of His own
choice promises! He
vouched that Saul would not
prevail. And then, a lovely
thing—the prince avowed
his loyalty to me, (for I not
he would wear
the crown)!

Abigail – Paran

My men and I have
faithfully observed the
rights of those upon the
land, not wishing any
enmity. But Nabal was an
evil man, uncouth in all his
wretched ways; he treated
us contemptuously. But,
Abigail, his wife did come
to us and intercede to save

the whole community. Her
deed impressed us so,
Though when she told
Nabal of this, he died of
shock immediately.
(Soon, Abigail became
my willing bride)!

King Saul – the Desert Lands

The two amazing instances
where Saul and I did meet
(unknown to him,) did place
the king within my power
to take his life. I'd have no
part of that; my loyalty
remained as unimpaired and
would be through his reign.
The yattered hem, and then
the spear and water jug
became the signs I'd spared
the king to hear my plea that
he should cease to doubt my
loyalty. The king, amazed,
at once concurred.
(Who'd know if whims
in him awoke)?

Achish – Gath

My safest sanctuary was
with the warring Philistines
who were our mortal
enemy. And yet they gave

to us a haven from incessant
hounding by King Saul.
And, Achish changed
his tune with me from when
we'd met before. I had no
need to act the fool;
he knew the enmity of Saul.
He gave to us the haven of
Ziklag where we'd abide in
peace. We proved our fealty
by raiding foes (though we
deceived)!

Abiathar of Ziklag
My faithful Abiathar, the
priest, and lone survivor of
the Nob atrocity, was with
us at Ziklag. Now, much
to my relief, though I did
feign a grief, the wily
Philistines refused our
company to terrorise Israel.
When we returned into our
homes, Our grief was real
for foes—Amalekites—had
plundered all: our wives,
our families and also, all our
goods. My men prepared
for murderous mutiny,
(distraught at this bleak
emptiness).

Rebellion and Reunion
This was my lowest ebb.

That they, my men, should
turn on me though I was
quite bereft as they. I
blamed it on their tragedy.
And then, my priest—
Abiathar—began to counsel
me. I found my strength
renewed in *YHVH*-LORD,
enquired of Him, and
trusted Him to bring us
victory! What joy it was,
retrieving all our loved-ones
and the booty too! My Clan
received a bounteous share
(and I, a guarantee of aid.)

SAUL – THE SÉANCE
1 Samuel 28

**All vestige of my hope is
lost! We mourn the death
of Samuel and I am as an
orphan in a storm of doubt
and stress. I fear my
incapacity to choose the
normal ways for kings
to act when faced with
real uncertainty. Where
do I turn? Who do I ask
in all this fertile land?**

**How do I calculate the
odds we'd win or lose**

against the Philistines?
I sought a sign from
YHVH-LORD, but He
is silent as the tomb!
No Samuel have I and
now I fear to trust
my son, my Jonathan.
I need to read the spirit-
powers and seek to see
beyond the grave.

My brain now troubles
me; I can't resume my
fleeting confidence.
It is as though I sink
into a slough of dark
despair. I'll go to her—
the witch near Endor at
her cave—entreating her,
enticing her to call up
Samuel, enlisting him
to speak from down in
nether-worlds beyond
the tomb of death.

I'll cast my kingly robes
aside and throw about
myself a veiling cloak of
anonymity. I choose the
night; the day betrays
the king. The drapes of
darkness suit my mood;
my spirit seems to cling
to glooms of night. No,
woman! Have no fear.

I'll pay you well,
be sure of that.

I would entreat the ghost
of Samuel, the faithful,
aged seer of Israel these
many years, just past.
Please, call him up for
me—I'll test your worth,
as witch, to see how well
you can oblige me with
your expertise this very
night: Engage the dead;
call up for me old Samuel!

I watch her weave her
potent spells within the
vapours of the night.
It is an eerie scene and
dark. I recognise that
voice: It's Samuel! The
witch is 'thralled in fear!
Now when he comes, she
all but faints and staggers
to the earth. What mortal
fright is in her face!

She called, entreated him
to rise! There's mystery,
stark terror in the air. She
points at me, accusingly.
She shrieks my name,
King Saul, you have
deceived; you want my

life! Fear not, you witch,
what do you see? What
can it be that you discern
right now?

A spirit forms from out
the ground and robed like
as the seer, I see! I fall
before Samuel, distraught.
Disturbed, the seer does
chide, reprove. I plead for
wise advice—he knows my
long-held malady of course.

Please, tell me what to do;
I am alone, the LORD's
departed far from me.
It's as predicted, and you
know what will be the
outcome of your wicked
ways: The *YHVH*–LORD
has torn the kingdom
from your grasp. As you
well know, it's David who
will take the crown. The
Philistines will cause a
rout: Tomorrow, you and
all your sons will be with
me. All help has gone!

SAUL–THE SUICIDE
1 Samuel 31; 1 Chron. 10

My failing eyes now glaze.

The pain, intense, does
burn into my very heart.
I come upon the throes of
death; its shadow falls. I
view with grief this battle
field. The Philistines do
now advance. My sons
are dead, my hope is lost,
Israel is lost! My throne,
my crown: all lost!

Come, armour-bearer,
please, thrust my sword
and save me from our
foes, at least… You
cannot, will not, do this
thing I ask? I see;
I'll take this sword:
Perhaps the peace that I
have yearned, that fled
from me, returns to me
in death...

DAVID: THE LAMENT
2 Samuel 1

O Israel, your glory fades;
It lies upon the heights;
Great lives are strewn upon
Your vast and hoary heights.

O, tell it not in Gath today;
Proclaim it not, our woe,
Lest they should dance upon

Our grief and gloat our woe.

O, Mountains of Gilboa's
heights,
May rains now cease to fall;
Fields cease to yield
their grain,
For here, Israel did fail.

O Saul, of Israel, I grieve
Your death, and Jonathan,
My own true friend, your bow
Lies low. O Jonathan.

How loved you were, the father
and the son; so gracious, too.
Far swifter than an eagle flight;
With strength of lions, too.

O, daughters of all Israel,
Now weep for Saul today;
He clothed you in your finery;
Now mourn for him today.

How mighty are the
fallen ones!
I grieve for you, my friend;
Your care for me was
wonderful,
My choice, my greatest friend.

O Israel, our grief is whole!
Your warrior king, his prince,
Has fallen with the mighty now;
We grieve for him and prince.

DAVID–THE CORONATION

2 Samuel 2 – 4; 1 Chron.
12:23-40

The crown is in my hands!
It's hardly in my heart,
I must confess, for I still
grieve for them, my liege
and prince. I am anointed,
chosen of the LORD. But,
how to prove it so this day,
confirm my kingship in
Israel? How will the nation
now react? The awesome
task compounds!

All Judah turns to me,
confirms allegiance—
they've sworn their faith-
fulness to me, their king, by
virtue of the choice that
YHVH-LORD has made!
There are immense intrigues
and the strategic purposing
as this, my reign begins this
very day. I am amazed.
The awesome kingly
task confounds.

Perceiving that the realm is
rent by choice of which king
should be lawful liege of
Israel, I speed to take
control and meld the Clans

once more to unity, to faith
in *YHVH*-LORD who really
is the King of all. Because
of this one thing, my
awesome, kingly
task compels.

DAVID:
THE RIVALRY

2 Samuel 2

The Pool of Gibeon was
stilled with sheen. It
mirrored well the men at
arms provoking all the
other side, opposing force,
with every spiteful glance.
Mistrust and malice, too,
were in their gaze.

And sitting down, we
glowered at them across
the shimmering pool,
determining intent—all
Israel was ranged against
Judah this day. The pool,
mirrored, did mock each
fighting force.

The rival generals—Joab,
Abner, son of Ner, decided
on a feat of strength by

well-selected men that day:
a wrestling match with all
their weapons drawn—
for malice or defence,
we little knew or cared.

The fighting was intense,
one side, and then, once
more, the other gained the
main ascendancy. The
men of Abner, though,
towards the end,
did weaken as our side
did bring about a rout
and victory won.

Now Asahel, the fleet of
foot, and brother of Joab,
set out to catch Abner who
had escaped the battle
scene. Abner did warn the
younger man to cease
pursuit of him in interest
of his very life!

Persisting, Asahel at last
did meet his fate on
Abner's sword. Joab,
Abishai, brothers too,
sought to avenge. But
then, we heard the cry:
Abner declared: It is
enough! No more blood-
shed: we're are together
brothers, everyone!

DAVID: THE TREACHERY
2 Samuel 3

He came to me!
He crossed from them
to us. He gave his sword
to me and vowed to me
allegiance now. Yes! It was
Abner, the general of
Ishbosheth, son of Saul!
I welcomed him and knew
at once that now the King
of Hebron would become
the King of all Israel. I'd
won the day, and crown:
At last! The kingdom
would be mine! But Joab
saw a rival in Abner, I'm
sure. But more, he grieved
the killing of his kin,
the well-known Asahel.

A treacherous thing: he
lured Abner into a trap of
death. I'm mortified that
this should happen now
when there was hope of
healing rifts and bringing
to Israel the hope of peace
and true prosperity.

I wept for him, for Abner,
newly loyal, now dead and
gone from us—it was truly

a wretched, treacherous
thing was done to him.
And cursed be, I say,
the house of Joab now!
Should Abner die as all
the lawless die, I ask you
now? His helpful hands,
unbonded, free, and on
his feet, no fetters yet; he
fell most wickedly by him,
a 'friend'. This is my
dark lament this day.

KING DAVID, THE ANOINTING

2 Samuel 5; 1 Chron. 11:1 – 3

Three times I've known the
oil to flow upon my head—
I'm thrice anointed king!
The first was in a field when
I was called to Samuel: I
bowed to take the sacred oil.
That was a day for all
remembrance. The LORD
did bless me in the oil,
anointing me via Samuel.
I felt I was truly the
'*messiah*–king' that day.

The oil at Hebron's heights
had also flowed upon my

head. All Judah hailed me
king. I called to mind the
words of Samuel and knew
that I was chosen of the
LORD. I ruled upon the
heights of Hebron in the
south—the heart of Judah's
land. And, all the while,
I thought: Next year,
Jerusalem, of course!
But, seven years then
passed.

The oils, again they flow!
I am anointed king once
more! The first was of the
LORD, the second, Judah's
choice. And now all Israel!
The delegation came to
represent all Clans. Their
formal speech was all
so moving to my mind. I'd
led them well. They knew,
they'd said, the LORD had
chosen me as king!

They recognised that I,
a humble shepherd, knew
just how to lead the 'sheep'
of Israel. They asked that I
would come to be their
king–their 'shepherd' king!
And there, I covenanted
with them all, on Hebron's
mount. The oil did flow

again upon my head. Above
the rest, I felt the *LIGHT* of
God upon my soul. Next
year, Jerusalem!

A BYSTANDER:
JERUSALEM!

2 Samuel 5; 1 Chron. 11:4 – 9

Jerusalem! King David's
home! The crown now
comes within your gates,
O beautiful Zion, the city
on the mountain height—
strategic fort which none
could conquer till he came
anointed of the LORD.

They entered via the water-
course. It wasn't all the
blind and lame who lost the
ground. It was the proudest
Jebusites who thought the
city was impregnable!
Yes, all brought to the dust
before the mighty men of
Israel. King David's throne
is set in Zion!

Jerusalem! The Home of
Peace: Your gates now open
wide—receive your king!
He rides a stallion,

the warrior, '*messiah*–king'.
See now, the conquering
hero comes. The children
wave their fronds. They sing
and strew their branch
before the stallion's path.
The king now rides in
splendour and the crowds
do chant his praise. The
king has brought salvation
near—the city grants its
greatest peace to him:
King David's throne
resides in Zion!

Jerusalem! *Messiah's* home.
A tethered donkey grazes
by the path, it raises up
its head to gaze upon
the spectacle. The donkey
dreams that he could,
chance, to carry such a king
as that—a king upon his
back! Imagine that—
the ass could not;
it munches grass!
The troop does pass; the
shadow of King David falls,
oblique, upon the donkey's
cross-marked back…
No king could come to Zion
upon an ass… It turns to
graze in peace, King David
now enters into Zion!

A PRIEST: THE ARK OF COVENANT

2 Samuel 5 – 6; 1 Chron. 13.

There was a sound of
marching in the trees; the
Wind of God did rustle in
the leaves—He signalled to
the king that victory was
near. The Philistines would
be vanquished.

The LORD gave all
the strategy;
The king then issued his
command; the foe did flee
forthwith. Then, from
the triumph of the
conquering of the wily
Philistines, King David
knew the time had come
to bring the holy Ark
into his Citadel.

Thus David called Israel to
participate by joining in the
grand procession of the Ark
by marching up to Zion's
heights, Jerusalem!

How gloriously they came,
the festive march and all so
jubilant and joyous of the

YHVH-LORD! The mighty
Name of God was praised;
all eyes were on the Ark,
resplendent in the brightest
noonday sun. The kneeling
cherubim did bow unto its
Caphah Lid–the sacred
Mercy Seat .

Although, why not the
priests? Ought not they
hoist the Ark upon the
poles, and shoulder it? The
Ark sat, precariously, upon
a cart. The oxen lurched
upon unstable ground,
the wheels descended in
a ditch; the Ark appeared
to fall to earth and Uzzah
placed his hand…

The Grand Procession
ceased for Uzzah lay upon
the ground. His heart had
failed for this outrageous
thing he did. He'd known
the rule: No hand must
touch the Ark! As if
the LORD should need
some help to stay erect!
Great fear then spread
throughout the host of
Israel: the priests and
all the commoners.

The king was in a rage at
first for this appalling thing
to happen to them all. But,
then, a fear stole over him.
How may the Ark now
come into the Citadel? He
dare not place Jerusalem
at risk; he'd have to find
alternatives—a suited place
to house the Ark and thus
placate the LORD.

Then, Obed-Edom, man
of Gad, was called into
the presence of the king.
Request was made that he
should take the Ark into his
home. The LORD did bless
the man and all his family.
His house became a shrine,
a holy place, where he and
all his family did worship
God, the *YHVH*–LORD.

The news from Obed-Edom
pleased the king. He
realised that God does bless
all those who honour Him,
who give first place to Him
in heart and home. The
LORD would have first
place within the heart
of our beloved Israel!

The king came down to
Obed-Edom's humble home
to speak with him.

Then out the house they
came, the Levi priests who
carried, on their shouldered
poles, the Ark of Covenant.
The whole procession
worshipped, sacrificed,
and danced most joyously
unto the LORD. The king
cast off his royal robe,
and ephod wore.
The trumpets set
the rhythm of
exuberant dance.

The Ark processed to
David's City on the Mount.
It entered through the
open gates, with David
dancing all the while
in joyous ecstasy. They
came unto the tent the king
had there prepared—
a 'tabernacle' where all
priests may serve and
worship there, and king
may praise the LORD.

· · · · · · ·

YHVH–LORD:
THE DIRECTION
2 Samuel 7; I Chron. 15 – 17

Are you the one, My son,
to build a 'Home' for God?
that I should dwell, as Man'
upon the Earth? I have no
'Home' on Earth, although
I closely dwell with you.

I've tabernacled with
the Clans through all their
years of pilgrimage. Where
did I ever say to one who
shepherded My 'sheep',
'I need a 'Home' In which
to dwell? Where is My own,
My cedar timbered 'Home',
where I'd abide?

I took you from the flocks,
from shepherd pastures in
the hills of Bethlehem; from
tending sheep, to tend My
precious people, Israel.

I've been with you all
through the years; your
name is praised throughout
the land. I've brought My
people to the City of My
Peace. No longer shall
oppressors foil. I shall

*establish your own house
eternally. Long after you
have gone to dust, a greater
Son shall rule in Kingdom
Peace! Your house endures
into Eternity!*

KING DAVID:
AT PRAYER
2 Samuel 7

O, who am I and what my
family, that You, O LORD,
do bless me so? You've
opened up the long
unknown of years to come
before my gaze. Is this Your
usual mode, to bless Your
chosen one, O *YHVH*-
LORD?

What can I say? You know
Your servant, Sovereign
LORD. According to Your
will, You make it known to
me. How great You are.
There is no god but You.
You chose Your people for
Yourself to bless Your
Name. You have established
well this holy nation,
blessed of God.

And now, O LORD, I pray
You keep these promises
that men may say, The
LORD Almighty rules
the holy tribes of Israel.
I'm bold to make this plea;
Your word I trust.

I meant to build a House
for You for why should I
in cedar dwell and You,
within a tent? But You
declare, instead, You'll
build a house for me and
mine that will remain
always! I am amazed
O *YHVH*–LORD
that You should care!

A COURTIER TO
MEPHIBOSHETH
2 Samuel 9

Mephibosheth! There's fear
upon your features now;
the king has called you up
to Zion, unto his courts that
he might question you.
Now, what is on your mind
but all of what King Saul
did plan to take his life,
annihilate his 'foe',

the minstrel shepherd lad
who sang so aptly for the
king. You fear he takes
revenge upon the one
grandson who yet remains,
to square the balances of
fate with you... You are a
crippled man, yet there's no
malice in your soul.

Mephibosheth, there's
LIGHT upon your painfilled
features now; You've come
from him, the king, and
courts of Zion to tell
amazing things. You speak
of how King David smiled
on you, inquired as to your
family and, how you've
fared these many years.

He's called you to his home,
his royal palace home,
to eat at table with the king?
He treats you as a prince, as
Jonathan, his dearest friend?
He's planned for your
economy? It's wonderful!
And you, a crippled man,
show awesome wonder in
your happy soul!

....

KING DAVID: THE STRATEGIES
2 Samuel 8, 10; 1 Chron. 14

The strategies of kings must
be both military and
conciliatory! There is a
certain skill in bringing
harmony to factions, fretting
tribes. The many Clans
of Israel have viewed
with dark mistrust those
years of inter-tribal strife,
for loyalties misplaced.

I sense the others have
no latent love for my own
Judah Clan but all have
merged for sake of me,
their king. It is my task
to heal the rifts and bring
cohesion to the Clans.

I praise the LORD that they
will follow me, the whole,
with loyalty and pride in
what has been achieved
for peace in Israel!
Conciliation now enables
me to plan, to strategize, the
wars which must be fought
against the enemies which
roam our precious,
Promised Land.

It's spring again, the season
when all kings set off for
battle where the strongest
will prevail. I praise the
LORD that we, within His
awesome plans, His
strategies, do win most
handsomely.

The Clans rejoice the
victories most hardly won
but, all convincingly.
Our homes we now
maintain at rest because
the power of God prevails.
He governs us
in glorious peace!

HALLELUJAH! LORD:
WE REST IN *SHALOM*
PEACE.

KING DAVID:
THE SEDUCTION
2 Samuel 11

**I saw her there–her home
pressed close against that
wall, my palace fence. I'd
risen from my bed for
breath of vale-cooled air
and, then, I saw her
lithesome frame was robed
in nought but the light of
moon. Its silvered rays**

**caressed her so and as she
tipped the earthen vase,
its waters flowed in
comely waves all down her
hair. Its raven tress did
shine within the kindly
moon. A stealthy cloud
did tempt the light;
in softest folds it draped
upon her milk-dew skin.**

**The rhythmic shapes
of light impelled my gaze,
her sensuous frame
enticed a lust; desire for
her increased. I knew a
passion then for her, the
wife of one who served
me well! I sent for her.**

**She came to me and I was
lost in her embrace. We
loved and hungered there
upon the bed of our
disgrace till she conceived,
my lovely one: Bathsheba,
my lusted, deep desire!**

**Our secret tryst, our
rendezvous, became a
grave affair when it was
told to me—she was 'with
child'! Her husband then
was called from out the**

battlefield. I'd thought to
have him come to her that
one could think the child
was his. Uriah was a
faithful man. I felt
alarmed when he
preferred to guard my
court for, why should he
enjoy the comfort of his
bed when all the army
rough did sleep on rocks!
He'd stay his guard to
serve his king! I really
should have owned
my sin but I compounded
it, instead unto my shame!

I sent Uriah to his death
to save the face of this,
the king! And, when the
days of mourning passed,
Bathsheba came to me
once more–the one I had
seduced became my
lovely bride!

NATHAN:
THE ADMONITION
2 Samuel 12

I bring to your attention,
Sire, a matter that repels
the mind, a drastic
circumstance, of which

you will recoil in utmost
horror of the blatant
crime that's done to one
so poor as him of whom
I now must speak.
Since you appointed me
as Royal Seer, your
servant Nathan has not
known a cruelty displayed
as is this thing I bring
before your awful gaze
this very day. I ask for
your own judgement on
this grim affair and mete
the proper punishment
that is appropriate for
such heinous crime.

There is, within your royal
realm, a prosperous man
whose wealth includes fine
flocks of lambs and sheep
which shepherds keep on
hills of home. And many
cattle, too, that do increase
considerably his massive
wealth beyond all means.

Now, in a humble village
by this rich man's fields,
there lives a humble man
whose only wealth was in
a small, but perfect lamb
the man adored. He raised
that lamb; he cherished it.

His children loved it so;
it shared the humble fare
they knew as food. It
drank out from the very
cup the poor man held!
It slept within his arms
on every winter's night.

A traveller came to spend
the night within the rich
man's home. And, as a
host is keen to do, the rich
man planned a feast on his
behalf. But when it came
to choose the lamb, a
fatted lamb, he loath did
look upon his flocks,
deplete his ample stocks!

He looked upon the lamb,
the one that grazed just by
the poor man's door. He
took the little lamb, the
ewe, and slaughtered it.
He grandly served it to his
guest with ne'er a thought
of grief his deed had
caused unto the poor man
and his family.

You're angry, Sire! I see
the fierce and righteous
rage you bear towards the
cruelty displayed unto the
poor, bereft of choicest
love. You say the man
deserves to die—how right
you are! You've judged
the wicked man,
determined punishment
to suit the crime. He must
repay fourfold because he
lacked in pity too! It is so
right that you should be so
furious at one who has
besmirched the Law. You
ask his name? My Sire,
I've come from *YHVH-*
LORD: The man is *YOU!*

I've sinned before the
LORD! I've sinned most
grievously. My sin is more
than I can bear! My wives!
My sons! My LORD!

A Hymn for Private Prayer

THE PENITENT'S PLEA
2 Samuel 12:13; Psalm 51
Tune: *Ellacombe*   D.C.M.

O LORD, Your faithfulness
is sure,
Your mercy ever flows;
Your lovingkindness never
fails,
You understand my woes.

O LORD, for pardon now
I come
For cleansing in Your stream,
Your healing stream of grace
that flows
To wash away sin's stains.

I know I've failed to honour You
In every deed and word;
Transgression's stains have
marred my soul,
Increased my guilt, O LORD.
Align my will unto Your own;
Come, LORD, to make
me whole,
Implant Your truth, Your
wisdom there,
Deep in my inmost soul.

Now wash away the stain of sin
That grieves You, LORD,
I pray;
My heart make pure as
whitest snow:
LORD, make me clean
this day!
Let joy replace the grief of sin
And gladness claim my life;
O, purify the hidden stains,
Forgive, and heal my strife.

Create in me the purest heart,
Renew my soul, my plea.
O, cast me not out from
Your care;

Sustain and strengthen me.
Restore me, LORD, unto
the joy
Which Your salvation gives;
Your Holy Spirit dwell with me:
In Him my spirit lives.

Grant me the grace to
lead the lost
Back to the ways of God,
To point poor sinners to
the One
Who saves within the Blood.
I'll sing of all Your
righteousness,
My lips shall sound
Your praise;
The broken, and the
contrite heart,
O LORD, You won't despise.

....

A Hymn for Public Worship

A PENITENT'S PRAYER
2 Samuel 12:13: Psalm 51
Tune: *Lloyd*   C.M.

O LORD, Your faithfulness
endures,
Your mercies ever flow,
Your lovingkindness
never fails;

With grace our souls endow.

We sorrow for our sins,
O LORD,
We've failed to honour You;
Impart Your truth, Your
wisdom, LORD,
To counsel and renew.

LORD, cleanse the soul,
our heart refine
Far whiter than the snow;
O, wash us in the
precious balm;
Let healing waters flow.

O LORD, create in us, we pray,
A heart that's pure and whole;
Renew a steadfast
spirit, LORD;
Come, sanctify the soul.

We seek Your presence
every hour:
O LORD, abide with us;
Restore to us our praising joy,
Renew our will and bless.

Sustain us by Your Grace,
O LORD,
We would declare Your praise;
We'll sing of all Your
righteousness
For You restore our peace.

A PROPHET
2 Samuel 13 – 19

The sins of David, king,
are visited upon his sons,
unprincely sons, who
almost brought the king
to nought for all their
spoiled and wicked ways.
Perhaps it was not, mostly,
fault of theirs! Ought not,
when each were youths,
the king have counselled
them, to rightly raise
them with some timely
discipline?

Where was that discipline
when David went to all
those wars? Who then did
counsel them about
integrity and honour,
ways that princes should
always behave, and, where
was suited punishment
when this was sadly
earned; no birch was laid
upon the flesh to chasten
them, I'm told.

Who guarded them and
guided them when
character was formed?
And, who instructed them
when David then, I'm told,

possessed Uriah's wife?
They learned the ways of
lustful men; but little did
they learn of choicest ways
to live as those who
followed *YHVH*-LORD's
chaste Laws.

The crime of Amnon was
unspeakable for he defiled
his sibling when his
senseless passion raped,
deprived her, Tamar, of
the one, most precious gift
a maid could bring to her
betrothed. There was no
discipline of self at all in
Amnon's awful, ignoble,
his foulest deed.

The handsome Absalom,
his father's choicest 'pet',
deprived his brother of
his life for this, his crime,
heinous crime, against
Tamar–as well, the king
and family. He took his
chance, repaid in blood
the dreadful sin that had
indeed besmirched
them all.

And as the prince–yes,
Absalom, the pride of

palace and the joy of
David's heart, did all but
rape the crown out from
his father's hands to make
it his. He planned, with
studied insolence and dark
contempt of him, the
greatest king of Israel,
to seize the crown and
father's throne.

And, loving him, the king
stood still for far too long
for fear he'd injure him,
his upstart son and
heinous heir. The sorrows
and the vilest, vicious
curses on the king did
leave him all but desolate.
The loss of palace, wives,
and all authority was grim
indeed and piteous to
ever see.

The griefs that David bore
from his own flesh and
blood did bring him grey
with age, the age that
sorrows bring. But then
Absalom's dark schemes
of rank impertinence did
bring him down for he
misread advice: The good

was bad to him, the bad
seemed good, so bad it
was. And Absalom
continued in his sins
with greater yet intrigue
and all the while, this
offered time unto the king,
allowing his own faithful
troops to group again,
advantage seize, and win
the day. The prince was
caught up, in his pride:
unruly hair. The oak tree
held him fast!

The tree became the
gallows till a swifter death
engulfed the prince by
force of Joab's spear.
Then all the messengers
did run. The one, the
darker lad, commenced
the race against the time
to tell the king of
Absalom's demise. But
another, fleet of foot,
outran the first.

The king received the
news from him so vaguely
put it proved a buffer till
the darker lad then told it
all—the death of Absalom.
Then David wept in grief,
in grief of him, the son

who'd sought his crown,
his life. O Absalom, if only
I had died this day instead
of you, my grief would be
erased in my own death!

AN OBSERVER:
THE FRIENDS
2 Samuel 14 – 23; 1 Chron. 11

The General
The champion–Joab, the
one who stood as general to
the king; the chief of all the
fighting force was cruel but
knew the skills of battle and
intrigue. He used them well.
Some exploits of this man
would horrify but he
maintained his oath
(or, so it seemed)!

The Guards
King David's loyal men!
Full strong, they were six
hundred men at arms.
They'd served him well
all through those years
they'd lived as fugitives
and stayed by him.
And then, they served as
well as palace guards. Yes!
all were loyal unto the very

end. They'd give their lives
(if needed to)!

Ithai

What loyalty was found
In Ithai–commander of
these men! The king did try
to save his loyal friend but
he preferred to chance his
life, be true to king and,
YHVH-LORD. All forded
then the Kidron Brook,
Jerusalem's deep valley
babbling brook,
(the darkest stream).

The Priests

Zadok the priest, a
colleague too, and also
Abithai, had joined the king
upon that sad retreat. It
came, with them, the
precious Ark. The king well
knew it should remain
within the Tabernacle Tent.
He sent them back with this
to place it in its rightful
place. He did do well in this
(He also planned their
aid as well).

Hushai

Maybe the bravest of them
all, the friend of David,
Israel's king, was Hushai

who, it seemed, betrayed his
Sire, as did the prince.
Or so it seemed to some.
Though, never did he see
the wiles by which this man
did ill advise and send all
the intelligence back unto
home base, (that is towards
his king and friend).

The Aliens

With what respect and
warmth of heart they cared
for David whilst he fled, in
hiding from his Absalom,
his son. Of these, the three
from Trans-Jordan: Shobi,
Machir, and Barzillai,
succoured king and troops.
He'd earned the king's kind
offer of the court and
(his son did gain)!

Mephibosheth

The one so wronged by
his own Ziba, yes, the
servant who had lied to gain
the goods—the wealth the
king had placed within his
hands. The prince of
Jonathan did mourn the
strife and proved his
worth in grace when he
forgave the wretched man

(he did prefer the king's
royal remand)!

The Mighty Men

Let all the records show
the king was served by
Mighty Men—as giants
among their own and
nearest kin. And, of the
army, they did lead in
strength, exampling the best
of feats and all the victories
they gained in serving him.
They finally won through,
indeed, it's true—
(beside the king)!

KING DAVID: THE OFFERING

2 Samuel 24; 1 Chron. 21

Upon a day when to the
Mount we came, my troops
and I, we paused just near
the threshing floor of one,
Araunah, loyal Jebusite.
These days were shadowed;
all the land was in the
throes of death's grim grip.
The pall of death hung low
upon the earth as ravaged by
a plague—a visitation of
despair that entered every

home and kin. Frail children
breathed their last, or saw
each parent come to death.

We'd come to Mount
Moriah this day, now
nestled by Jerusalem.
Oh! What a site this was!
Just right—an altar for an
offering. Young Isaac was
once tested here and, by the
knife of Abraham his father,
loved; until a substitute, a
lamb, was found for
offering, just near. Oh, what
a place for Temple, too,
if only *YHVH* would
allow it so.

Just near the Eastern gate
we paused for here, the
pestilence did cease, was
checked, upon direct
command of *YHVH*-LORD.
I sought the man, Araunah,
who did come to me.
He offered me a threshing
floor as gift unto his liege,
the king! But, surely, I
would never bring an
offering to *YHVH*-LORD
of that which cost me
nought at all. I offered that
most personal and sacrificial
to myself; yes, that most

suitable for Him, my
YHVH-LORD for worship
has its costs: in this, its
value is the stewardship
of self!

A Hymn of Testimony

A SONG OF PRAISE
2 Samuel 22; Psalm 18
Tune: *Vox Dilecti* D.C.M.

O LORD, You are the
Mighty Rock,
My sure foundation, LORD.
My trusting soul's deliverance,
My Refuge, by Your word.
I call upon Your mighty Name,
The Saviour of my life;
How worthy of my praise,
O LORD,
My Fortress in all strife.

I trust Your faithfulness,
O LORD,
Your righteous promise plead;
I call to You in my distress,
You come to meet my need.
You draw me from the
flowing depths,
Your hand does reach to me;
Deep waters surge upon
my soul,
But You deliver me!

I yearn to live in righteousness,
To walk the ways of God
That I would follow
blamelessly,
Made pure within the Blood.
You turn my darkness
into light,
You are a Lamp to me
And, all Your ways are perfect,
LORD;
Your word now comforts me.

You arm me with the Shield
of Faith,
Perfecting me in might;
You make my steps like as
the deer,
To stand upon the height.
I sing unto my Saviour, LORD,
My Rock, my Tower,
my God!
Exulted be Your precious
Name
Forever! Praise the LORD!

··········

KING DAVID:
THE EPILOGUE
2 Samuel 23; Genesis 49:10

The shepherd lad, the son
of Jesse, David—man
exalted of the LORD—
anointed as the king,

the poet of the hymns of
Israel: The king who rules
in Zion, declares: 'The
Spirit of the LORD has
moved my soul, inspiring
me to speak.
Thus says the Rock of
Israel:

Let righteousness be all
your aim in leading men
and living in the sight of
God as pure and whole.
Then, in the shadowed
vales, you'll be as light, as
sun upon the lofty mountain
face in dawn's pure glow.

The morning dew shall flee,
disperse before the golden
morn shall rise, your light
endow abounding joy to
Israel. You'll trace the bow,
the radiance, of purest light
upon the rainbow's glorious
arc after the rainfall on the
Earth in colours ever bright.

The LORD has made this
kingdom for Himself and on
this throne shall sit
the One anointed King—
Messiah—And He shall
reign eternally.

The LORD declared that
this would be an everlasting
Covenant through Judah's
own Davidic line:
this royal sceptre shall
forever stay.

God's Law remains until
Messiah comes;
all people will be drawn to
Him. His reign shall be of
shalom peace; He'll lead
us to Eternal day.

Messiah will conquer
Satan's power and thorns
that grow in evil lives
will perish in eternal fires.
Now speed that day,
O LORD, we pray.

. . . .

KING SOLOMON:
THE ACCESSION
1 Kings 1 – 2

The dynasty of David
stands! I now have known
the flowing oil, the blessed
anointing oil upon my head
and heart, its perfume still
is dew upon my wondering
brow. The holy invocation

of the priest and prophet
rings within my ears—
I am the man appointed king
throughout Israel.

My father, David's life is at
its ebb; the full tide of his
God-blessed days recedes
from on the shores of time,
his twilight hours close in
on him. His only warmth is
loaned to him yet he has
acted as a king unto the last,
rescinding Adonijah's
claims to throne and crown;
and so his will is done!

King David's line will never
end! The LORD has
promised this to him.
And, to my honour now,
God's choice to follow him
is here! I stand upon
the threshold of the throne:
responsibility is surely
joined with privilege.
I search my soul to find
Assurance in this role.
Now, David's sceptre's
given into my trembling
hands. How may I wear
the crown, so touched with
glory by my father's reign?
How may I wield this royal
sceptre to ensure the

dynasty will hold its equity,
its provenance? But, to
my crowning day:
King Solomon!

KING SOLOMON:
THE CHOICE
1 Kings 3; 2 Chron. 1

Am I at dreams of
consequence, or do I find
a fantasy of mind, that God
should come to me, address
my soul's desire for aid to
make my reign of Israel
so memorable and glorious?

But this is real to me,
I hear the cadence of Your
Voice, O LORD and I am
immersed in radiant *LIGHT*
where sight and sound are
fused together now in
regal visions rare
to me, the King of Israel!.
Such *LIGHT* and sight
as this enlightens me!
If I would see Eternity
stretched out to me, it is
Your hand that reaches
down to me. You hold
for me this gift of
soul-blessed choice.

And I may take,
as mine, a treasury
of wealth: the gold
of mastery that crowns
do bring, the silver of
security for me and mine.
What wealth is this,
what gain!

(I'd gain, as well, some
greed in me for this and
every that!)

But, in Your hand,
I also see the honour
that a throne does bring
if one is deft to handle Law
with equity. I see there is
a glory there for me and
all I see as mine.

(I'd gain, as well. some
pride in me for this and
every that!)

A power I see within
Your hand for me to wield
my sword of state to smite
the foe to bring them down
to death and so secure,
through my times, this
cherished dynasty
for me and mine.

(I'd gain, as well, some
cruelty through this and

every that!)

Within Your hand
I also see the health of
limb to climb the heights
to take me down the years
in glorious power always
beyond 'three score
and ten'.

(I'd gain, as well, more
tears in life for this and
every that)!

I've made my choice:
A wisdom, LORD, I ask
of You by which to rule
for good that benefits all the
people, LORD! Oh, counsel
me in kingly, kindly,
knowing ways.

I pray that I may serve
this people well because
these are Your own. LORD,
You have called me, as their
king, to shepherd them and
care for them. I have
gained much.

(I've gained, as well,
Your smile that blesses this
and every that)!

What good is wealth,
or pride? Or, either power

or added age if I should fail
to act as wise. It is Your gift
of grace to make it mine.
And, from this gift, the
others flow.

(I've gained, as well,
the overflow of this
and every that)!

KING SOLOMON:
THE WISDOM
1 Kings 3:16-28; 4:29-34

This case before the
Court of Solomon, it does
intrigue my mind; it calls
for wisdom in the choice I
make for one will know her
joy renewed, the other will
depart in pain and grief for
unrequited mother-love!

Observe the stance,
the face, the pain of
motherhood. The one who
holds the child–a sorrow's
written there upon her pallid
features and an inner grief!
The other one, I find
a fear beyond the surface
of her pain.

They, both of them, are

mothers, that's so surely
written there but which is
mother of the child? This is
the question now before
the court I hold. I must
determine which the mother
is. I search with hope for it.
Ah! That's the light of it–
I see the grief, the fear!

I make my judgement for
you each! I'll render now
the child in half and give
a half to each, then both
of you will be appeased!

I thought as much!
The one with hidden fear
can see some virtue in
a virtue in the choice:
she'd have the half of child
and be appeased,
(She grieves a child she's
lost by plague).

The other cedes
the choice–she would not
have it harmed. The child
is hers beyond all doubt.
I place it tenderly within
her loving care.

I thank You, LORD, for
wisdom far beyond my ken,
the wisdom granted me that

I may rule, with equity
this people in my care.

KING SOLOMON:
THE TEMPLE
1 Kings 5 – 7; 2 Chron. 2 – 5

Should *YHVH* dwell in
desert tents? We've settled
in our palaces! For desert
times a tent was pitched
upon the arid sands. Yet
Now we live in homes.

Our fathers left that
wilderness; they entered in
the Promised Land and
warred from 'Sheba up
to Dan. establishing this
for *YHVH*–LORD..

The populace is on home
ground, attending to their
flocks and herds, their olive
groves, the choice vineyard
and fruit of vines all ready
For the harvest now.

And I am in my palace
grand! I reign and rest
in luxury; I wine and dine
in opulence, yet *YHWH*
dwells within a tent.
It is not right, this tent!

My father, David, yearned
to build a Temple fit for
YHVH LORD, but God
deferred the structure and
He placed the challenge
in my ready hands

It is my destiny to set
in place a building fit for
Him, the like of which was
ne'er before or ever will be
seen again: the Temple that
I build for *YHVH*–LORD.

I scan the plans now made.
I'll build upon Moriah's
rock, within Jerusalem.
Perhaps the rock of
Abraham's sacrifice, when
by His grace, the LORD
provided him a lamb.

It now is David's rock!
He paid a price upon the
generous gift Araunah
offered him and there
he sacrificed, appeasing
God for sins he'd done.

We'll build the Holy
House of God just basically,
according to the Tabernacle
plan of old. It's *YHVH's*
plan–He patterned it
for His Abiding Place

I am pleased and honoured
much to build His own High
Home–a glorious edifice. It
will endure, outshine my
own, most glorious home:
The palace of the king!

We've Hiram's cedars from
the heights of Lebanon.
They'll stand on rock as
pillars in God's Temple fair;
so tall they'll stand and
durable, withstanding time.

There's gold we've offered
for the work and precious
jewels to enhance the many
artists' skills–exquisite
work! And cherubim will
fly in patterns on the wall.

The portico impressive
stands, adjacent rooms
surround the whole. No
hammer, chisel, iron for
tools, are used. The quarries
hold their noise.

Not only is the lateral plan
now set within a triad
scheme but, height as well
gives place to three in all
the measurements. The
whole is roofed beams.

Constructing the exterior,
the carpenters have panelled
all the walls with cedar,
floors with pine. The inner
Sanctuary–the rare, Most
Holy Place–is whole.

The Inner Sanctuary
receives the gold, the pure
and burnished gold, the altar
and the walls are gilt also.
It truly is unique–
the House of God!

Ten cubits high, the
cherubim are carved, each
are symmetrical. Together
here the cherubim do stand
their wings will guard the
glorious Covenant.

And, cherubim bedeck
the walls throughout the
Sanctuary, with trees of
palm and opened flowers–
all this to beautify the
Temple of the LORD.

The entrance to the
Sanctuary is gold on olive
wood, with palms and
flowers and cherubim–each
one adorned as ornamental
artistry; all flush with gold.

Three courses of selected
stone, and dressed to grace
the courtyard here, are laid
to take the tramping feet of
countless worshippers who
come to sing in praise.

The peasants and the priests
will mingle here each day
for both the giving and
receipt of doves, all
offerings, in ritual before
the LORD who watches all.

…..

Now seven years have
passed in peace as all the
plans have been fulfilled by
which the Dwelling Place
of God is right for endless
worship to the *YHVH*
LORD.

The sun does rise–its early
rays do strike upon the gold
and through the slim
clerestories and beams,
the richest rays of sun now
touch the burnished gold.

Sunlight, with awesome
radiance reveals the Home–
the Dwelling Place–of God.

The golden light now glows
on the worshippers each lost
in wonder of the LORD.

HE COMES TO BLESS
US HERE!

KING SOLOMON:
THE DEDICATION
1 Kings 8; 2 Chronicles 6 – 7

They came with singing out
of Zion, the elders, chiefs,
and heads of clans to
joyfully process the lifting
of the Ark into the Dwelling
Place within the Temple's
Holiest Place.

The priests did place
it reverently beneath
the shadowing wings
of cherubim, the guards
of this, the holiest of all.
Their wings did spread
above the Ark to shelter
utmost holiness.

The wondering priests
withdrew in awe: the Cloud
of Presence filled the room
pervading, silent, all
the Sanctuary. The Cloud
was still yet all-consuming

in its power and none could
countenance its glow, the
all-pervasive Cloud
does signal Him, the
YHVH–LORD!

He sanctifies this place!
The LORD has said that
He would dwell in such
a nimbus cloud–this Cloud
is deep and shadowing
and yet, an inner *LIGHT*
is there. The 'Cloud of
Presencing' confirms
His blessing of this
hallowed, sacred hour.

Emotion stirs my heart,
O LORD. I pray that You
would bless Your people
bowed in worship here.
Praise be to You,
O *YHVH*–LORD,
the God of Israel who has
fulfilled Your promises to
David, King, and all the
people of Israel!

My father had it in his heart
to build a Sanctuary unto
The Name of *YHVH*–
LORD, our God.
But, none-the-less, to me
was given the task and I
now sit on Israel's throne.

'"The Temple of
The Sacred Name'
is built; the LORD's eternal
Name is written on the
Stones of Law residing in
the golden Ark. His Finger
wrote The Name, the Law.

And now I pray this prayer,
O LORD: There is no other
like to You–You keep Your
Powerful Word, Your
Covenant of Love; You
keep Your wondrous
promises of old.

Your lips did speak, Your
hands have wrought the
deeds of all Your promises.
We trust and know that You
will also keep this pledge
You made to us:
The Sceptre shall not pass
from this Royal house if
we will walk within Your
holy, chosen ways.

But, will You surely dwell
on Earth? Not all the
heavens could e'er contain
Your 'Presencing'; much
less this holy Temple on the
Mount. Yet, LORD, attend
unto this prayer: O, may

Your Eye forever scan this
Holy Place–You said:

My Name is there!

O LORD, do hear: We
supplicate, the king and
people here, as now
we pray toward Your Face.
Though Heaven is Your
Home, come nigh to us and,
when You hear our prayer,

O LORD, our many
trespasses forgive.
For those who sin against
the Law by harming
neighbours, near and far,
but come to make an oath,
do hear and then, forgive.

For those defeated by a foe
because of sins against
Your Name, O *YHVH,*
yet come confessing all
that sin and calling on
The Name, do hear
and when You hear,
O LORD forgive.

For those who want,
by lack of rain, for food
and sustenance because
of sins against Your Name,
O LORD—if they should
pray towards this place,

confess Your Name
and turn from sin, respond,
then, when You hear,
this errant people then
forgive.

And, when disasters or
disease should scourge the
Promised Land, or blight
or scourge of locusts,
enemies, do raid, then
prayers ascend out from
Your suffering people who,
afflicted in the heart, do
stretch their hands to You
with pleas, and hear their
anxious prayer,
forgive.

And, when You hear,
forgive and act for You
will know the whole,
the burdens of their heart–
You read our hearts:
O LORD, we plead,
forgive.

For those who come from
far off lands as foreigners
who've heard the Name and
know Your holy hand,
responding to Your grace,
then hear and answer
foreign prayers. That all
the peoples of the Earth may

know Your holy Name
and serve but You
in faith, O LORD,
forgive.

When enemies should strike
and men must march to
battle cries but praying go,
then hear, O LORD; from in
Your holy Heaven,
uphold their heart-felt plea,
their worthy cause. Do hear,
and answer: LORD,
forgive.

When men would sin
against Your Name and stir
Your anger, LORD; if they,
repenting, turn their hearts
to You and pray towards
this Promised Land, this
City fair, this Temple,
glorious and rare,
then from Your Dwelling
Place, do hear and,
hearing us, O LORD,
forgive.

O, may Your eyes be open
to Your servant's prayer,
also the pleas of Israel, for
You have chosen us, from
all the nations of the earth
as Your inheritance, that
You would hear and, in

listening to our cry, You
will forgive.

I would my Benediction
bring to this assembled host:
O praise the LORD who
grants His rest unto all
Israel–not one of all
His promises has failed.

O, may the LORD be with
us as He was with burdened
Israel all through the
'Moses Pilgrimage'. O may
He never leave, forsake, but
turn our hearts to Him to
walk within His ways and
keep His wise decrees.

And, may my intercessory
words be near the Heart of
God always that He might
hold us in the hollow of His
hand, according to our need.
Do bless Your people,
LORD, then all the Earth
may know that
You are *YHVH*–LORD.

KING SOLOMON:
THE RESPONSE
1 Kings 9; 2 Chronicles 7

The lightning strikes! The

Fire from Heaven descends
upon the offering and the
sacrifice. The glory of
the LORD now fills the
Sanctuary. No priest can
come into The Holy Place
for glory glows of God
within this Holy Place.

And every man—the
Worshippers—saw fire
fall down from Heaven.
The glory of the LORD
outshone the Holy Place.
They bow with face toward
the ground. They worship
and give thanks to God–
The *YHVH, El Shaddai*:
The LORD is good,
His love endures,
forevermore!

The LORD comes down
to me! As I have done the
work I had in mind to do
for Him, and me within my
palaces. The LORD comes
down to me; He speaks:

I hear your prayer. I choose
this place you've built for
Me for Temple and for
sacrifice. When heaven is
closed to rain or when the
locusts land, devouring

grain, or plagues descend
upon My people here;
if they, the people called
by My own name, will
humbly pray and seek My
face, and turn from sin, then
I will hear and answer
them, forgiving them.

My eyes are on this people,
choice; My ears attend
their every prayer. I've
chosen, and I sanctify this
Temple to My Name. My
Heart is ever here!

And as for you–if you will
walk before My Face as
David did, obey My Law,
I'll bless your reign, your
royal throne. It was my
choice to covenant with
David, prove his place
throughout all time.

But, if you turn, forsake the
Law, forsake your LORD,
desert to base idolatry, then
I will turn from you and all
the land will be bereft of
you. The Temple, too–
for it is holy made, because
I dwell within and sanctify it
to My Name–will stand

bereft of Me, of LIGHT,
of Life! This edifice, this
Holy Place: it will become
a ridicule to all the world.
Appalled, they'll ask, why
has the LORD rejected His
own Dwelling Place.

They'll know the truth:
'Because they did forsake
the YHVH–LORD,
Embracing all subservient
gods, and bow to them
instead. And this is why
disaster will then come!

KING SOLOMON:
THE PROJECTS
1 Kings 9; 2 Chronicles 8

O, how does one repay
the likes of Hiram, King of
Tyre? He gave the gold, the
cedar and the pine for both
the Temple and my palaces.
Now, where is resource
found to pay for all of that?
Those towns! Those twenty
northern towns, they will
repay, and more, what
he has brought to us.

But, Hiram, King of Tyre,
is much displeased with
everyone. He calls them
each, you see, 'cabul', the
good-for-nothing towns
(they are)!

Now, how does one begin
to action out the plans of
buildings sketched so grand
as these? The labour was
immense through seven
years for all the Temple
plans and more, for me, my
palaces, my forts, my walls,
and many towns? I turned
to seek some slaves and
found them in the land–
the Ammonites, Hivites,
the Jebusites and more.
(I trust it won't be judged
a shadow on my reign!)

Conscripted to the site,
the slaves were forced to
work for not one Israelite
would be required to slave.
And, how does one
command the seas as well
as land? Great ships were
built to ply the ever-restless
waves. And, Hiram helped!
His seasoned sailors served
the fleets of Solomon!
At Ezion-Geber, the region
near to Eloth in Edom,

those ships were built to ply
the Red, and greater seas.
(I trust these projects won't
be judged a stain upon
the face of Israel!)

Those hardy sailors took
Their ships to foreign ports
and gathered there, the
spoils to grace my palaces!

KING SOLOMON:
THE VISITOR
1 Kings 10; 2 Chronicles 9

The clashing symbols and
the golden bells convey
the entry of the Queen
through Zion's massive
gates; the crowds enthralled
at all this glittering
spectacle I see. Oh look!
They grant her homage
and exultant welcome, too!

As Sheba's Queen arrives
in stately promenade with
pomp and splendour all
around, her guards, her
aides, her slaves, in courtly
mien do come in ordered
file. They pause before my

portico: all this is an
impressive retinue!

The palace doors swing
wide—my cue to take the
steps toward her carriage
and extend my royal hand to
hers. Her foot does claim
the steps. Somewhat to my
surprise, a striking beauty
here emerges gracefully
into the summer sun!

Her skin is of the deepest
hue but, radiant; her hair,
well groomed, is raven
black; her jewelled arms
and throat betray immense
resource of wealth. Her
garments shine in vivid
red and gold–I like
the sight of her!

She smiles. Her glance
conveys intelligence and,
deep within those olive eyes
are questions to be posed.
She fastens then her eyes on
me and I am man enough to
read that gaze and know
there is an interest felt.

We breach the first mute
glance with ease and, all at

once, fall into converse of
the days of journey from the
south. I ask how she has
fared along the way. She
smiles, and lightly claims
a robust health indeed!

The queen then paused;
She turned around in
gestures to her caravan.
The gifts of gold, of spice,
and precious stones,
are meant to emphasise her
wish for closest ties, for
pacts of peace from robust
provenance.

There's time for us to share
experience of kings and
queens, of good and ill, of
war and peace, of life and
death. All these and more,
the questions came. I'm
pleased to find a wisdom in
her comely company.

This beauteous Sheba
Queen, how well she graces
all the room. All eyes do
turn to her. She brings a
light most radiant into this
court; my palace is the
grander for these joyous
days of covenant!

The Queen then spoke of
her desire, when learning of
my reign, to see this King,
Solomon and tell of his
wisdom, test his wealth–she
finds (to my relief), that
what she sees is more than
all she'd heard and more
than she believed!

How happy all your aides,
she said, to stand before
your wisdom in this massive
court! How happy is the
YHVH–LORD your God,
for this, your reign. He must
delight in you. His love for
Israel is sure: He made
you King!

I'm fascinated by this
Queen. What grace is in her
speech, what wealth is in
her gifts. What love is in her
touch! I'd grant her all
desire; I'd give her every
gain. I'd spend my very life
for her. I mourn the day
she must depart!

I find I am bereft
of elegance and sure
delight and I will mourn
her memory.

KING SOLOMON:
THE VERDICT
1 Kings 10 – 11; 2 Chron.9

It's time for weighing
right within the balances
all things that do pertain
to me on Earth. My own
inheritance was David's
wealth–his crown, his
throne, his rule, his reign,
his land. And, more than
this, the oil anointed on
my brow as chosen of
the LORD to reign.

Yet, in my time, the reign
extends in wealth, in
opulence, in power and
splendour–all indicative
of how the *YHVH*–LORD
has blessed this dynasty.

If weighing in the balances
be judged, I cite for you
the Temple on the Mount.
How glorious! And then,
my palaces and each so
very splendid in the
golden light of Israel,
so grand you will agree.

Do look upon the throne.
There never was the like
of this, from the grand
steps to lions, to throne.
The world has sought its
audience with me for God
has placed a wisdom in my
heart and year on year a
seeker brings his gift.

So, if my rule should be
now weighed with these,
 I should be largely viewed
'the King of Peace'! It's
been a tranquil reign,
all told. Agreed? I've
fortified the boundaries,
I've made alliances
through all the many
marriages and through
all my great wealth.

There's been unrest of
late, but naught to offer
threat before my chariots–
my force is unassailable,
you must agree! Our
coffers are so large that
silver's thrown upon the
streets as stone!

How foolish are the wise,
King Solomon! My anger
stirs, for you have turned
your back on Me!
You know the way I'd
planned for you for–in your

Dedication Prayer–you
vowed to serve but Me
alone, not touch a god of
other lands and schemes.

You failed to keep your
word. Your foreign wives
have turned your heart
from Me. You worship
alien gods on highest hills.
For sin, division always
comes to curse the one
who sins—your kingdom
will be rent in twain.

ISRAEL:
THE SCHISM
1 Kings 12; 2 Chronicles 10

So! To your tents,
O Israel!
What share have we
in David's throne?
What part have we in
Jesse's son? Preserve
your own affairs,
your house, O Israel,
we now secede–we need
not golden crowns
to save ourselves!

That foolish prince,
the son of kings–of David
and of Solomon–that

Rehoboam is too brash,
he calls not on the wisdom
of the sage, the aged,
he takes the lead from
youthful fools who've
served him as a lad. He'd
break the yoke which
Solomon did place upon
our necks, our hearts?

But no! He listened to
advice so sure to break
our backs. What Solomon
had bled from us, his son
did dredge much more
than this. But now,
no blood remains to
bleed from us again.
Before our bones are
bleached, we turn
from him, from Judah,
and the crown! We turn
to hope that, in a full
future free from the
overwhelming greed
of kings, we will renew
our strength to live
within the *LIGHT*
of *YHVH*–LORD:
we'll be redeemed!

We'll have no part with
scorpions, with whips and
yokes to bend our wills to

vicious kings who listen
not unto our righteous
pleas, but–from our
meagre lot–take plunder,
yes, the lot today.
We like it not! We go
unto our homes!

JEROBOAM:
THE IDOLATER
1 Kings 12

It's I, 'King' Jeroboam,
who will be your 'saviour'
now! You've had your fill
of Judah and King
Rehoboam, his delinquent
entourage and their cruel,
avaricious schemes.
Jerusalem no longer cares
what burdens Israel's
sons do bear on backs.
But they are Two, and we
are Ten: What strength is
in our hands: We'll stand
our ground and theirs!

You'd pine in reverence
for all the Temple means
to you? You'd long to have
the priests present, upon
the brazen hearth, the
offerings of doves and

rams? Why take the
weary trail through
Judah's rough terrain?
Why traipse that arid,
barren path again?

I give alternatives for you!
Ascend to Jacob's Mount.
Go now to Bethel's height
and bow unto the new
hewn golden calf!

I've set up for all your
convenience, a golden calf
in Dan as well. Now, mark
the festive date for you
to celebrate at will.

Though Judah's sons
want all the ancient ways,
all Israel chooses not
to be confined to past
constraints on them.

Our sacrificial fires will
save you from yourselves
for you have need of
freedom now, each one,
to live carefree!

Though, why do I discern
a fear within my soul?
I see a shadow falls upon
the golden calves…
All Israel's prayers

and pleas placate their
need of *YHVH*–LORD.
They'll learn respect
for me instead of
Judah's king.

They'll then preserve
my place and power.
They'd have my head
if once they thought
the Temple would
Then call them back
to worship there.

The gold must fascinate
their gaze, a passion for
the heights and altars here
must turn their heads
and hearts from
YHVH–LORD!

A PROPHET: THE
VOICE
1 Kings 13

You ask my name, my
fame? It matters not. The
message you will hear
surpasses all that I, the
messenger, will be to you.
You stand upon that pile of
stones and ash. I cry a wail
against those stones, that
pile of rock on which you

sacrifice in blasphemy
of *YHVH*–LORD,
your God.
Now hear your fate:

O altar, altar, hear:
A son that's born of David's
line will sacrifice on you
the human bones of priests
who now perform their
sacrifice on your stained
stones. You'll have your
doom not far from hence in
time. Your stones will split
apart and gorge out all the
ashes of your sins against
the *YHVH*–LORD.

You stomp upon my words?
You'd have my head? See
now your hand and arm–
it's shrivelled up; so will
your power be gone. You
wish to plead with me?
Restore my hand, you cry?
See now the gracious gift–
the mercy–of the LORD:
Your hand is whole!
Now contemplate
that matchless grace.

Come home with me, you
ask? Not even if the half of
all you own you gave to me!

I would not countenance
your dark designs–I am
commanded by the Word
of God, to have no part with
you. I go, as I have come,
within the grace,
the ordinance of God.

A PROPHET: AHIJAH
1 Kings 14

You come within the night?
The queen, the tearful
spouse of Jeroboam, who
did send you, on a fear of
how your ailing son does
fare upon his bed?

Why come as to deceive?
A shrouding cloak hides not
identity of queens whose
palling grief outstrips their
royal dignity. The LORD
did say you'd come to ask
of me, to plead, the fate of
him, your failing son. And I,
the prophet Ahijah, at
Shiloh, the holy mount,
will speak his fate to you.
Go! Tell your husband that
the *YHVH*–LORD, says:

You were raised as leader
of My people, Mine! I tore
your kingdom from the

House of David, king.
I gave it unto you but you
have failed the LORD:
You've brought idolatry
and evil, blatant sins
to Israel's faulty homes
and wayward heart.

Disaster spreads upon all
Israel, She reels before your
blatant sins. Your House
Will fall because of this!

Go home! I hold no hope
for you. In sorrows such as
these, I find no word of
consolation for your son
will die just when your
shadow falls upon the
open gates of home.

A SCRIBE:
HISTORY OF THE
CLANS
1 Kings 14 – 16; 2 Chronicles
12 – 18

I follow in the train of holy
men who wrote the
Chronicles of Falsity and
Faith, of **shadows** and
the *LIGHT*, upon the path
of pilgrims in the past.
My task is set like those

who wrote such history.
The shadows come again
to Israel–that faithless
stock–and Judah, who
remain still true to God.

We trace the paths of
kings, of Rehoboam who
could act as wise, then fool:
He fell to shameful ways,
abandoning the Law of
YHVH–LORD.

Unfaithfulness did cause
a servitude of sorts to
Shishak, Egypt's king, who
all but razed our forts. Yes,
even to Jerusalem's so
proud strategic gates.

Then, Shemaiah, from
the LORD, did speak these
words of *YHVH*–LORD:

You all abandoned Me:
I now abandon you to
Shishak's troops!

The LORD is just. The
king agreed. We're have
been humbled by His words.
The LORD did see an
honest woe, decreed
deliverance, appeased.

But Shishak took the gold–
the Temple treasures and
the palace gems as well,
the golden shields of kings,
and Rehoboam mourned.

He duplicated each and
every shield, but all of
bronze instead of gold.
The bronze did stand for
gold when king and guards
advanced for prayer.

Though Rehoboam's reign
was like the bronze, not
gold, there was some good
in what he did, what he
achieved, through all of
Judah through his time.

When Abijah, the son of
Jeroboam, took the throne,
a war broke out between
Israel and Judah's Clans.
The king declared upon
the heights of Israel:

All Israel, and king, now
hearken unto me: Do not
you know that God, the
LORD, has given yet the
kingship of this land and
nation to His own?
Acknowledge that

the LORD, by covenant of
salt, decreed that David's
line should rule forever in
this land. Do not resist
His utmost rule!

Now, as for Judah, we
have not forsaken Him–
we serve the LORD and He
is with us still. O Israel,
now cease your ever
hopeless quest!

But while he spoke,
a plot was hatched to
ambush all of Judah's men
who cried out to the LORD;
He met their need—
all Israel fled!

'King' Jeroboam ruled
no more–he waned, while
Abijah increased In strength
and wisdom, too. He then
brought peace to all
the land of Israel.

Then, Asa took the throne
and perpetrated good before
the LORD. He smashed
all ghastly idol stones
and poles and cried:
O seek the LORD!

The kingdom found its
peace as Asa purified and
fortified the towns. When
Cushites sought the land,
he called upon the
LORD for aid.

The Spirit of the LORD
sent Azariah, then, with
words of challenge for the
king and all his troops:
When you seek God,
He will be found!

All Israel knows
distress; turmoil disturbs
their days. But, as for you,
be true; be strong, endure,
do not give up: the LORD
prevails always!

The king took courage
In these words. Detested
idols were destroyed. The
Temple's altar was then all
repaired and some in
Israel concurred.

All Judah then did make
a covenant in heart and soul.
They sought the LORD and
He was found. In grace, He
granted peace
anew to all.

In age, King Asa fell from
grace in fear of King Baasha
of Israel. He gifted all the
treasures of the LORD
And land to Ben-Hadad,
the king of Syria.

In treaty, Ben-Hadad
agreed to change his plans,
attacked Israel instead
because Asa relied on
Syria's king instead of
YHVH–LORD.

Hanani, seer, rebuked
the king: Because you've
not relied on *YHVH*–LORD,
you did a foolish thing!
You close your eyes to God
God sees, He knows!

He knows all those who
do commit their hearts to
Him. To those who do rely
on Him, He will deliver foes
into their hand! You're
now at war!

Enraged, the king did
cast the seer to jail and then
oppressed his people in his
sin! He failed in health but
also failed to seek
the LORD!

Jehoshaphat, his son,
succeeded to the throne.
And God was with this king
for—in his youth—he
walked as David walked,
obeyed the LORD!

Devoted as he was,
Jehoshaphat did cleanse the
heights from Asherah; he
channelled teachers through
the land, they taught in
YHVH's Law.

The fear of God did fall
on all the kingdoms round
about and wars did cease.
The Philistines brought gifts
of tribute to the king: yes,
King Jehoshaphat.

The words of *YHVH*–
LORD, also, were spoken
through Jehu, the son of
Hanani, against Baasha who
had despised the rule of
righteous Law:

*I lifted you from dust and
made you leader of My
people, Israel. But you have
walked as Jeroboam walked.
for all your sins, you will not
live your length of days!*

Elah, the son of Baasha,
then took the throne but,
Zimri's plot did send him to
the dust. And Zimri reigned
instead but, just for
seven days!

The army's great
commander, Omri then
became the king of Israel.
All Israel then was in a
schism until King Omri
conquered all.

King Omri formed
Samaria, but he was evil,
worse by far than those
who went before. And,
when he died, his son,
Ahab, was crowned.

Jehoshaphat allied
himself with Israel's king,
Ahab, and plotted for
expansion, warring in a
unison but, not without
the LORD's decree.

Seek first the counsel of the
LORD, Jehoshaphat did
warn and finally, Michaiah,
seer, was asked to voice
opinion there, so earning
voluminous wrath.

King Ahab heard
Michaiah's words: I see
them all, all Israel, scattered
on the hills like sheep with-
out a guide; no shepherds
will be found.

As payment for his
words of prophecy, the seer,
Michaiah, found him-self
behind strong prison bars.
He wavered not;
he trusted God!

Now, Ahab opted for
disguise. Jehoshaphat was
placed in jeopardy but God
did aid. It must be said
that Ahab most provoked
the LORD!

ELIJAH–THE PROPHET
1 Kings 17 – 18

I'm called to tell my story
now–Elijah, Tishbite, from
Gilead. I'd been to Ahab
with God's word:

*As I, The LORD do live,
there'll be no dew, no rain
upon this land except as by
My governing word:
REPENT!*

The LORD did counsel me
to go, from Israel, eastward
to the cleft–the Kerioth
Ravine across the Jordan's
winding stream. I knew I'd
find my sustenance for
there; the ravens came
to Kerioth Brook.

The parched earth lay
without respite, the brook
diminished, failed to flow.
And, from the ravished
river bed, the LORD
directed me along the path
to Zarapath where He'd
prepared a widow to
give ample aid.

At dawn and eve, the
birds brought bread like
offerings on 'altar' rock.
Who gave that bread, as
broken to sustain my life,
regain my strength?
The bread and brook, a
sacrament, became my
praise of *YHVH*–LORD.

I pleaded for some food,
a draught out from her store
and in her want,
without remorse, she
offered me to share the very
last of meals she had.

I challenged her to bake
some bread in faith of
further sustenance.

Nor will your jar of oil
deplete, I said, for every
day, sufficient will the jar
contain to meet our need
perennially. They will
suffice until this war of
wills is past and Ahab loses
face and fails at last!

The widow's son became
as one of those who quickly
fails when ill. His breath
had gone. I knew that God
could overcome this
tragedy. I pleaded both his
cause and hers and in God's
grace, his life returned.

When three years passed,
the time had come to cast
my challenge to the king.
Then, Obadiah, able man
of faith—though fearful—
bravely gave my message
to Ahab who took the bait
and came to me quite
late with angry rant.

You, troubler of all Israel,
he said. Can I be sure it's

really you? I'll take no
blame for trouble here,
I said. "But you, your
father's Clan, have much
transgressed–you each
abandoned God for
love of Baal!

Now, summon, if you will,
everyone in Israel
to come to Carmel on the
height. Ensure that all the
prophets of the Baal, also
of Asherah, parade
themselves!

The people came in droves
to view my challenge to the
king and Baal. How long,
this wavering between the
LORD and Baal? If God is
LORD then, worship him;
if Baal is god, content your-
selves with him instead.
No murmur came of yea,
or nay. The time had
surely come!

Go! Sacrifice a bull
to Baal! I said. But, light
no fire; inquire of Baal
if he will deign to send
some fire, today, consume
his altar pyre! The priests
did chant their many

liturgies and I did taunt
their frenzied prayers!

Still, no response. An
emptiness of silence from
their Baal did send the
priests to bloodied ire
In slashes with their swords
and spears. But, all in vain.
As evening came, I asked
for stones—all twelve—
and sacrificial bull.

Intrigued, the workers
built 'the stones of Israel'–
an altar for an offering. But,
why the trench as well? The
bull secured, deprived of
life, the kindling waiting
too. We need the fire,
consuming *Fire*!

Now, let the waters flow
right down, to douse all
earthly flames or spark. It's
time for God to act. O God
come down, receive my
prayer, consume this holy
offering–the bull, the wood,
the rocks and all!

O LORD, give answer now
so all this host will surely
know that You are God; that
You will turn their hearts

once more. Ah, now it falls,
the Fire of God! It burns the
sacrifice–Yes, all consumed
in furious fire!

The people worshipped!
Now they cry, The *YHVH*–
LORD, He is our LORD:
The God of Israel! Let none
escape who sought to
denigrate. So! Ahab, go on
home! I hear the sound
of falling rain.

ELIJAH:
THE RETREAT
1 Kings 19

The way before me
mortifies! What lies behind
lends greater fear! That
woman, Jezebel, is out
to claim my life in
consequence of losing all
her priests and pride. Her
threat to vanquish me
appals.

A refugee, to God I flee;
my only haven is the
YHVH–LORD.
I scan the desert's faint
mirage, the haze. How long,

before the height of Horeb
beckons me to Him, the
LORD who'd shelter me.
This shade of desert branch
would scarce a respite be.

I thirst; I've had enough.
I've fought for Him, the
LORD, against all odds.
I've stood my ground. I've
challenged king and priest.

O LORD, where is
Your certain aid?
I've proved the power of
God; I've seen the flooding
rain in consequence of
prayer. But now they seek
my life. LORD, help!

Get up, and eat.

The LORD has spoken unto
me! An angel ministers.
I am alive!

So! Why this flight of fear?
What are you doing here?

I'm shaken from my sleep;
I've reached and rested on
the holy Rock and now, He
speaks with me as once He
spoke to Moses here!

You know how zealous I
have been, *Adonai*, LORD,
my *El Shaddai*. Rejected is
Your Covenant, Your altars
crumble in the dust,
Your prophets are all slain
and only I am left.
They seek my life!

Go out and stand upon
the Mount, to stand within
the Presence of the LORD;
The Holy One now passes by.

A great and mighty wind
springs up, it sweeps the
mountain's face as rocks are
tumbling down.

But God is not within the
wind! An earthquake rends
the trembling earth, but God
is not within its wake!
And now, a Fire, consuming
all within its blazing,
hungry flames. But God is
not within its path.

And now… and now,
a still, small Voice. I listen
to His word, incline my ear,
my heart. I raise my cloak
upon my brow; I fear to
look upon the Face of Him
who counsels me:

Elijah! What are you
doing here? Go! Back
the way you came.
You've felt you were
alone, you've feared
your very life. You are
secure in Me!

You have a work to do,
a task to speak for Me.
You are My lips,
my hands, to Israel's
waiting clans.

Yes! I reserve a host
of men, full seven
thousand, who
have not bowed down
to Baal. Their mouths
are wholly pure;
no kiss they've given
to that mound
of sacrificial rock.
Now Go! Anoint
My chosen one.

KING AHAB:
THE COVETING
1 Kings 21

This greening of the land
will mean I can extend my
grounds beyond the palace
walls. I've half a mind to

grow some things–some
fruit or vegetables; I've
half a mind to spread
to broader bounds!

My neighbour, Naboth,
grows a vineyard there.
That land is prime, it suits
my garden scheme. I need
no further grapes of course;
I'll grab, then plough,
then till the soil for fruit,
no… vegetables, for me!
What? Do I hear you
right? You dare to take
a stand against Ahab,
your king's desire?
You say, to me, the king,
'The LORD forbid'?
The LORD forbid that
you should grant your
own inheritance
 unto the king?

I'll pay you well–
just what It's worth
or, better still, why not
select a better, verdant
plot of ground on which
to grow your crop
of grapes if you must
have it so. But, do
make up your mind.
I wait for your response!

You won't? You don't
desire to please
your sovereign king?
I like it not!
Beware for fear,
you place your feet
outside your boundaries!
I've ways and means
to make You pay for all
your wretched impudence!

…….

You ask me why I sulk,
My love? I cannot have
that piece of land!
That measly Naboth won't
release his plot to me!
I can't begin to grow my
fruit–no, vegetables; can't
extend my palace grounds!

Ah, now that's a scheme
outdoing all the rest
you've had! I think it's
sure to work to take that
Naboth from his land
and make it mine,
instead. You write;
I'll sign decrees at once!

We'll have the feast.
 I'll place that farmer,
Naboth, at the head of all

**the rest beside myself, of
course. What laughs he'll
bring; and then, the ones
who will but testify:
He scorns the king!**

**I take possession of this
land! That fool, old
Naboth, is no more. His
'treason' cost him all he
had–his worthless life!
And now, it's mine, this
pleasant land, to dig and
plant my vegetables.**

Now hear, King Ahab, you
who murdered him,
the owner of this ground.
Where Naboth's blood
was spilt upon the earth,
your blood will flow
un-staunched and dogs
will feast upon its stream.

MICHAIAH:
THE PROPHECY
1 Kings 22; 2 Chronicles 18

I stand alone, between
these warring kings–they
ask advice and then, they
rue the quest they had of
me, for truth lies ill between
their ears for they are kin
to lies, intrigue.
They'll hear a falsity with
pride–it bolsters their
morale, to fight a war with
omens told of great and
'noble' victories afield.

And now, they'll fight
again. They've asked
of me, what would the
outcome be–the King
Jehoshaphat and, too,
King Ahab who does hate
the ground on which
I stand or walk! But who
are they to judge the truth
that *YHVH*–LORD
has given me for them?
The others said,
'Attack! The LORD gives
land into your hands.'

Michaiah, tell the truth,
King Ahab said. He asks the
truth of me? Attack,
victorious be; the LORD
will fill your hand! He said,
alarmed: How many times
must I demand you tell the
truth? (Such words should
pass his lying lips?). I tell
it then. I saw all Israel
scattered on the hills
as sheep bereft!

No shepherd Israel has!
Let every man go to his
'fold' in peace. I see The
LORD upon His throne with
all the host of Heaven.

In plotting out your course,
you are enticed to war
but not for victory, for you
must surely know it now:
Disaster waits for you upon
the hills and vales of
Aram's killing fields.

JEHU, JAHAZIEL,
ELIEZER–PROPHETS
2 Chronicles 19 – 20

There is some good in you!
The wicked you have
helped and oft unloved all
those who place their trust
in God. And yet, there is
some good in you!

You've cleansed the land
and rid the earth of icon
poles. There is some good
in that, Jehoshaphat.
What's more, you've set
your heart to search
for *YHVH*-LORD!

There is some good in what
you've done. The judges
you did choose for Judah's
towns–your words of
counsel reached their hearts
that Judah's God
is wholly just!

There is some good in plans
you've made for Levites,
priests, and patriarchs,
to wield the Law and settle
all disputes that rise
within the city's gates.

There is some good in all
you've said to them, of how
to rule most faithfully,
to serve whole-heartedly,
to live upright and fear
the *YHVH*–LORD.

There was much good
In all your prayers when
threatened by all those
eastern hordes. You called
upon the LORD. You saw
that power and might
are in His hands.

There was some good
in how you threw the weight
of care upon the LORD—
you knew not what to do

through fear but raised
your prayers.

There is some good
in what you did. You sought
the LORD. The battle, then,
became the LORD's. You
saw, to your delight, there
was deliverance—The
LORD had heard your
prayers!

There was much good
in how you sang upon
the way to war, encouraging
your troops to sing in praise
of all the splendour of
the *YHVH*–LORD and of
His wondrous ways.

And, there was good
in how you praised the
LORD upon the march,
returning home with spoils
and laden down. You came
to Zion to dwell within
the courts of peace.

Oh, yes! There was some
good! But, those alliances of
ill repute; the ships you built
with alien kings: such
devious plans for gain have
brought you to the dust!

ELISHA:
THE SUCCESSOR
1 Kings 19; 2 Kings 2

His mantle fell on me!
My plough was stilled
awhile as he came marching
down the furrow I had cut
into the soil as straight as
any line (I had my pride;
I marked my goal and
stayed my eyes ahead).

Who was this man who
came, approaching at the
height of noon? I gazed into
his face. Ah, yes! It was
God's man! Elijah came
to me and stood awhile,
his gaze upon my face.
He smiled. God's *LIGHT*
was in his glowing eyes.

His mantle fell on me!
That I should be the one to
take his place–the thought
did overwhelm me then and
still it does. I threw the reins
aside and gave my beasts
to Him, the *YHVH*–LORD,
in evening sacrifice.

I turned my back on home;
my parents bade me go with
him, the man of God, for I

would learn His will,
apprenticed to the seer,
attending him to bide my
time by learning ways
of prayer, of praise.

We came to Bethel, then,
for I would stay by him,
Elijah—the aged saint. The
Prophets' School did warn
me of the day but, I already
knew it was his time. The
LORD was calling him into
His Heavenly 'Home' and
I would be alone!

Elijah asked that I would
stay behind while he should
onward go to Jericho. But I
accompanied him with grief
of what did lay ahead for us.
Again, the word of warning
came although I knew
already that, surely,
the end was near.

So! On to Jordan's tide.
The prophet's cloak did dip
in waves which parted there
and eddied back to form
a path for us to cross on
drying sand. He turned to
me and asked: "What may
I do for you?"

I would, I said, that I
could have a double part
of what your spirit is!
He said it was a hard
request, so difficult but if
I saw him go from off
this Earth, such would be
mine. My spirit warmed.
I found my faith in *YHVH*–
LORD was raised.

Then, suddenly, the sound
of racing chariots—but one,
and that of Fire, a Heavenly
Fire that lit the skies and
rendered them, the horses,
of a blazing Fire; their
hooves all thundering to
carry our Elijah 'Home'.

A whirlwind in the path of
Fire then snatched God's
man and took him to the
chariot. The horses turned
and galloped to the skies.
They took Elijah to His God
and I, Elisha, bowed in awe
of Heavenly views!

I rent my clothes in grief
of him, my mentor, aged,
but father-like to me. I
turned to go, but stooped
to grasp his mantle from

the sand. I draped its
honoured folds on me!
It seems to me that
somehow now, God's
Holy Spirit stirs within.

THE PROPHETS:
WATERS HEALED
2 Kings 2:19-22

He threw that salt into
our spring, our loathsome
spring where stagnant
waters lay.

Our town of Jericho is
placed in pleasant climes
but, useless was our bitter,
briny spring.

Bring me a bowl of purest
salt, Elisha said, and cast
that salt Into the salty,
brackish spring.

How could such salt,
a saline thing, bring
healing to a foul and
fetid spring?

But, healing came!
The water's pure–it is
made clean, our poisoned
water-spring!

Elisha, man of God, the
LORD, has made it fresh–
the whole–our putrid water-
spring!

THE WIDOW:
A MIRACLE!
2 Kings 4:1-7

It did not fail–
that flowing oil until
all earthen jars were filled!
Some secret source
increased its store,
that meagre mite of oil
that I had eked
so miserly.

A rich resource
I thus received to pay
my creditors then, with the
rest, Elisha said my sons
and I would gain our needed
sustenance for life,
our daily bread!

THE WIDOW:
A SON RESTORED
2 Kings 4:8-37

My promised son did come

when he, the man of God,
had said he would. I nursed
this child with all maternal
joy. My friends, they had
delighted in the child God
gave to us when hope of
him had passed.

My promised son then lay
in death upon his bed. I fled
in grief to seek the man
of God. How could that
promise come to nought?
How could the LORD now
take, snatch back, the joy
He'd given once to me?

Elisha came to us! He saw
the pale, the ashen pall of
death. He offered prayer
then stretched upon the boy
with mouth to mouth and
hands to hands, then
breathed the breath of life to
him. He lives!

NAAMAN:
THE HEALING
2 Kings 5

I'm not a man of fear, you
know, But, when the
lep'rous white did form

upon my skin, I shrank,
aghast at what this meant
for me and mine, you see.
Condemned to dwell outside
the bounds of home, alone,
and quite bereft I was;
I did despair of health
and any hope.

I'm not a man of pride, you
know, But, when our maid—
an Israelite—did quote
the powers of such a man
who knew the way to robust
health, I hastened to my
king for leave to seek Elisha
and his God and find
my health once more
restored.

I'm not a man who scorns
you know, but, when Elisha
showed no care, refusing
sight of me though sent
a servant to relay his terms,
I scarce could stay my ire!
That he should offer help in
Jordan's waves, I thought
it ludicrous! Just wash,
be cleansed, he said…
In flowing clay?

I'm not a man who doubts,
you know, But, when he

said that Jordan would all
the leper-white remove, I all
but laughed! Such thoughts
and, if that weren't enough,
to dip not once but seven
times! Upon advice, I took
the plunge. I now
am whole!

When faithful men do look
to God for aid, cry out to
Him, their eyes perceive the
sight that doubting men
shall never see: LORD,
open earth-bound eyes to
see angelic hosts come
down to shield our souls
from all that evil would
achieve for us.

ELISHA:
THE VISION
2 Kings 6 – 7

When evil men conspire
to take, imprison out of
spite, the innocent, their
powers would seem as
disproportionate. Disquiet
can rob a man of soul to
counter for deliverance.
Then fear enthrals and the
mind is clamped in chains.

When fearful men would
quake, impending doom no
doubt their fate, a vision
clear of what the LORD can
do instils new power to
stand firm, resolute, for all
the Hosts of Heaven are
near to win the war. The
LORD is at our side!

ELISHA:
FEATS OF FAITH
2 Kings 7 – 13

There have been times when
I have known the hand of
God take charge
of me. I knew, as from the
very day Elijah's cloak
enfolded me, God's Spirit
came to guard and
strengthen me always.

When famine struck, and
poverty encroached upon
our holy land, God used me
then to heal the wounds
of such catastrophes. And,
always, He was near to
guide and counsel me in
ways the Law demands.

I walked with kings,
chastised, or brought them
comfort as the need would
be. Yes! there were times
when mothers came to me
for aid. I saw their grief
transformed to joy, God
using me always.

I saw, not once, but many
times, amazing things: the
waters healed and meals
enlarged, the leper, too,
was cleansed. I saw the
flowing oil as well. Yes!
every need was met
by God empowering me.

THE SCRIBE:
THE REGAL RECORDS
2 Kings; 2 Chronicles

The sorry saga of our kings
does blunt my writing tool
but I am charged–as
chronicler– to tell the
whole: the good, the ill…

Where were we when I last
laid down my pen? Ah, yes!
With Israel and Ahab's gory
tale. There followed
Ahaziah and, in more than
one respect, this man did

fall and Joram ruled instead.
His end was steeped in
crimson blood (as all
the House of Ahab was,)
and Jehu reigned instead.

King Jehu, man of racing
chariots, did purge the land
of Ahab's House. He
vanquished Baal, though not
the golden calves; no longer
careful to, in any way,
retain the Law of God with
all his heart. So, Israel's
land declined because
of this failed stand.

Jehoahaz succeeded him;
a weak-willed man who
turned to God for, when
Aram—Syria—had
threatened all, Jehoash then
succeeded him—an
evil man who followed in
the ways of Nebat. Then,
the second Jeroboam took
the throne. He ruled for over
forty years, reclaiming land,
restoring Israel's broad
boundaries.

Then, Zachariah took the
throne—for half a year, no
more: he was assassinated
by Shallum who then

succeeded him as king—
for just one month, no
more! Then, Menahem,
from Tirzah, came with
bloodied sword to claim the
sullied throne. Compounded
were his sins by selling out
to Pul, Assyrian, for peace
at any price. Pekahiah,
his son, succeeded him.
He reigned for just two
years, no more. Then,
Remaliah's son,
Pekah, assassinated king
and friends to snatch
the tottering throne.

Just one more king for Israel
as all had followed in the
steps of wicked fathers who
had failed to turn from
all the sins of Nebat's ouse.
Now, in the time of Pekah's
reign, Tiglath-Pileser, bold
Assyrian, began his raping
of the land. Hoshea then
conspired against Pekah,
attacking then, ssassinating
him. He took the throne,
to no one's benefit.

Then, Shalmaneser, king
of all Assyria proved
Hoshea a traitor to Assyria
and so imprisoned him.

Invasion then ensued,
a siege was laid, the land
was razed and Israel
then was taken captive, led
to alien lands in chains.
In parallel to Israel's Royal
Roll, there ruled, in Judah,
to the south a train of
royalty more fitted in
their ways to serve the
LORD supremely
throughout their days.

When King Jehoshaphat
did pass into his royal
grave, Jehoram ruled
instead. He sinned by
taking, as a wife, the
daughter of Ahab, king of
Israel. But Judah was not
lost (for David's sake).
Ahaziah succeeded him.
He ruled one year, no more.

When Ahaziah, by intrigue
with Joram, king of Israel,
was inflicted with a mortal
wound, his wicked mother,
Athaliah, then conspired
to kill the royal heirs
(so she should rule instead).
Her sister saved Prince
Joash, hiding him until the
murderous queen was
ousted from the throne

when taken from the
Temple courts where Joash
was proclaimed as king.

Jehoiada, the priest, did
make a covenant for kings
and subjects, all to be
the people of the LORD.
The nation all rejoiced; the
city of Jerusalem retained
its peace. King Joash acted
right within the sight of
YHVH–LORD.

The Temple needed much
repair and finally,
the work was done. But
then, he disobeyed
the LORD's commands,
abandoning the Faith
to worship Asherah.
The LORD would see the
death of Zachariah in
the Temple courts.

..... oOo .....

THE TRANSCENDING YEARS
Wisdom—Language of the Soul

JOB
A GRIEF OBSERVED

THE DEBATERS:
THE ARGUMENT
Job 1:1-12

*From whence you've come,
you Satan one? Have you
observed My Job?*

**He has his reasons
You to fear!**

*My Job displays integrity,
He seeks to serve but Me.*

**You've thrown a hedge
around that man; it is not
fair—this thing You do!**

*My Job is strong in hope
and aim. He will not fall to
wily plans proposed by you!*

**You've blessed his kin,
his stock, his land! You've
spoiled the man!**

*Job's strength of soul
withstands your strife!*

**Stretch out Your hand
and strike him down and
he will fail to stand as
whole!**

*So, Satan, take his wealth;
but, save his life!*

**I'll do as You've allowed;
I'll prove his weakness,
test his worth!**

of life: I am alone!

I came as naked from
the womb, I'll naked be
when I depart.
The LORD has given,
then He takes, but I
will trust Him yet!

JOB: THE DISASTERS
Job 1:13-22

The day, it dawned as
others do,
no hint of ill was in the air
till people came, their news
to tell: what shock of loss
was mine to bear.

It seems the ill forebode
did creep across my life
as shadows do–
At first, a hint and then,
the mass:
My stock was gone
and servants too!

Then, blackest night!
A raging storm of loss:
my family dead in one
foul swooping gust
of hurricane! O, grief

THE DEBATERS:
THE DESPITE
Job 2:1-10

*From whence you come,
you Satan one?*

**I've roamed the Earth,
I've seen, I've heard!**

*Have you observed
what Job has done?*

**He yet has reasons
to be glad!**

*Still Job will shun your evil
ploy; he'd give his all for
his Eternal Life to gain!*

....

THE FRIENDLY
DISCOURSES

JOB AND 'FRIENDS'
Job 3 – 14

Job

I sit in sack and ash
bereft of comfort here–
of all I've lost, these have
I gained: my boils, and morbid
fear! I curse the day of birth!
That first day turn to night!
May light refuse to shine
on me, let shadows
shroud my plight.

Let morning stars be
dark and wait in vain for light;
the rays of dawn be dim as
night. Why was I born to blight?
Oh, why such weight on pain?
For bitterness of soul I weep.
Oh, why a life in sorrow's
night? My bitter well
is wide and deep!

Eliphaz
Chapters 4 – 5

We sit beside you now
to tend your soul in grief;
for seven days we've sat
as mute. It's time for
counsel brief with you.

You are the one to whom
we've looked–you've
counselled us, you've
strengthened feeble hands;
now, trouble is your loss!

Where is your courage,
man? Why give a grief such
endless scope? With trouble
near you are dismayed;
a blameless life your hope!
Consider now the fact:
the innocent don't die! Who
ploughs an evil, reaps an ill;
The upright find help nigh!

Can mortals be more right
than God, more pure than
He? If God can't trust His
own, how less the one who
lives in 'clay'? A fool takes
root but then, so suddenly,
his house does fall. His
richest harvest wastes: he
comes to gruesome woes!

If I were you, I'd take my
misery in to God; I'd lay
my cares upon His hands;
great wonders He has
wrought! How blessed is
the man whom God
God corrects. Don't e'er
despise His chastening,
His tests! He wounds;
His hands will then repair.
The LORD will ransom you!
He will protect you! Delve;
we have examined truth in
this, apply it to yourself!

Job
Chapters 6 – 7

If but my woes were weighed,
more weight they'd have
than sand upon the ground.
God's terrors are arraigned
at me, I've found!

Oh, that I could request
that God would grant my
'pride': If He should thrash
me, yet I'd find my joy:
I've not denied!

A grieving man should have
his friends around him. But,
even if I'd leave Him, still
my friends deny my grief,
no help instil.

So! teach me how, and when,
I've wronged the LORD. Now!
Prove my fault–correct me, if
you can; you friend today
you would reprove?

Just look at me! How could
I lie, deny the LORD
and speak profanity?
Don't be unjust Review
my own integrity!

LORD! What is man that You
should look upon his soul,
would seek to test and try,
examine him today and not
a moment look away?

What have I done? What is
my sin, am I a burden, LORD?
I ask, O Watcher Wise:
am I a person that You rue?
Forgive before demise!

Bildad
Chapter 8

How long must you
persist in this? The LORD
does not pervert. Your
blustering words are naught
but wind and better far:
His justice sought!

Your children sinned, of
course; God gave them up
to guilt. But, if you would
look unto Him, He will your
own estate rebuild.

Inquire of people past
to see what they have
learned: Our days on Earth
are but a shade; they've
nought to tell of worth.

Rely upon a hanging web
that spiders weave and lean

upon its fragile thread, you'll
find the web won't hold:
it will most certainly unfurl!

A life soon wilts and withers
if you will entwine your roots
around an unforgiving rock.
The wretched plant returns
to dust and ever mocks!

Most surely, God does not
neglect, and He did not
reject the blameless man
who sought to do His will
before your woes began!

Job
Chapters 9 – 10

Indeed, I know it so!
But, how may I be judged
as righteous to the LORD
and how fulfil His will as
pledged?

His wisdom is profound!
Who could resist His might?
His awesome power is
daily proved
as wondrous in His sight.

And, could I win disputes
with Him although I be
so innocent?
I'd plead, no less, His mercy,

still, for me!

He crushes in the storm
and multiplies my wounds;
my breath is spent
I am bereft,
no hope rebounds.

My days so swiftly ebb
and fly–as eagles soar-
away. No joy relieves
my plight,
I'm plunged in deep despair.

God is no man that I
could answer His indict.
If only one would come,
remove
the rod of God's debate.

I speak my soul's complaint
and tell my bitter woe;
I'd ask why God
oppresses me–
He knows I'm guiltless now.

Your hands, O LORD,
have shaped
my life: You'd make it waste?
You moulded me from
formless clay,
You'd turn me back to dust?

You gave me life, Your grace
endowed my spirit once;

but, was it in Your mind to find
    a guilt for innocence?

Then, why did You extract
me from my mother's womb?
Oh, that I'd died before
    my birth
for carriage to the tomb!

So soon, I'll find that place
within the deepest night
where all is darkness, shadows
    deep,
where light resembles night.

bounded limits over the
Almighty's wondrous ways?

Now, if you would devote
your heart and hands to Him
and put away all evil plans,
your 'night' will turn to dawn!

You'll find serenity if
you'd believe, hope clear!
Then most would seek
your utmost good!
You'd rest in safety, have
no dreadful fear.

Zophar
Chapter 11

Should your complaint
remain unchallenged In
the light?
You'd say to God, without
rebuke:
'I'm pure within Your sight'?
I wish that God would
speak,
revealing wisdom's ways.
Be sure of this, that God
forgets
just some of your sin's days!

Are you the one so prone
to fathom mysteries
of God and place some

Job
Chapters 12 – 14

Just listen now! I have
a mind as well as you!
I'm not inferior, though I'm
a laughing stock to you!

You have contempt for those
whose feet have slipped
in mire
but ask God's creatures–
they all know
His hand brought pain so dire!

To God belongs the power,
to Him, the victories. He rends,
He holds, He leads, He frees
and none withstands His ways.

I would but take my case
before my God and plead
my innocence, for you do not,
as would physicians, heed.

If you would cease your talk,
that's wisdom, for you'd hear
my argument, my plea, my
plight.
Don't argue as God's seer!

Keep silent now and let
me speak, then–come what
may!
Though God would slay me,
yet
I'll hope in Him alway!

Yes! I will speak my piece
for my deliverance–
no Godless man would dare
defy His awesome holiness!

Oh, grant me just two things,
O God: withdraw Your hand
And stay Your terrors from
my life.
Then, summon me; contend!

"Please, tell me LORD,
what are
the wrongs that I have done?
Reveal my sins, reveal Your
Face!
Do not, now, leave me 'lone!

The span of life is like
a flower that fades or, as
a shadow cast–just once,
then, gone!
You've set the limits, days.

There's hope for greening
trees!
If lopped they sprout
once more;
the roots may age, the stump
may die
but water will their life restore.

But when a man does breathe
his last, his life has ebbed;
it does not rouse, he does
not rise,
nor can his 'sleep' be waived!

If only You would hide
me in the grave, conceal
me till Your anger passed,
then You'd renew me well!

LORD, if a man should die,
tell, will he live anew?
For I would wait to be released:
You'd call, I'd answer You.

You'd count my steps but, now
to track my sins–You'd deign
to cover them. But LORD,
You take
my hope and leave but pain!"

THE FIERCE DEBATES

Eliphaz
Chapters 15 – 21

I say, the wise would not
an empty answer give
or fill himself with desert
winds—
by useless words you live!

Your sin does motivate
your mouth, your crafty
tongue
condemns you now; it's not
my own;
your lips confirm you're
wrong!

Are you the first of men—
the first created, rise
to listen in to Heaven's
plans?
Are you the only wise?

You'd know what we don't
know?
Your insights more than
sage?
The grey beards all agree
with us;
how dare you vent your rage!

If God should doubt His
aides,
if all the heavens fail

His test of purity, how less
would man, so frail?

So! Listen now to me:
The wise declare that, all
their days, the wicked writhe
in wretched torment to appal.

He fain would flee the dark,
he is but vulture's food;
distress and terror mark
his fears
as he defies his God.

He flees to wasted towns,
in crumbling rubble lives;
his wealth is sieved as sand,
he'll not escape the night
that grieves.

Be not deceived in this:
before his time, he's paid
in full;
like empty vines, or olives
shed,
of blossoms, barren still.

Job
Chapters 16 – 17

What misery! How could
you seek to comfort me
in such a way as this you
choose?

Please go, and leave me be!

If you were in my place,
yes, I could bring you grief;
but I'd prefer to comfort you,
encourage your relief!

'My God, it's You who wore
me out; You've bound me fast
and devastated all I had.
Now, here I stay, aghast.'

I am reviled, men jeer
and scorn me in my shame.
My God has thrown me to
their wiles;
I'm shattered in my prime.

I'm draped in sackcloth now,
my brow with ash is grimed
and streaming tears besmirch
my face
though pure I have remained.

My Witness be in Heaven,
my Advocate on High,
He'd plead my case, my sad
lament;
He'd heed my prayerful sigh.

My spirit's broken, all
is lost. The grave awaits;
and now my eyes are dim
with grief,
my frame, a shadow, faints.

Do try to ease my pain!
You'd share the night to save—
In deepest night, you'd say,
'The *LIGHT*
is near!" (My hope's the grave)!

Bildad
Chapter 18

**When will your speeches
end?
Be sensible so we may talk!
Why do you think us stupid
now?
At truth, you must not balk!**

**The lamp of evil men
is snuffed and such as they
will find a lighted tent as
dark
and, vigour snuffed at day.**

**Their scheming brings them
down,
entrapped within their snare;
calamity will hold them fast,
disaster they will bear.**

**From light to darkness
driven,
they're banished from the
land;
no offspring or survivor left;**

this is the fate they've found.

Job
Chapter 19

You crush me with your words;
reproachfully, you prod!
If this is true, I've gone astray;
These are the wounds of God.

I cry, 'injustice!' but
He does not answer me;
He shrouds my path in darkest
night,
There's no relief for me!

My hope is like a tree
uprooted, cast aside.
He's drawn the battlelines and
strikes;
My grief none could abide.

Have pity now, my friends,
for God's own hand has
wrought
this grief. Will you pursue
as He?
Oh, please, what has
He sought?

Yet this one thing I know—
that my Redeemer lives!
Engrave this on the rocks

and sacred scrolls–
that, in the end,
HE LIVES!

And, in the Latter Day,
He'll stand upon the Earth.
Though worms shall eat
my flesh,
*I WILL SEE GOD
ON EARTH!*

Zophar
Chapter 20

I've troubled thoughts
that prompt a dire
reaction to your speech,
your strong rebuke of God.
I must reply to what you do!

You surely know that mirth
of fools and foul will fly!
What joy they find is whisked
away to never find
though pride would reach
the sky!

Then, those who watch
will ask, in questioning,
now, where is his praise?
As dreams at dawn,
he fades into oblivion—
in woe he ends his days.

The sweetest bread he eats
will turn to gall and bring
a poison to his soul; his
massive wealth can't help,
won't staunch the viper's
deadly, mortal sting.

He'll not enjoy the streams
of honeyed cream; he'd fain
enjoy the profits of his pride
for greed has soiled his gain.

And no respite from grief
he'll find; his wealth will fail
to salve the misery of his mind
with terror, he will quail.

And, unfanned flames
will steal, with no rebate,
his last resourced estate.
His guilt will be exposed
at last by Heaven;
All vile men meet this fate!

Job
Chapter 21

Do bear with me until
I tell what's on my heart;
then, you can mock me if
you will,
inflict me with your dart.

Just place your hand across

your mouth! Just look upon
the pains which bring the
terror to
this trembling body's bone.

Just take another look
at what befalls all those
who dance to evil's tune
and win
the spoils–it's a disgrace!

They live their lives in great
prosperity; filled are their
days
with ease, their end, with
peace
and still they scorn God's
ways.

How often do you see
the lamps of evil are snuffed,
pray,
before their wicks had waned?
Where's their calamity?

But who could teach our God?
It's He who teaches each—
One dies in ease, the other,
pain:
Where does God's justice
reach?

I see what's on your mind,

you fail to see how well
the evil fare; you won't accept
that they are spared God's
knell.

And, who denounces those
whose conduct does appal?
Their tombs are housed in
grandeur:
You can't console at all!

THE FIERY DIATRIBES
Eliphaz
Chapter 22

How may a man begin
to benefit our God today?
What pleasures could you
give unto Almighty God,
YHVH, El Shaddai?

And, do you think that your
great piety would draw
a commendation from His
lips to ease your pain?
Your wickedness does soar!

I here condemn you for
the myriad ways you must
have hid your wealth from
those, the poorest men
in greatest need of trust.

Sure! This is why you find
such peril in the gloom
of your distress where
waves of grief untamed
in woe would sweep
you on to endless doom.

You'd challenge God?
Defy His majesty?
His perfect will?
Will you persist in
treading dangerous paths
of dark defiance still?

Submit to God and be at
peace with Him; you'll
find prosperity refined:
Just trust the LORD
with heart, and soul,
and all your mind.

Return to Him, your God,
He'll be to you as gold.
Delight in Him; lift up your
face, your mournful face
to Him, His grace behold.

Fulfil your vows and you
will find a light upon
your way. Then God will
 hear your heartfelt pleas;
He will your sins atone!

Job
Chapters 23 – 24

If only I could find
where He does dwell, I'd see
how He would answer my
complaint—
He'd hear my plaintive plea!

Would God oppose me to
my face? No! He would choose
to drop the charges; I'd present
my case and I'd not lose!

I search the east, I find
Him not, nor in the west;
the north, the south? I find Him
not!
Alone, I have no rest.

But: He does know the way
I take and, when my God
has tested me, I shall come
forth
as pure, unsullied gold!

My feet have followed in
the path He set for man;
I've kept His way, not turned
aside—
I've cherished His command.

But He opposes me!
I'm terrified of Him;

yet I'm not silenced in this
cloud
of shrouding **shadows** grim.

Why does not God now choose
a time for judging those whose
sins do crush the wretched,
poor?
Yet He does not oppose!

Such men as these rebel
against the *LIGHT*, design
to scorn its path, preferring
dark
to wreak their sordid sin.

They cling to dusk, their face
concealed; the **shadows** might
be friends in crime–evil is
cloaked
in terrors of the night.

Yet, sinners are but foam
afloat the water's wave
for won't the grave snatch at
the life:
God takes the life He gave.

They rest awhile, secure
it seems, but God still sees
their wickedness. As corn is
reaped,
so they're deprived of years.

Bildad
Chapter 25

Dominion and awe
belong unto God's Light.
It's He who sets in order all
of Heaven's glorious height.

Can any limit now be set
upon God's power?
Do any stand outside His
dawn to face the sun
and live without His dower?

How then could one pretend
as righteous, wholly good?
How can a man be pure,
if sun and moon and all
the stars are not, to God?

Job
Chapters 26 – 31

How well you guide me now
so helpless in my plight:
Such insight and advice—
such aid!
Much wisdom is implied!

Man stands as naked in
the sight of God whose power
is awesome still in every
realm—
in every field and flower.

The clouds do hold their dew
until He wills the flood;
the boundaries of **shadows**,
LIGHT
are set as to His good.

As surely as God lives,
He's brought me bitter blight
of soul. But, surely as I live,
I will not think you're right!

I'll not deny my own
integrity, my true
and utter righteousness
in all I think and do.

I'll teach you of God's power,
I'll not conceal His ways;
why all this fruitless talk?
You've seen God's
judgements; why, surprise?

For out of blackest night
there comes
from silver mines men's wealth.
He cuts his shafts down deep
to draw out gems with stealth.

Though, where is man to find
the well where wisdom dwells?
The deep does say, 'It's not
in me!
A treasure never tells!'

Our God alone knows where
all wisdom dwells; He sees
its road,
its winding and its ways—
the fear
of God is its abode.

I long for yesteryear
when God watched over me;
I found the *LIGHT* upon
my path,
His friendship ever near.

The days of yore allowed
my service to the poor,
to show my righteousness,
my good
intent to these and more.

My words were precious then
to all who sought to prove
my counsel and my grace
to them;
my face did shine in love.

But now they mock me, these
brash brats I would distain
this base and brainless brood
of sons
whose fathers were my bane.

My life now ebbs away,
the night does pierce
my bones;

I am reduced to dust and ash;
I cry to God my groans.

For, when I searched for good,
an evil came; I'd heed
the *LIGHT* but darkness falls
on me;
my path is dark indeed.

If I have walked in false
and lustful ways, my eyes
as leading heart, my hands
defiled,
then others: take my prize!

If I have once denied
a justice to my own,
and others too, then take
my hands,
my arms! I've harmed not one!

If I have placed my trust
in gold; if I would bless,
instead of God, the radiant sun,
then judge my faithlessness!

If strangers knocked in vain
for succour at my door,
I've left them lone, upon
the street,
then judge my sin, and more!

If my estate cries out,
its furrows wet with tears,

if I devoured its yield without
redress, let wheat be briars!

O give me One to hear
as I present my case.
Then, my accusers, try
me sore,
and God indict my days.

I place my signature
upon my bold defence;
I'd stand before my Judge
and win!
The word of Job now ends!

THE FINAL
DENOUNCEMENT
Elihu
Job 32 – 37

Three friends have spoken
now in wisdom's way!
You've said your piece,
and yet, to date,
you have no substance
of rebuke to fling
which could with Job
now meet!

My anger stirs; I'm young,
it's true, defer to you:
Let age and wisdom speak,
I said—remember it–

although, I've wisdom too!

Not one of you has proved
that Job has erred;
you are so very sure
that God, not you, should
challenge him. So I will take
the floor instead!

Now Job, do listen, pay
attention to my words!
My speech is from an upright
heart none can dispute;
Almighty God now girds.

You said–I heard you claim–
I'm pure, I'm clean, I'm free
from guilt yet God finds fault
with me. You thought it, too!
You're wrong! How wrong,
before too long, you'll see!

In dreams and visions God
does speak, preserving
all repentant souls
out from the pit; and also,
God, in loving-kindness
by beds of pain, consoles.

If one should mediate,
in grace, for you to spur
your soul and ransom you
from all your blatant sin,
you'd live in *LIGHT* by which
to see the scene once more.

God does these things,
you see, of course,
to turn a soul back from
the pit and make the *LIGHT*
of life for which he yearns
to shine upon his frame.

You three, now listen to
my wise and learned
discourse; together, let
us learn together now
what's good through what
we see from day to day.
Job says he's innocent!
Discern:

He says it profits nought
to please his God! Far be
it from the LORD to evil pay
for good. His justice see!

God's eyes are on the ways
of men. There is no night
to Him, there are–for him–
no shadows that could
shield in utmost gloom
all evils from their time!

But, Job does speak without
the insight known of him;
he answers as a wicked man,
rebelling in his awful sin.

Job, you have asked to be
absolved from what is past

by *YHVH*-LORD! And yet
you blithely say:
What profit is my purity,
what gain, to live
God's way each day?

What is your righteousness?
What can God gain from
your own hand?
Your open wickedness
affects you to your doom.

Men soon cry out whene'er
oppression dims their light
but, no one asks 'where is
my God, the *YHVH*–LORD
who gives me songs
within enshrouding night?'

God listens not to one
who brings his empty pleas;
much less He heeds your
empty talk, your lies;
you mouth but plaintive and
foreboding sighs.

Now, bear with me awhile;
there's more to say on God's
behalf. My knowledge knows
no end; the years have
taught me well: no falsehood
taints my helpful words!

Our God is mighty, yet
He'll not despise the wise:

His eyes are on the righteous
ones who are upright,
He will exalt their lives.

To those enchained by woes,
God tells them their disease
and calls them to repent
that they, in *shalom* peace
may end their days in ease.

Your God is wooing you
into a spacious place;
take care that wealth
does not entice,
nor evil's sustenance
when greed gives rise.

How great is God!
Take care to praise
His mighty power
for who can gauge His
wondrous works,
creation's expertise.

What awesome power,
what might to praise!
My heart leaps to God's
Praise, I joy in God;
The lightning strikes,
the thunder rolls;
how marvellous, His ways!

Now, listen to me, Job:
Consider well how God
 all things controls

the clouds, the skies,
the rolling seas
and how He quells the tolls.

Out from the north He comes
in golden splendour; He's
arrayed in great magnificence
in awesome majesty, beyond
our reach. He is revered
above all things, all ways!

YHVH–LORD
The Resolution
Chapters 38 – 39

*And who is this that deigns
to darken by your word of
ignorance, My counsel so?
I'll question you instead!*

*So! Where were you when
all foundations of the Earth
were laid? Who marked its
size? Do tell Me of its girth!*

*Who laid its cornerstone
while morning stars
did soar to fill the skies
and angels chanted joy and
bounded seas with shore?*

*How many orders have
you given to the morn?
And have you shown the*

dawn its place, the moment it
was born?

Where is the chief abode
of LIGHT? Where do the **shades**
of night now dwell? Who knows
the path where darkness fades
and from where the LIGHT
will swell each day?

And, have you entered in
the storehouse of the snow?
Where is the way of lightning
and where do winds wend now,
from whence, they come?

Still, could you bind the path
of stars, Orion's course?
And you would steer the
constellations in their space
and know their laws?

So, who endows the heart
with wisdom, or the mind
it's understanding yet?
Who counts the clouds,
who moulds the sand?

And do you know the times
of birth for creatures rare?
Their habitats, their fare, their
flair? Who goes
where all the eagles dare?

·······

Job
Chapter 40

How can I find reply?
Unworthy, I do find
myself! I put my hand upon
my mouth, my lips to bind!

YHVH–LORD

Now brace yourself for you
shall answer Me this day
Would you discredit Me, so as
to justify your way?

And, is your arm like Mine?
Adorn yourself with LIGHT,
with glory and with honour
here–you feel it is your right?

Unleash the venom of
your darts; bring proud men to
dust, then I'll admit to you
that you can save your own.

Observe the chief of all
the animals–what strength
he has, what power! He is
secure along the river's length.

Can you secure the lithe
and wily crocodile
with but a hook and bait, and
he so placid all the while?

*Perhaps you'd make a pet
of him? Subdue him, if
you can. You lay a hand on
him, you will remember it!*

*Who'd dare to prise his mouth
that flashes in the dawn.
He will not be subdued; You'd
rue the day that you were born!*

*He rises up; the men
of might do quail beside
his threshing tail; no javelin
or sword could pierce his hide!*

*He churns the ocean depths
and stirs the river's run
like boiling caldrons, and his
wake lies glistening in the sun.*

*There's nothing on the Earth
to equal his fierce jaws!
A creature without fear, he's
king of all the proud, of course.*

Job
Chapter 42

I know that You can do
all things—no plan of Yours
will ever be displaced.
You asked
who challenges Your Laws?

Most surely, I did speak

of things not understood,
too wonderful for me to know;
You questioned, right, my
word.

My ears have heard of You,
but now my eyes have seen
the LORD! Repenting,
I despise
myself. Your Truth I glean!

YHVH–LORD
Chapter 42

*I turn to you now, Eliphaz,
I vent My wrath on you
and on your friends:
You have not spoken as you
ought of Me; but Job repents!*

*You need to sacrifice, repent.
My servant Job will pray
for you. And I accept
his earnest prayers,
his intercession now, today!*

Job
I've prayed for these,
my friends,
O LORD, and now I speak
my prayer

of praise for You have blessed
me so;
You've brought prosperity
most rare.

I've found a consolation in
the comfort of my gracious
guests–
they understand me now,
and bless;
But, Lord, I praise for Your
bequests.

O LORD, You've blessed
my home
and heart beyond the
measure of
the past. I'm blessed far more
than I
deserve. I will Your mercy
prove!

..... oOo .....

THE TRANSCENDING YEARS
Continued

THE KING'S ANTHOLOGY
KING SOLOMON

WISDOM IN PROVERBS
Proverbs 1 – 9

THE WARNING

For wisdom and self-discipline,
come, lend a listening ear
to me:
Let all who would be truly wise,
acknowledge God most
reverently.

You seek the counsel of
your peers,
your peers of pain, enticing
youth?
Place not your feet in evil's
way,
this is a downward path
to death!

You search for wisdom all
your days?
She cries aloud upon
the street!
How far your blinded eyes
do search,

how long your foolish ways
repeat?

It's when distress would
overwhelm
that simple souls do seek the
truth.
It's only then you call; I'll
answer not:
You vainly search in all the
Earth.

THE MORALITY

Apply your heart to
wisdom's way—
it is as silver, treasure rare.
You'll find it from the
mouth of God,
true understanding's
always there.

It is the LORD who guards
the just,
protecting still His faithful
ones.
And wisdom enters in
the heart
that turns from sin,
its grief atones.

Shun all who tread in sin's
dark ways

delighting in perversity;
they always miss the Path
of Life,
their end is in adversity.

THE BENEFITS

Let love and faithfulness
remain
your constant company;
entwine
them through your life, engrave
them on your heart; with
no repine.

Trust in the LORD with all your
heart,
lean not upon your own self-
praise;
in all your ways acknowledge
God
who guards and guides
your paths.

Do not despise God's
discipline;
He will rebuke where sin
is prone;
The LORD will discipline
in love,
just as the parent to his son.

How blessed are they
discerning right

by understanding wisdom's
care.
More precious than the
purest gold

or jewels rare; nought can
compare!

True wisdom's ways are
pleasant ways,
her every route, a peaceful
path!
With wisdom you may
safely walk,
not stumbling on the path
of truth.

You'll rest in safety with no fear
of ruin found in wicked lairs;
the LORD is all your
confidence;
He keeps your feet from
sinful snares.

The LORD does bless the
holy home,
unto the humble grants His
grace;
the wise inherit honour's smile,
the fool is shamed by
sinfulness.

THE SUPREMACY

True wisdom is supreme; now
seek

until you find; though it may
cost
all that you have, gain
wisdom's ways:
do not forsake, but love
her most!

Esteem most high all
wisdom's ways,
she will exalt and honour you;
embrace, enfold her to
your heart,
she'll crown your life with
grace anew.

The way of righteous
men is like
the dawn that glows so bright
in fullest light of day, but know:
the wicked walk in blackest
night!

Above all else do guard
your heart,
it is the wellspring of your life;
look straight ahead, tread
level paths,
don't swerve and stumble
into strife.

THE DISCRETION

Attend to wisdom, tend
her words,

gain precious insight from
the wise;
that you would always be
discreet:
let knowledge be your
chosen prize.

Completely shun adulterous
ways–
such steps will lead you to
the grave;
lest strangers feed upon
your wealth,
through toil enrich what
others crave.

Do quench your thirst with what
is yours and covet not a base
desire.
Should you expect your
sustenance?
To purest love always aspire!

THE FOLLY

When you have acted foolishly
in pledging much beyond
your wealth,
go humbly to your neighbour,
seek
a freedom from this pact
for health.

Unto the sluggard I would say:

consider well the common
ants:
find your example in their
ways;
a lazy slumber ruin sends.

Flee scoundrels who corrupt
And plot their evil from the

and plot their evil from
the heart;
they stir dissention, reaping
lies.
Destruction is disaster's part.

Your parents' guidance, take
to heart:
their teaching is a steady light.
Take discipline—your daily
guide:
It ever shines in darkest night.

THE COMMANDS

Do keep these words as
offered now;
store my commands and you
will live–
do treat them as your inner
eye;
attend their will, for honour
strive.

In lacking judgement youth

can stray
as day does fade and night
sets in;
the temptress lurks within the
dark,
seduction comes in cloaking
sin.

Write all my teachings on
your heart
and bind them on your willing
hand;
see wisdom as your loved
sibling
and understanding, kin and
friend.

THE CALL

Hark, hear the urgent pleading,
call;
upon the height this voice does
sound
and at the crossroad wisdom
stands:
her voice is raised to
humankind.

To simple folk she calls,
'be wise',
to fools: 'be understanding,
bright!'
The call of wisdom worthy
sounds,

her lips proclaim the wrong,
the right!

All wisdom dwells with
prudence rare,
discretion, knowledge, hand
in hand
do walk. But pride and
arrogance
do creep with those in
evil's strand.

You search for wisdom?
You will find
her on the road of
righteousness.
With her is honour, wealth
supreme,
along the paths of justice,
peace.

The LORD delivered her
before
the dawn of Eden's day,
she was
appointed in Eternity
to come to birth for earthly
days.

How blessed is the one who
listens to
the voice of wisdom in the soul
and waits upon the threshold of
all truth, receiving life as whole.

THE INVITATIONS

See wisdom's hospitality;
she plans her menu, cooks
her food,
Invites her guests, all those
in need,
to choicest meals which
taste
quite luscious and so good.

'Let all the simple come to me,
all those who lack a judgement
wise
come eat and drink at
wisdom's home,
come, leave your foolish
fasting guise.'

All wisdom springs from
fear of God:
to know the LORD is
knowledge true!
Your years extend in
wisdom's ways
and wisdom grants reward
to you.

But, folly, too, invites her fools—
undisciplined and loud she'd
strive;
her stolen waters, treats,
are sweet!
(Her poison sends guests to
the grave).

....

THE EPIGRAMS
Selected from Proverbs 10–22

ON RIGHTEOUSNESS

No value find in treasure's
girth:
righteousness will save from
death.
The righteous are sustained by
God;
the wicked crave but are not
fed.

The righteous wear a blessed
crown
but violence will the wicked
own.

To think of righteousness
brings joy
but evil names will rust
away.

The righteous are the fount of
life,
the wicked are engulfed in
strife.

The righteous tongue's a silver
bell,
but wicked hearts their values
tell.

The lips of righteous men bring
peace
but fools will die for lack of
grace.

The righteous show a loving
care,
the wicked show a kindness
ne'er.
No harm befalls a righteous
man
but trouble stalks all evil
men.

A righteous man will know
his friend,
the wicked stray to evil's
end.

The righteous loathe a
falsity,
disgrace repays the evil's
fee.

The righteous guard
integrity,
the wicked reap
perversity.

The righteous' light is
burning bright
but faulty lamps are snuffed
by night.

True righteousness exalts
the land
but sin disgraces every
hand.

The righteous man a
treasure has
but trouble is the wickeds'
cash.

The righteous weighs a truth
as seen
but evil gushes from
the mean.

Much better is a mite with
right
than lack of justice with all
might.

ON INTEGRITY

Integrity does dwell
secure
but crooked paths to sin
would lure.

The LORD abhors dishonest
weight;
be accurate to gain His
rate.

Integrity will guide you
right,

unfaithfulness brings endless
night.

The good will surely
find goodwill
but evil comes to those
who will.

The good obtain God's
favour well
but crafty men, condemned,
do ill.

A good man leaves
inheritance
but sinful wealth, no
recompense.

The upright walk in fear
of God
but devious men despise
the LORD.

A truthful witness saves men's
lives;
a false report condemning
is.

A heart at peace redeems
the life
but envy rots the bones
in strife.

The healing tongue's a tree
of life,

deceitful tongues make
anguish rife.

The prayers of upright men
please God,
but He deserts sin's offered
hoard.

A man believes his
innocence
but, motive's in God's
balances.

The highway of the upright's
straight,
who guards his way will guide
his fate.

A humble soul among
the poor
is richer than with plunder's
store.

There is a way that seems like
truth
but, in the end, it leads to
death.

Far better is a crust of
peace
than feasting fools in much
disgrace.

A furnace tests the worth
of gold;

the LORD will test the heart
so bold.

The poor man pleads for mercy
still
but rich men scorn God's grace
for ill.

Man makes his plan within the
heart
but what prevails is God's own
part.

Unfailing love is chief
desire;
much better to be poor
than liar.

An honoured man will shun
sin's style,
a quarrelling fool will quickly
rile.

The fruit of fraud tastes honey
sweet;
against the truth, it's nought
but grit.

The LORD requires the truest
weights,
dishonest scales the LORD
berates.

The LORD declares the just
and right;

without, one's sacrifice
is blight.

A righteous act brings lasting
joys
but terror comes from evil
ploys.

Good names, more choice than
jewels,
a fool prefers the gold and
sells.

ON PRUDENCE

A wise son will rejoice his
father,
a foolish son will grieve his
mother.

The summer harvester is
wise;
a harvest sleeper brings
disgrace.

The wisest man will store up
wisdom,
a foolish gossip reaps his
ruin.

A man who holds his tongue
is wise,
malicious tongues have sinful
bias.

The fear of God adds length
to years,
the wickeds' time is brief,
with tears.

The one who gives will gain
the more;
unduly hoard, your purse is
poor.

In working land, the wise gain
food,
who chases wisps will lack the
good.

While wise men listen to
advice,
the fool will chase forbidden
ways.

In wisdom's words will healing
come,
but reckless words pierce
to the bone.

A prudent man will hold
his prize
but fools blurt out each
wilful craze.

Prudent men act out of
knowledge,
the simple fool exposes
garbage!

To walk with wise will make us
wise,
companion fools invite harm's
ways.

The wise will build a stable
house;
but fools destroy the house of
straws.

Wisdom seeks a wise
reception;
folly is the fool's
deception.

A prudent man will watch
his way
but foolish men believe
each sway.

A level-headed man keeps
rules,
but hot-heads are just reckless
fools.

The gentle answer turns a
wrath,
a harsh word spoken stirs up
froth.

A patient man will quell
a quarrel,
hot-headed men will stir
up trouble.

Who hates a bribe will live and
lead
but trouble comes to those of
greed.

Prefer the meek, with poor
abide,
don't share a plunder with
all pride.

Prefer great patience, self-
control,
avoiding evil's fierce
patrol.

Far better meet a cub-less
bear
than meet a fool of wisdom
bare.

Discerning men have clear
insight;
a fool's eyes wander and take
flight.

There is a friend more close
than kin
while many more would fail
to 'ken'.

To heed a discipline brings
life;
ignore correction, end in
strife.

Receive advice, the victory's
won;
for lack of guide, the nation's
gone.

Righteous are released
untarnished;
the wicked will not go
unpunished.

Love discipline and knowledge
rare;
who hates correction takes no
care.

A wise man listens to
advice,
a fool is caught within
a vice.

Respect instruction, be
rewarded,
scorn advice and be but
thwarted.

Respect instruction, be as
honoured,
resent correction, shame is
garnered.

Who loves his son will chastise
him,
but spare the rod and love grows
dim.

The lips of wise no safety
lack
but foolish talk means rod on
back.

The prudent son receives
correction,
a fool will spurn all
jurisdiction.

Heed wise advice, receive
instruction;
ignore correction, find
frustration.

Obey the good, life is
your prize;
contemptuous ways will bring
demise.

Do discipline your son; there's
hope!
Save him from death, the last
full-stop.

....

MORAL MAXIMS

Selections: Proverbs 22–24

Attention pay to sayings wise;
apply your mind to what I
teach,
do keep them safely, in your
heart, apply them aptly when
you preach.

In order that you trust the
LORD,
I teach you truly what to do;
I teach but sound, reliable
words
for I would guide and counsel
you.

Don't fret yourself to get rich
quick;
it cannot earn what wisdom
buys.
Such riches will but sprout their
wings and fly as eagles, to the
skies.

Now listen, son, be truly wise,
do keep your heart in wisdom's
ways.
Don't trust the sparkling wine—
it bites as vipers, blights your
days.

In wisdom is a great house
built,
in understanding it
is raised;
with knowledge all its rooms
are filled with treasures rare,
much praised.

A wise man has great power
my son;
men of knowledge increase
strength.

For waging war, you need wise
guides;
the wise will gauge a battle's
length.

Now, don't be partial as a
judge:
To show the guilty 'innocent'
will bring a curse on judge as
well—blessings flow where
truth is meant.

The sluggard teaches lessons
slow;
observing him, one sees great
woe.
a little sleep, with folded arms,
and poverty will pay
alarms!

....

THE PROVERBS

Selections: Chapters 25–29

ON KINGS

Remove the silver's dross
to find
what's pure for silversmiths
to bind.
Remove the wicked from
the king

for he does wear the righteous
ring!

Do not exalt before the throne,
the king may find you are
a drone!
What's seen, don't quickly
spread,
your neighbour may espy
you dead.

ON THE WEATHER

Like snow-cooled air at
harvest lent,
the trusted messenger
who's sent:
in faithfulness his word
is stressed;
his master's spirit is refreshed.

Like cloud and wind that bear
no rain,
the man who boasts his
generous gain
as gifts that are not wrapped
to give,
(nor planned to give,) he is a
thief!

ON FOOLS

Like lame men's legs that hang
so limp,

are proverbs by a fool, a wimp;
like tying stones in useless
slings,
the fool who all dishonour
brings.
Like thornbush in a drunkard's
hand,
are proverbs in a fool's
command;

like archers wounding
needlessly
are those who hire a fool with
fee.

ON FRIENDS

Trust wounds inflicted by
a friend,
it's foes who hide a vicious
rend;
as perfume spreads and joy
attends,
is counsel shared among
good friends.

The wise do not a friend
forsake;
no friends for fathers sadness
make.
Now bring no burden home
to bear,
true neighbours will a burden
share.

ON JUSTICE

The king who by oppression
reigns
is driving rain that leaves no
grains;
he does not practise justice fair
but men who seek the LORD
do care.

The man who deafens ears
to Law,
the LORD detests his plaintive
prayer.
And he who leads the just
to ruin,
will fall into the pit he's hewn.

In justice comes a nation's
strength
but greed will tear it down
at length;
The righteous do for justice
care,
The wicked no concerns
do bear.

Oppressors and the poor
share this:
the LORD gave eyes unto
them both;
one's eyes, dark wells
of greed;
the other pines: he sees
his need.

THE
COLLECTIONS
Chapters 30 – 31

THE ORACLE OF AGUR

I am a man most ignorant;
I lack, I do not understand:
who has ascended into
Heaven?
Who gathers up the winds
as given?
Who wraps the water in
his cloth?
And who has set in place
the Earth?
What is His name and, what
his Son?
Please tell–what have they
done?

Two things I ask of You,
O LORD, do not refuse me,
O my God!
Please make me neither rich
nor poor
but give me this: my bread,
no more.
Too much, I may disown
my LORD;
too sparse, if poor, I'd take
by fraud.
I would that no dishonour
comes
unto my God by these alarms.

Four things on Earth are very
small
and, seemingly, so
very frail:
The ant is such a tiny mite
yet stores his food as is
his right.
The rabbit has such little
powers
yet makes his home in rooted
bowers.
The locusts have no king of
rank,
yet they advance in rank on
rank.
The lizard can be caught with
ease
yet it is found in palaces.

THE ORACLE OF
LEMUEL'S MOTHER

O son, my son, the child
I bore,
spend not your night beside a
whore,
your vigour on unworthy men.
It's not for kings to crave
the wine;
it's prone to cloud your just
decrees.
Find character to mark
your days;

Speak up for those who stand
alone;
defend the rights of poor
and wan.

THE NOBLE WIFE

By searching, who can find
the wife
of noble character and worth?
Far more than rubies on
a strand,
she brings him good
as planned.

Selecting finest wool
and flax,
this woman works, is
never lax.
It seems as if a merchant boat
has brought her all the food
afloat!

From early dawn her actions
prove
that kith and kin reserve her
love.
Both home and field she
oversights,
her plans and actions store
delights.

Her trading all good profits
bring

and friends of all her goodness
sing.
Her light is ever burning bright,
her lamp does not exhaust
at night.

The distaff and the spindle fly,
she heeds the poor, their
plaintive cry.
When winter snows do fall and
chill,
her household is in comfort
still.

Warm coverlets with skill
are sewn
and clothing—linen, purple—
worn.
Her husband has respect
in town;
she sells her wares at market
time.

She is of beauteous character,
she has a dignity to
wear.
She speaks with wisdom's
faithfulness
and oversights the home's
affairs.

Her children bless her every
day,
her husband cherishes her
way.

THE ENLIGHTENMENT
Proverbs: The Book

The king has gathered to
his store
these precious proverbs
to explore;
when in his court is fierce
debate
and he would ponder well
a fate–
the quality of righteous
judgement made,
the sentence of the court
is laid.
He takes each half of it
to see
what one must prize and what
to flee.
And first, the right, the side
of *LIGHT*;
then, as a coin, he tosses it,
reversing, then, the
sentiment—
the grim, **dark** side to view a
sin:
the *LIGHT*, the **dark**, the
malcontent,
and thus he takes
enlightenment.
....

THE KING'S
PHILOSOPHY

THE QUEST FOR
ENLIGHTENMENT
Ecclesiastes 1:1-2

THE TEXT
Words of Solomon,
Son of David

Futile! Utterly futile!
All things are but a vain
reproach.
They're meaningless, yes,
everything.
Upon them would a sin
encroach.

PROBLEMS TO POSE
Chapter 1:3-11

What is the payment for
man's toil?
What is the gain, and what
the spoil?
The generations come and go,
the Earth remains, the sun
aglow;
the winds do rise, the winds
do wane,
all streams do flow, no seas
do gain.
Returning to the place
from whence
they came, all rivers go
on hence.

All things bring weariness,
it's true
and more than one could
ever rue.
The eye scans all and pleads
for more,
The ear is full yet yearns
a store.

All that has been will be
again
for nothing new the sun
has seen.
Is anything, yet possibly,
so new?
Already it is aged,
it's true!
And none remember men
of old;
forgotten all, no memory
is held.

THE QUEST ENGAGED
Chapter 1:12-18

As I have studied our domain,
a burden God has placed
on man,
I surely find I've seen
it all:
The thing that's done, it does
appal.
The twisted is not now made
Straight,

the lacking can't be counted
late.

(You'd think that I'd be wise,
but no!
I'm chasing wind that's
wayward bound)!

THE SEARCH IN PLEASURE
Chapter 2:1-11

Come now, here is a text
to heed:
Will pleasure spring
from greed?
Or laughter, will this bring
me joys?
(Strong wine is but a folly's
choice).

Great projects sate my own
desires,
all that to which the soul
aspires;
But, if it is surveyed, where's
LIGHT?
And where is meaning? Out
of sight!

THE SEARCH IN TRUTH
Chapter 2: 12-23

I searched in wisdom, folly,
care;
saw the wisdom and
the lair
and, just as day outshines
the night,
the wise have eyes but fools,
a blight.

The one has *LIGHT*, the other
gloom
but he will come at last to
doom.
What do I gain by being
wise?
The both do die, that's no
surprise.

A BRIEF SURMISE
Chapter 2:24-26

There's nothing better than
to drink,
to eat, to find one's joy
in work;
it all comes from the hand
of God:
Can wisdom give the best
reward?

(You'll think me to be wise;
instead,
I'm chasing wind that's
wayward bound).

THE SEARCH IN TIME
Chapters 3 – 5

There is a time for all our
days:
a season for all words and
ways:
a time to birth, a time to die,
a time to stand, a time to lie.
A time to scourge, a time to
praise,
a time to wreck, a time to
raise.
A time to weep, a time to
laugh,
a time to mourn, a time to
salve.
A time to cast, a time to
chase,
a time to kiss, a time to
pass.
A time to search, a time to
guess,
a time to keep, a time to
miss.
A time to tear, a time to
mend,
a time for quiet, a time for
sound.
A time to love, a time to
hate,
a time for war, a time to
wait.

The LORD has made, within
its time,
all things so beautiful
and prime;
He set Eternity in hearts—
and none can fathom where
He starts!

All things pertaining
unto God
endure forever, always
good;
with Him, nothing will add
to gain–
what is, has been, will
be again!

THE SEARCH IN
SOCIETY
Chapter 4

I looked and saw oppression's
ways,
the tears that flow if
comfortless
and I declared the dead
who'd died
are better off than life
supplied!

A fool will fold his hands
from work;
to ruin runs, yet still
he'll shirk;

But better fill one hand
with peace
than two hands full of toil,
disgrace.

THE SEARCH IN
WEALTH
Chapter 5:1-17

If you'd find the poor
oppressed,
have no surprise, they have
no rest.
The sleep of humble men
adore–
the slumber of the rich?
How poor!

A child brings nothing
In his hand
when he is birthed into
the land,
nor can he take what he
would save,
a meagre cent, beyond
the grave.

A BRIEF SURMISE
Chapter 5:18-20

I've come to realise
it so:

Take heart! Enjoy all that you
This man has gained
from God–
he doesn't fret, he's
occupied!

(You'd think that I'd be wise;
I've found
I'm chasing wind that's
wayward bound).

THE SEARCH IN LIFE
Chapter 6:1-6

A man, in lacking nought, has
gained
a rich supply for toil though
drained!
A still-born child is better
off—
no light, no night, it sees
enough!

A man, when bent on appetite
will never be quite satisfied.

(All life is meaningless I've
found,
I'm chasing wind that's
wayward bound)!

THE SEARCH IN
DEATH
Chapter 7

A worthy name is better
far
to be enjoyed than perfume
rare;
it's better far to mourn
I see
for death's our mutual
destiny.

I've seen the righteous man the
same
in death as is a wicked
man;
so why be overworked to
death,
for nothing gasp the last grim
breath?

THE SEARCH IN
THE FUTURE
Chapter 8

Who would obey correct
procedure
should stand as free within
the future!
But who can know that future
time,
or who can tell what is
to come?

No man has power on wind to
hold it,
no man has power on death to

stop it!
We'll see the day when 'lordly'
men
will come at last to death's
dark den.

When I applied my mind
to thought
observing man's so frequent
fraught,
I then saw all that God
had done
but knew not ought beneath
the sun!

(I've gained in wisdom but
I found
I'm chasing wind that's
wayward bound).

THE TRUTH ON
DESTINY
Chapter 9

As I reflected on man's
fate,
all that I saw at death's
grim gate:
All share a common
destiny,
the good, the bad:
Eternity.

The living know that they

will die,
the dead know not where they
do lie;
their love and hate have gone
to fate:
we all must join them soon
or late.

THE TRUTH ON
MAXIMS
Chapter 10

The heart of wise men guides
to right;
the heart of fools prefers
the night.
There is an evil 'neath
the sun
where rulers judge what is not
done.

Whoever digs a massive
pit
is prone to fall, headlong,
in it.
Snakes bite e'er they
are charmed,
what profit for the one who's
harmed?

A wise man's words are full of
grace,
a fool's consumed upon
his craze.

If men do laze, their rafters
creak,
if hands are idle, houses
leak.

And woe to you if kings
are slaves
but bless'd are you if they
are braves.
Berate your kind not even in
a thought,
a bird may whisper and you're
caught.

THE TRUTH ON
GOODNESS
Chapter 11

Cast all your bread on
waters deep,
in many days there's much
to reap;
Give portions of your gain
to some
lest a disaster comes to them.

Whoever watches winds
will weep,
or fears the clouds: you will
not reap.
As you can't tell the path
of winds,
you'll not explain what God
intends.

Though *LIGHT* will please
the eyes,
remember night, its tears,
its sighs.
Do follow in your heart's
true ways
or know God's judgement
weighs.

WARNINGS
Chapter 12

TO YOUTH

Remember your Creator now
while youth is on your
brow!
before the day of trouble
comes,
before a future danger looms.

TO THE STRONG

Before the light of sun,
or moon
and stars, no more will wax
or wane;
Before the clouds return f
rom rain,
the strong will stumble,
writhe in pain.

TO THE WEAK

When all the doors are

closed
and sounds of harvesting
reposed;
when men are frightened at
a bird,
the weak will crumble, fear
is stirred.

TO THE FAILING

In almond blossom e'er the
spring,
the creatures of the meadow
bring
no hope of joy, the soul
prepares
its final flight—the mourner
cares.

TO ALL

Remember Him, your God,
the LORD
before it's rent: life's silver
cord;
before the golden bowl is
smashed,
before the well-wheel's
dashed:

Before this human clay
returns
to dust from whence it
comes,

before the spirit flees to
God
who gave us breath within
this sod.

It's meaningless…
So meaningless?
The preacher stresses
'meaningless'!

(I've lost my wisdom, for
I've found
I'm chasing wind that's
wayward bound)!

…………

THE CONCLUSION
Chapter 12:9-14

Not only is the
preacher wise,
he shares his knowledge,
expertise;
he's searched his
many probes:
his words of wisdom act
like goads.

Now, all is spoken, all is
heard–conclusions come:
the mind now gird, have fear
of God and keep His ways

for judgement comes—the
soul it pays!

For ill, the **shadows**;
good: the *LIGHT*.
The LORD observes you
in His sight;
for every secret thing of life,
God has His will: it is
enough!

THOUGH FLEETING
SHADOWS MOODS HAVE
LENT, MY SOUL:
THIS IS *ENLIGHTENMENT!*

....

THE SEVEN
SONGS
OF LOVE
Canticles of Solomon

In the New Testament, the
Church is referred to as "The
Bride of Christ". The poems
appearing in this edition of
the Canticles, therefore, are
written as prayers for the
Church, The LORD
responds. Hymns may be
sung to tunes available in
most hymnals.

THE CHOICE
Chapter 1

I sing to my beloved LORD:
Your grace my trembling
soul becalms:
My heart is fixed on You alone,
O shield me in Your
loving arms.

I joy in my beloved LORD
Whose tender love is choice
to me;
How lovely is Your dwelling
place.
I come to You, Your
mercy see.

I worship my beloved LORD!
O, take me where Your
flocks do graze
and where Your sheep find
rest at night.
Now rest me in Your
wondrous grace.

The Groom–King
*I call you now, dear to My
Heart;
Come via the path you know of
old.
Now come to My most Holy
'Tent',
Come, fleet of foot, into My
fold.*

THE REQUEST
Chapter 2

O LORD, my King, haste
now to me
As perfume spreads its
fragrant tide.
O tender Shepherd of my soul,
Now draw me to Your
precious side.

You are the Rose of
Sharon fair
And Lily of the Valley rare.
O Flower of Beauty, hold
me there,
Within Your fragrant,
loving care.

You are my sustenance,
my joy;
You bring me to Your Banquet
Hall;
Your Banner o'er my soul
is love;
Your arms support me,
knowing all!

The Groom-King
*As doves that settle to
their nests
Within the mountain's
clefted lair,
So come to Me, your
Refuge here:*

*Show Me your face
and speak your prayer.*

THE SEARCH
Chapter 3

I've searched for You, Beloved
LORD,
Through days and nights of
fear;
I longed to find You e'er You'd
gone;
I find You now, my LORD,
most dear.

You come into my 'desert',
LORD,
With healing oil and choicest
balm.
Unto our union, LORD, my
King,
You come to claim my dream!

Awake, and haste, you zephyr
wind;
Come, freshly, to my garden
here;
Take this, the choicest
fragrance hence
My LORD, do heed and
answer prayer.

The Groom-King
*I see you now: how choice
you are!*

Your countenance is
ever clear;
How beautiful you
are to Me;
I'll hold you safe, always
secure.

THE DESIRE
Chapter 5

Awakened from the depths
of sleep,
My heart responds for You
are near!
I hear Your welcome Voice,
O LORD,
I will obey Your call
so clear.

I rise to meet You, LORD,
You bring
All purest love and joy to me.
How I adore your Presence,
LORD,
O, take my heart, Your
own to be.

My Shepherd-King is radiant,
fair,
His Eyes are doves, His Face
is gold.
He's altogether lovely and
He is the Tree of Life: Behold!

The Groom-King

How beautiful My
chosen "bride",
So pure, so holy in
your ways.
Adorned in a pure
'wedding' gown,
You are unique as sun's
pure rays.

THE LONGING
Chapter 7

O, Shepherd-King, receive
my joy
As wine that flows so
wholly sweet;
My heart belongs in troth
to You:

Come, walk with me, I'll be
complete!
Come early to my 'vineyard',
LORD,
To tend the growth of
early 'fruit'.
You are 'The Vine' to me,
O LORD,
Abide in me as from the 'root'.
O, seal me ever Yours,
dear LORD,
My love for You is ecstasy—
So strong, it passes
even death:
It is aflame with constancy.

THE GIFT
Chapter 8

I give You all my love,
dear LORD,
All that adoring hearts
could hold;
As fruit upon 'The Vine'
gives joy,
So I would yield my life:
the whole!

The Groom-King
Come dwell with Me in
Eden's bower
And stay with Me in love's
pure hour;
As whole do come: this is
your dower;
O, breath a prayer to
find My power.

THE CHOIR
Canticles–Selections

Rejoicing, we delight in You,
As fair as evening's silver
moon;
Appearing as the Dawn,
O 'bride',
And bright as summer sun
at noon.

You are arrayed in garments
white,
So pure and fair, you have

now come
to take Your rightful place
beside
the King of Love–the Heavenly
Groom!

..... oOo .....

THE TELLING YEARS

THE FIVE HYMN BOOKS OF ISRAEL
Each hymn is drawn from
selected Psalms

THE PSALMS: BOOK 1
GOD'S POWER IN CREATION
Songs of Praise: Psalms 1–41

THE BLESSED
Psalms 1, 16, 32, 33
A Hymn of the Blessed
Tune: *He leadeth me* D.L.M.

How blessed are the lives
of those
Who walk the righteous
paths of God,
Delighting in the holy Law
And meditating on His word;
For these are like the
verdant trees

By rivers of abundant grace.
The LORD will nurture
growing fruit
And thankful hearts rejoice
in praise.

How pleasant are the paths
of those
Whose ways are ordered by
the LORD;
The boundaries of grace
are wide,
Unmeasured as the love
of God.
The LORD reveals the Path
of Life,
Abounding joy marks all
His ways.
Eternal pleasures from
His hand,
Providing grace through all
our days.

How happy are the souls
redeemed,
Transgressions covered by
the Blood;
The past forgiven, the
present blest,
We sing for joy to praise
the LORD!
The word of God is right
and true;
His righteousness endures,
His love

Unfailingly pervades our lives
As we His mercies ever prove.

THE SEEKER
Psalms 6, 27, 38, 31: *A Hymn*
of Petition
Tune: *Lloyd*   C.M.

Be merciful to me, O LORD,
I seek Your guiding hand;
I come for healing by
Your grace
And in Your love, to stand.

You are as *LIGHT* unto my life;
In You all fear is gone;
You are my Stronghold, keep
me safe
Until the victory's won.

My heart lies open to Your
gaze,
My longings rest in You;
I wait upon Your
righteousness,
Now come, O LORD, renew.

In You, O LORD, I refuge find,
Deliver me from sin;
Into Your hands I place my life
And find my soul is clean.

THE WORSHIPPER
Psalms 24, 15, 27, 29, 30:
A Hymn of Consecration

Tune: *Saved by Grace*
D.L.M.

I would ascend the Hill
of God
To stand within Your Holy
Place;
LORD, cleanse my hands, my
heart make pure
And grant the blessing of
Your grace.
O LORD, I seek Your
Sanctuary
Wherein the pure in heart
may dwell,
To worship You in holiness
And all my vows to You fulfil.

One thing I seek, my soul's
desire:
LORD, to abide within
Your house,
To gaze upon Your beauty
there,
For Your great love my soul
endows.
I'm confident that I
shall see
The goodness of the LORD
to me;
I wait on You and find
my strength,
I seek Your Face, I find
You near.

I worship You, rejoicing in
The splendour of Your
holiness,
The glory of Your majesty,
For granting blessings of
Your peace.
I will exalt Your Name,
O LORD,
For You have lifted sorrow's
night:
I called Your Name, You
healed my soul;
Rejoicing came with
morning light.

THE PILGRIM
Psalms 23, 25, 26, 37:
A Hymn of Experience
Tune: *Melita*   8.8.8.8.8.8.

You are my loving Shepherd,
LORD,
You lead me through a
pastureland
Where paths of righteousness
abound;
My nourishment comes from
Your hand,
By gentle streams You lead
me on;
Restore my soul by Your
command.

O guide me in Your truth,
O LORD

And show me now Your
chosen ways
For all my hope I find in you,
Remembering Your love
always!
Your faithfulness is ever sure;
LORD, guard my soul through
all my days.

Now test me, LORD, and try
my heart,
Examine all my motive,
thought;
Your love is ever guiding me
As I Your perfect way have
sought.
You counsel me within
the truth,
Instruct my soul in paths
so straight.

I trust Your guiding hand,
O LORD,
Delighting in Your chosen path;
Committing all my ways to you,
The dawn shall rise within
my heart.
Your righteousness, reflect
its ray,
Your *LIGHT* illumine
every part.

BE AWARE
Psalms 4, 13, 17, 31, 34, 36:

A Hymn of Communion
Tune: *Warrington*   L.M.

O Love of God, reveal
Your Light,
Your searching *LIGHT* of
proffered grace;
Now fill my heart with praising
joy,
My peace is in Your shining
Face.

I search the night if I might find
Your quickening ray. Enlighten
me and lift my eyes
unto your Face;
You meet my need unfailingly.

I see the wonder of Your love,
You shelter me through soul
distress;
I seek Your Face in
righteousness.

My times are in Your hands,
O LORD,
For You redeem my soul
from care;
O may Your Presence shelter
me
For I have sought Your Face
in prayer.

Your Eye does guard my
pilgrim way,

Your Ear attends my urgent
pleas;
In joyful praise my ransomed
soul
Reflects the radiance of
Your Face.

How precious Your unfailing
Love
And deep Your Rivers of
delight;
You are the Fountain of my life
And in Your Face, I see the
LIGHT!

. . . .

THE PSALMS
BOOK TWO

RUIN AND
REDEMPTION

Songs of Experience
Psalms 42 – 72

THE PILGRIM PATH
Psalms 42, 43:
A hymn of Questing
Tune: *Rimington*   L.M.

My pilgrim path ascends
the heights;
Your mountain trail is steep
O LORD,
But I would seek to find
You there;

My soul aspires to God,
adored.
I thirst for You, O living LORD,
As deer that long for streams
so cool
When wearied in a desert
place;
O quench my thirst, renew
my soul.

But why should I so downcast
be?
My hope is in the LORD!
my praise
Shall yet ascend to You;
my heart
Rejoice: I walk within Your
Peace.

You are the Stronghold of
my life,
Send forth Your light, Your
truth, to guide
And lead me to your holy
Mount
That I may worship and abide.

THE REFUGE
Psalm 46:
A Hymn for Resting
Tune: *Martyrdom*   C.M.

O LORD, you are our Refuge
here,
Our Strength, our Hope,

Oh, hear;
We rest in You though waves
do surge
and mountains quake in fear.

Chorus:
*Be still, be still, be still
and know
I AM the LORD, your God;
Be still, be still, be still, exalt
The Name of YHVH–LORD!*

There is a river, LORD, whose
streams
Make glad your city fair;
That Holy Place where YHVH
dwells,
Transcends all earthly care.

We would ascend Your mount
for prayer
Within Your Presence here
(Your dwelling Place, Your
Holy Hill,)
And know Your blessing there.
The LORD Almighty, *El
Shaddai,*
Is always near, He guides;
He grants His grace and
deepest peace,
Within the heart abides.

THE TRIALS
Psalm 55:
A Hymn of Testing

Tune: *Take up Thy Cross*
10.8.10.8.

O for the wings, yes: the wings
of a dove,
I'd fly away and be at rest!
LORD lend Your ear unto my
humble plea;
In suffering, commend
Your love.

Chorus:
*I'd fly to You and be at rest,
To shelter in Your Haven there
And speak my need with You
in prayer;
O LORD, now bless me in
my quest.*

O for the wings, yes, the wings
of a dove,
I'd flee unto Your Sanctuary
And seek a shelter from the
raging storm;
To comfort me, extend Your love.
O for the wings, yes: the wings
of a dove,
I'd seek my Saviour, YHVH–
LORD!
Within the darkest night You
hear my cry;
You answer me in grace
and love.

O for the wings, yes: the wings
of a dove,

I'd cast my care upon the
LORD
For You sustain my soul
in righteousness;
And, as for me, I trust
Your love.

THE PRAISING HEART
Psalm 63:
A Hymn of Feasting
Tune: *Retreat*   L.M.

O LORD, You are the Living
God,
How earnestly I seek Your
Face;
O quench this thirsting of my
soul
And lead me from this desert
place.

I find You in the Sanctuary
And I behold Your glory there;

Your love is more than life
to me.
To You I lift my hands in
prayer.

I feast upon Your
righteousness,
My lips will glorify Your name;
You satisfy the hungry soul,
I shout my joy, my praise
proclaim.

I meditate upon Your word
Remembering Your living
springs;
You are my constant help,
I sing
Beneath the shadow of Your
wings.

My praise ascends the highest
heights,
In faith Your promises applaud;
Your hands uphold me lest
I fall—
My soul rejoices! Praise
the LORD!

THE BENEDICTION
Psalm 67
A Hymn of Blessing
Tune: *Turner*   8.6.8.6.8.6.

The blessing of the LORD
be yours:
The blessing of His shining
Face,
The blessing of His gracious
ways,
The blessing of His guiding
hand,
The blessing of His saving
power:
His blessings grant all joy and
peace.

....

THE PSALMS
BOOK THREE

THE HOLINESS
OF THE
SANCTUARY
Songs of Devotion
Psalms 73–89

THE SANCTUARY
Psalm 73:
A Hymn for Worship
Tune: *Maryton*   L.M.

There's blessing in the
Sanctuary!
My soul, adoring, draws apart;
The LORD is good, His
blessings flow
Unto His own, the pure in
heart.

There's comfort in the
Sanctuary
For those who falter on
the way;
The LORD encourages and
grants
His guardian care in this
our day.

There's knowledge in the
Sanctuary!
The mind that searches after
God

Shall find the path is bathed
in light
And know the counsel of
the LORD.

There's guidance in the
Sanctuary!
By His own hand the LORD
does lead;
In nights of grief, the deep
distress
is lost in God—He meets
each need,

I worship in the Sanctuary:
The *LIGHT* of God illumines
there;
Where is my hope but in the
LORD?
I find my sustenance in prayer.

THE EVENING HYMN
Psalm 77:
A Hymn of Faith
Tune: *Nuttall*   6.4.6.4.6.6.6.4.

When evening shadows fall
And night draw near,
I seek the Sanctuary
peace harbours me.
The LORD knows all
my need,
The burden of my prayer
In faith my all I cast

Into His care.

As evening shadows steal
Through twilight hours,
I meditate on God
Knowing my vows.
I find a song to sing
Within the depth of night;
Without a star to guide,
I walk in *LIGHT*.

Though evening **shadows** pall,
In deepest night,
I know the LORD is nigh,
He guides aright.
By His unfailing love,
The LORD my fear allays,
For He displays His power
By His own grace.

THE PROVISION
Psalms 78 – 80:
A Hymn of Praise
Tune: *Vox Dilecti* D.C.M.

The majesty of God is seen
Through all His wondrous
ways;
He calls His people unto prayer
And covenants His peace.
Where all His precious rivers
flow,
Abundant as the seas,
The floodtides of His
righteousness

Release redeeming grace.

The kindly hand of God
is seen
In meeting all our needs;
He opens Heaven's gates
to us,
Our souls with manna feeds.
His streams in arid desert
lands
Refresh where'er He leads;
And, all His paths are pleasant
paths,
His Presence yet abides.

The Shepherd staff of God
is seen,
Held by His own right hand;
We are His sheep who graze
in peace
In verdant pastureland.
We fill His Sanctuary with
praise,
His mercies sing. We stand,
Restored, before His shining
Face
And His salvation find.

THE PRAYER
Psalm 86:
A Hymn of Devotion
Tune: *Diademata* D.C.M.

I lift my soul in prayer

And speak the matchless
Name:
O, hear my humble pleading,
LORD,
You knew me e'er I came
To speak to You my need.
Bring joy where once was
shame;
Now may redeeming grace
abound;
I would Your mercy claim.

Forgiving ever, LORD,
Your love extends to me;
So faithfully You quickly come
In answer to my plea.
I worship only You,
By faith Your glory see!
How marvellous Your miracles,
Your wondrous grace to me.

O teach me, LORD, to walk
Within Your truth again;
Grant me an undivided heart,
Removing all sin's stain.
O LORD, my God, I praise
And glorify Your Name;
How great Your love enabling
me
To find my life again.

THE PRAISING HEART
Psalm 89:
A Hymn of Joy
Tune: *Silchester* S.M.

O LORD, Your love endures
Throughout all time and space;
Your righteousness a solid rock
Throughout our length of days.

We praise Your wonders,
LORD,
Your faithful constancy!
Who can compare the love
of God—
Unbounded, flowing free?

We walk in *LIGHT*—Your own
Dear presence, LORD, does
guard
Our path each day. You are
our Shield,
Our Life, our Hope, our Guide.

Your Covenant stands firm,
You are the Rock for us,
Our Saviour–LORD in whom
we trust,
Established in Your grace.

....

THE PSALMS
BOOK FOUR

GOD'S SOVEREIGN
KINGDOM

**Songs for the Sabbath:
Psalms 90 – 106**

THE DISCERNMENT
Psalm 90
A Hymn for Rejoicing
Tune: *Spohr* (Rep. last 2 lines)

O LORD, You've been our
dwelling high
Throughout the years of time;
Before the mountains pierced
the sky,
Before the world was born!
From everlasting You are nigh,
You are the Living LORD!

A thousand years within Your
sight
Are as a fleeting day
Or even as the passing night.
But, as for us, our years
Are as the dew-drenched
grass, its night
A brief and passing phase.

You grant to us a span of years
But sin would mar our day;
Your *LIGHT* reveals our fears,
our tears.
O, teach us, LORD, to know
And to discern all wisdom's
ways–
We plead Your guiding hand.

O, satisfy the yearning soul
With Your unfailing love
That all our songs would then
extol

Your wondrous Name; we see
The splendour of Your
presence now,
Your favour rests on us.

THE REFUGE
Psalm 91:
A Hymn of Trust
Tune: *Thy Welcome Voice* S.M.

There is a dwelling place
So near the Heart of God;
I find my shelter 'neath His
care,
My Refuge is the LORD!

Chorus:
God has rescued me,
Guarding me in love;
Walking in the way He leads,
Redeeming grace I prove.

Beneath His shadow here
I rest secure in peace;
He is my Fortress and
my God;
I trust in His embrace.

God covers me with grace,
I find my solace there;
His faithfulness allays
my fear;
He grants His strength
through prayer.

God is my Dwelling Place,
No terrors here appal;
His angels guard a treacherous
path,
Supporting lest I fall.

THE NEW SONG
Psalms 95 – 98:
A Hymn of Praise
Tune: *Maryland*   D.L.M.

Come, sing for joy unto
the LORD
The new song of your highest
praise;
Come, let us go unto the Rock,
The Rock of our salvation!
The LORD, He is our God
and King,
His hand has set the worlds
in place,
The mountains and the seas
are His:
Rejoice in His creation.

Come, let us bow before
the LORD
And kneel before our Maker,
God,
For He is God, He is the
LORD,
He rules the Earth in majesty!
Declare His glory through
all lands

And tell the peoples of His
deeds:

How great the LORD, worthy
of praise,
His splendour fills the
Sanctuary!

Ascribe to God the glory due,
O, come into His courts with
praise
And worship Him, the LORD,
within
The splendour of His holiness!

The LORD now reigns, He
rules the world
In justice and in truth. Let all
The peoples joy in God and all
Creation sing His
righteousness.

May all the distant shores
rejoice:
The LORD is King, He rules
supreme.
His reign is based on
righteousness,
His glory shines through
Heaven and Earth!

All joy unto the upright heart,
His *LIGHT* reveals the upward
path;
Rejoice in God all you who sing

In praising now His matchless
worth.

O, sing a new song to the
LORD
For He has done such
wondrous things;
His right hand and His holy arm
Have brought salvation nigh
to us.

The LORD remembers us
in love,
His faithfulness extends
in grace.
Be jubilant to sing of Him:
Jehovah rules in
righteousness.

THE THANKSGIVING
Psalm 100:
A Hymn of Joy
Tune: *Trentham* S.M.

O, shout your songs of joy,
Your praising joy to God;
Let all the Earth rejoice in Him,
Now, praise the LORD,
your God.

O, gladly sound your praise
And worship Him, the LORD;
Now come with joyful,
happy songs

And bow before the LORD.

Yes! Know that He is God,
He is Creator, LORD,
And we, His people, are
as sheep;
He is our Shepherd, LORD.

O, enter in His gates
With thanks unto the LORD
And enter in His courts
with praise,
Give thanks unto the LORD.

The LORD is good, His love
Endures. It is the LORD
Whose faithfulness endures
throughout
All time: He is the LORD!

THE PRAISE
Psalm 103:
A Hymn of Remembrance
Tune: *Warrington* L.M.

O praise the living LORD,
my soul;
Yes, all my inmost being,
praise
The LORD and bless His holy
Name.
Remember all His wondrous
grace.

O praise the loving LORD,
my soul,
Forgiving all your erring ways
And healing all your heart's
disease;

Remember all His wondrous
peace.
O praise the giving LORD,
my soul,
Who satisfies the heart's deep
need,
Restoring and renewing life;
Remember every wondrous
deed.

O praise the everlasting LORD;
His Kingdom rules
forevermore!
O praise the LORD, all Heaven
and Earth,
Remember to give thanks,
adore!

....

THE PSALMS
BOOK FIVE

THE SUFFICIENCY
OF GOD'S WORD

Songs of Praise:
Psalms 107–150

THE CHANT
Psalm 119
Setting relates to an acrostic
Psalm: the structure of the
poem relies on the alphabet.
(Music: *Background to chant*)

ALL those who walk within the
Law
of God, a pathway straight will
find;
BE mindful of the LORD, our
Guide,
forever righteous, ever kind.

CAN any keep the upward way
according to the LORD most
High?
DO any hide the Word of God
forever in the heart? Yes, I!

ENABLE me to see the Light,
the wonders of Your shining
Way;
FAITHFUL and true unto Your
word,
Lord, counsel me in truth this
day.

GOD, heal the sorrows of my
heart
and strengthen me within Your
grace;
HELP me to meditate upon

the ways of God in tranquil
peace.

IN all my ways, I follow You,
obedient to Your righteous
Laws;
JEHOVAH, LORD, O lift my
eyes
unto the Light my soul adores.

KNOW that salvation comes,
my soul,
by God's unfailing, matchless
love.
LORD, I will walk within Your
paths
and all Your mercies ever
prove.

MY comfort and my faith have
come
Remembering Your living word;
NIGHT'S shadows cover me
but still
I call upon Your Name, O
LORD.

O LORD, You are my portion
here,
I seek Your Face with all my
heart;
PLEASE shelter me within
Your Law
and guard my onward path
aright.

QUESTIONS are answered in
the Word
and knowing You will bring my
joys.

REMEMBERING Your
precious Word,
I follow, LORD, Your sound
advice.

SALVATION comes at Your
command
for You have found and
counselled me;
THERE'S hope for me within
Your word:
You're faithful, LORD, to me.

UNDER the shadow of Your
care,
my hope leans on Your
promises!
VICTORY is sure within Your
care;
eternal is Your faithfulness.

WONDROUS Your word unto
my taste
And, sweeter than the honey
bright;
(e)XAMINE now the way I take,
Your Word is as a lamp, a light.

YOU are my Refuge and my
Shield,

sustain me by Your promises;
ZEALOUS to follow Your
commands,
now shine on me in
righteousness.

THE ANTIPHONAL
THANKSGIVING
Psalm 136: *(Antiphonal)*
Music: *Selected, background*

Give thanks unto the LORD,
your God,
His love endures fore'er;
Give thanks unto His holy
Name,
His precious Name so dear.
Give thanks unto the LORD,
He lends
His ever-listening ear;
Give thanks for every
wondrous deed,
His watchful, tender care.

To Him give thanks, proclaim
in praise
His matchless grace so fair;
Who made the rays of Heaven
shine,
His wondrous LIGHT so clear,
The sun to rule the daytime
skies–
He takes the shade of fear,
The moon and stars to guard

the night
He checks the falling tear.

From Him redemption's plan
has come–
He pays the price so rare;
Who leads His people through
all trials,
He offers strength to dare!
He lends His mighty,
outstretched arm,
He frees us from the snare;
He takes us by His strong right
hand,
He will our burdens bear.

To Him all praise and thanks
are due,
He grants us choicest fare;
Providing rich inheritance,
His Presence ever near.
From Him all blessings ever
flow,
He all our griefs will share;
Give thanks unto the God of
Heaven:
His love endures for e'er.

THE
ACKNOWLEDGEMENT
Psalm 139:
A Hymn of Devotion
Tune: *Southport*   S.M.

O LORD, You've searched my
soul,
You know my inmost thoughts;
Discerning every deed, the
whole,
You know the way I take.

I find Your Presence near,
Your hand is placed on me;
You follow and precede me
here:
My LORD, how wonderful!

The wings of dawn can't dare
To carry me from You;
All time and space are in Your
care:
O LORD, You guard and guide.

When **shadows** seek
to hide
My face far from Your *LIGHT*,
The night will shine as day!
Abide,
The night is *LIGHT* to you.

Your hands once formed
my soul
And brought me, LORD,
to birth;
Amazing, Your creative skill,
You planned my life, my all.

How precious is Your thought,
How vast, Your love for me;

As dawn releases morning
light,
I waken to Your care.

O search me, LORD, and
cleanse
My heart, my inmost soul;
See if there be, in me, offence.
LORD, test me, make
me whole.

THE HALLELUJAH
SONG
Psalms 146 – 150
A Hymn of Joyous Praise
Tune: *Diademata*   D.S.M.

Sing Hallelu–Jah!
Yes, Hallelu–Jah!
Though all your days,
Sound forth His praise
Proclaim this truth with me:
He sets the prisoner free,
He gives the blind their sight,
He lifts the fallen, grants
His *LIGHT*;
He rules eternally!

Sing Hallelu–Jah!
Yes, Hallelu–Jah!
The Living LORD
Is God adored.
He heals the sin-sick soul,
He binds our wounds, His goal!
We'll praise Him all our days:

He tells the number of
the stars,
How great is God, the LORD!

Sing Hallelu–Jah!
Yes, Hallelu–Jah!
All Heaven's host
In God now boast
within the heights above;
Give praise on Earth with love.
His glorious works, proclaim
Let all creation now acclaim
The splendour of His love.

Sing Hallelu–Jah!
Yes, Hallelu–Jah!
O praise the LORD

with one accord;
Let all the people sing
And Earth the echo ring.
Rejoice, with praise applaud:
O glory to our Saviour–LORD,
He is, of kings, the King!

Sing Hallelu–Jah!
Yes, Hallelu–Jah!
Bring Him your praise
Your voice now raise
Within His Sanctuary.
Let everyone agree,
All creatures great and small,
With instruments and voices call
Your praise of God with me.

SHADOWS AND THE LIGHT

A COMPANION TO THE BIBLE

— EYE-WITNESS TESTIMONIES —

BOOK TWO

THE PROPHETS AND THEIR PURPOSES

Shadows And The Light

Lucille L. Turfrey

BACKGROUND

There are new songs to be sung! In 'turning the page', we are taking a significant step in moving from the books carrying the History and the Hymnology of the Old Testament, into the mindset of the Prophets of Israel. These men have turned their gaze from the **Past** and, standing firmly on the ground of their **Present** turbulent times, they begin their report on how their dramatic, God-given, visions relating to the **Future** offer hope to the discerning mind.

A prophet is one who *fore*tells what will certainly happen at a future time. But this is not the only remit of one who is called out from among his contemporaries to give form to seemingly unimaginable futuristic concepts. A prophet is also one who '*forth*tells' today's message! This is, indeed, the most profoundly important aspect of the entire mission! The prophet is set apart to become the LORD's spokesperson. He, or she, is to announce the great themes of judgement, warning, retribution, and consequence.

Set against this bleak backdrop, however, is the glorious news of God's love, mercy, grace, forgiveness, renewal, restoration and ultimate resolution. These are the factors that bring into focus the mind, the message, the meaning of what *YHVH*–LORD chooses to disclose to humankind. The *prospective* is balanced by the *proclamation*. Yes! Tomorrow is vital but how can one negotiate the yet unknown without knowing that the LORD is with us today, in the midst of our turmoil, as He maps out the parameters whereby the eternal issues of life will set us on the right path to Eternity!

Occasionally, a **shadow** will loom over the scene as an enemy makes his entry from 'left field'. On the whole, however, the messages of the Prophets are here presented in a form that offers access to the deep issues of Scripture by a window that lets in the *LIGHT* openly and effectively.

May this channel of grace be a blessing to you, the reader!

CONTENTS

THE PROPHETS AND THEIR PURPOSES

THE ROAD AHEAD
PROPHECIES AND PROMISES
Jeremiah 29:10 – 14

The *YHVH*–LORD now speaks to you:
> *I hold kind thoughts for you;*
> *I know the plans I have for you:*
> *They're for your benefit!*
> *My plans are not disastrous plans;*
> *I plan to give you hope! I plan*
> *a future that is manifest in grace.*
> *I'll listen to your prayers, your pleas.*
> *So, be wholehearted in your search*
> *for Me: I will be found by you!*
> *I will restore, I'll settle you:*
> *I'LL BRING YOU HOME!*

PROPHECIES AND PROCESSES
Micah 6:8

What does the LORD require of you?
> *I will explain all that is good*
> *as this is what I will require*
> *of those who choose to walk*
> *within the paths of righteousness:*
> *Choose right, abhor the wrong;*
> *be merciful—be kind to everyone*
> *for all are equal in My sight.*
> *You choose to walk the path*
> *that I have set for you?*
> *Stay at My side, in step with Me,*
> *and walk in deep humility:*
> *I AM THE YHVH–LORD!*

THE TESTING YEARS

ISAIAH

Greetings! My name is Isaiah. I rejoice in this as it is a continual reminder that *God saves*. I understand that—through my family line—I am related to the kings of Israel (Judah actually,) though I like to feel that I am more closely aligned with the people as a whole. My home is the city of Jerusalem.

My onerous role is to speak God's values to both king and commoner without fear or favour. We live in perilous times—my ministry began in the year that King Uzziah died. As prophet, I speak the prophecies as *YHVH*–LORD directs. This must be done without fear or favour.

Set against the nation's dire need, it is vital that I speak now to you the prophecies that *YHVH* shares:

WAKE UP, JUDAH!
Chapter 1

I sense the word of *YHVH*–
LORD
within the deep recess
of mind;
I see, in visions rare, His
will
revealing to my soul,
in kind,
the message I must bring
to all
His people–loved, yet
wandering far,
rebelling and recalcitrant.
O, open up your ears
and heart:
God's word is clear:

YHVH–LORD:
*The ox responds to
guiding reins
and donkeys know who
would control
but Judah's Clan, you're blind!
You do not recognise My Call!
Corruption seeps into the soul
of all dismissive of the LORD.
Why does rebellion haunt
your ways?
You need a balm to heal
the flawed.
Your sacrifices won't assuage
My sorrows for your sin
and, here,*

I find no pleasure in
your worshipping—
so bare without devotion's
prayer.
You've turned your sullen
backs on Me
so I respond in kind. I will
not gaze
upon your loathsome practices
where holiness you would
debase.

Go! Wash yourselves!
Be clean!
Seek goodness, holiness
and purity;
Reject all evil ways, let
justice reign
and peace will come
with surety.
Let equity now be your mould,
care for the orphans in
the land—
they stand alone where love
ne'er comes
and widows need your
helping hand!

Let reason speak!
Come, come to Me, hear
what I say.
Your sins are scarlet,
bloody, stained!
I'll cleanse you whole, you'll
be just like

the wool of lambs—as once
you yearned.
Obey My word, turn from
all paths
of wickedness and
blatant strife.
Alternatives? Destruction!
Death!

I've spoken! Hear My words
and live!
The worthless slag will be
removed—
Through righteousness
one learns
to be ashamed of past
misdeeds
as Zion is restored.
Repentance turns
the tide; You'll be revived.
Jerusalem
shall live again—the Home of
Holiness,
the faithful city, loved
by God—
as equity replaces
worthlessness.

ISAIAH'S VISION OF JERUSALEM
Chapter 2:1-5

Before the end of time, all Zion
will be the goal of the devout

pilgrims
who yearn to scale the
mountain's peak
to praise the *YHVH*–LORD
with hymns.

The Law of God will flow
out from
Jerusalem for God will rule.
All lands and peoples find
their peace:
the nations, all, at rest
and well.

The warring warriors will down
their weaponry, remoulding
them
from spears and swords
to tools
that will enhance their home.

No nation will desire to fight
the battles of the proud;
they'll be
at peace for, in this land,
they'll lay
aside all weaponry as *LIGHT*
they see.

ISAIAH: THE DAY OF THE LORD
Chapter 2

The day is gorged in waste!

You count it worth–the gold;
the idols here and everywhere
you bow to all so bold.

Go to your hiding place
in fear of glorious Majesty
for pride will be your malady–
make fear of God your
strategy!

There is a day in store
for all profane iniquity;
the lofty brought so low:
Be gone to dust, inequity!

The mighty trees of Lebanon,
the oaks on mountains tall,
and all exalted ships and kings
one day will, humbled, fall.

The LORD alone exalt;
the splendour of His might
and majesty proclaim.
Now, walk within His *LIGHT*.

ISAIAH: JUDGEMENT LOOMS
Chapters 3 – 4

O Judah, and Jerusalem,
your House will fall and soon.
All strength is drained, support
is gone. All water seeps,
is gone.

Your heroes, gone, your
judges, lost.
No craftsmen will remain,
the weak will lead the strong;
Ungainly youths will train.

(But tell the righteous all
will then
be well with them—they've
been abused.)

You seek for leaders yet
but there is none to hold
the rein
or testify to strength within
sufficient to suffice for gain.

The elders are despised
by youth
who lead their peers astray;
disaster lurks, will not
be passed,
oppression will the guides
betray.

(But tell the righteous all
will then
be well with them—they are
excused.)

The LORD as Judge returns
to court;
His gavel is employed;
all stand

before His gaze to hear
His rule
against the leaders of the land:

The poor are plundered,
vineyards bare;
God's people all are crushed
and bruised;
YHVH, El Shaddai*, Almighty
God,
has rendered all to blame:
none are excused.

(But tell the righteous all
will then
be well with them–none are
refused.)

The women grieve, they are
alone;
Yet, there will be a blossoming
Branch
so beautiful and glorious.
The fruit of this one Branch,
the Branch:

Yes, YHVH–LORD, will be the
glory of
all those who love His holy
Name;
He'll cleanse, make holy by His
love.
Nought then will bring the land
to shame.

(And tell the righteous all will
then
be well with them, their grief
defused.)

The LORD will wash away
the guilt
of those who mourn on heights
of Zion:
all stains He'll cleanse, make
pure;
by fire He will the soul refine.

The cloud of Presence–Fire
by night–
will be a canopy of grace
to shelter them within His care;
He'll be a Refuge there always.

(And, tell the righteous all will
then
be well with them–none are
recused.)

SONG OF THE
VINEYARD
Chapter 5

My song is for the one
I love—
about His vineyard perched
upon
a hillside, verdant, rare.
He tilled
the ground, removed

all stone
and planted vines that
flourished there.
My Loved One built a tower
and scanned
for enemies who would deface
the vineyard so well planned.

My Beloved dug a winepress
there–
He hoped for harvests rich,
immense.
But what is this? Contaminated
and
despoiled, His crop; a grim
offence!

The *YHVH*–LORD now speaks:

*Now judge you well: what
did betide
My vineyard and My crop?
I hope
for more than tainted grapes.
What can
I do? I'll tell you now how I
will cope!*

*I'll take away protecting walls–
the hedge will be destroyed;
My vineyard will become
a waste;
no pruning, cultivation
that is stored.
The ground will bear but
briars, thorns,*

*no rain shall grace this
fallow ground.
This vineyard is a parable: it is
all Israel! I looked for
justice: None!*

*So! Woe to you who spoil
the land!
Now YHVH–LORD, the
El Shaddai,
declares this condemnation for
your ears: Take heed, I cry:
your homes become
quite desolate,
your acreage will be despoiled
and ravaged by a wanton mob
as drunkards do, embroiled
in lust.*

You'll sing and dance with
tambourine
but care not for the nation's
pride.
Take note of this: An exile does
await where hunger, thirst
abide.

Another thing to note: the
YHVH–LORD
Will be exalted then as holy,
pray,
by His own glorious
righteousness
and sheep shall graze with
lambs at play.

ISAIAH: THE CALLING
Chapter 6

I've seen the *YHVH*–
LORD! Enthroned, exalted
in the heavenly heights!
The Temple was in majesty
immersed; Seraphim–each
six winged, outspread–
their faces were twice
covered and their feet, twice
hid. With two,
each flew… the Temple
was entranced! The
seraphim then sang in flight:
HOLY, HOLY, HOLY is
the LORD, The *YHVH*–
El Shaddai. His glory does
outshine all lights upon
the beauteous Earth!

The Temple shook upon
its frame as smoke then
filled the holy site. I saw
my sin: "Oh, woe is me!
I'm in remorse, my lips
unclean, my hands
besmirched, I live among
immoral Clans today!

What will become of me?
My eyes have gazed upon
the *YHVH*–LORD!
A seraph came to me
with tongs

that held some altar coal. He
touched my lips! He said,
By this, you are
made whole, your sin,
atoned! You stand now
cleansed before the *YHVH*–
LORD. And then, I heard
the Voice Divine: He spoke
to me, the *YHVH*–LORD:

Whom shall I send,
now, who will go for Me?

I spoke to Him, the *YHVH*–
LORD: LORD, I'll obey;
I'll go for You! Yes! Here
I stand: send me. He said:

Go! Tell this people:
You are forever hearing Me
but you will never truly learn!
You're ever looking, seeing,
but you never do discern.
You've calloused hearts, your
ears are deafened and you're
blind! You could have heard,
you could have seen, be
healed, peace find.

O LORD, I prayed, How
long, how long must this go
on? How long this most
distressing quandary?

Until the cities lie in dust,
bereft of citizens; no harvest
will be found upon the fields
of home but then an exile
intervenes at will and, though a
tithe remains, the land will be
laid bare, not heal.
Hear now: My promise is:
Just as the fallen forest trees
leave stumps within the
ground, My Holy One, will be
'The Stump' to heal!

WHAT'S IN A NAME?
Chapters 7 – 8

ISAIAH: *YHVH is my*
Helper
That's me, of course, the
son of Amoz who had
named me well. YHVH–
LORD is ALL to me: He is
my Helper–all I need to be
the man he asks of me–I'll
be His spokesman to
the nation now.

UZZIAH: *YHVH is strong*
The king of Judah, now
demised, he was a man
of note. His strength was in
the *YHVH*–LORD. The date
renowned is when he died—
I mention it

because it was the date
when YHVH called.

RESIN: *Dominion*
That's what he sought! e
was well named. He was the
king of Syria but, when he
died, that date did prove to
match the end of his great
dynasty: proving might may
not be right!

PEKAH: *Watchfulness*
He was alert, this king
but, sadly, he was watching
for a means to seize the
throne of Israel. He marched
with Syria up to
Jerusalem but failed his
quest. His grief would
know no bounds.

REMELIAH: *YHVH
increases*
This king, the father of
Pekah, expected God to
make him rich (if given
names are any guide).
The history of Israel did
plunge once Pekah took
the crown and flaunted
all his garish plans.

AHAZ: *He holds*
This king did reign in Judah
and Isaiah stood by him for,
when he heard the voice of
God (who 'held' this king,)
Isaiah went with son to bring
encouragement, to guide:
Don't give up hope.

SHEAR–JASHUB:
A remnant will return
Here is a prophecy indeed.
I understood how serious
the doom impending for
Israel (about to learn what
exile does to beaten Clans.
few would return)!

**MAHER–SHALAL–
HASH–BAZ**
Quick to plunder, swift spoil
The name meant much
when it was chosen for this
son, by name, would
emphasise that Israel's days
of glory hung by slender
threads. Their land would be
destroyed and soon!

SHILOAH: *Sending forth*
This fountain sweet was
choice indeed in sending
forth its stream,

refreshing, life-renewing,
wending through Jerusalem.
But Israel
cared little for its gentle
flow. Rejoicing, rather,
in that wretched man Resin.

URIAH: *YHVH is LIGHT*
Well named, this priest, his
aim was to be carrying the
LIGHT of *YHVH*–LORD.
He was respected for the
LORD called in Uriah and
the king to vouch for him,
reliable
in witnessing The Word.

ZECHARIAH: *YHVH is
renowned*
How worthy was this man!
He stood for righteousness,
he witnessed for the LORD,
Himself! What greater joy
is there than this: to be a
spokesman for the LORD;
to stand on holy ground,
proclaim that *YHVH* reigns!

IMMANUEL: *God is
with us*
This name is one of victory.
The title warns that those
who think that, bearing
arms, they're sure to win

to win all battle frays, be
they with God or man. But
sheltered are all those who
battle for the LORD.

YHVH, EL SHADDAI
*The LORD, the Almighty
One* I heard the Voice of
God advising me to hold
faith, pray, regard *YHVH*
as the Holy One. Fear God,
He'll be your Sanctuary.
For Israel, He'd be a
stumbling stone until they
placed their trust in Him.

JACOB: *Supplanter*
ISRAEL: *A prince ruling
with God*
How far the mighty fall
when they have tossed their
faith away and choose to
flirt with mediums. Why
will they yet consult the
dead to guide when *LIGHT*
from God would guide them
to the dawn?

MOUNT ZION: *Fortress*
JERUSALEM:
Possessing Peace
'A mighty Fortress is our
God'! and, those who dwell
in Zion—in looking to the

LORD to guide—will find a
fortress where they'd find
Jerusalem to be their safe
possession of 'Shalom'!

SHEAR–JASHUB
Chapter 7:3-9

I walked with Dad today!
It was a very special time
for me. You see, we went
to meet the king. We
walked up to the aqueduct
where water flows into
the Upper Pool–that's where
our clothes are washed–
and there
King Ahaz met with us.

My Dad said to the king
that he should cease his
worrying. The king,
you see,
was scared, I think, of the
fierce anger of Resin, the
king of Syria. And, Pekah,
Israel's king. He was a very
wicked man. You see,
Pekah assassinated his own
king and stole his crown—
or so I'm told. He must
not win
the day! The kings of Israel

and Syria were out to get
our king and seize his crown
as well—or so I'm told.

As I was saying, then
I stood
beside my Dad as he gave
words of comfort to our
king, Ahaz, I heard Dad say
to him that Syria and Israel
would never win the day!
I do remember well the
words Dad then conveyed to
King Ahaz: the words
of *YHVH*–LORD for him:

It just won't happen for
all Syria has no strength that
is greater than its capital and
Israel is no stronger than it's
faulty capital. You see,
Damascus and Samaria
could never conquer
YHVH–LORD! It's time
for faith! Stand firm!

I'm glad I walked with Dad
today. I hope to grow
just like my Dad–Isaiah:
he is the prophet for our
YHVH–LORD.

KING AHAZ
Chapter 7

I am the king you know!
It's I who gives direction as
to which would be the way
to go, the what to do, the
why it's done! Then, would
you know, Isaiah comes
to me with words he thought
that I'd obey. He did
explain that *YHVH*–LORD
requested that
I seek a sign significant,
a confirmation, if you like—
and He, the LORD, would
grant fulfilment of that sign.

I must say, this is quite
irregular! What type of
sign? And why the sign?
Isaiah then explained: the
sign could be most difficult
as I can conjure up. As high
as Heaven or as deep as
hell. He'd grant me even
that. I am perturbed.
I wonder if my faulty faith
is fine enough to then
believe what He would say.

He'd answer any quest?
I'm king but I can't tell
what God should do—
we are not quite
on friendly terms.
That's why I have relied

on what Isaiah prophesies.

Is this a trap for me?
You see, I've much upon
my mind. I know at once
what my reply must be:
No! Tell *YHVH* I can
not do this thing! I will
not, cannot, test or tempt
the YHVH–LORD.

How ill prepared I was
for what the prophet said:
I call upon the royal house
of David's dynasty to hear
God's word. How long will
you continue on to try the
patience of our God,
the *YHVH*–LORD?

Hark now! The LORD will
give a sign to you instead:
A virgin lass will bear a
Child. She will give birth
unto a son. This child
will be then named
IMMANUEL

There is a message in this
precious name, it is:
God is with us. This is
the sign but, with the sign,
a warning, too. The day
will come when Israel

will be shorn of all its
greatly valued worth.
Assyrian hordes will
pillage all the Holy Land.
I should have known!

THE BROTHERS
Chapters 7 – 9

We two will play and chat
together happily for we
are much alike—so like
our Dad in many ways.
(He is a special man, my
Dad—The king will come
to him for counselling from
time to time—at least,
that's what it seems.

I should explain that I am
known as Shear-Jashub and
my brother, Maher—that's
how I will speak of him—is
younger far than I. His
name is strange and I can
hardly roll it off my tongue
but here, today, I'll try it
out. You'll need to know
his name. It is–hear this–
Mahershalalhashbaz!

I told you so. It is a name
not once forgotten but, not

spoken much. I will explain.
One day, Maher and I sat in
the shade and while we
played with marbles
(or such a game, I think.)

We both began to wonder if
we'd ever fully know just
what our names could really
mean. We're old enough
and smart enough (because
of listening to our Dad),
to know just why
our Dad and Mum had
named us each as they did.

I'd better tell you what
each means or you'll be
wondering at our puzzling
at names so strange for boys
like us, you see.

So, first of all, there's me.
I'm Shear-Jashub and my
name means *a remnant
shall return.* And then, there
is my brother,
Mahershalalhashbaz–wait–
*the plunder will be swift
and quick the spoil will go*
(or words to that effect).
You'll see the reason why,
I'm sure, just as we spoke
of it together on that day.

Oh, think of it. I'd be '*a piece of rag*' but, I'd come home. But Maher–little brother–he could not understand why he must carry that grim name right from his lowly birth.

It was explained to me that this strange name has held a message for the king and country, too. You see, Israel would be plundered and its riches taken–all is gone before Maher could speak a word and, surely, not his special name!

Then, as we thought about the news our names implied, we whispered what we'd heard one day when Dad was speaking to the king. It was so strange, that conversation overheard that day.

King Ahaz had refused to ask a sign from *YHVH–* LORD. Our dad, he used his loud, authoritative voice, then said: A youthful woman will give birth unto a Son. His Name will be *IMMANUEL*.

Maher and me–we two–did wonder if Immanuel would be a brother for us both. How could this be? You see, we heard the meaning of that Name, it was, you see, *IMMANUEL*: *God with us.*

We'd love to be the brothers of a little boy who's teach us more about the *YHVH–*LORD. And this is what we overheard: A child is born to us—to us? He will be given to us—to us?

He'll bear the government, He will be called 'The Counsellor most wonderful', and '*El Shaddai*', 'The Everlasting Abba', and 'The Shalom* Prince'. WOW!

There is no other name like that! Our Dad has said that this boy would, one day, be born into *this* family: Our very own, ISRAEL!

*Shalom: Hebrew, *peace*

THE CHILD OF
PROMISE
Chapters 9 – 10

The day will come when
the debased
will find their gloom has
passed:
The Galilee will then be
honoured by
the *YHVH*–LORD. The
promise? Vast!

Those souls who walked
in gloom
have seen God's *Light* that
shines
upon those living in the
shade of death; for them,
the *Light* returns.

There is a joy that will erupt
from happy hearts when
harvests soar;
the yoke, the rod, all shattered
and all sullied garments
burned for gore.

All this because a child is born
to us! (*Messiah*–Christ*;)
all government shall rest upon
His shoulders: all applaud!

His Name shall be so
wonderful, The Counsellor,
the El Gibbor*!

Eternal Father from of old–
His people love Him evermore!

The child (Messiah–Christ*)
will be 'The Prince of Peace'.
His Kingdom Peace is
everlasting,
it will know no end; it
reaches us!

The Prince of Peace shall rule
on David's throne with justice,
righteousness and grace. The
El Gibbor* brings it to pass.

* Messiah–Christ: *Anointed*
*El Gibbor: *God Almighty*

ISAIAH
Recalcitrance
Chapters 9 – 10

A messenger will come to
preach
a woe to Israel. All, listen to
his words:
Your arrogance and pride
will be embroiled in woe.

Your bricks have fallen to
the ground,
the fig trees have been felled;
You'll plant tall cedars in
their place?

But Resin's gruesome plans
are bold.

God's anger in the midst of this
is poised, His hand upraised;
He gave Israel its chance
but now,
there's nothing to be praised.

The ire of *YHVH*–LORD is not
assuaged.
The Syrians, the Philistines,
conspired to rid the land
of your impertinent front lines.

There's no repenting, no relent!
You'll find that, in a single day,
your 'head and tail' will be
destroyed
and this for every evil ploy.

The LORD will find no
pleasure in
such wickedness abroad.
He challenged you to change
your ways but sin is all you
brought.

The unjust judges will have
qualms–
their ways are evil to the core.
To whom then can you turn?
Where may
you keep your treasure store?

YHVH, EL SHADDAI
Chapter 10

A word now for Assyrians:
You came against Israel,
you plan destruction rampant
but your pride
will surely fall.

You are but tools within My
plans: I'll stand against your
power;
your plans are to destroy the
land and vanquish kingdoms
near and far.

By My strong arm
I will rebuke
Assyria! There will be no
relent. The axe is not more
strong than He who
wields it so.

So, have you seen
a walking stick
parading by itself? Beware,
the Fire of God, the Holy One–
Myself– will be consuming Fire!

Your glory will be gone.
The nation bred of thorns
and briars
will be consumed one night;
there is no place for liars.

Yet there is hope: the remnant
In the land–Israel–will turn
from Godless ways. They will
come home; they'll build again.

Don't be afraid of the
Assyrians. Remember Gideon
who stood his ground,
and Horeb's rock,
and Moses when his staff was
raised and Egypt drowned.

The LORD still speaks to
Israel! All bondage will be
gone; your massive yoke
will shatter from your backs.
Take heart for soon
I'll rescue and revoke.

The lofty 'tree'–Assyria–
will soon be hewn,
cut down and chopped
for 'firewood'! So behold: the
Lebanon will fall to
YHWH, as you hoped.

ISAIAH
The 'Branch'
Chapter 11

Up from the stump of David's
line—
behold, a new 'Shoot' does
appear.
Up from the roots a 'Branch'
will bear much fruit so dear.
Upon this 'Branch' the Spirit of
the LORD will rest; so wise,
He'll know
just how to wield His power.
All those
who fear the LORD will bow.

He'll judge in righteousness—
that which He sees and hears
will each pertain.
in righteousness. He'll wield
His power
and faithfulness will be
His mien.

The world will find abiding
peace
in dwelling with the gentle
Lamb.
Leopards feeding with a calf
and lion,
a little child will lead them
home.

A babe will play near snakes,
the lions replete with
humble straw
for none shall seek to harm
a soul
upon Mount Zion without
one flaw.

In that day all will bow to Him,
the 'Branch'. He'll be

a Banner for
all nations, peoples, when the
time
is right: He'll claim His Land
and Law.

Those scattered far will then
return
out from all nations of the
world;
with scorching wind He'll
triumph then;
He'll build a highway, none
appalled.

....

ISAIAH 12: THE CHOIR
A Song of Praise
Tune: *Silchester* – S.M.
Chapter 12

My song of praise ascends!
The LORD speaks peace to
me;
Yes, *YHVH* is my Comforter:
I'll trust and fearless be.

The LORD becomes my song,
He is my strength each day!
From deep Salvation Wells
I draw;
My thirst is quenched in joy.

Sing to the LORD, my soul,

Proclaim each glorious deed;
Let all the world resound
in praise:
None can the LORD exceed!

ISAIAH
The Fall of Babylon
Chapter 13

Raise your banner high,
declare
the LORD will lead His mighty
force;
all those, the faithful, who
rejoice
in fighting for His worthy cause

Hark, hear a clamouring host
draw near: a multitude is
mustering:
the LORD, Commander of this
troop,
His weapons cause a
blustering.

Weep for the awesome day
is near;
all hands will wilt and fearful
hearts
will melt as terror grips in fear:
the day of vengeance yet
awaits;

See to it now, the day the
LORD

decrees is hastening on apace;
the land will be made desolate
as horrors meet men's awful
gaze.

The sun shall then be dark, the
moon
refuse to glow. The world will
see
its punishment; the arrogant,
the proud, the haughty, felled
shall be.

Pure gold shall be more
prevalent,
Mankind quite rare within
the land;
the heavens and the Earth
shall quake
as slaughter does expand.

Proud Babylon shall fall before
the Persians; Medes will
overthrow—
like Sodom and Gomorrah,
there,
the jewel of all powers brought
low.

The mighty kingdom, Babylon,
will never rise again; no man
will ever pitch his tent within
nor shepherd feed his flocks
anon.

ISAIAH
The Nation Will Return
Chapter 14

How great is the compassion of
The *YHVH*–LORD for, once
again,
Israel will be His choice and He
will settle them within their land
again.
The aliens will then align
themselves with Israel's best:
the captives, captors, as
they rule
the nations that oppressed:

God's chosen will His Law
enforce.
Proud Babylon will bear the
brunt
of taunts of victors for
its power is at an end!
The weapons of the wicked
smashed,
all lands will know a peace
profound.
Oh, how the mighty falls
to dust:

You shone just like the Morning
Star
but now, cast down to rise no
more;
you'd thought to rise to Heaven
by war!

You made the world a desert
place
and brought all cities to the
dust;
you thought to rise above the
clouds
but you'll decay just as all rust.
Enthroned, you'd sit to
captivate
the nations at your feet?
Instead,
you'll fall and none
commiserate.

YHVH–LORD
Proclamations of Doom
Chapters 14 – 21

ASSYRIA
*As I have planned
so it will be;
My purposes are ever firm.
Assyrian yokes will be
withdrawn—
this burden is
removed in time.
I stretch My hand upon
the Earth,
upon the world; none turns
its back.
My word determines it;
the enemy will be cast down:
I give no slack.*

PHILISTIA
*Now, take no heart, do
not rejoice
that broken is the rod
that struck!
The snake is vanquished,
but the asp
most venomous is primed
to strike.
The poorest in the land will find
respite, and rest in safety there
but you will be with
famine bound,
survivors then devoid
of care.*

MOAB
*Ruined! Ruined all, within
a night;
the people search the heights
in vain.
All wear a sack-cloth, ashed;
prostrate, they bow in
sorrow's bane.
All fugitives do flee afar,
lamenting for what's lost—
in flood
of grief—all nature sheds
its wealth
as waters stain with
flowing blood.*

DAMASCUS
A heap of ruins you'll become:

deserted, left to
desert sands.
Your royal power
will dissipate.
a remnant though, like
Israel, returns.
And when the harvest shall
be past,
the ears of standing corn,
yet good,
will then be gleaned; some
will remain
for, in that day, they'll trust
in God.

ETHIOPIA
Swift be the messenger of woe
to mighty Cush, long
feared but far!
Regard My banner in t
he breeze
and hasten to the
trumpets' blare
for this is what the LORD
declares:
'Before your harvest
blossom's gone,
before the ripening fruit,
the knife
will slay your vine till
all is gone.

.EGYPT
Upon the clouds so swift,

the LORD
invades Egypt; there is a
trembling fear
that's stirred within as
kingdoms fight
against themselves–they
cannot bear
to see the Nile decline;
none heeds.
No anglers in the reeds
will find
a flapping fish to fry–all,
gone. Where are your wise
men, knowing, kind?

BABYLON
A whirlwind sweeping
through the land,
so shall invaders come as
terror strikes.
A ghastly vision then
unfolds:
the traitor does betray, the
looter takes.
Go! Set the watchman;
be alert:
the message comes by
chariot—
'The mighty Babylon has
fallen, gone!'
The LORD has told me so:
my God.

EDOM

*O watchman there, what is now
left? How long must we endure
in grief
this endless, hopeless,
faithless night?
The bright new morning
comes. Believe!
The sun will rise and soon,
but then
the deep night will return again.
There is a woe upon this
arid land;
where is the balm to heal
its pain?*

ARABIA

*You travellers that live in
caravans
in camp grounds with no rest
in arid scrubland of Arabia:
bring water to assuage
the thirst,
bring food to aid the refugees.
Where is the one who
truly cares?
All flee from war, the
battleground.
Survivors: few, the LORD
declares.*

AN EGYPTIAN
Chapter 19.

I've heard the prophecies
that are now spoken by
Isaiah, the prophet of
Judah who's spokesman
for their God: the *YHVH*,
El Shaddai. God of
power? Mighty God? He
would destroy our land!

But why this onslaught on
our soil, our soul? I know,
I know we've made it
tough right from the time
when Israelites were slaves
that laboured at our kilns,
our pits, our pyramids
and such. But that is
history long past. What
have we done, deserving
such a recompense?

The land of Judah brings
a terror unto us. Our
rivers will dry up, our
reeds and rushes wilt for
want of water here; our
anglers will go back into
their homes: No fish to
fry! Our weavers will lose
hope—no linen cloth to
make for patterns nice
and neat? Our counsellors
are stupid? Fools?
There's something to be
said for that, at least.

Where are our wise men
now? There are no
cornerstones–there is no
base on which to build our
lives: we are debased.

But what is this? A word
of hope? Egyptians will
yet vow allegiance to their
LORD? The *YHVH, El
Shaddai*? When we cry out
to Him for help, we'll find
 a saviour, a defender, and
all Egypt will be rescued
yet? Oh yes! let's turn
unto the LORD: we will be
healed of all the many
things we've done and
failed to do for Israel.
And, In that day so far
away, we will be blessed.
I'll take that word by
faith and, hope!
Though, think a while
on this: when could
all Egypt come,
and bow before
the *YHVH*–LORD?

ISAIAH
A Prophecy for Jerusalem
Chapter 22

It's time to shed the burlap now

and sandals too; naked,
I'll wail for you:

Jerusalem, Jerusalem,
the city of the *YHVH*–LORD:
your frequent fear replaces
faith;
The tumult reaches fever pitch;
you're fleeing from the coming
wrath.

Jerusalem, Jerusalem,
I speak for *YHVH*–LORD
to you:
Do not begin now to console;
my people are destroyed;
so, turn
from me, my tears are real!

Jerusalem, Jerusalem,
there is a day marked out
for you—
a day of battering where
ramparts fall;
your defences are all stripped
away.
Where is the water, where
the wall?

Jerusalem, Jerusalem,
you failed the test to trust
in God—
there's no regard within your
heart:

you've chosen to rejoice:
'Let's eat,
and drink, be merry; death
can wait!'

Jerusalem, Jerusalem,
'Tomorrow we will die,'
you say.
There's no atonement for
such sin:
beware the coming Day of
Wrath–
this day for you will soon begin.

ISAIAH
A Word for Tyre
Chapter 23

The mighty ships of Tarshish
flail,
all Tyre has been destroyed.
Be silent now, O Sidon and
Cyprus,
you've been enriched;
deployed
all wealth from that great place.

But you should be ashamed
of this,
your merchant men were
'royalty'.
Your pride has brought you low
for you have shown no loyalty!

Your harbour is destroyed;
no more
the revelry. Take note of
Babylon:
its greatness is destroyed; a
ruin
has displaced its power: it's
flown!

Yet, after ten times seven
years,
the Tyre of old will ply its trade
across the world. But every
profit
will become a 'tithe' for God–
all paid!

ISAIAH
The Devastation
Chapter 24

The Earth will be laid waste in
time—
all citizens will fear this day:
the LORD decrees, because of
sin,
it all will languish, pine away.

Defiled, the Earth is harmed by
those
who bear the guilt of pride!
Their sin
has shaped their fall

from grace;
see now that dance with
tambourine.

The wine that flowed at will,
imbibed
by drunken men is, sudden,
stilled.
The city is in ruin now, its gates
are broken and its walls now
piled.

So will it be for all mankind:
though gleanings will be left
on vine,
inhabitants cry out for wine;
in gloom
they recognise that joy
becomes repine.

The harvest's past, the
summer gone
and singing in the streets
will not
assuage the grief of God.
beware,
The LORD will cleanse
this blot!

A flood will be unleashed in
that day,
the LORD will bring His
punishment.
Grim dungeons will reclaim

their own;
the sun and moon bow down.
Repent!

How glorious, the grace
of God!
Behold: the LORD will come
again;
He'll stand within Jerusalem,
The LORD Almighty then
will reign!

THE CHOIR
A Song of Praise
Chapter 25
Tune: "*Southport*" – S.M.

We will exalt You, LORD!
We praise Your holy Name;
In perfect faithfulness You act–
To cleanse from sin You came.

You are our Refuge, LORD!
The needy are made strong;
You are our shelter from
life's storm
Though fierce the gale
and long.

You are our Sovereign LORD!
You wipe away our tears;
The wrong made right,
the stain
made clean, You take away
our fears.

Most surely, You are LORD!
We trust You and rejoice;
This is the LORD whom we
adore,
The Source of all our joys.

THE CHOIR
Perfect Peace
Isaiah 26
Tune: "*Amazing Grace*"–C.M.

O LORD, we seek Your perfect
peace:
Come, calm our souls, we
pray;
We open now our hearts in
trust;
LORD, enter in today.

O LORD, mark out the path
to tread
For we would walk in trust;
Your guidance is our soul's
desire:
The LORD of Life be praised.

O LORD, as night descends
keep guard.
When morning comes, Your
grace;
Your peace profound
surrounds the soul:
Established are our days.

Our bodies rise once more;

We'll wake and shout for joy;
the soul,
Like dew of morn, shall soar.

ISAIAH
Deliverance
Chapter 27

Let Israel sing—her 'vineyard'
here
is guarded by the *YHVH*–
LORD;
He watches over Israel by day
and night so Israel is restored
here!

No enemy shall venture forth
to harm the ground of *YHVH*
there;
if they would come for refuge
now,
let them make peace at last,
here!

In days to come, Israel takes
root;
then blossoms will appear on
stems
that bud well into springtime
rare:
the world will fill with fruit from
here!

Your guilt will be atoned, Israel;
removal of your sin will be

like harvest of ripe fruit that's
gained
when you will turn from idols
here!

The day will come when Israel,
out from Euphrates and the
Nile,
are gathered one by one and,
then,
the trumpets sound for worship
here!

ISAIAH
Banes and Blessings
for Israel
Chapters 28 – 31

Ephraim is a fading flower—
his beauty is now gone
because of wine!
Like driving rain, hailstones
and wind,
your end will come and pride
will wane.

In that sad day, the YHVH,
El Shaddai
will be a glorious crown, the
'wreath'
that represents the remnant of
the People of the LORD,
bequeathed.

It comes to this—a foreign land

will order you: do this, do that,
obey our rules! You'll listen
then!
You'd take death's covenant?

Now, this is what God says
to you:
*'Behold! I lay a Cornerstone
in Zion! A tested Stone,
a 'Gem'.
He is the Sure foundation.
Done!
Your covenant with death
will be
annulled, agreements will
not stand.
Now, understand: there's terror
here;
to make the bread grain must
be ground'*

Jerusalem
Chapter 29

Jerusalem, Oh, Ariel:
The City of King David, hear:
the 'Lion of God' becomes 'the
hearth'!
The 'Lion' will find his 'nectar'
here.
Besieged, the city will lament
as on the Temple altar's
hearth.

And you will cry to *YHVH* from
the dust.
But then, the LORD will come,
the Wind of God will blow a
'dearth'
upon all enemies–they'll not
appear!
Just like a visioned dream,
a vision of
the night, the hordes are done
to death.

You will not read the signs,
will plead
to know the truth. You are
so blind!
You praise the LORD with
tongue
but all your hearts are far
from kind;
you worship nought but in
your ritual.
I will astound you once again.

Take note of this: your wisdom
will
not stand before the LORD;
despise
Him if you will but know
this well
for, is the Potter less than clays
he melds and will the clays
despise
the One who moulds?

Observe the LORD, discern
His own creative ways.

When Israel sees the works
He wrought
and will respect the Holy One,
in awe, then they shall gain
wisdom–
as they accept instruction,
it is won.

The Obstinate Children
Chapter 30

How obstinate! Like children
who—
Recalcitrant—defy their
parents and
escape from home. That's
Israel,
all traipsing off to Egypt's land.

There's no consulting *YHVH*–
LORD;
you think that Pharaoh will
protect
the disobedient? What shame
for Israel: the LORD they would
reject?

Go! Write upon a scroll for
them
the history of all Israel's
shame:

rebellions to the last deceit
will rule their every deed.

Who came to counsel them?
They would not hear
instructions from the LORD.
What blame
must be accrued to them.
They would
the pleasant things revere,
cast out
the words of discipline that
would
inform the mind and make
devout.
"Oh, leave us to ourselves,"
they say,
"and stop confronting us with
doubt!"

So! Listen to the word of God!
Because deceit seems right
for you,
because oppression is your
guide,
because you have rejected
truth,
this word of wisdom I'll confide.

Your sin becomes a crumbling
wall
collapsing suddenly as pottery:
there's nothing left of worth
retained

so listen to what *YHVH*–LORD
will say:
Repentance, and the rest of
soul
is your salvation evermore;
your strength is in serenity
and faithful trust, your power.

You still reject the *YHVH*–
LORD?
Yet He desires to share His
grace
with you for He's patient; He
will bless with justice and with
peace.

So! Weep no more, receive
His grace,
He hears your plaintive cry
today;
you've known adversity, take
hope–
you'll hear His voice: "*Walk in
My Way!*"

Then you will sing the songs
of Zion
akin to holy festivals
and you will come rejoicing to
the Mount, the Rock of Israel.

Israel's Salvation
Chapter 31

Do not rely upon the horse–
a thousand chariots would fail
before the power of *YHVH*–
LORD.
Spend not your hope in Egypt's
'all'.
King's horses, all king's men,
you see,
will falter for they are but
men—
how weak they are for flesh
will not
the conqueror be o'er Heaven!

The Lion of Judah, then, will
break
the chains of sins which do
appal.
The lion roars and foes do
quail,
the *YHVH*–LORD shall
conquer all;
the LORD will shield Jerusalem
just as an eagle hovering there
with wings outstretched will
cover them:
He shelters the oppressed with
care.

Comparisons
Chapter 32

Oh, see! Behold the King, the
LORD

who rules in righteousness:
His own,
who follow Him, take justice as
their guide.
They are a shelter from
the wind,
a refuge from the storm.
Such men are like a flowing
stream
in desert lands; a mighty rock
within a sun-baked land
so mean.

Then those who see, no longer
blind,
with ears unstopped, will hear
His word,
irrational minds will
understand,
stammering tongues be fluent,
heard!
But fools are seen for what
they are—
their wisdom is a folly and
they speak just as a wayward
soul:
the good is ill, the evil grand!

A fool acts on ungodliness,
he will not care for those in
need,
the hungry starve, the thirsty
wilt.

an evil man plants wicked
seed,
he loves to see the poor
destroyed,
he turns his eyes and ears
from need.

But, hear this now: A noble
man
will stand as just by every
deed.
The women, too, must be
appraised:
complacency does not achieve,
your bland security won't hold;
there's nought that can suffice,
relieve!
The harvest will in summer fail.
So! Don yourselves with
sackcloth for
your fortress will be gone;
bereft,
you'll cry for peace—there is
no law.

I bear a word of hope for you:
across the wasteland of the
years
where donkeys dwell in
pleasantness,
God's Spirit then will come.
Your tears
will cease for justice reigns
and righteousness shall
overflow

resulting in a calm serenity—
God's shalom peace will
settle you.

YHVH–LORD
A Word To The Wise
Chapter 33

Sorrow will come to you!
Assyria: you'll be destroyed.
Betray? You'll be betrayed-
as locusts strip the vines
Assyria will be no more.
Jerusalem you will adore!
It is the home of YHVH–
LORD.
There, righteousness and
peace
true justice will release.
I'll be your sure Foundation
and I'll grant salvation,
wisdom, by My open door.
Do come!

But view the land—where do
you see My calm abode?
Now, no one travels on
your road,
Assyria cares nothing for
their promises—those
plunderers. You'll see they
are but murderers.

Hear what I say, observe
My might:
who can survive consuming
fires?
All those who walk in
righteousness,
all honest souls, those fair
in trade
who turn from schemes
some crave.
I'll be your Fortress, strong
to save,

I'll ever keep you in My sight.
Your eyes will see the King
in all His beauty and also,
your land.
The day will come, so grand,
when you will see Jerusalem
at peace.
I am the LORD, the
El Shaddai:
I will protect where aliens lie.
You'll find a river deep
and wide;
no enemy will ride this breeze,
no ships invade your seas.
I am the LORD! I offer you
protection from all harm;
from all your sins there'll
be a balm.

So! feast your eyes upon
Jerusalem! This is
the city of great festivals.

Your eyes will see
your city fair.
This shall be 'The Home
of Peace'–
it is '*Jeru–shalom*'!
This city shall be a 'tent'
that's never moved. No one
shall pull its stakes. It will
remain.
The LORD shall be
our *El Shaddai.*
The LORD is Judge, the One
who is 'SHALOM'!

ISAIAH
A Judgement Made
Chapter 34

Come near, all peoples,
listen now!
The wrath of God will
surely flow:
destruction follows on
from hate,
upheaval claims the
godless foe.
The stars of heaven are
caught within
the closing 'scroll' that is
the sky.
The LORD will be avenged,
His wrath
against all evil not appeased:
all die

who thumb their nose at
YHVH–LORD.

Old Edom shall be lost, its
streams
will flow with pitch, its smoke
not quelled
as brambled scrub replaces
towns.
This land shall be the haunt of
owls,
The LORD shall take the toll
and quotes
all are accounted for, His Spirit
then
will gather all who have
possessed
this land for they will dwell
therein—
each generation settled,
blessed.

THE CHOIR
Song of The Redeemed
Chapter 35
Tune: "*Spohr*" 8.6.8.6.8.6.

The desert shall rejoice again,
The parched land praise once
more;
The desert rose will burst to
flower,
God's glory will be seen.
Throughout the Earth, all see,
applaud,

The splendour of the LORD.

Be strong, fear not, our Mighty
God
Will come to us in power;
The LORD will come to save
you now:
He casts out fear, grants
peace.
The LORD will come to bring
accord,
You'll be redeemed, restored.

Then will the blind be healed,
they'll see!
The deaf will hear, will pray;
The lamb shall leap like deer
at play.
The dumb will sing this song:
As streams flow through
a desert place,
The thirsty lands rejoice.

A highway shall be there,
a way;
Its name is 'Holiness'.
This highway is reserved
for those
Who walk the way of peace.
The unclean will not journey
there,
Redeemed souls walk
on there.

The ransomed of the LORD
return
To Zion with 'shalom' peace;
Their lips shall testify to grace,
Their heads with joy are
crowned;
Resounding joy their song
each day
As sorrow flees away.

SENNACHERIB
Chapters 36 – 37

Our time has come!
All troops in place, about
to start the onslaught of
this mighty fort.

The march was long,
my troops are tired
(and some have died
along the route.) There's
been great towns—all
fortified—and dangerous
for us but we've prevailed.
We've won! Now, soon,
the goal will be achieved:
Jerusalem will be our
best!

We sent the news to
Judah's king: Why are
you now so confident?
You have your plans
Strategically in place?

You think that Egypt will
give aid to you? What's
that you say? You trust
in God? Your *YHVH*–
LORD, no less?
How ludicrous!
Come now, be wise!
I'll make with you
a bargain grand. Here,
take this gift: one
thousand strong
the horses you may have
if you can put a man
upon a horse!

I'll tell you now:
Your *YHVH*–LORD
told us to come and take
this land! (That surely
will put fear into his
trembling heart!)
Then, after all the
verbiage thrown about,
cast about, new plans:
We shouted out to all
Upon the city walls:
Do not believe the words
your king would have
you think on it!

Now, hear this news:
Don't listen to Your king!
Believe us now; make
peace with us! We'll treat
you well. It is God's will.

**Our spies sent word
to us, The king has
gone to pray–he's
gone to 'Church'!
He's spoken ill of me
Before his God!? I will
not have it so! The battle
lines are drawn. We go!
Jerusalem will fall to us...**

**What's this I hear?
Our troops are ill? They're
falling to the ground?
They're dead? Break camp!
Return to Nineveh. This is
the end of it: we've failed!**

HEZEKIAH
The King's Dilemma
Chapters 36 – 39

Sennacherib came rattling
spears, attacking all our
towns; what grief!
His army then confronted
me just near the aqueduct.
This was a crucial place—
we needed water in the
Citadel! A confrontation
loomed on us.

On whom do you place
faith? he goaded me, You
trust in *YHVH*–LORD?

Now let me say that, if you
will
just trust in me, I'll see you
through, I'll give you horses
if you'd find a man
or two to handle them!

I'll have you know, he
prattled on: You think
the LORD is on your side.
Now think again! He's
called for us to come
to you, destroy your land!
So! Now you will be held,
besieged. Don't hide this
news, tell it abroad!

But when the envoys of
Sennacherib blared forth
this news, the people then
fell silent in accord with
what I had commanded
them: Don't give an answer
to these empty threats!
My men returned,
reporting many woes.

I knew it was due time
to ask the LORD what we
should do. How could we
conquer King Sennacherib?
Perhaps Isaiah could give
some words of guidance
now. Please, tell me what

to do! Isaiah's answer came:
he spoke the
Guidance of the LORD:

He spoke the guidance of
the LORD: Take heed of
what I say: God will now
move against Sennacherib
who will be called home to
Assyria–and he will be
assassinated there! He'd said,
Don't trust the LORD.

Upon this news I went up to
the Temple to commune
with God: O *YHVH*–LORD,
You rule the kingdoms of
the Earth: bend down to us,
allow Your eyes to see our
plight, please hear:
Assyria now threatens us.

O *YHVH*–LORD, please
rescue us, we know Assyria
wields awful power. They
purpose to destroy all gods
of wood and stone carved
by the hands of artisans
across the world. But You
are God. Alone, You stand.

Isaiah then communed with
me: Hark now to what the
YHVH–LORD reveals to

you. Because you prayed,
the LORD will let him
know, that king:
You are despised!
All Zion will laugh
at you for all your
men will flee away!

Whom do you think you
ridicule? To whom, you
shout abuse today? You
flaunt your power, believe
that none can conquer you.
Have you not heard how
long ago God planned
to lead you, by the nose,
back to Assyria?

Isaiah spoke again to me:
Here is the proof of what
I say, At first, a meagre
crop, but it will grow–as
seasons come and go.
A remnant will remain, send
down their roots, grow up
and flourish then.

For, this is what the LORD
decrees: The armies of
Assyria will not gain entry
to Jerusalem; no arrow will
take flight and hit its mark.
It's for His honour and
for King David's sake,

He will protect Israel.

About this time, I did
become
most gravely ill. Isaiah
came to me;
he counselled me. The
LORD declares:
Set all affairs in order now
for you will soon succumb–
you will
not gain your health: you'll
die!

I turned my face unto the
wall
and prayed this prayer:
Remember, LORD, I have
been faithful through
the years; I've served You
well, I tried
to please You single-
mindedly.
With that, I wept most
bitterly.

I am informed: another
word
came, via Isaiah, from the
LORD:

*Go back and tell the king
just what
I say: 'I've heard your
prayer,*

*I've seen Your tears. I'll
rescue you;
I will defend Jerusalem
right now.*

HEZEKIAH
A Hymn of Praise
Tune: "*Rimington*" – L.M.
Chapter 38:9-22

I'll trust the LORD from this day
on!
I'll walk the path He bids me
tread.
The challenges, the trials, I've
faced
Have taught me how to trust
His lead.

I'd thought my life was at an
end,
Just like a shepherd's tent in
wind
Or, cloth that's taken from the
loom,
But God is gracious, ever kind.

I'll live to serve You faithfully
For You have saved my soul,
O LORD;
I'll praise Your holy Name
always
Within the Temple of my God.

....

HEZEKIAH
The Great Regret
Chapter 39

Why did I take my guests
to see the treasures of my
palace here? Why did I open
up the vaults,
reveal the riches stored
away from prying eyes and
alien spies? One day the
consequence will come.

Isaiah came to me;
he asked of me, What did
those men require? And
where did they come from?
They came from Babylon;
they wished
to see my palace and, I
showed them everything.
They were amazed!

Oh, Hezekiah, Sire, he said;
Now listen to this word
from God:

*The time will come when
everything
within your palace walls
will be
removed and taken far
away:
They'll serve the king
of Babylon!*

THE CHOIR
The Comforter
Tune: "*Europe*"
8.7.8.7.8.7.8.7.
Chapter 40:1-11

Comfort, comfort, all God's
people,
Peace now flows, the past
forgiven,
Sorrow is replaced with
gladness!
Listen to the Voice from
Heaven:
'Clear the wasteland, drain the
marshes,
Raise the valleys, level
mounts;
Build a highway in the desert
For God's glory now resounds.'

Shout the Good News loudly,
clearly:
'Nature's beauty will not last:
As grass withers, so the
people—
Flowers will fade as seasons
pass.
But the word of God remains
true,
It will stand eternally.'
Tell the nations, 'God is
coming,
He will rule victoriously.'

As a shepherd feeds his flock,
so
God will tend His fragile lambs;
He will carry all the needy,
He our Guard and Guide
becomes
If we trust Him to receive us
As His flock for pasturing.
He will lead us gently onward,
Ever caring, nurturing.

YHWH–LORD
Chapter 40:12-31

To whom may I now be
compared?
For, have you seen a soul
who'd hold
the oceans in his hand and has
he measured all the
heavens, bold
to make his mighty
mark, proclaim
that he advises YHVH–LORD?
Now, harken to Me,
be instructed:
all the world cannot compare
or laud!

Have you not heard? Now,
understand
Eternity has known Him move
before the worlds were born.
Do not

be ignorant—God is ruler
through
creation. YHVH's Breath
will give
or take all life. To whom will
you compare the LORD? And
can you find
His equal anywhere?
Say, who?

So, search the Scriptures;
see the stars:
Who has created, known
their names?
How can you say, O Israel,
that God
ignores your rights, rejects
complaints?
No one can gauge God's
depth of care:
He will empower the weak,
He will
give strength to those who call
upon His Name. He
never faints.

Have you not heard? Have you
not seen?
The LORD will not grow
weary, tire
as youths are prone to do.
Trust God.
Like eagles flying high,
you'll soar!

The strongest may,
exhausted, fall,
But those that trust the LORD
each day
will run the course, will keep
right on.
So, walk God's way,
all sin abhor.

YHVH–LORD
Good News Is
On The Way
Chapter 41

Hush now, Hearken to
your God!
Keep silence in My
Presence now;
your case has come to court.
All lands,
who has stirred up the
Potentate?
Who activates His services,
permits His victories?
Who called
His people from the first
of days?
I am the One: await your fate.

The nations quake in fear;
they call
their artisans to craft a
graven god.
They steady it, adorn with paint

the thing and grant it powers
like sand!
But, as for you, O Israel,
I've chosen you; I'll not discard
My own beloved ones: I'll hold
you safe with My right hand.

Let no discouragement intrude
for I am with you, I will guide;
I'll bear you up, sustain
you with
My own victorious power!
Your enemies will go
to ground,
they have no strength to call
their own.
But I will hold you by your hand
and I'll be with you every hour.

I'm your Redeemer, Israel!
You'll be the 'threshing tool'
of God–
as grass is tossed within
the wind!
And you'll rejoice in
YHVH–LORD
for, when the needy search
the land
for water but in vain, I'll not
abandon you. Deep rivers then
will flow through desert lands:
this is My word!

This is the reason why I bring
new life to you. This miracle

is for your benefit, that you
will know the "I AM",
YHVH–LORD!
Present the hand-hewn rocks,
idols that you do worship now.
Yes! let them show what they
can do—
they'll tell you what the
future holds?

I have a Leader who will come
to gain the victory over all—
He'll trample enemies
like shards
are shattered under
careless foot.
But who predicted this,
you ask?
Will you admit God's word i
s true?
I'll send Jerusalem some news,
Yes! Good News! Idols are
all mute!

THE CHOSEN
SERVANT
Chapter 42:1-9
(1st of 4 Servant Songs)

Observe My Servant, if
you will;
He is My chosen One: I've put
My Spirit upon Him. He will
My justice bring to all the world.
He's gentle, never shouts,

is calm;
He'll never crush a
wounded soul.
No flickering candle will
He snuff
and distant lands He
will remould.

It is the YHVH–LORD who has
created all the heavens–t
hat vast
expanse. He grants the
Breath of life
to everyone who walks t
he Earth.
It is the LORD who says
to you:
"I AM", the One who calls
you to
reveal My righteousness
will take
your hand to guard and guide
forthwith.

I'll give You to my people,
Israel,
You are the symbol of
My love,
My lasting Covenant
with them
and You will be the
Guiding Light.
Through You the blind are
made to see,

the captives will be freed.
"I AM",
the LORD, this is My name,
and I
reveal the future by My might.

THE CHOIR
The New Song
Chapter 42:10-17
Tune: *Beethoven*   L.M.

O sing a new song to
the LORD,
Let praise ascend, make
known His name;
Sing to the LORD with joy
this day,
Tell the whole world: His news
proclaim.

Let all the Earth sing forth
His worth,
Join in the chorus, glorify
And sing His praises, He
is LORD;
Let Earth acclaim His power
on high.

He leads His people into Light,
The darkest valley will
be bright;
The LORD will straighten out
our path,
He'll lead us onward by
His might.

ISAIAH
Consequences
Chapter 42:18-25

Why don't you listen? Are
you deaf?
Watch out! Take care! Or are
you blind?
There's none so deaf as those
who block
their ears, nor blind if eyes
are closed!

The LORD exalts His glorious
Law;
His people are 'fair game'
to all!
But who will hear the lessons
past?
Who'll be alert to history's
prose?

The past, you see, foretells
the days
that are as yet to come.
Observe:
Look! See the massive
consequence
of disobedience. What woes!

YHWH-LORD
Recognise Your Saviour
Chapter 43:1-13

Good News is now declared

to you!
O Israel, hush the bluster,
hear:
"I AM"*. YHVH, I created you–
This is no time for fear for I,
the LORD
have ransomed you. I call
to you
by name for you belong to Me.
When grief assails in flood
or fire,
you'll not succumb. "I AM",
your God!

Yes! "I AM", YHVH–LORD,
Saviour!
You're precious in My sight;
Do not
be so afraid for "I AM" with you!
I'll gather you from lands afar:
I will demand the north,
the south,
to bring you home for "I AM",
He
who did create you, I preserved
and nurtured you,
a people rare.

There's those with eyes but do
not see
and some with ears who do
not hear;
so, ask the nations if their gods
could tell you what the
future holds.

But, you perceive My will
and ways,
You are My chosen,
precious ones
and you are witness to
this truth:
"I AM", the LORD, My power
enfolds.

* God's transcendence of any
limitation.   See Exodus 3:14.
God is inscrutable.

YHVH–LORD
I Promise You
Chapter 43:14-20

This message is for you,
My friends:
I am Redeemer, Holy One
of Israel;
I ask you to remember all
the ways that I have
nurtured you.
I made a path through
seas for you.
You found dry ground where
waves were bound,
but Egypt's army was
immersed:
they died at last, as
candles do.

But see, I am about to do
a new thing that has
now begun.

*Have you observed, have you
not seen?
There is a pathway set for you
across the wilderness where
streams
will then begin to flow; all will
rejoice as rivers run throughout
the desert lands–life
given anew.*

*Let it now be known: "I AM",
the One
who did create Israel f
or Myself.
one day, My chosen people will
begin to honour Me again
before the whole wide world
with joy!
But you have failed your
promises:
you've burdened me with
many sins–
I am prepared to cleanse
your stain!*

The "*I AM*" Signature
Chapters 44 – 49

*O My beloved Israel,
hear now the promises
I make
to you: you'll see great
rivers flow,
the arid ground will
celebrate.*

*"I AM", the LORD: the First
and Last.
The day will surely come
when "Ruach" (My Holy
Spirit), will refresh
your lives; you'll be renewed
like grass
in dew: Your children I
will bless.*

*"I AM", the LORD: this is
My Name.
The graven images
so prized
have no intrinsic worth:
the hand-hewn rock of
idols has
no power to claim as god
the Earth.*

*"I AM", the LORD: alone
I stand.
Now, pay attention, Israel,
I am Creator: you're in view;
I'll not forget you, know that I
have paid the price to
ransom you.*

*"I AM", the LORD; return
to Me.
No obstacle will block
My path*

and, when I come, I'll bring
to you
the treasures hidden in
the dark.
then you'll hear Me call to you.

"I AM", the LORD: I know
your name.
Who stood by Me if carved
in stone
to emulate the YHVH–LORD?
What have those idols done
to prove
they've strategies you could
applaud?

"I AM", the LORD: there is no
other god!
O, let the earth now open wide
that I may pour My
righteousness;
from heaven above,
salvation will
then coincide with holiness.

"I AM", the LORD, I will
transform.
Through everlasting ages I,
the YHVH Elohim, the LORD,
will shelter you: you will
be saved.
throughout Eternity: redeemed!

" I AM", the LORD, eternally.
Why argue with Creator,

LORD?
For can a clay pot argue with
the potter who has shaped
it so?
And would that pot proclaim
your worth?
"I AM", the LORD, I formed
you so.
My promises are bold, Israel,
I do not whisper in the night;
when you seek Me, I'll
be found.
My words are true, the future's
bright.

"I AM", the LORD, I'll nurture
you.
My promises stand by
My Name,
My word is sacrosanct: Believe
that I will not discard My word
(It is by faith you'll live!)

"I AM", the LORD: I cherish
you.
To whom will you compare
your LORD?
and who is equal? You've
moulded it
with gold and silver, formed
it whole
to worship it: misguided yet!

"I AM", the LORD: I rescue
you!

Now listen, children of Israel,
I've cared for you, I've nurtured
you;
I'll be your God throughout
your life–
to old age I will carry you.

"I AM", the LORD, I created
you.
So, listen to My promises
for I am ready to make right
and not in future years but now
I'll show My glory, grant
you Light!

"I AM", the LORD; I make
it known
But Zion, your promises
are filled with air, you call
yourself
God's city, yet you fail to keep
your word–it has no worth.

"I AM", the LORD: My words
stand firm!
Let it be known: Chaldea
(that is
grand Babylon), will end
in dread:
you'll grind your flour with
millstones yet.
Vengeance is Mine. So, be
prepared!

"I AM", the LORD: the LORD
of Hosts.
O Israel, it's for My sake
that I will hold My ire. I will
refine you in My furnaces—
through suffering, both pure
and well.

"I AM", the LORD, My
glory glows.
Have your idols told
you so—
those 'gods' of brass:
mute stone?
It's I who saves you from
Chaldea;
I have explained, this shall
be done!

"I AM", the LORD, your
teacher yet.
O listen now to My
commands
then peace will flow to you
as streams
of water, waves of
placid seas
will flow in peace beyond
your dreams.

"I AM", the LORD, the
Source of peace.

My Servant shall restore Israel,
what's more, He'll be a Light
for all
the world. The Gentiles will
rejoice:
salvation will extend to all!

"I AM", the LORD, I've chosen
you!
There is One, although
despised,
rejected by the nations and
a Servant unto all. And, when
He comes
all kings will bow to Him.
He'll stand!
"I AM", the LORD, your
faithful God!
Through My Servant I will give
protection via My Covenant:
the prisoners will be freed,
they'll come
into the Light—there'll be
no want.

"I AM", the LORD who
shepherds you!
Then I will lead by waters cool,
in mercy I will save Israel.
The mountains levelled,
valleys raised
My people will return in peace
to dwell.

"I AM", the LORD who guides

you home!
What's that you say,
Jerusalem?
the YHVH–LORD is fast
asleep?
He has deserted you, He has
forgotten you? Do think! I keep!

"I AM", the LORD; I stand
by you!
You think that I'd forget
you now?
Observe a mother's love—
her babe
is safe within her care and so
are you: I'll not forget, I'll save!

"I AM", the LORD who loves
you so!
O Israel, you are My signal to
the alien nations and
their kings;
they'll care for all your needs
and bow;
then you will know, through Me
you win!

"I AM", the LORD, Eternal
King!
Say, who can snatch the
plunder from
the hands of vicious warriors?
Who could demand a despot
free

his captives? It's the LORD
who cares!
"I AM", the LORD: the
El Shaddai of Israel.

YHVH and ISAIAH
Warnings, Woes, and
Wonders
Chapters 50 – 52

Why were you sold
as slaves?
Why was there none
responding to
My call? So, was My arm
too short?
I have no means to rescue
you?
I rule creation yet you doubt
that you I love, I've ever
sought?

YHVH plants His thoughts
that I may comfort you.
Each morning He
awakens me
and opens up my mind.
Yes, I have listened, heard;
I offered up myself
to mockery that I
may all His will now find.
Wake up! Keep watch!
Don't hide!

Justice He grants to me
so, will the Judge deride?
Who will declare my guilt?
The LORD is on my side!
Have you no fear of God?
Would you obey His word?
Walk out of darkness, look
into His Light: abide!
Wake up! Keep watch!
On guard!

Look to the mighty rock
from which you're formed.
Yes! think
of Abraham—God called,
He blessed! Abram became
the father of your Clans.
And He will come to you
again: the desert will
become your garden home.
Wake up! Keep watch!
Decide!

With mercy, justice, and
by right I'll reign; the world
will come to see how I
will bring new hope to all.
And distant lands will come
to know that I am just:
Salvation? Gift of grace
to those who heed My call.
Wake up! Keep watch!
I'll guide!

The ransomed of the LORD
will march with joy to Zion;
your sorrow will depart
for I will come to you.
I am the LORD, your God;
My words are in
your mouth,
I hold you in My hand;
you are Mine, I love you!
Wake up! Keep watch!
Confide!

You've known great
terror and
calamity. Who can
you find to sympathise?
But listen now to Me:
I've taken back the cup
of woe you drank; instead,
your enemies will know
My wrath and they will flee.
Wake up! Keep watch! Tears
dried!

Rise from the dust, O Zion,
remove those chains—
no more
will you be slaves of kings
for your redemption comes!
How beautiful the steps
of those who bring
Good News:
peace and salvation won,
the gift of grace becomes.
Wake up! Keep watch

on every tide!

Now let the choir rejoice
in songs of victory:
your slavery is past
when all return to Zion.
My Servant suffered for
your sake: His wounds
were deep
but aliens will see
and know that all are Mine!
Wake up! Keep watch!
Reside!

THE CHOIR
The Servant Song
Isaiah 53
Tune: *Southport* S.M.

He took those wounds for us,
Transgressions that were ours;
He was despised, rejected, and
With grief He bore our tears.

Who can believe this news?
The Servant of the LORD
Was unadorned with beauty
and
The roughest path He trod.

He carried all our sins,
Our sorrows laid on Him
And he was pierced for what

we did!
But we are healed through
Him!

Just like a sheep that strays,
We chose to walk a path
So far removed from Him,
yet God
Has laid on Him His wrath.

The suffering Servant, He
Was led just as a lamb
To slaughter where He,
silent, died
To take from us the blame.

This was the plan of God
To grant redemption, peace
Profound; because He bore
our sins,
He bought our soul's release.

ISAIAH and *YHVH*
Future Joy
Chapter 54

Jerusalem, O Zion—
the city of God's peace:
too long you've been bereft
of all the promises.
It's time for joyous song;
you've been a 'childless bride'
but soon your cradled sons
will then your praise prolong.
The LORD now calls

you home.
Fear not, your shame is past:
He is redeemer, LORD:

With everlasting love
I call for you: 'Come home;'
Though mountains sink to sand
My faithful love remains;
you will My mercy prove.
Bright jewels shall adorn
your firm foundations and
your walls and gates with gems
will show the worth of 'Home'.
Then you will live in peace,
no terror will come near,
no voices will be raised:
the voice of God calls 'Home'!

YHWH and ISAIAH
The Invitation
Chapter 55

You're thirsty? Come
and drink;
you're poor? This draught
is free!
Come with your ears attuned:
listen, for this feast is yours.
The covenant I made
with David is the one
I offer you in loving kindness
now:
you'll lead away from wars.

O, seek the LORD while He
is near, call to Him now!

Turn from all wrong, you'll find
in mercy He'll forgive you now.

*My thoughts are not your
thoughts,
My ways contrast your own;
Just as the heavens are high
My thoughts are high, alone!*

*All nature is a parable
to teach you how My word
will reproduce good fruit:
this will My nature prove.
I plan it so to do—
then, you will live in joy
and peace. All nature sings:
an everlasting sign of love.*

YHVH–LORD
Universal Blessings
Chapters 56 – 59

*Look to the way you live:
Be just and fair to all
For I am coming soon–
I'll come to rescue you.
How blessed are all who will
now honour Sabbath days
of rest and stay away
from sin. Be true!*

*Do not allow an alien
who trusts the LORD to feel
unloved, alone, bereft
of care. For I will bless*

*all those whose trust is in
My holy Name.
And I will give to them the right
to know eternal rest.*

*The name I'll give to them
will stand eternally
for they'll be known as Mine
by holding fast the Covenant.
They'll find true joy within
Jerusalem city's 'heart'—
My House of prayer. It will
become all nations' fount.*

*But know this too: all those
who lead My people must
adhere to covenants
for, if the shepherd is
so blind he cannot see,
he will then lead My sheep
astray in ignorance,
blaspheming all their days.*

*In the west, there'll be respect,
the east will worship Him,
the LORD. He will redeem
all those who turn from sin.
This is My covenant:
My Spirit will abide,
My words will be retained;
all generations: Mine!*

Future Glory
Chapter 60

O, see the new sunrise:
Jerusalem shall glow
with grace for I, the
YHVH–LORD,
have risen to bring you Light.
The nations of the world
are draped in darkness still
but glory shines on those
who Light will radiate.

Your families will then return,
you will rejoice, be glad;
The nations will restore
your wealth and know
your peace.
Tall ships will sail the seas
in from the ends of Earth;
they'll honour YHVH–LORD,
they'll know My mercy, grace.

The glory of the Lebanon
will beautify your home–
My Sanctuary. You'll be
the joy of nations here;
you'll know at last that
I am your Redeemer and
the Mighty One of Israel–
Salvation holds you here.

The sun no longer needs
to shine, nor moon by night,
for YHVH–LORD will be
your Light, your radiance.
The days of death will be
no more, your grief assuaged,

your people holy then—
there'll be a recompense!

CLIMACTIC EXCLAMATIONS
Chapters 61 – 66

THE PRE-EXISTENT MESSIAH
Good News!

God's Spirit is in Me,
I am 'The anointed' One–
Messiah–LORD!
I will be sent to preach
Good News to all the poor,
the broken-hearted heal.
I am to share God's peace,
bring beauty for the ash.
The ancient ruins will be
renewed and foreigners
will feed your flocks and tend
your vines and field.
You'll be My priests
who'll serve
within the Holy Place
for I love justice and
I'm faithful to My word.

ISAIAH

The *YHVH*–LORD has made
an everlasting covenant:
I'm overwhelmed with joy
for He has shown to me
His will, He's clothed me in

the robes of His delight:
His love extends to all;
His justice is a garden: See!.

A Prayer for Purity

Jerusalem! I love
you so! I need to speak,
to pray for you until
you shine just as the dawn.
All nations will take note
of you, observe your worth.
Your righteousness aglow;
a new name will be given you.
The watchmen scan the dawn
believing God will act;
now, open up your gates,
prepare the highway, call
your people to return.
Behold! Your Saviour comes,
He brings His great reward,
His city will enthral.

Say, who is this who comes
with robes all stained with
blood?
He wears His royal robes:
we see His power to save!
You want to know My Name?
"I AM", the YHVH–LORD,
and I announce today:
I will your sins forgive!

Why are You treading grapes
and all alone? Why are

Your robes all stained in red?
This is My blood shed in
the fight that right prevail.
It's time that I redeem
My people, ransom them:
I've shed My blood for them!

I'll tell of God's great love
unfolding in its grace
and I'll rejoice to see
His mercy, goodness, love.
Here is our salvation.
He has rescued us and He
has lifted us and He
has gifted us to live!

Remember now the days
long gone, when Moses came
lo lead The Exodus!
But where's my Shepherd
now?
Where is the Holy Spirit who
will come to bring new life?
Where is the One whose power
will with new life endow?

Prayer for Mercy

Look down from Heav'n
O LORD,
show us the passion now
You utilised in days
long past to comfort us.
You are our Redeemer still,

do not allow us now to stray
from paths You've set. Return,
O LORD and free us, save us!

Come down to us from Heaven
Like as You did of old;
since the creation days,
No ear has heard, eye seen,
another bring about
the wondrous deeds of God.
Like autumn leaves we fall
(But spring will come again!)

Do not remember, LORD,
our failures through the years.
Look to us now and see
that we're Your people yet.
Our city is a wilderness,
the Temple is destroyed;
do not refuse to aid,
do not be silent yet.

The Speech of God

I am so ready to respond
to you and yet I do
not hear petitions or
just one requesting aid.
Hark! Here I am today:
You know, don't call,
My Name—
I've opened out My arms
to you; now come; I've said!
I will repay the sin,

I'll not be silent while
you do persist in ways
so evil, deeds that will
insult My love for you.
A payment must be made
for sin! I will deliver all!

But, just as good grapes will
be found among the bad,
I will preserve the good—
a remnant will be saved.
These people will possess
My land.
Sharon will fill with flocks,
the valleys pasture herds
and I will cleanse,
sins laved!

I am creating all things new,
new heaven and earth.
You'll not be called to think
about the past. Rejoice!
The sounds of grief
will not be heard again!
You will not die before
your time—
age will be filled with grace.
Before you call, I'll hear
and answer you;
While you still think about
your needs
I'll come to you through prayer.
The wolf and lamb will be
good friends.; the lions will not

*give trouble and the snakes eat
dust!
No one will be harmed. I care!*

*You'll find My throne in
Heaven;
on Earth, My feet will rest!
I have created all:
and both belong to Me.
All those who honour Me,
contrite for all past sins,
will know deep blessings all
their lives. Indeed,
they're free!*

*So, when I call, take heed
and answer My request.
Before birth pangs: behold,
Jerusalem, your Son!
This is unique! No one
has seen a nation rise
in such a way as this:
I will deliver you: It's done!*

*Rejoice, Jerusalem!
Be glad all those
who've loved
and mourned for her;
drink deep,
the city of God's peace.
I give to Zion a stream
of peace, prosperity.
The wealth of nations, all
will flow to her by grace.
My glory will be seen*

*by those in darkness yet;
they'll bring the remnant home:
they will rejoice in Zion.
As surely as all Heaven
and Earth remain, you'll be
My people and your name
eternal will remain.*

....

THE SONG OF ISAIAH

Tune: *Aberystwyth*, 7.7.7.7. D.

Holy, holy is the LORD,
El Shaddai, Almighty God;
His, the glory that outshines
Sun and moon and stars:
Behold!
All who walk in darkness will
View God's Light and shout
for joy.
Bonds that hold us in the night
Shattered by that brilliant ray.

Wonderful, the Counsellor:
Mighty God and Father! Sing:
'Prince of Peace, Eternal One,
He's *Messiah*, Christ, the King'.
Desert lands will surge to life,
Blind made whole, the deaf
will hear.
God reserves the Holy Road,
Ransomed souls walk
without fear.

Suffering for our sin, He came,
Lamb led to the slaughter dies;
Bearing sins of the whole
world,
Lamb of God bought our
release.
Thirsty? Come, refresh
your soul;
Poor? The peace of God
is free!
Seek the LORD, His mercy
flows;
Plan of God: Redemption see!

Heaven is the throne of God,
Earth is His beloved land;
None could build a worthy
house
For the LORD as He has
planned.
His own home is in our heart:
All who listen to His voice,
Know His peace as streams
of grace;
They will praise Him and
rejoice.

..... oOo .....

THE TRAUMATIC YEARS

JEREMIAH

Allow me to introduce myself. You'll seek to know the meaning of my name–I will suggest to you that it's well-chosen for I serve *the LORD most High*. He's hurled me into the thick of the fray!

Our enemies were all but battering down our doors when He called me to become His voice, His prophet though I was a priest! The Lord declared that soon the sins of Judah would catch up with us. The end would come within our time. This, sadly, is the news I have for you! But YHVH will be exalted now as people see He does not lie!

YHVH–LORD and JEREMIAH
Chapter 1

O Jeremiah! Jeremiah!
You are the son of Hilkiah—
When Josiah ruled, I came
to you. You heard Me call

your name, well-chosen
name:

'YHVH is exalted' (by
your fame).
Before I placed you in
the womb
I knew you well! I saw, in you,
an aptitude—before
your birth—
that you'd fulfil My plans
for you:
before you breathed, set quite
apart
to prophesy, to preach
with worth.

But, LORD, I'm but a child!
I do not have the skill to speak
with clarity what You desire
of me. I do not have the means
within my soul to prophesy,
make known a doom so dire.

You must not see yourself
just as
a child for I have chosen you
to speak for Me. I will direct
you where to go and what
to say.
Don't be afraid of enemies:
for I am with you; I'll protect.

The *YHVH*–LORD then
reached to me,

He touched my lips and said
to me:

Now you've received the news
that I command you'll give.
You are appointed to proclaim
that—for sin—there's
no excuse!

YHVH–LORD and
JEREMIAH
Nature's Parable

What do you see,
O Jeremiah?

I see a branch of almond tree!
It's winter, LORD, but
this tree
sprouts before the spring.
What is
Your word through blossoms
rare?
What do You say through
these to me?

You are correct! This blossom
bears
strategic news for you!
Just as
the almond blossoms sprout
before
the spring arrives, so does
My word
come quickly! Let the nations
know

I'll hasten to fulfil My word.
Hear more:
What do you see now,
Jeremiah?

I see a boiling cauldron, LORD!
It's tilted from the northern
clime so far from here.

You have observed
My news:
it's from the north that fire
will come,
engulf the land, destroy
each home.
The eastern kings will come,
despoil the Promised Land
throughout Judah, and then
My people will be judged,
condemned.
Get ready now. Stand firm,
define!
Jeremiah: know
That I am with you now!

YHVH–LORD and
JEREMIAH
The Fate of Judah
Chapters 2 – 5

Now, Jeremiah, go! Proclaim
to Zion: I do remember you
how as a bride you loved
Me when I guided you all
through
the desert Exodus. Then, you

were holy–set apart,
well-proved.

What was the fault you found
in Me? I brought you to
the Promised Land but you
defiled that land. The priests
all failed to follow Me,
the lawyers failed, the
prophets, too!

My people then exchanged
the glory of the YHVH–LORD
for worthless idols, gold;
they have forsaken Me—
the Spring of Living Water—
for the cisterns that have failed.

You brought your brokenness
upon yourselves—
forsaking God
Who led you all the way.
You broke My yoke, you have
corrupted every quality
of life; you flung it all away.

I planted you a fruitful vine
but you desired a weed!
You say, 'I'm not defiled'
and yet you gaze in awe
on wood and stone so carved
that worthy worship is
despoiled.

O Jeremiah, have you not seen

what faithless Israel did?
Ascending every highest hill
and bowing under spreading
trees,
committing sins—a blasphemy,
thinking idols would their
dreams fulfil.

For all that Israel did
in faithlessness, they were
more righteous than
the south!
Go! Speak these words
to them:
'Return to Me, O Israel;
you'll find My grace
comes forth.'

And I will give to you
good shepherds that will then
display My love—they'll lead
you, understand your grief.
So, you've no need to look
towards an ark to plead
the Ark of Covenant.
Believe!

No longer I'll a focus give—
You'll not remember it
because—one day—
the Throne
of God will be in Zion,
all nations gathering in Light.

Return to Me and I will cure
backsliding, all your sin!
O, cast away your gods
of stone,
break up the fallow ground—
don't sow among the thorns
then, for your sins,
I will atone.

Oh, if indeed you will return
to Me, if you will cast aside
those idols made of stone
for worshipping and; if
you will be true to Me,
all nations can be won!

Disaster follows you!
The north will fall: Go! Flee!
Return to Zion, be safe.
The lion emerges from
his den, lays waste
your land.
The king, the priests,
can't save.

But LORD, You've spoken
peace
and now the sword is raised!
We're told of scorching wind;
this wind is strong, so strong
for winnowing: ruin! Woe!

Oh, Jerusalem, some

virtue find! I am in anguish,
LORD!
I can't be silent now:
I've heard the trumpet sound—
the land is ruined, done:
The battle cry is heard—
how long must this resound?

My people, use your brains!
Why don't you understand
the consequence of evil minds!
The Earth will mourn because
of you. I won't relent
the punishment for sins.

Go up, go down the
city streets,
search for a holy one—
an honest man who'll seek
the truth. Where can you find
one person without blame?
You've thrown away My yoke.

No harm will come to us!
you said. The prophets' words
are wind. Let failure fall
on them! Because you speak
like this, My words will be
a fire on you. They will appal!

O Israel! A distant
nation comes;
their language will be strange
to you. They will devour
your families, your flocks,

your herds, your crops;
their swords
will surely make you cower.

Yet, even then, I'll save—
a remnant shall remain.
You've served the alien gods
throughout your land and
in your family homes so, now
you'll serve those alien 'lords'.

You've eyes, but do not see;
you've ears, but do not hear.
Why do you not revere
the mighty works of God?
I've given fertile land;
your sin brought
drought severe.

A shocking thing, most horrible,
has happened to this land:
the prophets prophesied
their lies, the priests do rule
by their authority—
you've loved it, satisfied!

YHVH-LORD:
The Siege of Jerusalem
Chapter 6

O Benjamin, now flee,
seek safety far away;
disaster looms for Zion!
It will become the field

where shepherds tend
their flocks,
they'll pitch their tents, recline.

The enemy will build
their siege ramps against Zion;
like streams of water, here,
her wickedness does flow.
O Jerusalem, you're warned:
a desolation comes.
So, fear!

Who listens to My word?
Advice is so offensive to
My people there, they find
no pleasure in My words.
The nation is involved;
My wrath is not confined.

Peace! Peace! They plead.
But where is peace? I do
not find the shalom peace
to cover all their pride.
They'll fall. This nation's prone
to find their own 'release'.

Stand at the signpost;
search the crossroads and
request the ancient goals;
seek out the good way now;
walk in that path, for here
you'll find rest for your souls.

I sent you watchmen, words
of advice; you did not listen

and you rejected all the Law
set down for guidance and
for grace. Your sacrifice,
your offerings, I do deplore.

I made you to become the one
to test the metal and
and My people are the ore:
You see? The gold becomes
just bronze and iron—
they are refined no more.

JEREMIAH and
YHVH–LORD
False Faith
Chapters 7 – 9

Hear the word of *YHVH*–
LORD! You walk through
gates of Zion: Take heed!
This is God's word to you:

Reform your ways!
Let actions speak for you.
Don't be deceitful but,
instead, reform; take care of
aliens. Do not oppress an
orphan or a widow, do not
resort to idol worship. No!
If you'll fulfil these tenets,
live in peace! You think
you're safe within My house
yet you remain but robbers
still? I see your ways;
I'm watching you.

*Return to Shiloh and
observe what happens to
a wickedness. I have
repented of the ways
required of you. I called
to you, requested you
to seek My paths, and
walk within My ways,
but you declined.*

Observe your
waywardness—how you
provoke your LORD. It's
always been the same:
Since your escape from
Egypt's woes, you've tested
YHVH–LORD; you've tried
His patience. So, it's time
for every consequence!

All that He has required
of you was your obedience:
walk in His ways, be clean
in heart and soul. Instead,
you backward marched.

All truth has perished from
the face of Earth. Bring on
the dirge: lament what
might have been. The Vale
of Slaughter will be trod.
The sounds of joy no longer
heard as desolation
colours all the earth.

Your history's bones will
bleach within the sun, the
moon, the stars. You'll long
for death as life will ebb
from you in grief.

*How can you say you're
wise? ''The Law gives
wisdom yet and this we hold
most dear?'' Unworthy
scribes have penned
your lies–their quills
have dripped deceit
without a tear!*

*The 'wise' are put to shame,
a falsity can't keep you safe.
He is not wise who would
reject the Law of YHVH–
LORD. A greed replaces
generosity, the truth
you can't afford.*

*Peace! Peace! They do
proclaim. But where is
shalom peace? There is no
peace where there's no
shame. There is no joy when
prophets speak a lie; there
is no love in faulty prayers.*

O *YHVH*–LORD, I yearn
for comfort now; my heart
is faint—all Israel, deprived,

cry out. "Where is he
LORD?
Has He departed Zion?"
The harvest's past
and we're not saved.

Is there no balm in Gilead?
Is there no physician there?
Israel is crushed and so
am I,
I mourn for them, and for
their open wounds. Is there
no medicine? LORD, hear
my cry.

I long for tears that would
assuage this pain of grief.
Oh, that I could now flee into
a desert home and be
at rest; away from those
who've caused this abject woe.

I will refine and test
this people who have grieved
Me so. A punishment
must fit the crime. So then,
Jerusalem will be laid waste:
the haunt of jackals, desolate.

Let not the 'wise' now boast
of wisdom, or the strong
regard his strength as great,
or rich men boast their loot!
Let him who boasts, boast
that he knows My justice yet.

YHVH-LORD and
JEREMIAH
The LORD Reigns
Chapter 10

'Cut down this tree and carve
it in the shape of beauty and
for reverence. They go,
declare: "This is our god—
the one who understands
our grievances, our woe.

Adorned with silver and
with gold, made fast to spoil
a tottering, a fall.
It's like a scarecrow in
a pumpkin patch and mute;
a god that does appal.

O LORD, I look to You
from whom all blessings flow:
how great Your Name,
Your fame,
for there is none like You—
the King of nations, all
the Earth; of leaders: prime!

You formed the Earth in power,
Your wisdom laid its base.
All nature claps its hands
with lightning, thunder, and
the rain for You are God!
YHVH, El Shaddai commands.

O LORD, I bow to You;

You know my woe, my pain;
my life is in Your hands:
correct us now, let justice
flow—O LORD,
I know that punishment
arrives from alien lands.

YHVH-LORD
The Broken Covenant
Chapter 11

You know the terms
I've set—
The Covenant was made
in Exodus. The desert
promises hold true through
generations past and still
today. You know the terms.

Your fathers failed Me, so
have you. This is the word
you must convey to Israel.
Proclaim this news
throughout
Judah, Jerusalem: Disaster
follows on from
disobedience.

You've made a god to fit
in each and every town;
you send your sacrifice
to Baal–the branches of
your 'olive tree' are past
redemption, broken now!

JEREMIAH and *YHVH-LORD*
The Complaint
Chapter 12

O LORD, now bear with me:
I need to plead our cause
with You to bring my case
to You
Why do the evil prosper here?
Why do the faithless live
in ease?
O LORD, where is a justice
now?

You planted them, they grow,
bear fruit; You're on their lips
but far from in the heart.
You know to test my thoughts:
be done with them, they say,
'The LORD won't see our
dearth!'

The shepherds trample down
My field; they'll turn
My pleasant land
into a wasteland, desolate.
The whole land is laid waste:
There is no one who cares!
So, over all the barren height
their enemies will swarm,
they will
destroy the land. But My
sword will
swing to land's end for

their blame
They'll sow the seed and reap
no crop—just weeds.
Exhausted, they will
gain nothing;
the harvest will bring shame.
They seized Israel's
inheritance:
I will uproot them from
their lands.
And Judah, too, will be
uprooted then.
But, afterwards, I'll be
compassionate,
I'll bring them back to their
homeland:
Judah's inheritance they'll
find again.

JEREMIAH and *YHVH-*LORD
Sound Advice
Chapters 13 – 17

The LORD has given me
directions for the binding of
a belt. What parables of
truth He gives through me.
I will comply. Perhaps
I'll learn of His intent.
Ahh! I see it now: It is
the House of Israel that's
bound and, then, the
wineskins too. They must
be filled but, then,

they'll burst—like Israel!

Oh Israel, now take to heart
the message from the
LORD:
before the darkness comes,
give glory to the LORD.
You hope for light? Beware:
the darkness overwhelms.

Observe those coming from
the North: Where is the flock
entrusted to your care?
You wonder why all this
could happen to Israel?
Where is a man of prayer?

Look! Can the Ethiopian
entice a paler skin?
Or, can a leopard change
his vivid spots? No more
can you exchange
your ways;
you think that this
is strange?

And, neither can you change,
accustomed as you are to sin!
So! Here are My decrees:
you will be scattered as
the chaff that winnowed from
the grain: no longer, live
in peace.

You'll search the cisterns,

but you'll find no water
to refill the urns.
The ground is parched, the
farmers weep:

'Do something, LORD,
O Hope of Israel, our Saviour's
found.'
The time for prayer is past;
the offerings, the sacrifice,
I won't receive. The heart
of Israel is far from pure
and words will fail to ease
their temperament to part.

O LORD, I speak for them,
my people for we do admit
our faults and failings, yet
because of Your great name,
do not forsake us now—
our every sin we do regret.

A retribution waits
for blatant disregard of
justice and of righteousness.
But! Know that I am with
you, Jeremiah; you will
be saved, redeemed, no less.

Refrain from building for
yourself a family
as children that are born
into this nation now
will be bereft of peace,
prosperity. Disease

will overtake and cast
them to their death. Do not
then mourn the dead, there'll
be no pity for a people who
have blatantly besmirched
this nation in the grime of sin.
Do not partake in revelling—
there'll be an end to joy!
But, make reply to those
who query what they've done
to now deserve such pain
and suffering. It's plain
to see: 'you knew the way
to life yet you chose death.
You pleased yourselves,
forgetting Laws by which
to live. There is for each and
all, a consequence for this.
But, even now, My promise is:
I will restore once more
My people to this land!'

O LORD, my fortress, Strength
and Refuge in this time
of deep distress: I see a time
when Israel will return,
own up to depths of sin
that was their forebears' grime.

A flintstone has engraved
their sins upon the tablet of
the heart of Israel.
Each child is weaned to paths
of wantonness. There's none
escaping 'fires' of Hell.

Your true inheritance
is lost, for you have turned
your backs on YHVH–LORD.
There is a curse on such
as these who flaunt
their immorality, so soiled.

But blessed are all those
who trust in God for they
shall be like trees whose root
goes deep into the soil
of grace.
I see into the depths of
human souls:
I judge according to the fruit.

Heal me, O LORD, and I'll
be healed; save me, I will
be saved. I praise Your name,
I am Your shepherd yet;
You know what's in my heart,
You are my Refuge. LORD,
You came!

You ask Me what I do
require? Go, stand there—
at the city gate—and there
proclaim what I desire
of Israel: 'Remember now
the Sabbath Day. This is
a holy day. Set it apart.
Your forefathers forgot,
they listened not, did not
respond to discipline—
there is a consequence!

If only you'd obey, you'd see
the kings of Israel ride through
these gates and they would
rule in peace.

YHVH-LORD
The Potter's House
Chapters 18 – 19

What can a potter do?
He moulds the clay within
his artist hands; he shapes
the sodden mass to his
design. The clay responds
but, then, descends into a
mass of mud. It won't allow
the potter his intent for it.
See how, reshaped, the clay
becomes a vessel of a grace
that's fit to serve the king.

O Israel, can I not do
with you just what you see
upon the potter's wheel?
You are as clay within My
hands. What can I do when
'clay of Israel' prefers the
sodden mud? I would
remake, remould, transform
you as this vase if only you
were malleable, pliable,
formable. You're in My
hands–allow the shaping of
a vessel fit for holy things;
reveal the Potter's worth.

*So, take your pot with you
and, take the elders too
out through the Potsherd
Gate and there proclaim
what must be said to Israel.
Announce a doom on them
and then take up the pot and
smash it there where they'll
observe My plans for Judah
and Jerusalem. Then, go
into the Temple, there
proclaim the great disaster
for the wickedness for sin.*

JEREMIAH
Chapter 20

Now look, O LORD, what
has been done to me.
I'm mocked; insults are
flung at me. I've been
abused for words that
plainly came from You.
My grief is plain. LORD,
see!

And yet, I can't refuse
to speak. If silent, LORD,
Your words are as a fire
that burns within my bones!
The nation seeks revenge
and all now vent their ire.
Yct You are with
Yet, You are with me,
LORD.

Please work on my behalf
for I would sing unto the
LORD. But now, I curse the
day that I was born. Why
was I born to bear a
grief?

JEREMIAH
Chapters 21 – 22

The priest, Pashur, has
come requesting guidance
here. Nebuchadnezzar, King
of Babylon, has set his goal
upon Jerusalem. I had to say
that all the news has pointed
to recalcitrance. For all their
sin, Jerusalem's
inhabitants would know a
wrath commensurate with
what they'd done and failed
to do. 'This is God's
message to you all:
surrender now and save
your life. The king will take
the city and the state by fire!'

**KING ZEDEKIAH
It's time I had a word to
say on my behalf! For,
after all, I am the king—
I sit on David's throne!
My words, my laws,
should hold the sway**

before that upstart,
Jeremiah! I did revere
my dad—Josiah, king of
such repute throughout
the land. Yet I am now
the king and what I say
should be obeyed—not
antiquated Laws held
in such holy reverence
by some, you see,
though not by me!

I have been warned.
The King of Babylon
is marching to this land.
The cheek of him!
I'll have his head for this.
Perhaps, though first,
I should inquire of
Jeremiah now. Just what
is in his mind regarding
what the LORD would
have to say about this
horde of aliens. I do
detest him, but defer:
What's this, I hear?
My weapons will rebound
on me for Babylon is near
the city gates and they will
march right in? How dare
he speak such words
of woe, of fear, to me!

Hear the word of YHVH–
LORD: O Zedekiah, King,

you sit on David's throne:
do what is just and right,
take care of the oppressed
and shed no blood of
innocents. If you would
show a care for all, you'll
ride in victory.
But, if you scorn, do not
obey My just commands,
this city and your palace
will become a ruined mound.
You are just like Gilead to Me
but you'll become deserted
and succumb to death. Woe
to the one who builds his
palace on the base of pride,
injustice, sinfulness and
a dark unrighteousness.
The grandest palace does
not make a king. More wise
you'd be in faithfulness.
Your father showed you how
to lead—Josiah's rule was
just. To follow him you
would be blessed; since
youth you've not obeyed.
You listened not to sound
advice. You'll find no rest.

YHVH and JEREMIAH
The Righteous Branch
Chapter 23
Where are the shepherds
now? My flocks are

scattered far and wide.
My pastureland is bare.
I call each one—
the shepherds—to appear
before Me now. Indictment
must be heard. You have not
cared for them, My sheep.
Your punishment will come
without relent. Then I, the
LORD, will call the remnant
home. Good shepherds
will give care!

The day will come, I vow,
when I will raise a Branch'—
the Branch of David, King
of Israel. He'll be your King!
He'll reign in wisdom and in
righteousness and then all Israel
will sing! Through Him, all Judah
will be saved and Israel will live.
His Name? 'The Righteous King'!

Hark! This will be the new
'memorial'–no more the Egypt
saga; it will be: "The LORD has
now redeemed
us from all alien lands!

O LORD, my heart is rent!
I tremble 'neath the weight
of these, Your words
unleashed, announcing depths
of sin the nation has 'enjoyed'.

The prophets and the priests
have walked
a slippery slope, they tread a
treacherous trail–I've seen it
all: Most terrible!

Ungodliness abounds.
These leaders speak without
a thought of truth; they lie
with mindless mirth: 'Oh yes!
There's peace at hand for you!' It
is a peace they cannot buy!

Look! See the thunderstorm
approach. A whirlwind will
destroy the land, each. Am I
a God who does not see?
Could any hide their sin from
Me? I am the LORD: I will
impeach!

A PRIEST
A Mindless Query
Chapter 23:33 – 40

How can the LORD
think ill of me? I do my
duty yet; I serve Him well
within the Temple courts.
I do not hear Him speak
to me—I've listened,
never heard, except
old Jeremiah who rants
at city gates and stomps
in Temple halls.

What does he know?
I've said what I believe,
I've stated all the oracles
that come to mind. These
are my own words, true—
But when I'm asked for
oracles what can I say but
that which comes to mind.
This can't be a disgrace.
I represent the LORD.
Why does He not now
speak His holy word?

A PROPHET
Empty Words
Chapter 24

I'd speak a word
for Him—this is my role,
you see: I represent
the *YHVH*–LORD. If only
He would grant a word
of prophecy that I could
then repeat right at
the city gates. That
rancid Jeremiah takes
my rightful place.
It seems that *YHVH*–
LORD prefers his
raucous voice. He does
not grant to me a word
to speak. I lean towards
my Asteroth—Perhaps
she'll speak, my god. She's

silent yet and so is my own
precious idol carved from
stone. A better word from
it I'd get if He, the LORD,
would speak to me one day.

A PEASANT
Pathetic Pleas

Why don't they think of
me in all their mumblings
and their mutterings.
They do not look to me
to hear what's in my
weary heart! I want
to know, where is
the *YHVH*-LORD?
He does not speak to me.
And there: that Jeremiah
rants and raves of things
to come—he speaks of
woes and blows, of battles
lost and exile too! I do not
see it so, not me! I much
prefer the words of priests
and prophets, too.
Their plaintive pleas, their
promises and all their
prophecies, I take to heart.
What's more, I do delight
in gods that I can see. I'll
speak to them this day;
perhaps they will give
answer to my pleas.

Behold that lovely shape
That's formed from
stately wood! It does
delight me so—
It calms my fears.

JEREMIAH and
YHVH-LORD
Prophetic Figs
Chapter 24

All the artisans: gone!
Officials, king, and all
the craftsmen–gone from
home. The skilled of Judah:
gone to Nebuchadnezzar's
far off Babylon.

Just then, the *YHVH*–LORD
asked me what my vision
held. I saw—before the
Temple of the LORD—two
baskets full of figs. The one
held precious fruit; the
other? Over-ripe!

*What do you see here
Jeremiah, now?*

I see some figs, I said.
The good are very good,
the bad, so very bad!

*So! hear me well on this:
your vision's parable.*

*Those good figs represent
the exiles gone to Babylon.
I'll watch them, guard them,
Bring them home again. I'll
build, not tear them down. I'll
plant and not uproot. I'll give
them each a heart that will
then recognise I am the
LORD for they'll return to
Me with all their heart,
revived! But, just like rotten
figs, King Zedekiah and his
chiefs and cohorts, all will be
offensive to all kingdoms of
the world. They are abhorrent
now and then they'll be
destroyed!*

JEREMIAH and
YHVH-LORD
Seventy Years
Chapter 25

Threescore years and ten—
a lifetime length of years.
No child born now could
e'er perceive a time when
they'd come home. Is this
what it's to be? How can I
break such news to these,
my brethren? It's now
Jehoiakim that I must
face—Josiah's son, it's true,
but he is not the man that

his own father was!
But here I speak again:
It's time you listened to
my words. You are a people
that have disregarded all
the prophets *YHVH*–LORD
has sent to you! They've
counselled you, cajoled and
chastened you yet not a
'sorry' word you've said!
Therefore, this is the news:

Because of your
recalcitrance, the idols
flung into My face, I am to
summon Babylon! I'll
banish every sound of joy;
a wasteland the result—
for seventy years, no more!
But Babylon will be repaid
for slavery: their desolation
shall not cease: they
will all be repaid!

Now, Jeremiah, take
this cup—it's filled with all
the wine of wrath that all
marauding nations have
unleashed. The day will
come: all know the worst.

I took the cup and then
I handed its indictment
from the *YHVH*–LORD
to all the listed leaders and
I also took the news that He

required I should impart.
So weep, so wail, you men
who call yourselves, today,
the shepherds of the LORD!
This is the news He'd have
you know, digest,
and realise:

A storm of wrath descends
upon this weary Earth
by catastrophic sword!
You'll shatter like a pot
that's dropped. There is
no haven left for you. I hear
your deep distress but you
have led them all, the
people to disastrous fate.
Your fields will be laid waste,
there'll be no shalom peace:
My wrath is not assuaged!

THE RABBLE ROUSERS
Problems for the Prophet
Chapters 26 – 29

You'll pay for what you've
said! How dare you
preach what you now
claim to be the words, the
news, from *YHVH*–
LORD! We will report
you now. You stood up in
the court before the
Temple where you claimed
that, if we did not listen to

your vilest threats we
would become like Shiloh,
done to death, and we'd be
cursed above all nations.
Then you say that He'll
relent, the *YHVH*–LORD,
if we obey what you
decree. We are His holy
people yet so listen well!
Let it become quite clear:
you should receive the
death decree because you
prophesied against God's
holy city here–Jerusalem!

Court Officials:
We've heard the firm
defence. We see that
Jeremiah has but spoken
words we need to hear! The
people all agree. So! Listen,
all you priests and prophets
too: this man should not be
sent to die! He's spoken to
us all in the Name of
YHVH–LORD!

The Elders:
Remember Micah–
he came from Moresheth
to prophesy with blessings
from the king of Judah.
Yes! Hezekiah. This is what
the king proclaimed: The
city of

Jerusalem will be a heap
of rubble and Zion ploughed;
the Temple will become a
mound of brambles,
thickets, reeds!

Was Micah put to
death? Did not King
Hezekiah seek for true
forgiveness and the land
was saved. We are in peril
now. With such support
we do affirm that
Jeremiah lives!

YHVH–LORD:
*Jeremiah! Make a
yoke, secure it round your
neck. Send word to all
surrounding kings.
Through envoys preach this
news: With My great power,
I have created all the Earth.
But now, I give to Babylon
the blessings of
the Land of Israel. You'll
serve that king and, if you
do object to yokes he'll
place on you, you'll lose
your land, serve Babylon.
You will reside at home.*

Jeremiah:

I told King Zedekiah of
this rule of Law: Now serve
the king of Babylon and you
will live. Allow that king
his power. But! One day in
a future time, the LORD
will come, restore to you
all that is rightly yours
of Temple and of palaces.

Hananiah:
This is what the *YHVH*–
LORD would have you
know right now: Within
two years, you'll all come
home! The precious things
are yours for God will
break the yoke. The king,
Jehoiachin, will be once
more enthroned.

Jeremiah:
Amen! Amen! Of course
it all will be as you have said
it would—all, home! But!
Listen now to me: From early
times you've heard the words
of prophecy against great
kingdoms. Mark you well: the
prophet of your peace will be
known as such when all his
words come true!

Hananiah:

I'll take that yoke you've
draped around your neck!
I'll break it on those
rocks; for this is what the
LORD decrees: you'll all
be home within two years!

YHVH–LORD:
Go back to Hananiah, say:
"You broke the wooden
yoke but, in its place, you'll
find a yoke of iron about
the neck of nations for
they'll serve the King of
Babylon. The LORD did not
send you! You emphasised
all lies unto My people here.
For that, you'll surely die!"

Jeremiah:
I've sent a letter to
all exiles held in Babylon
(and this includes the king.)
Now hear the word of
YHVH–LORD: build houses
there, plant gardens, eat the
fruit. Yes! Settle down,
choose wives and husbands
for the children to be given
you. Seek peace, pray for
that land for, as it prospers,
so will you. Know this
—the word of God:

When seventy years are
through, I then will come to
you. I'll bring you home
for I have plans for you:
to give to you a future and
a hope. Then, you will call
upon My Name; you'll pray
and I will hear your plea.
And you will seek and find
Me when you search for Me
with all your heart. I will
be found by you.
I'll bring you home!

ISRAEL RESTORED
Jeremiah 30 – 31

Write down these things I've
spoken unto you, record them
in a book for this is what I say
to you: the day will surely come
when Israel shall come home—
they'll be renewed and
they'll obey.

Israel will know a day of strife
and like no other they have
faced—
a troubled time. But! They'll
be saved! I'll break their yokes,
I'll tear way their bonds; no more
they'll serve as slaves. It is
My will.

Israel will serve the YHVH-

LORD and 'David' I'll appoint
as king. So, do not fear, don't
be dismayed:
you will come home! The
distant land won't hold you
then. My peace you'll know, as
I've portrayed.

You'll know My discipline—
the rule of Law that's just;
you'll realise the consequence.
Your wounds: Incurable? There
is no healing for your sore?
I'll heal your wound: My
recompense!

Your homes will be restored;
I have compassion for your
land. Jerusalem will be rebuilt.
You'll see Jerusalem reborn
and from your glad, rejoicing
hearts the hymns of praise will
rise. You will come home and
you will shout your hallelujahs
to YHVH yet!

You ask Me why this gift of
grace? I've loved you with
eternal love, I've drawn you to
Myself.
You'll know My lovingkindness
and you'll be rebuilt. Your joy
will overflow in worship's
proof.

You'll come with weeping for
the blind, the lame, and you
will pray
as you return for I will lead you
by still waters and via level
paths; you will not stumble on
the way

JEREMIAH

Now, hear the word of God!
'All nations of the world, take
heed:
the LORD, who scattered Israel
will be their Shepherd,
watching,
guarding, guiding all His sheep.
He will ransom, He'll redeem
Israel.

'Then, all the Clans of Israel
will shout for joy, they'll be
just like a garden, watered and
renewed. And there will be
no sorrow then for joy will take
the place of mourning—by His
hand!

'A voice is heard in Ramah:
Rachel mourns for children
lost.
She finds no comfort—grief
o'erflows.
But wipe those tears, restrain
your grief, for there is hope:

there is a future after woes!

'Set up the right road signs,
put up guideposts on the path
you are to take. Return,
O Israel, how long will you
yet wander without faith?
The LORD renews the
Earth: re-learn!:

When I awoke, I knew my
sleep had been so pleasant for
the LORD assured me of
His care.
His promises re-echoed in
my mind: He would rebuild,
He would replant His
nation rare!

YHVH–LORD:
This is the Covenant that I
will make: I'll put My Law
into their minds; I'll write
it on their hearts. I'll be
their God and they'll rejoice.
I will forgive, so gain insight!

I have appointed sun and
moon their lights, their course,
their force: I am the YHVH–
El Shaddai.
It's only if they'd vanish from
My sight would I forget Israel.
Yes! I will always hear their cry!

JEREMIAH and
YHVH-LORD
Foreboding News
Chapters 32 – 36

The King of Babylon
besieged Jerusalem and I
was held a captive in the
Palace of Judah. The king—
that is, Zedekiah—he had
kept me under lock and key
for he despised the news I
had to tell. 'Why do you
prophesy in such a way?
The King of Babylon
cannot break down
these massive walls.
We are impregnable!'

My cousin came to me.
He said, It is your right
to buy my land—you can
redeem that field. I bought
that land because I knew
it was the will of God. I
signed and sealed the deeds
and gave them to Baruch,
explaining well:
Now put these deeds of
purchase in a jar of clay
for they must last. I had
explained that *YHVH*–
LORD revealed to me
the day would come this
land again would then
be ours to cultivate.

And then I prayed:

O Sovereign LORD, You
made the heavens and the
earth by Your creative
power, Your outstretched
hand. All things are possible
to You. How great Your
deeds, Your purposes will
be fulfilled. O great and
powerful One, the *YHVH*,
El Shaddai, we will give
witness to Your miracles.

The Exodus from Egypt
brought us to this land that
flows in milk and honey for
our benefit. Because we
failed in our commitment to
our LORD, we are brought
low for, even now, the siege
ramps are in place as
Babylon prepares
to conquer us.

O LORD, I hear Your
words
now spoken unto me. I
realise that this disaster
soon will fall on us.
Destruction looms—
Jerusalem, reduced to dust!
You've been provoked:
Idolatry, recalcitrance
replaced our loyalty.

But! Hear this news,
O Israel: the LORD will
gather us again. Israel shall
return and you will live in
peace. Your hearts will be
inclined to *YHVH*–LORD.

An everlasting Covenant
will bind you unto Him who
will inspire respect. God
will rejoice! This land
becomes a desert waste—It
will be born again, restored!
The Holy One has spoken it.

It happened yet again. The
LORD spoke deep within
my soul and I have
recorded it:

*Call unto Me and I will
answer you—I'll tell you of
mysterious things
You have not known. I'll
hide My Face from Zion for
wickedness. But! Know this
too: I will bring health
and healing into it.*

*My people will be healed
and they will know My
Shalom Peace, security.
They will be cleansed. Then
I will know their joy,
their praise*

*and honour through the
Earth. The song of Israel
shall be 'Give thanks unto
our YHVH, El Shaddai, for
He is good, His love
endures eternally.' They'll
sing The Shepherd's Psalm
once more for I will guard
and guide. They'll pass
beneath My hand into
the fold I build for them.*

*The day will come! I will
fulfil My gracious promises
to you and, at that time, a
special 'Branch of
Righteousness' will sprout
from David's Throne.
Jerusalem's new name,
renowned, shall be:
'the LORD, our
Righteousness'.*

*This throne will never fail
nor will the Levite priests
no longer stand before Me
to offer up their sacrifice.
This is My word to you. But,
if My covenant with day and
night is broken, only then
My word is broken. David's
line will stand and
countless be as stars above
and measureless as sand!*

*Now listen, Jeremiah, have
you not heard the gossip
here that I've rejected
Israel—that they are now of
no account? Again: if sun
and moon refuse to shine
then, it's only then, I will
reject the clans of Jacob,
David. True!
I will restore the fortunes of
Israel, I'll have compassion
on them all! The YHVH–
LORD presents this news:*

*I am about to give
Jerusalem into the hands of
Babylon. That king will then
command that it be burnt.
You'll not escape his power.
You'll see that king with
your own eyes and you will
go to Babylon. You'll die
upon an alien land. Your
people will lament your
death eventually.*

So Zedekiah set about
redeeming slaves in tune
with God's desire. No Jew
should now be held in
bondage. But then he
changed his mind. No
longer were they free.
Then, *YHVH* spoke of
this to me. He said:

*I made a covenant with
Israel that—every seventh
year—the slaves should be
set free. Six years they'd
serve, no more. Quite
recently the king repented,
set slaves free. But now he
has profaned My Name.
He's not obeyed. But,
freedom he shall have: a
'freedom' of the sword, of
famine and the plague. He'll
be the food of birds. The
towns of Judah will all be
laid waste... Now,
Jeremiah, go to Rechabites,
invite them to the Temple
courts to hear My word.*

They came, were offered
wine which they refused,
explaining that their lives
were those of self-denial;
they lived in tents and quite
content. They'd come into
Jerusalem escaping alien
armies now. Again, the
Voice of *YHVH*–LORD:

*Go to the men of Judah, say
to them, Why do you not
obey My voice? Will you not
learn the lesson here
displayed? Observe
the good example of*

the Rechabites as shown
to you and learn your
lessons now!
They'll never fail to serve as
I decree,
while clans of Judah leave
in chains.

When king Jehoiakim
ascended to the throne, the
LORD requested me to take
a scroll, record on it the
words I've shared with you
concerning Judah, Israel,
and all surrounding nations,
too. I was to set down all
events of King Josiah's
reign till now. Perhaps,
when Judah hears this news
proclaimed again, they'll
cease their wicked ways,
who knows?

I called my secretary,
Baruch, who set sown all
the history dictated for his
'pen'. When this was done,
I then explained, because of
my restriction, that he'd
need to go to read before
the people all the news as
written on the lengthy
scroll. Perhaps, I said, the
people that would hear

the things they'd done,
or failed to do, would then
repent, return to God
and pray!

My secretary, Baruch, did
as I required. I'm told
he read the news outlined
upon the scroll with great
integrity–right there, within
an upper courtyard room.
Micaiah then reported all
the news to the officials
who were gathered in the
royal room of the
secretaries. An errand boy
was sent to Baruch. He was
to bring the scroll to them.
Sit down, they said. Now,
read the news to all of us.
and Baruch did obey. When
this was done, they searched
each other's eyes
in fear. We must now tell
the king!

MICAIAH
So! Tell us first, is this
the work of Jeremiah or,
yourself?' I asked. These
words the prophet did
dictate to me. Baruch
had answered well.

All the officials then
declared: Go now to
Jeremiah. Both of you must
hide. Keep secret where you
are. With this advice,
we went, then, to the king
reporting all the news. The
king commanded that the
scroll be brought to him.
The news was read beside
the brazier fire because of
winter's evening chills.

When Jehudi read out three
or four parts of the history,
the king became enraged.
He sliced the scroll and cast
it to the brazier's flames.
He ordered then that certain
men should take captive
Baruch, Jeremiah too,
imprison them
(But *YHVH*–LORD had
hidden them). The *YHVH*–
LORD then asked
that Jeremiah take
another scroll.

Now, write upon this scroll
a repetition of the first
and then inform the king:
'This is what the LORD
declares: You burned that
scroll which bore the news
that you should hear.

Therefore, I will not have a
king to sit upon King
David's throne. A
punishment will fall upon
your heirs. Disaster looms!
All this because you did not
listen to My serious words!'

BARUCH

I am the great man's
secretary. Yes, Jeremiah
sought my help. It's been
amazing, what I've heard,
what I have seen, what I
was asked to do. I took the
'pen' he offered me, the
scroll on which I wrote the
news, the awesome news of
wondrous things, of
mysteries, catastrophes.
And too, there was the
glorious news—the
News of hope, of joy, a
Future blessed by *YHVH*–
LORD when all the Clans of
Israel, repenting, would
return with hearts renewed
by grace. I never thought to
be the preacher though!
Jeremiah could not go to
read the scroll to all the
people gathered there. So,
I must go instead. No, never
had I known experience like

this. I think I read it well
for, after all, I'd written all
the words he gave to me.
They listened well, all the
officials. How was I to
know
the king would be Incensed?
My mentor and this
quivering Scribe were
thrown into the stocks!

ZEDEKIAH
Chapter 37

I'm now the King of
Judah and I mean to rule
this land iron clad through
peace or war. I will be
conqueror of Babylon.
That wretched man! I'll
have his head for this! For
years I have
endeavoured to encourage
Israel to look upon the
brighter side. I say that
Babylon will be no match
for us. Jerusalem in
impregnable!

Yes! I shall sit upon my
throne while life shall last.
The crown will go then to
my son and heir—it is the
way of things for Israel.

We're not so prone a
people to be stickler to the
'rules and regs' of years
long past. They served
us well, of course, but we
have come of age.
Maturity
of mind allows a broader
range of pleasantness,
'Believe what you believe',
I say I have no fear of
consequence for any
worship of each form of
golden frames as carved
so gracefully. I've said a
prayer or two myself
before my own idol, a
commanding shape, to
honour it; to supplicate
my chief desires. Now,
look at me! In spite of
Jeremiah's raves and
rants,
I'm here, upon my throne
And here I'll stay. That
so-called prophet, though,
will find but prison bars
that he'll regret!

AN OFFICIAL
Chapter 38:1-6

We are the king's men and

we heard the prophecies
of Jeremiah that
forewarned of looming
doom: 'All those who stay
within these walls will die
by sword, by dire famine
or the plague. Though,
whosoever chooses
to step over to
the forces of the king
of Babylon shall live—
they will escape; they'll
live!' We talked of it,
reported it, then said,
This man should die!

He is discouraging the men
who fight for us. The
people, too, are listening
to his rants. He does
not seek our good; he'll
run us to the ground!
The king replied, He's in
your hands. Do what
you will with him.
I won't oppose
or threaten you. Be on
your way! We took that
wretched 'troubler'
and threw him in the
Prince's Pit. This is a
cistern in the yard
belonging to the guard.
So, Jeremiah can't
climb out of it.

It was a muddy pit with
slime so deep it was a
wonder that he did not
sink beneath the mud!

EBED-MELECH
Chapter 38:7-13

Good morning! I'm a
Cushite—Egypt is my home.
I'm part of this record for
I, too, serve King Zedekiah
as a loyal official in his
palace. Word has come to
me that Jeremiah has been
pushed into that pit—the
king had known of it.
I could not let this stand!

I went to Zedekiah—king—
and said to him, My lord,
the King, these men are
wicked; look at what
they've done! He'll starve
while down that putrid hole
for where will there be
bread for him?
The king then said to me:
Take thirty men and lift him
up out from that pit. I will
not let him die, though he's
no friend!

With orders then in hand,

I went into the Treasury;
I lifted up some worn-out
clothes and let them down
with ropes, helped by
the troop assisting me.

I shouted down that bleak,
black hole of certain death:
Now, Jeremiah, pad beneath
your arms; these rags will
help. Just set the rope in
place, we'll pull
You up. Then up, slowly up,
he came. He looked a sorry
sight (he smelt as well!)
From that time on,
my friend remained within
the courtyard of the
Garrison.

ZEDEKIAH, JEREMIAH
Chapter 38:14-20

**Things were getting out of
hand. I sent for Jeremiah
and the guard delivered him
right to the Temple gates.
I questioned him:
So, Jeremiah, son of
Hilkiah, I must question
you and you must not hide
one thing from me. But
he dared to question me!**

O King, if I'm to answer
you, you'll place me in the
pit again or worse, you'll
have my head. Even if I
counselled you, there'd be
no listening ear for me!

**I'm king! I make
the rules! I'll swear
an oath to you,
but secretly:
As surely as the *YHVH*–
LORD now lives—
the One who grants us
breath—I will not
kill you, nor will hand
you over to my guards
who seek to kill you now!
The prophet took
my word. He said,**

O King, I now proclaim
what *YHVH, El Shaddai*
has said:

*If you surrender to the King
of Babylon, your life is saved.
Also, this city will not burn.
You surely then would live.
But if you will refuse this
word, hold out against the
enemy, Jerusalem cannot be
saved: you'll not escape.*

This scared me and I said,

**But, Jeremiah, I'm afraid
that all the Jews who've
gone to Babylon will have
my hide, I'm sure of that!**

They will not hand you to
the men of Babylon. Obey
what *YHVH*–LORD
requires of you so all will
then be well with you.
Allow the LORD to spare
your life.
But, if you do refuse, it will
be said of you, You were
misled! Your family will be
given to the enemy. You
won't escape.

**I said, Now, Jeremiah, you
must keep this meeting
secret or you will not live.
Explain away the topic
shared! And this is what
he did. Though questioned
much, he kept his word. He
then was safe until the end.**

A GUARDSMAN
Chapter 39:1-4

They've broken through at
last! Our nation is no more.
We're lost the battle now.
Nebuchadnezzar's men are
storming through the fort.

Our wall is breached–the
aliens break through
to plunder us!

I see them now: officials of
the King of Babylon. They
take their seats within the
gate. I am ashamed to say
that, when they saw that the
invasion was complete, our
king and army, all
forsook their vital posts. I
saw them go out through the
gate near where
the garden grew.

It's time I fled as well! But
wait, I hear they have been
caught. I'll stay on guard
until they come to capture
me as well. Oh, why did we
refuse to hear the warnings
of the prophet Jeremiah? He
was right! We should
have heard, believed,
repented of our great
stupidity. We have
not pleased our LORD!

O LORD, now hear my
prayer: is it too late to heed
Your plea? I give myself
into Your hands.

ZEDEKIAH
Chapter 39:4-7

We got as far as Jericho.
How ignominious! Old
Jericho was Israel's finest
hour and now, our
bleakest day—the worst in
all our history. Here's
Jericho again. We have
no Joshua to guide us
now ahead.
Where's Jeremiah?
Perhaps he's dead...

The ghastly thing is done.
It's come to this. The last
thing I shall see—my sons,
my precious princes, loved
and lost. The swords have
swung at them, Iron—
plunged into their heart.
They are no more... Those
guards, I saw them slay
my sons and then, they
gouged my eyes. I see no
more... I'm blind and I
am bound in shackles for
the journey far: to
Babylon.

How different things
would be if I had heeded
Jeremiah and encouraged
all to hearken to the words

he spoke as prophet of
the *YHVH, El Shaddai.*
I mourn my sons, I mourn
my throne, my crown,
I mourn this land, bereft
of love, of life, of *LIGHT*
of God!

I wonder what's become
of him, the prophet,
Jeremiah, now?
Perhaps he's dead...

NEBUZARADAN
Chapter 39:8 – Chapter 41

Now! Let me introduce
myself: I'm Nebuzaradan,
Commander of the Imperial
Guard of Babylon. I have
them now in chains—all
those who have offended
Babylon by their attempts
to halt our massive march.
Jerusalem is ours—we
would not have it otherwise:
we won!

Before I give the order to
march on to Babylon, there
are some plans to set in
place. Oh yes, they'll come
with us—in chains—our
captives cowered at last

by mighty Babylon.

I've noted that there are,
within the ruined city here,
the poor, the handicapped.
None had a chance at life;
they'd die among the ruined
rocks of home.

We need to care for them.
I called the guard; I said:
Arrange for these poor folk
to now become the owners
of these farms, the
vineyards, home.
Allow them freedom to
sustain themselves by tilling
land and planting vines.
They'll be well fed; they'll
settle happily.

Also, I've remembered
what my king had asked
of me: Go, search for
Jeremiah, prophet of their
God. Take care of him,
ensure his safety through
the strife to come. Don't
harm this man in any way
and do what he will ask.

When he was found, I had
him handed over to the son
of Ahikam, Gedaliah, who
escorted him back home

where Jeremiah lives in
peace. And by the way he
asked, did Jeremiah, for the
safety of his friend, the
Cushite, Ebed-Melech, who
had saved his life. He said
that *YHVH, El Shaddai*, his
God, had said it would be
so. I made it so!

I will explain how this was
done: I found the prophet
bound among the captives
from Judah who were to
march to Babylon. I'd taken
well to heart the news that
Jeremiah and his God
were on good speaking
terms! I understood it was
decreed that all that all
Jerusalem and Judah would
fall to our superior force.

There was
a reason for this rout:
the nation failed to trust
their God. I gave him
options then: If you would
so desire, you will be
welcome in our Babylon.
I'd see you were kept safe
by my own interest in
yourself. If, on the other
hand, it is your will to stay,
the whole great country

spreads out before you now.
You're free to go
wherever you may please.

Before he left us, I gave
food—both fruit and wine—
to him. I did suggest that he
go on to Gedaliah at
Mizpah, there to stay with
him who was appointed
Governor, and live in
perfect safety there.

AN ATROCITY

Our men reported that,
when we'd departed from
Judah, the news went out
that all the land was free.

There was an influx of the
Clans as many came to
harvest crops—there was
abundance in the land.

And as for Gedaliah,
governor: It has been noised
abroad that one—
a man named Ishmael—was
bent on taking Gedaliah's
life. The governor could not
believe this thing could
happen on his watch. But

news has come that Ishmael,
with ten cohorts,
arrived at Mizpah, feasted
there and then attacked
the Governor. Yes! He was
slaughtered there with
others that included all
our soldiers there.

And then there was a
new atrocity: Ishmael
assassinated many who
had come to them in peace.
Ten of these men had asked
that they be spared. They
were, though Ishmael held
them captive with so many
more. We've been advised
that troops were called
were called to capture
Ishmael but he went to
the Ammonites.

Survivors of this dark
atrocity regrouped, decided
to depart due south to
Bethlehem before then
going on to Egypt to escape.

JOHANAN
The Egyptian Tragedy
Chapters 42 – 45

You look at me askance!
I am Johanan. So! Listen
up! I went to Jeremiah
with this plea: We seek
advice from you. As well
you know, once we were
many but now, so few.
Pray now for us that
YHVH–LORD will tell
us where to go and what
to do. Today, we need
His gracious aid!

The prophet prayed at
once and promised he
would tell us everything
the LORD advised. We
vowed allegiance to the
LORD. We would obey
We would obey His every
word! If it was good, we'd
follow Him And, if it's ill,
we'll still obey His word.

We waited far too long,
I feel. It took ten days
of wondering before the
prophet came to us. He
there proclaimed before
us all: If you remain in
Judah, you will be kept in
safety by the LORD. He'll
build you up, not tear
  you down. He'll plant you
  deep, He'll not uproot you

anymore. Don't be afraid;
the King of Babylon will
do no harm to you. He will
sustain and strengthen
you. He has compassion
on your deadly plight.

The prophet then went on
to say that, if we flee to
Egypt, to stay away from
conflicts, wars, and also all
that Babylon intends, the
sword you fear will
overtake you there
and you will surely die.
Then, Jeremiah pleaded,
saying: Don't go; remain!
But you have disobeyed–
already you are on your
way. Be sure of this—
there is no hope for you
in Egypt's future days.
This is the end for you!

I cannot well describe the
ire, the anger that we felt.
You're lying! Tell the
truth. We will be safe!
But Jeremiah stood s
tock-still. We would
not have it so. We took
the man, his friend,
in tow—they'd come
with us to Egypt now!

I have to set on record
this:
When we arrived in
Egypt, then that troubler
of our groups—he said it
was the LORD's
command—and he
requested that large stones
be buried at the entrance
to the palace grounds.
He then proclaimed to us
this news: The LORD,
YHVH El Shaddai,
The God of Israel, says:

> *I'll send King*
> *Nebuchadnezzar now*
> *to set his throne upon these*
> *very stones and when he*
> *comes, death and*
> *destruction follows in*
> *his wake. Be sure of that!*

I could have stoned that
man Jeremiah for all of
those remarks. The gods
of Eygpt are now doomed,
he said. And know this
now, that this was not
the last we heard from
him. It does appear that
YHVH loathes our daily
worshipping of Egypt's
gods. Why not, for this is
where we live! We must
assimilate or it will be:
'Return to slavery!'

We do delight in trusting
good in worshipping
'the queen of heaven'.
How good is that?
The cakes we bake,
the songs we sing,
the prayers ascending
to her very throne.
We can't believe the
words of utmost doom
that prophet rants. It's
here we'll live in peace–
why do we have to trust
in *YHVH*–LORD?
Look at what He's done
to us! His right-hand-man
has been rebuffed, I'm
told. He'd thought a word
would come to him that
YHVH–LORD would add
more sorrows to his soul.

I've heard it said that
YHVH spoke to him:
Should you now seek
great riches for yourself?
Don't search for gold—
it turns to crimson blood.
But know, Baruch, where
you will go, there *I AM*.
Be sure: you will escape,
you'll surely live!' So!

YHVH **will have promises**
for those who trust Him
still. How can this be?
I'll think awhile on that ...

YHVH–LORD
Promises of past and
Present
Chapters 46 – 52

Egypt

This is My word against Necho,
the King of Egypt, defeated at
the battle of Carchemish:
'Prepare your shields and
mount your steeds. Take up
positions with your helmets on.
I see an army in retreat. And
who is this but Egypt rising like
the waters of the Nile.
Charge on, march on: this day
belongs to Me. Entreat!
Egypt will turn, they'll flee–
they cannot stay their ground.
The day of punishment arrives:
here, dread and death
shall meet. But, do not fear,
Jacob, Israel: you will
be saved. You will come home,
back from that distant place.
You will be saved!

Philistia

Observe the waters rise:
they come in torrents from
the North. The land will be
submerged. The people weep.
The sounds of horses galloping
and rumbling chariots converge
on all of us .
A Father cannot save his
child—Philistia will know
that blood will seep.
Gaza will shave its head;
the mourning will be long.
The sword cannot be stilled
until the land lies in a heap.
How long until you rest
the sword that slashes
the sword that slashes,
thrusts, you ask?
Until your scabbard is
at rest, at peace, at last.

Moab

Moab will be praised no more:
your downfall is foretold.
Flee now, run now, to save
your life. Exist as desert
shrubs, so dry. Your pride and
arrogance has brought you
down to this.
My heart laments; how sad—
your capture is now nigh.
Look! See the eagle swoop;
it spreads its wings across
your land. There is no hope
for those who cherish dross.

Ammon

Has Israel no sons,
no heirs upon their lands?
The day will come when I
will sound the battle cry.
Put on your sackcloth then:
Molech will go to exile with
his priests, officials too.
Why don't you raise a sigh
for those in pain, in want? A
terror will befall your land; you
boast your power; it will be
done into the dust. You'll die.
Yet, afterwards, be sure
of this: I will restore to you
the land that you adore:
you'll find your peace anew.

Edom

Have you no wisdom left
by which to choose the right?
Have you no counsellor
to whom you'd turn for aid?
You are advised to flee
your country now. Hide deep
in caves to shelter you.
For crime, you will be paid!
You'll be a horror to all those
who pass you by, appalled
at what's become of you.
The hearts of warriors will fade.
Though each shall tremble
then and cries resound about,
do leave your orphans, widows
for I will protect them,

have no doubt.

Damascus

The strength you had has
failed, your people are
disheartened—all a troubled
people, like the sea that
pounds upon the rocks.
The city walls will be
consumed in flames and
Ben-Hadad will fall.
Why have you not abandoned
all the stocks?
This is a city that had once
delighted so in Me. So surely
will her youths be found in
death and, all the while, the
alien mocks.
Your feeble soul deserts you
now: dismay will ravage all
your thought.
Your anguish offers nought but
pain. Look what your hate
has wrought.

Kedar and Hazor

Your tents and flocks will be
no more. Nebuchadnezzar
will attack these lands.
They'll be destroyed. There'll
be no home
remaining as a shelter in
Kedar, Hazor. Your camels
and your wealth will be no

more. You've been so blind:
they'll come.
So confident, you failed to see
the peril that will plunder you.
No barricades? This is
your doom!
I'll scatter to the winds all those
who failed to plan and
did not care.
There is a consequence for laze;
a tragedy you're called to bear.

Elam

Your might is awesome but
a broken bow will be
your plight. The winds of north,
south, east and also, west,
will scatter you throughout
the Earth. So many seek
your lives, your livelihood.
You'll find no peace, no rest;
you'll be pursued by enemies
until I make an end to them.
One day you meet your quest.
I will restore your land;
I'll set My Throne within Elam
and, in the days to come,
I will restore to you your fame.

Babylon

This is My word that I
have given to the prophet that
I trust: Yes! Jeremiah! Hark,
this word concerns the great

and mighty Babylon.
Announce the doom of this
great empire, Babylon.
This nation will be put to
shame; their gods will
crumble, fold to dust.
A nation from the north
will raid, lay waste her land.
No one will live within this
'wonder of the world'.
Flee out from Babylon for I'll
prepare a great alliance of
two nations from the north,
the like of which has not
been told.
This nation will become
a wilderness, a desert land
a desolation never healed.
This nation won't expand.

JEREMIAH
Chapter 51:59-64

The LORD will vindicate
us now! I've written down
upon a scroll what *YHVH–*
LORD has done for us! He
cared for us! Now know:
The LORD fulfils what He
declares: Oh, you who live
by many waters and are rich
beyond belief, your end has
come; you'll be cut down:
the *YHVH*–LORD,

the Mighty El Shaddai,
will circumvent your days.
This is the message I have
sent and ordered that its
news be read in Babylon.
And when it's read, it must
be tied to stone so it will
sink into the River
Euphrates. This is the end!
Here's where my testimony
will cease—upon a
solemn note!

ZEDEKIAH
Chapter 52:1-30

You've heard the sorry
saga of my reign. I'll not
repeat the wretched news
again! I must admit my
infidelity to *YHVH*–ORD,
and to the prophet
Jeremiah. I wonder where
he is and if he now is safe.
He may be given a safe
recompense for how he
stood his ground against
the odds I placed on him.
The aliens could just
appreciate his skill, relent
and grant him peace. It's
more than I can say about
my treatment of the man.
Perhaps there'll be a

recompense for Jeremiah.
But, for me, it's all of it
a consequence of what I
did, and failed to do for
him, for Judah, and the
YHVH–LORD! One thing,
I cannot see the worst of it
for I'm blind—forever
seeing just that most
ghastly sight: the death of
my two sons. I'm spared
the flames that took
Jerusalem and all that
I held dear, of all for
which I had responsibility.
I mourn my inability to
listen, learn or lead.
Now I must follow on to
Babylon—one thing I will
see always, the worst
of tragedies. 10th day, 10th
month: the date forever
stamped upon my brain.
Jerusalem: No More!
The walls, the Temple,
palace, gone!

JEHOIACHIN
Chapter 52:31-34

What a surprise!
The last word comes from
me, the king! It's very

fitting for, look what's
happened now to me!
For over thirty years, I
found myself a prisoner.
At times, I'm clapped in
chains, no bread to ease
the hunger of my life.
I've tried to be the man
expected long of me. But
how can I retain the stance
a monarch must convey?
I have no crown, no throne.
At times, I sank in deep
Despair: where was *LIGHT*?

And then, they came for
me—the King of Babylon's
own guard! They freed me
from my chains, they
spruced me up. How long
was it since I had cleansed
myself—my body and, my
soul? They marched me, via
those Hanging Gardens—
I've never seen a sight like
that in all my life, so grand,
superb—to where the palace
gates then opened wide to
me! This was the year that
Evil-Merodach became the
King of Babylon. New man,
new ways, or so it seemed.

And there I was; I stood
before the king. He spoke so

kindly, smiled at me and
then began to ask how I was
feeling on this day.
I scarcely knew how to
respond! Then, think of this:
the most stupendous thing–
the king invited me to sup
with him! It's been like this,
each day since then. I sit at
meals—a throneless king
sat down each day
with king enthroned!

THE SONG OF JEREMIAH

Tune: *Hendon* (repeat last line)
7.7.7.7.

LORD, You've known us
from before
Birth had brought us into
LIGHT,
Plan of God before we
breathed,
Set apart to tell Your might.

See a branch of almond tree
Burst to life in beauty rare;
Spring comes soon to those
who trust,
Parable of Your great care.

There's a Balm in Gilead

Making wounded lives now
whole;
Medicine to cure life's pain,
Heals all wounds that harm
the soul.

Set up guideposts, mark
the path
That will lead to faith's
new start;
God will meet the seeking soul!
Stamp Your peace LORD, on
our heart.

Mould us as a potter forms
Clay within his skilful hand;
Shape us to Your pattern,
LORD.
Make us vessels whole, as
planned.

Blessing in abundance flows;
Great your name, Your power
is prime;
King of all the Earth, You rule.
LORD of all, You reign
supreme.

..... oOo .....

THE TRAGIC YEARS

JEREMIAH'S LAMENTS

THE SORROWS
Chapter 1

The once beloved city is
deserted now; Jerusalem,
a 'widow', once a 'queen',
among the nations: sold!
A tragedy of vacancy,
the city weeps her tears
and none can comfort her;
our people are exiled.

Judah dwells in alien lands;
the roads of Zion now mourn.
Where is a gate to welcome us?
The land is now engulfed
in slavery–her blatant sins
have brought her to the dust.
Where is her splendour now?
Where is her treasure 'pursed'?

The memories that hang
about our hearts reflect
her wealth, her welcoming,
her worshipping, her worth.
How blindly Zion went
her way and caring not
that filth now clung to her—
the rags that cloaked her 'health'.

Now there is none who will
give comfort, aid her deep
distress. Where is a crust
of bread, a bed for rest?
Is this but nothing yet to all
observers passing by?
Has suffering e'er been such
as this, the harshest test?

THE ABANDONMENT
Chapter 2

We are made desolate—
our sins have clamped
us in a yoke of death;
our strength has waned.
We have been trampled in
the dust, The fires that scourge
the Earth make known
just what our grief has gained.

Our *YHVH*–LORD now
silent stays,
dense shadows cloak
our hope.
'O LORD, look down upon
our grief, our deep distress.
Where is Your comfort now?
Israel's splendour is
hurled down;
You have forgotten us!
Our land
is dust in deep regress.
Your cloud of anger, LORD,

has draped us in despair;
our land is swallowed up.
You have withdrawn Your hand
of mercy from our heart.
We sense You are against
us now,
there is a dire destruction in
our wake. Where lies our land?

We bow in sorrow, LORD:
the Sanctuary has been
abandoned now. We find
You not. The enemy is bold.
We sit in ash with drapes
of sackcloth to proclaim
our grief. Our tears become
relief from pain untold.
Our starving families
now faint for want of bread.

What can I say for Judah now?
How may I comfort you,
my dear Jerusalem?
Your wounds are deep,
deep as the surging sea.
Who brings a cure to you?

All those who pass you by
now scoff at you, they clasp
their hands in scorn of you.
Is this the city that was known
for perfect beauty and the joy
of all the Earth? Where is
your beauty now; where is
your grace, O city of renown?

Arise! Let your lament
be heard deep in the night.
Pour out your heart
to *YHVH*–LORD, now raise
your hands to supplicate
your need for peace, asking
that this bleak slaughter will
now pass, assuaged, in peace.

THE AFFIRMATION
Chapter 3

LORD, I have seen the wrath
You have displayed and
now my flesh, my bones,
have aged. I am besieged
by all this bitterness.
I am imprisoned where
iron bars restrain: I live
without the *LIGHT* engaged.

It seems a jungle beast
encamps by me. I am
defenceless. I'm the target and
my grieving heart is pierced.
Affliction claims my
beaten soul.
Yet, this I call to mind—
it gives me hope—no more
forlorn, the LORD be praised:

This is because Your love
has granted us the grace
You bear for us for we are not

consumed. Your
compassion will
not fail. It is renewed
each dawn.
How great Your faithfulness!
O LORD! You are my portion;
I will wait reliant, still.

How good You are to those
whose hope remains in you,
to those who seek you now
with patience and with
quietness: We know that You
respond to faith, obedience
and You will never cast
us off from You in wrath!

Why should we groan,
complain,
when we are disciplined
for sins by which we've grieved
our LORD? Let us, at last,
acknowledge all we've done
and failed to do; rebellion is
the cause of tragedies
that leave us all aghast.

I called upon Your name,
O LORD. Up from the
deepest pit
You heard my prayer;
You came
to me. And, when I called,
You counselled, 'Do not fear.'
Do not now close your ears:

of every crime, you'd
be appalled!

You've seen the grievous
wrongs
the aliens have wrought;
You've heard the mocking and
their lies. They surely mean
my end. LORD, let there be
a recompense for hate.
Give to them what they
deserve—
Let Heaven's peace begin.

THE PENURY
Chapter 4

**I've seen the finest gold
become so dull, its lustre
gone;** all worth destroyed,
and precious gems
once sacred, scattered on
the city streets. Like Zion:
once worth their weight in gold
but now, a broken jar of clay;
the potter's joy now gone.

The punishment of Israel
is worse than Sodom and
Gomorrah: all reduced to ash.
Your princes once displayed
a purity, integrity,
but now they're blackened by
the soot of sin. Those slain
are better off when weighed.

No one believed that it
would come to this! It was
iniquity–by prophets, priests
and kings. The populace
then followed after them.
But now they grope in ash
to find a way to *LIGHT*–
we search in vain for grace.

Our end was near, our days
were short and none would aid
us in the streets of home.
And, swifter than a raid
where arrows, aimed,
would fly,
the chosen people of
the LORD
fell in the traps of aliens…
the exile passes, sin is paid.

THE CONSEQUENCE
Chapter 5

Remember us, O LORD,
See now the depth of our
disgrace. Inheritance is gone,
our homes: abode of aliens.
Those slaves now rule;
we're bound
and there is none to free
us from these chains; we risk
our lives for bread, our
only means. Our youths
now toil through all

their days at millstones, boys
are called to carry wood, all joy
has gone, no music calms
our fears, these woes for sin.
Our beasts are faint, our eyes
grow dim. Mount Zion is quite
desolate, a jackal's lair
becomes.

O LORD, You reign
through time
and evermore; Your Throne
endures always. Why do
You now forget Your Clans
so long? Renew us, LORD,
We long for restoration.
Restore our days just as
the days long past: Your Plans!

THE LAMENT OF
JEREMIAH
Tune: *Dominus Regit me*
8.7.8.7. Iambic

When shadows claim the
path ahead,
Sorrow enfolding darkness,
I search for answers to
life's quest—
God's shining *LIGHT* will
guide us.

When blindly we have sought
the path

To tread by faith now, always,
We need the comfort of
Your map,
Your searching *LIGHT*
to find us.

LORD, Your compassions
do not fail,
They are renewed each
morning;
How great Your faithfulness,
O LORD,
Guard, salient *LIGHT*, till
dawning.

O LORD, You are this dark
world's *LIGHT*,
Shine in our hearts, we
now pray:
Restore our soul, renew
our days;
Lead, saving *LIGHT*, each
new day.

..... oOo .....

THE TEMPESTUOUS YEARS

EZEKIEL

You have read much of Israel and Judah's history in these pages. As I now introduce myself to you, I must confess that you will be astounded at the news that I must convey to you. The 'Picture Parables' are spectacular, awesome!

I am Ezekiel. The LORD has called me to a high and holy vocation. However, the news that I must share with you is so tempestuous, I all but hesitate to stand my ground. But speak I must for Israel—Judah—is in exile.

The year is 597 BC. The Babylonian Empire has trampled us into the arid sands. Is this the end? I do have news for you! It will take time to tell it well. I must begin:

MY INITIAL VISION
Chapter 1

I am Ezekiel: *'God is Strong',*
You've heard of me, no doubt. My father was Buzi. I now reside in Babylon by Kebar, a major river in that land. As priest, my role had been to represent the worshippers before the LORD. But now, the role reversed, I am to represent the LORD, to be His spokesman, ready to proclaim His word to Israel.

I was arrested, halted, stilled, amazed—a vision splendid had transformed the Earth, the skies. A brilliant radiance beyond all worldly reasoning had trapped my startled gaze. And then, a windstorm came upon me unawares.

A fire burst from the lightning, glowing as of molten metal rare. One's mind is challenged by such awesomeness. The fire displayed four creatures. But, though their countenance resembled humans, each did reveal four faces and four wings.

Their feet seemed hooved
and underneath their wings,
on all four sides of them,
there were the hands of
active men. Those faces,
manly, yet had other
features quite remarkable:
one side, on the right, was
leonine and on the left, an
ox! Each also had an eagle's
face exposed. This was no
earthly sight. I was amazed
at what I saw that day.

The creatures' wings were
wide and upward spread. I
looked above, the sky then
shone as icicles. Two wings
on each, spread out to
touch—this spoke
to me of unity, cohesion,
too. The other wings
concealed their frame.

The movement of their
wings brought mighty
sounds to me of rushing
water, flooded streams.
This was, to me, just as
the Voice of *YHVH*,
El Shaddai.

I also saw some wheels—
What wheels they were,
those unique wheels. Those
wheels were each inside of
wheels and they were
moving in an 'every-which-
way' path as offered them.
Those wheels, they headed
north, south, east
and west. Those wheels had
eyes around their rims.
This very feature spoke to
me of *YHVH*–LORD!
He, the sovereign LORD,
was in control—He sees all
things and He abides in
every place!

I heard The Voice! It came
to me from high above.
I saw, in form, a man but
glowing as the molten metal
in the flames. A brilliant
Light suffused His being in
rays as of a rainbow's
radiance. This was too
glorious for me.
I fell before the LORD.

THE CALLING
Chapter 2

The *YHVH*–LORD
has called just now to me:

Come, son of man, stand up.
I'll take your hand to raise
you up. O son of man, be
strong; I'm sending you
unto My people, Israel. My
own rebellious clans—they
are so obstinate. The news
that you declare to them will
be such that, when it is
proclaimed, these words
will indicate My prophet
comes to them! And you, O
son of man, don't be afraid
though you will think that
scorpions, briars and thorns
surround you there.
Take now and eat what
I have given you.

I saw His hand stretched out
to me; He gave to me a
scroll and, when unrolled,
I read the dreaded words
of woe, also lament
and warning, too.

SWEET AND SOUR
Chapter 3

The *YHVH*–LORD
commanded me to eat that
scroll—so sweet until

I swallowed it! And then,
instructions came:

Go to the House of Israel.
I send you not to people of
strange tongues and alien
concepts of what's right and
wrong (you would be
welcomed, understood.)

I'm sending you to those
Israelis who have known of
Me yet fail to understand,
accept, My care, My love,
My will for them. They will
not heed your words for
they will not respond to Me.
So you must be as strong,
unyielding as they are. Do
not have fear! Yes! Be as
flint, unbreakable. Take
care to hear what I will say
and take it to your heart.
Go! Tell it well.

Then I was lifted up
and whisked away, across
it seemed, a large expanse.
I went with bitterness
(the scroll had this effect,)
but *YHVH* held me fast.
I found myself among
the Clans at Tel Abib; I sat
for seven days, entranced.

That solemn week complete,
I heard The Voice
once more:

Know, son of man, I have
prepared you for your task.
You are 'The Watchman'
now for Israel and I
will hold you as
accountable if you
should fail the task I give.
You are to warn all
Those so careless of the
consequence of sin. Be
sure you speak to offer
warnings of rebuke.

His hand again held me—
He took me to a plain and
there the Glory of the
LORD returned. I fell face
down again. The Spirit of
the LORD then lifted me.
He spoke:

Go, shut yourself inside
your house. And, tied with
ropes, mute, unapproached.
But! When I speak to you,
you'll be released, you'll
say: If you will listen, listen
now. If you refuse, you may
refuse; but know: there is an
awful consequence.

THE CLAY TABLET
Chapter 4

Now, son of man, take up
a tablet made of clay on
which you'll sketch
the city of Jerusalem.
Lay siege to it.
Then, take a pan of iron
and build it as a barricade.

When all is then in place,
lie down for you must bear
the sins of Israel. Then,
of Judah, for all of forty
days—a day to replicate a
year. First, left; then, right.
I'll tie you down. You will
not move until the 'Pictured
Parable' is done. Make sure
there is some wheat to bake
your bread; some beans and
lentils too. Each should be
weighed, sufficient for the
times that you'll recline.
Your food is cooked by your
own excrement—this is the
sign that Israel will eat a
food that is defiled
because of sin!

Not so, O LORD! I cannot
eat a meal that is defiled!
Is there no other way?

I hear your plea;
you'll bake your bread
the usual way each day.
But, know this, son of man,
the food supply for Zion's
city shall be cut. The people
will eat nought but rationed
meals of bread and water
with anxiety and deep
despair—they'll waste
away in want.

YHVH-LORD
Weighed in the Balance
Chapter 5

Now, son of man, take up
a sword and shave your ead
and beard. Then, take a set
of scales to weigh that hair.
Retain the hairs and place
them in three equal heaps:
when all the days of 'siege'
shall end, take up a third
and burn that hair. Then,
take a third and cast it to
the wind. But take the final
third then draw some
strands to secret them
within your robe. Next, cast
some of those threads
into the flames. This is, you
see, a 'Pictured Parable'
of Israel and its demise!

This is the lesson to be
heard: 'you've been unruly,
Israel; far worse than all
the aliens (you've known a
better Way but chose it not
to be). You see? I am
against you, Jerusalem,
your idols have besmirched
your worth; you've turned
from Me, so very far away.
For this dire circumstance:
a third will die by famine or
the plague; a third be cast
into the wind and smitten by
the sword. Though, some
are saved that they may be
renewed. Until the day when
exile is no more, you'll be a
ruin, a reproach, a warning
and a grief unbearable.
Hear now what I condemn:
"I AM", the YHVH–LORD,
has spoken now!

YHVH-LORD
The Mountains of Israel
Chapter 6

I need you, son of man, to
turn towards the mountain
heights of Israel. Declare
this news: O mountains of
Israel, now hear the words
of YHVH–LORD:

*this is what I will have to
say unto the hills, ravines,
the valley lands. A sword
will pierce your 'heart',
your Sanctuary will be
destroyed. Your people will
be slain at worship where
your idols are in pride
of place before My gaze.*

*Those idols will
come crashing down—
they'll turn to dust and you
will know I am the LORD,
the Holy One of Israel: the
YHVH, El Shaddai.*

*Begin to show remorse,
turn from your wickedness.
But! Know this too: there
will be some who will
escape the exile slaughter-
house then, they will once
again remember Me. They'll
know a sorrow in the soul
for every way they've
caused Me grief, your
suffering LORD. Begin now
to lament your wayward
ways and turn to Me again.
Then you will know I AM,
your LORD.*

*O may it be that, when you
see the slain upon the*

*mountains, under spreading
trees and every leafy oak,
you will remember,
turn to Me.*

YHVH-LORD
The End is Near
Chapter 7

*O son of man, the time has
come! The end is near.
From every place, all
compass points, the slain
reveal the recompense for
sin. This is disaster that
Israel has brought upon
themselves.
They hearkened not to
discipline; they turned their
backs on Zion's Sanctuary.
They closed their ears
against the prophecies that
warned of doom for all their
careless lack of faith.*

*The rod has burst to
bloom—this rod becomes a
punishment; its season
comes. The day has come,
arrived is Israel's doom.
Although the ram's horn
now will sound, they'll
hearken not.
All Israel will faint, strength*

failed. *All hands are limp
and knees will wilt for lack
of trust. The sackcloth will
be worn all grimy with its
ash. They'll cast aside their
treasury for it becomes a
plunder now. My Face is
turned from them. Mine is a
sorrow in a magnitude not
known to man.*

*The chains are now
employed as blood flows
in the streets. All pride
disintegrates as shame
replaces faith. They'll seek
My Shalom Peace but there
is none for them. What does
the prophet say?*

*They'll ask; How will the
priest now pray for us? The
house of God is desolate;
there are no priests who'll
pray for them. The king will
mourn his loss of crown, of
throne, of every power.*

*The people tremble as they
well realise, too late, that it
is all the standards owned
that their demise is certain,
sure. Know, I have judged
them now and they are
found without excuse.*

*It's then they'll know, as not
before, "I AM", The LORD.*

EZEKIEL
The Desecration
Chapter 8

Over a year has passed…
I am familiar now with how
it sounds, The Voice, the
LORD's amazing
resonance, to claim my 'rapt
attention when He speaks.
But, none-the-less, each
time He speaks to me, I am
entranced. He entered in my
vision's range, He spoke to
me once more while I
was sitting in my house with
all the Elders gathered there.
I felt His hand upon me.
When I looked, I saw a
person standing there.

Again, the brightness of His
form was like some molten
metal and His hand then
grasped my hair! He lifted,
carried me and—in
my vision then, I travelled
so it seemed, right to
Jerusalem. And then I stood
there, in the precincts of the
Temple, where a

gaudy idol held the pride of place. So, how detestable was this? The 'Glory of the LORD' shone round. He 'took' my gaze to where a hole was gouged into the Temple wall. He said, Now dig! And so I did. I saw a door. Go through that door, He said. Observe the ghastly things now perpetrated in this place.

How could this be? I saw a host of unclean animals portrayed on all the walls and crawling things detestable. To my dismay, I saw them all, Elders– seventy at least–each paying homage mid the cloud of incense rising there. What shame!

'The Man' then said to me: O son of man, you see what they have done? They think that, in the gloom of darkness, they'll be hid from Me. Besides, these sins are not the worst you'll see within the Sanctuary.

He took me to the north side where there was a group of women who were bowing in respect for Tummuz (the god of all fertility), whom they discovered via the hordes of Babylonia. How deep the grief of *YHVH*–LORD, Creator and Preserver of all things–the one true God on whom to cast all praise.

I then saw men who faced the sun, the object of their wonder worship now.

'The Man' then spoke again to me: Is this a trivial pursuit for men whose lives were dedicated once to *YHVH*–LORD? I can't forget this blatant sin, this putrid perfidy!

EZEKIEL
The Saving Sign
Chapter 9

I heard Him call the guards—they came with weapons drawn. These men were in the company of one—a scribe—whose garb was linen, pure. He had

a kit for writing purposes
in hand. 'The Glory of the
LORD' arose and moved
right to the threshold of the
Temple there. He gave
instructions to the scribe:
Go through this city and
prepare to place the letter
tav—so like a cross*.

How strange, the final letter
of the Hebrew alphabet—
upon the heads of all who
grieve, lamenting all the
things that are detestable
within this place. The duty
of the guards was then
to slay all those who did not
wear that 'cross' sign on
their foreheads there. Has
this significance for us?

He said: Begin within the
Sanctuary. I fell down on
the ground. O Sovereign
LORD, will You destroy the
remnant of Israel without
relent, with no one saved?
He answered me in
Solemn words:

*The sins of Israel are so
great, immense beyond
degree, I can't now stay My
hand–the land is swamped*

*in blood; injustice stains in
depth the streets of all
Jerusalem. The people gloat
that I have left this land and
do not see their sin!*

* ancient form of Hebrew
letter *tav*: a cross!

EZEKIEL
The Glory Departs
Chapter 10

The Sapphire throne now
glowed above as *YHVH–*
LORD declared unto
The scribe:

*Go in among the wheels,
the wheels within the wheels
under the winged cherubim.
Take burning coals from
them and scatter them.*

'The Glory of the LORD'
then moved up to the
threshold of the Temple and
a cloud loomed all
about. The court was filled
with radiance. God's voice
was heard:

*Take fire and place
it now within the hands
of the good scribe.*

He took the fire and walked
beneath the cherubim
wings. Here were those
wheels once more, the
wheels within those wheels;
they did reside beside the
cherubim.

The wheels went 'every-
which-way' of the cherubim
and each of them were
covered with some
searching eyes—as were the
wheels, all four, and
cherubim, all four—all, full
of eyes: all seeing, viewing,
as they moved. The
cherubim, all four
had faces, yes—each: four!
The wheels remained apace
with all the cherubim—they
moved as one. 'The Glory
of the LORD' remained
with them. I'd seen these
splendid creatures at Kebar.

EZEKIEL, *YHVH*-LORD
Judgement Falls
Chapter 11:1-15

The Spirit of the LORD
then came and lifted me. He
brought me to the Eastern
gate. I saw there just

twenty-five men—these
were the leaders of Israel—
now all these men stood as
condemned. The LORD
requested that I prophesy
against these men.
Now, listen to God's word:

*O House of Israel, I read
your mind. You've
slaughtered all
your kin. You've filled these
streets with all the slain.
You fear the sword–it is
the sword that I will wield
against you all. Then
you will know "I AM",
the YHVH, El Shaddai.*

O Sovereign LORD, I cried,
will You annihilate Israel–
its remnant, those of worth?

YHVH-LORD,
EZEKIEL
The Promise Gained
Chapter 11:16-25

*Though I have sent them far
away, and scattered them
among the aliens, I've been
for them a Sanctuary.
Therefore, I will gather
them and lead them back to
Home! They will return.*

*They will remove all idols
from their midst. I'll give to
them an undivided heart.
I'll give to them a spirit that
is new. Their hearts of stone
I will remove; they'll gain a
heart of flesh. Then they will
follow My decrees;
they will take care to keep
the Law for they'll be Mine,
"I AM" Eternal God,
the YHVH–LORD.*

The cherubim beside the
wheels spread out their
wings and 'The Glory of the
LORD' was above them.
Then He moved eastward,
above the Mount of Olives.
The Spirit lifted me and
brought me to the exiles in
old Babylon. And then the
vision I had seen was gone.
I told the exiles everything.

YHVH-LORD
The Symbols of Exile
Chapter 12

*Know, son of man, you live
among a people so
rebellious that they've eyes
to see but they are blind;*

*they've ears to hear, they do
not hear, they dig
their heels into the ground,
won't budge to save
themselves! I need you to
portray for Me An exile of
the direst ilk. Pack up your
bags while all the others
watch and then you must
set out upon a 'march' to
exile now. In daytime, pack
your bags; at night,
commence to dig into the
wall: 'set out' upon
the journey, carrying the
load. And place a cover on
your face—You'll be a sign.*

I did as I was asked with
care to show intent to all
who saw the 'sign'.

*Did that rebellious House
of Israel ask, What's this,
why have you packed your
bags? Then, say to them:
I am a sign to you of what
will happen to you all e'er
long for what's displayed in
'Picture Parables' will
surely come to you. It's by
this way they'll know
"I AM", the YHVH–LORD,
when I disperse them far*

abroad. A few are spared
so they, one day, will then
acknowledge Me and
change their wayward
minds. O son of man, now
tremble, show a fear when
eating food. Explain that
Israel will live in deep
anxiety when they are then
confronted with exile.

And when Israel begins to
taunt, to gloat that nothing
happens of your prophecy,
make sure they realise that
it is rebellion that ensures;
the end will come. I will
fulfil all that I say. All Israel
thinks these visions rare
will speak of future days.
Indeed, my words are not
delayed. The host of
Babylon returns to gather
up the rest of you!

YHVH-LORD
The Condemnation
Chapter 13.

You'll prophesy to prophets
now. Their prophecies—
imagined—have no place in
Truth. Woe to those foolish
prattlers! They speak of
what they do not know.

Prophets have not
investigated all the signs
of coming disarray. Their
truth is falsehood, their
divinations—blatant lies!

Now, say to them: I am
against you and My hand
is raised against your lies.
You will not stand among
the Council of My people
and you'll be forgotten
in the annuls of the
nation's history.

You still declare a 'shalom'
peace where peace no
longer dwells! You
whitewash flimsy walls—
when rain begins to fall in
floods and hailstones hurtle
down upon your towns,
you'll wonder why those
walls collapse. The white-
wash is the strength of your
great argument. It will
disintegrate just like
your inane prophecies.

I offer now a prophecy
against conniving women
who sew magic charms to
gowns. How could you thus
entrap your people while
you save yourselves? You

*need to know I will set free
those you ensnare like birds.
The honest people will no
longer fall as prey to you.
Because you have beset the
righteous with your lies,
now: hear the Truth–they
will be saved, you will not!
I'll save My people from
your hands. Then you will
know "I AM", The LORD!*

EZEKIEL and
YHVH-LORD
Inescapable Justice
Chapter 14

Some elders came to me—
to sit and chat, inquire of me
just what the LORD would
say. The *YHVH*–LORD
then spoke to me:

*These men have set up idols
in their hearts—they have
no place for Me. I'll not
give you a word to speak for
Me. I'll speak to them
Myself! When these, My
people
set up idols in their hearts,
do not expect encouraging
response from Me! This is
what I have to say: I will*

*answer you in words that so
condemn your ways. Hear
now: My purpose is to shake
you wide awake, proclaim
to you: repent! Turn from
your idols and
renounce your wickedness.
You separate yourselves
from Me and place a
worthless stump, a
stumbling block against
My sound advice. Know now
that you will be cut off from
Israel. Admit your guilt for,
when My people do return,
they'll not defile themselves
because of vile advice!*

*Now, son of man, I'll share
with you the strength
of Truth, of goodness and
of righteousness: If so, and
where, I see a nation near
and bathing in
unrighteousness.*

*Even if old Noah, Daniel
or Job, should wallow with
them there—I'll not excuse
an action of rebellion. Know
this, O son of man, there are
now four dire judgements
that await all
those who choose to follow*

*evil paths: the sword, the
plague and famine and wild
beasts. But, son of man,
you'll be consoled when you
observe the deeds of holy
people—those who do not
bow the bended knee to
Godlessness. You'll know
there is a purpose in the
judgements now
proclaimed to you.*

YHVH-LORD
The Wilting Vine
Chapter 15

*O son of man, I'll question
you: why is the wood that
holds a vine in place
thought better than the
wood of any other tree?
The vine's wood is not taken
for a home or furniture and
is it useful as a tool
when burned to ash?*

*Now, learn the lesson of the
vine and other trees: the
vine will stand for Israel.
The forest trees are alien to
the vine. The vine will hold
no special relevance
if it is rotten at its heart!*

*Therefore, as I have given
wood of the vine among the
forest giants as fuel for
flames, so will I treat the
people living in Jerusalem.
The land is desolate for the
people's unfaithfulness.*

YHVH-LORD
Unfaithfulness
Chapter 16

*Confront Jerusalem, these
people once accounted as
My own. Now say to them,
declare: You know your
history. You've no one
who'll take pity now. Yet I,
your sovereign LORD, have
pitied you. I took the 'babe'
rejected, 'lone, and helped
you grow just like a plant
out in the fields of Israel.*

*You grew up to maturity—
a jewel beautiful and
sought—a lovely 'virgin
bride'. I made a lasting
covenant with you; your
fame spread far and wide.
You were revered until, in
time, you then succumbed to
pride. A prostitute you*

then became, O Israel. A
woe, a woe to you! Those
lofty shrines degraded you.
Weak-willed and ever so
promiscuous, you have
preferred the stranger to the
One who gave you love.

Know this: I gather all the
evil, lewd, and lawless louts
to gaze upon your blatant
nakedness because you have
forgotten all your own
heritage, also the One who
brought you out of slavery
and set your feet towards
My Sanctuary. You have
profaned the Holy Place,
became depraved far worse
than aliens. As Sodom and
Gomorrah did give up their
life to compromise and
more wicked than Samaria,
how can you think there
is no consequence? You
brought this on yourselves.
Learn now! I'll deal with
you as you deserve because
you have despised your
precious covenant.

Yet I, the LORD,
remember well the past—
your will to learn, to love!

I will establish a pure,
Lasting covenant. Then you
will know, remember, too,
I am the YHVH–LORD.
My promise is (hold on to
it)—I'll make an everlasting
covenant: ATONEMENT
FOR YOUR SINS, that you
may be AT-ONE with Me—
I will become the 'Caphah'
[cover] for your sin,
your blatant waywardness.

YHVH-LORD
'Picture Parables'
Chapter 17

The *YHVH*–LORD had
come again:

O son of man, I want you
now to illustrate a parable
that Israel will understand
just what it is that they must
know: An eagle, so majestic,
with long feathers, a full
plumage and
such powerful wings
displayed bright rainbow
colours for the populace to
see. The eagle flew to
Lebanon and seized a
topmost cedar branch so
strong and carried it, then

*planted it within a merchant
city there. And then the
branch became a splendid
vine. This eagle planted
fertile seeds by flowing
streams and glens.
Another eagle, flying high
was mighty in the lofty
heights. The vine stretched
out each branch and asked
for water, sustenance.*

*I question Israel: Will this
strong vine then survive? Its
fruit has been purloined, it
withers; soon the vine could
die. Now, if one takes,
transplants the vine, then
will it thrive? The east wind
spoils the verdant growth.*

*O son of man, now say to
Israel: "The King of
Babylon has taken to his
land the vine of Israel and,
if the vine should cling to
Egypt still, to find support,
the vine will surely wilt.
Therefore, be sure of this,
for broken covenants,
your vine, displaced,
shall surely fail.
The fleeing troops
of Israel's king will fall,
slain by the sword.*

*Survivors will be scattered
to the wind. You'll know, I
am the LORD. I promise
you that I will take a branch
of cedar, plant, and nurture
it upon the lofty height of
Israel. It will produce its
fruit—a splendid cedar tree.*

*The birds from near and far
shall rest in it and all the
trees in this fair field will
know I am the LORD. I
bring down tall trees but I'll
help the low to grow so tall
The 'green tree' will dry up,
The 'dry tree' flourish well.
So I, the YHVH–LORD,
have spoken and I will fulfil
these fateful words!*

YHVH-LORD: SIN'S CONSEQUENCE
–A Lament–
Chapter 18

The *YHVH*–LORD
now speaks:

*What do you mean by
mouthing proverbs without
wisdom still? It seems the only
adage you recall: "The fathers
eat sour grapes*

and so the children's teeth
are set on edge (with
utter bitterness)'. Your
obstinance I will not bear!
You'll hear now My Lament:
It's time you saw the Truth
of it. Hear now My word of it:
Yes, every soul belongs to Me:
the father, mother and, the
child. It's everyone, not this or
that: 'The soul that sins
shall die!'

All are alike, so each must bear
sin's consequence–all, in that
mould. Suppose you find a
citizen who will remain
unstained by sin. He will not
bow to idols placed
at worship shrines.

He treats his neighbours with
respect; he does not rob, he
does no harm, he follows My
decrees, is faithful, shines!
Suppose his son defied his
dad, he sins prolifically. Will he
be saved because his dad
has lived a holy life?
He won't!
Suppose his son then has a
son who sees the sins his dad
commits and, though he
sees, to copy them,
he won't!

This son of son will surely live.
His father dies for his own sins;
why does the son not share his
guilt? The son remains
untainted by the sins his father
perpetrates. The son has lived
a holy life, not rent.
True righteousness is credited;
the wrong is noted–sinners die!
Why do you choose to die,
O Israel? I take no pleasure in
your rampant sins. Repent!

YHVH-LORD
The Royal Lament
Chapter 19

Now, hear another 'Picture
Parable': How gracious is the
lioness—so well respected by
all lions. She raised her cubs
with care.
One cub was raised to be
a lion that tore its victims and
devouring all that challenged
him. The nations heard, they
planned revenge, entrapped
him there.
The lioness was much
distressed. She took another
cub and trained him well to be
a powerful lion.
He learned how to devour his
prey. Men's strongholds were
destroyed for he devoured all

towns. *The nations mobilized
their troops, they spread their
nets and won the day.
The mighty lion was tamed—
entrapped, within a pit, placed
within a cage and dragged
to Babylon.
He was imprisoned there.
The lion's roar was heard no
more, his wilful ways were
rectified; the terror, then,
was gone.*

*Your mother, 'Israel', was like
a fruitful vine—its branches
spread afar;
abundant waters nurtured her.
Her branch was strong, fit for
the sceptre of a king. But it was
uprooted and the 'east wind'
wilted her.*

*And now the fruitful vine
that was, is planted deep within
an arid land, a dry and thirsty
land where fire
spread through the branch,
consuming all the fruit.
There are no branches now
fit for the sceptre
of the sire.*

EZEKIEL 20:
The Rebellious Nation
Chapter 20:1-29

The elders came again to sit
with me and chew with me
upon a meagre meal. They
came for all desired to quiz
me all about the dire distress
we knew.
The *YHVH*–LORD then
spoke to me:

*As surely as I live, I won't
allow them to inquire of Me!
I challenge you, O son of
man, to judge them, tell
them all the reason why
they've earned My wrath.
I chose the clans of Israel.
I then revealed Myself, My
ways, My will, to them. They
did not listen, then or now! I
found for them a verdant
land where 'milk and
honey' flow. I gave
them aid, I nurtured them,
discipled them—they would
not understand that
waywardness has
consequence. They have
rebelled, so justice must be
done. I pitied them, I
counselled them to follow
each and every guideline
that was offered them: keep
Sabbaths, Laws, as holy as
My Name: you'll know
"I AM", the YHVH–LORD.*

They have rebelled, through
All the year——in every
circumstance of life; they
failed to live as whole.
They have forgotten Me;
they've each turned to their
own, their evil ways.

Judgement–Choice–Restoration
Chapter 20:30-49

O son of man, now say to
Israel: Will you defile
yourselves just as your
forebears did throughout
their lives! Your sacrifice of
sons is most abominable!
A sacrilege!

It's your desire to emulate
the nations round about. So,
I declare to you that I will
rule you with a mighty hand
with arm outstretched
in wrath
for every sin you have
employed. I've taken note of
each as you pass by. Know
this: My punishment
will be a purging of
your souls.

Go now! Go! Serve
your idols—each and

every one. But, after that,
you'll listen, learn, and lean
on Me for, on the holy
mount, Jerusalem, one day
this nation will return
to Me. And I will, at that
time, return you to your
land and you will be a holy
nation serving Me.

O son of man, now set your
face towards the south.
Speak to the forests there.
Beware, a fire shall
suddenly descend to claim
all trees—both green and
dry. This fire will search the
land and people too!
They'll know I kindled
all those flames.

O Sovereign LORD, I said,
they are responding now, all
those who visited. The
Elders say, Ezekiel, we
know you speak in 'Picture
Parables' so, what you say
just can't be true!

The Sword of Judgement
Chapter 21

O son of man, it's time to
preach against Jerusalem

and Israel, against the
Sanctuary. Proclaim:
I am against you now;
I draw My sword to cut
you off forthwith from holy
things. Unsheathed,
My sword and aimed from
north to south. You'll know
it's drawn. Groan, son of
man, reveal to all your
sorrowed, broken heart.

Now, listen, when
they ask the reason why,
explain to them it is because
the news is coming now.
Then at its tidings, hearts
will melt, all hands grow
limp, the knees succumb.
They'll feel the force of
grief: it's unassuaged.

A sword descends; it's
sharp, it glints against the
sun, it's grasped within the
hand. Cry out; wail for the
wickedness of princes who
will profess their hope
in devious ways to free
the land. Therefore, they
will be slain; it's time
to weep, to beat your
breast!"

The LORD has spoken

yet again:

Mark out two roads the
King of Babylon may take.
Set up a signpost to the City
then. One route leads into
Rabbah Ammon, the other
heads towards Jerusalem.
The King of Babylon will
cast his lots, consult his
many gods; he'll see it is
Jerusalem to which his
army moves forthwith.

Because of all your guilt of
sin, profane and wicked
prince of Israel, your day
has come. Take off your
turban and remove the
crown. You will not see the
like again. From this day
forth, exalted are brought
low! Ruin, until He comes,
the only One to whom it
rightfully belongs. It shall
be His, the righteous One!

The City of Sin
Chapter 22

O son of man, you'll
prophesy about My
judgement of Jerusalem.
Confront her with the many

ways that she has
perpetrated sins detestable.
The city's blood runs
deep—it is not quenched.
You've closed the gates
on steadfast faith
so, you have also closed
your days: your end of years
has come—you'll be a
laughing stock to all your
foes. They'll mock

O son of man, the House of
Israel becomes but dross to
Me—all are as copper, iron,
the tin, the lead now smelted
in a furnace violent.
Just as the molten metal,
Israel, you'll all be melted
down. Then you
will know that I have judged
you and you have not
passed the test.

You've seen their wicked
ways, O son of man. I've
searched for one to build
a wall, to stand within
the open gap to intercede
for all My people, Israel.
I've found not one
who'd pray for them that
there would be no need
to judge, destroy the land.
Not one to intercede!

THE SISTERS:
Oholah And Oholibah
Chapter 23

We'll chat awhile with
you, so listen in:
we are so much alike—
two peas within a pod,
they say. Yes, we were just
like twins: As kin as keen
as we, we chose to make
our merry way through
life by seeing which of us
two twins could more
than match the other at
our play. Our play,
you dare to ask?
Well, we are prostitutes!
We lusted after lovers all
the while, our riches piled
on high. The guys were
grand in Egypt's haunts
and we did flaunt
ourselves with them!

The ways of men, for us,
would sometimes be
quite ill and fraught
with dangers but
we both conspired
to make the most of it,
those years; this was
our wayward way.

I am Oholah and as if

you didn't know, I
represent Samaria: the
Israel of old! My day has
surely come; I'm naked
now, I lay in want, bereft
of kindness anywhere,
the victim of my helpless
circumstance: I am about
to die for this. Assyria has
knocked; I go to them!

I am the sister of Samaria:
That's right, Oholah, gone
from me. You see, Israel—
my sister—was then
taken, all by force,
into the great Assyria.
Now I, Oholibah—her
sister, who pursued her
chosen way of life, have
performed outlandish acts.
I prostituted, in my lust,
all that had been my
heritage. I am, you see,
Jerusalem! I took no note
of what became of Oholah
in her promiscuous ways.
I chose to walk all the
identical paths she took,
my lust beyond her own!

The *YHVH*–LORD has
spoken now. He has
confronted me with all
my sins. He said to me:

I will stir up your lovers! Yes,
the ones from whom you
turned. But! Now they will
return, they will repay you for
your wilful ways;
they'll strip you of your finery,
your sons and daughters will
be taken from your care;
you're left a destitute
all your days.
Your lewdness and your lust
caused aliens to take you from
the YHVH–LORD.
You'll drink your sister's bitter
cup. I have spoken: "I AM",
YHVH says.

I heard that *YHVH's*
man–Ezekiel–will
challenge us for YHVH
now: I fear the outcome of
that speech!

AN ELDER
The Cooking Pot
Chapter 24

Oh, look at him! What is
he up to now, our prophet
man? Him, and his
'Picture-Parables'! I ask
you, what is he up to with
that pot? Is he about to
cook a scrumptious meal

for us, a meal to satisfy?

We came upon him
unawares—as elders,
we've a right to this.
I will say this of him—
He is a gracious host
and wise.

He's cooking simple soup
it seems and by the sound
of things, this soup will
lead to grouches once
again for us! Grudge
Soup, that's it!
We've been frustrated,
true. So many issues on
our list to fling at him.

He full well knows the
why and where of it
so why won't he accept
that he's at fault?
Harangues all have
their place, of course,
but we are sick of them
and of his measly soup,
no doubt…
Aromas fill the air.
Hmmm,
perhaps his soup will be
more to our taste today.

The cooking pot is on the
coals And into it goes all

the meat. What meat, the
very best there is! He'll
need to watch that pot;
Be sure it doesn't fry the
meat! The flames conspire
to spoil the food I'm sure
he had in mind. What
now? He mutters in his
beard. I do not like the
sound of it at all!

EZEKIEL, *YHVH*–LORD

It was the ninth year, tenth
day, the tenth month too:
the *YHWH*–LORD
instructed me to note the
date and said:

*This is the very day that
Babylon lays siege against
Jerusalem so, use this 'Picture-
Parable': Put on the
cooking pot
and pour some water in
the pot; cut up some meat—
the choicest cuts—prime lamb,
leg and shoulder,
in the pot.*

*Make sure the bones
are best, the pick of all
the precious flock,
then pile the wood to cook*

the lot upon the coals.
Why cook these bones?

Take note:
There is a woe upon the land
for there is bloodshed in
the street. Jerusalem now
stands condemned;
The blood she shed surrounds
her now. She poured that blood
upon the Rock—no dust can
cover it, that blood will not
be stemmed.

Woe to the city on the height,
the 'caldron' of her bones is
now alight; the wood is kindled
and the flames hold heat
profound to cook all well.
The meat is spiced, the bones
are charred. The pot is empty.
Now, set it on the fiery coals–
The copper glows, is melted:
at the last, it's ground!

EZEKIEL
My Beloved's Death

How may I hold a wordless
grief deep in my heart?
There are no channels for a
falling tear, no access for
the woe I hold within my
tortured soul. My own
beloved one, my wife,
the sunshine of my life,
passed on this eve to be
with *YHVH*-LORD.

Yet, while
I know a joy for her
(now in the presence of
the King of kings),
the sorrows that
surrounded me these exiled
years, the grief I know
has no respite. The LORD
requested me to hold within
my heart all that I feel for
her, my wife. There's no
respite away from woe,
yet I'll obey—the LORD
knows why the muteness of
my grief will, somehow,
bring a solace now to
someone else.

Who could it be, or what, I
ask? What is His word for
me, for Israel? Here is
God's word to all:

My Sanctuary will be
no more! Your greatest
pride, the object of your
love: the Holy Place of
comfort there.

You will not weep, no woe
shall pass your lips. This
day, the desecration of the

*Sanctuary will be because
you sinned without respite,
regret, repine. Your prophet
here, Ezekiel, will be a sign
for you. Now see how
silently he bears his grief.
And when you hear the
news, you'll know "I AM",
the YHVH–LORD.*

*Ezekiel, O son of man,
now know that, on the day
that the delight of Israel
has been destroyed, a
fugitive will trek to you to
bring the news. And, on that
day you'll find your speech
again, your silence will
have passed. They'll know
"I AM", the LORD.*

YHVH–LORD
The Surrounding Nations
Chapters 25 – 32

*These are the prophecies
that you must speak, O son
of man, against the nations
that surround all Israel.
Proclaim the news
with power from now:
All, hear the word of
YHVH–LORD: because you
gloated with 'Aha!' when*

*you espied the Sanctuary
laid waste when Judah went
to Babylon as exiles, so
the peoples of the East will
come, invade your land.
Your city will be pastureland
for camels. And you clapped
your hands, you stamped
your feet with joy—a glee
despicable. Because of this,
My hand is out-stretched
to judge you all.*

Against Moab:
*Because you made great
news of it: you scorned
Israel, proclaiming its
demise—as other nations
so; your flanks will be
exposed, beginning with
your bold frontiers.
You'll be possessed
by aliens. And in
your punishment, you'll
know that YHVH is the
Sovereign LORD!*

Against Edom:
*You took revenge upon
a people decimated, shorn
of all their wealth, their
land. You're guilty for this
crime. Therefore: I'll
stretch My hand upon your
nation now. I'll lay it waste*

*that day. There is no justice
where an evil heart remains
immune from a regret or
fear of consequence. You'll
know My vengeance now!*

Against Philistia:

*You acted with a malice in
your heart and you have
sought, with ancient
hatreds, to destroy Judah.
Therefore: I'll stretch My
hand against you now in
consequence. I find a wrath
against all sinfulness.
I am the YHVH–LORD!*

Against Tyre:

*I am against you, Tyre!
You were so glad to see
a nation broken, on its
knees. Therefore: you'll find
that all the nations round
about will fall on you like
waves upon the shore. Your
city, prized, will then
become a place where
fishermen will spread
their nets. You'll be a
plunder for all nations. I
have now ruled against you
and it will be done!*

YHVH-LORD

A Lament for Tyre
Ezekiel 27 – 28

*You think within your heart
your beauty's perfect, that
there is no other like to it.
You were magnificent.
Your true domain,
the mighty sea, saw all your
ships come sailing by. Of
cedar, oak, your decks of ivory,
your sails of linen finery.
You had much gain.
The nations near and far
applauded all your wealth,
all carried by the oarsmen, by
the breeze and waves.
But be afraid, I say to you:
great nation of a maritime
intent, your wealth, your wares,
will sink in salty seas!*

*Your shipwreck is immense;
how great will be the mourning
of your mighty mariners for you
will be submerged in cruel seas.
The depth of many waters will
obliterate you all. All those who
witness your demise will be
appalled at pride's decrease.*

*I prophesy against Tyre's king:
It was because the pride you
held in thinking you were 'god',
at last your ruin came. You*

thought your throne the place
for ruling all the seas.
Know this: you are no 'god',
you are a measly man!
You think you're wise?
The pride of wishful
thought is your disease.
Therefore, because you think
your wisdom far outweighs
the strength of all and giving
you the right to plunder
as you wrongly willed,
the foreigners will take your
life. Then, all the nations that
had once applauded you,
will be appalled.

I am the Sovereign LORD!

A PHOENICIAN
SAILOR
Ezekiel 27

We've plied the Seven
Seas! Our ships are
mighty ships—their sails
top all the rest and taller
than the cedars of all
Lebanon! We've crafted
all our ships from cedars
and the oaks. How grand
they look upon the waters,
even when
the waves are harsh and
high. But, we are used to
wind and wave. We have
amassed great wealth.
Phoenicia is renowned for
mightiness. The winds, the
waves, have carried us to
far-off lands where money
changes hands for all our
wares and worth. We've
heard some whispers
on the wind that trouble
brews. We have no fear of
that—we are the mighty
mariners. What's this?
There is a great west wind
that's beating up the surf.
The fiercest storm I've
seen. Take down those
sails, secure the anchor
and hold fast to all the
oars… The waves, they
reach new heights I fear
what will befall us in this
gale. What will become
of all our mighty ships ?

YHVH-LORD
Against Sidon
Ezekiel 28

I am against you, Sidon, and
I'll gain great glory in your
streets and alleyways—
Your people then will know
I am the LORD, the Holy
One. There'll be a plague

*upon your people, such that
blood will flow, the slain
will fall by sharpened
swords: it will be done!
I am against you, Pharaoh,
great, the king of Egypt. You
are powerful, a 'monster of
the deep' for all
your wicked ways. You say,
The Nile is mine, I made it
mine. But! Know this now:
beware, the angler's hook.
You will become the
'food' for all the fray!*

*idols, too, will go; your king
will lose his crown though
he will speak denial.
So, son of man, know this:
I've broken the strong arm
of Egypt's king. He cannot
wield his bloodied sword.
His word is weak for
Babylon has now begun to
brandish all their power
and Egypt is dispersed
among the countries of the
Earth. Then: all will know
"I AM", the LORD!*

A Lament For Egypt
Ezekiel 30

*Alas for Egypt, 'Queen of
all the South'. Your day is
near; the dawn of death will
soon appear—dense cloud
portends the gloom for
swords will come upon your
peoples—Cush as well.
Arabia and Libya will fall.
Nought can dismiss their
doom. The King of Babylon
will send his troops—those
ruthless men—to take
control, destroy the land.
The streams that feed the
Nile will cease to flow. A
wasteland now awaits. Your*

The 'Cedar' of Lebanon
Ezekiel 31

*Proclaim this news, O son of
man: "What majesty: the
'Cedar Tree'!
What tree in all the forest can
now be compared to you,
the 'Tree'?
There was, of course, Assyria.
Now, what a 'Tree' was she!
That nation towered on high,
its branches covered all
the 'forest' round, much drier.*

*But waters nurtured well
the 'Cedar Tree'. It grew
beyond all trees that*

sheltered there under its
canopy for care.
And all the forest's birds
would nest high in its boughs:
the animals would
shelter there—
majestic, beautiful this
'Tree' so rare.

No 'trees' could rival this,
the 'Cedar Tree'. Therefore,
a judgement comes unto
the 'Tree' of Lebanon: Because
it towers high, it will be lopped.
Those sheltering will flee for
life. The deep springs are in
mourning now: the 'Cedar'
disregarded flaws!

A LAMENT FOR
PHARAOH
Ezekiel 32

You are the 'roaring lion':
your power was manifest
through all the Earth. How
goes it with your soul today?
You are 'leviathan', the mighty
monster of the sea; I'll cast My
net upon you now. You'll be
entangled, die.

At your demise, the moon,
the stars, will hide their light;

the sun enshrouded in a cloud:
the earth grows dim in grief
because of you. All hearts
will sorrow, so appalled at such
tremendous loss. Your land
becomes quite desolate
with no reprieve.

This is the lament all those
who witness the demise will
chant: now, wail for them,
O son of man, all Egypt and
Assyria, Elam, Meshech and
Tubal, Edom too; the princes of
the North—Sidon, Phoenicia,
and now: the king of Egypt,
all with blame.

YHVH–LORD and
EZEKIEL
The Watchman
Ezekiel 33:1 – 20

O son of man, these are My
plans: Assess each situation
on its merit as you move
among the captives through
this land. I have apportioned
you to be activities for good
or ill. My watchman!
Be alert to all,

He said, the YHVH-LORD
to me, this news:

The whole responsibility,
is on my shoulders
and that I will bear the
blame if, when someone
has acted quite unwisely,
and besmirched the Holy
Name. But I must turn
my back without a word
of reprimand nor call to
account the deed; I'll bear
responsibility! Or, if a man
who acts in righteousness
would think his righteous
deed would earn him points
with God, that man should
not escape the judgement
that would come upon him
in this alien land. The
watchman's task is crucial
now for everyone will wait
to hear the ram's horn
sounding out a warning to
take care, take cover, seek
a refuge and be safe.

He calls me 'son of man':
I've heard that call again—
He said to me, He'd made
me watchman for the Clans
of Israel. I'll hear the words
I must convey. He said
that I must carry them to all
the captives for they must
be told what to expect when
they transgress His

righteous Law. He said I'd
be accountable. But if—
He said—I will fulfil this
task, I would be saved!

THE MESSENGER
Ezekiel 33:21 – 33

I've travelled far with this
sad news; my feet are
blistered and my back cries
out in pain for each and
every mile I've sped to tell
of it. My health's worn to a
frazzle and just how I did
escape I cannot tell. It is
a mighty miracle!

I'll find Ezekiel if I must
search for him all night. He
is the one who'll know just
how to break this tragic
news to all our people
captive in this hell-hole
named bold Babylon.
My weariness caught up
with me. I'll rest awhile…
But no! I cannot give up
now—I'm in his street!
Ezekiel: Jerusalem, our city
fair, has gone! It's shattered,
on the ground; it's fallen to
our powerful enemy!
I faint… Something to

drink I crave, to cast away
my thirst, renew me from
the gaping grave!

EZEKIEL
The Aftermath
Ezekiel 33

The Sovereign LORD
requires I speak again on
His behalf. I am His
watchman-prophet and
I will fulfil this dreaded
task. I must relay the
consequence of blatant sins!
All Israel had placed their
trust in Abraham's
bequest—the land was
given to possess always.
The land becomes a desert
waste; the pride of Israel
lies in the bloodied dust!
I know that Israel is
whispering behind the hand,
Let's go to hear
what he will say: Ezekiel!
Oh yes, you listen to my
words, you act devotedly
but, in your heart, your
greed has been the downfall
of the mighty Clans. You'll
realise, one day, there's
been a prophet here today!

EZEKIEL and *YHVH–* LORD
The Shepherds
Ezekiel 34

I'm asked once more by
YHVH-LORD to prophesy
to Israel's Elders here—
those who are shepherds of
the 'flock' of Israel, all
those
within their special care.
He said:

*A woe to you, the shepherds
who lavish on themselves all
care while leaving all the
flock to fend for very life in
fields so barren that they
faint for food that feeds your
greedy gluttony!*

*When have you shown a pity
for the weak, or where have
you set out to heal the sick,
where have you searched
for 'strays'? And when have
you once eased the rod? The
sheep are scattered now, the
food for creatures that
would dare to make them
meat!*
*The sheep of YHVH-LORD
have wandered far across
the hills, the mountains*

*rough and bare. When will
you search for them?
Therefore, you shepherds,
hear the word of YHVH–
LORD: I am against the
shepherds for they are
accountable for all the
flock. Know this: I'll rescue
them! I'll search for them,
I'll care for them; I'll bring
them back from all the
nations and they will come
home to their own fold. I'll
tend them in green fields.
They'll lie beside still
waters and I'll care for
them each day with
matchless grace.
I'll guard, eradicating
beasts that prowl in search
of meat. I'll bless My flock
upon My Holy Hill. I will
send showers in their
season so the trees of every
field will yield their fruit,
the ground will yield its
crops. The people then will
be secure—they'll surely
know beyond all doubt,
"I AM", the YHVH–LORD!
You are My sheep, O Israel,
you are the sheep of My
home pasture: You are My
people, I am your God.*

AN EDOMITE
Ezekiel 35

It's time to make a fuss
right now! You see, I've
heard the gossip round
the tracks, the inuendoes
of that man, Ezekiel. I
hear he's at it once again,
the prattler! My land?
Become a waste? A bleak
expanse of desolated
desert sand? What right
has he to say such things?

As if he'd know—I hear
he's clamped in stocks
or something of that
brand, or, maybe not.
The fact remains he is a
captive of bold Babylon!
What does he know of
Edom's lands? I'll say just
what I like about Israel—
they will all be gone for
good! We'll now take
over all their land—their
'precious Holy Land'!

And as for what their so-
called *YHVH*–LORD has
been reported to have said
(ha ha): Oh yes! We will
rejoice, and soon!

**We'll be the lords of all.
What's that you dare
to say? There'll be a
consequence for all we
seek to do in Israel? I do
defy their *YHVH* now…
What's this? I see a
cloud of dust. Is this
our destiny, at last…**

YHVH–LORD
The Mountain Kingdom
Ezekiel 36

*O son of man, it's time to
bring a word of comfort to
Israel: I've heard the
gloating glee of nations
round about (with Edom in
the midst.) I will proclaim
the true outcome of every
grasping hand that dares to
ravage Israel's soil!*

*Ezekiel: tell all the world
that they will each be
vanquished at the last
because of every vile and
vicious, hateful
ploy to take My land. I
swear, with hand upraised,
that Israel will come Home!
They'll occupy their land*

*once more. New fruit will
form on every spreading
tree. The people will
increase. They'll be
renewed—not for their
sakes, but for My Holy
Name. Then all will know,
yes, every citizen from first
to last, the foremost citizen,
the least: "I AM", the
YHVH Elohim. O Israel,
now hear My promises:*

*I'll take you back from all
the nations, gather you and
bring you into your home-
land again. I'll sprinkle you
with water that is pure:
you'll be made clean. All
your impurities, and all
your idol blasphemies,
will be removed. I'll give a
heart that's new, I'll place
in you a spirit true; I will
remove your heart of stone,
replacing it with tenderness.
My Spirit shall reside in you
enabling you to live in peace
with justice as your theme.
You'll be My people and I'll
be your God, removing all
impurities from you—your
land will be like pristine*

*Eden then; you'll walk
within My ways.*

EZEKIEL, *YHVH*-LORD
Dry Bones
Ezekiel 37

Dry bones, dry bones,
within an arid place, a
valley of despair where life
ne'er comes! The desert
sands exposed its dearth.

The Spirit of the *YHVH*–
LORD had brought me to
this barrenness. He
Spoke to me:

*O son of man, could these
bones, dry bones, live?*

How could I answer Him?
I ceded to His wisdom, said:
O Sovereign LORD, alone,
You know!

*So! son of man, now prophesy
to these bleached bones: 'Dry
bones, now hear the word
of YHVH–LORD:*

'Hark! Listen, bones, dry
bones: the LORD will send
His Spirit-Breath to you

to enter in and you
will live. New tendons will
attach to flesh, the bones
will be aligned to bone.'
Then, as I looked, I saw
indeed, a miracle take form
before my startled gaze. The
form was there but, where
was life?

*O son of man, now
prophesy, this is what
YHVH–LORD declares:*

Come from the winds, four
winds, of Earth. O Spirit-
Breath, now breathe
upon these slain that they
may live'… Then, as I
gazed, those lifeless forms
began to move, they stood
upon their feet. They danced
with joy; this army lived!

*O son of man, observe:
here stands the House of
Israel renewed, made whole
once more! Now, say to
Israel: 'Your graves will
open and I'll bring you up
from them. You'll live
again!*

*My Spirit will reside in you,
you'll settle in your land—
the land of Israel. Then,*

you will know "I AM", the
LORD… Now, take a stick,
Ezekiel, and name it
'Judah'; then, one more and
name it 'Ephraim'—
(Israel.) Ply them together;
so entwine those sticks that
they can then become one
'branch'.
When asked what this
conveys, declare: I'll make
of all the scattered Clans
one nation and there'll be
one king to unify the whole
so they will be My people,
cleansed and free; made
whole: I am the LORD!

EZEKIEL
Gog And Magog
Ezekiel 38 – 39

The word of God has come
again to me. He's told me
now so many things about
the hordes I knew not of. He
gave to them a title that I
greatly fear: 'Gog and
Magog'. I think of them and
mull upon the names—
what could they mean?
I sit and mull; I ponder
both of them.

These are the thoughts filter
through my brain: Gog
comes from Magog—that is
a clue at least. What can I
say of one named Gog? He
is the 'chief prince' of
Magog. I see another clue:
the word that *YHVH*–LORD
has used is 'Rosh'—this
word means 'head' of
course. Gog is the king, he's
'Rosh'. He comes
from northern lands of
Rosh: Magog! Meshech
and Tubal, too!

This information sits now in
my muddled mind. What
can I make of it? The 'chief
man' from a land far to the
north is he of whom the
YHVH speaks: 'Rosh'
comes from 'Rosh-ia'; he
has, with him, consorts as
well!

O *YHVH*–LORD,
I do not like at all
the sound of this! These
names, Gog and Magog,
reach on into far future
days. They'll be a force
to reckon with.

Write on, the *YHVH*–LORD
requests of me.
I take my pen. He then
disclosed to me most
startling things:
Gog, from Roshia, would
come —upon a fateful,
future day—toward
Jerusalem and in a
conflagration so intense
that many men would fall
by sword and arrow too:

An all-out war, a flying
death along with hand-to-
hand combat. And then, the
end became quite clear–
I do rejoice, for all Roshia
and cohorts too, would
be defeated on the hills
of Jerusalem.

The thing quite manifest
to me, the outcome of this
stark disclosure from the
LORD, is that it matters not
—to me—the name and
place—Gog and Magog.

I know these hordes will
come upon us from the
north. It matters not! What
is the word I must convey?
It's this: the *YHVH*–LORD

is in control. He moves to
save His people; He'll
protect us, He will save us
from our sin in every
circumstance!

His Holy Name will be
exalted in the heights as all
the people bow to Him in
praise. The *YHVH*–LORD
declares:

*No longer will they need
to search for Me, My people
who are faithful to the end!
No longer will I hide
My Face from them for I
will pour My Holy Spirit on
the House of Israel: They'll
know "I AM", the LORD!*

EZEKIEL
A Temple For Israel
Ezekiel 40 – 48

These are the plans He
gave, the *YHVH*–LORD—
the many plans,
specifications, for the
Temple to be built on our
return from
Babylonia. It's true! The
Exile will, one day, be
passed in peace.

I'll tabulate all the designs
He's given to my hands.
You'll find these in the
Annals of our History
—This is a 'bible' of His
plans!—I'll list them now,
a ready reference for
the artisans.

A Strategic Meeting
The *YHVH*–LORD
transported me by means
I cannot tell, except to say,
this was a vision grand.
You see, there was a
'man'—I cannot tell his
name—I knew he was no
ordinary personage. His
garb was linen, white, he
held a rod for measurement
in his able hand.

He called to me as 'son of
man'. I recognised he came
from God! He said, You
must record all that
you see today.

The Wall
There was a wall.
The 'man' disclosed
its measurements;
it did surround the Outer
Court. He measured all

the length, the alcoves,
portico, the gateways,
too, and all the many
parapets around.

The Outer Court
I saw some rooms; the
'man' then went to measure
all their distances, returned
confirming
all went well.

The North Gate
I saw the massive wall,
Its openings, its porticos,
All measured now.

The South Gate
He found, the 'man of
bronze', that all the
measurements
were each identical.

The Inner Court Gates
His measuring rod was
very busy now, with many
ins-and-outs. He found
that all the measurements
combined with all the rest.

The Rooms for Sacrifice
The annals will describe
the walls, the tables, slabs.
I saw utensils that were fit

to slaughter sacrifice.

The Rooms for Priests
Inside the inner Gate, two
rooms—The 'man' then did
describe their use: The
Temple Priests, the Altar
Priests, the sons of Zadok
who, alone, drew near to
YHVH–LORD to minister
His utmost Grace.

The Temple
I stood with him, the 'man';
the measurements were
made of every section of the
Holy Sanctuary. I saw, with
him, the Holy Place, also,
the Place Most Holy
to the YHVH–LORD.

The Priestly Rooms
There was a row of rooms;
the 'man' accounted for
them all. I set this down.
And, then:

The Glory Returns!
The 'man' directed me to go
with him out to the east—
the Gate that faced the
morning sun.
I saw the Glory of
the YHVH–LORD
—Shekinah Glory! True—

His Voice as rushing
streams in flood. I fell face
down. The Glory of the
LORD now went towards
the Holy Sanctuary. I
followed Him. I heard
His voice—I know it well!

*O son of man, this is the
Place where I will set My
throne and where My feet
shall rest; I'll live among
My people here for Israel
will not again defile My
Holy Name, "I AM" YHVH!*

*O son of man, describe
this Temple to the people of
Israel. Let them consider
it—the whole design—also,
the Law that will apply to
all. Now, write it down
for all Israel to keep.*

The Altar
It was the YHVH–LORD
who spoke to me. The many
measurements were all
applied to parchment then:
the measurements, the
Laws—by these, the people
everyone, will be acceptable
to Him.

The Prince, the Priests,
Levites: There were some

regulations special for all
those who would be *YHVH–*
LORD's own ministers of
grace. The ordinance of all
these men is very intricate.
You'll find them in the
Annals of our History—
it is set out there.

Division of the Land
The measurements were
made within my visioned
trance. The cubits given
were precise. In later years,
new ways to measure land
and length will be
devised—dynamics will be
changed. For now, the cubit
is the gauge assessing all.
But here, suffice to say that
one day, every Clan could
claim its ground in Israel.

Holy Days and Offerings
Of ephahs, tenths, of
homers and the rest are
noted down with carefulness
as tithes
and offerings are integral
to Temple needs—the
ministry of grace is such
that it requires men's trust
and open pockets, too,
especially at Passover
for this speaks of

ATONEMENT
for us with the *YHVH–*
LORD
who out-gives all with love.

The Sovereign LORD,
again,
spoke words of wisdom to
my soul regarding all the
regulations that concern
the Sabbath when the
Temple gates that face the
eastern side will open to the
worshippers. The guidelines
for the seasons
and offerings were all
recorded then.

EZEKIEL
The Stream of Grace
Ezekiel 47

The 'man' who had been
sent from God—arrayed in
linen garb and, with his
measuring rod—then led me
to the entrance of
the Temple where I saw
some water trickling down,
out from the threshold of
the Sanctuary. He took
me through the north gate
and he led me round
towards the east. I saw

that stream once more!
Some measurements
were made again and I made
note of them.

The sight I saw led me in
awe through water that was
ankle deep. A thousand
cubits further on, the water
was knee deep. And then,
a thousand more, the water
was waist deep. Then, yet
another yet, a thousand:

Here was a river that was
streaming gently down
the mountainside. I could
not cross this wondrous
stream! Its waters had now
risen high, far deeper than
I'd ever cross.

The 'man' then asked of
me: O son of man, what do
you see? He led me back
towards the brimming bank,
explaining that
this stream flowed down
via arid land into the Sea
of Salt and as this water
flows, the sea becomes quite
fresh! It lives! The
fishermen will ply their
trade and everywhere the
water flows, all things will

grow again. They'll live!

All kinds of fruit trees then
will flourish there. Both
banks will give support to
them. Their leaves will not
succumb to summer sun, the
fruit won't fail. These trees
will bear their fruit each
month for all the water will
flow down, on from the
Sanctuary to bless the land.
The leaves of every tree will
be for healing all the while.

This is the Stream of Grace
that from God's Presence
flows—a fountain pure and
wide, unmeasured and
available to all who plunge
into its mighty tide that
covers all our sins and
circumstance.

EZEKIEL and
YHVH–LORD
The Boundaries of Israel
Ezekiel 47:13 – chapter 48

The sovereign LORD
then said:

*O son of man, record the
outer rim, the boundaries of
Israel. The Clans will then
receive their very own*

*inheritance. The land will
be divided equally. Allot
the land according to the
needs of Israel and for the
aliens too that settle down
in holiness and peace.*
I've listed all the Clans

You'll see them once again
within the Annals of our
History. This portioning
includes the land that's
given to the Priests. There
is, also, some land set by
that will belong unto the
king who reigns.

The Gates of the City
There'll be the exits,
entrances, on each and
every side of this the Holy
City and It shall be named,
from that day on:

"THE LORD IS THERE"

I now lay down my pen!

**THE SONG OF
EZEKIEL**
Tune: *Saved by Grace*
D.C.M.

The LORD's great promises
to bring

His people Home, to heal
their wounds,
Provide soul sustenance,
are true!
To all who seek, His grace
abounds.
*God brings Good News to all
who trust,
We'll be restored, renewed,
made whole;
The heart of stone will be
transformed,
Made tender as a reclaimed
soul.*

Observe a scene of scattered
bones
All bleached and bare—this is
a scene
Where hope is lost. Where is
the faith
By which to live? Where is trust
seen?
*The Spirit of the LORD
brings hope,
He breathes new life within
the soul;
The sorrows of past days re
lost:
This new beginning makes s
whole.*

At times when ease floats all
around,

We fail to gauge our true
complaint;
For, without faith, we stand
alone,
There is no strength, our heart
grows faint.
*Come, Holy Spirit, breathe
in us,
Turn all our sorrows to
a song;
Come, Spirit come, reside
in us,
We joy in God, our praise
prolong.*

A river flows from God's
own Home,
A boundless stream of endless
grace;
It flows on down to desert
lands
Renewing life, restoring peace.
*A river deep and wide, it flows
Unmeasured and available
To all who plunge within its
tide:
Come, Tide of God, and make
us whole!*

..... oOo .....

THE TURBULENT
YEARS

DANIEL

You will have heard of me
as many aspects of my life's
story are quite renowned
throughout the world. I have
lived in turbulent times,
that's true. The king,
Nebuchadnezzar, was the
mighty man of Babylon but
there were many occasions
when I found it difficult to
gauge his mood.

There were occurrences
where my friends and I
feared for our lives! Then,
you'll be familiar with that
gruesome period relating to
the lion's den! There'd been
a regime change! You'll
need to be aware of this.
Babylonia has been routed in
the coup that saw the Medes
and Persians steal, by night,
into the very heart of the
once proud kingdom, the
most magnificent empire the
world had ever seen (if you
will discount the greatness of
Israel).
We'll rise from the ashes of
The Exile but we must wait

awhile until the *YHVH–LORD* will save us from ourselves. Meantime, we will remain in servitude to Medo-Persian powers! But let's begin in Babylon:

THE INTRODUCTIONS
Daniel 1 – 2

We Four—I am the penman here—are now in service to the king: Nebuchadnezzar, ruler of all Babylonia. We're named Shadrach, Meshach, Abednego; and I, Daniel, was named Belteshazzar— although I do prefer Daniel. You'll know me by that name so I will stay with it. We're working for the king. We're told—perhaps it's true—it was because we had an aptitude well qualified to serve him well.

I must admit that things went well until an order came for us to eat the soggy mush of Babylon. We would not be defiled by it! But what to do? We thought on it, decided that

we'd take a test and eat just fruit and vegetables. We stood the test for, after just ten days, we came up much the better than the rest. This diet was selected then. Our standing in the court became a valued thing by all who noted that our wisdom and our under-standing of the literature and learning of bold Babylon surpassed all else.

My 'reading' of a dream or vision has proved our worth at times. The king and court ruled in our favour more than all the rest. We entered then into the court of Babylon and we were sought to solve problems, prove a point.

DANIEL
The King's Dream
Daniel 2

The King of Babylon was in a 'stew'—he'd dreamed a dream but could not think what it foretold. He knew it was so real, surreal, so vital for his rule. But what was it? Who could he ask? He called to him the wisest men—magicians, all the soothsayers, and all the men who 'read' the stars.

He told of his dilemma and demanded that they bring to him an answer swift and sure. They asked, of course, for clues. The king displayed his ire at this. They were the men that knew the ins-and-outs of wisdom things. So, get on with it and tell me well before the dawn or heads will surely roll!

The men complained. There was no man who could reveal to him a mystery without a clue. That was it! The king then ruled the execution of these men must be fulfilled. Now, Shadrach, Meshach and Abednego and I were in great peril too. I had to act for everyone. On being told the reason why the edict had gone out, I sought an audience with the king. I asked for time as I must pray. I'd wait upon the YHVH–LORD to tell the meaning of the dream. The king complied. I went on home. Then, in the middle of the night, the answer came. I knew it all!

Praise be, O YHVH–LORD, You rule eternally and over all! All wisdom and all power are Yours. You plan all the affairs of kings and courtiers, of people in all circumstance. You have revealed the deep and hidden things of mystery.

You know what lies within the night and all is brought to light what You disclose. By You, O YHVH–LORD, the mighty source of *LIGHT*, all mystery will unfold: You've granted me to know what's asked of You. You have revealed the Truth tonight of ages yet to come!

I went at once unto the king who quizzed me on his his dream. You can reveal to me what I have seen, you'll tell me what it means and so dismiss my fear? No man, your Majesty,

could tell you of the
mystery without a given
clue. But I have trusted in
the LORD of all the
universe, the One, the only
One, who knows all things,
reveals them now:

As you were resting in the
night, your mind began to
see great visions of all
future time. This vision was
revealed to me though not
because my wisdom is far
greater than the rest. It is
because you need to hear
the dream interpreted so you
may know God's ways.

You looked, O king, and
there you saw a statue
standing tall. So dazzling,
awesome, was this edifice
that you were then amazed
by brilliance rare. The
statue's head was gold,
Its chest and arms of silver
And the torso was of
brightest bronze; the legs
were iron, the feet—a
mixture of the iron with
clay. Then, as you looked in
awe, a Rock, uncut by
human hands, came hurtling
through the air.

It struck the statue at its feet
of iron and clay. The feet
then crumbled, smashed.
The clay, the iron, the
bronze, the silver and the
gold, all gone; all smashed
beyond repair.
Then, as you viewed the
scene, the Rock, O king,
became a mountain
filling all the Earth!

This was your dream,
O king, and now I
will interpret it:
Nebuchadnezzar, you are
the greatest of all kings:
pure gold! You hold
dominion, power; your
glory is immense. You are
that head of gold. Another
king will come to follow
you; he'll be inferior to you:
the 'silver' man and in
and in two parts—
the chest and arms.

So then, a kingdom cast
in bronze will follow but
inferior again. And finally,
a kingdom strong as iron
and ruthless too, will come
to rule the Earth. This
kingdom, too, will be
divided—just as iron

that's mixed with clay, so
weak this kingdom will
not, cannot meld.

Now hear, O king, that it
will be within the time of
both the iron and clay, that
YHVH–LORD will instigate
a Kingdom that will never
be destroyed. Nor will
it come into the hands of
those that seek its sure
demise. All other kingdoms
then will cease ascendency.
The Rock—not made with
human hands—will break
the iron and clay, the
bronze, the silver and the
gold. This dream is true and
you can trust this
explanation of what, one
day, comes to pass.
The king fell down before
me then and ordered
offerings be sent. He spoke
just then, declared: Most
surely as the sun shall rise,
your God is God of gods;
He's King of kings, and
Lord of lords: He has
revealed
to you, my dream.

The offshoot of this incident
is such that I am held in
high esteem in all the land.
I have become the ruler of
the province of bold
Babylon. I did request that
Shadrach, Meshach, and
Abednego be given high
positions too: to be
administrators of all
Babylon while I remain at
court to serve the king.

THE THREE FRIENDS
The Fiery Furnace
Daniel 3

How do we tell this story,
lads? There has been
nothing like it in the Annals
of our History! In looking
back on the event, we see
we see it now, the hand of
God our *YHVH*–LORD, was
on our lives. He meant it
unto good! I'm Shadrach
and I'll have my friends
participate for we three men
were all involved from the
beginning to the end.

Oh, hi! I'm Meshach. So,
my friends and I had known
for months that there were
jealousies—we were
administrators for Daniel

who was required at Court
(the king relies on him).
It's never really good, you
see, for slaves to take the
'reins', enforce the rules
while all the Babylonians
had need to carry out these
rules. They then began to
plot for us to be removed.

Some bright spark saw
our prayers and practices
were so unlike their own,
they set a plan, went to the
king (who was quite partial
to us three), with a surprise.
Abednego, you saw what
happened then to further the
intrigue. Oh yes,

Oh yes, the plotters came
and stated what was in their
mind. You see, the king had
ordered that
an image of himself—
immense and grand in gold
be set and, on the
Dedication Day—(to him),
when music makers all
chimed in with perfect
harmony, all people must
bow down towards the man
of gold. All did as they were
told! Shadrach, tell all our
part in this. Well, it was

such that all the men
who came to end our
ministry informed the king
that we refused to bow to
golden men! O king, they
said, Such men should be as
you decreed, cast to a fire!

The king then vented rage!
He questioned us and,
With affirmatives in place,
he ordered that we three
should 'go to hell!'
Meshach, go on. You tell
it well! It was our chance
to witness To our faith
in *YHVH*–LORD! O king,
now throw us to the flames
for we are guilty as you
rightly said to us.

But we believe that *YHVH*–
LORD will not abandon us.
He'll keep us safe. If he
decides not to step in, we'll
have you know we can do
nothing but to serve the
YHVH–LORD above
all else on Earth!
Abednego: You've got the
best of it. now tell it all.

The king was furious. He
had the flames increased
then cast us to the furnace

there. You see what did
become of us: there's not
a singe upon our healthy
skins! How could that
furnace fail to do its work to
bring our end? Why not
allow the king to tell

it all! You see, the king
observed what happened in
those flames! There never
was the like of it, nor will
there be again! He said:
There are not three men in
that furnace now; there's
four! And, look at Him:
He's like The LORD's
own cherished Son.

Never a moment so
profound! As flames
roared high, roared on, He
came to us, He smiled at us!
Our fears were gone. He
stood with us. He saved us
from the deadly flames.

I guess the final word
belongs to me—Shadrach.
The king gave praise in
honour of the *YHVH*-LORD
and ruled that any who
defiled His Holy Name
would be dismissed,
reviled, and set aside.

The king was pleased to
find some men so willing
to give up their life to serve
the *YHVH*-LORD no matter
what the cost to them!

NEBUCHADNEZZAR
Daniel 4

This is an edict from your
king! I write to tell my
subjects that are scattered
over all the Earth. Goodwill
to you! It's my desire to tell
you all about the signs and
wonders sent to me from
YHVH–LORD, Most High!

I am your ruler and I realise
you need to be aware
that He, the Most High God,
will reign for all Eternity;
His Kingdom will endure
through all our time and
generations yet to come.

Unique events have led me
to take up my 'pen' to write
to you. I seek to show what
has occurred when I was
sound asleep. A dream
profound awakened me or,
was I still asleep? I saw a

massive tree, a tree of such
enormous height. It touched
the sky, was seen
through all the Earth. I saw
a 'messenger', a holy man,
descend from Heaven.

He called, Cut down the tree
and strip it; then, scatter all
its luscious fruit. Send off
the animals from under it,
the birds that shelter there.
But let the stump remain.
Let him be drenched with
heaven's dew and live with
all the animals among the
plants of Earth. Let him no
longer act as men; give him
the mind of animals
until this period shall end.

I now report that I requested
that my aide,
Belteshazzar—who
is also known as Daniel—
to come, explain the whole.

When I had shared the
whole with him, all aspects
of my dream, I saw that
Belteshazzar became
perplexed. He seemed quite
terrified. I counselled him
then into calm: Don't be
afraid, my friend, tell all

to me. He answered then:

The tree you saw is you,
O king. Your greatness
covers all the Earth. You
saw a holy 'messenger'—
he was an angel sent
from *YHVH*–LORD.

You took to heart all that he
said. The news for you is
not so good, your Majesty.
The time will come, so
swiftly now, when you will
leave your palaces to live
among the animals, the
birds. Your food will be but
grass, just like the cattle
there. All will be drenched
with dews from heaven.
And full seven 'seasons'
will elapse before you'll be
restored again as king.

Your need is an
acknowledgement
That *YHVH*-LORD is
Sovereign and rules all
nations of the world.
I am most pleased to say
The stump you saw ensures
that you'll return to rule;
all will be then restored.
advice: renounce your
wickedness; do only what

is right; be kind to the
oppressed, revere the
YHVH–LORD.

I need to now report
that all has happened as
my aide had prophesied.
I went too far with pride—
it goes before a fall. I'd tell
of my experience out in the
fields of Babylon; you know
it well so I'll desist, except
to say my sanity has been
restored to me. I praise the
LORD Most High; I honour
and revere the LORD.

BELSHAZZAR
The Writing on The Wall
Daniel 5

I am the king!
I rule now in
the hallowed place
of Nebuchadnezzar, king
of all the Babylonian
Empire! It must be said,
I do enjoy a feast or two
each month. I like to
celebrate receiving both
my throne and crown;
Also, all my constituency.
I would explain not all

are happy with the state
of things outside the city
walls. But let us eat,
and let us drink,
let us be merry as we
eat this fare tonight.
It is enough to feed
a multitude!

What's that? A hand?
A human hand? What is
it doing on the wall?
That hand is writing
something on my
plastered wall.

I watch as it
spells out a ghastly
message for us all.
So! Who can read
all this graffiti on
my palace wall?

No one? Oh, surely,
there's a man
who'll know
the Script, recite
it for us now?

My queen says,
don't be so afraid;
don't look so pale—
there is a man
renowned within
the times your

predecessor ruled.
His name is Daniel.
Sire, send for him;
he'll tell it all!

He turned up with
alacrity! He glared at me!
Are you the man, I asked,
who will explain just what
an insight gives to you?
If you will tell us what
this script conveys to us,
I'll gift you mightily,
I said. Sire, keep your
gifts, he said and then
went on. Yes, I will tell
what news for you
is on the wall!

The message on the wall
has come because of your
great pride: because you
set yourself against the
YHVH–LORD of
Heaven and Earth;
because you desecrated
all the Temple artefacts;
because you drank your
wine from them; because
you praise idols that
are scattered through
the land;
because you've proudly
here dishonoured God!
He sent this message

down to you. This is
the stark inscription
written here:

'MENE, MENE, TEKEL,
PARSIN'

And, this is what it reads:

MENE: 'Numbered'
God has numbered all the
days that you will reign:
they're at a sorry end!

TEKEL: 'Weighed'
You have been weighed
upon God's justice scales;
you have been found in
abject peril, want!

PARSIN: 'Broken
fragments'
Your kingdom is divided
now: It goes into the hands
of Medes and Persian
troops–you will find out!

I gave to Belteshazzar,
Daniel, a gown of purple
and a chain of gold that
indicates he is one of the
high rulers in the land.
What now? The Medes
and Persians are now
banging on the door?

They come for me?
They'll take my
They come for me? They
take my kingdom and my
crown? This is the end
of mighty Babylon**!**

DARIUS
Daniel 6

I state my case as
emperor—in partnership
with Cyrus now. The
Medo–Persian powers are in
our hands. I feel I rule all
things with sensitivity—
quite liberal. I follow in the
steps of mighty men.

I have an aged friend:
Daniel; he was the first
of all the greatest men,
important presidents at
Court. This man had served
past kings and conquerors
quite well. Indeed, he is
a loyal aide.

He has a certain way
with him, an excellence
well pleasing in my view of
things. He gives advice
from time to time. Although
his years are now far spent,

his eyes are keen.
I'm well aware that
Daniel's fidelity sets him
at odds with schemers in my
court. I found, too late, that
they conspired my Daniel
down into the dust.
There was one way,
just one.

Here he was
vulnerable. The man
stood firm in his belief in
the Most High—he named
Him *YHVH, El Shaddai:*
this name means, 'The
LORD, the Mighty God'.
I saw no harm.

When next I stood
up to receive the adulation
of the peasantry, my aide
was seen at prayer—on
knees, three times! Three
times, to offer thanks
to *El Shaddai!*

The plotting princes
came to me, made their
report, demanding that
I act compliant with the law.
This was a legal trap
without a doubt.
I had to act.

I then decreed
a den of lions would
be prepared, set up to be
the means of ample
punishment!

With sadness in
my heart, I gave the order
for the punishment. Daniel
was sealed inside the den
with my own royal seal. I
prayed yes, prayed, that
El Shaddai whom he has
worshipped faithfully
would tame the lions
to save this man.

I fasted through the
night. I could not sleep.
When dawn appeared,
I rushed on down toward
the den where all
was quiet.

O Daniel, I cried
in anguish then. You are
the loyal servant of your
God, the living God. Has He
stepped in, delivered you
from all those lions?

O Sire, may you live
always! Yes! My *YHVH*-
LORD, the *El Shaddai*, has
sent His angel to protect me

by the closing of
their hungry mouths!
At once, that edict was
erased. All those who
planned this great atrocity
got just desserts!
I then commanded all
respect be given to the
YHVH-LORD.

I'll say this now:
The God of Daniel is the
one Eternal LORD of all.
His rule shall never end. It
will not be destroyed for His
dominion is complete. He
rescues and delivers all who
trust in Him. His signs and
wonders are unique!
I rest my case!

DANIEL
Apocalyptic* Avenues
(**A revelation*) Daniel 7

I've need to leave our
history's page where signs
and wonders were quite
obvious, though sent
to test our trust, our
faithfulness.

I turn to inner turmoils
now to set the record

straight on what I've seen
of all that is to be. The
YHVH–LORD has given
to me exceeding great
disclosures of a world that's
yet to be. I'll do my best to
set it down so you may
focus on its worth and know
what He has planned for all
that is to be in time–beyond
it too! While resting on
my bed, a dream
occurred that must
be written down.

The winds of heaven came
down to churn an angry,
storm-tossed sea. Then they
emerged: A lion: with
eagle-wings then torn,
A bear: a lumbering thing
with power, A leopard: with
four wings and heads,
A terror beast: ten-horned
and fuming, furious.

Then, while I thought on
this, a horn,
a smaller horn emerged
from it. This horn had
searching eyes, a mouth
that roared most boastfully.
They ranted and they raved
in turn, These fearsome,
raucous beasts. Then, as

I looked, considered all,
there stood, before me,
YHVH–LORD, 'Ancient of
Days', He sat down on the
Judgement throne. His robe
was pristine white, His hair
was white as wool. The
throne was all aflame and
fire proceeded as a stream
as countless thousands stood
with Him. The Record Book
was opened then.

The horn continued on
so boastfully until its life
was taken and destroyed!
The other beasts, all three,
were stripped of all
authority.

And then He came!
How may I best describe
this 'Man' though coming
on the clouds of heaven? He
stood before the 'Ancient of
Days' and here The 'Man',
the Son of Man, was given
authority, all glory, and all
power. All peoples, nations
of the world, bowed down
to worship Him. The Son
of Man's dominion is
to be for everlasting,
evermore; it will not
pass away and never be

destroyed! This vision
troubled me. How could
I understand the nature of
this dream? I then
approached a 'visionary'
to ask of it. The answer
came. This being said:
Four kingdoms will arise
in turn then cease to be.

The saints of 'The Most
High' will all possess the
Kingdom and through
time—all time, that is!
It is the 'Ancient of Days'
who is victorious. He gave
to me the explanation of
'ten horns': these represent
ten kings who'll try to
change the course of
history. They'll not
succeed—they'll rule for
time, for times, and half a
time, before demise.

Remember this: God's
Kingdom is eternal and you
are a citizen. This news has
deeply troubled me;
I've not discussed it since.

DANIEL
The Ram And The Goat
Daniel 8

Another vision came to me,
much like the one described
above. I 'saw' myself at
Susa in Elam. Before me
stood a ram with horns.
The ram charged north,
south, west and none could
counter his attacks. Then, as
I looked, a goat charged
from the west—his horn
was all most prominent.

The goat attacked the ram
and won. The ram enlarged
his power until his horn
was smashed. And in its
place, four horns emerged.
On one, another grew, quite
small but then enlarged
in mighty power to all
the compass points.

So powerful was he that
none could stand against
him then. He thought that he
out-classed the Prince! He
prospered well; in every-
thing outdid all else. All
truth was crushed in sand.

A question came: the Holy
One inquired, How long
before his sin, his wicked-
Ness against the LORD's

own Holy Place will be
curtailed, at end? A time
was given then. I tried to
understand but had to ask
the sense of it. The One like
to 'The Son of Man'
requested Gabriel, the
Angel of the LORD, to tell
of all it surely meant to me.

This vision does relate unto
the end of time. I'd been
asleep—he roused me to my
feet. This two-horned ram?
It represents the Medo-
Persian days. The shaggy
goat belongs to Greece.
The horns are kings.

Take note: four kingdoms
will emerge as time draws
to an eventual end.
A wicked king will come.
He will succeed in all he
does. He will destroy God's
holy people, try to outwit
Heaven's own Prince.
But he will be destroyed.

The vision of the length of
days: the evenings and the
mornings: true. But! Seal
this vision: It concerns
The end of future time.

I lay exhausted then.
But then I rose
soon after rest, to serve
the king—yet, still appalled.
I yet had much to learn.

DANIEL'S PRAYER
Daniel 9

I'd counted up the years,
remembered that it was
the prophet Jeremiah who
had once proclaimed that
Israel would be exiled for
full on seventy years before
all's done. I turned to
YHVH-LORD. By prayer,
by fasting and petition,
draped in sackcloth and
the mourning ash,
I prayed for peace.

O LORD, You always keep
Your Covenant of Love for
all who love Your Law: our
sin has caused great grief;
we turned our backs in
disobedience. We know that
You are merciful;
You will forgive the
penitent. The judgement
laid on us was right and just.
It was because
unrighteousness had

clouded all our will and
way. Yet, LORD, we did
not seek Your favour, we
withstood Your grace,
Your gracious kindliness.

O LORD, I lay before You
now our utmost need. The
wrath of God has sorely
tested us. O LORD, I pray
for us, Your people here, in
Babylon. In keeping with
Your righteousness, turn
from Your anger now and
smile on us. For Your sake,
LORD, give ear to us, and
turn Your eyes on us
to see our deep despair.

I ask You not because of
our own righteousness but
LORD, because of grace
that ever flows to us
because Your mercy does
extend to even us.

While I yet spoke my
prayer, God's messenger,
Gabriel, had come to me.
He spoke to me these
words: Daniel, I come to
give insight for you to
understand that, when you
began to pray, the answer
came. I'm with you now,

confirming that you are
beloved of God. Here is
the vision and its message
too: Full seventy years were
all decreed for Israel,
Jerusalem, to finish all their
sin, to be atoned for
wickedness, to usher in true
righteousness, to seal up
vision, prophecy and to
anoint the Holy One.

Then Gabriel gave to me
the calculations—based on
'7'—Oh, how appropriate:
70, 7, 7 x 7.

He told of the 'Anointed
One'—in Greek, this is 'the
Christ'. He spoke of when
the end would come—like
streams in flood. He spoke
of wars that would continue
through all time. And then,
with great solemnity, he
spoke of an abomination
that would cause great
desolation and then
continue to the end as is
decreed by *YHVH*–LORD.

I am amazed at what I heard
and yet, I know it's true! O
LORD, do not delay—Your
People bear Your Name.

DANIEL
The End Times
Daniel 10 – 12

How can I tell of this
great mystery? I'm told to
hold its truth unto myself.
It must be sealed until the
end of time—far down the
future years. How does one
lay before you now
the basic gist of it?

It will become quite plain,
I'm told when all is set in
place for final things. I'll set
the scene then, when it
comes to pass, Earth's
citizens will then say, Yes,
old Daniel spoke of it—we
know just what he said!

But first, the meeting like
no other I'd experienced:
I'm standing at the Tigress
shore when suddenly a light
shone bright; I'd never seen
the like of it before.
'A Man' appeared,
apparelled in
white linen with a belt
of gold. He shone like
chrysolite; His body bright
as bronze. His eyes, a torch,
searched mine; His voice

was resonant. My name
My name was called; I had
no strength to stand—I fell
entranced, right to the
ground. His hand touched
me—it sent me trembling to
my knees. Daniel, He spoke
to me: You are beloved by
YHVH–LORD.

The words that I now speak
must be considered well.
Stand up; I have been sent
to you." I, trembling, stood.

Don't be afraid, beloved of
God—since you began to
set your life in tune with
Him, your words, your
prayers, were heard. The
struggles of these years
detained Me with those
kings. You know what now
is past; I'll tell you now
of future certainties.

I bowed my face before
Him now, this Majesty from
God. He came to me, He
touched my lips. I then
began to speak: "O, see my
anguish, Lord, I am so
helpless in the sight of You.
Breathless, strength gone.

Again, He touched me and
I found my strength return.
Do not, now, be afraid, O
man esteemed of God. His
peace will strengthen you.
Be strong! Speak, Lord,
I hear You now!

He said, Soon things will
change. You know why I
have come? Soon, I'll
depart for Persian rule
will end and Greece will
come to take the reins of
power. I'll tell you carefully
what's in the Book of Truth.
So, hear it from Me now.

This 'visitation' of the
Being—the Man from out
of Heaven has set the scene
for me to clarify what may
be said of what was there
disclosed then sealed and
closed to all. This is the
very truth of it:

Four Persian kings would
reign before Greece takes
the reins. The king of
Greece will please himself.
Then he will crumble to
the dust. Four winds from
Heaven—that is, all
compass points—and then

will cast the rest away.

The southern king will then
wax strong while there will
be alliances to strengthen
ties—the south with north.
This will not last. The north
invades the south but then
the south retaliates and
ousts that king. The
northern king enlarges all
his armies and he'll build
great ramps to capture all
the vulnerable who vied.

He will establish power
within the 'Lovely Land'.
He plans alliances again.
These fail to work. He'll
turn again to his own land
and will be seen no more.

A king shall then arise
imposing heavy taxes on
the land. He's followed by
a man contemptuous—
he has no royal claim but he
will seize the crown by
great intrigue. Then watch,
for in his path, a man then
comes to power, he will
assassinate a 'prince of
Israel's covenant'. Deceit is
his foul weapon of
conquest. With all secure,

he then invades—his wealth
distributed among his
thankful men.

It's only for a time.
The king of all the south
will wage a war but his own
army will be swept away.
The kings of north
and south shall feast
together but will lie
regarding all they plan,
though all will fail.

The northern king
will then set out to ruin
all the Holy Covenant.
He acts and then returns
at once northward before
deciding to engage in war
against the south. This time,
he will lose heart. He'll
vent his fury on the Holy
Covenant. He'll favour
those who follow him.

The Temple then is set
for desecration and also for
abolishing the holy
sacrifice. He will corrupt all
those who turned from holy
covenants. God's people,
though, will all resist and
turn from him finally.

The wise will give advice
though many love their life.
Some wise will stumble but
this is so they'll be refined,
made pure and sanctified
until the time appointed for
the final end of everything.
The king shall please
himself.

He'll be successful too,
Until the time of wrath is at
an end. He'll dally with the
gods all set before him to
adore though he will think
himself above them all!

Then, at the time when all
shall end, the kings of north
and south will then invade
the Holy Land and sweep
across vast tracks of Earth,
extending power supreme.
The treasuries will be in his
control—all others are
subservient until he hears
until he hears alarming
news. He'll place himself
within The Holy Land. His
end will surely come apace
for no one grants him aid.

At this time Michael,
the Angel of the LORD,

arrives for there will be
a time of deep distress.
Then, it will be this very
time our people are
delivered whole—that is,
all those whose names
are written in 'The Book'!
And multitudes of those
long dead will rise—some
to eternal, everlasting life
and others to a surely
devastating end.

The wise shall shine like
To the brightness of the
heavens and those who lead
another on to righteousness
will glow like stars above
for evermore. Now, Daniel,
seal the sacred scroll!

Then, I became aware of
two more 'men'. One asked
the 'Man', How long, O
Lord, before the end? He
then replied in grace to me:

*For time, and times, and
half a time!*

What could such timing
mean? This was a mystery to
me. I asked the 'Man',
O Lord, What will the
outcome be? He said to me:

Now go your way,
O Daniel.
The scroll is sealed until
The time of the
Apocalypse.* Yes, many
will be saved, made pure
and holy, though the wicked
will not know. Yet, all the
wise will know—they'll
understand the strange
meaning of the mystery
dates of time. Yes, you will
rest and then, when time
shall end, you will arise,
receive your just reward.
This is my final word—
my pen is now at rest.

*Greek: unveiling, revealing

DANIEL'S SONG
Tune: *Arizona* L.M.

All earthly kingdoms rise and
fall:
They rise in power, they fall by
pride
Which blocks the path that
leads to peace;
Trust in His grace, the LORD
will guide.

When shadows veil the
pilgrim's path,

We search for meaning from
the wise.
In seeking wisdom, learn
to trust
In God, be righteous in
His eyes.

At times a fear becomes just
like
A fiery furnace set for us;
By trusting God when trials
arise
We find release: the LORD
grants grace!

When faith is ebbing, trust
departs;
The quandaries of life
bring fear:
The way ahead, a 'den
of lions'!
Trust God! He sets us free,
He's near.

The 'writing is upon the wall'

For those who worship self,
instead
Of trusting in the LORD for
grace;
Have faith in God, be safely
led.

..... oOo .....

THE
TRIUMPHANT
YEARS

INSERT: HISTORICAL
RECORDS
RELATING TO THE
EXILE

EZRA

Allow me to introduce
myself. These are my
credentials: I am Ezra and
I'm pleased to announce that
my name means *help*! This is
what I have sought to do
throughout my life. I am
chief among the priests who
accompanied Zerubbabel
upon the epic journey from
Babylon to the Holy Land as
the Exile was coming to its
inevitable end.

You will realize,
therefore, that I live in a time
of great transition. I am
aligned closely with
Nehemiah whom you will
meet shortly. It has been
said, and I do not deny it, that
my pen was active through
the recording of Chronicles
so I am well fitted for the
task of recording events

relating to our return from Exile to the Promised Land.

EZRA: INTRODUCTIONS
Ezra 1

My greetings to you all:
I'm Ezra, priest of Israel.
My testimony is out of place
perhaps, but it was thought
applicable to fit it in the
Annals of our History
associated with those years
of exile—that is, first to
Babylon and then the
later Persian years.

I am no prophet but I share
a close affinity with Daniel,
Ezekiel and others who
have worn the chains of
slavery. Because our current
news relates to this, we
thought it wise to set
the records all in place.

You see, it has begun! Full
seventy years is in the
wings. The edict has been
signed, repatriation has
begun! We're homeward
bound! I'll set the recent
history down:

In the first year, King Cyrus
of Persia, saw it, set it out—
the plan. A proclamation
from the king is written
down: The *YHVH*–LORD,
the God of Heaven, has
given to me the kingdoms of
the Earth. He has appointed
me to build a Temple in
Jerusalem.

Therefore, if any feel
inclined to be involved in
this, I give permission for
its plan to be fulfilled. This
royal edict is concerned
with Israel's God. Also, our
people are to provide the
silver and the gold required,
the livestock, goods, for all
the Temple—as a gift.

Just so, it was the family
heads of Judah, Benjamin,
The priests and everyone
whose heart was moved,
who packed their bags to
travel to Jerusalem to build
God's Holy Temple there.
Our neighbours, friends,
assisted with the necessary
items needed for the
enterprise. What's more,
King Cyrus then returned

the Temple treasures taken
all those many tiresome
years ago. Inventories
were taken, saved.

EZRA:
THE ARRIVAL
Ezra 2

You'll find the total list of
names recorded for
posterity, of those who
made the journey home.
You'll see that thousands
were involved: the priests,
Levites, the servants, added
to the list of travelling costs;
all told, 42,360 comprised
the company—without
the extras added on.

Upon arrival, some then
gave a freewill offering,
with thanks, towards the
building of God's House
in gratitude for their new
circumstance. Then, all the
travellers went home to
their own villages of old.

On the due date arranged,
all then assembled in
Jerusalem. It was upon
this very day Zerubbabel—

the son of Shealtiel, and his
associates began the work.

They built an altar for the
gifts of sacrifice according
to our heritage. When this
was done, all celebrated in
the Feast of Tabernacles
with each act of worship
done according to the Law.
As yet, the foundations of
the House of God—the
Temple—were not laid.

EZRA:
MY REPORT
Chapter 3

Note: By the second month,
the second year, all things
were set in place as planned.
Materials supplied, the men
began to work to the design.
Zerubbabel and
Jeshua, together with the
priests and Levites too,
began appointing adult men
to supervise the work.

When the foundations were
in place, a celebration then
took place: full vestments
worn, and trumpets all
engaged, all took their

place, exalting *YHVH*–
LORD with praise:
The LORD is good!
His love endures for e'er:
The LORD's own grace
Will bless our best
endeavour here!

It must be said that many
priests—the older school—
had wept aloud at such a
sight as this: Foundations
that did not approach
the excellence of what
the former Temple had.
The sounds of weeping,
sounds of joy, were
intermingled so no one
could say the sound
was other than the jubilant.

ZERUBBABEL
Ezra 4

**Our home-grown enemies
began a plot to foil our
plans. They sought to join
the staff at work but to
disrupt it all. We were
quite adamant: You have
no part with us in building
YHVH–LORD's own
House! It is our work**

**alone. They then set out
to place discouragement
among the workers.
Brooding fear set in,
the work was paused.**

**So, nothing of much merit
was accomplished through
the reign of Cyrus, Persian
monarch, then. After this,
Xerxes came to power. An
accusation—unjust lies—
about Jerusalem was sent.**

**And in the days of the
successor, Artaxerxes,
a letter in the Aramaic
script was sent to him. It
read: The king should
know that Jews who had
returned are building up
the place: the walls, and
the foundations, all!
You need to know, your
Majesty, that once this
work is done, you won't
the taxes due. It is not
proper that we don't
inform your Majesty
about
the mad rebellions of the
past. We rest our case!**

**The king sent this reply:
I thank you for this news.**

Time has been taken now
to check the records of the
past. It's found to be quite
true. Therefore: All work
must cease. The city will
not be rebuilt till so
decreed. Do not neglect to
follow through! The Royal
Seal was then affixed.

TATTENAI
Ezra 5

My friend and fellow
prophet Zechariah and I
were tested with rallying the
workers in the Name of
YHVH–LORD. Zerubbabel
and Jeshua had led the work
and we gave all
encouragement to them.
There were concerns and we
negotiated with the
governor who queried our
authority. We knew the Eye
of God was on our quest.
There was a letter sent unto
Darius, now the Medo-
Persian king, and it
contained this news:
Upon the word of Jewish
men, the leaders of the
work, we give you this

report: It does appear
the men are keen to build
again all that has lain
in ruin. A great king did
achieve the first
great edifice. However,
Jews rebelled so lost
their right to worship in
the Temple of their *YHVH*–
LORD. In consequence,
the nation was deported
into Babylon.

Reminders of the edict of
King Cyrus who allowed
the Jews to go back home—
their plundered treasures
were returned to them—
were then included in the
letter's length. If it should
please your Majesty, we do
advise a search be made
to ascertain the truth of it.
The letter, sealed, was sent
post haste unto the Persian
king who opened it.

DARIUS
Ezra 6.

As Medo-Persia's king,
I speak the words of law—
remember: laws of Medo-
Persia can't be changed—

as now I speak, it will be so,
upon my word! I have
requested that a search be
made to check the facts!
When the exact records
were found, a truthful
memorandum was
compiled affirming history
of Israel's past was true.
Let it be known that I am
pleased for work to now
commence again within
the Holy Land! The Temple
and the city would be built
again forthwith!

I have word that my favour
in this enterprise has been
received most heartily for I
decreed that all the costs be
met, ensuring the
continuance of planning
building, furnishing,
the whole. The bottom line
on my decree now reads:
May God, who has caused
His Name to dwell within
Jerusalem, be pleased
to overthrow all
enemies who lift a hand
to alter this Decree or to
destroy the Holy Temple in
Jerusalem. I, Darius, so
decrees! Let it be carried out
with all due diligence!

EZRA:
THE DEDICATION
Ezra 6

As priest, I—Ezra—will
relate the happenings that
did eventuate, resulting
from the edict of Darius,
King. The governor of
Trans Euphrates ensured
that all the men worked with
a diligence that saw the
work completed as the
preaching of Haggai and
Zechariah had continued on.

By now, Darius had been
king for six whole years.
this date was marked by the
most holy day when all the
when all the building was
complete. Now was the time
for the great dedication
of the Temple and we sang
for rapturous joy.

We worshipped *YHVH*–
LORD. We sacrificed our
offerings of animals—such
is the way since Moses
formed it so. The *YHVH*–
LORD Is pleased. Then,
when the Passover was due,
the day was set aside for
sacrifice, for prayer, and for
atonement for our soul.

EZRA
Ezra 7 - 8

Much time has passed.
I have endeavoured to
keep up with everything
according to the edicts,
orders, subterfuge, and how
the kings of Persia aided us
in the most holy work of
restoration of the Temple
and Jerusalem.

I should confirm that my
recording of this history is
accepted well because of
my ancestry. You see,
I stand descendant to Aaron,
the first High Priest. The
kings of Persia have valued
my input to all
the machinations of
the Persian Court.

At times, they sought my
counsel and they took my
word. They acted on its
worth. In consequence,
it was decided that
my presence in Jerusalem
would help the cause of
peace, prosperity and for
posterity at large.

I had received a letter from
King Artaxerxes and it read:

To Ezra, priest and rabbi of
The *YHVH*–LORD:

Greetings
from the King and
Council—
Ezra: hereby, you now
receive my gratitude,
goodwill and all my good
encouragement for your trek
onward to Jerusalem.
I'm now appointing you
to travel there to then
investigate the situation
concerning all the
happenings and every
circumstance of all
the people, plans, and
problems in the City of
Jerusalem. You are to take
with you the personnel who
wish to go with you. I place
within your hands the silver
and the gold as offered for
this splendid enterprise.

I have decreed that all you
need by way of resources,
finance, is hereby made
available to you. Let
everything be done with
diligence and due regard.
Upon arrival, you are to
then appoint the judges,
magistrates, who will

administer true justice to all
peoples there who know the
Law of *YHVH*–LORD.
Those ignorant of this Law,
you take good care to teach,
to counsel in the ways of
YHVH–LORD.

I praise the LORD for this
edict and evidence of the
goodwill between the king
and I. It is because the
YHVH–LORD has placed
within his heart a just desire
to honour God.

Because God's hand was on
my life, to guard and guide
me well, I take the courage
needed for the task and
chose the men who would
accompany me. Their
names are listed in the
Annals of our History.
And then, when every-
thing was organised, the
journey was begun.

EZRA: THE PRAYER
Ezra 9

The lot of leaders is
lamentable! I find that I
must arbitrate between so

many rights and wrongs.
The situation that concerned
so many Jews was what to
do with foreign wives. It's
ever been the case. When
will there be an end to it?

A change of mind? A choice
of what is right? I take my
time to hear the long
confessions of the kind
that would provoke a saint
to wrath! I sit appalled at all
this gross unfaithfulness.
And then, I realised my only
course: I fall upon my knees
to pray! O LORD, I weep
for this disgrace. We're
meant to be a people who
are holy, choice of
YHVH–LORD.

Our guilt betrays our fault—
We've suffered punishment
for disobedience, rebellion,
too. And yet we do not learn
the utter sin of it. How You
must grieve
our waywardness!

You brought us home. You
grant to us a friendship
that's unique and yet we
have betrayed Your trust yet

once again. This people is
corrupted, LORD, the land
has been polluted and we
need a cleansing now.

You are the God of Israel!
You've kept Your promise
that a remnant would return.
Not one of us is worthy of
Your precious love, your
grace…

What is that noise? I hear
the sound of weeping,
wailing. Why? In looking
up, I see a crowd
approaching me.
Then Shechaniah spoke
for all: We've been
unfaithful and we are in
great distress because of it.
But we have hope!
We hope in God!
We want to make
a covenant.

When all had been arranged,
the people sat before the
House of God. Their deep
distress was plainly seen
and heard for rain was also
falling there.

I stood before the penitents
and challenged them

to make confession and
commit themselves to do
God's will, stay true to
Him—a holy people,
dedicated: whole! They did
agree and planned the
means to solve the sin.

And so the exiles did as was
proposed. The family heads
each supervised the plans
whereby each case was
solved. On New Year's
Day we found a great
accomplishment!

….. oOo …..

THE TENACIOUS YEARS

HISTORICAL RECORDS CONTINUED

NEHEMIAH

I need to introduce
myself! You see, I am, it
would appear, included with
the prophets of Israel. This
cannot be for I am but a
servant of the king of Persia!
I am the one designated to
test his food, ensure its
quality. I 'bear the cup' into

King Artaxerxes—on the whole, a kindly man to me.

To my surprise, the king has now requested that I travel to Jerusalem to check the work for I received disquieting reports. At least, my name has a meaning to my liking. My name means *The LORD Comforts.* I've found that this is really so. I serve the LORD! I think it is the LORD who calls me to this task. Perhaps, I'll be a prophet yet!

My task right now is to set down the facts, as history, that led me to my task and good grace. This is the news:

NEHEMIAH: CUP BEARER
Chapters 1 – 2

You'll see my main report: it's placed within the pages of the Annals of our History.
I'm Nehemiah and I need to give my testimony as part of this inserted History relating to the final years of Exile and repatriation from the Medo-Persian

lands. The date is well defined—how could I once forget—it was the month of Kislev (the twentieth year) while I remained in Susa's lavish Citadel.

My brother came from Israel; I loaded him with questions all the while. How does the remnant fare? What of Jerusalem? The Temple, too?

I sorrowed at the news, so ill, he brought to me. There is, it seems, great trouble and there's much disgrace. The walls of our Jerusalem have fallen down. The gates, destroyed.

I mourned and fasted at his words. I found myself in tears. I prayed: O LORD, You keep Your covenant of Love; please, listen to my earnest plea.
I'm praying for Jerusalem, for Israel, Your chosen people, LORD. On their behalf, I do confess our sin.
Your laws, decrees, commands are trampled on.
It is the sin of self that

countermands the justice,
ordinance, of *YHVH*–
LORD.

I do remember, LORD, how
You instructed Moses as to
why Your will for us was
vital to well-being of the
Clans; that—in events that
prove unfaithfulness—
we would be scattered all
abroad without a hope.

But! If we'd turn to You,
You'd turn to us, You'd
gather us back from
beyond the far horizons of
the Earth. You'd bring us
'Home'! These are Your
people, LORD; You have
redeemed us by Your love,
Your power, Your mighty
hand. O LORD, now hear
my prayer and grant me
good success in my petition
to the king. Please, give me
strength: I will obey.

I am appointed 'Keeper of
the Cup'—ensuring that the
king was safe from all
onslaught. I know the king
respected me, relied on me
to keep him safe. He is
the king, of course!

I know my place.
So, now I fear to
look into his face for I
am grieving at the news
of happenstance at 'Home'.
Jerusalem cries out for help:
how may I tread the ground
whereby I ask for help
from him, King Artaxerxes,
with the face that I
must turn to him?

ARTAXERXES
Nehemiah 2

I do appreciate this man—
there's something different
in his stance, demeanour,
and his just behaviour when
I'm not around or, seated on
my throne. There is
no subterfuge, no under-
hand exploits I hear of him.
I see him now approach.
Did I say 'different'?
There's something new
today in Nehemiah's stance!

I call to him and ask of him
the reason why he looks so
sad. Now, Nehemiah,
you're not ill. There is, no
doubt, a reason why you
turn a sorrowed face to me!

You're sad at heart,
I think, perhaps?

He told me then how
matters stood: His heritage
was ruined—there is no
home, no fortresses
whereby some safety would
be sure. I said to him, What
is your will about this grief?
What may I do to ease your
pain? I'll hear from you.

He is respectful to the
throne—he prefaced all he
said with if I have found
some favour in your sight,
please, let me go to
oversight the building once
again of all my heritage.

I could not disagree with
him! How long, I asked,
would you be gone? What
do you need? I'll see that all
is done forthwith by edict
and with force!

I set down edicts for the
men who governed Trans-
Euphrates land ensuring his
safe-conduct and some
letters to the overseers of
the forest, thus providing
needs for building once

again his 'Home'.
Ensuring safety on the trek,
I ordered that a large cohort
of cavalry escort,
accompany him. I waved
my man goodbye,
'Godspeed'!

SANBALLAT
Chapter 2

Tobiah,—he's the
Ammonite—Tobiah, we
will have to think on this.
From all I hear, this is
a great catastrophe!
This wretched man—
yes, Nehemiah—
will arrive with cavalry
and such in toe, to take
control of all the things
we have undone!
We've set in place
a new regime, you know.
How dare this man
prepare to foil all we
have done to date!

NEHEMIAH
The Arrival

I've just arrived. Three days
it took to settle in and view

the great disaster at our feet.

I took the 'cloak' of
darkness with a few
assistants too, to guide.
And, in surveying all the
site, I was appalled at what
Our enemies had wrought.

I called officials, priests,
the noblemen and others
who would be inclined to
offer help. I said, You see
the trouble we are in—
come, let us now begin!

Let us rebuild what could
have been. Too long,
disgrace has been the theme
of all we've thought of it—
the ruins of smashed rock,
burned gates and sheltered
homes. Without
pause, they rolled up
sleeves, began the work
with all good enterprise.

ELIASHIB
Chapter 3

I'm High Priest and elated
at the work that we've
begun. Our full report will
be outlined within the

Annals of our History.
Suffice to say, I testify to
what we've done thus far:

The Fish Gate was rebuilt
and sections of the wall
around it raised forthwith.
And then, The Jeshanah
Gate, the Valley Gate,
the Dung Gate, Fountain
Gate with walls erected on
each side. The Horse Gate
was erected too and all the
men at work with will!

These men were organised
by rote in sections so the
whole could be erected with
the greatest skill
and timely, too! It was a joy
to see such bold activity!

SANBALLAT
Chapter 4

**This can't go on! We must
attack! We tried to mock,
to ridicule. This did not
work. We'll need to act
before the Gates are
closed. A battle must be
fought or we will lose the
ground we've won. We
need to stir up trouble**

**here. The enemy must now
deplete what they will
need to finish all the work.
That's when we'll strike
and win! Before they see
us come, we'll strike them
down. They won't know
what has hit them by
the end of every blow!**

NEHEMIAH

The Jews who lived nearby
were spreading rumours,
too, that Sanballat, Tobiah,
and the rest of them will
kill us all and no mistake.
It's time to act!

I called the leaders to my
side, encouraged them,
explained my plans. All
were agreed. This did
frustrate the foe! We all
returned to work upon
the outer walls.

From that day on,
half of the men were set to
watch and half to lay the
bricks so that the wall was
raised. The workers all wore
swords at work—they were

prepared for Sanballat. And
when a trouble loomed, the
trumpeters would sound
alarms so all were ready for
the fray. All came together
when a threat would loom.

The work progressed. We
paused not day nor night—
the work by day, the guard
at night—all did their part.
We kept our day clothes on
also at night and each
with weapon too.

NEHEMIAH
Chapter 5

At times, our people were
without sufficient food. The
cry went up, their needs
were met though difficult to
fathom why it should be so.
Upon my test of them, it
was discovered that our
leaders were extracting from
the workers, guards, yes, all
the populace
the populace, a tax that was
obscene! When challenged,
they were speechless with
regret. Should not you walk
within the ways that
YHVH–LORD decrees?

I said. You should avoid
reproach when all our foes
surround us day and night.
Give back to each all you
extracted from their
meagre means. We will
comply. Taxes, now,
will be returned to all.

The priests were then all
summoned up to then
extract an oath that would
confirm the promises being
made. I shook my robes
then to imply that any man
that fails his word would
then be shaken out from all
and emptied of his lot.
Amen! the host replied
with one accord.

Through all the time the
wall was being rebuilt, I did
not take what could have
been my lot. Instead, I did
ensure that all did eat their
fill—the poor, as well as
Foreigners who came to
shelter in our kindest care.
At last, the walls were
built—not one small crack
was found in all of it!

TOBIAH
Chapter 6

Sanballat, Geshem and I
have viewed all this with
great distain. We then
devised a plot. Sanballat,
feigning piety, sent word
to Nehemiah that they
should meet right at
a site that was immune
from vicious spite.

A message was returned
forthwith that Nehemiah
wrote to us: I'm in the
middle of a mighty work.
I have no time to come
to you. I cannot stop
the work just for
a meeting far away.

Of course, we did repeat
our invite to the man.
In fact, four times we sent
the invite and four times
we got the same response
from him! Then Sanballat
sent his man to Nehemiah
and repeated all that had
been sent before to him,

Five now, the times of
these communications.
This was our ruse—we're
proud of it: It is reported
that you plan revolt,
that you'll appoint a king

instead of Persia's mighty
potentate. You are
informed this news will go
to Persia's ruler now!
Nehemiah would have no
plan to work with us,
comply with us. We've
reached impasse again!

NEHEMIAH
Chapters 6 – 7

Sanballat, Tobiah and the
rest of them were trying to
put fear within the heart of
Israel. I prayed to *YHVH*–
LORD for strength.

One day, I was advised to
flee into the Temple for my
enemies were seeking to
demand my life. I then
replied, Should I be one
who'd run away and should
I flee to Temple ground? I
will not go! I realised that
Sanballat had hired his man.

The work at last was done
so swiftly and so well. We
came to the completion
date. Our enemies forsook
us then. They realised that
YHVH–LORD was on

our side! The time had come
to make our plans for
Dedication Day!

The doors were set in place;
appointments then were
made—my brother, Hanani,
was placed in charge of all
Jerusalem and Hananiah—
he was a man of great
integrity—became
Commander of the Citadel.
The rules required for safety
and the guards to post in
each locality were allocated
then to our delight.

The city was prepared for
all who would return back
to their heritage. We
checked the records, found
them all in place for each
and every town. When all
was ready on the day, the
people all assembled at
the City Square to celebrate.

EZRA
Chapter 8

When all was set in place,
I was requested—as the
Priest and Scribe—to bring
the Book of Moses' Law

before the host. I read
from it without a break,
all through the morn till
noon, I read "The Law"!

The people listened most
attentively. As I'd begun
to read, they all stood up,
remaining so throughout
with due 'Amens' in tune
exclaimed. They bowed
and then they worshipped
YHVH–LORD. It was
unique, this great assembled
group, devout in worship of
the *YHVH*–LORD.

NEHEMIAH

This day is sacred to the
LORD: enjoy your food and
drinks while making sure
that those without a meal
can join in too. Don't
grieve. Now know with all
assurance that it is the joy
of *YHVH*–LORD that is
your daily strength. Rejoice!

Then, on the second day,
Ezra had continued with
The Law. He read again, at
length. It was discovered—
in the Book of Law—

that people were to live in
booths within the seventh
month. They shall proclaim,
throughout the land, this
holy ordinance. Returning
home, they were to bring
back branches from the
trees to make their booths.

The people did respond so
well. The Festival of Booths
had now begun once more
in Israel. The Festival had
not been e'er so joyful as
this celebration! And, day
after day, Ezra would open
once again the Book of
Moses' Law and read from
it. This was a time most
blessed indeed!

A CITIZEN
Chapters 9 – 10

It was the twenty-fifth day
of the month when there
were great hosts of people
gathered there. I stood with
them that Holy Day!

We stood in our allotted
place, each wearing
sackcloth with fine ash dust
scattered on our heads.

The Law was read.
We stood enthralled, then,
all together we resolved to
make confession of our sins
before, together, all were
worshipping the LORD:

O blessed be Your Holy
Name For You alone are
YHVH–LORD. You made
the heavens and the Earth.
Your power we do applaud.
You've given life to
everyone: We worship you,
O *YHVH*–LORD!

The Annals of our History
were then relayed to us
by spoken word. We were
reminded of the mounts of
praise, the valleys of deep
grief where we betrayed the
LORD in many ways.

We prayed that *YHVH*–
LORD who keeps His
Covenant of Love, would
keep us through the years
to come, would guide,
direct, our ways, that we'd
remain true to our word
before the LORD:

O LORD, protect us as a
host once slaves because of
sins the past has offered us
and taken, too. We live in
deep distress, regret. O
LORD, we make this
solemn vow to serve You
whole, and holy as we sign
and seal before You now
these promises so surely
made.

A RESIDENT
Chapter 11

What a surprise it was for
us! First, all the leaders
settled in Jerusalem and
then we all cast lots to settle
one in ten within the City
walls. This was a tithe of all
the population as all that
missed the tithe were
counted nine of ten! There
is a chapter given to the
allocations made within
the Annals of our History.
I won't account, therefore,
those records here. At least,
I'm counted in the Tithe!

A LEVITE
Chapter 12

The time has come for all

of us—the Levites—to assemble in Jerusalem that we may join in celebration on the day the City walls are dedicated to the *YHVH*–LORD. There'll be a great thanksgiving, psalms of praise accompanied by the instruments: the cymbals, harps and lyres. Oh yes, the choir, comprised of choristers from near and far are brought together now.

I see the leaders of Judah up there, atop the City walls. The choir is now divided into two. They, too, are on the City wall. One walked to right and one walked to the left. Oh! Listen to the harmonies surrounding us!

They've done the circuit now—they are processing on towards the holy Temple of the LORD to offer sacrifice together now. I do declare that all the sound Is echoing around the city walls. Each man, appointed to a task— to fill the storerooms to ensure the sustenance of

priests—fulfilled their roles before the benediction!

ALL IS DONE!

NEHEMIAH
Chapter 13

Upon the day the Holy Book—the Law of Moses— was then read within the hearing of the host, the story of old Balaam and his ass, it was there acknowledged that our land should now be rid of aliens; that we should be a nation wholly one and pure within the sight of *YHVH*–LORD.

Our leaders noted that Tobiah still was implicated in the plans relating to our stores. This was against our principles. I was not present not present at the time. When news arrived concerning this, I was incensed that such could be allowed. I had, of course, returned to Artaxerxes and my role as servant to the king. I asked once more for leave, was granted it.

Upon arrival at the scene
of such disgust, I took upon
myself the task of
extricating all Tobiah's
'goods' from Temple
courts.

When this was finalised,
we purified the rooms,
returned equipment that
belonged. Because of other
matters, too, concerning
Levites who forsook their
great responsibilities,
I did rebuke officials who
had oversight: Why are your
tasks relating to the Temple,
House of God, neglected
so? I gave the order they
remain at
their appointed tasks.

So, things began to level
out... Again, I went to
prayer: O LORD, do not
forget the work that I have
done to make Your house to
be as You desire.

Some further areas of care
not taken for the Sabbath
Day had need to be
addressed. I did not fail to
order all necessities to be
fulfilled. I'm glad that God

has called me to this task.
At times, I find the burden
is too great but realise He
needs me here!

Remember me, O LORD,
and show Your mercy now,
according to the love You
have displayed to me.
Remember me, O LORD,
because the priests must be
made pure. Remember me,
O *YHVH*–LORD.

..... oOo .....

**HISTORICAL
RECORDS
CONTINUED**

ESTHER

Mine is an awesome task
for I must walk a narrow
path. I am, you see, the
chosen queen of Xerxes,
new king of the Medo-
Persian Empire. Though yet

little does he know that I am Jewish through and through.

Perhaps you'll know Mordecai, my uncle, better than you know myself. I follow his advice though tentatively at times. Your own assumption that my story is set during the Jewish Exile is sound. You will note that I bring no emphasis to *YHVH*–LORD as we choose to draw no specific attention to the many ways He guards and guides our daily lives.

We continue to trust in Him in our heart, our soul! Whatever be the end of our commitment to the LORD, I must stand for the right against the subterfuge of Haman who must be defeated. We'll trust in God.

XERXES
Chapter 1

Bring in the best \hIc/ booze! We need to supplement all *(hic)* **supplies of wine fit for the king! Where are the servants now? Why aren't** (hiC) **drinks now poured?**

You see, we're partying *(HIC)* **now! We've been at it, full on, oh yes, for more** \Hic/ **days than I can count;**
the wine *(HIC)* **flowed, no restraint. My friends deserve the very best from me, Xerxes, Persia's King. I rule a vast empire! See: from India to Egypt I rule** \hIc/.

Where is the Queen? Go, (hic) **fetch the Queen! My Vashti must be part of this great feast. Come, Vashti** (HIC) **my turtle dove. What's this you say? She will not come to me? She has refused my company? Since when have Queens ruled over kings? She will not sit with drunken** \hIc/ **clowns? I'll have her golden** *(HIC)* **crown for this atrocity!**

Go! Take from her the royal robes and all her jewellery. *(Hic)* **Then, lead her down into the darkest Persian night! I will not**

look on her again through all my \hic hic/ **reign!**

MORDECAI
Chapter 2

I am a Jew—keep hush of
it—and I'm informed of
happenings up in the 'ivory
palaces'. It does appear that
Xerxes needs to find
another queen for him!
(The harem does not
suit his tastes).

I have devised a scheme that
will—if things go right—be
helpful to
our cause. My cousin,
Hadassah, (whom I am
pleased to call 'Esther')
is more beautiful than all
who live at Court, of any
in the Eastern realm.
Perhaps the king could be
inclined to look on her
with 'kindly' gaze!

I worked my plan and things
went well. My cousin Esther
is accepted as a worthy
'applicant'. Before she left
my guardianship, I did
advise most strongly that

she never mention anything
of her own heritage—such
would be viewed with
arrogance (at best, she
would be shunned).

All applicants had need to
be prepared through many
months of beautifying,
educating, in the ways of
king and court. When Esther
was in readiness
to be presented to the king,
she went with grace and all
the beauty of her race. She
smiled. The king, Xerxes
was entranced with her.
He made his choice without
a pause. Esther became the
'Persian' Queen!

Just near to these events
I heard of a conspiracy
to soon assassinate the king.
I so informed Queen Esther
who then told His Majesty
what was afoot.
The queen gave credit to my
role. The courtiers
responsible were hanged.

HAMAN
Chapter 3

I'm Haman, favoured
courtier of King Xerxes
and I keep my eyes and
ears alert for all that
would bring grief to him
(or me,
if I'd be honest once).
I have discovered that
some Jews have infiltrated
to the Court (I have my
ways and means)!

I mean to do away with
them—they're prone to so
ingratiate themselves with
king and queen and I'll
have none of that intrigue!
They could usurp my
powerful plans.

Your majesty, it comes to
my attention that some
activities are now afoot
that places you in jeopardy.
If it will please you, Sire,
let it be said that Mordecai
has not obeyed your
strong edict to kneel
whenever I pass by.
It is outrageous Sir!

MORDECAI

The matter was then was
checked. The king complied

with Haman's guile that, by
the Purim Festival—the first
conducted by all Jews—his
plot would seal the coffin
of us all—and me of course!

HAMAN

The king took off his
signet ring and gave it to
me, together with these
words, Do what you
please: Be done with
Jews forthwith!

The edict then went out to
all the governors that Jews
would grieve: This is the
Signature, the Seal, of
Xerxes, King of Medo-
Persia (at my expressed
request of course.)
This Act will happen on
Adar Day—with
plundering of goods
at once allowed!

THE QUEEN
Chapters 4 – 5

I had been told of Mordecai
and of his plight. I knew
that I must act at once.

But how? My aides were
asked to change his clothes
but he would not comply,
explaining then that all
the evil Haman wrought
to wipe the Jews from off
the face of Earth. I sent him
word that I would seek to
rectify the circumstance of
doom for us. I ordered
Mordecai to gather all the
Jews of Susa to fast for me,
that all my plans would
work. Three days from now,
I'd go into the presence of
the king. This was forbidden
but I'd place myself into
his care with love.

I donned my royal robes
and stood before the throne.
I touched the sceptre in his
hand; He knew I'd need
to speak with him.

If it will give a pleasure to
the King, I've planned a
feast for you and your chief
courtier—Haman—I wish
to honour both.

Xerxes sent for Haman then,
requesting he present
himself for special plans to
celebrate the worth

of Haman to the king. So,
according to my plan, as
we would eat the feast
prepared, Xerxes asked the
reason why this feast was
planned for them. If you
regard your Queen, my
King, I do request that you
and Haman will then come,
partake another feast
to honour you. I'll then
reply to your request for
explanation then.

I noticed Haman was
delighted with the thought
of further banquets that
would honour him. I heard
him boast of all the honours
given to him. He firmed up
plans to hang the Jews
(He knew not I would be
involved! Haman, I'm sure,
will be surprised)!

ESTHER
Chapter 6

The king was restless in the
night; he felt the need to
check his work. He noted
once again how he was
saved by wise old Mordecai.
What had been done

to honour him
and recognise his worth to
me? His courtiers explained
it was not done. The king
then saw that Haman stood
within the court. Haman
was summoned and the king
inquired, What should
be done for one that I
delight to honour. Tell me
now, Haman!

Haman, of course, thought
of himself so offered this
advice: Let him receive a
royal robe, a horse the king
has ridden on for then
the honoured man would
ride the city streets for
adulation there! the king
agreed and said at once:
Go now, Haman, to
Mordecai—the Jew that sits
at city gates. Do all that you
suggest for him. Do not
neglect one thing I've said!

What pain this was for him
but Haman knew he must
fulfil the edict of Xerxes,
King. He placed the robe on
Mordecai and mounted him
upon the horse then Haman
led the animal while
chanting all the while:

This is what Xerxes, King,
decrees for one in whom
he takes delight!

How Haman hated the
parade! His cohorts then
advised the man that
Mordecai be hanged quite
soon. Before this plan could
be advanced, Haman was
ushered to the most
delicious banquet I'd
Prepared for king and him.

ESTHER
Chapter 7

The time had come for me
to stand up for the Jews
about to die. Queen Esther,
what is your request?
It will be given you. Speak
now: Up to half the
Kingdom, it is yours!

I spoke the solemn words,
as planned: If it will please
Your Majesty, please, spare
my life, and spare the lives
of all my people, Sire.
You see, I am a Jew and all
my people—yes, including
me are to be sold for
laughter and to be

destroyed, annihilated, all!
Who is the man who's
planned this ghastly thing?
Who dares to perpetrate
such slaughter here?

O Sire, the enemy,
adversary, is with us now:
Haman, 'the Horrible'!
The king was in a rage. He
went out to the palace
grounds. But Haman,
knowing peril near,
remained to plead
his cause with me.

He fell upon my couch with
pleas. The king returned,
misread the act: Molest the
Queen, would you? Away
with him and let him swing
upon the gallows built for
Jews! Only then Xerxes'
fury did subside and every
Jew sighed with relief.

XERXES
Chapters 8 – 9

At last I know of Haman's
guilt of subterfuge, blind
hatred for a people vaguely
understood. I must admit

my Queen has been of great
assistance. First, I must
acknowledge her great
grace. Esther has led me to
confirm that Jews are folk
of high regard,
integrity and
wholesomeness!

Esther will have my word—
I swear by sceptre, crown,
that I'll regard the lives
of all those sentenced to
the gallows and they
will be repaid for evil done
to them. I'll send this news
from India to Egypt now!
None will molest those
humble Jews!

I've ordered Mordecai to
wear the royal gowns of
blue and white, a crown
of gold, a purple robe.
The news has reached,
now, my placated ears
of celebrations far and wide.
Much happiness and joy
abounds throughout the
royal realm. I am so well
impressed. In fact, I know
of some non-Jews who have
decided to now switch
allegiances—they have

become new Jews!

It was decreed the thirteenth
day of Adar—the self-same
day that fool,
Haman, had planned
eradication of all Jews—the
tables would be turned.
All governors, satraps and
noblemen assisted all the
Jews—they knew what
side to spread the butter on!

And all the while, I have
observed the worth of
Mordecai. He is a man on
whom I can rely. He now is
elevated in responsibility.
We did eradicate the
perpetrators of the evil
scheme until, at last,
all rested from their
heavy, onerous tasks.

My acts of power and might
are well recorded in the
Annals of our History and,
theirs, the Jews. I have
included words that do
acclaim the worth of
Mordecai. He is pre-
eminent among the Jews
and held in high esteem for
he did—with my Queen—

work for the good, the
welfare of all Jews and, us!

MORDECAI
Chapters 9 – 10

The fifteenth day of Adar
came with celebrations,
feasts, to mark the passing
of our fears—the fears
we Jews had held for many
moons. I've set up records
of the happenings of recent
days. Together, then, we
instigated Purim. Yes! This
feast would remember every
happening concerning
Esther's saving of the Jews
in Persia, exiled from
Jerusalem, our Home.
Queen Esther did confirm
all the decrees relating to
each year's remembrance of
Purim. (We joy in God
for all His grace)!

HERE ENDS THE
HISTORICAL NEWS!

….. oOo …..

THE TRYING YEARS

....

THE MINOR PROPHETS

HOSEA

My name is Hosea. I do rejoice in this! You see, the great Joshua and I may stand together by this name: it means *salvation*—Joshua, *Jeshua* (some would say, also, *Jesus*—a derivation, it is true.) But here I also stand. Hosea: *salvation!* Oh, that I might be a *saviour* too!

Uniquely, I'm the only prophet, of all those entered in these records, whose home is in the north: Israel, the northern Kingdom! What I have to say will be directed to the Northern Clans.
I date my work quite early in the writings of the lesser prophets. You will hear of Amos soon although he lives in southern climes just now.

And, you'll want to know the identity of the enemy that is the focus of my 'parable'. By chapter 7 you'll recognise Assyria: our great foe.

YHVH–LORD
Chapter 1

Hosea! Listen for I have in mind for you a most perplexing parable: a task that will require all that your trust in Me will need for this is not an easy thing a man of faith can contemplate. Hosea, you're to take a wife, a whore, for I would have you 'paint' a bleak picture of Israel's adultery against all they were taught about integrity, credulity and faithfulness: Israel has taken to adultery!

HOSEA

How can He ask this thing of me, the vilest deed an honest man would dare to do among his friends, the villagers, the nation, too?

Yet, He would have His
reasons and He knows I will
obey. I trust Him so. I know
Him so. I know that *YHVH–*
LORD will keep me whole
and true to Him. I searched
for one, a whore and found
Gomer; proposed, then took
her to my home, a man now
married to a wife who has
displayed herself without
restraint. (How can I show
my face to anyone?)

We have a son. His name,
'Jezreel', reveals that
Israel's due for punishment;
for massacres just near this
place. Israel will come to
grief within the Valley
of Jezreel!

We have a daughter now.
The LORD decreed her
chosen name should tell
of broken partnerships
between Israel and *YHVH–*
LORD. The baby's name is
'Lo-Ruhamah'. How
terrible the news contained
within that name. It means
I'll show no love to Israel
(and they are not
forgiven now.)

Hosea, now let it be
Made known I'll now
love Judah, Benjamin.

Another child to grace our
home: The LORD instructed
that his name would be 'Lo-
Ammi' which means:

You're not My people and
I am no longer your YHVH–
LORD, Israel!

She's gone! My Gomer's
gone from me. I learned to
love her so. She has
preferred an alien love:
her children miss her so.

She's gone! My Israel's
gone from me I learned to
love her so. She chose
instead an alien god.
I yearn for her.

Hosea, know that Israel
will yet become a mighty
race. Just where they heard
the news they were no
longer Mine, they will, one
day, be called 'the sons of
YHVH–LORD'. And there
will be reunion of Judah
and Israel. They'll have

once more one leader and
one land. They'll be My own
beloved ones—Israel—
one family and beloved!

YHVH-LORD:
THE REBUKE
Chapter 2

Hosea, this is the Parable:
Rebuke Gomer (Israel,) I'm
not the One who is her
husband. No! It's time she cast
away all her adultery,
unfaithfulness.
Unless she'll change her
wicked ways, she'll find a
desert place. Her children will
become as orphans for her
carelessness.

Her wantonness has caused
distress, she searches for the
riches of this world. I'll block
her path; I'll wall her in her way
confine.
She'll search in vain for love
and will decide her husband
gave the better circumstance
for her. This is no basis for
return.

Without repentance, all is vain,
resources will be lost to her.

The vines, the figs, deprived
bring famine then
for thorns and thickets grow
where once the fertile land
produced abundant crops.
These are laid bare for sin.

But know this too, Hosea:
The day will come when I'll
restore her wealth. Out in the
desert, yet, I'll give to her
a door of hope.
She'll sing as in her youthful
days. O Israel, then you will
call Me 'Husband' and your lips
will praise the one true God:
I am your Hope!

I'll make a covenant with Israel:
I will betroth you to Myself
in righteousness and justice,
love, compassion and My
faithfulness.
In that day I'll respond as skies
respond to earth, as earth
responds to need throughout
the land, rejoicing in its
fruitfulness.

I'll show My love to Israel:
the land once known: 'Not
Loved'; those known as 'Not
My People' will reveal their love
for Me then prove.

Israel will know "I AM", the
LORD. In that great day, I'll
prove My love; that, though
they strayed, I welcome them,
My faithfulness I'll prove.

HOSEA
Reconciliation
Chapter 3

The LORD has spoken
once again:

*Go now to Gomer, show your
love though she forsook you
for her wanton loves. Go,
love her well as I love Israel.
This act of love will
demonstrate My love for
Israel. I do not fail My love
for them though far they rove.*

I went to her with confidence
in re-awakened love. This will
reveal to Israel a parable:
the Israelites will live without
a king for many years, without
the rituals and worship's ways.
Then, they will return with
trembling and remorse. They
will no longer doubt.

THE CHARGE
Chapters 4 – 7

I am the YHVH–LORD who
speaks, O Israel, for I must
bring this charge: there is no
faithfulness, no love. You live
degraded lives of lewdness,
of adultery and drunkenness,
brawls, murder, theft—what
graft! The people waste in
penury, the land is mourning
for your sinfulness.

You stumble in the dark,
your priests and prophets too.
You have rejected wisdom, live
in ignorance—priests in
disgrace the glory now discard
with mirthless glee.

Your prophets prattle,
disregard—with no account for
right—the truth of current
circumstance; You choose to
bow to idols every day.
Yours is a whoredom that is
vile: it's wholly spiritual! And
you, O Judah, know your
harvest comes!

Whenever I would move to
heal Israel, her sin is still
exposed. It's set before My
face, Israel, deceit and theft
your evil crimes,

*The king delights in
wickedness; adulterous fires
burn on—they need no stoking
now. Men fall but no one
cries out their pain to Me.
Ephraim is a cake not turned
(it's burned;) his strength of
grace is gone—you're like a
senseless dove. You run to
aliens: so, let it be!*

*I long to be Redeemer, Israel;
though you cry out, it's not
to Me.
You gather to your yearly
feasts
but turn from Me with careless
words.
You're like a faulty bow that
won't allow an arrow's flight
that's straight. The nation—
all—will know, too late, that
they will fall by slashing
swords.*

THE CONSEQUENCES
Chapter 8

*Now sound the trumpets for
an eagle swoops upon its prey:
My people have defied their
LORD, they failed to keep the
Covenant,
rebelled against My Holy Law.*

*They cry to Me, they plead
their cause but they have not
obeyed My word: How long,
Israel, still unrepentant?*

*All those that sow a wily wind
will find they reap whirlwind.
A stalk that has no head
cannot produce some flour!
The grain that's grown will
be devoured by alien
soldiers here. Israel is
Israel is worthless in extreme,
they're donkeys none can steer
though with power.*

*I had their laws all written down
on plates of stone that will
remain all through the years of
time. these were regarded as
all mean;
their sacrifice was utter gall.
I am not pleased with them at
all. I will remember their past
sins—a worthy man I cannot
glean!*

THE PUNISHMENT
Chapters 9 – 10

*Do not rejoice, O Israel!
Do not be jubilant: You are
unfaithful to your LORD. So,
know your winepress,*

battered threshing floor,
will fail to yield what you desire.
And as for you: return to Egypt
is the route for you—it's alien
gods that you adore.

What will you do when seasons
come for festivals and fasting,
too? Your treasures will be lost
in briars and thorns will then
infest your tents.
A reckoning is in the arid wind;
there will be no reward for
you—you've ridiculed the man
of God: no watchman
made you tense.

When I first found Israel,
it was like finding grapes within
a desert place, like early fruit.
But you disintegrated to
sour grapes and tasteless figs.
So! You'll be barren too; with-
out a grace, you'll be bereft;
much woe will come to you.

What you should sow is
righteousness and reap the
fruit of perfect love! Break up
the fallow ground today: it's
time to seek the YHVH–LORD.
You'll find that that I will come
and shower My righteousness
on you. No longer seek a
wickedness nor reap the evil,

worthless grain to hoard.

THE LOVE OF GOD
Chapter 11

When Israel was a tender child,
I loved him as a father would. I
called My son from Egypt's
clasp but Israel strayed away.
I taught Ephraim (Israel) to
walk—a toddler in My loving
arms—but he refused to realise
that it was I who loved alway!

I led Israel with cords of love
with special kindness all the
way; I lifted up the yoke that
choked and knelt to feed
them and to love all.
How can I give you up,
Ephraim and can I disregard
you, Israel? All My compassion
is aroused: I'll settle you again
within the land of Israel.

I act this way for I am God,
not man—"I AM", the Holy One;
I'll come to you. I do not carry
wrath to you. With Me,
you'll come back 'Home'.
You'll tremble like a frightened
bird: behold the gentle dove,
her fear; you'll know Me then,
you'll follow Me. So come!

re-join My Family:
I'll settle you at Home.

REBELLION
Chapter 12

Ephraim has long pursued his
ways, unruly and deceitful,
violent. He feeds upon the
Eastern wind, he courts
Assyria with 'hay'.
I have a charge to bring
against Judah and Jacob will
be punished for his wicked
deeds. Assyria receives
his 'oil' today!

You do remember Jacob well?
God found him at Bethel,
alone. He met with God, the *El
Shaddai*—the Mighty God—
that night.
It's up to Jacob now: return
unto The *YHVH*–LORD,
maintain your love. Remember
to act justly now and wait for
God to act with might.

Acknowledge sinful ways:
you merchant men—your
scales are rigged; dishonesty
pervades—you would defraud
your dearest friend!
You boast of your great wealth,
you say that none know of your

sin. So! Know the "I AM": God,
the LORD. On Him always
you can depend.

THE WRATH OF GOD
Chapter 13

*When Ephraim, Israel, was
strong in faith, integrity and
grace, he was exalted… guilt
seeped in! O you who kiss the
brazen calf,
please know your circumstance
and where sin leads you now.
You're like evaporating dew,
Like chaff swept to a gulf.*

*But! Know this truth: I am the
LORD who led you from Egypt.
I cared for you through Sinai,
that desert-land of searing,
unrelenting heat.
I satisfied your hunger, thirst;
I gave you guidelines, Laws to
love, but you betrayed My trust
in you. Who will you trust
to be replete?*

*I make My Covenant with
Israel: I'll ransom you out from
your tomb; I will redeem you
from your 'death'. So! Where,
O Death, your plague?
And, where O Grave, your*

power? won't look kindly on
your sin. There's no
compassion for your wrong;
there is no life where
sin would drag.

REPENTANCE
Chapter 14

Return, O Israel, unto the
LORD; your downfall is
because of sin! Come to the
LORD on bended knee,
with due repentance, prayer.
Now make your plea: 'Forgive
us, LORD, receive us
graciously that we may serve
You all our days and treat all
else with care.'

I'll heal your waywardness,
Israel, and love you freely for
My ire is turned from you. I will
refresh as would dew. You'll
blossom then
like lilies rare; like cedar trees,
your roots will dig deep into soil
that's fertile as your branches
grow with splendour, whole
and clean.

All people will then dwell within
the shade that's granted them.
All Israel will flourish as the

corn; their fame will spread for
all to see!
O Ephraim, let idols crash.
I'll care for you, I'll nurture you;
Your fruitfulness will come from
Me. You are discerning? Walk
with Me!

. . . .

THE SONG OF HOSEA
Tune: *Deep Harmony, Old*
Hundredth LM

The *YHVH*–LORD, the *El*
Shaddai,
Almighty God, the LORD is He;
This is His Name, His holy
Name;
Allow Him now your Guide
to be.

Return to God, receive His love
And wait upon Him, trust in
God;
His ways are just, let yours be
too;
Maintain your love for all things
good.

The LORD has promised to
redeem
His people from the grave. So,
where

O Death is now your sting, your
plague?
And where, O Grave, your
waiting lair?

O seek the LORD, now turn to
Him,
He will forgive the penitent;
The LORD will heal your
wayward ways,
He'll love you freely, be your
Friend.

..... oOo .....

THE TREMULOUS YEARS

JOEL

Allow me to introduce myself. I'm one of many Joels, it's true, but you'll soon sort me out. As 'minor' as I am, I'll rate a mention further on when things fall into place. *Messiah* sees to that!

You'll probably work out that I'm a resident of Judah for that's where my burden lies! Don't worry about a lack of provable dates. What's more important is the message I bring to God's own people in this locust and drought plagued land! You want to rid yourselves of plagues and droughts, Israel? Clean up your act! Repent, return to God! Come clean!

WAKE UP!
Chapter 1

Hear this, you Elders, listen all
who hear my voice.

my voice. Has anything
like this been said before today
or in the past? Relate
this to
your children so they'll tell,
in turn, what must be known.
Wake up, you drunkards, time
to weep. Beware of what
you do!

The locust swarm is here to
steal! What could be left of
grain-filled fields? What they
have left, their spawn comes in
to plunder gleanings left.
There is a grain or two still on a
stalk (so few). More locusts
swoop. The locusts? See, a
nation comes marauding
through a land in debt

With teeth of lions, long fangs
just like a lioness, this army—
so numberless—lays waste the
drooping vines, the figs.
The bark has gone;
the branches bare, will surely
die. It's time for mourning,
sackcloth, ask. This grief is like
a husband's death; the land is
bare despair—all, gone!

The *YHVH*–LORD now calls
you to put on your grieving

Yes! You: the priests who
minister before the LORD
at altar, deep in prayer.
Declare a holy fast; assemble
all who name the Name
of *YHVH*–LORD. All come.
This is a sacred gathering.
Come to the LORD, cry out
your prayer.

Alas! The Day of *YHVH*–LORD
is near. It comes! Destruction
comes. The *YHVH El
Shaddai*—the One
Almighty God—His House
vacates!
Your food has been cut off, the
seeds are lifeless, storehouses
are bare,
the cattle moan, the herds
stand in a barren field. All joy
evaporates.

To You, O *YHVH*–LORD,
I call: as fire consumes
the barren land,
our pastureland is smouldering
ash. The fires have devastated
verdant, virile trees—
our forests are aflame. We are
laid bare. I see a wild beast
there now panting for some
water from a dried-up stream.
….. It dies …..

THE LOCUST ARMY
Chapter 2:1-17

Now! Blow the trumpet, let
its sound reverberate through
Zion. It's time for trembling
now. The Day of *YHVH*-LORD
approaches now,
so very near, so very
threatening! It is a day of
darkness as deep gloom
descends. You see that nimbus
cloud engulf the Mount of God?
Men howl!

Where can they flee? Fire is
before and flames at rear,
devouring where was once an
Eden bower but now, it is
a desert waste. The locusts
swarm, appearing as an army
bent on slaughter of all
enemies. With sound of
chariots they leap across
the land, A trauma with much
anguish grips the nations as all
watch for their advance. They
march. They charge. They act
as one great force
that's unified. They plunge into
the fray as no defence can hold
the march. They rush into the
fields, the towns. Fear soars.

The earth quakes as the
locusts tear the fabric of
society. All nature wilts
at their advance. The moon is
dark, the stars go dim as night
descends.
It does appear the *YHVH*–
LORD is leading this advance.
The LORD is mighty—He is
the *El Shaddai*—What might!
We wait in much
suspense!

At this late hour, return to God!
Return to Him with all your
heart. Your heartfelt mourning
would be heard. You tear
your garments in
great fear—why not the
rending of your hearts? Return
unto the LORD, you'll find He is
compassionate: His is
abounding love! With God,
victorious; you win!

You'll find He will relent. He
turns to pity you, to bring His
blessing to repentant hearts
and earnest souls. So! come
together now, declare
a holy fast. Assemble in
the Sacred Place. No matter
what your circumstance, all
come to pray; with penitence
enwrap your prayer.
……….

YHWH-LORD
Chapter 2:18 - 32

*I'll meet your need for grain,
for food: enough to feed your
families. I'll move to take away
the scorn that's tossed into
your penury.
That northern army will remove
itself to parched and barren
land; it's stench shall rise
perennially*

*Be not afraid, O Israel,
your LORD has done great
things. Rejoice with Me: Don't
be afraid, the arid earth is
turning green!
Look, see the trees are bearing
fruit: be glad, rejoice,
Jerusalem for, see, I come to
you today—here is
the autumn rain, the
righteous rain!*

*Now know: "I AM", the YHVH–
LORD. Remember I am with
Israel. I will repay you for those
years the locust swarms
destroyed,
wrought havoc in your land.
Your barns will be refilled.
I will work wonders in your
midst. I say to you:
Don't be afraid!*

*Know, in the future I will pour
My Holy Spirit on you all.
Your sons, your daughters too,
will prophesy with grace;
they'll teach My way.
Old men will dream, the young
will see clear visions of My
messages. My servants, too,
both men, women, will be
renewed from day to day.*

*You'll see great wonders in the
sky and, on the earth, you'll
see the signs of blood, fire,
smoke, the sun a darkened
face will show,
the moon's deep glow will be of
blood before the fateful day
when I will intervene on
troubled Earth. Then: call on
Me, I will save you!*

YHVH-LORD
Chapter 3

*Know, in these coming days
and at that very time, I will
restore Judah, Jerusalem;
I'll gather all the nations to
the Valley of Jehoshaphat.
I'll enter into judgement there
concerning Israel for they are
My inheritance. You'll now!*

So! what have you against
Your LORD, you people that
Surround Jerusalem, and all
Israel? He'll place your hatred
on your heads:
you took all things that were
of worth and hoarded them.
You sold His people into
alien hands
that they'd be cast in chains,
transported far from home.
So! Know God's plans, you
alien fiends.
He'll rouse His people from
those lands to which you sold
and left them there. He'll bring
them home and place upon
your heads
what you have done
so painfully to them. Know that
it is the YHVH–LORD who
speaks.

Proclaim this news! Prepare for
war, rouse all the warriors.
Take up your ploughshares,
make them swords, make
all your pruning hooks
a spear.
And let the weak know He is
strong. Come you nations march
to war. It's in Jehoshaphat you'll
meet your fate. The outcome is
quite clear!

Come, trample on the grapes
of wrath until the winepress
overflows. This is because of
wickedness the multitudes
appear so soon. This is
the Valley of Decision now:
The Day of YHVH–LORD is
near. Hark, hear His thunder
out of Zion. Know this: the
LORD your Refuge is.

THE BLESSING
Chapter 3:17 – 21

When you accept the
YHVH–LORD to be your
Stronghold and your Peace,
O Israel, you'll find Him on
His Holy, sacred, Hill.
The foreigners are gone for
good, Jerusalem will be the
place where holiness will
then be shown: a fountain
flows to make you whole!

………

THE SONG OF JOEL
Tune: *Arizona*   L.M.

Rejoice all people of
the LORD,

He has poured out His
righteousness
On those who trust His
holy Name;
The thirsty soul He satisfies.

The LORD forgives the past by
grace,
His bonds will be the cords of
love.
He brings the recompense of
years
For chains of sin had bound
the slave.

The LORD has promised that
one day,
He'll pour His Spirit on
mankind;
The young will testify
of Him,
See visions and redemption
find.

The day of YHVH–LORD
is near:
This is our time; don't be afraid.
God is our Refuge and
our Friend;
He is our Stronghold: trust in
God!

..... oOo .....

THE TREACHEROUS YEARS

AMOS

Greetings to you all. My news must be told so let me introduce myself. I'm Amos. I live in Tekoa, just a few miles south of Jerusalem. I cared for sycamore fig trees. All was at peace, life seemed good. I've taken care to educate myself being near to rabbis who trained me in the Law and all that it entails.

You may think I'm just a peasant—perhaps I am but, living on the land did not preclude my study of our history. I know its rights and wrongs. Perhaps it was because of this that I was called to speak the values and the will and ways of *YHVH*–LORD and His purposes for His people.

King Uzziah rules in Jerusalem where Isaiah also dwells. The nation is corrupt and I must speak to Israel. The news is far from good!

AMOS: THE INDICTMENT
Chapters 1 - 2

Oh, hear what *YHVH* has to say: For three sins, perhaps just four, I'll not turn back My wrath. You may be sure I'll smash the gates Damascus built
because of sin against Gilead. The fortress Ben-Hadad will fall and Gaza too has sealed her fate; Ashdod and Ashkelon will wilt.

For three sins, perhaps just four, old Edom feels My wrath. You did pursue your brother with a sword, without a due compassion for you took his life.
For three sins, four, Ammon will fall. You slaughtered pregnant wives! Your walls will burn with fire; exile will extend your strife.

For three sins, perhaps just four, Moab will fall: Your lime destroyed the bones of Edom's king. For this your fort will be consumed by blazing, fuming fire.
Moab will be destroyed, along with war cries, trumpet blasts.

The fortress of old Kerioth will burn, her ruler and officials: to the flames of ire!

For three sins, perhaps just four, for Judah's sins I'll not turn back My wrath. You have rejected *YHVH's* Law, Decrees, forsaken Him— false gods have entered in your life! The fires of judgement fall on you. Oh yes, a fire will fall on Judah too: It will consume Jerusalem!

For three sins perhaps just four O Israel, I'll not turn back My wrath: you sell your people out for wealth—your silver means much more than life.
You trample on the heads of those who have no strength; you did profane My holy Name; you have disgraced the Holy Place by drunkards' strife.

Remember how I sought and won the nation from Ammon; I brought you out of Egypt, sheltered you in desert lands for forty years.
I raised up prophets from your sons and Nazarites—the 'holy ones'. Is this not true? Did you forget, discard, the holy men

without some tears?

There is a punishment laid
down for such as you. You will
be crushed, your wagons
overladen, smashed.
The swift will not escape;
the strong
will find no strength, the archer
lose his stance; the warrior
vanquished; the horseman
won't his life prolong.

YHVH:
THE WITNESSES
Chapter 3

*You only have I chosen from
all nations of the Earth to be
My people, Israel. Where is
your trust? There is a
punishment for sin;
can two men walk in step
unless they can agree on
strategy? And will the lion roar
loud unless he spots a tasty
prey to win?*

*Will birds fall in a lethal trap
where not a snare is laid for
them?
And if the trumpet sounds,
will not the city quake
in fear?*

*The YHVH–LORD will not
fulfil His plans unless He first
announces it? You'll know
when He will act to right each
with care.*

*The lion has roared, the bird
will fall into the trap that's set;
the trumpet sounds. I've
spoken so the prophet now
must prophesy.
An enemy will overrun
the land. The strongholds are
to be destroyed; your
fortresses will know a plunder
as you die!*

*Just two bones from the hide
is saved out from the lion's
jaws. This is the parable of
Israel. How much is saved
though now you laze at ease
within Samaria? Hear Me, O
Israel, I am YHVH, El Shaddai:
on that day I'll destroy the altar,
homes, your very house!*

YHVH–LORD
Recalcitrant Israel
Chapter 4

*Hear this, all you who sit at
ease on Mount Samaria, all
you who still oppress the poor:*

Yes! I have sworn by My own
Holiness,
the time will come; you will be
led away by hooks, via
crumbling walls around you all.
Yet you will still perform your
rituals. Go on, now brag your
power: a mess!

I've tried the path of penury,
you would not turn to Me. I
have withheld
the rain to no avail. You
searched the streams for water
but you did
not turn to Me to be refreshed
in soul. Your gardens failed
and then the locusts came. No
one returned to Me. Instead,
from Me you hid!

The plagues upon you did not
win your trust. Your young men
died, you've shown no care.
You are a burning branch
snatched from a fire
yet you refuse My open arms.
Because of this, prepare to
meet with God—the one,
Creator LORD, all powerful El
Shaddai. It's dire!

THE LORD'S LAMENT
Chapter 5

You've fallen, Israel, once
great. I do lament your
wretched state: now no one
stands to pick you up; You're
destitute yet no one learns.
You march a thousand strong:
nought but a 'tithe' is left.
A thousand marches to the
fray; one hundred men,
a 'tithe', returns.

Now this is what I say to you:
seek after Me and you will live.
Don't yearn for Bethel or Gilgal
for they will go to exile—lost!
Seek after Me, you'll surely
live. Alternatives are bleak: a
fire on Joseph—Israel—it will
devour with none that's left
to boast.

I speak to those who turn
a blessing into bitterness,
the righteous tossed to dust.
You wonder who I am to speak
a doom upon you all. I am
the One who calls the dawn,
the One who turns the day to
night. You loathe justice,
no longer meek.

You trample on the poor, you
force My hand to give you
grain; you've built your
mansions where you will not

dwell, grown vineyards but
you'll drink no wine.
And where is justice in your
courts? The prudent man
refrains from speech!
Seek good that you may dwell
in grace. The YHVH–LORD will
come, refine.

YHVH–LORD
The Day of The LORD

Deep woe to those who long
for God to act, who plead
the Day of the LORD. Why
don't you understand that
Day brings darkness, not
the Light.
You're like a man who runs
from lions only to meet a
raging bear, to run back
home to find a snake that
bites. The Day of the LORD
won't be so bright.

I hate, despise your holy
feasts, I loathe assemblies
that feign allegiance,
holiness and grace.
I won't accept your tainted
offerings;
away with noisy hymns

and songs and cast away
the harps and lyres.
Let justice flow as rivers
wide and goodness like
perennial streams.

Woe to the Complacent
Chapter 6

You live complacently—
a woe upon you now. All you
who think you are secure on
Mount Samaria. Observe the
cities that surround
you now: are they much
better off than you? Look at
yourselves: you live in luxury
but you don't grieve for any
who have fallen down.

Observe it, if you will: I ask,
just think of how your
sinfulness has grieved your
YHVH–LORD. Consider how
I do abhor
your pride, your arrogance.
Know this: the House of
Israel will fall, it's castings
will be small: a nation comes
with greater power.

AMOS

The Plumbline
Chapter 7

The sovereign LORD
revealed to me the
preparations for 'rebuke':
a swarm of locusts that
would reap the
the harvesting. O LORD, I
bowed; forgive these foolish
people for all Israel is so
small, he won't survive. The
LORD relented and This
won't happen now! He
vowed.

The LORD then showed a
fire that would devour the
land. I pleaded, Sovereign
LORD, I beg You, how
would Israel survive? He is
so small. The fire won't
burn Israel. I will relent this
direst punishment for I will
show you something else.

I saw Him standing by a
wall. The wall was built
quite true to plumb but then
he held a plumbline there.
He asked, What do you see,
Amos? I said, I see a
plumbline, LORD. He said,
I place this plumbline right
among My people, Israel.
I saw that Israel was not
truly right. The LORD
declared that Israel would
fall; its sanctuaries as well.

Just at this time, the priest
of Bethel sent a message to
the king of Israel—yes,
Jeroboam! Amos is
preaching insurrection in
the very heart of Israel. He
says that you will die and
Israel will go to exile in a
land so far away. He turned
on me: Get out, you seer!
Go back to Judah! Go and
preach your doom and
gloom and eat your bread
back there. Be gone,
for Jeroboam's Sanctuary is
here! I turned then to the
priest: Now hear me out.

I'm just a shepherd,
orchardist, but it is the
YHVH–LORD who called
me to this task. I left my
flock to warn of danger
immanent to Israel.
Your families have broken
down, your sons and
daughters will be lost in
battles soon to come
and you, yourself, will die
far out from home, far
out from Israel!

YHVH– LORD
The Parable of the Fruit
Chapters 8 – 9

The LORD then showed
some fruit to me—a basket
filled with fruit, a summer
crop—so ripe, the fruit
would fail to keep beyond
a week. What do you see,
Amos? Some fruit;
it's ripe O LORD.

Just so! Israel is ripe. I cannot
spare them long: the fruit is
much too soft for it has
no strength; it soon is
squashed and it is rotten to
the very core of it.

When that day comes, the
songs you hear at Temple
turns to wailing in
the street for Israel has
trampled all the poor and
judgement falls upon their sin.

All you that hear these solemn
words should know the reason
for your doom:
you sell the sweepings with the
wheat; you skimp the measure
of your loom.
You cheat, you sell your soul
for what you'd fill your pockets:
pence and dime.

Weighed in the balances, you
fail. The land will tremble for
your crime.

The nation rose, but sinks in
sand. The scene is set at noon
but e'er long,
the night descends, the feasts
will turn to mourning and your
ribald song,
to tears. A famine is about to
fall: it's not a famine of
your food,
nor yet of water slaking thirst, it
is a famine of God's word—
there's not one tittle,
not one jot.

The nation's best will faint, for
thirst will spread throughout
the land. You have relied on
graven gods—where are they
now to lend a hand?
The pillars of your palaces will
not remain intact—they'll fall
upon idolaters and scheming
foes of YHVH–LORD,
at My command!

There is nowhere to hide from
wrath that is legitimate; there is
resultant consequence for sin
in every guise. You cannot hide
the evil of your ways. It comes

*to light as I pass by
the 'grave' that you have dug.
But don't you know, it's for
your good to 'bide.*

*You should recall the eyes of
God, the Sovereign LORD. Do
not neglect the smallest crime
against humanity. The sinful
kingdom will have gone
and it will never rise again. Yet
I will not destroy 'Jacob'
(Israel). The House of Israel
shall shake as in a sieve but
all, it is not done!*

YHVH–LORD
Restoration
Chapter 9:11 – 15

*I will restore King David's 'tent':
the broken, mended and
restored. Rebuilt, its glory will
return; the Remnant
will be found!
My people will return to Me,
to Israel. The ruined towns
rebuilt, they'll plat their crops,
rejoice: they're planted in their
land, their ground!*

THE SONG OF AMOS
Tune: *Rimington* L.M.

The LORD Almighty is Your
name,
O *YHVH*–LORD, the *El
Shaddai;*
Creator of the universe,
You formed the mountains and
the sky.

You call me, LORD, to seek
Your Face,
No longer search for worthless
gain;
You challenge me to ask
of You
To cleanse the soul, remove
sin's stain.

Let justice flow on like a
stream,
A river that supplies God's
peace;
Let righteousness flow from
the heart,
A never-failing stream of grace.

It is the LORD who does
restore,
His people's brokenness make
whole
The day will come when all
shall find
His healing for the sin-sick
soul.

And as for me, I stand on
grace;
The LORD my peace shall
surely be!
My hope is in the YHVH–
LORD;
He is my Saviour, He healed
me!

..... oOo .....

THE TERROR
YEARS

OBADIAH

You've heard of me, no
doubt although the news I
leave with you is very brief.
However, I'll take a moment
just to say that my name
holds rich meanings and you
may take your pick: it's
either *'a servant'* or *'a
worshipper'* of *YHVH*–
LORD. I do rejoice in that.
You'll have to set the dating
of my life yourself.

It's said that I am
contemporary with Elisha
though I do have need to
emphasise that the later date
is more precise: I share a link
with Jeremiah!

OBADIAH
My Testimony

*I'm just a breath upon a
breeze—I'm hardly here before
I'm gone. But you'd be wise to
listen to my testimony
for I will speak for Him:
the YHVH–LORD this day.
I'll share with you His words
to me about the state of things
today. The Sovereign LORD
would have you know just
what I have to say.*

*There is a message from
the LORD—an envoy comes to
preach His word to nations
near at hand. He said:*

*Rise up for war descends,
Edom.
I'll cut you down to size and
you
will be despised for you
degrade
My Israel. Your pride has let
you down: from height to depth
you've gone.
You soar like eagles in the sky,*

you make your rest among the stars. From there you will descend to crash. As thieves come in the night to rob the unprepared, so you will find your chasm cache made bare. Your closest friends will set a trap for you—you'll fail to see the mob!

Your wise men sit with pride today, their knowledge is supreme, they think you're emblematic of all those that do aspire to greatest heights by harsh, abysmal treachery on those who live to please the YHVH– LORD. The day will come when you will know your shame; you stand aloof: you crash!

Remember now the day you stood aside while Israel's enemies cast lots to take Jerusalem and you rejoiced to see their pain. You boasted their destruction and you marched through Zion's gates to steal their wealth and wait to take the lives of fugitives. What gain?

The Day of YHVH–LORD is near! I speak to all the nations that denied Israel their livelihood. You sat, imbibed upon the Mount most holy to Israel. Your deeds one day will turn on you. You'll find destruction in your path. You doubt?

The House of Esau (Edom) will disintegrate. Though 'Jacob' burns, the House of Esau will be stalks of grain, the flames consuming it. Take note: one day your fate will find that Jacob's people will return, take up the ground that you will lose, they'll take possession, win their right.

My final message to you is: Deliverers will march to Zion; they'll govern all your lands for then the Kingdom will be God's: His Zion!

THE SONG OF OBADIAH
Tune: *Silchester* S.M.

There is a day set down
When God will come at last
As Judge of Heaven and Earth,

He'll come
To deal with all that's past.

The ledgers will be seen:
What has been done—
the good,
The ill, will be accounted then
For all is known to God.

There is a holy hill
Where all may be forgiven;
There is deliverance from sin
Where God's own love is
given.

God's people know the way;
His Holy Hill brings peace!
The heavenly Kingdom is
the Lord's,
Receive His gifts of grace.

..... oOo .....

THE TIDAL
YEARS

JONAH

It is a sad and sorry thing
that you have known so very
little of the story of my life!

In the testimony that I will
give, I'll seek to rectify the
limitations of your thoughts
for I have striven, through
most of my younger life, to
live as *YHVH*–LORD
decrees.

First things first: My name
in Hebrew means a *dove*.
Yes! That is what I really
am—a gentle dove! I live in
tremulous times—including
those of Jeroboam ll.
Damascus sought to
capitalise upon Israel's lack
of strength.

Our king however managed
to restore our borders but
Assyria remained a dire
threat to Israel (that is, the
Northern Kingdom.) In fact,
I prophesied it would be so.
But, would you know, Israel
began to gloat.

We would remain
inviolate from further
conflicts for *YHVH*–LORD
was on our side! I echoed
Elisha's prophecies. At this
time, also, Amos and Hosea
were sent by the LORD to
counsel Israel.

I stood with them; I felt I
had 'arrived' as a prophet of
the LORD! But the LORD

took hold of me, instructed
me to go to Nineveh to warn
that nation of impending
doom. Me? To Nineveh?
The gentle *dove* could not
face up to it. My troubles
then began.

JONAH
Chapters 1 – 2

Oh yes! You've heard of
me: Jonah, more famous
than I'd want to be. My
name is on the lips of all
who wish to denigrate a soul
in trouble on the sea
or land. The things you do
not know could be
investigated, known and
shown! I am a prophet of
the *YHVH*–LORD.

And, yes,
I disobeyed but what
I did reluctantly should be
accredited. Yes! I am Jonah.
I'm 'the dove'. It's as a
dove I chose to live my life
from day to day, you see.

I'm Jonah—dove—the son
of Amittai. The *YHVH*-
LORD has called to me:

*Come, Jonah, you're to go
to Ninevah, I need you there
to preach My word
against that city's
wretched wickedness.*

But LORD, You know
That Ninevah is wicked and
I'll lose my life if I would
take this task 'on board'!
Oh yes, I ran from Him, the
LORD! At least, I sailed
from Him. I went on board a
boat intent on flight from
anywhere that led to that
'hell-hole' of Ninevah.
I'd paid my way—a first
class passenger was I.

A balmy breeze arose and
we set sail towards the
Earth's extremities. It's
'westward ho!' until, that
placid breeze quite suddenly
became a hurricane. The
sailors toiled, took down the
sails and battened down the
hatches while I went below
to ride it out. The storm
increased. Those waves
crashed down upon
our fragile barque like
mountains from above.

It did appear that we would

fail to find some land—a
harbour fit to save us from
the fiercest force of gales
I'd ever faced till then.
I then began to realise it
Was my disobedience that
caused the ghastly, dire
predicament we all were in.
I am a man of God and,
though so disobedient about
the task the LORD had
given me, I would own up.
I'd save the souls
of sailors innocent of crime.

Meanwhile, the sailors cast
their lots—they were a
superstitious bunch—
they thought the 'chips'
would tell who was
responsible for this
catastrophe. And yes, the lot
did fall on me. They
inquisitioned me: who is
responsible? Tell all!

What is your craft, what is
your land? What is your
nationality? I am Hebrew
and I worship God, the
YHVH–LORD, Creator of
the Earth and sky. They all
were shocked, afraid. The
sea rose higher, my soul

sank lower! What have you
done? What can we do?
What do? Just throw me
overboard! The sea will
cease its angry threats. It's
all my fault. I do own up!

Those sailors were such
worthy men—they all
refused and rowed the more.
But still the hurricane
increased. At last they took
me up and cast me to the
waves. How could that sea
become so placid suddenly?

But as for me, I sank into
the sea. I realised that none
but *YHVH*–LORD could
save my skin! I asked of
Him that very thing while
gulping down the sea
and kicking at the waves.

Just then, a fish—I cannot
tell the make of it, I saw it
from inside—rose up and
swallowed me! I'm down
its throat and there I've
stayed for three whole days
and nights. Of course,
I prayed: the LORD
had sent that fish!

JONAH
My Prayer

From ocean depths I pleaded
with the LORD who'd nurtured
me always. I'd run from Him,
my Guard and Guide. Oh
LORD, it's like a grave but You
have rescued me. I'm in this
fish—I could be dead but you
have saved my life. You heard
my cry for help: from wind and
wave I'm saved anew.

Your waves and billows have
engulfed my life. I have been
banished from Your sight. Yet I
will look again towards Your
holy Temple, ask
for help among the seaweed,
salt. Oh LORD, You bring me
from the pit. My life was ebbing
fast. You heard my plea!
LORD: I accept the task!

JONAH
My Response
Chapter 3

I heard the Voice of *YHVH*–
LORD once more; He said
again to me:

Now, go to Nineveh,
proclaim the message
I will give through you!

And yes! I did obey the
LORD! You know of
course, that Nineveh is vast,
important, powerful.
The trek across would take
three days! This message
was proclaimed: In forty
days, all Nineveh will be
then overturned. Beware!
The people heard, believed,
declared and put on
mourning garb.

The king heard what had
happened. He took off his
royal robes and then put on
the mourning garb and sat
down in the dust. He then
proclaimed a fast that
everyone must then obey.
All Nineveh must change
its evil ways. Who knows?
The LORD may yet relent,
take pity on our woes.

The LORD observed how
Nineveh reacted to the
warning given. He had
compassion on them all
and all the people thus were
duly saved!

JONAH
My Reaction
Chapter 4

I was irate at this. How
could the *YHVH*–LORD
relent upon so great
a sinfulness as that
displayed throughout all
Nineveh? I cried:
Is this not the very thing
why I was quick to flee, oh
LORD? I've seen Your
grace before today. You're
slow to anger, quick to love.
I came to warn of coming
doom, I'm left a laughing
stock! So, LORD, You can
now take my life. I don't
want, any more, to live with
this embarrassment!

Jonah! Jonah! Have you
a right to vent your anger
on My work?

I didn't want to hear! I went
right out and found some
shade within the hut that I
had built just east of where
the city stands. I'd watch
from here to see what would
eventuate.

I saw a vine—a gift from
God to ease discomfort in
the heat. My happiness was
so short-lived; a worm ate
all the vine that night.
Next day; I swear it was

the LORD who sent that
blistering heat! I feared
sunstroke would take my
life, I longed for death—far
better than to live amid
this ghastly mess! The
YHVH–LORD spoke
to me again:

Jonah! Jonah! What right
have you to have a care
about the vine, the worm?

I'm angry, LORD, enough
to die! The LORD replied:

You showed concern about
a vine; you failed to tend it,
help it grow—it died
without your aid. Observe
the city there: the citizens of
Nineveh can't tell the left
hand from their right; they
have just two hands for the
work. They need our help!
Why can I not now show
concern for Nineveh?

It took a while for me to see
just how to recognise why
YHVH–LORD involves
Himself with needy folk—
like me, in fact. God's final
word becomes the reason
for the whole report. We
need to recognise its worth.

THE SONG OF JONAH
Tune: *Retreat* L.M.

LORD, all Your waves and
billows now
Have plunged my soul beneath
the wave
That overwhelms my very life;
I cannot rise, I am not brave.

LORD, from the depths I cry
to You;
I do believe You'll take
my hand.
I call to You for help—You'll
hear!
LORD, lift me up, I'll take
Your Hand.

You brought me from the
throes of death
When I remembered You,
Your grace,
Your love that would not let
me go!
You are my Hope, my Joy,
my Peace.

LORD, when I doubt Your way
for me,
Your will to make me whole
once more
And what You do require
of me,
LORD grant me grace my soul
to soar.

..... oOo .....

THE THREATENING YEARS

MICAH

I'm what you'd call a 'minor man'. I do have friends in high places, though. Well, at least one: Isaiah! I live within his shadow and that's where I prefer to be. We've shared our notes at times and you will see the results of this for our styles are much the same.

Most certainly, the prophecies we must relate will focus on Judah's wonts and wills and our fears for Israel as you will see when I unleash all the burden of my news wrapped up within the testimonies. The social conditions of the land were indeed most dire before the king, Hezekiah, instigated wide reforms.

I've set the scene for you; let us get under way as I set my quill to poetry.

MICAH
Chapter 1

I'm honoured to be friend
of the great doyen of the
prophets. Me, the friend
of our Isaiah: wonderful!
Though he associates
with kings—
Jotham, Ahaz, Hezekiah
too, he's never lost his
friendliness with common
country folk like me.
Isaiah is my mentor; that's
for sure. He prophesies
within Jerusalem while I'm
a voice for *YHVH*–LORD
in lesser climes but vital in
God's scheme of things.

The LORD showed me
a vision that I must declare
to both Samaria and all
Jerusalem. He authorised:

The LORD is coming down to
tread the mounds and mounts
of Israel. An earthquake greets
His footfall on the ground of
earth. This is because
of Jacob's (that is, Israel's)
sins. Look now, Samaria,
transgressions see. Observe,
Jerusalem, the site of sin—
on *YHVH* you have closed
your massive doors.

Tears for Mourning

That heap of rubble and the
stones that were foundations
call to God: idolatry has
brought you down, your
prostitutes are thieves. Cry on!
I weep for you. My mourning is
intense. Your mounds are
putrid now. In from Samaria,
these sins have beaten down
the gates of Zion.

God's Plans, Man's Plans
Chapter 2

A woe to those who plan
iniquity; they carry out
the ploys of night.
At dawning of the day,
they seize what they have
coveted, defraud
their friends' inheritance.
Therefore, disaster will confront
the proud, calamity will fall for
all the evils people
hoard.

MICAH and
YHVH–LORD
False Prophets

Calm down, you say, stay
quiet; how can one know of
future things? Disgrace won't

fall on us! You say: should it
be said the LORD will come,
wreak havoc on Israel? How
can the LORD be angry when
we are His people, loved by
God? Will He now turn on
Judah, Israel? It's Home!

I must reply to ignorant pride!
Do not My words encourage
those who live a righteous, holy
life? My people have become,
to Me, an enemy! You steal
from those
who pass, expecting safety
here. You rob the mothers of
their homes, you have deprived
My children, so! Get up! Be
gone! Go with your
faithless foes!

YHVH–LORD
Deliverance

I'll gather you, My people,
then. A remnant will return to
Home; you'll come as sheep
into the fold, you'll come like
flocks to pastureland.
There will be one who goes
before to open up the way.
Oh, yes! The gates of Home
will open then, the king will
lead (by My own hand).

MICAH
The Rebuke
Chapter 3

Listen, you proud heads of
Israel, should you not know
and show justice? All you
who love evil, turn from good,
you tear Israel from limb
to tattered limb.
You'll seek God's help one
day—He will be 'far away' from
you. You led God's people
all astray; out from your pit
you cannot climb.

But, as for me, He gives me
strength—His Holy Spirit
breathes in me. I know His
justice and His might;

The LORD empowers
so hear me speak
all you who show disgust for
right, distorting righteousness
with bribes and, still, you'd lean
upon the LORD refusing to
believe. Be meek!

MICAH and YHVH–
LORD
The Mountain of the
LORD
Chapter 4

I speak to you today about
the Mountain of the *YHVH–*
LORD: The day will come,
His temple will be known
abroad; all nations will
then stream to it. Come, let us
go to worship *YHVH*-LORD of
Israel: He'll teach us of true
righteousness that me may
tread His Holy Hill.

The LORD will be our Judge,
He'll rule the nations far and
wide in peace. All swords
become ploughshares and
spears become a pruning rod.
No nation will engage in wars;
each man will live at home
beneath his vines, his figs and
sycamores. All fear will pass;
we'll walk with God.

In that Day I, the YHVH–LORD
will gather all the weak, the
lame; all those exiled in grief
will come, a remnant, back
into their homes.
I'll rule in Zion; they'll know My
ways. My Kingdom is
perennial! You will be rescued
from exile; you'll be redeemed;
behold: God comes!

MICAH
The Promised Messiah
Chapter 5

O Bethlehem, O Ephrathah!
You are so small among the
clans But out of you shall come
the One—the Ruler of Israel.
His worth,
His origin before the past!
Out from the ancient times,
Messiah comes. Israel will be
bereft until the virgin comes to
give Him birth.

Messiah will be a Shepherd
For His flock—His strength is
of the LORD, His majesty is in
the Name of God. All then will
be secure for He's of God.
His power shall reach right to
the very ends of Earth. There'll
be no boundary to fence Him
in: Messiah is, for all,
our Peace!

Deliverance—Destruction

Assyria will come, invade
our land, smash down our
fortresses; we'll raise our
shepherds to defend.
One day, the LORD
delivers us!
The remnant of Israel will be,
amid the many nations of the
world, like God's refreshing
dew, like showers on the
withered grass.

The remnant will become
just like a lion amid your flocks
of sheep. Applauding hands
will then be raised
in victory, the foes embroiled.
The LORD will then remove
from you all that has marred
your faithfulness, your icons,
strongholds, cities too:
the power of Asherah
is foiled.

YHVH–LORD
The Court is in Session
Chapter 6

*I stand before you to
condemn all sin. The case
I'll make—Attorney now—
will cause the very ground to
quake. My people, hear: what
have I done?
How have I burdened you, I
ask? Respond to Me now, if
you can. I brought you out of
Egypt and redeemed you from
all slavery: gone!.*

*I sent Moses, Aaron and
Miriam to you and Moses led
you, Aaron has taught you,
Miriam loved you. Remember
all the ways I led
you then and brought you to*

*this land that you could know
My righteousness.
You wonder how you could
return to faithfulness, what can
make glad?*

*The LORD has shown you
what is good! What does the
LORD require of you? It's this:
act justly and love mercy too
and walk most humbly with
your God.
But you have not complied.
You walk in arrogance, your
gains have gone. Your ruin
comes as your deceit has now
negated all the good.*

MICAH
My Misery
Chapter 7

What misery comes to me
today; I see the depth to which
you've plunged, the godly have
been swept away, the best of
you none can applaud
as upright men descend to
briars. The Day of *YHVH*–
LORD has come: trust no one,
even families fail. But as for
me, my hope is in the LORD!

Resurgence

Don't gloat, my enemy! You
see I'm 'Israel'. I sit in
darkness, yet the LORD is my
eternal *LIGHT*. I know the
wrath of God for sin
but He will plead my case; He'll
bring me to the *LIGHT*. I'll see
His worth, His righteousness,
and this will shame my foes.
Who loves the LORD will win!

Prayer and Praise

O LORD, You are the
Shepherd of the flock of Your
inheritance; LORD, guide me
to rich pastureland that You
prepare for Your own sheep.
All those who scorned us then
will see the worth of
righteousness. Who is a God
like You? You pardon us; Your
mercy flows our souls to keep.

You promised, LORD, to
save our souls,
In You we find our peace;
With weapons shaped for
harvesting,
Then all world wars will
cease.

You've shown us what is
good in life;
What You require, O LORD:
Act justly and love mercy
now
And humbly walk with God.

THE SONG OF MICAH

Tune: *Amazing Grace*   C.M.

You are, for us, the
Shepherd LORD
And we will follow You;
The Gate is open, LORD,
we come
To find Your pastures new.

..... oOo .....

THE TENDER YEARS

NAHUM

Welcome! My name is Nahum which, I'm pleased to say, means *comforter*. I have hope that you will find some comfort in the prophecy I am bound to convey.

It's difficult to find a date in time for me but, as my words relate to the eventual fall of Nineveh, this places me in the time when Assyria flung its might about. Samaria (the northern kingdom of Israel) had been taken into exile. Assyria was looming large upon the borders of Judah.

Briefly, the related history takes in Sennacherib's amazing defeat at the gates of Jerusalem. Assyria's eventual fall came in the jurisdiction of the brutal Ashurbanipal.

The *comfort* (just as surely as this means *to come with* strength,) that I will bring to God's people is just this: Assyria will fall!

....

NAHUM:
Introduction
Chapters 1 – 3

My name is Nahum and you
will be pleased to know it
means *comfort*. I hope to be
a 'comforter' to you.
I like to think of how the
name I bear means

'to come with strength'!

You'll need your strength
for what I'll testify to you
from *YHVH*–LORD who
called me from Elkosh—
oh yes, diminutive at best—
a village in my land of birth.
I stand to speak as
prophet of the LORD .

NAHUM
The enemy: Ninevah

The *YHVH*–LORD will take
revenge
upon the might of Nineveh.
He's slow to anger, great in
strength; the guilty cannot
freely go
about their business at no cost.
The mountains quake before
the LORD; you can't withstand
His judgement or His wrath
outpoured to be brought low.

The LORD is good to those
that trust; He is their refuge
and their strength. His care for
all the righteous means that
evil must forego its crime.
You plot and plan against the
good; though allies stand by
you, they won't remain a
threat—they'll be cut off—but
Judah: know God's love in time.

Look to the mountains, see the
One Who publishes Good
news today! See now the feet
of Him who comes
proclaiming peace. So,
celebrate!
Fulfil your vows, O Judah, for
the wicked won't invade again.
Your festivals will bring you joy,
your enemies have met
their fate!

You'll guard the fortress, watch
the road and marshal all your
strength. On guard!
You need to know the YHVH–
LORD restores the splendours
of Israel.
They've suffered, been laid
waste, their vineyards have
been stripped but they will live
again with joy for they'll return
back home to dwell.

Great chariots storm through
the streets and gates are open
wide for none can save the day
for Nineveh. The plunderers
seek all the gold,
the city's silver, mighty wealth.
Hearts melt, the troops grow
faint. Your youth—young
lions—will melt. Where now
is Nineveh's stronghold?

A woe to you, great Nineveh
where streams of blood will
flow for horses, chariots and
cavalry—those flashing swords
bring casualties;
the bodies without number
now. God is against you,
Nineveh—Your shame will be
your nakedness. All Nineveh's
a ruin none pities!

Are you much better than the
Thebes and Egypt, Libya and
Cush? Your fortress is just like
the fig—shake trees, the fruit
will fall, all gone!
Your gates are open wide to
enemies: draw water, work the
clay, repair the brickwork now.
But fire consumes as locusts
strip your land to bone.

O king of vast Assyria,

your shepherds are asleep,
your flock (your people,)
scatter on the hills. There's no
one left to gather them.
No one can now bring healing
to your fatal injury and who will
care for you? They'll clap their
hands for all have felt your
cruel crime.

THE SONG OF NAHUM

Tune: *Southport* S.M.

How patient is the LORD!
So slow to anger, praise
His power: He comes in
strength to all
Who ask for saving grace.

How loving is the LORD!
He is our Refuge: He
Will care for all who trust
in Him:
Have faith: He'll set you free!

How thoughtful is the LORD!
He comes to tend the wounds
Of those afflicted by life's
storms:
His mercy has no bounds.

How wonderful to see
The tread of One who'll speak
Good News, proclaiming
'shalom' peace;

His grace makes strong
the weak.

..... oOo .....

THE TORRID
YEARS

HABAKKUK

Allow me to introduce myself. You will struggle to recall the details of my work as prophet of *YHVH*–LORD. But this will help: I am contemporary with one of the greatest prophets of all.

Yes, Jeremiah! That very fact will set the scene of those traumatic, tragic years when *YHVH* did require of us a faithfulness to speak His values into the evil shadows falling over us.

My name—Habakkuk— is so very special though: for its meaning most of all. You see, it gives expression to *love's embrace*! As you now read my testimony, you'll soon observe that I am held in the embrace of *YHVH*– LORD who gives direction

and protection to my very
life!

HABAKKUK
Chapter 1

How long, O *YHVH*–LORD,
must I persist in prayer when I
hear nought from You? You're
silent as the tomb! Why is
it that I must observe
such violence? How can you
stand aside and tolerate such
wrong? All justice is perverted
here—such sinfulness without
reprieve.

YHVH–LORD

*Observe the nations and watch
all. Be utterly amazed. I am
involved in work that will
restore your hope. I know you
won't believe it's true
and fear, far worse, that I have
raised a ruthless people—
Babylonians—far fiercer than
the ravening wolves. Their god
is their own military cue!*

HABAKKUK

O LORD, You are the
Everlasting One,

my God, my holy *YHVH*–
LORD. You have appointed
ruthless men to do Your work
for You. You will
not tolerate a wrong. Why,
then, accept the treacherous?
Why are You silent while
the righteous die?
The aliens throw nets at will!

(I'll stand upon my watch,
observe—from these tall
ramparts—look to see
what *YHVH*–LORD will say
to me—I wonder how
He'll answer me?)

YHVH–LORD
Chapter 2

*Write down what you observe,
make plain on tablets written
clear, then send this news by
heralds as My words will be a
revelation for
they speak of an appointed
time. My word is true although
it is delayed.*

*Be patient yet: it tells
of End Times.
Could you ask for more?*

The righteous live by faith!

All those who disobey My ordinance, those greedy as the grave, what woe will then arrive. Those building on an unjust means of gain, who think they will escape their just reward, they shame their families, soon gone!

A woe will come to those who build their cities on the blood of all the innocents. The day will come when all the earth will joyfully be filled with knowledge of the LORD. My glory—glory that will fill the Earth as water floods the sea—will show that grace flows gloriously.

A woe to those who give no care to neighbours—they'll be exposed. What they have done to Lebanon will overwhelm. Destruction looms for those who shed much blood with ease. What value is an idol to the wood carver? The LORD observes. Be still, for now He comes!

HABAKKUK
My Prayer
Chapter 3

O LORD, I worship You,
I stand in awe of Your accomplishments.
Renew Your deeds in this, our day and make them known to us, I pray.
LORD, in the midst of wrath, please do remember all Your mercy now.
Your glory covers all the heavens,
Your praise can fill the Earth today.

Your splendour, LORD, does rise each day as sunrise floods the Earth with joy. Your power is manifest in all the Earth.
Creator, LORD, in wrath You did convulse the Earth and crush the mountains, flood the seas as streams all torrenting swept by. Your power is seen in all the Earth.

You came to save Your people, LORD: You crush all sinfulness, You bend the sword of wrath and break the bow of sinfulness. The sun and moon stood still to see You take control. You thresh the nations, sorting 'grain' of worth;

You toss away the 'chaff'.
I hear Your news: with You
we've won!

LORD, I will wait with patience
now; I tremble at Your
awesome power yet I will wait
Your Day to come. And, though
the fig tree yields no bud,
no grapes appear upon the
vine, though olives will refuse
their yield, no sheep, no cattle
in their stalls, yet still I will
rejoice, trust You! Rejoice, my
soul, I trust the LORD:

He is my Saviour and my joy.
The sovereign LORD is all my
strength, He makes my feet
like those of deer—
the doe that climbs up to the
heights; its hind feet correlating
with the fore, won't stumble on
the way. Just so, I trust my
LORD most dear.

THE SONG OF
HABAKKUK

Tune: *He Leadeth Me*   L.M.

How long, O LORD, this night—
no stars
Bring comfort to my downcast
soul.

I long for *LIGHT*, a star to
guide;
Must sorrow's test be still my
goal?

Chorus:
I know of God's eternal love,
On Him I can rely; the LORD
Gives hope when challenged,
weak;
Be now my strength today,
O God.

The LORD is God, He is the
LIGHT
That shines within the deepest
night;
He comes to meet us in our
grief:
He'll be our Guide, He leads to
LIGHT.

His written word will bring you
hope,
The LORD will comfort,
counsel where
All paths are hidden, goals
obscured:
He'll come to cheer,
encourage, care!

The LORD, who made all
Heaven and Earth,
Made known to us His
matchless grace;
Though all around would fail

its worth,
We find in God our perfect
peace.

One day God's glory will
embrace
The whole wide world, His
splendour shine
As sunshine floods the Earth
at dawn;
Shine in my heart, my soul
refine.

..... oOo .....

THE TROUBLED YEARS

ZEPHANIAH

Now, let's see, how should I introduce myself? Ah, yes, let me draw your attention to the final syllable of my name. There is a clue, you see, that links me with such towering figures as Isaiah, Jeremiah, Hezekiah! This is a hint that we each are linked to royalty.

You'll take note of the fact that this is pointed out in my initial statement so you can rely upon its veracity.

The *YHVH*–LORD has delegated me to speak regarding issues that pertain to the ruling class. I do reveal that I am quite familiar with the issues of the day. I could also say that I am contemporary with Jeremiah, Nahum and even Habakkuk.

My words relate, in particular, to all the conditions that apply to the reasons why King Josiah brought about reform.

YHVH–LORD
The Warnings
Chapter 1

All creation, please take note:
God's broom will sweep away
all seen
in consequence of sinfulness.
The face of Earth will be swept
clean.

Regarding Judah
I'll raise My hand against
Judah: all living in Jerusalem
will know My wrath. Your idols
are a blasphemy.
Your priests do sin.

*From rooftops you bow down
to stars! You have adored
Molech and Baal; you neither
seek nor ask for Me,
the YHVH–LORD, if you are
clean.*

*You fill the Temple with your
gods and with your violence
and deceit. On My great
sacrificial day a cry will soar up
from the depths;
your wailing will be heard
across the market place:
all goods have gone! I'll take
a lamp to search you
out from all the city's
darkest clefts.*

ZEPHANIAH
The Day of the LORD

The day the LORD foretold is
near; your grief upon that day
will be most bitter for it is a day
of wrath, of darkness and
deep gloom,
a day when clouds obscure
the sun. You'll hear the trumpet
sound, the cry of battle ring
within your ears; the Day of
great distress will come.

ZEPHANIAH

The Challenge
Chapter 2

So! Gather now, all Judah,
come together, come! Allow
your shame to tell you how you
grieved the LORD. Before the
broom sweeps through:
Oh, seek Him now all you who
still obey the Law; my hope is
that you'll be sheltered well;
trust Him now.

YHVH–LORD
The Surrounding Nations
Chapter 2

*Now listen, Gaza, you will be
abandoned, left in ruins.
Midday will see you emptied,
rooted out. A woe upon you,
Canaan, now
I've heard your insults, Moab,
and the Ammonites as well:
take heed! You have insulted
Judah, So, as surely as I live,
you'll go!*

*And you, the Cushites by the
sea of northern Africa, you all
will feel My anger at your
gain—ill-gotten gain: by
swords, all slain.
Assyria, My hand is raised
against your land—an empire*

*cruel, with no attempt at
justice, carefulness. You will be
desolate: no gain!*

*You will become an arid land;
The desert owl will haunt your
homes. You are the city
carefree, safe! You've vaunted
up your empire grand.
But what a ghastly ruin will
befall your great fortress! Wild
animals will roam your palaces
and all who pass will raise a
scornful hand.*

ZEPHANIAH
The Future of Jerusalem
Chapter 3

Jerusalem! Look to yourselves!
You lack the wisdom of a true
obedience. You do not trust
the *YHVH*–LORD, you show
no grace,
you don't draw near to worship
God. Officials: roaring lions.
The rulers: vicious wolves.
The prophets: arrogant
while priests profane the
Holy Place.

But in the midst of your
disgrace, the LORD who dwells
within, reveals His
righteousness. As morning
comes each day, the LORD
dispenses, to
you all, His justice and He does
not fail. And yet—as you
receive all that His mercy
showers, there is
no shame in what you do.

YHVH–LORD

*I am the YHVH–LORD. I have
demolished nations, left their
streets deserted; cities, all
destroyed. They had their
warnings but did not
react repentantly; corrupt until
the end. Therefore, I say to
you: I'll bring together nations
so all sin will be consumed:
in consequence: the lot!
Then I will come to purify
the lips, the hands, the hearts
of all that they may call upon
the name of YHVH–LORD to
serve Me whole.
The remnant of Israel will do
no wrong and none make them
afraid. Then sing, Jerusalem,
be glad! Rejoice: the LORD will
make you whole.*

ZEPHANIAH

The LORD is with you, do not
fear; the LORD will hear you,

He's your God! The LORD is
mighty: *El Shaddai*—He takes
delight in how you live
by grace. He'll quiet you with
His love. The LORD rejoices,
sings to you! You'll know the
truth: you are alive!

YHVH–LORD
*The sorrows of the past will be
removed from you; this burden
will be lifted, you'll be free!!
My Day will be the time
when I will deal
with all oppression and all
dread. I'll rescue all the lame
and grant you praise and
honour everywhere and in
that Day, all will be well!*

SONG OF ZEPHANIAH
Tune: *Colne* C.M.

The LORD is with us, this
our song:
He reigns eternally!
The LORD is great, mighty
to save;
The LORD has set us free!

He quiets us with all His
love,
He gives to us a song;

We walk His way, we are
alive,
We will His praise prolong.

In sorrow, He's our
Comforter,
He lifts the burden from
Our heart; He rescued us to
live
For Him. All doubt has gone!

He promised to restore our
peace,
He leads us safely 'Home'!
We praise and honour all the
LORD
Has done. Will you now
come?

..... oOo .....

THE TORTUOUS
YEARS

HAGGAI

Our nation has come
'Home' from Exile and the
YHVH–LORD requires that I
stand up to give strong
encouragement so that the
rebuilding could commence.

The Temple is a ruin. Its resurrection, without delay, must commence. You'll find my testimonies are brief but I do encourage you to delve into the depths so that you may understand what the *YHVH*–LORD does desire, require of us in these strategic times. Rise up and get involved! The "Desire of all Nations" will come.

Let the nation prepare for His coming. We have our enemies and they will work to thwart our plans.

Trust the LORD and expect Him to work on your behalf. It is His will that Israel does well each day.

HAGGAI
Chapter 1

Oh yes, I am a prophet too—a very minor one in fact. Best known for my encouragement to exiles coming home from climes in distant lands. I am a friend of Zechariah who you'll meet when he contributes to the words of testimony each prophet gives. Now, if you'll take

the meaning of my name: *the festive one*, you'd think I'd dance my way into this book but such is not always the case!

My work is fraught with difficulty. I speak what God would have me say; my words are brief but what I say has resonance, significance! I testify to history now:

Darius, king of Medes and Persia, had ascended to the throne two years ago and, half-way through that year, the LORD revealed to me what must be said to leaders meant to keep good watch on renovative work.

The LORD declared through me: it seems not time to build the Temple once again. He asked that I convey a message, questioning the stance of Zerubbabel and of Joshua. It must be said!

YHVH–**LORD**
Is it a time for you to be residing in your homes

*while My House remains a
forlorn ruin? Give careful
thought to this: you planted
but the harvests small;
you eat but never have
enough, you drink but never
satisfied. You dress
yourselves, remain too cold;
you pay your way, the purse
has holes! Give careful
thought to what you do:
go to the mountains and
bring down good timber for
the builders all to use in
reconstructing My own
sacred House in Zion.*

*You have expected much but
see how small are the
results. The work has yet
to bring a pleasure and
you do not honour Me. You
have neglected Me while all
your homes are adequate;
they're safe and warm.
You wonder why there is a
dearth of an achievement
in your Temple plans.*

HAGGAI

I can report with joy this
news: the remnant—led
by Zerubbabel and Joshua,
the High Priest's son—
obeyed the LORD without
undue delay to stall.
Yes, all the people did so
readily comply with the
instructions given by
my words, dictated by
the LORD. They knew
that I was sent by God—
They all respected
YHVH–LORD.
As all the work was
underway, the LORD spoke
once again to me. I then
conveyed His words to all:

*I am with you! Know this:
" I AM" the YHVH–LORD!*

The governor, Zerubbabel
was deeply moved—his
spirit stirred to work with
to work with zeal, obey the
LORD. And all the remnant
too then knew the Spirit of
the LORD endowed them
with the zeal they saw each
day in Zerubbabel, Joshua,
the men who led them in the
work set down by God to
build His Temple there.

HAGGAI
The Glory Promised
Chapter 2

I do remember it so well—
the date lodged in my mind.
It was the twenty-seventh,
seventh month, that *YHVH*–
LORD then spoke to me.

I was to go up to the
Governor—yes, to him:
Zerubbabel—and to Joshua
and also to the remnant of
the people, asking them just
who were left who saw
God's Temple there before
its ruin. Recall the past
glory, consider how it looks
today and does it seem too
poor beside the Temple of
King Solomon? Be strong,
Zerubbabel, God declares.
And Joshua, be strong.

Be strong you people of the
YHVH–LORD: He does
require that you will work
with knowledge of His
presence with you
constantly. He says to you:

I am the YHVH, El Shaddai:
think of My covenant that I
proposed to you, accepted
too, when coming out from
Egypt all those years ago.
Remember now: My Spirit
still remains with you.

"I AM" is here— don't fear.
The time will surely come
when I will cause all heaven
and Earth to tremble—all
the sea, the land: all nations
will be shaken. Then, the
One desired by everyone
will come. My House will
once again be filled with all
the glory of the YHVH, El
Shaddai. The glory of the
House will be far greater
than the former House for,
in My House, I grant peace.

HAGGAI
The Nature of Holiness

And I, the prophet Haggai,
asks: why is a holy thing
deemed holy now? And
how is anyone defiled? Do
learn this lesson well: Be
whole! It is in learning of
God's will and ways and
keeping to His path that
you'll be blessed within
your inmost soul.

So! Finally, the *YHVH*–
LORD
declared that I should go
to Zerubbabel, governor,
inform him that the Signet

Ring (the seal,) will come
to him for he is chosen of
the *YHVH, El Shaddai!*

THE SONG OF HAGGAI
Tune: *Beethoven* L.M.

You call Your people to
be whole;
O LORD, this is our soul's
desire.
We ask that You will cleanse
us now;
To live for You we now aspire.

You have a task for us to do?
LORD, grant us strength to
follow You!

O LORD, reveal Your perfect
plan;
We see the need: our souls
renew.

The glory of the LORD gives
light
To shine upon our chosen way.
LORD, lead us to Your Holy
Hill:
We'll worship at Your altar,
pray.

O, place Your seal upon our
lives

That we may share the word
of God
And testify to Your great grace,
Revealing now Your peace,
dear LORD.

..... oOo .....

THE
TUMULTUOUS
YEARS

ZECHARIAH

You may remember that
Haggai gave some mention
of the fact that I'd be
testifying quite soon. You
see, I work in tandem, so to
speak, with him for our work
refers to the post-exilic times
soon after our nation's return
from alien lands.

It may be of more than
passing interest that, while
my mission is to prophesy, I
am also a priest so this dual
responsibility was handled
in the daily strength given to
me by *YHVH*–LORD. I was
quite young when I 'took up
the reins' to be God's man
through these most
tumultuous times. So, I have

continued in my dual task for quite some years as you will discover through the content of the messages I bring to the nation on behalf of *YHVH*– LORD.

ZECHARIAH

I'm Zechariah, friend to Haggai. Because he made God's message clear and plain, I will not fear that you won't 'hear' the news I have to share. Give heed once more! See, as my name suggests, I'm linked to kings. However, close is that relationship, my calling is to be both priest and prophet now. As priest, I speak to *YHVH*–LORD for people through my many parishes; I am the one who intercedes for them before God's awesome Throne. As prophet, I now represent the LORD to all. Mine is a dual role, you see, with quite divergent tasks.

ZECHARIAH and *YHVH*–LORD
A Call to Return to God
Chapter 1

My testimony is clear and plain: as prophet I will speak for Him, the *YHVH, El Shaddai* (the One known as Almighty God.) His news I will proclaim:

Return to Me: I'll come to you; don't emulate those gone before! 'Turn from your wicked ways,' I asked; they blocked their ears and didn't heed. Where are they now? Eternal? Safe? My words at last were powerful, enough for them to take some note. Look now at what I've done!

ZECHARIAH
The First Vision

I couldn't sleep; I wondered why and then I saw what seemed a dream. But I was wide awake. This was a vision clear! I saw a man who stood among the myrtle trees deep in a great ravine. I saw near him, three horses: red, brown, white. I had to ask the man… I realised just then, an angel stood by me; he could disclose the gist of it.

He said, These are the ones
that are prepared by *YHVH*–
LORD to go throughout the
Earth to ascertain its worth.
They have returned to say:
We've searched the Earth
and found the whole wide
world to be at peace.

The angel of the LORD then
asked: O LORD, the *El
Shaddai*, how long will You
withhold Your mercy now,
for seventy years have
passed? The LORD
responded with great grace.

The angel turned to me and
said, *YHVH*–LORD, the *El
Shaddai*, wants Jerusalem to
know His care for them, for
Zion! The ruthlessness
of evil men has caused
much harm. He will return
to Zion; His House shall be
rebuilt. He will bring peace
and comfort to Jerusalem!

The Second Vision

I looked again and then
I saw four horns confronting
me! What is
this vision, sir? I did
enquire. His answer came as

a surprise: These are
symbolic of great strength
and these are they that sent
Judah, Israel—scattered
Judah, Jerusalem—to
distant lands. But now they
come: the craftsmen who
will terrify, cut down the
horns. Then: peace.

The Third Vision
Chapter 2

I then looked up. There
stood by me a man with
measuring tape. What is
the use of tape? He said:
I am to measure all
Jerusalem. Another angel
then appeared with startling
news: Quick, run to that
young man, explain to him
that all Jerusalem will be a
place that has no walls for it
will be too large to house
all those who flock
to it. Instead, hear this:

*"I AM" will be its walls,
I will secure its peace. "I
AM", the YHVH–LORD, the
El Shaddai: Almighty God!
Come! Come! Flee from the
North, all who have been*

scattered by the four winds
sent from Heaven.

Come now, O Zion, out
from the lands that held you
captive; come back 'Home'
then you will know the *El
Shaddai* has sent me to
redeem you all.

Shout and be glad for
YHVH–LORD declares
He'll come to dwell
with you always!
Then you will know the
LORD has sent me to
redeem you all. Rejoice!
Be still before the LORD!
Know peace!

The Fourth Vision
Chapter 3

The angel spoke to me
of him, the High Priest,
Joshua. His name of course,
means *'YHVH saves'*.
I saw, in vision, Joshua
who stood before the angel
of the LORD; but at His
side slinked Satan then.
He stood to be accuser of
the priest. He was rebuked:
The LORD Himself rebukes
you, evil one! The LORD

has chosen Zion—
Jerusalem.
Is not this man you see a
'brand' plucked from
consuming fire?

It should be said that Joshua
was garbed in filthy clothes.
He was commanded by
the angel to disrobe, remove
those measly rags.
You see, your sins
have been forgiven;
you will be cleansed and
robed anew. This is my
charge to you: the LORD,
the *El Shaddai*, now says
to you that, if you'll walk
within His ways and keep
all ordinance, then you
will have control of all
God's House.

Now listen, Joshua, High
Priest, the *YHVH, El
Shaddai*, will bring
the Chosen One: 'The
branch'. He'll be 'The
Rock' to all who will
receive Him. Note: 'The
Rock' has seven eyes (this
is the symbol of
omniscience.) His name
will be inscribed on it. I will
remove sin from My people

then. I'll do it in a single
day and on that Day, you'll
find, each one, a perfect
peace.

The Fifth Vision
Chapter 4

The angel shook me,
startled me—like one
like one aroused from
sleep—but I was wide
awake. What do you see?
he asked. I see a lampstand,
gold, with seven lights
above its base. Each has a
channel feeding its own
light. As well, I see two
trees—these olive trees
stand tall, they grow one
each side of the lamp. I
could not tell the meaning
of the lamp or olive trees.
I questioned him. He was
incredulous. Do not you
know their meaning yet?
These represent the word
of God to Zerubbabel:

Not by might, nor yet by
power, but by My own Spirit

says *YHVH, El Shaddai.*
The mountain will be level
ground when *YHVH* comes

to claim His Home! The
hands of Zerubbabel laid
foundations here, his hands
also will finish it. Then you
will know that *YHVH–*
LORD sent me to you.
Recall the visions you have
seen; don't let them be
of little note.

Excuse me, Sir, I do not
know the import of the olive
trees. Please, tell me now, I
asked. Have you not
realised their worth? he
asked. Oh no, I cannot say!
He said, These are the two
that are anointed now to
serve the LORD. I realised
'anointing' represents
the Spirit (Oil) of God. But
who are they that represent
the two that serve the
LORD? A king and priest,
perhaps—the dual role of
leadership—I wondered if
just one could be both king
and priest. I cannot tell.

The Sixth Vision
Chapter 5

I then looked up to see
again a vision—open eyed

I was, I swear! A flying
scroll came floating by,
immense in size—full thirty
feet by fifteen feet.
The angel said:
This is the solemn news
to be relayed throughout
the land. It's written on both
sides, you see. The one
Proclaims that thieves
won't last. The other side
declares that liars are
banished from the Holy
Land. This news will bring
destruction to their very
house—both timbers and all
stone, cut down!

The Seventh Vision

Look up, the angel said,
Observe what now appears.
Oh! what is it? I asked. It is
a basket meant for careful
measurement. It will reveal
how great the sins that
spread throughout the land.
When opening it we found a
woman cramped inside.
I was then introduced to
wickedness. The lid
slammed down, was locked.
As I looked up, two angels
came with wings out-
stretched. They took the

basket, lifted it and flew
away. Where will they go? I
asked. They fly to Babylon:
that is its most fit place!

The Eighth Vision
Chapter 6

Four chariots appeared.
How strange! They flew
between two mounts of
bronze. Four teams of
horses pulled them on. The
first: red; second: black; the
third was white; the fourth:
a dappled steed. So, what's
the meaning of those
chariots? I asked. These are
the four winds that will flow
from *YHVH's* Presence and
the black heads north, the
white, due west, the dappled
gallops south.
(Is this the last we'll see of
them? They sound like an
apocalypse—strange word,
it means: *reveal*!)

The angel then continued:
Take some silver also gold
to form a crown. This crown
will sit upon the head of
Joshua for he will build the
Temple of the LORD and he
will be a priest enthroned.

This crown will stand memorial in the Temple. You will know the *YHVH–*LORD sent me to you.

ZECHARIAH and *YHVH–*LORD
Justice and Mercy
Chapter 7

The *YHVH–*LORD has spoken now to me once more. His words were a response to questioning by men of Bethel. Is our fasting still required? We've fasted now for seventy years! The LORD's reply was clear:

Was it indeed that you engaged in fasting and was this for Me? This is My word to you: you must administer true justice and reveal your mercy to the poor. Do not oppress the widows or the aliens. Think good, not evil things at all. You have not listened in the past: men turned their backs on Me, have not observed My ordinance; they plugged their ears and turned their backs. I turned My back!

The Blessing
Chapter 8

The LORD has promised to return for He cannot forget His love for all Jerusalem:

I will return and dwell with you. The city will be labelled 'Truth', the mount known as 'The Holy Mount'. The elders will return, they'll sit together and at ease and boys and girls will play at will—no fear will enter there. I'll save My people and they'll come from east and west; they'll live in peace: I will be faithful as their God.

So! Let your hands be strong; bend to the work of building up the House of YHVH–LORD. I'll dwell therein! Your plants will be fertile, the vine will yield its crops, the sky will drop its dew, refreshing all the land. I give you this inheritance. I'll save you all: you will be blessed

there and abundantly.
Be true!

Now this will be required
of you: the truth is to
be spoken, give sound
judgement in your courts;
do not plan evil nor speak
falsely: these are the sins
these are the sins I loathe.
be true!

It's time for joy. Rejoice at
all your festivals. Love truth
and peace for many people
then will come to seek the
LORD, request His aid;
they'll plead the presence of
a Jew, walk up with him
to worship God!

The Judgements
Chapter 9

The eyes of all are on the
LORD.
They look also to fortresses
but *YHVH*–LORD, all-powerful,
deprives the proud of their
increase.
The nations then will writhe
in pain,
the remnant will belong to God;
they'll be the leaders in Judah.

He will keep watch and save
by grace!

The Coming of the King

Rejoice, O daughter of
Jerusalem;
Shout loudly, sing to Zion!
Your King is coming now
to you.
The King is righteous and
He'll save.
He comes to you upon an ass
(which is the symbol of His
peace,)
He will proclaim His peace
to all;
His rule will shelter us.
Believe!

The LORD's Assurance

The sovereign LORD now
sends His word: He sounds the
trumpet, He will come.
The *YHVH, El Shaddai*
will shield all those who stand
with Him by faith.
The LORD, their God, will save
them on that Day as His own
flock; the flock of His own
people then will shine like
jewels in His crown, in truth!

The LORD's Care
Chapter 10

It's spring! You need the rain?
Then ask the *YHVH*–LORD
to send upon you now
His blessed showers;
He'll tend the grain, revitalise
the fields to yield His harvest
here as are His powers.

Diviners show deceit and lie,
therefore, God's people
wonder why there is no
guidance, care. Like sheep
they stray; they lack a
shepherd who will know!

My anger burns against all
those who lead My sheep in
arid paths! "I AM", the YHVH,
El Shaddai: I'll care for you, My
flock. Come now,
for out of Judah comes a Rock
known as 'The Corner-stone',
the One who'll set the whole
House right for I am with you
always now!

I will redeem My people, Israel
(the House of Joseph and
Judah!) I will restore you, make
you whole; I'll have
compassion and I'll act
to save you all. Then it will
seem as though we've never
been apart Your children shall
rejoice; I will redeem My

people, bring you back!

The Reckoning
Chapter 11

It's time for wailing, far and
wide: The time has come for
recompense. I give the
word: pasture the flock—
their buyers slaughter them
without regret. The
salesmen dance, so rich.
The flock become distanced
from Me, preferring tracts
of land that set them free. So
I, the Good Shepherd,
did turn from them. They
went their way so wilful to
the end. The staff so named
'favour' was broken. Then
the reckoning for pay was
just a 'slave' price:
thirty silver coins!

The LORD requested that
I throw the thirty pieces to
the field the potter owned.
The second staff, 'union'
was broken then. This was
the time when the Israeli-
Judah family was breached,
the schism wide. Woe to the
worthless shepherd who
deserts his flock for richer,
glittering gain!

YHVH–LORD
Enemies Destroyed
Chapter 12

"I AM", the YHVH–LORD,
My word to Israel is: I am
the One who laid all the
foundations for the world.
I have created man's own
spirit—soul. I'll make
Jerusalem a 'cup' so
powerful, surrounding it,
all peoples will recoil for
Zion will be a 'Rock'
unmoveable. My eye will
watch Jerusalem and keep
you safe from cavalry. Then,
Zion will say: The people of
Jerusalem are strong!
This is because the YHVH
El Shaddai is our God. On
Him we do rely. The LORD
will guard Jerusalem and
make her strong once more.
The weakest will be strong,
just like King David who
did trust the LORD!

I'll pour upon King David's
House and all inhabitants of
Zion a Spirit of pure grace.
And they will look on Me,
the One they pierced, and
mourn for Him as for their
child. And on that Day

they'll grieve the One
who's slain, as for
a first-born Son.

Spiritual Cleansing
Chapter 13

A fountain will be opened
on that Day upon King
David's House—yes, on
inhabitants of Zion to
cleanse from sin and all
impurity. All idols will be
gone. All that reveals
impurity and sins will be
remembered never more—
I will remove all the unclean.
If one should ask a prophet,
What are those wounds your
body bears? He'll answer
him: The wounds
I bear were gained in the
house of friends!

Shepherd Struck, Sheep
Gone

Awake, O sword, against
My Shepherd who is close to
me, My very own! The
Shepherd's struck! His
sheep will flee. So many will
be lost. A third will live,
they'll be brought through

the fire; they'll be refined as
gold; they'll call upon My
Name and I will answer
their distress: I've heard!

ZECHARIAH
The Reign of God
Chapter 14

The Day will come when
YHVH–LORD will gather
all the nations that rebel.
He'll fight against invading
troops intent on doing harm
to Zion. And on that Day,
His feet—the feet
of 'The anointed One'—will
stand upon Mount Olivet.
The mount will quake and
break in two from east to
west. A valley will be
formed. All armies: flee the
wrath for then, the LORD,
my God will come, His holy
ones will follow him!

On that great Day, the sun
will cease to shine—no
cold, no heat—a Day
unique, of God's design.
When night descends, there
will be *LIGHT*! On that
great Day, a fountain will
begin to flow out from

Jerusalem to reach the ends
of east and west. On that
great Day, the LORD will
reign. There'll be one
LORD, His name the one
and only Name: *YHVH–*
*El Shadda*i

Jerusalem will be secure.
Then, in the End Time, all
who will survive from
nations that attacked
Jerusalem will climb the
Mountain of the LORD
to give due honour to
the *YHVH, El Shaddai.*
He is the King! They'll
worship Him, the *YHVH–*
LORD, the *El Shaddai.*
The horse bells ringing loud
and clear will be inscribed
as 'Holy to the LORD'!

THE SONG OF
ZECHARIAH
Tune: *Chalvey* D.S.M.

I'll sing of One today,
Anointed of the LORD;
He is the 'Rock of Ages' and
We know that He is God!
His Name, the YHVH–LORD
Will be inscribed upon
Our heart for He makes
known to us

His own beloved One!

It's not by might, and not
By power, but by My own
Eternal Spirit, says the LORD,
His saving work is done.
A fountain flows today:
God's cleansing stream
of grace
Makes clean the sin-sick soul
He grants our soul's release.

It's time to sing! Rejoice!
Shout loudly, sing of grace:
Your King is coming now
to you—
He will proclaim His peace.
The LORD is Saviour, He
Redeems, restores the soul
And as our Shepherd tends
our wounds:
The LORD will make us whole.

The people of the LORD
Will come from east and west
And they'll sit down together in
The Kingdom of God's peace.
The LORD will save His own
And make us whole to live
By grace. The LORD is
faithful and
His love extends to us!

.....oOo .....

THE TWILIGHT YEARS

MALACHI

I see the need to emphasise my identity as some imply that, as my name, Malachi, means *my messenger*, it is merely a pseudonym and my actual name remains a mystery. I therefore wish to say that I, Malachi, am the messenger of *YHVH*–LORD!

I come to you in times where **shadows** cloud the land. The faith of many fades and I am requested by the LORD to emphasise that promises He made through Haggai and Zechariah remain inviolate. Morale was high in Ezra's day and Nehemiah set the seal on that. But when he fulfilled his promise to return to the service of Persia's king, the nation, all, crumbled into spiritual decay.

You can rightly imagine Nehemiah's despair when he came back to find that sin had seeped once more into the fabric of society. I stand upon the verge of the Silent Years: my words convey the last of the prophetic utterances of the First Testament.

My remit is to emphasise the hope that the Promised One will come, dispel your doubts and reiterate that *YHVH*–LORD will finally right the wrongs of humankind. In the **shadows**, we await a new dawn, the *LIGHT* that will shine on us all whose hope is in the LORD!

YHVH–LORD
Shortcomings
Chapter 1

I've loved you with eternal love but yet you ask, have You loved us? This is My answer to you all: I truly loved Jacob (Israel). His mountain is a wasteland now—the jackals ate inheritance! Though Edom has rebuilding plans, My answer is, An end to it! You'll see this with your own two eyes and say,

How great is God? See now! You question: there's contempt. You query, how could this be so? You have defiled the Holy Place and yet you ask, how could this be? Reflect upon the wrongs the past has seen you perpetrate. Am I now pleased with you? My Name will be revered around the world and great among all nations and from sunrise to sunset interminably. But still you do profane My name, the YHVH–ORD. Your offerings have failed the test of faithfulness. I won't accept your sacrifice!

The Admonition
Chapter 2

I challenge you, the priests, to live according to the precepts of the LORD. Have you as yet not set your heart to honour Me, fulfil your role? You need to hear this challenge now: I made a covenant with Levi, Israel's priest—all priests are chosen from this tribe–

*Levi revered, respected Me.
He stood in awe and spoke
the truth; he walked with
Me upright and turned away
from sin. All Levite priests
should follow in
the steps of holy Levite
priests. You've turned from
holiness, despised the
qualities laid down for life!*

MALACHI
Unfaithfulness

The question must be asked,
Why do you yet profane the
Covenant
the *YHVH*–LORD has made
with you? Your Father is the
YHVH–LORD, Creator of
the universe. You fail to
honour Him, break faith
with one another and distain
the Holy Law of *YHVH*–
LORD!

You treat with disrespect
the love that once you
showed your wives. The
LORD declares He hates
divorce! Has He not made
'one', betrothed? So guard
your soul–do not break your
faith in Me!

MALACHI
Final Judgement
Chapter 3

Behold! He sends His
'*messenger*', yes: '*Malachi*'
to you. He will prepare the
way for you. The LORD
you seek will come (and
suddenly,) to God's most
Holy House! But who can
stand secure when He
appears? The LORD is like
refining fire and cleansing
soap and He will judge—
refining, bringing forth pure
gold—untainted priests
to serve Him whole.

YHVH–LORD
The Immutable

*"I AM", the YHVH–LORD,
I do not change: I am
immutable. Throughout all
time you came up short:
return to Me, I'll come to
you. You ask, How may we
now return? You do not
realise that you have robbed
Me. Bring your tithes into
My House. Yes! Test Me
now and see how I
will open up the stores*

of Heaven and pour My blessings as a flood that you will have no room for them, so great will be your joy! No pests will eat your crops and fruit upon the vine will hold till harvesting. Observing this, all nations will be drawn to you—My blessings bring delight! Believe Me: "I AM", God!

You said harsh things with no regret; you doubted Me and failed to count Me Friend. You felt all worship brings a mourning in the heart. Why should we listen to the LORD, obey His Law? Why can't we please ourselves, each one?

But there are those who turn to Me, they covenanted with their LORD! They will be Mine when I return to choose the jewels for My crown. You then will see how I decide between the righteous, evil—those who serve the LORD and all who don't.

The Day of the LORD
Chapter 4

The Day of YHVH–LORD will come. It is of furnace heat! It will consume the stubble of all deemed of ill-repute. No twig, no branch of such will then be saved. To you, of Israel, who do revere My name, 'The Sun of Righteousness' will rise; there will be healing in His wings.

Then you will dance for joy. All wickedness will be destroyed. Remember all the Law—Decrees—of Moses now. I'll send to you a prophet: Yes! 'Elijah' comes before the Day when YHVH moves to right the wrongs of humankind and bring you Home! He'll turn the hearts of fathers to their children and the hearts of children to their Abba, Dads—Don't let the **SHADOWS** *fall again!*

THE SONG OF MALACHI
Tune: *Rimington* L.M.

The LORD now calls us to His side

To speak of Him and of
His love,
To be a messenger of Truth
And share the Gospel:
'God is Love'.

The Name of God will be
revered
Throughout the whole wide
world;
We'll celebrate His saving
grace:
Come share with all the Faith
we hold.

The LORD has challenged us
to walk
The paths of holiness, to live
For Him each day, aspire to be
His messengers of peace
through life.

God's word decrees His Day
will come:
'The Sun of Righteousness will rise
With healing in His wings.'
LORD, be
Our strength in witnessing
for Christ.

SHADOWS AND THE LIGHT

Jerusalem, late afternoon

The lengthening shadows fall about Jerusalem;
it is late afternoon and with declining might
of sun on Zion's lofty heights, they call for the
encroaching night. By this, the sun cedes *LIGHT*?

But night is when the glorious stars shine bright above
the sleeping Earth. The day is done though lambent light
shines on. And when a star outshone all else to guide
those eastern pilgrims from afar, behold: delight!

That star, it paused o'er Bethlehem's bless'd hills
where shepherds watched their sheep by night.
And wise men learned that light will overcome,
will bring bright hope in darkest, sin-held blight.

The Earth is draped in night by grief profound
but Death will never overcome the Dawn. It's right!
It's Gospel News—a King born to be Man, Messiah:
the Saviour of the world and all is bathed in *LIGHT*!

SHADOWS AND THE LIGHT

A COMPANION TO THE BIBLE

— EYE-WITNESS TESTIMONIES —

BOOK THREE

PART ONE: THE GOSPELS
THE PERSONNEL AND THEIR POTENTIAL

New Life via the Cross-bound Route

Lucille L. Turfrey

BACKGROUND

There's been a new awakening! Four hundred long, dark, silent years in depth of night, were peppered by the horrors associated with Antiochus Epiphanes, thwarted by the magnificent exploits of the Maccabees... There is a stirring in the trees and undergrowth. New life is taking its first breath.

A new world is emerging. The ancient languages have all but gone into the dust of history. Greek becomes the *lingua franca* though another mighty empire is flexing its muscles—an empire of iron, Yet there is a flaw: the iron is mixed with clay.

Rome will play out its day. Rome will subjugate the nations of the world. It will conqueror be. The **shadows** cast are long, so very long, so deep, so dark. And 'middled' there by mighty mounts, a beaten people bowed to Rome. What hope have they?

Herod sits upon his throne but he, the 'king' of Israel, has no power—Tiberius will see to that. What of the High Priest in his tower, guarding what is left of holy things? These potentates will make their peace with Rome at any price. From whence will hope come? From Temple courts? From Palace power? That stirring in the trees and undergrowth intensifies as the breeze now gathers strength up in the hills, west of Galilee.

The page is turning on the saga of the centuries. The past is in its place, firmly cemented in the history of the ages. There are **shadows** but these cannot obliterate the *LIGHT*. Together, they give form to the story of the ageless Community of Faith which has triumphed over all that wickedness has thrown at them.

As we leave the Hebrew text for the Greek, though the poetic style remains basically rhythmic, the addition of rhyme will be employed when the writer decides to burst into a song of praise, thanksgiving, devotion, petition, intercession, and of awe. This will provide an avenue for private or corporate worship.

The poems, again, will be highlighted by the use of this specific font.

Come with me now: the door is open...

CONTENTS
PART ONE: THE GOSPELS
THE PERSONNEL AND THEIR POTENTIAL

PART TWO: THE CHRISTIAN CHURCH
THE PROCLAIMERS AND THEIR PROGRAM

THE TRAINING YEARS
MATTHEW: "LION OF JUDAH"

Matthew, that's my name. I've nought to recommend about what's past in the story of my life. Scum of the earth, that was me. At least, that's what the villagers, my neighbours, thought of me. I was a tax collector—need I say more? But, one day in the midst of it (money on the table, and a little under, just for me), He came to me, the Rabbi who opened to our eyes the Kingdom of Heaven. He called to me... I am transformed. I am His man! I walk with Him!

My task is to set upon a scroll the record of the years—of all the Training Years—where He made a man of me. I've organised the contents of my scroll to focus on the ways He emphasised the Kingdom of Heaven. I am drawn to '*The Lion of Judah*', the first mentioned of all: the Genesis scroll (49:9) and in the last of Bible books (Revelation 5:5). You'll see within my work the things He said and how He exampled all He taught as He trained His twelve associates to be His men through all of life. The story begins in Nazareth. Let me lead you there:

MARY
The Visitation
Chapter 1:1 – 18

How swift the valley fog
is lifting from our ancient
hills. There is a freshening
breeze now wafting in the
dawn. The shadows of the
night are chased from view.
The sun announces that a
new day has begun with
all things new.

How beautiful the dawn
today! I'm Mary, just a
village maid, a teenager
so blessed with joy. I am
betrothed and soon I'll don
the bridal gown and go to
him, my Joseph. He's a
man of grace.

Our ancient town has reason
to be thankful for this man,
the well-known carpenter
of Nazareth!

Was that a knock upon my
door? I think it cannot be.
And yet… He stands within
the room, this man, his
entrance well beyond the
norm of visitors who meet
to chat with me. He smiles
at me; I am entranced…

I am a messenger from
YHVH–LORD! I've come to
bring to you Good News.
You are to bear a Son.
God's Time has come. The
Light of Heaven shines upon
you now. You'll carry
Him—you'll nurture Him;
you'll grieve for Him;
you'll glory in His word!
He speaks His will to you.

JOSEPH
Chapter 1:19 – 25

The strangest thing has
happened here. I met with
Mary yesterday. Her news
was so amazing yet it broke
my heart! I am a man who
strives to do what's right.

what's right. I grieve it all
but I have cared for her and
must do what is best for her.
Her story is so weird
yet there seems a truth in it.
I take her at her word. The
Holy Spirit came with news
that she—a virgin—would
conceive and bear a Son. I
choose to hide her and to
leave her be.

What can you think of this?
Just now when I had nodded
off the while,
(I had been thinking what
to do for making wrong
things right,) he came to
me—a man from God—
he spoke to me giving
encouragement:

Fear not! Don't be afraid of
me. You've been asleep;
I've wakened you to ease
your mind and give to you a
confidence to marry Mary
now. The Holy Spirit gave
to her the Son who will be
Saviour of the world.

You've known, as Joseph,
kin of kings—the ancestor
of David—throughout your
life that one day a virgin

would conceive and bear a
Son. His Name will be
'Immanuel' (God with us,)
The meaning of the
Saviour's Name confirms
that God is with you,
He will care for you, for
Mary and the whole wide
world eternally!

When I woke up, I made
swift plans to marry my
belov'd. A joyous night
It was though I became in
truest sense her husband,
fully so, after the Child
was born. I named Him
Yeshua–Jesus, the Saviour
of the world.

HEROD and THE MAGI
Chapter 2:1 – 12

**What's this I hear? The
'grapevine' natters on!
How do I seek the truth
of this, the right from
wrong? I hear they
entered into town last
night, inquiring as to
where
the 'Prince of Israel' has
been born! What do they
mean, these men of alien
tongue and eastern garb?**

**I am the king and I should
know if princes squawk
within the night!**

**I must inquire of them…
Bring now these men to
me.' I'll get to rights of it!
It really is off-putting and
our citizens are rushing
'to and fro' with unrest in
their peasant minds. We
can't condone uproars like
this… You've found the
visitors? Well bring them
in before my throne.
I will demand the source
of this disquiet.**

**Good evening, gentlemen!
You've come from far
afield: What is your aim?
Oh do tell me: I'll help.**

We seek the Baby born
a King—the King of all
the Jews. We saw His star
ascend one night (the star
was new, quite out of
place.) We understand
the wisdom of the stars.

We knew at once a king was
born and we must follow in
its course to find the Prince

of Peace. We've come to
worship Him!

I needed to take counsel
then—What is the
meaning of this news?
And why am
I the king—Herod—not
yet informed? I'll call my
own wise men and glean
the truth from them…
They came, the priests in
finery and teachers of
the Law with tomes that
weighed them down to
Earth! They rolled apart
a scroll—it creaked and
groaned—no doubt
unused.

I see it is the ancient scroll
of Micah, minor prophet
at the most. And what is
this I hear? It's
Bethlehem, the birthplace
of a Child born King? The
Levites read
the prophecy:

*O Bethlehem in Judah's
land, You are by no means
least of all the leading cities
of Judah: it is from you the
Greatest Leader comes*

*to guide and guard My
people, Israel.*

I need a plan in order to
placate Magi but also to
secure my throne! Ah yes,
I'll go to them in warmth
selected for the trickery.

You will be pleased to
know that we have
answers for your quest.
But first, do tell me more
about the star, the one
ascending in the east
and then onward towards
the western skies.

When did you first
observe its transit through
the skies? So! We are of
one mind. Yes! It is the
'Regal Star' and it will
come to rest by Bethlehem
Judea.

One thing: when you
have paid your homage to
the newborn king, do
come to me, report to me
all you have seen. I wish
to go to Bethlehem
to also worship Him.

THE MAGI—FIRST MAN
Chapter 2:1 – 12

The longest journey of our
lives this is and only yet
half done. That star, that
radiant star, has called us to
a pilgrimage the like of
which has spurred us on.
We've been to palaces,
to flapping tents out in
the wilderness where rock
gives way to shifting
windblown sand. A swaying
palm at times ensures we
are *en route* to an oasis
where our thirst is
quenched; a respite that
revives the body and the
soul. We travel light; the
camels roar displeasure
when overburdened on
the route. We carry gold—
that's heavy right enough.
The jars of frankincense are
ample but the myrrh is light
enough. Each gift will bring
their import for the prince.

The gold? It's for life's
circumstance as pennies in
the purse are not sufficient
to replenish food and
clothing for the body has its
many needs to satisfy.

The frankincense?
It's for the mind.
A fragrance rare, it is
conducive to serenity, a
clarity of thought that will
be able, in all circumstance,
to cope with life's demands.
The brain, also, has many
needs to satisfy.

The myrrh? It is for pain,
for death comes to us all.
The challenges that life will
fling towards the
unsuspecting will demand
all that life's circumstance
requires to keep the soul
quite whole.

The soul also has needs
to satisfy. These gifts, the
three, are as a prayer
for Him, the Child born to
be King: that, for the whole
of life, He will be whole in
body, mind and soul.

THE MAGI—SECOND MAN
We reached our goal with
no problems: our guiding
star had led us on to
Bethlehem, a hamlet in the

hills. This is no place for
kings or palaces! Who'd
think that we could find
a prince to rule the world
herein… We did! A humble
house it was and also
homespun folk did welcome
us. Then, as we entered in,
we found a peacefulness
profound. The Child, He
smiled at us. This was
indeed the goal we'd set.
The star above was now at
rest and so were we! We
bowed to Him, presented
Him with gifts wrapped
most purposefully.

THE MAGI—THIRD MAN

We must depart without
delay! I've had a restless
night; I tossed and turned in
dreams that warned of
threats to come when on the
homeward route without
a star to guide.
I say, I did not like the
attitude King Herod had
displayed to us—a man
most sinister. He meant no
kindness nor Israeli
hospitality. A Voice spoke
in my dream. He warned:

Go home another route; the
king has laid some plans
to see you dead!
Make ready now the
camels; we must
be on our way. Our quest
has been fulfilled; our
pilgrimage complete.

YHVH–LORD
Chapter 2:14 – 14

*Joseph! Wake up! You must
not tarry now in Bethlehem.
Herod, the king, is thwarted
in his plans but means to
kill the Child. There is a
route whereby you will
escape. Get up! Pack up!
Depart before the dawn.
Go! Head due south
towards Egypt where you
will stay awhile until
I give you word that all is
clear. You'll know My care
throughout this 'exodus' for
you're the guardian now.*

JOSEPH
Chapter 2:15

I see it all! How truly
wonderful! The word that
came to me has saved

our lives. I am the guardian
of a Child born to be King.
a Child born to be King.
He is 'The Chosen One'
as promised through
all ages past. The LORD
has deemed me fit to guard
Him, guide Him. So! It is
due south to Egypt now.
All this because the written
word of *YHVH*–LORD
has perfect clarity:

Take note: It's out of Egypt
that I'll call My own
beloved Son!

HEROD
Matthew 2:16 – 18

I've waited long enough!
Where are those Magi
from the east? I should
have sent a guard with
them, right to the crib of
One who dares to take
my place upon the throne
of Israel! An upstart,
snatching up my crown,
my sceptre and my
royal, Israeli throne:
I will not stand for this!
I'll call the guards!
I'll put an end to it!

I must admit my men did
look askance at orders
thrust at them. I know!
I know! I know! But kings
must take some iron-clad
steps lest men usurp the
throne. The edict given
solves the problem given
me. Two years? It's taken
two whole years for them
to enter in my realm.

That's when that loath-
some star dislodged them
from their alien land and
led them all the way to
Bethlehem. I do not know
just where the Child was
found. But this one thing
I know: a slaughter of all
boys born from that time
will fix the problem now!

Yes! Yes! I know! 'Rachel
now cries this morn for all
her children born in
Ramah' and I all but hear
the sobbing and the
sighing for the Rachels
can't be comforted
because the children are
all dead. It is a pall!

But what is that to me?
The rules I make are for the

greater good of all my government. I must ensure stability of monarch, throne.

JOSEPH and *YHVH–LORD*
Chapter 2:19 – 20

I suddenly awoke, my dream was real!

Joseph! Wake up! Get up! It's time to pack your bags once more! Herod is dead. He can't harm you or Mary and the Child. Return to Israel. All those instructed to do harm to you are dead. Return in peace.

We took no time to pack up all. Our donkey was well fed. He'd see us through— he's such a sturdy beast. A wave or two, a hurried handshake, goodbye, shalom, and we're gone.

In taking rest, I found one night, a traveller with solemn news: Archelaus had now succeeded to the throne. He would provide no haven for the mother or the Child. I went to bed that night with troubled mind. Near dawn, the LORD came near to comfort me:

Now do not be afraid, I care for you! You are to take the road due north and on to Nazareth. You'll find it's written in the Holy Scrolls that He, the Saviour Yeshua–Jesus shall be, to all, known as 'The Nazarene'.

JOHN THE BAPTIST
The Kingdom of Heaven announced
Chapter 3:1 – 12

I've come upon the scene quite suddenly. My name is John. The desert is my home. I'm rough-shod and the cloth I wear is camel's hair. My menu is quite frugal but it will suffice for me—a locust for my lunch but honey for my evening meal. It is enough for me. I am robust and need to be. You see, the words that I convey are most inflammatory. There is good reason: I am known as 'the Prophet of

the wilderness'.
You'll find me near
Qumran, quite near where
Jordan's stream empties
into the sea of salt.
They come from near and
far—there are some lads
from Galilee (I hold great
hopes for them.) But,
sprinkled in the crowds
who come to be baptised
as proselytes, I see them
there: those who must bear
the brunt of vitriol—from
me! It's time they lifted up
their sights; it's time they
changed their ways, those
Pharisees and Sadducees.

Beware, you vipers,
slithering snakes; why do
you think you can escape
the wrath of *YHVH*–LORD
for all your blatant
sinfulness? Be sure, old
Abraham can't help you
now. Your massive
'spreading tree' is rotten at
the roots. The axe is now
about to strike. Be sure
you bear good fruit. So!
change your ways. You
think this stream of water's
able to make clean your
soul. It's more than water

you will need to be made
whole. I baptise in Jordan's
in Jordan's flow but know
this truth: Here is Good
News! There's One who
follows me who will
baptise with Fire, the Holy
Spirit fire! He is the greater;
I'm the one who uses
Jordan's water to baptise;
I am not worthy to be
carrying His boots. He is
about to reap a harvest for
the tools are in His hand.
Now, hear my words: He
comes, Messiah comes to
gather to His barn the
worthy wheat. The chaff
will feed the flames of
wrath. Be warned!

I have Good News for you:
The Kingdom of the LORD
is near! You know the truth:
Isaiah said it well so
hearken to his words:
'There is a prophet in the
desert who declares the
coming of the LORD.
The road must be
prepared—a path that's
straight for He is travelling
on to you. Yes!
Yeshua—Jesus:
The Saviour of the world.'

JOHN THE BAPTIST
Chapter 3:13 – 17

Look! See! He comes to us
across the desert sand.
There's purpose in His
steps, a regal Man, yet
clothed in humble garb,
it's true. A northerner?

But, no! It cannot be! I'd
know Him anywhere. I have
not seen Him many years,
but yes,
it is my cousin *Yeshua*–
Jesus! I went to Him to
glean some news. How's
Mary and the family since
Joseph's death? You've
taken care of all? How is the
carpentry business?

Greetings, Cousin John!
I've come to be baptised.
No, don't deter Me John;
allow it to be done so I'll
fulfil all that is now
required of Me.
My Time has come!

I led Him then into the
Jordan's stream. I prayed
for Him as, dipping in the
flow, this Man of Grace was
giving of Himself to carry
all the burdens He would
face in this, His time.
Just then the sky grew
bright. It was as though it
drew apart to give a glimpse
of glory to my soul. A dove
then fluttered down and
hovered there. Is this the
Holy Spirit's sacred
confirmation that His
offering of life to do God's
will is now accepted from
the Throne in Heaven? I
heard it then, the Voice:

John! This is Yeshua–Jesus:
He is My own beloved Son.
He has rejoiced my heart—
I'm very pleased with Him!

I felt an awe within my soul.
My cousin, *Jeshua*–Jesus, is
true unto His name. This is
the Saviour of the world:
Messiah—the Anointed
One, the *Christ*—Anointed.
Promised: here!

SATAN VERSUS THE SON OF MAN
Chapter 4:1 – 11

I've watched Him there
for many days. He surely
knows some stringent

ways to fast. I've seen Him
move about the mount. He
Does not stagger, does not
It's all of forty days and
nights He's pestered me
with purity. He does not
bow to lies, deceit or
camouflage. The day will
come... I think it's NOW:
the hunger pangs are
troubling Him! Good
morning, Sir. Can I be
of help to You? A bite
to eat, perhaps?

*What is it that you've
packed away for Me to be
beguiled with smiles, by
which you mean to capture
Me? I know you well. We've
met before! I hold no fear
Of you. What gives?*

You must be starving, Sir.
I'm here to check Your
powers, try Your will to
see how You can meet
the test I have in mind
for You. Here are some
stones: I know Your
giftedness, if You want
bread, why not just pray
a Grace that these become
for You some bread just
freshly baked for You.

Go for it Man! Now test
Your power, confirm
Ability to answer all
life's challenges. You
think You are the Son of
God? So, prove it now!

*You're living up to your
Satanic wiles! You knew the
Truth and yet you turned
your back to live the lie. I
will remind you that one
does not live by bread
alone but by the words
proceeding from the Mind
of God! (I am the Bread of
Life! I will provide life's
sustenance for humankind!)*

Come, walk awhile with
me! You think you are so
smart in fending off the
easy ways to bake Your
bread. I have another test
for You. So come, it's up
the mountain trail we'll go
to Royal David's City in
the heights. Jerusalem will
surely open up her gates
to You. The trek is tiring,
it is true but You've had
bread I know not of.
There's strength enough
in You. It's Temple time.
You'll hear the chanting
and the ranting of the

Psalms right now.
Come to the highest point
of your own precious
place—the Temple! What
an edifice! Look down.
It's not so far to ground.
So, I will challenge You
to take a leap. Just see
what You can do.
You'll be quite safe
For I can quote the verse
of Scripture bound to
comfort You. You know
the holy Scripture too—
you know it all in greater
depth than I…
You know that *YHVH–*
LORD has squads of
angels guarding You.
They won't allow so much
as a stubbed toe. They'll
hold You in their hands.
It's really quite obscene
how they have nurtured
You. But I have ways
and means to counteract
all they have planned for
You. Go to it now! Jump
off! You'll be quite safe:
 it will confirm what
Scripture states.

The Scripture also states:
don't tempt the YHVH–
LORD. Go now, you Satan,

evil challenger of all that's
good. You would presume
to test My range of wisdom
here on earth. You'd have
Me done to death before My
time! You think to claim My
mind; I'll stand your
tempting test today!
(I am the Light that's come
into the world.)
Enlightenment will now
reveal the true extent of how
you've plagued all
humankind. My Light will
shine upon the path that
leads God's family 'Home'!

All right! You've read
my mind. Forget the leap
of faith. You failed that
test! Let bygones all be
bygones for I've
something serious
for You. I have a scene
for You to scan and then
to contemplate. Come now
away with me. The air
is clear; we'll see for miles
out there beyond beyond!

I know Your eyes take in
the longer, wider view.
You see them now? The
kingdoms of the world

come into closest range—
they're all laid out before
You now. I have no need
to be reminding You that
they are mine! They all
belong to me! I've earned
them all as You well know.
But these I offer You!
They're Yours—
just ask, but bow to me,
acknowledge my
ascendancy in things
akin to time and space.

*Now, Satan, you would try
the soul of Me. So! I should
bow to your 'almightiness',
consider you to be the one
outclassing YHVH–LORD?*

*There's One Supreme, to
whom all worship should
ascend and I will serve Him,
cherish Him though death
may intervene! (I am 'The
Door' that gives access
to God.) You'd have the
soul of Me but it belongs to
YHVH–LORD. You've tried
to conquer Me via Body,
Mind and Soul but you have
failed once more. Be gone
from Me. The Guardian
Angels come to nurture Me*

*right now! You failed! Your
time is short. Be gone!*

A FRIEND
The Kingdom of Heaven
is Near
Chapter 4:12 – 17

The news is bad! The
Baptist has been thrown into
the prison stocks!
No doubt his words were
judged inflammatory though
he'd said nought
but the truth to all that
hearkened to his words. You
are aware that I am
delegated to set down the
words and deeds of *Yeshua*–
Jesus. Take note of this:
He's on the move.

He is returning north. But a
surprise for you: He settles
by Capernaum just by the
banks of Galilee. He's gone
to where He will be near
the Gentile world. All those
whose lives have been
immersed in 'night' are to
behold His *LIGHT*. This
LIGHT will shine upon all
those who live within

the deepest shadows of the
'night'. It's now He walks
into our 'night' to share
this *LIGHT* with
humankind. Isaiah told us
this would be when *Yeshua*
will come to us. He brings
this news: Good News—
It's Gospel News. The
Kingdom of The YHVH–
LORD is near you now!

SIMON PETER
Chapter 4:18 – 22

These pesky nets do trouble
me! No sooner do I set
them free from tangles than
they're caught up once
again. At least, there is a
fish or two in them. I'll have
their heads and they'll be
fresh for sale today.

Now who is that who walks
along the path by Galilee?
I've seen that Man before. It
is the Nazarene! How come
He moves this way?
He calls to me and Andrew
too—my brother who has
joined me in this toilsome
task. We're overboard!
We wade towards the shore,

our eyes on Him.
He staggers us!

*Come! Follow Me! I know
you love your work. You are
good fishermen but now I
challenge you to leave your
nets and come with Me. I'll
teach you how to catch
another brand of fish.
You'll fish for men afar!*

We left our nets at once,
amazed that He would think
us able now to cast our nets
upon Capernaum,
Jerusalem and wider worlds
afar to catch the 'fish'
who'll swim to Him.

Before we'd caught our
breath He called again. This
time our friends—
young James and John—
had dropped their nets,
splashed out of Galilee
and sloshed their way to
where we stood: we are the
first four men to follow Him
and be His 'fishermen'
for human souls. And from
the boat, our father,
Zebedee, did bid farewell.

....

ANDREW
Chapter 4: 23 – 25

We've tramped through all
the towns by Galilee.
The synagogues were full,
the marketplace astir with
news about the 'Rabbi from
Obscurity' who makes good
sense. His News is new!

He's told us many things.
The Kingdom is so very
near to us, He said.
We knew that this was true:
His words were matched by
deeds, amazing deeds.

Diseases were dispatched,
the sick made whole, the
weak made strong. We went
to them, the poor,
encouraged them by giving
hope. The Good News
spread to Syria and people
flocked to hear His words,
the 'Rabbi of the Galilee'.

You'd be surprised, I know,
but travellers came from
everywhere—Jerusalem,
the Ten Towns (Decapolis,)
across the Jordan and also
far afield. His healing
ministry is changing lives!

A PILGRIM
The Kingdom of Heaven
Chapter 5:1 – 16

I've travelled many miles to
meet this Man, the 'Rabbi
of the Galilee'. I am a man
steeped in all the culture of
the Hebrew Clans. The Holy
Scrolls have been my meat
and drink. I honour well the
words of *YHVH*–LORD in
following His Law. But this
is something new. I've
never heard the like of it.
Here is a new take on the
verities of life! See what
you make of this—I heard
it all today:

YESHUA–JESUS

*How bless'd you are if you
do realise how poor you are
within your soul—your
wealth is great: The
Kingdom of the LORD
belongs to you!*

*How bless'd you are with
true humility—you will
receive the gifts that
YHVH–LORD now grants.*

How bless'd you are if your

desire is to fulfil the will
of YHVH–LORD:
You will be truly satisfied!

How bless'd you are if mercy
flows from your own heart
and hands—you'll find
God's mercy giv'n to you!

How bless'd you are when
you are pure within your
heart for you will see the
YHVH–LORD!

How bless'd you are if you
display the God's peace and
work to bring that peace to
all—you are God's family!

How bless'd you are if
persecution stalks your path
because you strive to do what
YHVH–LORD requires:
God's Kingdom now
belongs to you!

So when you are insulted for
your faith; when lies are
flung at you and you are
under siege because you
trust in YHVH–LORD, be
glad of it! If persecuted
because of your desire
to follow Me, rejoice!
You will receive your

recompense—it's yours,
awaiting you in Heaven.
This is no new phenomenon!
The prophets of the past
were treated just like you!

That did it all for me!
The Holy Law which I
have loved since Bar
Mitzvah is now translated
into life! I am enthralled.
This Rabbi is about to make
all things quite new! I am
convinced! I wait for more!

YESHUA–JESUS
Chapter 5:17 – 20

Please! Don't think that I
have come to smash the law
of Moses into dust!
I've come to now fulfil those
very codes, ensure the
will of YHVH–LORD
remains precise, intact.
No chips or cracks
I will allow!

The Law of God won't be
demised though earth or sky
should cease to be.
So! hear Me now: don't
treat the Law of God as of
no worth. If you would

enter in God's Kingdom
now, obey His word and
will. Be faithful, diligent!

THE TRAVELLER
Chapters 5:21 – 48, 6:1 – 4

I'm settling in to this
dramatic news! It's Gospel
News: Good News! This
Rabbi's rattling all my
brains and what I've learned
from Him is re-arranging all
my outlook and my *in*-look
on what *YHVH*–LORD
would have me know
and do. I feel that I am
being re-born—I'm me
but in a new and gracious
way for I am holding to
the Rabbi's thoughts: they
are the words of life to me.
See what you make of this:

On Personal Behaviour

To do an evil deed—like
murder— has its rightful
consequence, but think
those evil thoughts
and you are guilty too!
If someone angers you and
It is not resolved, your altar
Gift is not of any worth.

Make peace and then
return to worship God.

And when disputes are
brought to court, make
sure there's settlement
before that looming day.

You know the punishment
when caught up in adultery.
Be sure of this: the leer of
lust has caused adultery
within the heart: know
consequence.

It is too easy to divorce—
just write it down, present it
to your wife! But know:
it is unfaithfulness alone
that will demand the
severing ultimate.

You know it well: the law
laid down for making vows.
Don't do it now! Don't
swear by Heaven or
anything on Earth. A simple
'yes' or 'no' will do.

Too long it's been 'an eye
for eye, a tooth for tooth'.
Revenge should be no part
of consequence. Demands
on you should be always
fulfilled in peace.

You love your families,
your friends and neighbours
too but loathe your enemies.
Do good to them; they'll be
surprised and change.

You ask, what is the rule for
life? Be perfect! Yes, in
other words, fulfil what
YHVH–LORD requires of
you. Just walk within His
ways: look to the LORD,
be pure, be true!

Don't strut about with
'holier than thou' outlook.
Go, flaunt your wealth
and there will be no medals
in Eternity. Try kindliness
instead of harm!

YESHUA–JESUS
Chapter 6:5 – 15

*You ask for guidelines
regarding prayer: The
YHVH–LORD does not
count up your weighty
words, your eloquence, or
care
to mention everything that
comes to mind. The LORD
knows all your needs before
you ask one thing! It is
simplicity that really counts!*

*So, let your prayers be as
according to this plan:*

Acknowledge YHVH–LORD
*'Dear Father, LORD of
Heaven, Your precious
Name is honoured
in my heart'*

Request the Kingdom rule
*I pray that Your own
Kingdom will be
recognised, that humankind
will activate Your will on
Earth
just like it's done in Heaven.*

Ask for your need to be met
*LORD, grant today the food
we need to keep us well.
Help us to know a daily
sustenance.*

Confess wrongs you've done
*Forgive us, LORD, for any
wrongs we've done and
rights not done. As we
forgive each other now,
LORD, please forgive
us too.*

*Request God's help to
guard the soul*
*LORD, guard us when
temptation strikes and*

*shield us from all Satan's
evil power. We need
Your help. Let no
temptation turn to
evil deeds.*

*Know this: If you can find it
in your heart to say to
someone who has harmed
your body, mind or soul, I
do forgive what you have
done, You'll find most
surely that the LORD
forgives the faults you
carry too!*

The Kingdom of Heaven's Treasury
Matthew 6:16 – 34, 7:1 – 6

How do you think we can
remember what He's said
today? What say we call His
words, 'The Sermon on
the Mount'. He speaks
again; we'll take some notes
so we'll recall the gist
of what He teaches us
today. Here is a word about
the riches some folks hoard.
What sound advice:

*Don't hoard the coin to put
in banks beneath the pillow,*

*underground. Why store up
wealth where moths can eat
it all or rust erode its
worth? Store up your
wealth, your worth, in
Heaven for no moth or rust
can touch it there. No
robbers come at night to
steal it from Heaven's
'Bank'! Know this: Your
heart will always be just
where your valuables are!*

We've been enlightened,
one and all. He speaks,
'the Rabbi Rare', of eyes
that let in light to view
the scenes which please
the mind and heart. He says
our eyes are like a lamp—
they give you light. How
sad it is when folk go blind
and darkness is
their home. Know this,
He said, if *LIGHT* that
we've allowed to seep
into the soul is really
darkness yet, how terrible
that night will be!

And now he speaks
about possessions and
of self-possession too!
We hear:

*You cannot serve two
masters for you'll choose
the one you like and then
despise the other man.
Just so: It is impossible to
serve both YHVH–LORD
and worldly wealth.
Why must you be
concerned so much
about your food, your
clothes? Look up, see how
the birds are free to fly.
They do not hoard, they
have no wardrobes filled
with finery. Yet YHVH–
LORD does care for them!
Are you not each
of greater worth
than doves that fly?*

*And look around you here:
take note of all the lilies of
the field now swaying in the
breeze. King Solomon had
not a robe like any one of
them. So! If your Heavenly
Father dresses all the fields
in beauty with the flowers,
won't He take care of you?
You have such little faith.*

*So quit your worrying; take
note of how your Heavenly
Father cares for you. Do*

*take Him at His word. Place
your concerns within the
Kingdom of the LORD and
what He does require of
you. There are sufficient
cares that crowd our lives
disturbing peace so why
reach out to worry all about
tomorrow too? Tomorrow
has its horde of troubles
without you carrying any
one of them today!*

*You do not wish a
judgement on your soul?
Refrain from placing one
upon another even though
he grieves you so. You may
expect that YHVH–LORD
will judge you too in just the
self-same way you lay down
judgements here and there.*

*You are so prone to point to
specks within another's eye
yet have not seen nor felt
the plank within your own.
How dare you offer to
remove that speck while
blinded by a log! Such is the
way of hypocrites. Clean up
your own eyesight before
you judge the vision of your
friend! You hold some*

*precious pearls within your
life; don't fling them off to
pigs. They have no need of
them—they'll 'trotter' them
within their mouldy mud!*

The day is now far spent;
the Rabbi's words are
almost done. But now
we find He changes tack—
He speaks of opportunity.
Come, listen in:

*What lies ahead of you?
You are excited yet you
wonder what the future
holds? Take courage in
to your own hands! Now!
Seize the day ahead of you.
You are in need? Just ask:
it's kindness that will fill
your hand. You've lost the
precious things of life?*

*Just open up your eyes and
you will find the greater and
the lesser things awaiting
you. All doors are closed to
you? They will be opened
unto you with hospitality.
You do not think that this
could be the outcome of
your quest? Think now: a
child asks food from Dad—
what kind of father gives a*

*stone instead? 'Dad, give
me just one fish.' What
father parcels up a snake?*

*You may be evil in your
heart yet you will know how
to fulfil the needs of
children. If you'd nurture
all the children in your
care, then how much more
will YHVH–LORD grant all
our needs with grace.*

*If you would know, fulfil,
the Law of Moses faithfully,
here is the 'key': Act kindly;
do to all what you would
have them do to you. This is
the Law in its entirety.*

*You seek the route to Life?
Don't look for paths until
you find the gate that opens
into pilgrimage. Make your
decision now! It is the
mountain or the valley path
you wish to take? The
mountain brings its
challenges to faith;*

*the valley leads you down
to shadows and to death.
There are two gates, you
see. The one will bring its
challenges: it is the gate*

*called 'Faith'. The second
gate will bring you ease and
comfort you away from
strife. It is the gate called
'Freedom'. Such a carefree
route, you think. You'll take
the easy route? Take note of
this: Your destination must
be well in mind before you
open up the chosen gate!*

*A warning as you set your
course: The road to Hell is
very wide and many travel
on that route. It is the valley
route where shadows cloud
the path. The Road to Life is
narrow and there are but
few that travel on that
chosen path. But come: for I
will be your Guide to Life.*

We find the Rabbi speaking
of 'bewares'. The things He
shares now with the crowds
that still refuse to go on
home will be life-changing
for us all. Our notes are
lengthy now!

*Beware of wolves that look
like sheep; their bleat may
cloak a roar of hate. You
wonder how to gauge how
they are what they seem to*

*be. How do you recognise a
wolf in wool? It's not so
difficult to pick the fault:
just watch the things they
do—the sheep, the wolf, the
man who walks so
'blamelessly' will be
exposed by what they do
and how they live.*

*You recognise a thorn bush
and you'll know it never will
grow grapes. There'll never
be a fig upon a briar. It is
the healthy tree that bears
good fruit—the thorn, the
briar, will be cut down and
cast into the flames. In just
the way that you decide
what's good fruit or the
bad, you may discern what's
false, what's good.*

*A prophet will be judged not
by his words but by his daily
what's good. A prophet will
be judged not by his words
but by his daily walk.
The fruit he bears: is it of
worth, is it good fruit? This
is the gauge. It is the
attitude and 'altitude' at
which you set your sights
that count with YHVH–
LORD. You think that when*

it comes right to the crunch,
a quick cast prayer will
prove your hold on faith:
LORD, LORD, You know
me well—just look at what
I've done; my whole life's
been exemplary. I've
preached all sermons from
'The Book'; I've done some
mighty miracles at times...

Take note of this: it won't
be what you say, nor mighty
acts spectacular, that win
your way to Heaven. The ne
criterion is faithfulness,
fulfilling what the YHVH–
LORD requires of you.
This is your opening to
Eternal Joy!

O what a way to end His
talks with us today! It is the
carpenter in Him. It's basic
stuff but we declare that
no one else has thought of it
in quite the way 'The Rabbi
from the Builder's Bench'
has laid out all His plans for
us. The basic matter is that
bricks have no stability if
laid upon
the shifting sand. It's rock
the builder needs: the bricks
must lay upon the rock as

this will give foundations
that will last. It is the same
with us! Go! Build your life
on solid rock
if you would live eternally.
It's foolishness to try
another plan: suffice on
sand then drift to dust!

ON CHRIST,
THE 'SOLID ROCK'
WE STAND!

MATTHEW with 'THE SON OF MAN'

A Place in the Kingdom of Heaven
Chapter 8:1 – 22

I've taken up some space
and time to let you know the
Gospel News that *Yeshua*–
Jesus is sharing with the
crowds that throng
the crowds that throng
around Him every day. This
is the major task I have been
given. I am to set down all
His teaching on the
Kingdom of the LORD.
These early chapters of
the scroll have caught,
I trust, the tenor of amazing
things He says—the basic

things that will direct our
paths to live His way.

And on the path—on His
itinerary—He meets with
many who are caught up in
the clutches of the 'evil one'
or in some desperate need
for Him to help, give aid or
counsel on the way ahead.
For instance, there's the
speeches that He gives.

The verdict is: He speaks
with great authority. The
Law is opened up to us in
simple yet amazing ways.
And on the road a leper is
made clean. The Gentile
world is not dismissed—
they're welcomed to His
ministry. He said many
would enter and sit down
in Heaven's Kingdom then.

Just think of it: when
officers of note take
opportunity to seek His aid
and even they aren't turned
away. I'll tell you what,
though, even He can be
amazed at the extent that faith
is spoken, trust is shown—
'Just say the word, Lord, it's
all we need to see my servant
is made well.' And by
the time that Roman reached
his home, his lad was seen
to be quite well!

There was that day in
Capernaum when Simon
Peter's mother-in-law
became unwell. He went
into their humble home and
took her hand. I tell you
now, she got right up and
served a meal for them!

Not only were the sick made
well, but many came to Him
to ask if they might follow
Him. He warned
them then and there that
though they did desire to
follow on each road He
trod, the route
would not lend any ease…

I heard it then, the name
He gave Himself: He said:

*THE SON OF MAN
will have no place to lay
His head. If you would
follow Me, you'll need
to leave the past back in
the past; your future is
with Me. I'll show the way.*

ANDREW
Chapter 8:23 – 34

We got into a boat last night
to take a respite journey on
the Lake. The day had been
so very long,
the challenges He faces are
so stark: the Son of Man
had need of rest as well as
us. He went right off to
sleep but you know how
it is on Galilee, a wisp of
wind can blow itself into a
storm before the sails are set
for it. We did our best.

We're used to them, the
waves on Galilee. But there
He was, so sound asleep. He
could not help us though
those waves were bound to
see the end of us! Go! Wake
Him up! Get Him to lend a
hand! What do you know?
He stood right up and steady
as a rock, He then
commanded all the waves
to be at peace. A *shalom*
peace it was indeed. The
wind abated, waves sat
down upon the deep! There
came amazing calm. What
kind of Man is in this boat?
Nature bows to Him. He is

the Lord of wind and wave!

Then, what we met on the
next day in landing at
Gadara on the eastern shore
will really turn the 'tide'
of how you think of Him,
the 'Rabbi of Renewal',
for there we met two men
who lived among
the caves—their mental
powers were gone. Insanity
beset them, took from them
all reasoning. They
screamed invective at
the Lord. He calmly went to
them with words of grace:

*Your minds are stolen from
you but I'll see that powers
of darkness
will no longer rule your
lives! You see those swine?
The darkness you've endured
will be replaced. The swine
will carry all your woe
into the rolling sea!*

Well, look at that! Would
you believe what we then
saw? The pigs fled to the
sea! I must say this, that—
when the men who owned
the pigs saw what had

happened there—they each ran home to spread the news. No one would welcome *Yeshua*–Jesus then. All begged Him to depart: they'd have no part with One who came disrupting everything!

We all got back into the boat to sail back home. Oh, what a time of it we'd had. We surely needed time to rest, curl up and sleep in peace. But no! We were once more engaged in ministry—His ministry and we were learning fast. The followers of *Yeshua*–Jesus must always be quite ready for the tasks each day.

A LEVITE
Chapter 9:1 – 8

Look! Here He comes, the upstart from that backward town of Nazareth. What could commend Him to my mind, I ask you now. We'll wait and see what happens next. See! They're bringing up a man on stretcher—

he can't move his arms or legs. What? Surely they don't mean to get 'the Rabbi of the Nondescript' to wave His wand and make him well? I don't believe my ears! How dare that rugged Rabbi say such things! This is a blasphemy! I tell you now, I heard it with my own ears:

> *Have faith: your sins*
> *Are all forgiven!*

So! Who is this who dares to stand in place of God? I'll have His head! So now He comes this way: He speaks. How did He read my thoughts? I do not like what He implies! It's I who should be challenging what He has done this day!

> *Why do you think such evil*
> *thoughts? For, is it not as*
> *easy to be saying now:*
> *'your sins are all forgiven,'*
> *or challenge him to get right*
> *up and walk today?*
> *Let me confirm that I, the*
> *Son of Man, have the*

authority to cleanse sin's
stains, forgiving him of all!

He turned, the Nazarene,
and said right then and
there: Get up! Pick up
your bed and walk on
home!'
I must confess when all
had seen and heard what
He had done they were
amazed and praised the
LORD. And as for me? I
know not how He did
what's done with a word!

MATTHEW
The Kingdom of Heaven,
Open Now!
Chapter 9:9 – 38

It is about the time that I
should speak of how things
fell into their place for me:
the day when I was made,
remade indeed! So, there
was I, just minding all the
government business as I
should—demanding tax was
paid (and a little left for me
to spend.) Life rattled on
quite well until… He came
my way; He looked into my
eyes, He smiled and called

me by my name; how did
He know it to be so?

'Matthew, come: now follow
Me—you'll find true
treasure on the road that
leads you into Life. Come!'

I packed right up and came
without regret to meet with
Andrew, James, Peter and
John. Oh, what a team we
made. I did invite them all
to come and share a meal
with me… It was a change
of scenery, of mode, but so
much more. It was, you see,
a new beginning that
renewed my soul. Some
think a change of clothes,
vocation or address is all
it needs to start afresh.

I know it now: renewal
starts within. The *in*-look
then the outlook is remade.
I'm ready for the road! I'll
walk with Him—He is
my Rabbi and my
Guide to Life.

I thought it was a joke—
the way the Pharisees
and cohorts pointed to
our entourage and

questioned why the Rabbi
would sit down to eat
with us, the 'riff-raff' of
my own home town.

The answer that He gave
was quite enough to quell
their blustering. He
challenged them with logic
then: He pointed out that,
when one's well there is no
need to call a doctor here.
Likewise, He had not come
to those who think there is
no wrong in them. He came
to heal the sick at heart
(like me). What is the worth
of worship where there is
no kindliness within a soul!

Another thing that came up
soon. The Baptist's men
inquired as to the reason
why our group did not
engage in fasting as they
did. *Jeshua*–Jesus replied
When the groom and bride
are present, it is not time to
fast... One does not put a
patch that's new upon a
ragged gown—it makes a
bigger hole! One does not
pour new wine into the old
wine sacks—they'll burst

and make a mess. One
needs to realise it's time to
make all things quite new.
Accept the truth when it is
demonstrated unto you!

I tell you now, one thing is
happening upon another all
the while. Just when those
Pharisees went off all in a
huff, a Jewish leader came
to *Yeshua*–Jesus. He knelt
and spoke with certitude:
Rabbi, my daughter has just
died—please come and
place Your hand on her.
I know she'll then be well
again. He rose at once to
come without delay.

But on the way,
a woman came to seek
His help, knelt down and
grasped the hem of Rabbi's
garment for she realised
this act of faith would
Then suffice to see her well
Again. We were amazed to
see that *Yeshua*–Jesus had
felt that healing flowed
from Him that day:

*Who touched My gown just
then? No, not those milling*

*crowds; there was a grasp
of faith. Come to Me: take
courage for you are whole.*

There seems no end to it,
the miracles, the mysteries,
the masteries, that mark
each day with goodness and
His matchless grace.

Oh, yes! I must report as
well that when 'the Rabbi of
the Healing Hands' arrived
within the house of
mourning, He explained at
once the little girl was yet
alive! I must admit that He
was laughed to scorn but
when the child ran out to
play all were in awe of
Him!

What's more, two blind men
came and pleaded for their
sight. He asked if they
believed it could be so.
O Rabbi, yes, we truly do.
He touched their eyes and
they rejoiced in new-found
sight: They saw Him clearly
face to Face that day!

As *Yeshua*–Jesus then
turned to leave, some men
came up to Him

accompanied by a mute man
and they pleaded for his
cause. The touch was all
he needed to speak out
in praise of *YHVH*–LORD.

The visitation of all towns
around the Galilee included
teaching in the synagogue.
'The Kingdom' was His
theme. Healings continued
but we saw a grief upon the
brow of *Yeshua*–Jesus. He
did explain that people were
like sheep scattered in
a wilderness without a
shepherd that would truly
care. He said to them:

*The harvest is so large but
where are the sufficient
harvesters prepared to
gather in the ripened
sheaves? Pray for some
happy harvesters today!*

MATTHEW
**Teaching on the Kingdom
of Heaven**
Chapter 10:1 – 15

The team is now
complete—all twelve of us
in training for the ministry.

There's Simon (known as
'Peter'—solid rock you
see,) his brother Andrew,
James and John (the sons
of Zebedee,) then Philip and
Bartholomew, Thomas and
a second James, then
Thaddaeus, another Simon
too and then, Iscariot. Oh,
and I must not forget
just me: Matthew.

The Rabbi gave to us
authority to be assistants
then, to aid Him in His
massive ministry. We are
instructed well just in the
way He goes about His
wondrous work each day.
Our guidelines are to care
for those, the wandering
sheep of Israel.

We are to preach God's
Kingdom News with clarity,
to use our hands to heal the
sick and ease the pain of
poor and rich alike. There is
no need to carry silver in
our sacks and He is right!
Our needs are met—our
satisfaction soars! We pray
for Shalom Peace to be
received in every home.
If any turn their back on us,

we are to leave them be.
They'll know the drastic
consequence of saying
'No!' to God and we're to
dust
our shoes and move right on
to those who'll welcome us,
He said to each of us.

THE SON OF MAN
Chapter 10:16 – 42

*Come, listen now, My
friends, the way ahead is
fraught with many troubles
for you are lambs before a
pack of wolves. Take care:
They'll lie in wait for you.
They'll take you into court,
reject the Truth you tell.
Much blame will come to
you for breaking Holy Law,
for subterfuge. Take care
in what you do!*

*Be wise—as serpents are—
but also gentle as a dove:
the day will come when you
will be required to preach
to kings and conquerors
and, in this way, you'll take
the Gospel to the world.
You'll wonder what to say
but have no fear—you will
be given what to say. Your*

words will not be yours: the
Spirit of the YHVH–LORD
will speak through you the
Word of Truth. The world
will hate the words you
speak, the deeds you do, but
keep on keeping on: you will
rejoice, you will be saved!
My friends, dispel your fear:
the hidden things will be
made clear. I speak to you in
privacy but all these things
will be revealed most openly.

Don't fear the one who seeks
to rob your body of its life—
such cannot harm your soul,
your 'Home' is in Eternity!
Look! See this penny now:
You'd buy two sparrows for
this coin; but know this too:
Not one small bird will fall
to earth without My Father
knows. You are of much
more value than the birds.
He cares for you—He knows
each hair upon your head.

Confess your faith, your
trust in Me, I will declare
your faithfulness before My
Father's Throne in Heaven!
You think I've come to grant
the Shalom Peace of Heaven.
Don't be surprised: it is to be

a sword that severs aged
fidelities. All those who love
their family far more than
YHVH–LORD hold wrong
priorities (deep love for
God brings love that will
not die.) I've come to bear
a cross, and those who
follow Me must lift the cross
that's in their path. If you
will seek to save your life
above all else you'll lose
that life. But if you are
prepared to lose your life
for My sake then you'll gain
Eternal Life.

All those who welcome you
will welcome Me and when
they welcome Me, they will bid
welcome then to YHVH–LORD.
The one that offers just one
glass of water to the least of
these My followers and in
acknowledgement of Me will be
recognised for that deed.

JOHN THE BAPTIST'S DISCIPLE
The Least in the Kingdom of Heaven
Chapter 11:1 – 19

I've come to make inquiries

for my rabbi John the
Baptist for he's heard of
what the Nazarene has done
in recent days throughout
the Galilee.

He wants to know if this
is proof that He's in truth
the Promised One—
Messiah. Can you confirm
that *Yeshua*–Jesus is really
"Him", the Promised One?
What do you know! Just
then it was the Man Himself
who did reply to me:

*Go back to your rabbi, give
him my warmest greetings,
then report what you have
seen yourself: the blind can
see, the deaf can hear, the
lepers are made clean, the
dead receive new life! The
Gospel is proclaimed. Good
News has come. You can
remove your doubts today.*

Then, as I turned to go, 'the
Rabbi from the Northern
Climes' began to speak of
John in glowing terms:

*What did you go to desert
lands to see? A blade of
grass that bends with every*

*puff of wind? You thought
he'd wear all fancy clothes?
What did you see out there?
You saw the greatest prophet
of them all. He is the one who
has announced the coming of
My Time with you:
'The Kingdom now is here!'*

*As great as John the
prophet is, the least in all
My Kingdom is far greater
still than he: for him, it was
the hope—for you, reality!*

*With what would I compare
the folk who live today?
They're just like children who
will play about within the
market-place. They'll dance a
wedding jig but you refuse to
dance and then, a funeral
dirge; you will not mourn.
When John appeared he
fasted, went without the wine:
you shouted, He's possessed!*

*But when I came and sat
at feasts with you,
You labelled Me a glutton
and a drunkard too: just
look at those who are His
friends, you blithely say!
Take note of this: The
wisdom that is real can be*

determined by results an
action brings always.

A VILLAGER
Chapter 11:20 – 24

I heard Him there today,
at Chorazim. He did
berate us for our attitudes.
What right has He, 'the
Rabbi from Old Nazareth'
to tell us all about our
faults? So! what about
His own? He takes short
shrift of those who live
by Law alone (it's true,
I have not seen how Law
alone has changed a life,)
but who is He to judge?
He has condemned
Bethsaida in the same
breath as berating us.

He reckons Tyre and
Sidon (well I ask you now!)
would live much more
within God's Law if given
half the chance. They'll
get more mercy on 'The
Day of Judgement' (can
you tell me when that's
bound to be?) Capernaum
has not escaped His vitriol.
He says we'll all go down
to Hell. How dare He treat
us so?! Sodom gets more
grace than us—how can
He think it so? He'll have
to go! We can't abide
His ghastly vitriol!

A VILLAGER
Chapter 11:25 – 30

You do not realise the worth
of Him, 'the Rabbi of
Renewal'! I heard Him pray
today. He speaks so well to
YHVH–LORD. He prayed
just now, 'Father…' (I am
surprised He speaks in such
familiar ways unto the
LORD; how could He truly
be 'The Son'?) But let me
share His words:

Father, I thank You for
revealing to unlearned folk
what You have hidden from
the so-called wise.

He then went on
to say to us:

My Father has now given to
Me the things I need for all
Eternity. But no one truly
knows the One who, as the
who, as the YHVH–LORD,
is also Father too. The Son

well knows and those to
whom the Father is
revealed as YHVH–LORD!

Come to Me now, all you
who are weighed down with
burdens that your
circumstance has laid on
you. Come now to Me, I'll
give you rest, respite from
all your care. Put on the
yoke I've brought to you
for you will find it very
comfortable so all your
burdens will be bearable.

A HARVESTER
Chapter 12

They came right by my
field of corn. It was the
Sabbath day when all
must take their rest.
His men did not
obey. They took some
sheaths and rubbed them
well between their hands.
The grain was eaten then.
I was amused. You see,
some 'know-all' Pharisees
rebuked loudly such
breaking of the sacred
Law. No work today!
I laughed out loud when

He reminded them of long
lost history when vital
laws were laid aside to
right a wrong. Why were
those priests not guilty
when they broke the
Sabbath Law? He asked
and then, surprisingly,
He said:

The Scriptures say that
kindness is the Law that
earns the smile of God! It is
not sacrifice that stands
instead. If you can work out
what I say, and then you
won't condemn the
innocent! Know this: the
Son of Man Is Governor of
the sacred Sabbath Day!

The Rabbi left. I followed
Him—the argument
regarding Sabbath rules
was not resolved. He went
into a synagogue where
whispering took over all
proceedings there. They
pointed fingers at the Man
as in their midst He healed
someone who could
not lift his arm or hand.
Well! Look at that! It is
not right to heal a man

upon the Sabbath Day!
The day is holy, we know
that! How dare He come
this way to prove the point
He makes. 'The Son of
Man' indeed! He should
be gone from us!
I saw the Pharisees.
The 'whisper' is they will
make plans to stop Him in
His tracks, restore things
as the Law demands.
They'll do it, too!

MATTHEW
Isaiah's Prophecy
Chapter 12:15 – 21
With Isaiah 42:1 – 4

The news was out and
fluttered all about. The
Pharisees were out to rob
the Rabbi of His life. The
Man is dangerous, He
must not be forever given
a free rein to say and do just
what He likes!

We moved on then to safer
ground but still the crowds
came too! They could not be
persuaded to go home.
He warned that what
they said of Him should be

confined, keep all the
miracles to self, in fact. We
saw, His men, just what He
meant: Isaiah's poem of
YHVH's words were
emphasised:

This is My Servant,
He's the Chosen One,
the One I love, He is
My joy: I place My Spirit
upon Him for He will judge
the nations of the world.
He does not cause
commotion in the streets;
He will not break a reed
nor douse a flickering
flame. He will establish
justice everywhere. The
islands then will place
their hope on Him,
they will behold His feats!

A BYSTANDER
Matthew 12:22 – 32

Things are getting mighty
strange right now. Some
people brought a blind
man to the Rabbi Healer
to be made quite well
again. He could not speak.
His muteness blamed on
demons—there was no
other cause; my eyes and

ears were not deceiving me—I saw and heard it all myself! You would expect them all, the Pharisees, to lurk nearby. They hugged the shadows, looked about to find the slightest doubt of good in what He did.

Someone had blurted out that, surely, He is the Messiah—the Expected One. That's all we need to throw the fuel into the flames! He drives out all those demons for He is the son of Beelzebub who is the source of all these powers! He does belong to Satan's kingdom, that's for sure! The Nazarene then gave reply:

So! Do I call on Beelzebub
to iron out all the woes of
humankind?! I ask you then:
who gives to you the powers
to chase the demons off? All
those who speak ill of My
work now need to know that
you can be forgiven of your
sins except when you
defame the Holy Spirit of
the LORD.
Say what you will but know:

It is the Spirit who
Gives eternal life!

Beware you snakes that
slither through the grass:
you cannot bear a witness to
the truth if faulty hearts are
steeped in evil thoughts.
You cannot speak
of good when evil lurks
within. The mouth is not the
master, it's the servant of
the heart. If you would bear
good fruit, you must make
sure the tree is healthy from
its roots. A tree is known by
all the fruit it bears and so
are you! What's in your
treasure store? Pure gold?
or counterfeit and dross?

Let's see what You can do: Perform a miracle for us!

You ask a miracle?! The
only one you will observe is
that of Jonah! Do know this:
just as he spent three days
and nights inside that fish
and then disgorged, heaved
up to live again, so will it
be: the Son of Man
will be three days and
nights deep in the Earth.
Now! Go and see what you

*can make of that. You faun
upon your history, revere
King Solomon—there is One
greater still than he! You
revel in the mysteries of evil
spirits keen to conquer all
susceptible to them. If they
depart, the heart swept bare
but nothing to replace
it there, they will return
with seven more to wreck
the 'home' of sanity. It's not
enough to rout all evil from
the soul: replace
the evil with the good!*

MARY, THE MOTHER
Chapter 12:46 – 50

I do not understand my Son
at times. I've waited here
for hours; the family as well
has come to visit Him. Why
does He not appear and eat
with us, inquire as to our
health; relax the while?
I heard Him speaking with
His friends, those men in
training at His side.
Someone had told Him we
are here. You'd think that it
would be enough to have
Him come right up to us.
What's that He said? How

strange the answer given:

*Who are my Mother and My
family? Whoever does what
YHVH–LORD, My Father,
does require of them is
brother, sister and My
Mother, too. All who fulfil
His will are 'family'.*

I see it now… I understand!
There are no borders in
God's family. I yet have
much to learn from Him,
the Son I bore, Son for the
world: He gives Himself!

MATTHEW
The Kingdom of Heaven:
It's Growth
Chapter 13

I have for you some pithy
parables. They speak the
truth far better than the
pulpit preachments rabbis
rant! There is a wisdom
seeping through the
windows of these parables.
today. You'll see they speak
of Kingdom Truth. That's
my remit: these Kingdom
values must be written
down, recorded now:

'The Rabbi for the whole
wide world' does speak of
ordinary things:

*A man sowed wheat upon
the soil; some fell where
birds were fed. On shallow
soil, the sprouts dried up.
Some fell in thorns, were
choked. The seed that fell in
fertile soil became a
harvest; So! Learn well.*

We had to ask His purpose
for the parables—why not
explain them all?

*These people look but do
not learn, they listen but
they do not hear. Isaiah's
words apply to them:*

The people listen, do not
heed;
they look at truth but do not
see.
Their minds are dull, you
see!
They've blocked their ears
and closed
their eyes. They cannot bear
to know their true condition
now.
If they would open up their
eyes,

healing would come, God
praised!

*You want to know about the
seeds? These are the truths
of YHVH–LORD.
The seeds that fall upon the
path are gobbled up by
evil's grasp. The seeds that
fall among the rocks spring
up with joy but have no
depth: the heat of
persecution comes then they
are shrivelled up and die.*

*The seeds that fall in thorns
will soon be strangled by
the cares of life. The seeds
that fall in fertile soil will
bear abundant harvests
then. The Kingdom yields
such joyous harvesting!*

Now, think on this as well:
*The weeds that grow among
the crop that's sown in
YHVH's field: the men
asked if they could uproot
the weeds. Pull out the
weeds, He said, and you
will damage all the crop.
We will abide with them
until the harvest time. then
they'll be taken out and
burned. The wheat will come*

*into My barn! The Kingdom
has no place for evil men!*

*Now, see this mustard seed: it
is the smallest of the small.
But when it grows it will
become the largest plant of
all. The birds will find their
home within the branches of
that plant. This is the
Kingdom's rate of growth!*

*Oh! Look right here: you
see the one who bakes her
bread upon the hob. She
measures out the flour and
mingles yeast within the
dough. Look at the
scrumptious bread she
bakes. The Kingdom works
just as that yeast!*

*I say unto you now that I
will speak in parables.
This is My way of sharing
all the mysteries of life right
from Creation's day until
the present time. For
instance: think of treasure
now: a man discovers gold
within a field. He rushes on
to buy that field. It cost him
all he had. The Kingdom
will require life's very best!
The oyster yields its pearls*

*and when the pearl of
greatest lustre shows its
worth, the one who buys
must give up all he has to
make it his. The Kingdom
will require the whole!*

*James, John: Look at
your Dad—Yes, Zebedee.
See how he tends the nets
that you have left? He takes
the fish caught in the ropes:
the best is readied to be
sold, the scraggy tiddlers
cast aside. The Kingdom
harvest time will be the time
of judgement made between
the good and evil souls!*

*Do you now understand
these things? You are
disciples in God's Kingdom
and discernment is required.
You'll find old truths, new
truths, combined within
God's Holy Law
You'll find My Word
is written there .*

MATTHEW
Chapter 13:53 – 58

We'd come to His home
town, 'the Rabbi of old

Nazareth', and He was
asked to take the pulpit,
say a word. His listeners
were amazed.

Is this the upstart
Carpenter of Nazareth
we hear today? How come
He knows so much? From
whence comes wisdom
such as He proclaims?
And what about those
many miracles? How
come, we ask? He's
Mary's Son. I went
to school with Him.

It can't be Bible truth
He preaches here! We
can't have Him declare
His wayward words!
He'll have to go:
Begone from us!

He left them then for He
assessed they had no faith,
no trust, in Him.

SALOME
Matthew 14:1 – 12

I'd heard so much about
the Baptist and we wanted
to be rid of him. He'd
us out for playing with
the Law of God. What use
is Law when we can't play
or please ourselves in
come what may?! My
Mother hatched a plan
to kill the wretched man.
A party was arranged and
Mother dear, Herodias,
prepared me well to dance
before the king. She knew
that Herod would be lost
to beauty and my charm.
I danced the dance of
veils. The last one cast,
I stood before the king.
He couldn't help himself!

He said, I'll give you
anything you ask my dear;
just do that dance for me
again. I swoon! I am
bemused! My Mother
knew he couldn't stand
against my wiles. She'd
planned with me the
perfect ruse: So Father,
dear, give me the ugly
head of John the Baptist
on a plate! Oh yes, the
king was shocked. We had
him in a trap. He had to
keep his word before the
guests that sat with him.
The deed was done,
we had our man!

ANDREW
Chapter 14:13 – 21

It's hard to tell how many
sat with us that day. So
many men, their wives and
children playing all around.
The sun was growing
tired—well past the time
they should be gone.
O Rabbi, don't You think
we should pack up? These
people all need food.
There are no shops; much
better to go home and rest
their weary legs.

There is no bread, you say,
to feed this crowd? How
many loaves have you? Go!
See what you can do.

Here are five loaves, Lord,
and two fish. It's nothing
but a crumb to feed this
crowd. He took the loaves
and gently blessed and then
began to feed the host—
of all five thousand men
plus families. We helped
Him there distribute more
than was enough for
everyone. When they went
home, we gathered up the
scraps more than enough to
spare. We had our fill!

PETER
Chapter 14:22 – 36

He told us He would meet
us there, across the Lake.
We hopped into the boat
and bade farewell—we'd
see Him soon enough, He
said, before He strode up to
the hills to be alone. It was
the way He was when it was
time for prayer. The day
was far more spent than
realised. The sun was
sinking fast. The sea was
calm—the Galilee serene.

What's that I see?
A silhouette on sea? It is
indeed a man. It's Him—
the 'Rabbi of the Galilee'.
At least, I think it's He but
cannot be! It is impossible
and yet it *is the* Lord!

I'll go to him… Just see…
It must be possible for there,
He walks upon the water—
I must go to Him.
The team tried to restrain
me but I leapt out from the
boat and, while I looked to
Him, I walked on top of
waves! Could it be true?
I looked down at my feet,
lost sight of *Yeshua*–Jesus

And sank. I nearly drowned.
He took my hand and
smiled but with a gentle,
calm rebuke, He said:

*O Peter, you have dropped
your gaze. You failed your
faltering faith! Now come,
get in the boat, take breath
and rest awhile!*

All were amazed but then
we settled down to think of
what had really made this
mystery a miracle. You can
imagine what we shared!
One said, It's easily
explained! He found a
sandbar, walked across
without a dampening of His
clothes. And you, Peter—
you must have felt the sand
between your toes.

Oh yes, I scorned. If I and
He were walking on a
sandbar there, why was the
boat still floating by?
The Master, *Yeshua*–Jesus,
just smiled! We made our
mind up then! You truly are
the Son of God! we said.

It was not long before we
reached the town of old

Gennesaret. The news
was spread abroad and soon
we all were in the thick of
it. The people came in
droves to be made well—
just touching was enough!

A PHARISEE
Chapter 15:1 – 9

**That Man has no respect
for Law! We came, you
see, to just point out that
His disciples were a rag-
tag mob. There is no way
those men should eat their
meals with dirty hands.
There is a proper way
to do it right, prepare
the meals quite ritually—
we've seen them munching
buns. We can't condone
such blatant sin!
We were within the rules
but He swung back at us in
rudest terms! He did
accuse us of a disobedience
to God! He asked us why
we did not live up to the
things we've taught!**

**What shocking
accusations came our way
in terms of basic rules**

concerning families.
Perhaps we've been
a little lax in how we
honour parents; it is no
concern to Him what we
will do or not! How dare
He treat us in this way—
He points the finger now
at us, recites Isaiah too.
We're blatant hypocrites?
No way! He said:

Remember what Isaiah
wrote:
'These people think they
honour Me
by speaking words most
eloquent
but actions speak much louder
than
devout worship of those whose
hearts
are far from Me and spend
their days
constructing human rules
instead
of honouring the Law I gave
to man'

AN OBSERVER
Matthew 15:10 – 20

I've listened avidly to this
debate! Fantastic, how He
put them in their place.
They did retire, those men
who came to set a trap for
Him—the Rabbi and His
faithful followers. When all
was settled down again,
He called the crowds to Him
once more. What sense He
makes of simple words!

*Now listen! Mark My
words: It's not what goes
into your mouth; it's what
comes out of it that is the
test of cleanliness. Of what
good are the cleanest hands
if what you say is utter
trash? A filthy tongue is
worse by far than dirty
hands and feet! Be clean
in what you say!*

His twelve assistants came
to Him—They seemed quite
tense to me. Rabbi, You've
made those Pharisees
quite angry now—we fear
their wretched plans!

*A plant My Father did not
place within the ground
will be pulled up. Do not be
fearful of those men—they
are but blind men leading
blind men and they'll both*

fall in the ditch!

He then explained to them
all that He meant by stories
shared concerning clean
hands, faulty hearts.

THE TESTED WOMAN
Chapter 15:21 – 28

I did what any Mother does
when children are in need,
near death! He didn't seem
to care; His men asked why.
He turned to them, not me,
explaining what His silence
meant. He spoke of sheep,
Israeli sheep: such were His
sole priority. I listened in
and pleaded then for help.

He spoke of children's food
being cast to dogs. I spoke
again: That's true, but even
dogs can take the left-overs
that fall onto the floor! He
smiled at me! He'd tested
me! My faith had won the
day. Right then my child
was healed. He is the Lord!

THE CROWD MEMBER
Chapter 15:29 – 39

That's us! The lame, blind,
dumb, the crippled, sick
and suffering. Our carers
brought us to His feet.
He touched us and we're
well. Our carers were
amazed and they joined in
our joyous throng!
We'd travelled far to seek
His aid; the hunger pangs
began to bite. He organised
the whole great feast:
amazing from the first to
last. We were all fed—I
cannot tell you how except
to say it was, for us, a
mighty miracle! He called
His men who brought, I
think, a meal or two. He
blessed the gift. It was
Remarkable, to think that all
four thousand, more,
did eat enough!

A SADDUCEE
Chapter 16:1 – 4

**You don't hear quite as
much from us: we are at
odds with Pharisees in
Terms of interpretation of
in terms of interpretation
of the Law. But! We're
together on this quest:**

this Rabbi must be gone
from us! We asked the
Man to show us how
He wrought His so-called
'miracles'. Just one would
do, we asked—it would
confirm God had
approved!

*You tell the weather from
the sky: red sky at night,
tomorrow bright! red sky at
dawn, you'll be forlorn! You
do quite well all weather-
wise but you can't read the
signs of times! You do not
see the evil done, the good
omitted from your lives.
You ask of me a miracle?
The one I give to you is that
of Jonah. Think on that!
Discern the truth of it!*

He left us then and just as
well—we'd sink Him in
the sea as well, without
delay!

THE TEAM
Chapter 16:5 – 15

We went to sea and not
before the sails were up,
we thought of it: the lack

of victuals for the trip. No
bread have we—we'd better
keep it quiet. But He had
read our thoughts.

*Take care what yeast you
choose when baking
bread of Pharisees!*

We thought at once He gave
the hint He knew our lack of
bread today.

*You worry about no bread
today? What little faith you
have right now: You've just
observed how people may
be fed. How many baskets
were made full? How do
you not discern that I was
speaking not about
the bread we eat?*

*I give to you
a warning to beware of
what the Pharisees and
Sadducees will do with
'yeast', that what
they say is teaching far
adrift of YHVH's way.
Take heed of this!*

PETER
Chapter 16:13 – 20

We journeyed on to
Caesarea at Philippi, just
near the spring where Pan,
a famous god, was quite
revered. It was appropriate
to ask of us just who the
people thought our Rabbi
was. The area was rife
with wooden 'gods'.

We offered Him some
thoughts. We did come up
with many names: Some
think the Baptist, John,
Elijah, said another. Then
one said, Old Jeremiah,
come again! No, it is not
him but one of the prophets,
that's for sure.
He looked at me, right
in the eye, inquired :

And you: who do
You say I am?

I looked right back into His
eyes for I now know just
who He is! You are
Messiah, Lord, the One who
is the Son of YHVH–
LORD!

Well done! Simon Peter,
you have thought it out,
observed, believed.

This truth was not explained
to you by anyone but JHVH
–LORD, the One who is My
Father, El Shaddai! That's
why I call you 'Peter'
For you stand upon the rock
on which My Church will
find a firm foundation.
True! Not even death
will overcome such faith.

I'll place within your hand
a key to open up the door
where those of faith may
enter in. For now: hold to
this truth and wait the time
when you can tell of it. The
Gospel will be heard! But
first, there'll be 'a Calvary'.
The Lord of Life would then
be called to die!

There's been a postscript:
I had then chastised Him
for His morbid thoughts:
such things could not be
done to Him! I was 'put in
my place' for this. It seems
I tempted Him to take an
easier path than that marked
out for Him. I have yet
much to learn! It does
appear we each will have
a cross to bear: O, help!

PETER, JAMES and JOHN
Chapter 17:1 – 21

We three went mountain climbing yesterday with *Yeshua*–Jesus. As things turned out we were the witnesses of a stupendous vision far, so further 'out' than anything a human could expect to see. It was no trick of light. We saw and recognised not only *Yeshua*–Jesus but, wait for it: Elijah walking there with Moses too, in conversation with our Lord. How could it be? We were amazed.

Well, Peter (me), just had to say: this is a very special day for us. We must remember it always. We'll build three tents—three tabernacles—Lord. One for each one—Your friends and You! It's left to me (John Bar Zebedee), to tell you just what happened next. A bright light lit the sky above! And then we heard a Voice the like of which was quite beyond a sound of Earth. The Voice then spoke clearly to us:

This is My own dear Son! I am so pleased with Him. Take care and listen to His words. He will reveal great truths to you!

I'm James. I am still scraping off the soil from all my clothes! You see, we fell right to the ground for such a terror filled our hearts, our souls! He came to us, 'the Rabbi from Eternity'. He touched us each:

Don't speak of this until you see the Son of God raised from the dead!

Well, Peter (me,) just had to ask: Why do the teachers of the Law suggest Elijah will come first?

Indeed, they're right about this truth. Elijah has come already and He remained unrecognised, like Me.

Yes! We now understand what He, the Son of Man, revealed. He spoke to us of John the Baptist's worth!

I'm John. I must report
what then occurred. As we
descended, there we found
the other nine, perplexed.
They couldn't heal a lad
'possessed'. Frustrated then,
He did give vent to
disappointment at this
most sorry lapse.

How long must I step in for
you? Just bring the boy to
Me… Go now, you demons.
Go! And leave the boy
alone! Return his sanity!

O Lord, the team then
asked, Why could we not
fulfil the task? We tried but
sadly failed our task!

It takes much prayer, much
focus on the nature of this
circumstance. Know this,
My friends, if you could
have a faith as small as just
one seed, a mustard seed,
you could command a
mountain to remove itself
and it would. Have faith!

MATTIIEW
Chapter 17:22 – 23

These matters quite

remarkable were capped
with dreadful news. It was
disquieting that *Yeshua*–
Jesus would soon be handed
over to His foes
and He would lose His life.
He said a thing most
strange. He said he would
be raised to life. What could
He mean? How strange that
He would know of this!

MATTHEW
Chapter 17:24 – 27

I know a thing or two, of
course, about the heavy
taxes that were ever due.
My friend, Peter, was
fronted by the Temple men
who came with hand held
out. So! does your Rabbi
pay the tax? they asked. Of
course He does! He pays
whatever's due each year'
When Peter went to tell of
this, our Rabbi asked,
instead, Just who should pay
a tax—should citizens or
foreigners pay tax to kings
or emperors?

Our Peter was quite
adamant: The foreigners!

This may be so, our Rabbi
then replied. But we must
not offend, He said. Go to
the Lake and catch some
fish. You'll gain the coinage
that's required for tax.

A CHILD
Citizens of the Kingdom
of Heaven
Chapter 18:1 – 5

I went to see the Rabbi Man
today. I'm just a little kid
but, Mummy, Dad, He
called to me. I ran right up.
He placed me on His lap.
He was so kind to me. He
said peculiar things. Dad,
can you tell me now, what
does this mean?

*Unless you will become just
like this child, you cannot
enter Heaven. The greatest
in My Kingdom is a humble
person like this child.
If you will welcome in My
Name a child like this,
you'll welcome Me!
Dad, what did he mean?*

MATTHEW
Chapter 18:6 – 14

I've jotted down that
precious thing the Rabbi
said about a child but now
I must add on what He
directed at us all. I've never
heard the like of it. A child
is foremost in the Kingdom
He initiates. He made it
plain. If anyone should
harm a child, it would for
him be better to be thrown
into the sea, a millstone tied
around the neck!

How terrible to be the cause
of one small child to lose its
faith. A hand, a foot, an eye
that was a cause of faltering
of faith should be
cut off, struck out for, far
the better with the one than
go to Hell with all!

He then went on to prove
His point. He chose to tell
a parable about a lamb—
well, just one sheep—
that sadly went astray.
The shepherd showed
his worth, securing all
of ninety-nine, he then went
off to find that lamb—
the one that went astray.
The flock was grazing
safely but that lamb was

nowhere to be seen until
he sighted it, caught up
in dangerous terrain. The
shepherd took it in his arms
and happily went home to
reunite the lamb with flock.
You get the point?

The shepherd loved that
wayward lamb as well
as all the flock that stayed
secure. He emphasised
that our Eternal Father
does not want
just one to stray.

I must not fail to tell you
Of just how the Rabbi
challenged us to act when
in a sharp dispute:

*Don't make a song or dance
of it: just go and sort things
out—no fuss! Each share
the problem quietly; you'll
see things working out.*

*Do not allow your strong
adversaries to act outside
the Law. Just go before the
LORD in prayer. If two or
three can solve their pains,
acknowledging the LORD,
He then will stand with them
and they will find His*

wondrous shalom peace.

Another parable confronted
us: Indeed, it had some bite
to it for it described the way
we act at times between
ourselves. I guess it is
because of this we
took the valued point.

How many times should we
forgive a wretched man that
does us wrong?
Peter asked the question,
adding on the possibility of
seven times. He got his
answer sure enough—
enough to make us wilt!

How could we meet the test
of seven multiplied
by seventy? He saw our
shock, decided to relate
this parable:

*A king is wronged by
servants who were prone to
steal from him. A million
dollars one owed him!
A punishment was meted
out. The servant begged
for leniency. The king
relented and forgave.
But then, the stupid man
beset another servant owing*

him a paltry piece of cash
not missed. He showed no
mercy, threw the man
into a prison, there to rot
until he paid the lot! The
king got wind of it. How
terrible, that you should
act like this. I showed you
grace; you turned your
back. You have no care for
anyone except yourself.
You'll get what you deserve!
Just so! Find a forgiveness in
your heart. It is God's way!

A PHARISEE
Chapter 19:1 – 9

I hear 'the Rabbi from
Obscurity' is coming
south. He's soon to set
His foot within Judea.
Let's see if we can help
Him 'put his foot
right in His mouth'.
We'll trap Him yet!

O Rabbi, if You will,
please help us settle our
dispute. We have a man
who thinks
that he can do just as he
wills if wanting a divorce:
Just say the word, it's

done, he says. What is
Your take on his ideas?

You know your Scripture;
from the first the YHVH–
LORD created man and
wife to be as 'one' through
life. No more the two—just
one. What God has
joined let no man part!

We've got Him now,
I think! Well, Sir, how can
it be that You are right?
Did not Moses set the Law
down straight, allowing
for the man to serve
the writ on his own
erring wife!

The law of Moses was then
given because the sin in
humankind was such that
they no longer took the
guidance of the LORD.
Man's sin requires the Law:
adultery must have an
active guard placed on it for
all humankind no longer
acts as in the garden bower
of Eden's deepest purity.

THE DISCIPLES
Chapter 19:10 – 15

We butted in right there—
we had to ask, if what You
say is true, is it not better
if we would remain
quite celibate?

There are quite different
reasons why some men will
not be married and there
are some who see it is
God's will for them.

Some will be born that way
and some are eunuchs;
some because they so decide
for sake of Kingdom aims. If
you can now accept this
path, so let it be: the
blessing's yours!

We've put our foot in it
again. We knew that He was
tired and when those crowds
came hurrying on
with children round their
feet, we thought is was our
duty then to stop them in
their dusty tracks.

No! Let them come to Me—
it is to people just like these
that I have come to set them
free! They represent the
very folk to whom the
Kingdom does belong.

He called them all to Him,
He placed His hands
on them; He prayed
and blessed them all.
We then retired for sleep.

A RICH YOUNG RULER
Chapter 19:16 – 22

I had to come. Oh, don't
you see? For all my wealth,
I'm destitute inside of me.
There is an emptiness;
I am not whole. I've heard
Him speak of life—Eternal
Life. I have to know just
what He means by that.

O Rabbi, what is it that I
Must do to gain a real
inheritance in things
pertaining to Eternal Life?

You ask Me what is good for
you? You know the rules—
the Law concerning this.

But, Rabbi, which of these
will give me life? How will
I find that special life?

You know them all so well:
don't kill, honour your wife,
don't steal, don't lie, and do
respect your parents always.

Well, Rabbi, all these laws
I've kept from youth. Why
am I 'empty' still?

*If you would be most truly
whole, then be prepared to
give up what you most
treasure in your life. If
you're prepared to give up
what you value most to gain
Eternal Life, if you can give
up worldly wealth,
you'll find the treasure
of Eternal Life.*

Why, Rabbi? Why do You
ask me what I cannot give?
You see, I'm rich. I must
retain what I can't give.
I leave with heavy heart.

PETER
Entrance to the Kingdom
of Heaven
Chapter 19:23 – 30

The Rabbi did reveal how
grieved He was to see that
man depart.
I heard His sad soliloquy:

*How difficult it is for any
rich man who desires to live
his life according to the*

*Kingdom's reign. It is far
easier for camels laden with
a load to make their way
through the old 'Eye of
Needle' gate than for a rich
man to enter Heaven's gate.*

Lord who then can be
saved? I asked.

*Impossible if taken from
the human point of view.
But know this Kingdom truth:
what is impossible to man is
quite possible to God!*

Lord we have given of
our best for You.

*You'll sit with Me one day
in Heaven. Consider this:
all those who give up what
they cannot keep to
gather gifts they cannot lose
will find their gain is
multiplied. But know this
truth as well: all those that
count self to be first will be
last. In Heaven's terms
the last will be the FIRST!*

YESHUA–JESUS
The Kingdom of Heaven
Chapter 20:1 – 16

*You wish to know the nature
of Heaven's Kingdom. I will
tell you now in parables:*

*There was a man who
wished to hire some worthy
labourers to work for him.
His vineyard needed men
prepared to work from
dawn to dusk. He was a man
who'd pay his men
the wage expected. Yes, top
range. He found some idlers
standing by and asked their
help. They did oblige.*

*At given times throughout
the day, he hired more men,
would pay them quite as
well. Then, just on evening,
more men took up the task.*

*When day was done and
work complete, he paid
each man the same fair
wage. The workers hired
that morn began to whine
about the fact that they
had worked all day but had
received not one fair
penny more than those
late-comers had! Their
grumblings overheard,
they were reminded of the pay
to which they had agreed.*

*'You have no right
to question My own
generosity. A fair day's
work: a fair day's pay.
There is no place for envy
here. You think that you are
first? You shall be last in
Kingdom terms assessed
in Heaven!*

THE SON OF MAN
Chapter 20:17 – 19

*We've all but reached our
goal to be in Zion by
Passover. I need to make it
clear to you that all will not
be well this year for I will
be, here, handed over to
Chief Priests and men who
teach the Law. I'll be
condemned to death.*

*The Gentiles, Rome's men,
will then ridicule the Son of
Man. I'll be their 'whipping
boy' before they nail Me to
a cross. Please hear Me
now, remember well:
within three days I will
be raised from death!*

ZEBEDEE'S WIFE
Chapter 20:20 – 28

I thought it high time that
I spoke up for my sons, my
James and John, for never
were there any boys
more suited than my sons to
take a leader's role. I all but
dragged them by the ears
but they at last
complied (a Mother has
some power beyond the
norm to get her sons
to do her will.) They came
with me to Him.

The Rabbi queried me.
I came right to the point:
O Rabbi, all I ask is for my
boys to take their seats to
left and right of You within
the Kingdom when it comes.
You know not what you
ask, He said. Then, looking
at my sons, this question
came: Can you both be
prepared to drink, with Me,
the cup of suffering?
Oh yes, we can!

You will indeed drink from
that cup but, as for
'Kingdom seats', this
Choice the YHVH–LORD,
My Father, makes.

I must admit the other men

were riled up, come what
may! There was a heated
argument about the 'firsts
and lasts' of it. Then
Yeshua–Jesus began to calm
His men. He said:

In worldly terms, a leader
has authority but this is not
the Kingdom way. Take
heed, the leader must be
servant of the rest. Please,
take My cue: I did not come
to laud it over you, I came
to serve you all and be for
you, and all the world,
Redeemer–Servant who
will give His all for you!

MEN OF JERICHO
Chapter 20:29 – 34

We heard they'd come to
Jericho, the 'Rabbi from the
Galilee', and the twelve that
followed Him.
We'd heard much more!
He was a healer of the blind.
'O come, let's find our way.
Perhaps He will take pity on
our plight. He must be in
that crowd. Mercy! Mercy!
Take some pity on us here.
What do you ask of Me?

He asked. Sir, give us
our sight, please, do! He
touched our eyes. At once,
we saw Him face to Face.
We followed in the way
He took up to Jerusalem.

A DONKEY'S OWNER
Chapter 21:1 – 11

Yes, it had been arranged.
He had a reason for the
hiring of the ass. And I
was happy that He asked.
When He came by and
settled on the donkey's
back, a wondrous thing took
place. The crowd enlarged
forthwith and they began
to chant the theme: Hosanna
(*Yeshua–na,*)
Hosanna: Save us NOW!

They then proclaimed His
praise: How blessed is the
One who comes to us
prepared to set us free!
They're chopping down the
Palm trees there—well, just
the fronds. Their purpose is
to garland all the path
before Him now. He's
treated like a King of Peace.
Perhaps He is! In answer to
some questioners, we say,
'He is the Rabbi from
old Nazareth!'

A MONEY-CHANGER
Matthew 21:12 – 17

**How dare the Man! He
came right in; He looked
me in the eye, then upped
the table right in front of
me! My coinage rolled
both here and there
quite lost to me. That
upstart from the north—
yes, *Nazareth* at that—
has no respect for
businesses that are run
efficiently, above the
board
(I'll vouch for that!)
What's this? He's taking
to the whip! What utter
gall! What's that He says?**

*This is My Father's House
of Prayer; You've made it to
become a den of thieves. I
will not stand for it!*

*Take this! Take that! Clean
up your act! Be gone from
Me! Depart Clear out!
The Temple is for Holiness!*

YESHUA–JESUS
Chapter 21:18 – 22

*So! fig tree: Here, I came to
you to seek a fig but, though
your leaves seem lustrous,
there's no fig. I am
convinced you've had your
day, so die. My team: you
ask now would that tree
just wither up and die? No
more can it bear fruit? It's
past its day. Faith works
this way when used aright.
Its time has come. I just
confirm. Soon you will need
to work by faith, so learn
the signs, confirm the truth.*

AN ELDER
Chapter 21:23 – 27

**It's time to put that Man
and all His meddling right
in their place—the refuse
bin. The Man's a maniac!
It is affrontery to speak
to us the way He does,
that so-called Rabbi from
the north. What right has
He to speak to us in just
the way He does? We are
the true authorities, the
guardians of the Law. He
cannot just decry the fact.**

**He's put us in a plight
with just one query: we
can't answer it.**

*Was John the Baptist's
desert work His own
initiative or did the YHVH–
LORD give him the
mandate? Well?*

**There is no answer that
will keep our rule intact—
you see, if God-given, why
did we not obey? But if we
say 'by others' we are in
real strife: that mob attacks!
We cannot say for sure.**

*Then neither will I
answer you. Go, work
it out yourselves!*

A LISTENER
Chapter 21:28 – 46

The parables came thick and
fast. Let me explain—
I think I can: a son says
says 'no' to dad who asks
for help. The other son
said, 'right away!' but ran
off with his pals. The first
son changed his mind and
'bent his back' for Dad.
Which of the two received

Dad's smile? You're right!
The first who had a change
of mind. It's time you also
changed your mind!

Another parable I can't
wipe from my mind: A
vineyard owner set
about preparing for a trip.
Before he left he did ensure
that all was set in place. His
workers had a surety that all
was well. They smiled.
Then off he went and they
eased off the duties left to
them. At time of harvest,
men were sent to gain
the owner's share and they
were killed! The owner in
great grief, then said:
I'll send my son, my only
son, for, surely, they will
heed his call! What did they
do but kill him then. So,
what will happen to them
all? Upon their question,
Rabbi said:

*Have you not read what
Scripture says? 'There is a
Stone, a Rock, rejected by
the careless mob who did
not see its worth. This Stone
turned out to be the Stone
of greatest value for the*

*YHVH–LORD had chosen
it:' (the Rock of Ages cleft
for all the world!)*

The rulers knew He spoke of
them; They did not act to
bring Him down—they were
afraid: He is a Prophet too!

MATTHEW
Illustrating the Kingdom
of Heaven
Chapter 22:1 – 14

Whoever heard the like of
it? The Rabbi was in utmost
form today—He spoke of
kings and sons (I think He
spoke of *YHVH*–LORD
and Him, of course.) Still,
the story is magnificent:
The king prepared a
wedding feast for son and
heir. He sent his many
invitations out, but none
agreed to come! Some slew
the postmen, too. The king
became quite angry then.

He sent more men, this time
to highways, byways,
with his invitations to, yes,
everyone. The folk then
came in droves though one

refused to wear some decent clothes. He was ejected from the feast. The Rabbi then explained:

Although the many are invited to the Kingdom Feast, so few prepare themselves and miss out on all Heaven's joy!

A PHARISEE
Chapter 22:15 – 22

This is the plan: these questions will entrap the Man and that's for sure! So, hear what I've to say to Him: Rabbi, we know you speak the truth on all occasions come what may. Do tell us, now, what has the Law to say regarding taxes paid to Rome?

You hypocrites! I am aware Of evil plans you have in store for Me. This is a trap. Hear Me: do look at this small piece of pence: whose face and name appear on it?

Well, anyone can see the etching is the Emperor of Rome, his name also.

Well, pay to Rome what does belong to Rome and pay to YHVH–LORD what rightfully belongs to Him!

He set us on our heels with that but we will live to fight another day!

A SADDUCEE
Matthew 22:23 – 33

You know full well we don't believe in all that twaddle that a man will rise again after he is demised! Not like the Pharisees, we have our heads screwed on all right. The dead are dead! They will not breathe again. On this one thing, we'll toss the Rabbi out...
Oh, Rabbi, please inform us now: You know that Moses said the brother of the dead must marry the widow so that the children would belong to the deceased. What happens If there are, within the family, all seven brothers and the same thing happens to them all.

**Now then, when all are
raised from death whose
wife then will the widow
be, we ask of you?**

*And what stupidity you do
display! You show an
ignorance of what the
Scripture says: When all are
raised to life, they'll be as
angels and there'll be no
marriage then. Have you
forgotten: YHVH–LORD is
God, the God of Abraham,
his son—Isaac; his son—
Jacob (Israel). He is the
God of living, not the dead!*

**He's done it once again!
We're done (for now! But
wait the *coup de gras*)!**

A PHARISEE
Chapter 22:34 – 46

**That fixed the Sadducee.
Wow! How great was that!
Let's see what we can do.
Rabbi, we need to know:
what is the greatest of
all the Mosaic Laws?**

*So simple! Why do you not
know? Love God with all
your heart, your soul, and*

*with your mind. That is the
Law deemed greatest of
them all. And the second is
so like it—Know: you are to
love your neighbour as
yourself. On these the whole
Law rests. So, let Me ask of
you a question now:
You speak of the Messiah—
Who is His forebear? From
whom does He descend?*

**That's easy, Rabbi, we're
surprised You have no
knowledge of His line! He is
descended from David, king.**

*Then why did David call
Him 'Lord'? The LORD
said to my Lord, sit here
until... If David called him
'Lord', How can Messiah be
descended from David,
our king, king long past?*

**What answer can we give
to that? That's it!
It's time for us to act!**

YESHUA–JESUS
**Serving in the Kingdom of
Heaven**
Chapter 23:1 – 12

Now, in regard to Moses'
Law, you must take heed of
all your rabbis preach to
you. Do hear what they've
to say, but do not do as they
now do! For they do not,
and never will, just practise
what they preach; their
words are vain! They'll tie
you down with burdens that
you need not bear. You see
them all with their
phylacteries—the laws they
wear tied on with string.

They faun on your respect
of them; they'll bind you up
with half a chance. Recall:
I've said so many times
that those who are
indeed the 'great' in
Heaven's Kingdom truly
are the servants. All who
are quite humble are
the truly great.

YESHUA–JESUS
Chapter 23:13 – 24:2

How terrible, the coming
purge for you, the teachers
of the Law—you hypocrites!
You'd lock the Gates of
Heaven in the face of people

who are all sincere. How
terrible for you, blind
leaders of the blind! Why
place your faith in Temple
gold? Why place
restrictions on the altar gift
but not
the altar that will need a
complete cleansing there?

How terrible for you! The
Day of Judgement looms.
You weigh your tithe yet you
neglect all justice, mercy,
grace. You are so blind,
you'd spit out flies but
swallow laden camels yet.
You polish up your cup and
plate so that the outside is
quite clean but, from the
inside, utter fifth
is swallowed wantonly.

How blind you are! Repent!
Clean up your inner cup
then what you swallow will
be pure. How terrible for
How terrible for you! You
are so like a white-washed
tomb that looks so good but
you are full of putrid flesh
and rotting bones. You look
so good but you are
hypocrites; you live on lies!

How terrible for you! You hypocrites! You are descendants of the very ones who killed so many prophets, spilled their blood. You slithering snakes! You can't escape the retribution that's awaiting you. The punishment for evil deeds will fall on you with no delay.

Jerusalem! Jerusalem! The City of God's Peace— there is no peace within your gates… Jerusalem! Jerusalem! How often I've desired to come to you and comfort you, I'd gather you to shelter you beneath My out- stretched arms to shield you from all harm. You have no will for this to be. You've closed your gates on Me.

My tears for you have no avail. You do not see that you will be abandoned and quite destitute again. You won't see Me until you welcome Me.

Oh yes, you've said how splendid do those Temple buildings now appear. How sad it is for Me to say that, one day soon, not one small stone will stay in place, not one remain in peace. The Temple will be gone!

THE TEAM
Gospel of the Kingdom
of Heaven
Chapter 24

We can report it here for we can see quite clearly now that what the Rabbi said makes utmost sense. We asked, you see, just what He meant by saying that Jerusalem would fall.

And sitting there with us on Olivet as we looked down upon Jerusalem with Temple still resplendent in the sun. He warned us to be watchful lest anyone should make a fool of us. He said that many men would come to proudly state, I am Messiah, hear me out! This will not mean The End has come for nations will then crumble, totter, kingdoms rise and fall as famine, fear, and mighty

earthquakes will increase.
Then you, My friends, are
caught and punished, put to
death. So many then will
cast their faith aside. Evil
will spread, the love of
many will run cold. But
those who hold out to The
End will all be saved. The
Kingdom News will reach
the very ends of Earth and
then The End will come.

You will remember David's
words, He said then spoke
of horror that will come to
stand within the Holy Place.
This is the time, He said,
when all must flee. Rush to
the hills! Do not delay for
lives will be at stake!

The ghastly scenes of which
He spoke would be more
terrible than all the wicked-
ness of past histories.
In fact, He said that these
days would be worse than
anything recorded yet. The
mother and the child will
feel it most. Just hope it
won't be winter time.
But *YHVH*–LORD will
intervene lest nothing, no
one will be left.

Then we were warned not
to expect the truth of fingers
pointing to reputed
'Christs'—Messiahs—on
the road. When I return,
that Day will suddenly
be known by all in lightning
flashes, thunder bolts, said
He, the One we know as the
Eternal *LIGHT*!

There'll be strong signs,
He said, the sun will lose
its brightness and the moon
will cease to shine. Great
stars will fall; the universe
will lose its paths, its orbits
be askew. It's then
Messiah's Sign will be
revealed across the heavens,
all humanity will weep—
they'll recognise, too late,
it is the LORD that they've
denied, dismissed, decried.
His power and glory will be
seen. The trumpet will
resound as angels gather the
beloved, the faithful saints,
from off the Earth.

You want to know the day
and hour? No one but
YHVH–LORD now knows
when it will be. You may be
sure of this: just look at how

things were in Noah's day—
much feasting, drinking, and
without a care of right
or wrong, of justice and
God's peace. Too late
to change their ways after
the Flood had washed them
all away! So, be alert!
Watch out—the Son of Man
will come when none are
ready for the trumpet call!
How happy will the faithful
servant be when his
inspection comes, but
hypocrites will wail.

THE TEN BRIDESMAIDS
Readiness for the Kingdom
Matthew 25:1 – 30

Let's hurry now or we'll
be late; the sun is sinking,
moon is up! We're all quite
ready now! Let's go: the
bridegroom won't delay
this special night!

The night drags on. How
long must we ten
bridesmaids amuse
ourselves tonight? Oh no!
My lamp's gone out!
And mine! I did forget
the extra oil!

We're in a fix for sure.
Look at the other five. Their
lamps are quite alight. Let's
ask if they can help us out,
fill up our lamps with oil.

We've just enough to suit
ourselves—go back and buy
some oil right now. And
hurry now, the groom will
come no doubt quite
very soon tonight.

Why does the groom delay?
Let's all relax a while. A
little nap will help. A little
Snooze will do no harm;
A little snooze will do no
harm; no doubt the groom
will wake us up!

So, five were gone to get
some oil, the other five were
fast asleep. The bridegroom
was disturbed indeed to find
the chosen gone, or fast
asleep!

How like My Church, My
chosen few: when I return—
the half are gone, the other
half, asleep. It is a matter of
the oil: the Holy Spirit Oil!

The Church must know it is
to you I'll come again.
Prepare for when the
Bridegroom comes: No Oil?
Asleep? I'll lock the door!

We learned so much from
this story that challenged us
to keep our lights all shining
brightly in the darkness of
the night where people
stumble, lose their way and
miss the 'Open Door'!

The Rabbi also spoke of
other things, of servants
carrying responsibilities and
others merely idling their
days away. We learned from
this that
there is a recompense,
a consequence!

THE FINAL
SEPARATION
Inheriting the Kingdom
of Heaven
Chapter 25:31 – 46

The Rabbi loved to speak of
sheep and goats. He knew
that we could see how we're
so prone to value sheep
above the goats!
He emphasised that, on

the Day of Judgement, there
would be a final separation
of the good from evil in
God's searching sight.
Decisions would be made.
Who are the sheep, the
goats? we asked. He then
replied that 'sheep' and
'goats' are people classified
as one or other of the
multitudes. And on that
Day, He'd say to those who
are the 'sheep': Come, for
you each are blessed: inherit
all the Kingdom offers you.
The 'goats' must
hear the solemn news of
their rejection for their
faithlessness. The Door is
shut. So why should such
things be, you ask?

The Kingdom folk are those
who care: to grant the
hungry food, to give a glass
of water to the thirsty in My
Name, to open up the doors
of hospitality, to clothe the
poor, to soothe the sick and
visit those in gaol. You'll be
surprised, but know today
that, in–as–much as those,
the very least received your
care, you did it all for Me.
The 'goats' will realise,

too late, that, in–as–much
as they neglected those in
need, they've by-passed Me.
The Kingdom has no place
for those, the blind
to every human need.

SIMON THE LEPER
Chapter 26:1 – 16

The rumours were quite
rife that plots were being
made to trap the Rabbi
but I had invited Him
into my home. The Rabbi
and His men came to the
feast I had prepared.
We sat at meat, discussing
news of this and that
when, spare my days, we
saw that woman come
and open up an alabaster
box of spikenard, a strong
perfume. That scent
pervaded all the room.
It must have cost a pretty
pound. The most amusing
thing to me was how the
Rabbi's team reacted to
the fact that she began
to bathe His feet before
anointing Him with all
that scent. It's just not
done! They said: The very

scent, if sold, would give
enough for us to feed
the poor among us all.

The Rabbi heard and
challenged them. He said,
Why are you bothering
this woman? Can't you see
that this is a most gracious
act? My body now is
ready for the tomb. Her
deed will be remembered
down the years. Oh, by
the way, I've heard that
one of those twelve men
has slipped away,
infuriated with the waste
of precious perfume on
those feet! He was the
treasurer, I hear! I do
believe he means to do
away with anything, or
anyone, who foils total
collection of his coins!

THE SON OF MAN
Passover and The
Kingdom Feast
Chapter 26:17 – 30

My team had asked just
where to set the scene for
the Passover Meal. I have
instructed them to seek

the hospitality of one who'll
aid us by the opening of his
home to us. When this was
done and plans were all in
place, we sat at meal.

Then, as I broke the bread
with them, the men expected
me to speak
of all the history this meal
involves. I knew that it was
now the time when a new
history would be involved.
But first, they needed to be
made aware that one of
them would sell Me out to
evil men this night! I saw
their deep distress; one
asked who could perform
this act. The clue was given:
The one who dips his bread
into My cup will be the one
who will betray His Lord,
the Son of Man tonight.

Yes, I will die but better far
for him if never born at all.
How could he with such
innocence then ask the
question, Surely Lord, You
cannot mean that I... It's as
you say—I do mean you!
This precious time must not
be lost. I took some bread
and blessed the loaf then

broke it, passing to each
man a piece. Now take this
'Bread of Life' I freely give;
it represents My body so
do each partake of it.
Likewise, the glass of wine.

When blessing it, I say, this
deep red wine now
represents the blood I'll
shed for you that all may be
forgiven by My sacrifice.
We'll share this in the
Kingdom Feast. We sang
the Psalms of Passover
then went out in the night
towards Gethsemane.
I'll give Myself tonight!

PETER
Chapter 26:31 – 35

I'm horrified to think of
what we've heard tonight. I
promised Him I would be
true to all my promises.
His answer left me stunned.
How could He even think
that I'd forsake Him to His
foes? He answered me by
ghastly words. You see,
He'd said that we would
flee from Him before the
night was through. How

could He think that we'd
forsake Him in His hour of
need. I said as much to Him
to which He then replied:
My friend, before the Cock
Crow hour—the early
morning trumpet call—
you will deny that you know
Me. I hardly heard the
rest—what He then said
of sheep that scatter for
the Shepherd will
be killed forthwith.

PETER, JAMES and JOHN
26:36 – 56

I cannot bear to see His
grief! There is a depth of
agony that can't be
plumbed. Why does He cry
to *YHVH*–LORD such
pleas?
His heart is crushed. James,
what was it that He prayed?
He spoke of God as Father;
we had heard Him speak
like that before but not in
agony! He pleaded with His
Abba there: Abba, is it
possible for You to take
This cup of sorrow from My
hands? But, not My will,

I want always to do Your
will. This was the last we
heard for then we slept…
John, look. He's moving
now. He comes… He
staggers so, as if in pain.
What did He ask?

Please, do not go to sleep. I
need to know you are alert
to pray for Me. Don't let the
tiredness of the day now
drag you into sleep.

He's moved right back
beyond us now and
kneels just by that olive
tree. We hear Him groan—
much as before; He asks for
grace to drink the cup of
suffering. John, do you
know what He could mean
by that? He's spoken much
of many things tonight… I
am so tired, I can't stay on
my feet. Perhaps He'll tell
us when He's finished with
His agonising prayer.

You could not watch for
longer here, you've settled
down to sleep again? Too
late! The time has come.
The Son of Man will be
attacked tonight. Get up!

Come, let us go to meet the
man who is betraying Me.

I am appalled! It's Judas,
the Iscariot. He marches up
to *Yeshua*–Jesus and kisses
Him! A traitor's kiss it is
for now those soldiers know
the One to be constrained,
in clanking chains,
to go with them. Not while
I'm Peter! No, they won't!
I'll grab this sword, I'll save
our Master, Friend. Take
that! The Rabbi, though,
spoke, so quietly:

Restrain yourself, Peter.
The man who takes the
sword will die by it.
My Father could control
this ghastly scene
with hosts of angels, saving
life. But then how could the
Scriptures be fulfilled which
point to sacrifice of life
to save ALL life? Just so,
My death occurs because
all that the prophets wrote
must be fulfilled and now.

That's it! We've failed!
Let's go, get out of here.
Gethsemane's a vale of
woe! We cannot help Him

now! What does He mean
by His words 'sacrifice that
is the way to save all life?'

CAIAPHAS
Chapter 26:57 – 68

That Man must die!
He'll go to Hell! for
blasphemy and disrespect
of holy things (including
me!) It is convenient,
Iscariot's defection from
the team. We certainly can
spare those thirty pieces
right enough—it's cheap
at twice the price! Give it
to him and send him off—
no need to have him
standing round the
Holy Temple courts.

Bring Him before me for
the main harangue. The
hour is late but better now
than when the day puts all
on view: explanations are
so difficult.

Well! Tell me now, what
answer do You give to
accusations flung at You?
We have two witnesses
to testify that You will tear

the Temple down and then
rebuild in just three days!
What do You say? The
Man glared back at me
refusing to confirm, deny.
In the name of *YHVH*–
LORD, no less, remember,
You are under oath!
Repeat the blasphemy
that You are who You say:
Messiah, Son of God
whom we obey with heart
and soul—yes, all of us!

You have said it now!
"I AM"! What I will say
is this to you: The time will
come when you will see the
Son of Man sit on the right
of YHVH–El Shaddai's
great Throne and coming on
the clouds of heaven.

Blasphemy! I rend my
clothes! We have no need
of further men to testify to
this Man's subterfuge.
I call upon you all:
exponents of the Law—
what is your verdict now?
The Man is guilty. He
must die! I've no regrets
for the maltreatment then
received by Him. He'd

earned it all! The bruises
are too few for Him!

PETER
Chapter 26:69 – 75

Oh yes, I fled with all the
rest. What else could we
have done? He would not
have me wield that sword;
but I then followed on,
though in the shadows
now. I took a seat outside
the court—there was a fire
so I kept very warm.

Then, would you know,
a girl, known as a servant of
Caiaphas came up and
challenged me. You're one
of those who stay by Him,
the Galilean now on trial.
I do not know the Man! Just
let me rest a while to warm
my hands. I do not know
what you imply. I thought to
leave the courtyard
but another challenged me.

I swear, I do not know the
Man! The lies I told leave
me ashamed, especially
when a man declared,

Of course! You are His
friend. Your Galilean accent
tells me so! I shouted back
at him. I swear, I don't
know Him! May God now
punish me if I am telling
lies—I do not know the
Man! The cock then
crowed—the time of 'Cock
crow' had occurred. I knew
at once my sin, my deadly
cowardice. Three times
I had denied my Lord.
I went out into the gloom
and wept most bitterly.

JUDAS
Chapter 27:1 – 10

What have I done? It was
my plan to force His hand
and instigate the time of
Israel's triumph over
Rome. He used the word
'betray'; it's furthest from
my mind. But now I see
that all my plans have
failed! Those godless
priests have trapped the
One I held in high esteem.

These thirty silver pieces
are like lead within my
pouch. I'll right the wrong
I've done this night.

I entered in the court
where they stood gloating
in the gloom. I have
betrayed the innocent
to death. Release Him
now. Here are your filthy,
loathsome coins!

So, what is that to us?
He's gone to Pilate now.
What He has said is
blasphemy. You are too
late to save Him now!
I threw the coins at evil
men. I left the room…
It is the end…

PILATE
Chapter 27:11 – 31

Who have we here?
Do tell me now: Surely not
the Galilean! I've heard
so much of You. Where
shall we start? Oh yes:
are You the King of Jews?

It's you who testify it's so!

Hmm, yes. Well said. I
hold some dire words—
some accusations from the
priests. What do You say
to these accusations now?
You answer not? I am

surprised. Surely you have
something worthy and so
beneficial for me? I am
impressed by You!

I have a ruse. It is the
custom at Passover to
release one prisoner
to show good faith to
priests. Here is Bar-Abbas
(*son of dad*). Which of
The two should I release:
Bar-Abbas, murderer,
or the 'Son of Man'?

I know the reason why this
  Man is in those chains—
they hated Him; I'll set Him
  free with half a chance.

Bar-Abbas—he is the
man! We choose that he
should be set free. Then,
what should I now do with
Yeshua–Jesus the
Messiah?

We want Him crucified!
they yelled. There's
nothing more that I can
do. Bring me a basin;
fill it up with water for
I'll wash my hands of this
foul deed. Let it be known:
I'm not responsible for
what you do. This is

your deed, not mine, it is
your doing, I am innocent!
Yes, be it as you say. Let
full responsibility—all—
rest on us and on the
children we will bear!

Indeed, I did release
Bar-Abbas and to
emphasise His foul fate,
I had the Galilean flogged
and sent Him off to die,
to bear a cross to Calvary.
I wipe my hands of wrong
today—I am absolved!

SIMON OF CYRENE
Chapter 27:32 – 33

The tramp of soldiers' feet
along this Dolorosa path
resounds with Rome's
imperial power. I see the
Prisoner now. He falls;
they prod Him up again.
The gore, it flows across his
brow. That plank He hauls
is clearly meant to bring
Him down. I hear the
groaning of this Man. He
falls again, just near my
fcct. IIc'll
die before His Calvary!

What's that you say? I am

to lift that plank? Yes! I will
carry it for Him. He's done
enough for us though who
would recognise His worth
today? Look there! Those
vicious welts! He has
been whipped! How could
He bear this plank?

The plank gets heavier each
step I take... I see Golgotha
now: the *skull* it grins at
us this hour! In words that
Rome would use, it is a
'Calvary'. This is the place
of death, outside the city
walls. At last! I drop the
plank and soldiers nail it to
a larger plank. A cross is
formed upon the ground.
The Nazarene is nailed to it
and then, uplifted to the sky
to breathe His last! The
'Son of Man' is crucified.

CROWD COMMENTS
Chapter 27:34 – 44

Here, have some wine. It
helps one through the
pain. Bitter though? Hey,
look at His garb. The
cloak
is fine, but there are some
blood-stains here. I'll have

it though—just meant for
me. You think it's yours?
Well, throw a dice; let it
decide whose back will
bear the 'saviour's' cloak!

That jerk when planks go
down into the hole would
hurt. But, look at that,
there is a sign above His
head: 'Here hangs a king!'
That's put Him in His
place! A 'crown' of thorns,
a royal 'robe', a 'throne'
of sorts... There is a
bandit 'courtier'
on either side. They yell
abuse at Him, fling scorn!

You thought You'd tear
the Temple down, rebuild
it in three days. Just how
will You achieve this stunt
with hands nailed to
that deadly cross?
So! Save Yourself—
You say You are God's
Son! Come down, we call,
come down, right now!

We priests and lawyers
know this Man's ungodly
ways, His blasphemy,
His tricks to please the
crowds. He 'saved' them

all but cannot save
Himself. Come down!
Do that, O Nazarene,
and we will give You
deference. We will
believe, make You
our king! Let's see
what God will do…
We won the day!

YESHUA–**JESUS**
Chapter 27:45 – 50, Psalm 22
(The prophetic Psalm)

*Eloi, Eloi, lama
sabachthani?
My God! Oh, why have You
abandoned Me? Oh, why
are You so far away?
I plead for help… Eloi,
come to Me: I'm scorned,
despised; they mock and
sneer. They challenge You
to save Me now. Don't hide
Your Face from Me… My
enemies are 'herds of
bulls'; like lions, they roar
for blood, My life is poured
as water flows in streams;*

*My bones dislodged, My
heart like wax. My strength
has gone. You've laid me in
the dust and left Me for the*

*dead… They've pierced My
hands, My feet. My garments
have been gambled, gone…
Yet, You're My strength;
Eloi, come…*

*The day will come; I will
give praise, the poor, at
last, be satisfied. And all
who seek the LORD will
praise Your Name: All
power belongs to You.*

*O LORD, the future
generations then will hear
of You, Your righteous acts.
Make of this hour what You
desire. Praise God!
IT'S FINISHED NOW!*

A ROMAN SOLDIER
Matthew 27:51 – 56

I've stood this ground so
many times but never have I
witnessed such as this!
Some news has come
that when the Nazarene had
breathed His last, the
Temple veil was torn—from
head of it to foot—no
carthly hands did that!
There's been a long eclipse
as well—for three hours,

give or take. Unearthly,
that's what I will say of it.
I'm sure those women
standing there agree.
They are His friends
and His own Mother,
standing still, with them.
The ground is rumbling
now—an earthquake in
the city of Jerusalem?
Absurd! The ground is
shifting though—as if all
nature bares its anger on
this day. And some have
Said there's ghosts at large;
they're roaming through
the lanes of old Jerusalem.
I have a fear upon me now.
But something else: I look
up to that cross and know
this was the Son of God!

JOSEPH OF ARIMATHEA
Chapter 27:57 – 61

I can't keep secret anymore
that I'm His very secret
friend—a true disciple yet
well cloaked in anonymity.
It's time to get involved—
too late, I fear, yet I will
dedicate my tomb to be His
resting place. I'll go right
now to Pilate, Roman
Governor, and ask to take
the body and inter it in my
sepulchre. There was no
problem with my plan.
The body of the Rabbi,
Nazarene, 'the Son of Man',
He liked to say, was placed
within my care. I took
Him, wrapped Him in pure
linen and then took Him to
my new-hewn tomb. The
nearby stone was rolled
across to seal the entrance
where two other friends,
both Mary by name,
sat there to mourn.

PILATE
Chapter 27:62 – 66

**They came to me, those
snivelling priests, to
ascertain what had
been done to make the
tomb of the crucified One
quite safe. It seemed to me
that they were ever so
perplexed. Whatever did
they mean with their
suggestion that He'd said
'within three days' He'd
rise again? Were they
afraid He'd do just as**

He said? He'd rise again?
Alive? Those superstitious
fools! And yet... I've never
known a man like Him.
That gaze upon my
verdict—I can't erase it
from my mind. Perhaps...
But still, I turned to them
most scornfully, derisively:
His men might take the
body in the depth of night
and surreptitiously dispose
of it. So! hear my words:
Go! Set a guard upon the
tomb. Yes, go and make
that site secure as you can
make it. Try your best!
Then, we'll see what we
shall see. Perhaps...

MARY MAGDALINE
Matthew 28:1 – 7

There are no words I can
convey that could describe
the depth of pain I'm
suffering. I stood with
Mary, mother of the Lord—
the One known as 'the
Nazarene'. Another one
of us—Martha's sister,
Mary too, stood with bar
Zebedee—his mother too.
We could not leave before

the end. Joseph, the rich
man, came and had
explained the gift of his own
tomb. I sit here now,
observing that these fiends
from Temple courts have set
a guard. So what? He's
beyond their meddling now!

I must have fallen fast
asleep. The sun's come up.
Let's check the tomb. The
earth is rumbling yet again.

Look there, Mary, a man
In garb I've never seen is
rolling back the stone. He
sits on it! Look now! He
came with lightning and his
garb is white as snow.

Those guards just don't
know what to do. They are
appalled. That man now
speaks to us: Don't be
afraid! I know that you are
here because of *Yeshua*–
Jesus. He is not here!
He is alive!

Come, look into His tomb;
you'll see it's empty now.
Go to His men, for His
disciples are in grief. Go
with the news that He's

been raised from death.
He will be up in Galilee.
Go; meet together there.

What joy to know He is
alive! Do listen now for we,
the Marys, have such tidings
of abounding joy!
We shared our news with
them. Then, suddenly,
He stood with us!

*My Peace be with you
now, always!*

We heard again His well-
Loved words; we came to
Him, we worshipped Him.

*Go! Tell our friends to meet
with Me up in the Galilee.
We'll share Good News!*

THE GUARD
Chapter 28:11 – 15

**Sir! What we say is true!
We saw it all with our own
eyes. One can't withstand
an earthquake at the dawn
and not arouse from sleep.
The sun's glare made the
garments of that man—a
stranger, that's for sure—
to shine as though he'd**
**come down from the
heavens. The Nazarene
then stood before us too!
We were amazed, we were
appalled! There's nothing
we could do to take Him
into custody…
But sirs, we *WERE* awake!**

CAIAPHAS
**This happening cannot be
told to anyone. It will be
secret to ourselves. We'll
pay you well. Just keep
your vow of silence on
this news. You are to
testify that His own men
had come at night to steal
His body while you slept.
We will convince the
Governor of your own
innocence. Don't worry
so! I do demand of you!**

YESHUA–JESUS
Matthew 28:16 – 20

*Peace be with you! How
good it is to meet with you
in Galilee. You've honoured
Me although some doubts
remain. It's natural for you
have witnessed an event*

beyond what any could expect. You see Me as the Son of Man—now know Me as the Son of God! I have been given all authority in Heaven above and on the Earth. I give you now My Great Commission: Go! You are to preach the Gospel to people everywhere, through all the world. All nations are to hear this News and know they too may be My own disciples dedicated to the YHVH–LORD.

Go then and teach them well and do remember this: I will be with you all the way, through every day!

..... oOo .....

MARK: "THE SACRIFICIAL SERVANT"

I am John Mark. I grew up in Jerusalem. My education was the very best for I was tutored in the history of Israel. I came, as a lad, to be quite sensitive to all the hints held in the ancient scrolls concerning the Messiah, the One anointed by the *YHVH–* LORD to be the Saviour of the world. I was hungry to learn more of Him. As a Jew who believed in, and tried to please *YHVH*–LORD, I felt drawn particularly to the way He offered up His life as a sacrifice that, by His death, we may find Eternal Life. He has given point to my quill for it was Jesus who made a path for me beside Saul of Tarsus (you know him as St Paul) who was quite disappointed in me at first though, later in life, Saul—Paul—asked for my assistance again for he said that I would be useful to him and, to the LORD !

It was with Peter, though, that I found my greatest fulfilment for I now may ascertain today that Peter filled up all the gaps in my firsthand accounting of the story of *Yeshua*–Jesus in the book that bears my name though I must say that in reality it is the biography of the *Messiah*! I learned so much from Peter in Rome before his life was taken, inverted on that infamous cross.

I had some personal knowledge of *Yeshua*–Jesus (I choose to use His Hebrew Name: it means *Saviour,*) as He would visit our home at Passover. You'll see from my testimony that I present to you 'the Saviour of the World', the One who—like the ox that gives its strength, its all, its very life to serve— so *Yeshua*-Jesus has given all to set His people free from bondage and provide the way to life!

INTRODUCTION

It was my friend, mentor, known as Simon Peter that encouraged me to set on record what he knew, and I also, of *Yeshua*–Jesus, the One disclosed as the promised *Messiah* (*Yeshua*– *Saviour* to my mind). The time was near for Peter to depart this life—in Rome where we had sought to bring Good News into the very heart of Empire and fulfil the Great Commission to spread the Gospel News.

I took the reed and scroll to tell of all the Lord set out to do on Earth. Some people say my records are the first, that Matthew, also Luke, were aided in their work by what Peter disclosed to me in Rome. You'll find I do not 'beat about the bush'. Mine is the Gospel filled with action from the first till last. It's as it ought to be as I convey the story of 'the Saviour of the World'. (We Jews know much of sacrifice!)

From this point on, I cede the story lines to Matthew for he stands right at the head of the New Testament. He's comprehensive in his coverage of everything that Jesus has said and done while with us in His ministry to humankind. Therefore, I choose to set down in this edition of my Gospel records, Three Great Themes that will present to you the Good News in a quite selective way.

You'll find the full story will be addressed though I'll present it by means of a unique outline. You'll come to know that I have been immersed in letting people know that *Yeshua*– Jesus had come to us to show us that His very life led to His saving act and we may know, ourselves, it is through *Yeshua* that we are saved. He came into this world that we may be prepared to live eternally.

He came to live with us that we, one day, will live with Him! It is my firm desire, my one intent, to emphasise how *Yeshua*–Jesus has won our hearts to live for Him.

The three great Themes I'll emphasise throughout my 'testament' are these:

COME: **The Imperative**

MISSION: The Saviour

FAITH: **The Response**

There are, within the first (original) edition of my own records, twelve instances where *Yeshua*–Jesus makes use of that quite simple word: COME.

Also we find recorded here twelve instances where His great MISSION is outlined plainly (via a symbolic ***oxen*** * calf perhaps?)

Twelve instances are also stated where response is then required of everyone who dares to follow in His steps. This will demand our FAITH— acceptance of His Truth.

Belief is for the mind. *Faith* is the soul's resolve. By *Trust* we activate them both for truth.

*The ox: symbol of St Mark!

SECTION ONE

COME:
THE IMPERATIVE

One simple word, repeated
here in twelve strategic
ways, brings home the Good
News so emphatically.
The word is '**COME**'—
a word that offers life
renewed, restored, reborn—
a gentle word
but an imperative!

1.
I HAVE COME
Chapter 2:13 – 17

I set the scene right now.
Our Levi—known to you as
Matthew—heard the call.
Just near the shore of
Galilee, he'd been in his
taxation booth when he
responded with alacrity to
Follow, be My disciple
from this day on.

As you will know from
Matthew's News, the Rabbi
was invited to his home.
The Pharisees were
scandalised and made a
point of questioning
Peter, Andrew, James and

John as to why the Rabbi sat
with rabble there?

The Rabbi heard these rude
remarks and took the
opportunity to state His
modus operandi then:

*None call a doctor to lend
aid if hale and hearty. No! It
is the sick and suffering who
ask for help that they'll be
well again. Likewise, I have
not come to those who think
their souls are well:*

*I'VE COME TO HEAL THE
SIN-SICK SOUL!*

2.
THE DAY WILL COME
Chapter 2:18 – 22

There was a feast—
the party in full swing—
when some turned up to ask
what was the meaning of
such revelry. They knew
that John the Baptist and the
Pharisees were all devoutly
fasting. So, what was the
Rabbi and His team now
thinking of for their
behaviour was appalling
and quite out of place!

Well, *Yeshua*–Jesus had heard it all! He asked a question that did set them on their heels. He asked the inquisitors:

Do wedding guests decide to fast when celebrating the event? Oh, no they don't! How could they fast— refrain from dainty dishes— when the Bridegroom sits with them! But you will need to keep in mind:

THE DAY WILL COME WHEN HE'LL BE TAKEN, THEN YOU'LL FAST!

3.
COME AFTER ME
Chapter 8:27 – 34
In leaving Galilee and trekking to the villages near Caesarea, the Rabbi asked quite suddenly:

Who do the people say I am? His men gave answers in some varied ways: Well, some say You're the Baptist; others say You are none other than Elijah and still others that You are the promised prophet who'll prepare Messiah's Way.

But you! Who do you say I am? What are your thoughts concerning Me?

It was Peter (Simon, don't you know,) who then replied: You are *Messiah*— Christ, the Anointed One!

I ask you now to keep this conversation to yourselves. It's not the time to spread such news abroad. You see, the 'Ben Adam' (the Son of Man,) must suffer much. He'll be rejected, slain! But He will rise again in just three days!

Peter stepped up, decried His words, rebuking Him for such remarks. The Rabbi turned to him:

Do not endeavour to deter My path— It's what you feel, but not God's will!

IF YOU DESIRE TO COME WITH ME YOU MUST FORGET YOURSELF, TAKE UP YOUR CROSS

AND FOLLOW IN MY WAY.

4.
THE WORLD TO COME
Chapter 8:35 – 38

The Caesarean discourse was not yet done! Some aspects of His words were staggering. For instance, this:

If you are out to save your life, you'll surely lose your life. But if you're willing to lay down your life for My sake and the Gospel that I preach, you'll surely save your life! What would you really gain if you would seek to win the world but lose your life? Don't be ashamed of Me:

I'D BE ASHAMED OF YOU THEN, WHEN I COME IN GLORY OF ABBA WITH ALL HEAVEN'S ANGELS TOO.

5.
LET THE CHILDREN COME
Chapter 10:13 – 16

When all returned to Capernaum, the Rabbi challenged them about their arguments along the road. They said, We had not thought He'd hear us there—our words just floated on the wind. It's hard to keep the slightest thing away from His perceptive mind.

There, it was out! We had been prone to wonder who was deemed to be the best in all our team. No harm in that. It would be good to know, we thought. Yet once again our thoughts, our paltry plots, were scanned. He took a little child and stood him up before us all. He said to us, His friends:

Whoever wants to be the leader in our team must be the one who serves the rest. Whoever welcomes one small child welcomes Me.

What's more, some people brought their children to be blessed. We stepped right in to save Him from all things unnecessary, spoiling His

respite. Our actions were
not welcomed and we were
admonished, and with ire:

*LET LITTLE CHILDREN
COME TO ME; DO NOT
DEBAR THE LEAST,
NOT ONE FROM ME.*

*the Gospel's sake will each
receive much greater gifts
(and persecution too,)
but know this truth today:*

*IN THE AGE TO COME
YOU WILL RECEIVE
ETERNAL LIFE, IT IS
MY GIFT FOR YOU.*

6.
THE AGE TO COME
Chapter 10:23 – 31

This was most difficult for
all the Rabbi's men. Yet
they had been with Him for
some time now. Yes, they
had given up the comforts
of their homes and families
but they had heard Him say
how difficult for rich people
to enter in the Kingdom of
the Lord—more so than

laden camels struggling
through Jerusalem's most
narrow gate. Whoever can
be saved if this is so? they
asked. Lord, we have left
our everything behind...
He had Good News:

*Oh yes! all that have left the
past behind for Me and for*

7.
REASON TO COME
Chapter 10:35 – 45

I have heard tell that James
and John, the sons of
Zebedee, came privately
to *Yeshua*–Jesus to ask of
Him a special privilege:
Jesus, please, there's
something we would ask
of You. You speak of when
Your Kingdom comes. We
know it will be glorious.
Because we've been

with You right from the
start, Lord, could You
contemplate that we both sit
beside You there? One on
each side—Lord, we ask
You, may it be?

You know not what you ask.

*Could you partake of the
same cup that I will be
required to drink? Can your
baptism be your death?*

Oh yes we can Rabbi!
Depend on us!

*Yes! you will drink the cup
of suffering, of death... But
as for Kingdom seats; it's
for My Abba, Father, to
decide. Yes, He will choose.*

I'll have you know the other
ten were quite enraged! Hot
anger had a need to be
replaced with peace.

*You know what leaders will
expect: they'll take the
topmost chair. Their
underlings must serve
them well and bend to rules
enforced at will. But such is
not the way with you. If you
desire to be the leader most
respected and with true
authority, you'll gain that
mastery by this eternal plan.
Yes! you must be the one
that serves the rest. If you'd
be first, you must be slave to
all. The Ben–Adam*

(the Son of Man) reveals:

*I DID NOT COME TO
BE SERVED BY YOU—
I CAME TO SERVE YOU
ALL; TO GIVE MY LIFE
FOR YOU: I AM THE
SAVIOUR OF THE ORLD.*

**8.
THE ONE WHO COMES**
Chapter 11:11 –10

The Rabbi and His twelve
associates were drawing
near Jerusalem. He called
just two aside and gave
to them instructions to take
charge of it, an untamed
donkey—just a colt.
When questioned, they
explained that Yeshua–
Jesus had need of it that
day. The colt came placidly,
allowed the Lord to sit upon
its cross-marked* back. The
people sensed that here they
witnessed wonderful
events. The 'Ben-Adam'
was recognised as Christ—
Messiah. Praise God! they
shouted. "Blessed is the One
who comes today in
YHVH's Name." They

threw their cloaks down at His feet while others waved some palm fronds in His path, rejoicing as He came. Yet others saw a deeper meaning: Here's '*The Lion King*'! His Kingdom now was here. Messiah comes to claim His crown. All Rome will crumble into dust right now! Hosanna! (*YESHUA-NA*: Saviour, *now*!) Oh, save us *Yeshua, NOW!*

HOW BLESSED IS HE WHO COMES IN THE NAME OF *YHVH*–LORD.

*All donkeys bear the distinctive sign of a cross on the back and shoulders.

9.
MANY WILL COME
Chapter 13:6

His men had been exclaiming just How wonderfully the Temple bricks enhanced the edifice. How beautiful those stones! What masonry! He looked at them and at the stones— there was a sorrow in His gaze.

You compliment this building but I say to you, before too long, it all will be erased for not one stone will then remain upon another here. All will come crashing down!

His men were sore amazed and, as they sat together on Mount Olivet, His four main men came privately to Him to ask, Lord, when will all the things of which You speak become reality? What time is left to us?

Be on your guard, keep watch My friends. Do not be fooled. There will be many who'll proclaim they are Messiah, 'Christ': applaud:

SOME FALSE MESSIAH'S WILL COME TO SAY THAT THEY WILL SAVE THE WORLD, DON'T BE DECEIVED.

10.
'*BEN–ADAM*' WILL COME
Chapter 13:1 – 31

As Peter, Andrew, James

and John sat with their
Rabbi on the Mount that
overlooked Jerusalem, His
words sank deep within
their soul. They heard of
future days where final
things would then impinge
on the world's peace:

*Don't be deceived! Battles
will come and battles go!
Kingdoms come, kingdoms
go into oblivion. Earthquakes
shudder here and there.
Much persecution will break
out; you'll stand before the
powers that be.*

*Don't be perturbed—
the Spirit of the YHVH–
LORD will then inspire your
words, your deeds and
testimony. You will be hated
and despised.*

*You'll witness the most
'awful horror' standing in
the Sacred Place. Take
heed: it is the time for you
to flee! The troubles of that
time will be far greater than
all history has told before.
But know this too: It's at
this very time the YHVH–
LORD will act. The powers*

*of all the heavens will be
suppressed—the sun grow
dark, the moon not shine;
the stars will fall—the
universe be 'out-of-place'.
It's at that time, the
'Ben–Adam' returns:*

*I'LL COME AGAIN
TO YOU UPON
THE CLOUDS IN POWER
AND GLORY THEN.*

11.
THE HOUR HAS COME
Chapter 14:32 – 42

This night is etched upon
my memory. Just hours
before the prayers heard
in Gethsemane, the Rabbi
and His men had first
partaken of the Feast of
Passover in a room set there
for them by my own Mum
and Dad within Jerusalem.
I'd listened in to much of
what was said and done that
night. It's written up in all
our records of the Gospel
News of which
you are aware. But then
the men went out into the
night, across Kidron, the

deep 'dark stream', into
Gethsemane, within the
lovely olive grove.

I watched them there—
you'll find a brief report
that's all but veiled beyond
eyesight because of all that
happened there. You'll hear
of it—the deed most
dastardly of Judas, also
Peter's rash act, brave
though misplaced, the
guards who came and
everything was lost for they
had taken Him in chains.

And I? You ask me how I
know of this? Well, Peter
told me much but did you
not observe the youth who
fled quite naked through
the grove, leaving his cloak
behind? I was afraid. I fled.
But there is one thing that I
must declare. He'd gone
into the olive grove to pray.

His men were tired. They
went to sleep. I heard Him
groaning in the night:

O Abba, if it be your will,
all things are possible to
You: if there could be

some other way, O please,
do let this up of suffering
now pass from Me. If it must
be, Abba: Your will be done.

He came back to His men
again and found them
snoring still. Three times He
came to them, asked them to
pray for Him, keep watch
with Him. They had no
words to say to Him. Then:

It's time. 'Ben-Adam' will
now be handed over into
evil hands. Get up! The one
who now betrays draws
near with Temple guards.

MY HOUR HAS COME:
WE GO TO MEET ALL
THAT MANKIND CAN DO.

12.
YOU'LL SEE ME COME
Chapter 14:53 – 65

It's Peter now who did
explain to me what
happened next. He told me
that he followed from afar
And found that he could
he followed from afar and
found that he could

overhear much that
was said and done that
dreadful night before
Messiah—Christ of God,
our *Yeshua*, the Saviour of
the world—was taken to
Golgotha, that place
so like a skull-faced hill
where He was crucified.
The twelve reports
regarding 'COME' are
climaxed in the darkest hall
of Caiaphas, High Priest and
keeper of the Holy Things
but blind unto the holy One!

He searched for evidence,
found none but lies he
counted on. Our Rabbi
stood before him silently.
Then, finally: 'Why don't
You answer me? Are You
Messiah, the '*Ben*' of God?'
Then *Yeshua*, the '*Ben–
Adam*', (the name He loved
to use Himself)
looked straight into
Caiaphas' eyes:

*I AM! ONE DAY YOU'LL
SEE ME SEATED AT THE
THRONE OF YHWH EL
SHADDAI: I WILL COME
UPON THE CLOUDS.*
....

SECTION TWO

MISSION: THE SAVIOUR

We come now to the second
of the three great Themes
that emphasise the focus
that my Gospel places on
the Ministry of *Yeshua*–
Jesus. We will observe
how actively He set about
His awesome task.
The Rabbi makes it clear
and plain: He'll give His life
to save all those who will
believe. There are twelve
avenues through which
we'll trek to find Him
at His mighty task.

1.
CONFIRMATION
Chapter 1:1 – 13

I've chosen to commence
my notes down near the
Dead Sea where we find the
Rabbi walking up to meet
with John the Baptist who is
quite o'erwhelmed when
Yeshua–Jesus requests
baptism in the stream.

The deed was done.

And then all were amazed
to hear a Voice resounding
But, from where? Also
there was a dove just
hovering. The sky appeared
as though parting.
With this the Confirmation
came: It was the *YHVH*–
LORD who spoke:

YOU ARE MY SON.
YOU ARE BELOVED.
I AM SO VERY PLEASED
WITH YOU, MY SON!

2.
TIMING
Chapter 1:14 – 20

When John the Baptist was
interred in prison, *Yeshua*–
Jesus went on to Galilee.
This was the start of all
His teaching, healing
ministry. The first
announcement that He made
was adamant, dramatic,
clear:

THE KINGDOM OF
THE LORD IS NEAR.
TURN FROM YOUR SIN,
BELIEVE THE GOSPEL
THAT I PREACH.

3.
TEACHING
Chapter 1:21 – 22

When *Yeshua*–Jesus and
His first disciples came to
Capernaum, He went into
the synagogue to preach.
The congregation was
amazed at what He said.
His News was different.
He spoke of *YHVH*, it was
true but in refreshing ways.
His preaching was as if the
News was all quite new. He
spoke with great authority.
Folk hung upon His words!

THIS WAS THE GOSPEL
NEWS! THE PEOPLE
UNDERSTOOD AND
SOUGHT TO CHANGE
THEIR WAYS.

4.
POWERFUL DEEDS
Chapter 1:23 – 34

All had remained within
the synagogue when
suddenly a troubled man
burst in to plead for help.
The man was demonised—
possessed—his mind
controlled by Satan's

power. He cried as demons
screamed, What do You
want? Will You destroy us
now? We know Your true
identity—You are...

*Be quiet! Depart! Let
this man be at peace!*

The poor man shuddered
with the strain of powers
possessing him. They
screamed but could not
thwart the power of *Yeshua*.
They then
departed and the man was
healed! The people were
in awe and asked:

WHAT KIND OF
TEACHING HAVE WE
HERE? THIS RABBI HAS
AUTHORITY TO GIVE
COMMANDS TO EVIL
SPIRITS AND THEY
WILL THEN OBEY!

5.
HEALING
Chapter 1:40 – 45

News of the Rabbi's coming
to a town would set the
residents into a hopeful

expectation that His words
and deeds would be
remarkable. The blind, the
deaf, the dumb would flock
to Him to plead His help,
believing that they could be
made quite well! One man
declared his trust this way:
Rabbi, if You would like to,
You can make we well.
Then *Yeshua*–Jesus
reached out to him and
touched him, Yes! I do
desire you to be well!

AT ONCE THE MAN'S
DISEASE WAS GONE!
THE NEWS SPREAD ALL
AROUND. PEOPLE
FLOCKED TO HIM.

6.
FORGIVING SIN
Chapter 2:1 – 12

I should begin this new
report by conveying that the
Pharisees and their cohorts
could not forgive
the Rabbi for the words He
spoke when healing all the
suffering souls that came to
Him for aid. There was that
day when *Yeshua*–Jesus

spoke not of healing a disease of body, or the mind. Rather, He set those Pharisees ablaze with 'righteous anger' as He said unto a man who had been lowered down from rafters by his close friends:

YOUR SINS ARE NOW FORGIVEN, INSTEAD OF SOMETHING LIKE: I'LL HEAL YOU NOW— BE WELL!

7.
OUTCASTS
Chapter 2:13 – 17

On the very day that Levi— Matthew—had been called to be discipled by the Rabbi, there were some disputes among the Pharisees who were all scandalised because the Rabbi came into the house and sat with all the 'riff raff' of the town—it's not what righteous folk would do! They questioned Rabbi's team: Why does the Man befriend such men? The Rabbi overheard and then replied to those that dared to listen in:

THOSE WHO ARE WELL DON'T NEED A DOCTOR, ONLY THE SICK. I HAVE NOT COME TO THE RESPECTABLES, I CAME TO SEEK AND SAVE THE WORLD'S OUTCASTS!

8.
PARABLES
Chapter 4:1 – 33

As *Yeshua*–Jesus taught beside Lake Galilee, the crowds were thronging round. He sat within a fishing boat to ease the scrum. He chose to emphasise His themes— the Gospel News—by telling stories set within the everyday. Even the most unlettered minds could comprehend the points He made. At story's end, He'd challenge them:

LISTEN IF YOU HAVE EARS: SO MANY LOOK BUT FAIL TO SEE AND THOSE WHO HEAR

BUT DO NOT LEARN
FOR, IF THEY DID,
THEY'D TURN UNTO
THE LORD!

9.
CONTROLLING
CREATION
Chapter 4:35 – 41, 6:45 – 52

There are amazing things
that did occur when
Yeshua–Jesus came by
to speak, to heal, to act
beyond the norm. I speak
of nature's rules all being
surpassed at times when
people were in need. For
instance, take this news
of storms that, suddenly,
are stilled because of His
command. His men have
seen it happen more
than once when they'd been
toiling on Lake Galilee.

The storm intensified.
A wreck was immanent...
They'd all but sunk; He was
asleep. When called upon,
He stood right up and spoke
first to the waves, the wind:

Peace! Be still!

The Lake at once was calm.
They were in awe of Him.
Yet more amazing was the
night they saw Him walking
on the crest of waves and,
do believe it, Peter got
a taste of it until he lost
his trust and sank. He took
the out-stretched hand of
Yeshua, was saved. They
feared Him then. He spoke:

DON'T BE AFRAID, IT'S
ME. I'LL COME INTO
YOUR BOAT
RIGHT NOW, TODAY.

10.
REJECTION
Chapter 6:1 – 6

The Rabbi then went home
to Nazareth to meet with
family and friends. He
preached within the
synagogue but those who
heard His words—
amazing though they
were—could not believe
that One who grew up in the
village there could gain the
wisdom they did hear. It
can't be true! He's just a
carpenter—we've known

Him since a lad. We'll
not stay here to hear him
out! The Rabbi was rejected
in His home, Nazareth.

HE KNEW THAT
PROPHETS WEREN'T
RESPECTED BY THEIR
OWN AND HE WAS
SADDENED BY
THE LACK
OF FAITH THAT
HE DISCERNED.

11.
WORLD MISSION
Chapter 7:24 – 30

The Rabbi visited Tyre's

The Rabbi visited Tyre's
territory and it was noised
abroad that He had come to
town. A villager in deep
distress because her child
was gravely ill, besought
His aid. This woman was a
Syrian Gentile.

*I came to aid the people of
Israel—folk don't take the
family's bread and feed
it to the dogs instead.*

She said, the dogs will catch
the scraps that fall beneath

the table, Sir. I'll be content
with scraps!" The Rabbi
smiled at her; His test to see
her faith was won!

*You may go home, your
child is well.*

*YOUR FAITH HAS BEEN
THE FACTOR THAT
ENSURED RETURNING
HEALTH.*

12.
THE REASON

I will select twelve
instances
which underline
emphatically the reason
why *Yeshua*–Jesus came
to Earth to give Himself so
wholly to the Mission He
fulfilled for us! What was
the purpose of His work?
Why do you ask? It's so
apparent if you will take
the time to contemplate
twelve REASONS why He
came. It's here the symbolic
oxen of a sacrifice comes to
the fore—the ashes of this
sacrifice (this *qorbanot*)

being used in ritual when
purifying a dead body:
how appropriate!

i.
Instruction
Chapter 8:31 – 38

Upon retreat from Caesarea
Philippi where Peter had
proclaimed that He,
the Rabbi, was in fact,
MESSIAH He then began to
teach His team that He
would suffer much and be
rejected by the leaders of
the Jews. He would be put
to death. And, even more
astounding, hear this news:

WITHIN THREE DAYS
BEYOND HIS DEATH,
THE *YESHUA*–JESUS
WOULD RISE TO LIFE
AGAIN!

ii.
Rising from Death
Chapter 9:9, 30 – 32

Peter, James and John had
gone with *Yeshua*–Jesus
trekking up a mountain
where they witnessed

a most glorious sight.
The Rabbi underwent
an awesome change and
then was seen to walk
on with two famous, ancient
men, no less than Moses
and Elijah, there. They
heard the voice of *YHVH*–
LORD confirming *Yeshua*
to be His Son! Then, when
this wondrous sight
concluded, Rabbi
counselled them:

Do not disclose what you
have seen until I have been
raised from death!

The three dazed men began
to think about their own
Rabbi being raised to life.
What do You mean by that?

I WILL BE HANDED OVER
TO MY EXECUTIONERS,
I'LL SUFFER MUCH,
BUT I WILL RISE
FROM DEATH TO LIFE.

iii.
Foretelling Death
Chapter 10:32 – 34

The occasion which

I mention now is the third
time that the Rabbi shared
His coming agonies and
death. The group were on
their way towards
Jerusalem. His disciples
were amazed and all who
followed them, afraid!
He took His team aside to
counsel them again for they
must realise what would
eventuate as now, the
Passover was nigh. It was
the time for sacrifice where
sins would be forgiven
according to the ritual
so honoured by them all.

THE SON OF MAN
WILL BE BETRAYED
BY THE CHIEF PRIESTS
AND TEACHERS OF
THE LAW. HE WILL
BE GIVEN INTO GENTILE
HANDS: MOCKING,
KILL-ING HIM. BUT HE
WOULD RISE GAIN.

iv.
The Cup of Suffering
Chapter 10:35 – 45

You'll know of the occasion
when both James and John
had asked the Rabbi to give
precedence to them when
seated on His glorious
throne in Heaven. With
kindness He rebuked
His men for they did not
discern the gravity of their
request to sit on either side
of Him. He asked:

CAN YOU PARTAKE MY
CUP OF SUFFERING?
THOSE WHO'D BE FIRST
ARE LAST FOR EVEN I
DID NOT COME HERE TO
BE SERVED BY YOU—
I CAME TO SERVE,
TO GIVE MY LIFE:
I WILL REDEEM!

v.
A Pointed Parable
Chapter 12:1 – 12

The Rabbi chose to tell a
parable that outlined His
predicament. He described a
vineyard owner setting out
his vines, his press,
a watchtower, then
deciding to depart for
regions new. He placed
some tenants to control his
land. At harvest time he sent

a servant to receive
remuneration for the crop.
The servant was maltreated
so another man was sent
but he was treated
shamefully, then killed!

At last, the owner had no
one left but his own son to
claim the dues. Those
tenants will respect my son.
The tenants realised that, if
the son was killed, the
vineyard would be theirs.
The deed was done!
The son was killed, thrown
out. What will the grieving
owner do? The tenants
would receive their 'due'!

THE STONE REJECTED
WAS REVEALED TO BE,
IN FACT, THE CORNER-
STONE—THE STONE
THAT WILL ENSURE THE
BUILDING IS ALIGNED,
KEPT TRUE UNTO THE
ARCHITECT'S DESIGN!

vi.
The Passover Prediction
Chapter 14:12 – 26

It was the fateful evening

and as they sat together at
the Passover meal, the
Rabbi shocked the men
with His dire news that one
of them would soon betray
Him—one who sat with
them. Surely no, not me?
Nor me? Nor me?
They were told the one
who dips his bread
within this dish is he.

THE BEN–ADAM WILL DIE
JUST AS THE SCRIPTURE
DOES PREDICT; BUT WOE
TO HIM THAT DOES
THE GHASTLY DEED.

vii.
Death of 'The Shepherd'
Chapter 14:27 – 31

Simon Peter was quite
horrified for his own
beloved Rabbi made an
accusation that he would
forsake Him e'er the 'Cock
Crow' on the following day!
He had implied that all
would leave Him, run away!
Peter exclaimed, Though all
the rest desert You, Rabbi, I
will surely stay with You—
I will not run from You,

no, even if I have to die
with You!

*YOU ALL WILL
SURELY RUN BECAUSE
THE HOLY SCRIPTURES
SAY THE SHEPHERD
WILL BE KILLED, THE
SHEEP WILL SCATTER
EVERYWHERE.*

viii.
The Gethsemane Betrayal
Chapter 14:32 – 50

Following the meal of
Passover, the Rabbi and His
men moved on into the olive
grove—Gethsemane.
In depth of night, He prayed
in agony. His men fell fast
asleep. He came to them
at times, requesting aid
through prayer. Fatigue
deterred them yet, upon
awakening, they were
perturbed at what
was heard of groanings,
pleadings to be saved
from what was looming
through the mist. In coming
back to them again, He then
expressed His pain that they
should be asleep. And then

His time had come:

*ENOUGH! MY TIME HAS
COME! THE BEN–ADAM
IS HANDED OVER TO
THE POWERS OF SIN.
LOOK: SEE THE MAN
BETRAYING ME.*

ix.
The Sanhedrin: "Death!"
Chapter 14:53 – 65

Caiaphas had gloated in his
glee that, finally, that
infamous Rabbi was in his
grasp! The Man was there,
condemned before the trial!
In fact, the sentence came
before the court,
unscheduled, was convened!
The whole Sanhedrin
scanned the evidence, could
find no proof that would
condemn Him to His death.
At last a man stood to
his fumbling feet,
accused the Rabbi of a
promise to destroy the
Temple and within three
days, rebuild the whole!
Yet, even then, the court
could not agree. Caiaphas
rose and asked, Are You

'*Messiah*', the promised One? The Son of God?

"I AM" And you will see Me sitting at the YHVH– LORD's Right Hand and coming on the clouds!

Caiaphas rent his clothes with rage! We've all the proof we need: this Man blasphemes. I see there is no further need of any witnesses!

THE RABBI WAS THERE CONDEMNED, WORTHY OF DEATH. HE WAS BRUISED AND SCORNED, THEN HANDED TO GENTILES.

x.
The Roman Governor: "Death!"
Chapter 15:1 – 15

The Roman Governor was intrigued. Why bring the Man to me, he thought; surely, He's done no wrong! He is quite circumspect, in fact. Still, we shall see what we shall see. Are You the King of all the Jews? Yes!

It's as you say, the Man replied. I see no harm in that. What are the wrongs of which You are accused? The man was silent then. Why so? I wondered and began to probe. I was amazed at His demeanour. I could find no fault and said as much! Just then, I had remembered that each year, at this great Feast, it was our custom to release a prisoner to please the Jews.

There was imprisoned at the time, a murderer. His name—amusing, I did find— was none other than Barabbas—*son of father!* I then addressed the crowd requesting that they choose between the two—the murderer or *Yeshua.* Give to us Barabbas, sir! What shall I do with *Yeshua?* You should have Him crucified! Why? What has He done? We want Him crucified!

I'VE WASHED MY HANDS OF THE WHOLE THING! CRUCIFY? I'D LIKE TO CRUCIFY THAT MOB!

TAKE HIM, DO WHAT
YOU WILL WITH HIM!
I FIND NO FAULT.

xi.
A Rabble Rouser:
"Death!"
Chapter 15:6 – 20

I, Mark, have said it all but
this must be recorded here.
There were, indeed, three
times *Yeshua*–Jesus was
condemned to die that day!

Though Caiaphas had done
his worst and Pilate finally
gave in, the coward that he
was, it was—in fact—those
crowds, unruly mobs, that
sealed the Rabbi's fate for
they were granted
options: say the 'yea' or
'nay' on Christ, the Rabbi
who was innocent!

Whom is it you prefer?
Barabbas, or the One who
calls Himself 'The Son of
Man'? There was no way
back from this questioning!

WE WANT HIM
CRUCIFIED!
YES, CRUCIFY 'THE
CHRIST'!

xii.
"It is finished!"
Chapter 15:33 – 39

His was not a cry of
desolation! It was
triumphant though, with it,
Yeshua–Jesus arrived at the
dark moment of His death.
His death. Oh yes! That
dastard's deed had reached
its culminating point.

Finished was that foulest
crime. But *Yeshua*–Jesus
most certainly had thoughts
beyond the deeds of
humankind! He knew that
God's Eternal Plan had been
fulfilled: The 'AT-ONE-
MENT' was achieved.
By sacrifice, the Sinless
One could now eradicate
all sin; yes, through His
blood, atoning blood!
And there was one who,
through the darkness of
that bleakest day, then saw
the Light, proclaimed his
powerful testimony:

I AM THE CENTURION
WHO HAS ORGANISED
THE HAPPENINGS HERE
AND AS I CONSIDER

ALL THAT I'VE HEARD
AND SEEN, I MUST ADD
THIS: TRULY, I TESTIFY:
THIS MAN WAS
INDEED THE SON OF
GOD!

....

SECTION THREE

FAITH: THE
RESPONSE

MARK

In moving to the third great
theme enclosed in my
report, you'll find that we
approach the crucial aspect:
FAITH! We have observed
the imperative to 'COME'.
Then, within the MISSION
theme, what the Rabbi did
achieve is our salvation.
And, inherent in this great
Redemption Plan, is the
required response of all who
would be saved: we must
BELIEVE that, by
His death, we may choose
Life! The twelve disciples
each received the challenge
to believe, have faith (even

if no larger than a seed—a
mustard seed.) We are to
trust His word. This is a
matter for the will!
We now pursue the twelve
accounts where faith is
duly emphasised.

1.
FAITH THAT IS
NOTICED
Chapter 2:1 – 5

Right near the early days
when Rabbi had begun His
ministry, so many came in
the belief that He could heal
their many woes. The news
was out! He was in town.

Capernaum was all agog.
Folk came in droves to
watch Him work and listen
to Good News.
Four men arrived to seek
His aid—they carried on a
stretcher, one poor man in
need of help. He could not
walk… There was no way
they could get near—the
house was crowded out.
These men were not
deterred. They climbed up
on the roof and made a hole

that did allow the stretcher
to 'float' down on ropes,
the ailing man secured.
The Rabbi saw what they
had done and knew it was
by faith in Him they'd dared
to break right in.

MY SON, THROUGH
FAITH YOUR SINS ARE
GONE! TO PUT YOUR
TRUST IN ME BRINGS
ANSWERS FOR LIFE'S
NEED, YOUR HEALTH
RETURNS TO YOU
TODAY.

2.
FAITH CAN STILL
LIFE'S STORMS
Chapter 4:35 –41

The drama of that night
can't be forgotten by those
men who were engaged in
sailing on the lake of
Galilee. A storm can bluster
up so fast as gully gales
whip up the waves. The
men were very much
afraid—they found the wind
was more than sails could
bear. They struggled with
the ropes but fear was in

their hearts. Just look at
Him! He's fast asleep! Go!
Wake Him up to lend a
hand. Rabbi! Don't You
care? We're sure to die!
He stood right up without
an aid and then He took
command: *Be calm!*
The wind abated suddenly.
The waves then settled
down—just like a mill pond.
Peace returned. All were in
awe of Him. They wondered
then, who is this Man that
even wind and waves obey
His voice? He spoke:

WHY ARE YOU SO
AFRAID? HAVE YOU
STILL TO FIND YOUR
FAITH IN ME?

3.
FAITH THAT CASTS
OUT FEAR
Chapter 5:21 – 43

While on His way to where
Jairus lived, a woman
who'd been ill for many
years approached the Rabbi
seeking aid. She saw the
throng but thought that just
one touch of His long robe

would be sufficient to
regain her usual health.

She reached to Him.
The Rabbi realised some
power had seeped from
Him.

Who touched My cloak?

How strange: there were so
many bustling round and
bumping into Him! He
asked again. The woman
explained her actions then.

*DEAR WOMAN: YOUR
FAITH HAS HEALED YOU
SO BE FREE FROM
SUFFERING. NOW,
GO IN PEACE.*

You will remember that the
daughter of Jairus was so ill.
In fact, she died before He
could arrive. When news
came, then the Rabbi
calmed her pleading dad.

*DON'T BE AFRAID,
ONLY BELIEVE!*

The crowd then laughed at
Him but, after He'd arrived,
He then exclaimed

the child, not dead, was
sleeping there. He took the
matter well in hand so that
the little girl ran out to play.
All learned a lesson well
on that amazing day!

*DO NOT FEAR,
HAVE FAITH!*

4.
CAN YOU BELIEVE
IN ME?
Chapter 9:14 – 32

He saw the Rabbi with three
men descending
from the mountain and
then went to Him. The other
nine had tried their best but
they could not deliver his
poor son from all the
anguish plaguing him. He
was 'possessed' and no
one eased his suffering.

He'd heard this Rabbi was
renowned for miracles. He
had a need of miracles
today! He brought the boy,
beseeched the Healer: Help!
The Rabbi questioned him
and he explained each
dreadful instance where

the youth had almost died
at times. Have pity on us,
help us now! You have
your part to play, He said:
Do you believe it's
possible? I do believe.
Oh, help my unbelief.
The Rabbi took the boy's
right hand and lifted him.
He stood, was healed!

ALL THINGS ARE
POSSIBLE TO THOSE
WHO WILL BELIEVE IT
CAN BE DONE!

5.
ENCOURAGE FAITH
Chapter 9:39 – 50

A most surprising thing
occurred when the
disciples did admonish

one just man who was
endeavouring to solve the
ills of humankind
enslaved to Satan's power.
They told their Rabbi how
they had commanded him to
stop his work because he
did not work with them.

Do not enforce this man to
stop his work. All those who

aren't against us are indeed
for us! If anyone should
cause another to lose faith
in Me, it would be better for
a millstone to sink him
to the bottom of the sea.

DO NOT ALLOW FALSE
ATTITUDES TO MAKE
FOLK LOSE THEIR
EARNEST FAITH.

6.
FAITH TO SEE
Chapter 10:46 – 52

The Rabbi and His men
were on their way towards
Jerusalem. The mountain
route to Zion would soon
be faced. They'd reached
the town of Jericho.

As usual, many followed on
and as the Rabbi turned
to leave, a blind man,
Bartimaeus, heard the loud
commotion, asked what was
astir. On being told, he
realised that here, today,
the possibility of sight
was his. He laid aside
his begging bowl and
moved towards the crowd.

Son of David, do have
mercy on me. Hush now!
Do be quiet, the Rabbi is
just passing through. He
cannot stop for such as you!
Do know your place. The
Rabbi halted, turned to ask
that Bartimaeus would be
brought to Him. Get up!
He's calling you! He cast
his cloak, rushed up to Him
in hope. The Rabbi asked,
What do you want that I
should do for you? Rabbi,
I want to see the light, I
want to see! You're healed!
It is your faith that makes
you well again. Look up!

TAKE HOLD OF FAITH;
BELIEVE THAT IT IS
POSSIBLE. LOOK TO
THE LIGHT, IT BRINGS
THE DAWN OF YOUR
NEW DAY!

7.
EXPECT GREAT
THINGS
Chapter 11:20 – 26

The disciples were
impressed when they had
heard their Rabbi speaking
to a fig tree that was ailing
fast. There was not one fig
found on that poor tree. One
does expect the fruit of figs
when green leaves do
provide the canopy even if
the harvest's past.

I'm sorry, fig tree; you are
at your last. You'll never
grow another fig.

Well, on the next day,
Yeshua's men observed the
fig tree to be withering!
They pointed out its plight.

My friends, you have not
learned as yet the power of
faith. If you could just
believe, you'd say unto this
hill: get up and throw your-
self into the sea. It would be
done. I merely illustrate, but
see what faith can do!

WHEN YOU PRAY,
BELIEVE THE ANSWER
WILL THEN COME.
HAVE FAITH IN GOD!

8.
WHAT TO BELIEVE
Chapter 11:27 – 33

In coming to Jerusalem, the
Rabbi and His men had
gone into the precincts of
the Temple where He was
challenged by the priests
and teachers of the Law.

What right have You, a
Nazarene, to do and say the
things You do? I'll ask of
you a question too. If you
will answer it sincerely, I
will tell you of what right
I have. My question is: you
know about My cousin,
John Baptist.

Do tell Me by what
authority did he baptise?
Was it from God or was it
man? This set them in a
quandary. They knew that,
if they said, John gained his
authority from God, He then
would ask, why did they not
believe in him? If they said,
from humanity, the people
would object and cause
an awful uproar there.

They chose a coward's way.
We do not know! Then
neither will I tell you of
My right to act!

*WHY FIND IT VERY
DIFFICULT TO HAVE
FAITH IN WHAT'S
OBVIOUS?*

**9.
THE SCORN OF
UNBELIEF**
Chapter 15:21 – 42

How easy it will seem to
mock the truth—indeed, the
Source of Truth when evil
would appear to gain
ascendancy. That afternoon,
as death loomed near, and
Truth hung on a cross on
Calvary (the skull-faced
hill,) a chant rang out, Come
down! You need not hang
upon that cross, You
Worker of those many
miracles! Just show us how
it's done; come, save
Yourself—it can be done!

Oh! You who saved so
many, save Yourself! Come
down! We will believe.
Let's see the great Messiah,
the King of Israel, save
Himself and all
of Israel this day!

WHAT DO YOU NOW
BELIEVE? BECAUSE
CHRIST CHOSE TO DIE,
HE MADE IT POSSIBLE
TO SAVE US ALL!

10.
FAITH COMES BY
*IN*SIGHT
Chapter 16:9 – 14

How hard it is to trust
another's word when all the
news states otherwise. The
Rabbi had been hung upon
that cross until He died. He
then was placed within a
tomb and it was sealed.
What's more, a guard was
set to make quite sure that
no one stole the Rabbi's
body in the night. There
were some rumours floating
round that He would rise
again—He'd said as much
Himself.

Against the strength of
arguments like these, how
could His friends believe
against the doubts, denials
too? For instance, Mary
Magdalene had rushed to
tell the news that she had

seen the Lord that very day!
How can this sight be so?

A FAITH THAT'S REAL
DOES NOT NEED EYES!
THE NEED IS FOR
A SOUL ALIGNED WITH
TRUTH THAT'S BORN
OF LIVING FAITH.

11.
DOUBT VERSUS FAITH
Chapter 16

The day was quite
remarkable! How could the
news be true? All wanted, in
their hearts, to hope against
all hope but one cannot
deny the power of death to
hold its prey.
As evening shadows fell,
the friends were sharing a
communal meal when,
suddenly, the Rabbi stood
there, in their midst. How
could you not believe the
news of those who'd met
Him early in the day. You
need *in*sight to see truth.

DOUBT IS THE TEST TO
OVERCOME IF FAITH
WOULD WIN THE DAY.

ALL THOSE WHO WAIT
FOR SIGHT WILL MISS
THE STRENGTH OF
TRUST.

WORLD AND DEDICATE
THEIR LIFE, RECEIVE
ETERNAL LIFE.

….. oOo …..

12.
FAITH TO ALL THE
WORLD
Chapter 12

When the disciples'
grieving turned to joy as
startled eyes confirmed
what they had heard, their
open ears and hearts were
ready to absorb all that the
Rabbi shared with them.
And after all the happy
chatter had been calmed the
Ben–Adam and more *the
Son of God* stood tall among
His team. He gave to them
the Great Commission
they'd uphold:

*Go now throughout the
world to share the Good
News that, through faith in
Yeshua, all may be saved.*

WHOEVER WILL
BELIEVE THAT
YESHUA–JESUS IS
SAVIOUR OF THE

LUKE:
"THE SON
OF MAN"

Greetings! I am Dr Lucas,
known to you as Luke.
Because my nationality will
be known as Greek, I am
also known as a Gentile
(being not of Jewish blood).
Because of this, you will be
wondering why I have found
a place within the original
records relating to the story
of 'The Son of Man'.

Well, yes, much of my
evidence is second-hand,
gained from Paul for I had
accompanied him through
many of his journeys to the
Gentile world.

Because of his rough
treatment through the years,
the medical attention that I
could give at times kept Paul

alive! I am blessed that he expressed his gratitude by naming me, 'The Beloved Physician'.

You'd be quite adamant that I had never met nor conversed with the Man of Galilee while He lived on Earth. I do, however, have a strong claim to first-hand information for I have also relied on Mark to some degree. However, there are more important sources, all first-hand, for my original treatise.

You will remember that Paul was imprisoned at Caesarea in Israel for a lengthy period and much of what I write was told verbatim to me, for example, by the Marys—yes, including the Mother of our Lord. You will note, therefore, that all my introductory remarks in the original work are, most certainly, first-hand! At first, my script was private being addressed to Theophilus, a Greek of excellent status whom I am pleased to call my personal friend.

More importantly, his very name speaks of friendship more profound. His name means, *the friend of God.* Oh, to bear a name like that! But still, my name means *'light'* and this is fine with me for it is my hope that this companion edition of my original report will bring enlightenment to you.

Someone has said, indeed, that my rendition of the Gospel is one of the literary masterpieces of all time' and, another, that the work is 'the most beautiful book in the world.' I do not sit easily with such accolades!

In this edition of the greatest story of all time, there is no need to be repeating all that Matthew has recorded in his Gospel via this book. I therefore, now present to you the One who liked to refer to Himself as 'the Son of Man' via a most selective means. I will also use the Greek name, Christ, *Christos*, liberally. My emphasis relates to that *symbolic* figure known traditionally to be a 'man'. In light of the matchless nature of this story, I choose to present the many testimonies in the mode of formal poetry:

THE SON OF GOD BECOMES THE SON OF MAN

A CHILD IS ANNOUNCED

The Magnificat of Mary
Chapter 1:46 – 55

My soul will magnify the Lord!
How glorious is my Saviour,
God; to grant His perfect peace
He came:
I will rejoice in His great Name.
The Lord is mindful of our grief,
How blessed are those who
now believe;
The Lord is God, great things
His aim And holy is His
precious Name.
God's mercy flows to every
land: All nations shall His fame
expand. He will destroy sin's
evil claim,
For mighty is His powerful
Name. All peoples shall God's
glory see, His grace is flowing,
ever free; He comes to us
when want would maim.

And we will truly bless
His matchless Name.
The Lord is merciful and just,
His promises we still can trust;
Our God indeed, always the
same, And we will glory in His
name.

A FATHER'S JOY
Zechariah's Testimony
Chapter 1:68 – 79

Praise to the Lord for He
has come Fulfilling God's
Redemptive Plan.
His people now are blessed
indeed: This news proclaim to
every land!

The prophets in their ancient
times Announced that God
would intervene;
This promise ever stands
as truth And is fulfilled where
grace is seen!

Prepare the way for Christ,
the King! Make straight His
path for God is good;
Let people know forgiveness
comes In tender mercy
from the Lord.

In darkest night the people
mourned! The rising sun

will spread its ray;
All those who dwell in death's
dark vale May find the way
to life this day!

CHRIST HAS COME
The Bethlehem Birth
Chapter 2:4 – 20

Behold the stable scene
With cradled hay so mean,
Mother and Child serene:
Here Christ the Lord was born!
The Mother and her Child at
peace When Christ, Messiah–
Lord was born!

With hope not faltering,
The shepherds hastening,
Drew near in worshipping
The Baby, Christ, the Lord:
The shepherds all adored
Him there, The Child was born
both King and Lord.

Snowflakes had fallen low,
New lambs were calling now,
The angels sang their vow
That Christ the Lord had come;
The angels were rejoicing there
For Christ, our Saviour-Lord
had come.

To grant us inner peace,
All humankind embrace

And bring redeeming grace
He came, the Son of God!
The Child born in the hay
adore For He is Jesus Christ,
the Lord!

HEAVEN'S ANNOUNCEMENT
The Angels' Choir
Chapter 2:8 –14

Glory, glory, in the highest,
Peace has come to all the
Earth;
Now take heart, the Lord is
reigning,
We proclaim Messiah's birth.
In the darkness light is shining,
Darkest night gives way to
dawn,
God's own *LIGHT* is never
waning,
We declare that Christ is born.

Glory, glory, to the Saviour,
Christ has come! The Lord is
here!
God still loves you, shows His
favour;
This is news for all to hear!
Christ the King will never
waver,
He's your hope, you need not
fear;
He gives courage to be braver,

Jesus is the Lord so dear.

Glory, glory, Hallelujah!
Christ, the heavenly Prince
of Peace
Comes to bless His people
ever;
From your bondage He'll
release.
He abides, He'll leave you
never
And one day you'll see
His face;
His great Kingdom stands
forever:
Jesus' reign will never cease!

THE SHEPHERD'S JOY
The Bethlehem Trek
Chapter 2:8 – 20

Let us now go to Bethlehem,
We've seen a glorious sight;
Outshining stars, the angels
came,
Their light transcended night.

Let us now go to Bethlehem,
We've heard the angels' word;
Our Saviour has been born,
His Name
Is Jesus Christ, the Lord!

Let us now go to Bethlehem,
God's Son we there shall find;

The Baby is of heavenly fame
Though born as humankind.

Let us now go to Bethlehem,
The angels gave new hope,
They told us peace to all
would come,
Goodwill of worldwide scope.

Let us now go to Bethlehem,
God's wondrous grace
applaud.
To save this needy world He
came;
He is the King, the Lord!

SIMEON'S ACKNOWLEDGEMENT
The Saviour is Recognised
Chapter 2:25 – 35

I rest my soul in perfect peace:
I've seen the glory of the Lord
Upon the Face of Jesus Christ;
My hope is now fulfilled in God.

He is our peace though tears
may flow,
When bound by grief, He
brings release,
He is our peace when fears
appal;
When shadows fall, He is
our peace.

He is the *LIGHT* dispelling
night,
Revealing to a waiting world
Salvation is for humankind,
The peace of God in grace
extolled.

The peace of God can calm
the soul;
If clouds may weep and storms
Arise,

In tranquil strength He holds
us still:
He is our peace, our sure
repose.

THE MAN WHO LIVED THE WORD OF GOD

LUKE: GOOD NEWS
The Gospel is Proclaimed
Chapter 1:1 – 4

I would proclaim the word
of God
Fulfilled in Jesus Christ,
the Lord,
For those who saw Him day
by day,
All saw His glorious love
outpoured.

I would now claim the ways
of God

Are clearly seen in Jesus
Christ:
Good News I have for you
today,
He came to Earth to save
the lost.

I would exclaim our wondrous
Lord,
The Great Physician to us
came;
He healed the sick and raised
the dead,
O glory to His precious Name.

I would reclaim the world
for God!
Jesus alone has paid sin's
price;
He conquered death on
Calvary
By His atoning sacrifice.

I would acclaim the will of God!
Be certain of His mighty word,
Redemption's Plan gives
endless life
To you and all who call Him
Lord.

JESUS: A BOY'S QUESTION
"Did you not know?"
Chapter 2:41 – 52

Did you not know that
I would be
Within My Father's House?
He calls Me to His presence
here:
These are My choicest hours.

Did you not know that
I would read
The precious word of God?
Its open page brings truth
to light
Revealing Christ, the Lord!

Did you not know that
I would ask
For guidance and for care?
My Father is the Lord of Life,
His matchless love I share.

Did you not know that
I would seek
To do My Father's will?
I learn from Him the way
I'll take
His purpose to fulfil.

Did you not know that
I would pray
Within this holy place?
Communing with My Father
here
Brings strength to walk
His ways.

．．．．．．．

JOHN THE BAPTIST
The Prophet Speaks
Chapter 3:1 – 20

Prepare the way for Christ,
the Lord!
The desert lands will soon
rejoice.
The path is straight that leads
to God;
Prepare your heart, amend
your ways!

Come, raise the valleys of
remorse,
Cast down the mountains of
despair!
Step out of sin, walk on
in grace:
Select His way and meet
Him there.

Grind down the paths of
poverty,
Make smooth the rubble of
regret;
It is the road to Calvary
Where every need in Christ
is met.

It is the Lord who comes
to heal,
In love He will your heart
enfold.
It is the lord! Before him kneel,
He is the Saviour of the world.

AN OBSERVER
The Dove of Peace
Chapter 3:21 – 22

The Dove of Peace has
hovered o'er
God's Son, Messiah, Lord,
The King born to be Man!
John said,
"Behold, the Lamb of God!"

The Dove of Power disclosed
the One
Who would for sin atone;
When tempted in the
wilderness,
God's word the victory won.

The Dove of Prayer sustained
Him in
The midst of human care;
Alone, upon the mountainside,
He met His Father there.

O Dove of Promise, rest on me
May I Your power reveal;
Let peace attend my daily path,
Now, Lord, Your purpose seal.

DARKNESS AND *THE LIGHT*
Evil Vanquished
Chapter 4:1 – 13

It's written in God's holy word:

'One cannot live by bread
alone';
A hunger in the soul for good
Brings constant peace till
Heaven is won.

How precious is God's word
to those
Accepting His unbounded love;
It maps the path that leads to
Heaven,
Its promises I daily prove.

I'm counselled in God's living
word
To worship Him, serve Him
alone.
I lift my heart in praise to Him,
My hands to serve till day
is done.

It's written in God's mighty
word:
'Don't put the Lord unto
the test';
He has the power to heal
all pain,
Acknowledge Him, the
Heavenly Guest.

We're shown within God's
timeless word
Temptation can be overcome!
The darkest night of sin
is gone:

There's *LIGHT* to guide all
safely 'Home'!

A NAZARENE
The Manifesto
Chapter 4:14 – 22

When Jesus came to Nazareth
To share the love of God,
He chose Isaiah's sacred scroll
That magnifies the Lord.

He read, "The Spirit of the Lord
Is in this holy place;
This day He has anointed Me
To preach the word of grace.

He said, 'Good News there is
for all,
The poor and those who
mourn;
He sends Me forth to bring
release
To shackled souls forlorn.

Good News there is for
everyone:
The blind receive their sight
And the oppressed will surely
know
That freedom is their right.'

The Spirit of the Lord is near,
He comes to set us free
To tell the world His day
will come;

His glory we shall see.

THE MAN WHO
HEALED
BY FAITH
A GALILEAN
Walking and Talking
Chapters 4 – 8

When Jesus came to Galilee,
Good News He preached
in power;
He came to set the prisoners
free,
His words brought hope to all.

When Jesus walked by Galilee
He healed the halt, the lame,
By grace the blind were made
to see
And walk in *LIGHT* and love.

When Jesus talked by Galilee,
He shared the words of life;
The people saw authority
And trusted in the Lord.

When Jesus went to Calvary,
He walked that path alone;
Redeeming love His only plea,
And in that love we live!

WITNESSES

Miracles Confirmed
Chapters 4 – 8

He touched my eyes, now I
can see!
New insights are God's gift
to me
As He reveals Eternity:
This is a mighty miracle!

He touched my lips, now I
can speak
Of how He lifted me from sin
To grace: this is faith's
mountain peak;
Oh yes, this is a miracle.

He touched my mind and now
I know
His calm can permeate
the soul.
In grief, He shall His peace
bestow;
I find this is a miracle!

He touched my heart, my soul
is freed
From depths of night to paths
of *LIGHT*!
And day by day my Lord
will lead;
For me this is a miracle!

He touched my life, I am
made whole;
He takes my hand and leads
me now,
A new dawn breaks upon
my soul:
This is a wondrous miracle!

THE THRONG
Healing
Chapters 4 – 9

Jesus, see us in our need,
We would trust each day
to You;
You alone this work can do!
For Your gracious care
we plead,
We will follow where You lead,
You restore our strength anew.

Jesus, heed our soul's great
pain,
We are lost without Your aid;
In Your healing hand our gain,
All our sin on You is laid.
You can cleanse sin's deepest
stain,
Its great cost Your death
has paid.

Jesus, Great Physician, come,
Cleanse us from our sin
and woe,
Be our Guard through all
the gloom,
Be our Guide, Your peace
bestow;

You can lead us safely "Home"
Trusting as we onward go.

Jesus, in our weakest plight,
We have come to seek
Your hand;
For our blindness, grant
us sight,
For our lameness, help
us stand,
For our doubting, bring
us *LIGHT*,
Lead us to Your Promised
Land.

THE MAN WHO OFFERS ABUNDANT LIFE
JESUS, CHRIST

The Call to Follow
Chapters 5 – 6

Come, follow Me, the Saviour
said,
And I will make you to become
Ambassadors of grace to share
Good News! Take up your
cross .and come.

Come, follow Me the Saviour
called,
Give up the nets entangling
you;
Think not of cost to find
life's best,
Launch out today to make
life new!

Come, follow Me, the Saviour's
plea,
Now walk with Me, observe
My way
And share with Me life's heavy
load;
Now trust Me, find your faith
today'

'Come, follow Me,' the Saviour
leads;
'Come with Me now, your
name is called,
Come, take your cross and
walk My road,
Reveal My love to all the world.

THE DISCIPLES
The Response
Chapter 6:12 – 19

You call us to Your presence,
Lord,
And we have come with joyful
hearts;
You bid us welcome, draw
us near,
To know Your will we come
apart.

You call us to Your side,

O Lord,
You are the Lord of Heaven
and Earth;
We worship in this holy place,
We honour and adore Your
worth.

You call us to attend now,
Lord,
And be instructed in
God's word;
You will inform the trusting
mind
In how to live in one accord.

You call us to be whole,
dear Lord,
For you redeem and sanctify;
Now make us ready for
the task
For we would follow faithfully.

You call us to Your service,
Lord,
Renewed, transformed by
a great grace;
We dedicate our hearts to love,
Our hands, to serve You all
our days.

You call us to adventure, Lord;
To know Your will and walk
Your ways
Is now our soul's supreme
desire

And from its depths we sing
Your praise.

THE STUDENTS
The Beatitudes
Chapter 6:20 – 23

How blest you are, the Saviour
said,
You're Heaven's child! Though
poor you are,
You're rich! Within your soul
be glad;
In Heaven's Kingdom now
you share!

How blest you are, the Saviour
cried,
You are sustained by grace
and love;
The hungry will be satisfied,
My Father's giving you
will prove'
How blest you are! the Saviour
knew
That those who mourn may
find His peace!
He'll comfort you, accompany
you;
From deepest grief, He'll bring
release.

. . . .

How blest you are! the Lord
declared.
When persecuted for your faith,
Look unto Him, for He
has dared:
He'll lead you on the Heaven-
ward path.

How blest you are. The
victory's won!
Rejoice with all your mind
and soul.
Your Heavenly recompense
is known:
Through Christ, you are
made whole.

JESUS, THE CHRIST
Spiritual Guidance
Chapter 12:22 – 34

Be calm within your soul,
Fear not what might befall,
Your life is more than daily
bread!
Consider well the birds,
They gather not, nor reap,
And yet by God's own hand
they're fed.

Your value is much more
Than birds! No cares can add
To life a single hour or day!
Think of the lilies fair,
They do not labour on

Yet what can equal their
display?

If God so clothe the field,
The splendid wayside flower,
Though here today, tomorrow
done,
Then how much more shall He
Take care of you each day?
Increase your faith, let doubt
be gone!

You are the flock of God,
He shepherds you each day;
It is His pleasure from 'Above'
To grant you utmost joy:
He opens now to you
The glorious Kingdom of
His love.

Your treasure is in Heaven!
Secure the riches given,
Be sure your wealth will not
wear out
For none can take from you
The treasures of the soul;
So! Where's your treasure?
There, your heart!

A LOST SOUL
The Narrow Gate
Chapter 13.22 – 30

Lord, why is it we miss
the way

That leads us to the Narrow
Gate?
We have Your word to guide
our path
With heart alert to what
You say.

Lord, we would find that
Narrow Gate
So near at hand but hidden yet;
The way ahead is dark indeed,
Your light reveals the path
is straight.

Lord, what is it that we must do
For You to recognise our face
When we are called to stand
with You.
Lord, help us; mould our lives
anew.

Lord, we would join the faithful
throng,
All those that come from east
and west
To sit down at Your Kingdom
Feast
And hear the Heavenly
welcome song.

Lord, only You can show
the road
That leads from Earth to
Heaven's Gate;
Lord, be our Guide and walk
with us;

We find in You our true abode.

A QUESTIONER
Questions Answered
Chapter 17:20 – 37

The Kingdom of the Lord
Will not be found by those
Who scan the farthest skies;
Nor will it come because
Of subtle hints that it is near:
The Kingdom of the Lord
is here!

The Kingdom of the Lord
Comes not in worldly ways
Where kings and queens
are prone
To rule throughout their days
With force, their subjects' trust
to win;
God's mighty Kingdom
is within!

The kingdom of the Lord
Will come in glorious *LIGHT*
When Jesus, King of kings
Returns to rule by right!
Eternally, always the same,

His Kingdom will transcend
all time!
The kingdom of the Lord
Will come when Christ,
the Son,

Returns at ages' end
To rule in glorious peace.
And all will bow before
him then,
His reign enfolds all Earth
and Heaven.

THE MAN WHO CHALLENGES ALL TO FAITH

THE SEARCHER
A Living faith
Chapter 7:1 – 10

Where is there found a vibrant
faith
Within a weary land?
Not worthy of the grace of God,
It's true, but we believe
His loving care we will receive:
A living faith will stand!

Where can be found an active
faith
Within a pagan land?
When trust is energised
by hope,
Eroding fears are gone.
Just say the word, Lord, it
is done!
Your word is my command.

Where is there found a living
faith

Within a grieving land?
Though shadows fall, He hears
our call
And in the grief of loss,
We find the Counsellor
because
He takes our trembling hand.

There can be found a steadfast
faith
Within a burdened land!
For, where the sorrows of
the heart
By grace have been
transformed,
A fragile faith will be reformed,
And joy needs no demand!

CHRIST, PETER
Who am I?
Chapter 9:18 – 27

Who do you say I am?
The Lord requests of me;
Let others speak their
thoughts,
I ask, what do you see?

Who do you say I am?
A holy man you see?
A teacher sent from God?
What will your answer be?

Who do you say I am?
A kindly man I'd be?

A man of grace and peace?
How will you answer Me?"

I've found You, Lord of Life!
You are the Christ, 'The Way'!
And I will take my cross
To follow You today!

A WOULD-BE
DISCIPLE
Take Up Your Cross
Chapter 14:25 – 27

I'm standing at the
crossroads, Lord,
Which way, the way for me?
There is no sign except
this cross,
What could its challenge be?

Take up your cross, the Lord
declares,
And follow Me today;
I'll tread the future's path
with you
My *LIGHT*t will show
the way.

I've scanned the pleasant
paths of Earth,
The choice is mine, you see;
Where is there ease upon
this way,
The road to Calvary?

I'm weighing up the
circumstance,
Which way, the worthy way?
Is there no better
consequence,
What is His will for me?

He bids me not to think of cost
The greater good to find;
I'll follow in His cross-bound
way,
My will with His aligned.

I'll take the challenge offered
me,
I grieve the human strife;
Christ walked the Calvary road
for me,
He leads me into life.

A LISTENER
The Lost is Found
Chapter 15:3 – 32

Once, Jesus told of many
things,
Of precious things like sheep
astray;
He said, A shepherd tending
tending sheep
Became aware that one
was lost;
At once he plunged into
the night

To bring that sheep home to
the fold.
And, as The Shepherd, Jesus
seeks
His own, to save at utmost
cost.

Our Rabbi Lord told stories
bold
To teach the deeper things
behind
The parables of Earth
and time:
Of rich and poor, of loss
and gain.
He said, A woman in despair
Because her precious coin
'was lost,
Then lit her lamp and there
it was;
The light revealed where it
had lain.

As Jesus shared the love
of God,
He said, When someone strays
from home
And family nurturing, to walk
A heedless path, he's bound
to roam.
When cast aside and hope
has flown,
Then *LIGHT* can come, resolve
may form;
A wandering son returns to find

His loving father's welcome
home'

THE GREATEST
STORY-TELLER
Challenge to Unbelievers
Chapter 16:14 – 17

The glorious Gospel is
proclaimed
Throughout the world today!
Good News is shared in every
land,
It is hope's shining ray.
From the beginning of
the world,
God has set forth His truth;
With Eden lost, He then
revealed
His promise and its worth.

When Moses trod the
wilderness,
And in the king's own court,
He spoke God's values for
all time,
His nation's freedom brought.
The prophets took God at
His word,
Foretold Messiah's birth;
The Promised One would then
expend
His life for all the Earth.

And when He came,
Redeemer-Lord,
All glory to His Name,
He brought God's Kingdom
into view;
To heal Earth's woe He came.
Far easier for Earth to fade,
And Heaven to recede
Than this Good News to be
destroyed;
His saving power our creed!

THE RICH YOUNG
RULER
Eternal Life
Luke 18:18 –25

What shall I do to merit life
That reaches to Eternity?
What could I give to seal
my fate—
What treasures from my whole
estate?

I keep the Law, I'm
circumspect,
What is the thing that I
yet lack?
Lord, why should I give up
my all,
Your challenge would my heart
appal!

Life's greatest gain is in
God's will;
No one has left behind
true wealth
Who won't receive a greater
store
Both here and now, and
evermore!'

God's Kingdom is the wealth
supreme,
And Jesus, His Eternal Son,
Is King of kings and Lord
of lords:
His gifts of grace: beyond
all words!

THE MAN WHO
GIFTS
HIS GRACE AND
PEACE

THE WORSHIPPER
The Anointing
Chapter 7:26 – 50

I wept the bitter tears of grief,
Acknowledging my need;
I came with perfume rare
to him
And bathed His weary feet.

They named me 'sinner', saw
my pain,
Yet not e'en one was kind,

They scorned the One who
knew my grief;
all, in their pride, were blind.

If two should owe you anything
And one the more with dread,
Which is the one most grateful
when
Forgiveness comes? He said.

The greater sin, the greater
love
When I forgive the debt!
He looked at me and touched
me then;
I knew my sins were dead!

Then Jesus looked into
my heart,
Jesus, the Lord of grace;
He said, Your faith has saved
your soul,
now you may go in peace.

THE SAILORS
Peace, Be Still!
Chapter 8:22 – 25

The storm clouds gather
round us,
The gales so fiercely blow;
They fling the raging waters
Across our troubled bow.
O Master, lest we perish,
Come, take our fragile helm;

Our faith is bound to falter,
The waves would overwhelm.

All nature bows before You,
You understand our fear;
And, when the storm is raging,
We find that You are near.
You call us to have faith now,
You grant the soul's release;
With wind and waves prevailing
all the while,
Lord, gift Your perfect peace.

The Heavenly hosts obey You,
Their song of praise resounds
For, in your awesome
presence,
Amazing grace abounds!
We honour Your great power,
Lord,
And seek to do Your will
For You will calm the
tempest as
You whisper, Peace, be still!

THE 'PACIFIED'
How Peace is Found
Chapter 10:1 – 11

I praise Your holy Name,
O Lord,
You came to me, You healed
my pain;
From deep despair You

rescued me
You came to give me life again.

I will exalt You, living Lord!
You touched my life, You
lifted me;
I called to You from sin's
dark night,
You heard my cry and set me
free.

I sing of Your great love,
my Lord,
You healed my soul in tender
grace;
From vales of night to planes
of light,
From fear to joy; You brought
me peace.

I give You thanks for saving
me,
Your faithfulness remains
the same;
I know Your mercy day by day,
I glory in Your precious Name.

Your love is still the same
today,
Your grace has pardoned
even me;
Your peace transforms the
troubled heart;
I'll praise Your Name eternally.

....

CITIZENS OF ZION
He Rides in Peace
Chapter 19:28 – 44

He rides in peace! He comes
to save!
From Zion's lofty view
Jerusalem will welcome Him,
Her gates are open now.

He rides as King, though not
to wear
A crown of worldly worth;
The King of kings, His regal
power
And yet of humble birth.

He rides with palms laid at
His feet!
The crowd prays, Save
Your own!
And yet His own receive
Him not
When all His work is done!

He rides to face His Calvary
Redeeming grace to bring,
He'll die, God's purpose
to fulfil:
Hosanna, let us sing!

He rides through valleys waste
and wild,
And on the mountain height
His banner is unfurled.

He comes
To save us from sin's blight.

He'll ride in victory one day
When He returns to reign
All peoples then shall bow
to Him
With endless life our gain.

Hosanna, Lord, the blest,
We long for peace today;
Hosanna, Lord, O save
us now*,
Your Kingdom come, we pray.

*Hosanna: Hebrew, 'save NOW'

THE MAN WHO
EXAMPLES PRAYER
THE WORSHIPPERS
How to Pray
Chapter 11:1 – 4

Lord, we would learn to
simply pray;
How may we worship You?
How should we speak, what
can we say?
Lord, teach us how to pray.
"O Abba, Father, come
what may,
We hallow Your great Name;

Lord, may Your Kingdom
come to stay,

Your will be done on Earth.
Provide our food from Your
own hand,
Grant us our daily bread;
When famine strikes an
arid land,
Teach us our wealth to share.

Forgive us for our sins, O Lord:
Wrongs done or good undone,
For we would seek the ways
of God,
Forgiving others here.
Lord, keep us from
temptation's dream,
Save us from evil's wrath.

Grant us the wisdom to reclaim
The power of God today.
We worship and adore
You, Lord,
Rule in our hearts, we pray;
We will Your power and
glory laud
And hail Your Kingdom reign.

PETER, JAMES
AND JOHN
The Transfiguration
Chapter 9:28 – 36

Jesus, lead me up the mount,
Walking step by step with
You, Lord;
Till I reach the hallowed ground

Where the *LIGHT* of God
grants glory.

Jesus, hold my hand, I pray,
Lead me to the utmost
heights, Lord;
I will walk with You today,
Bear me up or I'd fall
from glory.

Jesus, show me God is near,
Here with all His power
and blessing;
May I see with vision clear,
As I gaze on Heaven's glory.

Jesus, I have seen Your face
Glowing with the *LIGHT*
of Heaven;
Now I know You come in grace
With transforming, radiant
glory!

THE MAN WHO
OPENS
THE FUTURE

THE DISCIPLES
and CHRIST
The Age to Come
Chapter 21:5 – 31

Lord, Lord of Life, when will
You be returning?

For we expect that glorious
Day is near;
What are the signs? We would
be ever learning
How to perceive the time You
will appear.
*Watch for the seasons, they
know their time!*
*Watch when the winter has bid
its last farewell;*
*Where all the fruit is, the
blossom will foretell.*

Lord, Lord, we ask, how may
we be discerning,
How can we read the signs that
You'll disclose?
For, one day soon, the
seasons will be turning,
Though raging storms the sun
does yet oppose.
*Wait for the reason God bides
His time,*
*Wait for the winter to clothe
itself in spring;*
*God intervenes then, Eternal
Life to bring.*

Lord, Lord, we pray, O listen to
our yearning,
The time of our distress is
hastening on;
The Earth seems doomed, this
warring world is burning,

We long for when the battles
will be done.
*When in the tempest, God
shelters you,*
*When all seems hopeless, He
aids you in the strife;*
*Hold to your faith now, it is the
way to Life!*

Lord, Lord, we seek to know
Your plan concerning
What is in store when You
return to reign;
Then we will know
Redemption's span confirming
That, in Your grace, we find
eternal gain.
*Then, in the Glory Land, all will
be free,*
*Though earth and heavens will
surely cease to be,*
*God's ageless Gospel will
never pass away.*

THE MAN WHO DIED THAT WE MAY LIVE

THE 'ORCHARDIST'
Chapter 20:9 – 18

The choicest vineyard of
the Lord
Was planted in a fertile land;
He watered it, prepared it well,
With His own hand.

This valued vineyard was
then let
To tenants who despised
the land
And harmed God's servants,
sent them on with empty hand.

At Harvest time the Lord
reviewed
What was entrusted to
their care;
He'd send His Son, His only
Son, His all to dare.

From Heaven's glory
Jesus came
God's precious vineyard
to redeem;
He was rejected, left to die,
Love was His aim.

The 'Stone' the builders did
reject
Became the chief, the
'Cornerstone';
He is 'The Rock', He will
prevail: The Lord, alone!

THE DISCIPLES
The Passover
Chapter 22:7 –30

An upper room, a quiet place,
A scene of prayer and offered
grace;
Here feet were washed by Him
who knelt
To serve His friends whose
pain He felt.

That cherished meal, a feast
ordained,
Gave focus to a lamb
once slain;
The broken bread was food
for thought;
The gift of blood Salvation
Brought.

In memory of exodus
The Lord became 'The Lamb'
for us!
By Him death's curse has
passed us by
To save the world He came
to die!

He promised in that evening
hour,
His Spirit would remain,
empower;
He prayed that we, His friends,
would bear
The unity His own may share.

They sang a hymn just at
the end,

A psalm of joy though death
would rend;
Then, out into the deepening
night,
He crossed the stream to heal
sin's blight.

THE DISCIPLES
Gethsemane
Chapter 22:38 – 46

Down from the mountain
heights He came
To dark Gethsemane.
He crossed the surging Kidron
stream,
To meet with God His goad.

His friends walked with Him on
that road
But they would sleep in peace;
They found no means to
comfort Him,
They could not take His load.

Gethsemane, the olive grove
Where fruit was crushed,
became
A scene of sorrow: Christ
would bear
The burden of His love.

Gethsemane, that vale of grief
Where Jesus came to pray;

He knew the blight of sin
required
The sacrifice of self.

O Abba, Father, take from Me
This cup of grief, He prayed;
Yet I will walk the Calvary
track;
I choose Your will for Me.

Lord, when I face Gethsemane,
The night of dark despair,
Grant me the strength, for good
or ill,
To choose Your will for me.

PETER
The Verdict
Chapters 22 – 23

He stood the testing whole,
my Lord!
The cruel barbs, the scorn
Flung in His face, His silence
there
The proof of courage borne.

He stood the scourging pain,
my Lord,
He wore the robe of kings,
The crown of thorns thrust on
His brow,
With grace which valour brings.

He stood the judgement's

crime, my Lord,
But Rome's great power
was gone!
The king, the priest, the
governor,
Would soon be called
to mourn!

He stood the verdict 'Death',
my Lord,
Upon that fateful morn;
Because He went to Calvary,
Now we can face The Dawn!

SIMON OF CYRENE
A rugged Cross
Chapter 23:26 – 56

His cross was borne to
Calvary,
The Lord of Life was called
to die!
He counselled those along
the way
Who wept for Him in grief
that day,
The King born to be Man.

His cross was raised on
Calvary,
A scaffold for the world to see;
He came to set the prisoner
free
And gave His life for you
and me,

Redeemer, Friend and Guide.

His cross was meant for
Calvary
For there a thief put in his plea;
He found the Kingdom's
shining ray.
In Paradise that day he'd see
The Saviour of the world.

Christ's cross enhances
Calvary,
For it became the place
where we
May come to seek His pardon
free
Then, at His side, forever stay
With our Eternal Lord.

MARY MAGDALENE
The Resurrection
Chapter 24:1 – 12

How glorious is this morning
LIGHT;
The sun announces a new day!
There is a garden here
where life
Will triumph over death's
dark ray!

As we have come to mourn
the dead,
We wonder at this open tomb:
That grave was sealed two
nights ago!
To grieve our Friend
we've come.

The tomb is empty, grave
clothes cast,
Where is the body of our Lord?
A stranger, glowing in the mist,
Then smiled at us; hark at
his word:

The Lord is risen! He's alive!
Why are you searching for
the dead?
Jesus now lives: He conquered
death!
This is the Truth: it's as
He said:

He would be slain by evil men,
Be crucified. Within three dews
He would arise. Go now
to them,
His grieving friends: tell the
Good News!

CLEOPAS
The Emmaus Road
Chapter 24:13 –32

They walked that day upon
a road
To hopeless thoughts resigned,
For sadness claimed their
converse there,

Dark Calvary on their mind.
And then He came! He
counselled them;
They felt their hearts would
rend!

The Scriptures had foretold
a day
Where death is not the end!
He reasoned there that God so
loved The world, He gave
His Son
That all may walk the upward
path
And find God's Kingdom won!

He made as though He would
go on
As they came home to rest;
But needing still His presence
there,
They bid Him be their Guest.
He came right in and sat
with them;
He blessed their daily bread.

They saw His hands and nail-
print scars,
It is the Lord! they said.
Come, stay with us, abide
with us,
The night is hastening on;
Remain with us and guide
us, Lord,
Till travelling days are done.

LUKE
Good News!
Chapter 24:33 – 53

The Gospel News is here
proclaimed!
It is Good News indeed:
Christ Jesus gave His
precious life
That, from our sin we're freed!

This Gospel News is for
This sin-stained world:
The sinless Son of God
Came to this Earth,
His damaged clime,
Reclaimed it for the
YHVH–LORD!

..... oOo .....

JOHN:
"THE SOARING
EAGLE"

Good morning! I'm John,
once a Galilean sailor
apprenticed unto my father,

Zebedee. I was schooled—together with my brother James—in the Jewish tradition by attending the local synagogue on the northern shore of Lake Galilee.

James and I were with Andrew and Simon (Peter, that is) down near the Dead Sea, not far from the lowest reaches of the Jordan River where John the Baptist was engaged in his ministry. It could also be ascertained that we had more than a passing interest in the Essene Community of Qumran—there were many who visited that commune by the Dead Sea to 'drink in' much of what 'the teacher of light' disclosed.

It was during a baptismal ceremony conducted by John the Baptist that we were introduced to *Yeshua*–Jesus, the One I came to know as "*The Word made Flesh*". It was not long after we received the invitation to come, see where He dwelt, that my friends and I took up His invitation to become His disciples.

You may wonder why the Gospel that bears my name is so significantly different from those of Matthew, Mark and Luke. These are known as the Synoptic Gospels in that their work is quite similar, focussing on the records of *Yeshua's* earthly ministry.

My first edition, however, centred on theology within a lyrical frame.

Mine is 'the journal of *LIGHT, LIFE* and *LOVE'*. These motifs permeate the whole. I have heard the cadenzas of the Gospel, the music of the soul, expressed in the Person of Christ and I have found them resonating in my mind. It appears appropriate, therefore, to endeavour to set down the melodies that flow through my soul.

I will provide you with the Gospel by this outline:

Psalms of Praise 3:16 10:10
Poetry of Prayer Ch. 14 –17
Peans of Primacy 1:1–5

Then:
7 "I AM" statements:

Because Matthew has presented the whole story of *Yeshua's* earthly life, I choose, in this edition, to provide the Gospel that bears my name in the form of a hymnbook. I present to you: "ST JOHN'S PSALMS"*.

You will find there is joy in these Psalms, there is pathos, hope, victory, wonder, there is quandary, yearning, wise instruction, there is wisdom, testimony and prayer.

I here provide you with a hymnbook for your prayers and also for a worshipping congregation. A song is a psalm when its music flows through the channel of the soul. Allow this stream of grace to express *your* personal TESTIMONIES.

* The author has published these hymns in a previous production, 'St John's Psalms', holds copyright.

CREATOR GOD

Tune: *Europe* 8.7.8.7. D.
Trochaic
Chapter 1:1 – 5

Word of God in the beginning,
Called the formless void
to *LIGHT*;
Voice of God commanding
order
In the chaos of the night.
Dawn has come in golden
glory,
Christ has formed the universe;
He began creation's story:
Spoken is the Mind of God!

Son of God, the Lord Eternal,
Once was clothed in human
clay;
Co-existent with the Father,
He displayed life's brightest
ray.
LIGHT that shone on Earth's
first morning
Has revealed hope for
the world;
Christ has brought us faith's
new dawning:
Open is the heart of God!

LIGHT of God forever shining
Through the gloom of sin's
dark night,
Glowing with the joy of Heaven
Shining on the human plight.

Radiant splendour not
declining,
LIGHT that night can't
overcome,
All our human life refining,
Token of the grace of God!

Power of God with life
abundant
Moved to heal the human
blight;
Mighty Word of God declaring
Evil's curse has had its night!
He's the *LIGHT* now
intervening
Giving all to set us free;
All our bonds have lost their
meaning,
Broken by the love of God!

LET THERE BE *LIGHT*!

Tune: *Holy Spirit, Faithful
Guide* 7.7.7.7. D.
Chapter 1:1 – 5

From before all time began
And no worlds were set
In space,
There was God, the *YHVH–
LORD*,
Planning for the dawn of days.
When the Earth was set
in place
And the day burst from
the night,

Yet God gave an evening glow:
Moon and stars were shining
bright.

Yes! 'The Word', the Joy
of Heaven,
Lit the flame that kindled light;
He has spoken to the night,
He has spoken, He is *LIGHT*!
Jesus formed the universe;
He has broken powers of night:
He commanded light to shine;
He has brought the Earth
to sight.

Word of Truth and Word
of Power,
He who is the Daystar bright,
Lord o'er all the universe
He has brought God's love
to sight.
Word of *LIGHT* and *LIFE*
and *LOVE*,
Jesus: God, the precious Son,
With the Father, He is Lord
As all earthly ages run.

Word of hope, revealing grace,
Jesus voiced the Mind of God;
He declared *LIGHT* for
the world:
God is known through Christ
the Lord!
For 'The Word' has come to us:
Jesus, Saviour, Christ adored.

Now He guards and guides
each day
Lighting all the way to God.

WORLD VALUES
Tune: *He Wipes the Tear*
D.L.M.
Chapter 1:1 – 14

The peoples of the Earth
can find
Faint hope on which to build
their life,
The values of the world
conspire,
Enclosing minds in earthly
strife.
O Lord, we pray that *LIGHT*
may shine
Into the **shadows** of the soul;
Lord come, transform despair
to joy;
O cast out care and make
us whole.

The nations, in their
restlessness
To gain life's best by selfish
Greed,
Neglect the virtues of
Your word
And find no guide your Law
to heed.
Lord, come into our troubled
world

Where hate displaces human
good;
Equip Your messengers
with grace
That, by their lives, the Christ
is heard.

Our world's adrift from what
You plan,
By colour, clime, by class
and creed;
Though *LIGHT* still shines
upon Your word,
The world prefers the darkest
deed!

THE WORD OF GOD
Tune: *Martyrdom*　C.M.
John 1:9 – 14

Lord, we would pray for every
land:
Turn all our **shadows** into
LIGHT,
Disperse the clouds of graft
and greed
That in our world peace comes
to sight!

'The Word' of God who walked
on Earth,
From Heaven's glory came;
A stable scene had marked
His birth
And hidden was His fame.

The Word was clothed in
human frame,
His dwelling was with us;
That we might learn to live
He came,
The Man of truth and grace.

He is the well-beloved Son,
The Man who came from God;
He and the Father, truly One:
He is 'The Word' of God!

Such wondrous love, abundant
grace
And truth for all to see,
The Son of God made known
His peace For all Eternity.

And we have seen His glory
now,
With radiance of our God.
One day, before Him, all
will bow
Proclaiming Him as Lord!

MATCHLESS GRACE

Tune: *Amazing Grace*   C.M.
Chapter 1:15 – 18

The grace of God, so rich
and free,
Outpoured so lavishly,
His matchless grace, how
could it be,

Such grace reserved for me?

All grace and truth have come
from Him,
The Lord of *LIGHT* and peace;
Now of His fullness we receive
And grace outpoured on grace.

When fear intrudes where
shadows lay,
His grace will cover me;
Though I may falter on
the way,
His grace will nurture me.

When all my cherished hopes
have fled,
His grace still reaches me;
And when my heart is filled
with dread
There's grace enough for me!

His wondrous grace, beyond
degree,
This grace He gifted me;
Grace multiplied abundantly,
For me, yes, even me!

His grace still flows from
Calvary,
Its stream now cleanses me;
The grace that floods Eternity
Has been outpoured on me!

THE VOICE

Tune: *Lydia* C.M. (Rep. last
line)
Chapter 1:6 – 15, 19 – 34

There was a man who came
from God
That walked the desert sand;
While not 'the *LIGHT*', he saw
its glow:
Messiah was at hand!

There was a voice of one
who called
Within the wilderness:
Make straight a pathway for
our God,
The 'Road of Righteousness'.

The Lord is near, make way
for Him;
Let valleys now be raised;
Tear down the barriers of
today,
Let mountains be erased!

Behold Him now, the 'Lamb
of God';
He takes the world's great sin;
The Saviour's blood will flow
for us,
He comes to make us clean!

'The Spirit–Dove' has come
from Heav'n,
It rests on Him, the Christ;

He is the Chosen One of God,
The only Son, most prized.

There is a Voice that calls
today
Into our wilderness;
Come, walk the Highway of
our God,
The Lord of Righteousness.

THE CALL

Tune: *Come, Ye Thankful
People* 7.7.7.7. D.
John 1:29 – 51

Come and see Him, Christ
the Lord,
Look! Behold the Lamb of God!
See Him now, He comes
this way;
In the desert, mark His road.

Come for guidance, come
for grace,
See the desert lands rejoice!
As He treads the earthly path,
Come to Him, now make
your choice.

Come and hear Him, Christ
the Lord,
Words of Life He speaks,
it's true!
Hear His challenge, heed
its worth;

What's your need? He asks
of you.

Come, Messiah–Christ is near!
Come and walk with Him
today;
He will guard and guide
you here;
Stay with Him, now watch
and pray.

Come and follow Christ,
the Lord,
He's the chosen One! Awake,
Are you yet as crumbling clay?
He will make you 'solid rock'!

Come, commit your life to Him:
Walk in *LIGHT*, He knows
your need.
Come! You'll see He is
the King;
He will make you free indeed!

I SAW JESUS
Tune: *Ellan Vannin*   8.7.8.7.
D. Trochaic
Chapter 2:1 –12

I saw Jesus on the pathway
Leading to the silvery sea;
There was purpose in His
footsteps
As He walked by Galilee.
There was beauty on

the hillside,
Great delight by Jordan's
stream,
Sparkling waters so inviting,
Yet at once, I turned to Him.

I met Jesus in the market
As I sought my daily wares,
Then, encumbered by life's
luggage,
Overburdened with my cares,
There He took my hand and
led me
And His peace spread all
around;
As He lifted all my burdens,
I was then no longer bound.

I told Jesus of my longing
To be free from all my sin;
I had thirsted for life's
treasures,
They were arid, miraging!
He renewed my life completely:
Living water, pure and free,
Came as nectar straight from
Heaven,
Flowing so abundantly.

Now I walk and talk with Jesus
On the road of victory
And He tells me of His
purpose,
How He brought new life to me.
I find joy upon the highway,

There is *LIGHT* His path
to prove;
There is love and tender
kindness,
There is life, eternal life!

JERUSALEM
Tune: *Rest* 8.6.8.8.6.
Chapter 2:13 – 25 with Ps. 24

Jerusalem, Jerusalem,
The city of God's peace,
Your ancient walls still stand
today;
Your gates are guarded and
we pray
This day for your release.

Great city of the mountain
heights,
The prophets spoke of you,
That one day you would
welcome Him,
The Chosen One, the Lord
supreme
And trust His word for you.

O city of that glorious past,
You have despised your own;
He preached the Gospel to
the poor
Where greed defiled the
holy Law
And love was never shown.

Great city of this troubled world
Where many learn to hate,
Where war and anguish rage
within:
When will you bid Christ
enter in?
Soon, it may be too late.

God's Temple was defiled
by sin,
Its purity profaned;
He sent His own beloved Son
To cleanse the Sanctuary
and won!
Such cleansing was ordained.

To peoples where all hope
has died,
Yet still the psalmist sings:
One day your hearts will
open wide,
The King of Glory will reside,
The Lord, the King of kings.

BORN ANEW
Tune: *Sweet Hour of Prayer*
Chapter 3:1 – 15

O Lord of Life, I seek Your
LIGHT,
The night is long and I can find
No answers for life's
circumstance;

Renew my anxious, questing
mind.
As freshening wind announces
spring,
You must be born now, from
'Above';
The Kingdom of God's grace
is yours:
In faith receive His gift of love.

O Master, teach me now
Your ways,
I search for *LIGHT*, for Life,
for Love,
Illumine all the darkest night;
Display Your wisdom from
'Above'.
The dawn may bear the
rustling wind,
But none can comprehend
from where
It comes or goes and, as
the wind,
The Spirit comes to answer
prayer.

O Holy Spirit, be my Guide
And, as the wind, display
Your power.
Now lead me to the brightest
day,
Infill my life this very hour.
Eternal Life is in the Son
Who came to turn your night
to day;

Now walk within the LIGHT
of God,
The Lord is with you all
the way.

THE RUSTLING WIND

Tune: *Diademata* DSM
Chapter 3:1 – 15

Oh, listen for the wind,
It stirs the fragile grass,
It ripples on the restless waves,
The clouds will trace its paths.
Just so, the Spirit stirs
The human soul to life
Inspiring us to trust in God,
Infusing faith's belief.

Oh, listen to the wind,
From whence it comes or goes;
No one could ever choose
its ways
Nor tell of where it flows.
Just so, the Spirit-Breath
Will move deep in the soul
Investing it with blessed hope,
Inviting to be whole.

Oh, listen in the wind!
The rustling, gale-swept trees
Reveal its presence in
the leaves
As nature lifts the breeze.
Just so, the Spirit's power
Encourages the soul.

Inducing inner fortitude,
Increasing power to all.

Oh, listen! Here's the wind;
Now hear its lilting voice,
It whispers on its wending way,
It bids us to rejoice.
Just so, the Spirit's course
Will guide us and sustain,
Invigorating every aim
Immortal life to gain.

GOD LOVES THIS WORLD

Tune: *Crimond* C.M.
John 1:1, 3:5 – 21

The LORD created all
things well
With Eden fair and bright;
The beauty of the universe
Bathed Earth in radiant light.

God loved this troubled world
so much
He gave His own dear Son
That all who do believe
shall live;
The vict'ry has been won.

From Heaven above God's
cherished Son
Once came to set us free
From chains of sin; He gave
His all

To die on Calvary.

But God sent not His own
loved Son
Into this world to blame
Or to condemn; indeed, to save
This sin-stained world
He came.

The answer is that *LIGHT*
has come
Though we have loved
sin's night;
And those who live in truth
may stand
Within God's gracious sight.

TRUTH FROM GOD

Tune: *Llanfair* 7.6.7.6. D.
Trochaic
Chapter 3:22 – 36

Christ came down from
Heaven's Throne,
This the wondrous story:
Earth belongs to Earth,
it's said,
He belongs to Glory!
Jesus is pre-eminent;
Earthly truth is transient.
He is Truth, from Heaven sent:
HALLELUJAH!

Who will now believe His word,

Trust His timeless Scripture?
Know that Truth's both heard
and seen;
View the larger picture!
Christ is ever paramount,
Hear God's word resounding:
Jesus is of Truth the Fount:
HALLELUJAH!

God immortal kept His word,
His is Love unending!
As the Father loved the Son,
He the Son was sending
Healing life's impediments,
Gifting Life eternal!
Now our joy has luminance:
HALLELUJAH!

Christ displays the Spirit's
power,
Limitless, abounding;
We can trust Him every hour,
Evil's grip confounding!
Word of truth so permanent,
Timeless and unchanging;
His return is immanent:
HALLELUJAH!

A PRAYER FOR GRACE
Tune: *Even Me* 8.7.8.7.
Trochaic
Chapter 4:1 – 15

I have come in search of grace,
Lord,
Finding nought to quench
my thirst;
Where's the life-stream,
where's the Fountain
Where my soul may be
resourced?
Lord, for me, let it be:
May Your grace now flow
to me.

I have tasted streams of
gladness
In the changing scenes of life;
All I've found are transient
flavours,
Nought has helped my soul
revive.
Lord, for me, let it be:
May Your grace now flow
to me.

Where's the well-spring of
God's mercy?
Where's the source of joy's
release?
Where may I be truly nurtured?
Lord, I come to You for grace.
Lord, for me, let it be:
May Your grace now flow
to me.

Here's the Fount of Living
Water

All my soul to satisfy;
Calvary's stream is flowing
freely
And my Lord now welcomes
me.
Lord, for me, I can see
That Your grace now flows
to me!

FIELDS WHITE TO HARVEST

Tune: *Blaenwern* 8.7.8.7. D.
Trochaic
Chapter 4:27 – 42

See the fields are white
to harvest
And the summer's at its height!
Take your place now in the
reaping,
See the sheaves and lift
your sight.
When the Lord spoke of
the harvest
And referred to ripened grain,
He observed a world of people
Longing to be born again.

Jesus saw a world of pathos
Saddened by encumbered
years;
People in chaotic darkness,
Struggling with unnumbered
fears.
While the sun is brightly
shining
And the whitened wheat
is new,
Let us take our place
beside Him
For the labourers are few.

Now the Gospel is resounding,
There's Good News for you
today,
For the 'harvest' is abounding;
Christ now calls, He's on
His way!
Soon the reaping will be over,
Winter's night is hastening on;
Oh, be gathered to God's
Garner
Where Eternal Life is won!

BETHESDA

Tune: *Bullinger* 8.5.8.3.
Chapter 5:1 –15

Lord, I come to healing waters
And I make my plea;
Though I linger, there's
no healing,
Not for me!

Healing comes to those
who seek it,
Surely this means me?
Even though the angels
touch it,

Not for me!

Lord, You ask if I want healing;
Saviour, hear my plea,
Is there yet a grace in Heaven,
Lord, for me?

Lord, I come to You for healing,
Healing yet for me;
Healing for my mind and spirit,
Even me!

Lord, I plunge into the ocean
Of Your love for me;
Now its waves my soul
is cleansing:
I am free!

I AM AMAZED
Tune: *Retreat* L.M.
Chapter 5:16 – 47

I am amazed! The Lord
declared
His works are still the Father's
deeds;
The Son has seen that though
He acts,
It is the LORD* who meets
our needs.

I am amazed! Yet greater
works
The Son will do and I believe,
Just as the Father will renew,

The Son will raise the dead
to life!

I am amazed, for He is Judge!
The Father placed within
His hands
The power to set us free
from sin;
I'll daily follow His commands.

I am amazed! All who believe
The Father and His Son today
Already have Eternal Life,
Already death has passed
them by!

I am amazed! Believe His word
And live by faith in Christ,
the Lord
For now Eternal Life is giv'n
To those who trust the One
adored.

*English translation of *YHVH*:
(Yahweh)

BREAD FOR THE
MULTITUDES
Tune: *Sweet Hour of Prayer*
D.L.M.
Chapter 6:1 – 24

I came one day to find
the Christ,
The crowds were thronging,
faint with heat

And then they cried, Who has
    some bread?
We're hungry Lord, what can
    we eat?

Chorus:
What could I bring to offer Him,
    The Rabbi from Eternity?
The need is great, beyond
    supply,
Yet He can use a gift from me.

I heard Him ask, What do
    you have,
How many loaves have you
    today?
What can you do to ease
    Earth's pain,
What will you give to help
    this day?

The beauty of the Galilee,
The peace that flowed through
    Jordan's stream,
Had filled my heart with joy
    that day;
When Jesus called, I came
    to Him.

He took my loaves and blessed
    them there
By Galilee, the silvery sea;
Then, breaking each, He
    shared the loaves;

From His own hand, bread
    came to me.

They gathered up the overflow,
Abundant resource from
    His hands.
This is the miracle of grace
That Jesus places in
    our hands.

I AM "THE BREAD OF LIFE"
Tune: *Ellers*   10.10.10.10.
Iambic
John 6:25 – 59

Why do I search for Him,
    the Christ of God?
Why do I yearn for Him,
    for Jesus plead?
Is it because I'm drawn to
    more than bread
To truly satisfy my daily need?

What will He do, the living
    Christ today?
How will He move to meet this
    world's great need?
In ancient times the manna fell
    each day,
So could it be that Bread from
    Heaven I'd plead?

The Lord has said, 'I am the
Bread of Life';
Whoever comes to Me this
Bread to gain
Will never hunger for Earth's
sustenance;
Those who believe in Me won't
thirst again!

Christ is the Living Bread that
came from Heav'n
To do the Father's will, the
Bread that came
Down from celestial heights
to give us Life;
Lord grant this Bread, I pray,
in Your great Name.

*Whoever comes to Me, I'll not
cast out!*
*I came to do the Father's will,
He cries;*
*And everyone who looks to Me
will have*
*Eternal Life; they will from
death arise!*

*"I am the Bread of Life", the
Living Bread;*
*Whoever will partake of Me
shall live!*
*The Bread I give is My own life;
this Bread*
*Will save the world unto
Eternal Life!*

WORDS OF LIFE

Tune: *Diademata* D.S.M.
Chapter 6:60 – 71 with 1:1,
8:31

Where may I go to find
The way that leads to life?
How may I know which road
to tread
That leads to soul's relief?
There is a narrow path,
The way is straight, believe:
It leads you to the only One
Who heals the heart's
deep grief.

Where may I hear the words
That will this truth declare?
How may I know the Lord
of Life
Who will my sorrow bear?
The truth you seek is real,
It tells of Christ whose care
Will bring God's precious Word
to light
For He is Truth, He's near!

Where may I hear the truth
God speaks into the soul?
How may I be released today
From sin's ensnaring shoal?
The truth you seek is in
The Lord, 'The Word'!
Yes, know
The Living Word who sets
you free;

By Him you are made whole.

You say, He is 'The Truth'
That sets us free from sin,
He is the Lord, He is the One
Who came to cleanse
sin's stain?
Christ is the Lord of Life,
He is the One whose reign
In Heaven will never know
an end,
His truth will never wane.

THE MESSIAH
Tune: *Lydia*   C.M.
Chapter 7:1 – 36

What is 'Messiah'?
'Anointed', you claim?
Who has this blessed balm,
What can He do to heal
the maimed?
He is 'Messiah–Christ'!
God's Son, to heal He came.

Who is 'Messiah',
The Chosen of God?
What is His role today?
He comes, revealing God,
the LORD!
He is the Living Christ,
The precious Son adored'

Where is 'Messiah'
Who sets us free?

How could He be the One
And would He go to Calvary
To bring us life today?
His cross signs life for me!

Why is 'Messiah'
Not worshipped today
Throughout the whole
wide world?
Most fear His *LIGHT*, will
not obey.
His guidelines for new life…
Come, walk with Him today!'

THE WATER OF LIFE
Tune: *Behold the Saviour*
(with chorus)
Chapter 7:37 – 53

Where may I go to quench
my thirst?
I long to satisfy
The deepest yearnings of
my soul;
Where is the Source of joy?

Chorus:
It is the Lord, He speaks to me:
Now look to Me and live!
I am the One who is the
Source
Where springs Eternal Life!

Where may I find the deepest
well

Where purest waters flow?
My cup is empty and I crave
To be replenished now.

I've heard there is a mighty
Source
Where Living Water streams
Out from the reservoirs
of grace;
This is beyond my dreams!

Christ is the Water gifting Life
To those who trust in Him;
Just as the Scriptures boldly
state,
This water flows within!

I AM "THE *LIGHT* OF THE WORLD"

Tune: *Europe*   8.7.8.7. D.
Trochaic
Chapter 8:1 – 30

In a whirl of twisted concepts,
Millions seek a path to tread
Searching for a light to guide
them,
Needing to be safely led.
Light the world, Lord, souls
are dying
In the darkest realms
of night;
You still hold the *LIGHT*
of Heaven,

Saviour, lead us to this *LIGHT*.

In this world where terror
surges
And the nations rise in war,
Where's the peace-plan,
What's the answer for our
basic human flaw?
Light our world, Lord, none
denying
On the road where grace
can heal.
You still bear the torch of
You will bear the torch of
freedom,
Saviour, now Your *LIGHT*
reveal.

In a well of heartfelt sorrows,
Grievous pain invades
the soul;
Where is hope for our
tomorrows,
Where is help to make
us whole?
Light this world, Lord, none
decrying
In the gloom of abject woe,
Jesus, bring the *LIGHT* of
gladness;
Saviour, light our candle now.

In the waste of shattered
precepts,
Maxims once held high

have flown;
In the depths we search
for meaning,
Where are virtues we
could own?
Light Your world, Lord, Hell
defying!
In the vales where **shadows**
lay,
Lord, you are the *LIGHT*
we search for;
Saviour, be our *LIGHT*
today!

FINDING TRUTH

Tune: *Troyte* 8.8.8.8.
Chapter 8:31 – 36

I sought for truth in scripture's
page,
Turned to the ancient prophet
sage
Who spoke of One in future
age
Who truth would bear.

I sought for truth in Gospels
rare,
They spoke of Christ with
reverent care
and, as I read, I saw Him there
who lived the truth.

I sought for truth at Jesus' feet
Where He revealed the Source

of *LIGHT*;
and as I pondered life
complete,
I knew the Truth!

His promise is,Now come
to Me,
You'll know the Truth, you shall
be free;
Receive My words, believe
in Me,
Know Truth indeed.

I found the Truth, now I
am free,
Free from the doubts that
hindered me:
Yes! I shall live eternally
For Christ is Truth!

NOW I CAN SEE

Tune: *Calabar*
(African Traditional)
Chapter 9:1-35

How wonderful, the Lord
of creation,
For His beauty outshines
the stars;
Darkness is going, morning
is glowing
Night shall depart and dawn
shall arise.
Sun on the mountains, dew in
the valleys;

Now I can see His glorious
LIGHT
Wakening the Earth and I will
praise Him
For this miracle of sight!

It's wonderful, God's
re-creation
Of the soul once held in night;
I am reviewing the Lord's
renewing:
Once I was blind but now
I have sight!
Mine is a vision: glory and
grandeur
And I can see that all who
believe
Share Life Eternal and I
revere Him
For His miracle of life!

Oh! wonderful, this new
creation,
Far beyond Earth's treasure
trove.
Lofty the mountains, deep are
the Earth's mines,
Higher yet, the scope of
God's love.
Deeper still the depth of
His mercy!
Now I can see it with my
own eyes:
Salvation's story, and I
adore Him

For this miracle of grace!

YOU ASK ME HOW
Tune: *Ein' Feste Burg*
Chapter 9:13 – 41

You ask me how could I
be healed,
A miracle curtailing?
You wonder why with joy
I'm filled?
The power of God's prevailing!
The Lord has walked my road,
Today He took my load!
I'll praise Him for I see
New *LIGHT* has come to me;
My night has turned to
morning.

You question what's my life's
true gain,
And why this path I'm
choosing?
I know that I've been born
again;
God's ways are not confusing.
His will is plain to me,
His follower I will be
For I have found release,
The reason for my peace
As this new day is dawning.

You query who is this
who cares
To answer all my yearning?

I know it is the Lord who bears
My burdens and I'm learning
How great His love for me;
The blind is made to see!
He cleansed my soul
from blame;
I'll glory in His Name,
He scattered all my mourning!

You ponder how could these
things be?
I cannot tell the reason why
That Jesus Christ would stoop
to me
And why He did not pass
me by.
But, this one thing I know:
Once I was blind and now
I see! Yes, all is *LIGHT*
For I have gained insight,
My soul His *LIGHT* adorning.

I AM "THE GATE"

Tune: *Belmont* C.M.
Chapter 10:1 – 9

I've found the access into 'Life':
The way is open though
The Gate is narrow, hard
to find:
Christ welcomes me: Come
through!

I've found the opening to 'Life',
Eternal Life beyond

The grave: The Lord has
guided me
To tread where Love is bound!

I've found the Gateway
into 'Life:
'The Gate' personified,
For Christ it is who offers me
New life because He died!

I AM "THE GOOD SHEPHERD"

Tune: *Crimond* C.M.
Chapter 10:1 – 21, Psalm 23

My Shepherd is the living Lord,
His goodness draws me near;
He walks the path of
righteousness
And I will meet Him there.
I follow in the path He takes
And listen to His voice.
He knows and calls me by
my name;
In Him I will rejoice.

My gracious Shepherd comes
to me,
The gate is open now;
By Him I enter and go on
To where green pastures grow.

My kindly Shepherd nurtures
me,
I'm fed from His own hand;

I drink from crystal fountains
and
I rest on hallowed ground.

My gentle Shepherd comforts
me
In grief I could not bear;
When walking through the
shadowed vale,
I'm mindful of His care.

My Shepherd Saviour gifted
life, abundant life to me;
He chose to walk the Calvary
track
That I may know Eternity!

WE KNOW YOU ARE THE CHRIST
Tune: *Chalvey* D.S.M.
Chapter 11

We know You are the Christ,
You are the Friend of all;
You enter in our daily care
And lift us when we fall.
You've walked the human road
And we have met You there;
You call us to Your presence
now
To hear our earnest prayer.

We claim You are the Christ,
You understand our joys;
We converse with
our living Lord,
We worship and rejoice.
You know our human ties,
The choicest bonds we share;
Our kinship with You now
becomes
A foretaste of Heaven's care.

Oh yes, You are the Christ,
You love us so! In grief
We find you near and for
our peace,
Your tender touch receive.
You help us bear the pain
For you have wept Your tears;
In reaching sorrow's sombre
depths,
You've mellowed all our fears.
We worship You, the Christ!
You took Redemption's Plan
And came to Earth to place
Yourself
Within the schemes of man.
How can it be that One
Could die to save the world?
But we believe the victory's
won,
The greatest story told!

I AM "THE RESURRECTION AND THE LIFE"
Tune: *Ellers* 10.10.10.10.
Chapter 11 and 5:24 – 29

(1 Corinthians, chapter 15)

I am 'The Resurrection and
the Life!'
All those who place their trust
in Me shall live
And, though they die, they'll
pass from death," Christ said.
Faith is the door that leads us
into Life!

Now roll away the stone of
unbelief,
You'll see the glory of the Lord
most prized;
Take off the grave clothes of
the past and find
The garments of a life renewed
in Christ.

This is your day, rejoice while
day shall last,
For those who walk the way of
Christ, The *LIGHT*,
Won't falter on the upward path
of life;
Those with no light will stumble
in the night.

His word is truth: whoever
will believe
in Me and in My Father too,
shall live!
Eternal Life comes into glorious
view:

The faithful have now passed
from death to life!

The dead in Christ shall rise,
O wondrous dawn!
The Lord's own glory shines
when death is lost.
We bear the image of the
earthly life
In Heaven we'll bear the form
endowed by Christ.

Our death shall be completely
swallowed up!
So, where's death's sting, or
victory of the grave?
Once clothed in dust, the soul
will be transformed;
Then we shall live with Him
who came to save.

THE GIFT
Tune: *Lloyd* C.M.
Chapter 12:1 – 11

How natural, that one
should come
To bow before the Lord,
To bathe His feet with tears
then take
The towel of servanthood.

How beautiful the perfume rare
A broken bowl may give;
Aromas of the gift released

Are redolent of love.

How wonderful that Christ
should stoop
To lift the penitent;
His gentle grace will touch
the heart
Of those who call Him friend.

How beautiful the gift of love
That Jesus offers now;
With every blessing of
His grace,
He will our soul endow.

How graceful is the living Christ
That He should call me friend,
For I would serve him from
my heart
And love Him past the end.

"HOSANNA"*
Tune: *Cwm Rhonda*
8.7.8.7.8.7. Trochaic
Chapter 12:12 – 19
*Hebrew: 'Save us *NOW*!'

Save us now, "Hosanna",
save us!
Blessed is the One who came
In the precious Name
of Yahweh,
We revere that holy Name.
He is LORD, the King of Glory;
We will sing of His great fame:
Now save us, "Hosanna"!

Do not fear, "Hosanna",
find peace,
Do not be afraid, you see:
Jesus is our Sovereign
Saviour;
He will ride to victory!
Peace comes in through Christ
who saves us;
See, He comes your peace
to be:
Let peace come, "Hosanna".

He is near, "Hosanna",
near now,
Let us go to welcome Christ;
Jesus is the great Redeemer,
Saviour of the world once lost;
He will bring His people
freedom,
Calvary would be the cost!
"Hosanna", save us NOW!

THE HOUR HAS COME
Tune: *Some Glad, Sweet Day*
Chapter 12:20, 36 – 50

The hour has come to glorify
Our Lord and Saviour,
For He has come from Heaven
to Earth
To show God's favour.
But those who cherish their
own life
Beyond all else will never know
That those who give up all

shall find
New life to savour.

Chorus:

Christ's road has led
to Calvary!
Just as a seed will fall to earth
And, dying, shall produce
new life,
So is God's mercy.

The time has come to quantify
What we are planning;
Are we prepared to follow Him,
Ourselves denying?
And will we take the cross-
bound way?
Are we prepared to serve
Him well?
Do we expect to stand
with Him,
Our zeal not waning?

Chorus:

Christ's path led through
Gethsemane,
And, though He prayed
in agony,
He chose to face the
darkest hour;
He knew God's mercy.

The day has come to satisfy
Our deepest yearning.
When Christ our Lord was
lifted up,

There was no turning
For, when He came to Calvary,
He knew that one day all
would bow,
Drawn to their Saviour's
wounded side,
His purpose learning.

Chorus:

Christ's path leads on
from Calvary,
His *LIGHT* is shining through
the night;
His challenge is to trust
that *LIGHT*:
It shines in mercy.

THE UPPER ROOM

Tune: *Rest*   C.M.
Chapters 13 – 17

Lord, I have found Your Upper
room;
I've come from deepening
care.
You meet me here to comfort
me,
You nurture me, encourage me
In this, the place of prayer.

In turning from the scenes
of Earth,
I come, my soul laid bare.
Acknowledging Your power
to save,

Your inner cleansing now
I crave;
Lord, meet my need through
prayer.

The words You speak are life
to me,
Enriching every thought;
For every question of the mind,
For every fetter that would
bind,
You are the answer sought!

You give me courage, Lord,
to trust,
Each daily task to bear
And where the path has
steep incline,
I claim the strength You offer in
This sacred hour of prayer.

Descending from these lofty
heights
Where I have shared in prayer,
I've found the faith your way
to see:
If I must face 'Gethsemane',
Lord, still Your will I'll dare.

Where fear is lost in grace;
Christ speaks within our hearts
in love:
Our hope becomes our praise!

The place of prayer is blessed
As heads and hearts are
bowed,
Acknowledging the Lord of Life,
With love we are endowed.

The home of prayer is joy;
Surpassing happiness,
Joy gives assurance when
all else
Would fail to grant us rest.

The quest of prayer is peace
Profound amid distress;
The Lord has gifted His
own peace:
Not of the world, His peace!

The path of prayer grants life:
The Way? He plans our path!
The Truth? He has revealed
the LORD!
The life? His death grants life!

THE ROOM OF PRAYER

Tune: *Trentham*   S.M.
Chapters 13 – 17

The room of prayer is calm

A SACRAMENTAL LIFE

Tune: *Martyrdom*   C.M.
Chapter 13:1 – 20

It is a sacred work of grace

Where Jesus takes a towel,
The sacrament of servanthood,
Then lifts the cleansing bowl.

It is a sacred task of grace
That Jesus demonstrates,
A sacrament of selfless love;
For my response He waits.

It is a sacred tryst of grace
Where Jesus hears my prayer
His sacrament of 'shalom'
peace
I celebrate this hour.

It is a sacred gift of grace
That Jesus brings today;
His sacrament of deepest joy
That streams upon my way.

It is a sacred act of love
That Jesus offers me;
His sacrament of saving grace
Flows down from Calvary.

He ministers in mercy
Where purest waters flow
And, at the fountainhead
of grace,
He stoops to cleanse me now.

DON'T BE AFRAID
Tune: *Mozart*   8.8.8.8.8.8.
Chapter 14:1 – 4

The Lord has said, Don't be
afraid,
Don't be disturbed or worry;
Do not allow an anxious
thought
To take you from Heaven's
Glory.
My Father's Realm has many
homes,
There's room for all His family.

I go before you to prepare
Your dwelling place in Glory.
Yes, I will go to set
your place
And to prepare your entry.
I promise to return again
And take you home to Glory.

You know the way that I
now take:
This is the wondrous story;
Now trust in God and trust
in Me,
It is the way to Glory.
My Spirit will be with you here
To lead you on to Glory.

I AM "THE WAY, THE TRUTH, THE LIFE"
Tune: *Hendon* 7.7.7.7.
Chapter 14:1 – 10

Jesus said, I am The Way:

I'm the 'Road' for travelling!
You'll not falter on this path;
Walk by faith, soul free and
finding
All My joy along the way

Jesus said, I am The Truth:
I'm the 'Word', declaring
What is in the Mind of God
Wisdom for your faith's bold
daring;
Now discern the power
of Truth.

Jesus said, I am the Life:
Offer me your striving;
Find in Me the Breath of God
For your dormant soul's
reviving:
It is yours, the gift of Life
.

I'm The Way, The Truth,
the Life,
Here you'll find life's meaning.
Jesus is the Lord of Life,
He brings virtue for our
gleaning:
All our needs are met in Him.

THE COUNSELLOR
Tune: *Healing Stream*
7.6.7.6.
Chapter 14:15 – 26

If you love Me, live My words,

Trust Me, do not waver;
I will ask for One to guide,
Holy Spirit, Helper,
Holy Spirit, Power!
Advocate, Paraclete*
Comforter and Counsellor.
*Greek: *One called alongside to
help*

You will know the One
who stands
Close beside to help you;
He's the Spirit, Source of truth.
Holy Spirit, come now,
Holy Spirit, guide now;
Advocate, Paraclete,
Comforter and Counsellor .

You will not be left alone,
Orphans in life's tempest;
I will come in power to you.
Holy Spirit, soul's Guest,
Holy Spirit, faith's quest;
Advocate, Paraclete,
Comforter and Counsellor.

This, My promise ever true,
You will know I'm with you
And, because I live, you'll live:
Holy Spirit with you,
Holy Spirit in you:
Advocate, Paraclete,
Comforter and Counsellor.

··········

THE DOVE OF PEACE
Tune: *Buckland*   7.7.7.7.
Ch. 14:15–18, 25–27, 16:5–16

Holy Spirit, come to us
As the promised Dove
of Peace;
Settle in our hearts, we pray,
In Your calm is fear's release.

Peaceful Spirit, gently come,
Satisfy our soul's deep need;
Magnify Heaven's gift in us,
Holy Spirit, come we plead.

Gracious Spirit, tend
our wounds,
Cleanse our hearts, renew
the soul;
Teach us from the Living Word,
Hear our prayer and make
us whole.

Powerful Spirit, energise,
Fire from Heaven, glow within;
Sanctify, refine, remould,
Fit us now for Heaven's gain.

Awesome Spirit, fill
our hearts,
Dwell within, enhance
our days;
Spirit of the Living God,
Stay with us, abide always.

....

I AM "THE TRUE VINE"
Tune: *Toplady*   7.7.7.7.7.7.
John 15:1 – 10

Jesus is the one 'True Vine'
God, the Father, planted here'
Pruning, cleansing making
clear
All the way 'The Vine' would
grow.
We're the branches and
we know
All our life comes from
'The Vine'.

We remain within 'The Vine',
We cannot abide alone;
If with Jesus, we're at one,
We will bear for Him much fruit!
Branches have no living root
Isolated from 'The Vine'.

Branches of 'The Living Vine',
None can sever our accord,
We're united with the Lord!
Jesus said, Abide in Me,
I'll remain with you each day,
For your life is in 'The Vine'

Fruitful branches of
'The Vine',
His disciples we would be,
Learning how to grow each day
Fruit that ever will remain;
Love and joy and peace

our gain
As they ripen on 'The Vine'.

NO GREATER LOVE
Tune: *Vox Dilecti* D.C.M.
Chapter 15:9 – 17

The Lord said, There's
no greater love,
To give up all to be
Prepared to die that one
should live,
Denying self today.
Allow My joy to flood
your soul
Where heart and mind
shall meet
And in My own abounding joy,
Your joy will be complete.

You are My friends, I care
for you
With all the love of God;
I do not call you servants now
For friends will share
each load.
You did not choose Me as
your Lord,
For I have chosen you
And I appointed you to bear
Much fruit that will endure.

Whatever you may ask of Me
In keeping with My Name,

My Father will supply
that need;
It was for this I came!
Love one another deeply now
As I have loved you all;
Remain within My love for you,
This is My earnest call.

THE GIFT OF THE SPIRIT
Tune: *Nuttall* 6.4.6.4.6.6.6.4.
Chapter 16:1 –15

Come, Holy Spirit, come,
Keen Breath of Heav'n;
Come, gentle Spirit, come,
Calm as 'The Dove';
Bring us Your counsel, Lord,
Comfort and care, O God,
Grant us Your solace now,
Gift from 'Above'.

Life-giving Spirit, come,
Wafting from Heav'n;
Come, powerful Spirit, come,
Strong as 'The Wind'.
Grant us true courage, Lord,
Prove now Your promises;
We seek Your power, O Lord,
New strength to find.

Come, righteous Spirit, come,
Sent now from Heav'n;
Refining Spirit, come,

Come as 'The Fire';
Melt all the hardness, Lord,
Taking the dross from Earth,
Mould to Christ's likeness here,
As You desire.

Come, cleansing Spirit, come,
Outpoured from Heav'n.
Quench all our thirsting, come,
Make us anew;
Just as a river flows
Streaming so pure and free;
Cleanse us, refresh us, Lord,
In Your pure flow.

TRANSCENDENT JOY
Tune: *Easter Hymn* 7.7.7.7.
Chapter 16:16 – 33

Jesus, all transcendent joy,
Hallelujah!
We are freed from sin's alloy,
Hallelujah!
There'll be grief along life's way
But our strife will turn to joy—
He is with us all the way,
Hallelujah!

Jesus' soul-renewing joy,
Hallelujah:
Grants us peace nought can
destroy,
Hallelujah!
Present pain may yet disturb,
Sorrows may the soul perturb,

But our joy no ill can curb;
Hallelujah!

Jesus, life's abounding joy,
Hallelujah:
This is now our soul's employ,
Hallelujah!
None can take this joy from us,
No satanic evil ruse,
Nor can any fierce abuse,
Hallelujah!

Jesus' deep abiding joy,
Hallelujah:
There's no need to wonder
why;
Hallelujah!
What we ask Him, He will give;
In His Name we do believe
And our joy is full: we live!
Hallelujah!

INTERCESSION
Tune: *Lloyd* C.M.
Chapter 17

O Lord, You call us to this
place
Where we may share with You
The secrets of Eternity:
We seek Your face anew.

The mystery of cosmic grace
Has opened up to us
As with Your Father You

have prayed
That we may know
Your peace.

You pray for us before
God's throne
For You have loved Your own;
In You, we see His glory so
Our doubts are overthrown.

You pray for our protection in
A world where Truth
grows dim;
That truth may be revealed
as we
Would live at one with Him.

You prayed that we'd be
sanctified
By truth found in God's word;
You sanctified Yourself for us:
Let Christ be glorified!

GETHSEMANE
Tune: *Belmont* C.M.
Chapter 18:1 – 11

Gethsemane, the vale
of grief
Across dark Kidron's stream;
The ancient olive grove
allowed
No place to seek reprieve.

Gethsemane, the garden
where

Its fruit for oil was crushed;
How like the crushing of a soul
Weighed down with grievous
care.

Gethsemane, where moonlight
blends
With deepening **shadows**
there
For night has fallen on despair
To grip a heart that rends.

Gethsemane, where tears
like blood
Bare agony of soul
As death's own **shadow**
hovers near
To grieve the Son of God.

Gethsemane, the ground
of prayer
Where Jesus found the
strength
To vow God's will not Mine
be done!
The victory's won right there!

THE GARDEN
Tune: *Spohr* 8.6.8.6.8.6.
Chapter 18:1 – 11

A garden is a silent place
And one may enter here
To claim serenity of soul,
Absorb its beauties rare,

Aware the heart may speak
When knowing God
draws near.

A garden is a secret place
Where one may come to pray;
A sanctuary of quietness
To seek life's noble way
Yet fear the burdens it
may bring
And still God's will obey.

A garden is a sombre place
As winter's rain descends;
The flowers will flee when
grief comes in
But now, as prayer ascends,
And God's own balm restores
the soul,
The chill of 'loneness ends.

A garden is a sacred place
And perfume lingers there
When sorrow finds its
true repose
In joy that conquers care;
The soul receives its strength
to stand
In finding God is there.

Have I grieved my Lord today,
Does He turn to look on me
Silent in His sad regret?
Fire betrays my agony.

Chorus:
Have I pleased my Lord today,
Sought forgiveness for denial?
Now I see Him meet me here;
I know Jesus loves me now!

Have I harmed my Lord today,
Failed to witness to His worth,
Caused my steadfast faith
to wane?
Flickering flames depict
my dearth.

Have I pained my Lord today,
Do I own that I'm to blame,
Know remorse that
overwhelms?
Glowing coal unmasks
my shame.

Have I asked His help through
prayer?
Do I find Him standing by?
Will I stand with Him today?
Warming embers heal me now.

THE DENIAL
Tune: *Will Ye No Come Back
Again?* 7.7.7.7.
Chapter 18:12 – 27, Ch.21

WHAT IS TRUTH?
Tune: *Ten Thousand SoulS*
Chapter 18:28 – 40

You ask me what is truth
today?
Now look at Jesus Christ:
He is the answer for
our age,
He meets life's greatest test.
So, what is truth? You may
well ask!
The answer for life's test,
The proven principle of life,
Is found in Jesus Christ.

You query where is truth?
The way
Of truth is found in Him;
Christ has validity, His word
Will stand the test of time.
You ponder why truth is
so rare?
Depend on Christ; His ways
Reveal a faithfulness that lasts:
The constancy of grace.

You challenge how can faith
be found?
The Lord is genuine!
Integrity, fidelity,
Will ever be His sign.
You want to know the clearest
truth?
Observe the Christ; He is
The Ultimate Reality;
He leads to righteousness.

....

THE JUDGEMENT
Tune: *Come, Ye Thankful
People* 7.7.7.7. D.
Chapter 19:1 – 16

Jesus! Hail the King of kings!
Crown of thorns upon Your
head,
Splendid in Your royal robe!
Hail to Christ! The mockers
said:
Crucify Him, crucify!
I don't know the reason why
Scorn betrayed the judgement
scene;
Why was Christ condemned
to die?

Here's the 'Man born to
be King',
There's no basis in your
charge;
There's no evil in this Man!
Pilate judged by Rome's
cruel gauge:
Crucify Him! Crucify!
Priestly men from Temple's
height
Judged the Lord by subterfuge;
Christ would be condemned
to death!

Pilate cited power to judge
Whether one should die or live,
Yet he chose to take
Christ's side:

He's your King, allegiance give!
Crucify Him! Crucify!
Crowds defied the judge's cry;
Hatred hid the Truth from sight,
Christ was then condemned
to die.

Jesus! Hail the King of kings;
He is Lord and God's own Son!
Praise Him for His grace
and love:
Standing in our place, He won!
Crucified, once crucified,
Christ has conquered death's
dark day;
He has saved us from
sin's blight:
That's why He was called
to die!

THE VIA DOLOROSA

Tune: *Aberystwyth*   7.7.7.7. D.
Chapter 19:17 & The 4
Gospels

Hear the tramp of marching
feet
Down the Dolorosa Lane;
Crack of whips blaspheme
the Lord,
Bleeding back reveals His pain.

Chorus:

Jesus, Lord and Saviour now,
You can save this very hour

For You went to Calvary,
You were crucified for me!

Slow, that march on cobbled
stone,
Roman soldiers, by their law,
Ordered to obey its rules
And all agony ignore.

Thrusting back the frenzied
throng,
Guardsmen urged the Prisoner
on;
Stumbling, falling to the
ground,
Frail His frame, all strength
was gone.

Then a stranger, standing near,
Bent to Jesus and arose
Shouldering the fallen beam:
Wood to make a rugged cross.

Do not falter on this road,
Would you lift a cross
for Christ?
There's the cross He took
for you,
Follow Him to Calvary's crest.

THE CRUCIFIXION

Tune: *Norwood*   7.7.7.7.7.7.
Chapter 19:17 – 37

Golgotha, the 'Horror Hill',

Skull face shadowed in
the gloom;
Crowds are hushed for awe
has seeped
To their very heart. They'd
come
Witness to an abject scene
That would end within a tomb.

Calvary, the height of shame,
Garments gambled, sharing
gain;
Virtue done to death this day!
Who is this in mortal pain,
On a rugged cross impaled?
Would this Martyr die in vain?

Crucified on either side,
One held scorn, the law
decried,
But the other hope portrayed.
Prayer was heard and Christ
replied!
While there is a hope in
Heaven,
Pleading souls are not denied.

Nailed above that sacred head,
Read a sign, 'King of the Jews',
Added there, 'The Nazarene'.
Named just so, men hurled
abuse;
Those who loved Him knew
the truth—
They one day would spread

this news!

Love predominant that noon,
Faithful friends stood near
the Lord.
Jesus spoke from His
rude cross,
"It is finished!" Love outpoured
Had fulfilled Redemption's
Plan:
Death is vanquished: Praise
the Lord!

SHADOW OF DEATH
Tune: *Toplady* 7.7.7.7.7.7.
Chapter 19:17 – 37 & 3:16, 17

Darkness **shadowed** all the
Earth
When our Lord was crucified;
Day became the darkest night,
Nature sorrowed in the gloom:
Sun and moon retired
to grieve,
Veiled from the Eternal *LIGHT*.

Death had entered in this
scene,
Strident in its rampant might;
Purity was slaughtered here,
Righteousness was overthrown
By satanic powers unleashed:
Gone from us our Saviour dear.

Christ was taken to the cross,

Raised upon its awful frame;
Who selected such a death
For a Man so innocent?
Who willed Jesus Christ to die?
Who? The LORD of Heaven
and Earth!

God sent not His only Son
To the world there to condemn
Earth in every passing phase;
His great gift would save
the world!
Calvary was meant for me,
But, in grace, Christ took
my place.

When He cried, *Abba! It's
done!,*
Jesus knew accomplishment;
Satan would not claim this day;
Not the victor, death was done!
Never would it conqueror be,
Never dim God's radiant day!

CHRIST IS RISEN!
Tune: *Austria* 8.7.8.7. D.
Chapter 20

Rise the sun in radiant
splendour,
Clothe the sky in peerless blue,
Dress the world in shining
garments,
Celebrate a dawn that's new!
Never has there been rejoicing

Such as this that greets
the dawn;
Christ is risen, Hallelujah!
All the world has been reborn!

Claim the dawn! It's light
resplendent
Greets the valley of despair
Where a garden, lovely garden,
Waits its glorious news
to share.
Rock is rending, burst asunder,
Death cannot its Victim hold:
Christ is risen! Hallelujah!
All the world sees joy unfold.

Morning breaks on visions
splendid,
Glowing colours paint
the Earth;
A new day has dawned
upon us,
Day of grace, the day for faith!
Hope has come that knows
no ending,
Knowledge of Eternity.
Christ has risen! Hallelujah!
All the world may now go free!

GLORIOUS, THE
MORNING *LIGHT*
Tune: *Will Ye No' Come Back
Again?* 7.7.7.7. D.
Chapter 20

Glorious is the morning *LIGHT*,
Rising sun with golden glow,
Dew on garden shining bright;
Here is wondrous life today.

Chorus:

Hallelujah! Jesus lives!
From the grave He rose
in power;
Hallelujah, Jesus gives
Hope for all eternity!

See, the great stone slab
is rent,
Where's the precious body
now?
Grave clothes cast, their need
is spent,
Neatly folded in the Tomb.

Angels in bright garments said,
Christ the Lord is risen indeed!
Why then search among
the dead?
Jesus lives! He conquered
death!

When alert to this Good news,
Those who knew Him would
rejoice!
Faith has come: Christ heals
our woes,
Joyful hearts will sing
His praise!

....

GOOD NEWS!
Tune: *Saved by Grace* C.M.
Chapter 20

The news is out! The lord
is raised!
Yes, Jesus lives today!
He came to us, He walks
with us,
He gives us hope today!

The news is great! The Lord's
alive,
He left the tomb today!
In tender love, He brings
His peace
And near us He will stay.

The news is true, Christ
Jesus lives!
He walks our road today
Our needs are met and
burdens eased,
He's with us all the way.

This news is yours so trust
Him now,
The Lord gives life today!
Believe His word and be
set free
To live for Him each day.

PEACE BE WITH YOU
Tune: *Saved by Grace* C.M.
John 20:19 – 29

He came to them in twilight
hour,
His radiance filled the room
with *LIGHT*;
When Jesus stood among
His friends,
He spoke His blessing to
each heart.

Chorus:
Let peace be yours as dawn
returns
And peace attend the noonday
heat;
May peace remain in evening
hours,
My peace surround you
through the night..

Their fears were great, they'd
hid from view;
Christ knew His friends, their
deepest plight;
The doors were locked yet
here He was;
He stood with them, His
wounds in sight!

Receive My Spirit, Jesus said;
As I was sent, I send alike.
He breathed on them the
breath of God;
His Spirit gave them strength
that night.

As joy erupted in the room,

Their faith returned, their fears
took flight;
The Lord commissioned them
to spread
Good News: Go now, reveal
God's LIGHT!

DO YOU LOVE ME?
Tune: *Blessed Assurance*
Chapter 21

Come from your toiling, in from
the sea,
Come and now bring the gifts
that you bear;
Come from your trials, the
waves of despair,
Come to Me, rest, unburden
your care.

Chorus:
You know I love you, Lord
You can tell
I am Your friend and I'll walk
with You;
Be my Companion down
the long years,
Guide me each day till
Heaven's in view.

Say, do you love Me more than
all these—
Things that would bind you
close to the Earth?
Love has its reasons where

e'er it's cast;
What are your values, what is
of worth?

Share all your longings as we
converse,
I have supplied your needs for
the day;
Share with Me now your aims
and desires;
Do you intend My word
to obey?

Stir up the coals, rekindle
the flame,
Find your vocation, pastor
My sheep,
Shepherd My lambs, they're
going astray;
Lead them to safety. the path
is steep.

You're My disciples, learning
from Me,
Finding your faith in God's
precious word;
Time has now come to share
what you've seen,
Time for declaring what you
have heard.

GOD'S WORD

Tune: *He Leadeth Me*   L.M.
Chapter 20:30 – 31, 21:24 – 25

The Bible is a testament,

A written record of the Lord,
Explaining why the Christ
was sent;
From the beginning, Son
of God.

Chorus:
The written records of our Lord
Are given so we could believe
His word, the testament to God
And all His promises receive.

The sacred Script sets down
His worth
For Jesus Christ has truth
displayed
By word and deed, His
gracious life
The splendid *LIGHT* of God
conveyed.

The Scriptures say Christ is
'The Word'!
As words express our deepest
thought,
Our Lord revealed the Mind
of God
In all the precious truths
He taught.

The prophets in the past
revealed
That He would come,
the Christ of God;

The Truth of God no longer
sealed,
The faithful sing: He is
the Lord!

THE EAGLE
Tune: *Lloyd* C.M.
The Gospel of John

Lord, lift me up on eagle's
wings,
Above Earth's binding care;
You carry me, encourage me,
Within the realm of prayer.

You stir my soul, entreat
me now
Far greater heights to dare;
You challenge me to trust
Your grace
In the abode of prayer.

I hear Your words of Life,
dear Lord,

Oh, lead me now to where
Your Spirit breath restores
the soul
as I engage in prayer.

Released to soar on wings
of joy,
Into the heights so rare;
Your Holy Spirit bears me up,
Up to the Light in prayer.

Transcending earthly sight
and sound,
Of hallowed peace aware;
My utmost aim to seek
Your Face;
Commune with You in prayer.

Descending from the heights
sublime,
The daily task to bear,
I claim the strength imparted in
This sacred hour of prayer.

THE NEW DAWN

Greeting The New Dawn

THE NEW BEGINNING

Wonderful, God's mighty power, dawning light on Earth's first hour!
His great Spirit breathed upon ocean depths and life was born.
Holy Spirit, breathe on me, make me all I ought to be;
For my **darkness** shine Your *LIGHT*, for my weakness grant Your might.

Awesome is the Spirit's power! Through the years at every hour,
Breathing insights of the LORD as recorded in God's word.
Energising, holy power, strength is given for the hour.
In God's time His Spirit came bearing Pentecostal *LIGHT*.

Life transforming, Spirit power, make me ready for this hour;
Holy Spirit, move in me, fit me for Eternity.
Holy Spirit, breathe in me, More like Jesus I would be;
In the **darkness** shine as *LIGHT*, for my blindness grant insight.

SHADOWS AND THE LIGHT

A COMPANION TO THE BIBLE
—EYE-WITNESS TESTIMONIES—

BOOK THREE
PART TWO: THE CHRISTIAN CHURCH

THE PROCLAIMERS AND THEIR PROGRAM

Open Road Into All The World

Lucille L. Turfrey

THE TRAVELLING YEARS

THE ACTS OF THE APOSTLES

BIRTH OF THE CHRISTIAN CHURCH

Luke

Circa AD 63

My Dear Theophilus,

I've taken up my pen again for there is much to say of what eventuated from the death and resurrection of *Yeshua*–Jesus, the Saviour, Messiah: known in Greek, as *Christos*–Christ.

Your response to the Gospel that bears my name encourages me to provide you now with the on-going story of the King born to be Man. My second volume, therefore, leads on from what Jesus began to do and teach into the ministry of the Apostles (*the 'sent' ones*) and the establishment of the Christian Church.

Many have asked the question as to who 'Luke' really is. It must be said that I am mentioned on three occasions only in the entire Scriptures—not much on which to stake my claim to provide you with the *bone fide* story of Christ. But surely, it's enough to say that the great apostle Paul refers to me as "Luke, the beloved physician." When others abandoned him, I remained Paul's travelling companion and personal doctor, tending his wounds and worries.

I stand in a strategic position in the recording of the testimonies of those who knew Christ personally (I will often use the Greek rendition of His name).

I am writing to you and to the Gentile world at large in recording all the many testimonies regarding the faith occurring through these earliest years. There are also instances of some wrongful conduct by many who conspired to put a halt to all the happenings proceeding from that most memorable Passover Feast in Jerusalem.

Not the least of these was Saul of Tarsus who, transformed, became the great St Paul. I now commence my task with the aid of those who will testify to the events that gave rise to the Early Church, first called Christians at Antioch:

LUKE TO THEOPHILUS
Chapter 1

You've read, within
my previous account,
the records of what Christ
began to do and teach.
And then, of course, the
matchless story of His
death and resurrection and
the day when He ascended
into Heaven. Those forty
days He shared with all His
followers were rare, unique,
as He appeared to them
to reinforce eternal life.

Yeshua promised that, quite
soon, the Holy Spirit would
descend, would come to
make of weakness strength,
to grant them courage for
the task, to fill their hearts
with peace profound, to give
them reason for their faith.

He said to them:

*You will receive new power
after the Holy Spirit comes
and you will be My
witnesses for you will testify
of Me within Jerusalem and
then Samaria and to the
ends of Earth.*

His Team observed the Lord
ascending into Heaven and,
as the clouds obscured the
scene, two white-robed men
stood by their side.
Oh men of Galilee, they
said, why do you stare into
the heavens? You've seen
Yeshua–Jesus ascend but,
someday, He'll return to
Earth the self-same way
as seen today!

PETER
Chapter 1:12 – 26

Since our return from Olivet
it's right that we should
meet within this upstairs
room. We're all together
here and plans must be
in place for future
witnessing unto the faith we
hold in *Yeshua*–Jesus, our
Lord. And let us be at

prayer for by this means,
we'll find the strength
for what is yet to be.

The final steps of Judas
Iscariot to slay Messiah
can't be erased but we have
need to choose a man to
take his place, to be
prepared! Justus and
Matthias will now stand
and we'll decide, after
some prayer…The lot is
cast… Results assessed:

JESUS' MOTHER, MARY
Chapter 2:1 – 41

Matthias is the man!
All things are now made
new! He promised us before
His own farewell that
Heaven's power
would fall on us. His Holy
spirit came to us, and He
transformed the weak,
that we would be inbreathed
just as the Eden's dawn,
invigorated by
the Breath that God alone
imparts: the Spirit, Holy
Spirit, came. He breathed
in us. Yes, all the faithful

waited there: the men, the
women too—there's no
exclusions when the Spirit
comes to grant His power—
there is a ministry for ALL
His followers! It was a
wondrous hour!

There was a rushing, mighty
wind and fiery tongues split
into speech that alien ears
could hear and understand.
The Gospel is for ALL!
Those walls could not
contain our joy. We sped
into the streets (yes, me as
well at my great age!) The
news was out! the Lord
spoke through us there.

Then someone queried what
was going on: How come
I hear this News in my own
language, here? I found that
I could speak the Gospel
News myself!

Then Peter stood right up;
he spoke so well, explaining
that what all the people saw
was not our drunkenness!
It's what the prophet Joel
declared those
many years ago: The
YHVH–LORD will pour

His Spirit on your sons and daughters, who'll proclaim the Gospel and your young men will see visions, older men will dream new dreams. Great miracles will then occur over the skies and wonders in the Earth below… Whoever will request His help, the *YHVH*–LORD will save! Now, hear God's word, the Gospel News: Each one must turn to Him to be forgiven of your sins. Before the day was done, three thousand souls came to believe in my dear Son!

THE COMMUNITY OF FAITH
Chapter 2: 42 – 47

Come, mingle and enjoy our fellowship; we are the new Community of Faith.
Our lives have been transformed because of the Immortal One who came to live as one of us, to suffer death for us. And now He lives again! He is the resurrected *Yeshua*–Jesus, the Christ, the Son of God who came to set us free from sin! Oh yes, we live together in community. We gain instruction from the team who shared His earthly ministry. Ours is indeed a happy fellowship, we've learned to share our meals and means, helping the poor. What's more, we share in prayer and this is more than bread!

THE BEGGAR
Chapter 3:1 – 26, 4:1 – 22

I've sat before this gate for years to rake in pennies, ruing there's no pounds. How many years? I cannot tell but this I know, it has been 'hell'. There's been no strength in hands, or arms, or legs—until today, that is!

All things have changed for me! I asked that man I asked that man (a friend he's been of *Yeshua,* the Nazarene,) for just a coin or two to help me with the simple needs of life. He said, I have no silver and no gold but what I have, I give

to you: In *Yeshua*–Jesus'
Name: rise, walk! I felt it
right away–what faith can
do! A flow of feeling surged
all through my arms, my
legs. I stood right up and
then, I walked! Oh yes, I
could have laughed at those
who stared! They knew
that I had sat at this Gate
Beautiful those many years.

No! They could not believe
what they now saw. The
man, named Peter, by the
way, stood to explain that it
was done because the God
of Abraham had intervened
by sending the Messiah to
save. Though you rejected
Him! Yes, He was crucified
because of you. Receive this
news: He lives today.
By Him, this man is healed!
Repent. Believe in Him!
Take hold of faith...
And then they came, those
Temple guards, to take Peter
and John—
his friend—by force.
They were arrested, placed
in stocks because of what
was done to me!

Ridiculous! How dare

they treat these men with
haughty disrespect?

All this had happened
yesterday. I am informed
that both the men were
brought before the
Council—that is, the
Sanhedrin—where they
were there interrogated by
Annas, Caiaphas and the
rest of them. It was
reported that Peter then
stood to say what they were
loath to hear although they
knew it was the truth.

They were the men who
claimed the Christ was
guilty of horrific crimes
though innocent. They were
reminded of the Scriptures
relevant to the Messiah's
sacrificial death.
The climax of the case was
reached as Peter said, You

all should know that this
man stood before you
healed through all the power
of *Yeshua*, the Nazarene: the
One you crucified and
Whom God raised from
death. You will recall the
prophet's words:

'The Stone the builders did
reject turned out to be the
chief stone, Cornerstone:
the most important of them
all!' You need to know:
salvation is now found in
Yeshua alone." It was with
joy I heard the Sanhedrin
was much amazed at these
unlearned men. They
realised the Truth they held
came from the Christ.

The judges chose to set both
free but counselled them
to silence on the subject of
the Lord, Messiah! The men
rejected this and said to
them: You judge
yourselves: what is the right
in God's own sight—
obeying Him or what you
ask? They then walked free
from court! And me? Well,
after forty years, I'd like to
dance the streets today!

SAPPHIRA
Chapter 5:1 – 11

**My husband and myself
had joined with the
Community of Faith. We
are more 'moneyed' than
the rest and like to fling
our funds about. You see,
we have aspired to take
command before too long.
We bide our time. Now,
something has come up;
there is a need for
diligence in caring for the
poor, bereaved and
handicapped. We talked
between ourselves, you
understand, Ananias and
myself. We have this
property; it's not
required. We'd put it on
the market, take as much
as we could get for it.**

**We'd keep some proceeds
for ourselves of course,
but then the greater
portion shall be placed
within 'the purse' of the
Community of Faith. We
gathered up a mighty
price for it and most went
in that purse. Then we
were roundly thanked for
were roundly thanked for
such great generosity.
But Peter challenged my
dear one. It does appear
he saw right through our
ruse. Why did you both**

conspire to lie to God?
The funds
you earned were yours
and you were free to
portion out the proceeds.
Why did you lie about
your gift?
'The wages of all sin is
death...' I heard it all and
smitten with regret for
him but still persisting in
the lie, I heard the same
remark. I'll die...

THE HIGH PRIEST
Chapter 5:12 – 42

This really has to stop!
Now Solomon's own Porch
is being defiled. The people
gathered here all claim to
be transformed. What's
more, they give allegiance:
their pennies and their
praise to that dead
Nazarene. It has to stop!

We'll lose control of all
Jerusalem and all the
people too... How very
laughable, they're laying
all the sick in line on mats
so that the shadow of the
Galilean fisherman might

fall on them. There's
something going on that I
don't understand. Surely
there is no magic in their
hands. I don't approve.
It's time that all the men
in charge of that
Community of 'so-called'
Faith are placed in gaol...

I don't believe the gates
just swung apart.
Somebody had the keys!
They have escaped!
They're in the Temple
now. Interrogate the
guards. What's that? The
gates are closed but
there's no one inside? Be
circumspect! The people
will revolt if we hurt hide
or hair of them. But bring
them here.

The Sanhedrin is in place.
So, let the case begin.
These men appeared to
hold no fear as they
outlined their quaint
response to questioning.

We will obey the Lord, not
what you would demand.
The *YHVH*–LORD has
raised *Yeshua*–Jesus up

from death. You killed Him;
had Him nailed upon a
cross. Death could not hold
the King born to be Man.
The LORD has used your
most ignoble deeds
to grant to Israel the
opportunity to seek Him and
to have their sins forgiven.
And now we have received
power from 'Above'. The
Holy Spirit guards and
surely guides us now.
We are His witnesses!

**We knew a fury then!
These men, these upstarts,
unlearned Galileans were
preaching to the powerful.
Let's do away with them!
Kill them! First, we'll
listen to Gamaliel, he
speaks sound wisdom yet.
Perhaps he's right… So!
flog them all and warn
them once again to hold
their livid tongues.
We'll have no more
preaching or that
prattling! Just look at
them! The welts upon
their wounded backs,
the blood. But they seem
happy men; they find
themselves to be made**

**worthy men for Jesus'
sake. I like it not! It is
by no means yet, the
end of this, the new
'Community of Faith'!**

STEPHEN
Chapters 6:8 — 7:60

I have been richly blessed
by God! I know the surge of
Holy Spirit power course
through my heart and soul.
My seven friends and I are
privileged men for we've
been asked to shoulder the
responsibility of caring for
the poor. The distribution of
the funds was in our care.
The Lord had said
that he who would be great
would be the one called into
servanthood.
Amazing though it seems,
I have been energised to
bring about some
miracles among us too.

Now, some disputes have
broken out and lies were
told to the effect I'd
slandered Moses, even God!
The outcome was arrest and
gaol. The Sanhedrin sat to

judge my case. Oh, I was
given opportunity to prove
my innocence. I doubt if
they could change their
minds though I have
outlined, via the word of
God—at great depth—
all the history
of Israel up to this time.

I chose to climax all that I
had quoted there by rightly
laying blame to the
adversaries that challenged
me: You stubborn men!
Your hearts are hard.
You're like your ancestors.
Was there any prophet who
escaped your vitriol, your
hate, your crime? To cap it
all, you sentenced Christ to
death, rejoiced that He was
crucified! You are the men
who have received God's
Law: you mangled it!

I saw their wrath and heard
it all—their hate, their fury,
anger's heat. I raised my
eyes to see, with joy,
a vision of the *YHVH*–
LORD and there, beside
Him, was *Yeshua*–Jesus,
The Christ.
Look! I see all Heaven

opened to my eyes: the Son
of Man is at God's own
right hand in Heaven!

The Sanhedrin was
scandalised! They rushed at
me, they pulled me forth
and cast me from the city
gates. The stones begin their
dread assault:
Lord, now receive me and
don't lay a blame on hem—
they do not understand...

SAUL OF TARSUS
Chapter 8:1 – 25

**I'm still quite young, a
student yet—Gamaliel, the
doyen of Israel's rabbis—
is my mentor, tutor,
patron too. He holds great
wisdom it is true–perhaps
too much at times! He
turned the tide most
recently and then those
Galilean fishermen
were freed at once.
Not so today! I'm not
surprised. None could
abide the blatant words,
the blasphemy, cast on our
great Sanhedrin sage—
Our Caiaphas and his**

Dad, Annas. I've followed
all the throng. I am so
furious at how the Law—
the Holy Law—was
flouted in the court. These
stones will find their
mark. I am required to
stand close by to guard
the gowns of those
who bring that outlaw
down—I'd fling a stone
or two myself!

You can mark it well, this
day! It was from this time
on that all who testified
the vanquished Nazarene
had left the opened tomb
miraculously, that some
persecution broke out.
We found them easily.
They did not cease their
wilful words or ways.

We threw as many as we
could into the
overcrowded gaols. I'm
proud to say I dragged a
few to gaol myself. You
see, we knew that this
'Community of Faith'
must, at all costs, be
destroyed at once.

They scattered

everywhere but, as they
went, those would-be
preachers testified and
wrought their miracles.
How strange—the more
the trouble, there were
more in number who
professed their faith in
Yeshua–Jesus. Samaria
became involved. I heard
that Peter and his good pal
John then went to
organise a new commune.

Of course, they preached;
the groups burgeoned. It's
getting out of hand! I'm
on my way up to
Damascus and I'm
breathing fire and fumes
on them the while. There's
more of that anon!

THE ETHIOPIAN
Chapter 8:26 – 40

I was returning from
Jerusalem. A eunuch, I'm
the Queen of Ethiopia's
treasurer. I had important
matters to convey but,
most of all, I also found
an opportunity to worship
God. I have some

knowledge of the Faith
of Israel and have a copy
of Isaiah's scroll. As my
chariot did rock and roll
across the desert sands,
I wondered at
these most amazing words
I read: This Man was like
a sheep, so silent as the
slaughterers took hold of
Him. He was abused,
denied fair trial. His life
has been cut off...

Now, this is strange: there is
a man approaching near my
chariot. He's out of place in
desert sands! The reins were
pulled, the horse
stood quiet. The stranger
introduced himself as
Philip. He then remarked
that he had heard me
reading from the scroll a
famous passage from
the Jewish prophet, Isaiah.

I asked, Do you know what
these words could mean? Of
whom does Isaiah speak—
himself, or is
it someone else?
And then, he told me all!
Beginning with Isaiah's

words, he then declared:
Isaiah refers, in prophecy,
to One I know so well. Yes!
Yeshua–Jesus the Nazarene;
once dead but now most
gloriously alive! I asked my
questions, he complied!
The chariot was stilled.
I said, There is an oasis
nearby, may I be baptised
there? When this was done,
Philip departed and I went
upon my way with
overwhelming joy: This
Gospel will be preached
in far-off Ethiopia!

SAUL OF TARSUS
Acts 9:1 – 6

I'm flabbergasted! Blind!
I'm utterly bowed down!
Well on my way to cleanse
the Earth of every stain left
by 'The Nazarene',
Damascus was my aim.
I carried documents which
gave me right to smite His
followers and plunge them
into gaol or stocks or other
means that pains me to
repeat! His strike was
sudden and the power
of *LIGHT* had stopped me

in my tracks. That Light
was luminous within my
shattered brain: it did appear
as though in human form
and, yet, divine for here was
LIGHT that shone into the
darkness of my soul. I had
been hurtling headlong
toward Damascus with a
murderous intent.

But now the hate was gone!
What's this I feel? Though I
am blind, I *see* what I have
been! I know what I must
do. Who are You, Lord?

I am Yeshua–Jesus: You've
persecuted all My followers,
What will you do with Me?

O Lord,
lead me from my **darkness**
into *LIGHT*!

THE CHALLENGE
Chapter 9:5 – 6
(Tune: *Harton-Lea* L.M.)

'Come, follow Me today,'
Christ said;

'Come, walk the path that
leads to life;
You'll share Good News
and work with Me
Now live your faith,
make known belief.'

'Come, follow Me,' the
Saviour called.
'What is your aim, to live
or die?
Think not of cost to find
life's best;
Take courage, all your
fears defy.'

'Come, follow Me,' the
Saviour's plea;
'Come, walk with Me,
observe My way
And share with Me life's
heavy load;
Trust Me to guide you
every day.'

'Come, follow Me,' the
Saviour urged;
Take heart, trust Me, do not
delay.
Act now to live the faith
you've found;
What is your goal?
Decide today!'

'Come, follow Me,' the
Saviour says;
'Come with Me now, your
name is called!

Come, take your cross and
walk My road,
Reveal My love to all the
world.'

ANANIAS
Chapter 9:10 –19

He spoke to me! I should
not be surprised but there I
was, at prayer when all
turned 'up-side-down' for
me. I heard my name. "O,
here I am, Lord." "So, get
ready now and go on down
to Straight Street in the
centre of Damascus. You
will find—in Juda's house,
a man named Saul of
Tarsus. He is at prayer.
He knows that you will
come to him." "O Lord, ask
what You will of me except
that I should meet this man!
He's murdering Your
followers. I am afraid.
He's authorised to do
away with us!"

*Go to him, Ananias, for I've
selected him to introduce
Me to the Gentile world
He'll suffer much for he's
prepared to serve Me whole,
throughout the years to come.*

I WENT!

My brother, Saul, (did I say
that)? The Lord has sent me
so you may regain your
sight, receive the Holy
Spirit of the *YHVH*–LORD.
How very strange! Some
scales fell from his eyes. He
looked at me with sight
renewed (and *in*sight too);
He'd come from
darkness into *LIGHT*!

A BELIEVER
Chapter 9:19 – 25

He came into the room.
We'd all been so afraid of
him. Look at him now,
this Saul of Tarsus: if this is
what the Lord can do, I'll
serve Him all my days!
I am amazed. He speaks
of *Yeshua*–Jesus with joy.
He went down to the
synagogue. He spoke with
power and so much so that
some of the Jews conspired
to kill the man. They set a
constant guard upon the
City Gates to apprehend the
'new-made' man of God!
We of The Faith determined

to allow Saul to escape. One night, we placed him in a basket and secured some ropes to ease the basket down by the Damascus walls. He has escaped!

THE COMMUNITY OF FAITH
Chapter 9:26 – 31

There's many stories thrown about that Saul of Tarsus— yes, that man who studied at the feet of old Gamaliel— has now returned into Jerusalem. It has been said he's had a 'turn-about'. We can't believe this news for, can a leopard change its spots? We live in fear of him; we cannot welcome him. Then, could you believe, our good friend Barnabas stepped in…

BARNABAS
Chapter 9:27 – 30
Excuse me for this interruption but I have some news for you. This man you know as 'Saul the Slayer' is no more—that is, he is a new man: born again.

He's seen the *LIGHT*! He had been blinded by the awesome *LIGHT* who met him on his way to foreclose all our operations in Damascus. He met with *Yeshua*–Jesus on the road. His **darkness** turned to *LIGHT!*

He's now Christ's man. He's boldly preached among the Community of Faith within that town. We must allow him now to preach and teach us as the Lord requires of him. If there is trouble we'll secure his safety and ensure his swift return to Tarsus until all peace has been restored.

PETER
Chapter 9:32 – 43

Who would have thought there'd be another turning point in the great saga of these glorious years when we—the students of *Yeshua*–Jesus became apostles (yes, 'sent' ones). We are ambassadors to take the Gospel to the world. I must admit that I believed

the world belonged to Jews!
We placed ourselves in
the front line to boldly
speak of life abundant
through His Name.
Jerusalem was in turmoil.
We'd been incarcerated,
exonerated, warned and
watched. We lost Stephen!
And then there was that
weird event as Saul of
Tarsus (who had vowed,
declared he'd wipe out
every trace of us), became
reborn! He's one of us!
Magnificent! We've come
to terms with all his news
and finally arranged escape
to save his life.

I've come to Joppa by the
sea. My journey was via
Lydda where Aeneas was
revitalised by faith in
Yeshua, our Risen Lord.
Upon my entry to Joppa, I
met Tabitha (known as
Dorcas by her friends). Here
was a gracious woman of
good works who suddenly
fell ill and died. The news
about Aeneas at Lydda had
compelled her friends to ask
that I would come to pray a
miracle for her. I came.

Through faith, I found
the strength to say, Tabitha,
stand upon your feet! The
grace of God is great! I
called her friends and we
rejoiced to see she was
renewed: she lived!

I stayed for many days at
Simon's house. You may
not think this was
significant but barriers were
breaking down. How so?
Here's Simon Peter now
residing with Simon, the
tanner—he treated hides
of tainted animals!
Unclean! Unclean!
We broke the rules of
Judaism. Wake up, before
it is too late: there are some
bridges that are much too
far to cross. I should not
break the rules so sacrosanct
throughout our history.
I must be true!

CORNELIUS
Chapter 10

My story must be told.
You'll find it quite amazing
for I don't sit rightly in the
Jewish frame of references!
I am a Roman officer but,

surprisingly, I do believe
in *YHVH*–LORD. I've tried
my best to take good care of
Jews within this Caesarean
community. I was at prayer
one afternoon when I
received a heavenly visitor.
An angel spoke with me!
The LORD is pleased with
what you do. He is about to
answer your requests. It is
imperative that you and two
cohorts now journey down
to Joppa and seek out
a man known well as Simon
Peter—You'll be guided
all the way.

PETER
Chapter 10 – 11

At Simon's house in Joppa,
I had found it quite
conducive to my prayers to
go up to the roof, all flat,
look out across the sea and
here to contemplate the
vastness of God's love for
you and me. In staying there
to meditate so long, I
needed food but fell into a
trance, I think, or was it but
a dream? It floated in above
the sea, a massive sheet

from far away, held at
the North, the East, the
West, the South, containing
every kind of unclean beast
the world could offer
anyone—from snakes
to jungle beasts!

Arise, come Peter,
kill and eat!

O no, Lord! Never those. I'd
rather starve! No unclean
meat that is defiled will
ever pass my lips. Please
do not ask!

Peter, do not presume to
name 'unclean' what God
has cleansed!

Three times, the vision
challenged me! What could
it mean? I was confused.
The Holy Spirit spoke again
to me:

An angel has directed
Gentiles to visit you. They
are downstairs awaiting
you. Each are in need of
guidance. You can help.
You'll find they love the
Lord. They need to hear the
Gospel. What will you do?

The men were then invited

in to come and sit with me.
We talked the night away!
Next day, I packed my bags
and headed north to
Caesarea with my new
friends, Cornelius and
cohorts. I entered in.

At last I understood the
meaning of that vision by
the sea. At last I see the
truth that God will have no
favourites: He treats all
people as equal despite the
race and colour of the skin.
What He requires of all
is faithfulness. All people
have an equal right to
share the peace of Jesus.

The Holy Spirit came upon
all those with whom I
spoke—my Jewish
company and Gentiles too
were fully blessed. All were
received as 'Family': those
of Faith in Christ!

I then went back into
Jerusalem to share all this
amazing news. There was
some criticism but when all
had heard the details of the
vision and the challenge,
how I came to realise how

great the grace of God—
He treats us all alike—
the matter was resolved!
We are the 'Family of God'
through faith in *Yeshua*,
the Christ. The praises then
rang out: all Gentiles share
the right to voice their faith
in God and live for Him!

BARNABAS
Chapter 11:

When persecution troubled
all the faithful in Judea, it
seemed advisable to move
away from all the threats
for there was danger
everywhere. Some of the
Community of Faith went
all the way to Antioch and
there proclaimed the Gospel
News. Great power was
evident. There was an
avalanche of people who
believed. Much help was
needed so I was dispatched
northward to Antioch.

The work progressed apace.
I knew I needed aid to
manage all that was
occurring there. I thought of
Saul, so promptly went to
Tarsus and he needed no

encouragement! He came at
once with me forthwith to
Antioch where we observed
Agabus who prophesied a
famine would afflict the
world. The disciples
understood the truth of it
and knew they must make
plans to help all the
believers in Judea. Just so,
a 'Social Service' ministry
began as Saul and I
distributed the funds
where needed most.

RHODA
Chapter 12

Some drastic things were
happening. King Herod had
James, John's brother,
killed. Because it pleased
the populace, he then
arranged for Peter to be
gaoled in preparation for
Passover, so to be tried, then
hung (or something worse!)
But we were praying for
Peter! All the Community
of Faith besought the Lord
for his release.

We have the story now of
how Peter was wakened in
the night. Between his
guards, he had no room to
move. Yet there he was, an
angel straight from Heaven!
"Peter, get up!" His chains
fell off! "Put on your cloak
and come with me." Peter
obeyed but thought he
dreamed and walked in
sleep! I must confess, I got
a shock! You see,
we all were praying at John
Mark's house for deliverance.

There was a knock upon
the outer door. I went
to see just who had called so
late. I opened up the door
and slammed it back again!
I thought I saw Peter there!
He'd smiled at me! I nearly
fainted with the shock of it!
I ran back in the house with
this amazing news (I left
poor Peter standing at
the outer door).
You must be crazy, girl!
He's in the gaol. Oh, no!
He's not! Alas, he must be
dead! It's his own angel at
the door, they said.

Meanwhile, Peter kept on
tapping at the door. At last
we opened it. Then
everyone was so amazed.

Hush now, let all be quiet.
Go back to James—the
Lord's brother—explaining
my release. I am departing
now to ease your strain.
But, can you learn to
exercise more faith? True
prayer will bring results.

King Herod Antipas was
furious when all the news
seeped out. He had those
guards all put to death!
Then he began to strut about
as though he owned all
things. He made a speech—
he'd donned his robes,
sceptre and crown, I hear,
but he was struck mid-
speech. He died that day.
But! We live on!
The number of the followers
expands as the Gospel News
spreads on through all
the land.

MANAEN
Chapter 13

You wonder who on Earth
I am? There is no doubt
you'd rack your brains
without result for I
am mentioned just this once
in all of Scripture for, you
see, my *persona* is most
tenuous. I'll dare to say
it here! My name is
Manaen. I grew up in the
palace with young Herod
Antipas. I learned
my lessons at his side.
There was no friendship
forged between
us two—he'd wear the
crown, I guessed that I
would polish up his boots!
However, praise the Lord,
I broke quite free of him
and now I do rejoice for I
am now accepted in the
Community of Faith!

I met within the group
that prayed as they
commissioned Saul and
Barnabas to go, fulfil the
work to which they had
been called: to take the
gospel to the Gentile world.
The Holy Spirit is
empowering them as they
take ship to Cyprus to
commence what is reported
as the First Missionary
Journey to the wider Gentile
world. John Mark is at
their side. Oh, what
a team they make!

JOHN MARK
Chapter 13

It was indeed a privilege to
sail in company with Saul
and Uncle Barnabas. We're
on a journey with a mission
to fulfil. We had begun the
work on Cyprus Isle,
an ideal starting place. We
did encounter trouble with a
sorcerer, Elymas, but found
a true friend in the Roman
Proconsul, Sergius Paulus
who, when he observed the
power so evident in Saul
and Uncle Barnabas,
requested that he interview
them, listening with due
respect then taking to
himself the Faith we hold.

He believed, in Greek
parlance, in *Christos*, the
Anointed One! Yes, Jesus
Christ! He became a notable
convert. Saul of Tarsus,
a free-born citizen of Rome
(though Jewish to the core,)
became known to us all as
'Paul'. This was the Roman
version of his name. It fitted
best within the wider world.
Also, he was so well
respected everywhere

that he became accepted as
the leader of our company.

Things had become quite
tense when I decided that a
journey home would ease
my yearning for my family.
You'll understand, I hope,
because I am quite young—
I'm barely out of teens. I am
so immature. The going had
been tough at times. I felt I
needed some respite. But I
am sorry to report that Paul
is not impressed. Yet I'll
go home, for just a while,
I hope they will agree!

BARNABAS
Chapters 13 – 14

Saul… Paul… When will
I find an ease in
'Romanising' Saul? But it
is right! It's understood—
as Jewish as he is–that Paul
is recognised as a free-man
for he can walk with ease in
any company throughout the
Gentile world. As I was just
about to say to you,
now that our Paul has full
responsibility for the
planning and for organising

everything, I've time
to make some notes:

My nephew Mark departed
at Perga in Pamphylia and
we journeyed on to Antioch
in Pisidia where leaders of
the synagogue invited us
to speak. Paul did so well,
outlining all the history of
Israel right up to John
the Baptist's ministry. Paul
then launched in with power
to speak of *Yeshua,* the
Christ (you have become
familiar with this term—
Christos, Anointed One, the
Greek form of Messiah).
Paul spoke of God's
Redemption Plan:
achieved on Calvary,
ratified at the open tomb,
activated by the Holy
Spirit's Power.

Paul then announced to all:
We are His witnesses. We
come to you to share the
Gospel News as God had
promised to our ancestors.
As we departed from the
synagogue, the people
pleaded that we come again
next Sabbath Day to speak.
The following Sabbath Day,

near to everyone turned up
to hear our witnessing.
The Gentiles were in the
majority within the
company and so much
so that all the Jews became
quite envious! Insults were
flung about and angry
words disgorged! The
situation here demanded
that we speak more boldly
and, at last, Paul said:
It was most necessary that
we came at first to speak
with you, the Jews, but you
rejected us. Therefore do
not consider that you're
worthy of the Life
Abundant *Yeshua* imparts.
We turn from you to heed
God's words:

*I have prepared you to
become a light to shine
upon the Gentiles so the
whole world may be saved.*

With these 'landmark'
words in mind, we turn now
to the Gentile world.
The situation showed itself
to be quite similar in
Iconium. At first, both Jews
and Gentiles listened gladly
to the Gospel News.

Some Jews who had
rejected all
our witnessing, stirred up
the Gentile crowd. But we
remained, did not curtail our
ministry. Some citizens
were for us, others were
against. So, finally, a group
of Jews and Gentiles too,
conspired to do away with
us. They planned to pick up
stones and fling them in our
face. We found it
circumspect to leave and go
on into Lystra, Derbe and
surrounding territories
to share the Word.

At Lystra, things got out
of hand when Paul
commanded that a crippled
man stand to his feet.
He did, with the belief he
could be healed by faith in
Christ. That's when the
crowd became obsessed:
The gods have come to us;
they're with us here today!
Then I was dubbed 'Zeus'
and Paul became 'Hermes'.
The Priest of Zeus brought
gifts: all were about to offer
sacrifice to us! How could
this happen? How could our
work disintegrate?

Paul raced into the centre of
the crowd: Don't pay this
homage unto us! We're
human, just like you! We
came to you to bring Good
News; we speak of Him, the
Living God who grants all
things to you; He cares!

But even Paul could hardly
still the adulating host. Just
then, some enemies from
Pisidian Antioch arrived and
turned the tide. Some took
up stones, slung them at us
and then left us for dead
outside the city walls.
Believers came to help us
there. They tended all our
wounds; we were revived
and journeyed on to Derbe.

Many people came to faith,
became disciples, grew in
grace. We stayed among
them for some time. Here
was a new Community of
Faith. When it was time for
us to go back home, we did
not search for other routes
but chose instead to retrace
steps via Lystra, Iconium
and Antioch, to strengthen
and encourage those who
had so recently received

the Lord. Some elders were
appointed and with prayers
of faith, all were
commended to the Lord.
At last we made it back,
arriving at our home-based
Antioch, rejoicing in
each circumstance.

THE PHARISEE
BELIEVER
Chapter 15

I can't believe how Saul
behaves! (Oh yes, I'm now
to call him by the Roman
connotation of his name).
So! Paul it is. He always
was a man so sure of
self—it's what Gamaliel
instilled in him in student
days of long ago.

There's been an attitude
of laxity that's creeping
into our Community of
Faith. We sent some
friends right up to Antioch
in Syria to let it there be
known in no uncertain
terms that no one can be
saved unless they're
circumcised, obeying
Moses' sacred rules.

And wouldn't you just
know, all the discussion
did become inflamed for
Paul put down his foot
with a firm hand (if you
will get my drift). There is
a greater freedom now to
which we should adhere!
he said without regret.

Both he and Barnabas
came all the way into
Jerusalem for some
discussions that would
solve the vexing, taxing,
circumstance. There was a
'to do' (if you gather what
I mean), but everyone
expressed delight in how
the Community of Faith
has grown. Though we of
the Pharisee persuasion
then took umbrage at
the lack of countenancing
Holy Law laid down by
Moses all those years ago.

Tradition, that's the thing!
It cannot be gainsaid. All
listened most attentively.
Discussion was intense.
Then Peter spoke. He took
the time to then remind
us all of his experience

at Joppa and the lesson
he had learned about
accepting those who had
been steeped in alien ways
but had received the Lord
as their Redeemer–Friend.
He emphasised this had
precedence over all the
'rules and regs' that, in
the end, can save no one!
Don't test the Lord by
laying all those heavy
burdens on their backs,
I ask! Remember this:
we're saved by grace
and not by massive works
we've done for Him!

The Council listened,
after this harangue,
to Barnabas and Paul.
So, finally, James (the
Lord's own brother and
the leader of us all,) spoke
up, reminding us of Amos
who declared that David's
Kingdom would, one day,
be rebuilt… the Gentiles
would be called 'God's
own'. In my opinion,
James declared, we should
not trouble Gentiles who
have turned to God! Let's
just explain that thorough
cleanliness in body, mind

and soul, and faithfulness
are what's required.
The Lord will bless
them then, for sure!

Addendum:

Our James spoke wisdom
and I do regret my frowning
countenance! A letter was
composed and taken up to
Antioch by Judah and Silas.
Upon arrival there, the letter
was then read. The
immediate response was joy
and determination made to
heed the edict from
Jerusalem. I must say here
that I concurred.

SILAS
Chapters 15 – 16

There's been a parting of
the ways: John Mark
returned, expecting to take
up where he left off. But
Paul believed that
immaturity would make the
going much too tough for
him. As Barnabas then
disagreed, he chose to take
his nephew, Mark, with him
in setting sail once more for
Cyprus in order to renew
the bond with all the

island's faithful souls.

I'd come, as you will know,
up to Syrian Antioch with
Judah (named Barsabbas). I
stayed, associating with the
great apostle Paul. This
gave some opportunity for
him to see some worth in
me that would sustain me on
a mission trail. His invite
was accepted with a joy.

We came to Lystra where
a youth named Timothy
then joined us in this
gladsome task: to carry
Gospel truth to all the
world. We took with us
the guidelines laid down
in Jerusalem whereby the
Gentiles could be received
without rancour, concern,
and fully saved!

We travelled through
the Phrygian region and on
into Galatia. How very
interesting however, that the
Holy Spirit would not allow
our entry into Asia at that
constraining time.

Instead, Paul was advised
(by this, well on the way to

Mysia and Troas), by means
of a strong vision of what
next to do.

Paul 'saw' a man of
Macedonia who called to
him, Come over to us for
we need your help so much!
Immediately, we three were
on our way—the new
course set, we pack:
we're on our way
to Macedonia!

DR. LUKE
Chapter 16

Have you now taken note?
The 'they' has turned to
'we'! How come, you ask?
Of course! I joined the
mission here, I've joined the
company! Some think the
'vision' Paul had seen was
the doctor he had sought to
gain some help—he was at
times quite ill for, after all,
he had been stoned
and flogged you may recall.

In taking stock of this, I like
to think that, when
I asked if he would journey
into Macedonia, he gained

the impetus—gained not
of me but from the One
known as the Holy Spirit
of the Lord! Our group has
grown: there's Paul,
accompanied by Timothy,
there's Silas and yes,
Dr. Luke. That's me!

We've taken ship, via
Samothrace, Neapolis and
from here, inland to
Philippi, a town in far
off Macedonia.
When the Sabbath Day
arrived, we hiked down to
the river bank—we thought
to find some Jews. We
found, instead, the lovely
Lydia, a merchant in fine
purple cloth. We found that
Lydia already worshipped
God and was prepared
to hear us out. She was
convinced and was baptised.

We were, what's more,
invited to her house where
we could rest and be
refreshed. Soon strife
accosted us—a woman who
had been restored to sanity
no longer would be making
money for her owners who
then flung Paul and Silas

into gaol. False testimony
was given. The 'guilty' men
were stripped, then flogged,
then strapped in stocks.
When clocks struck
midnight, Paul and Silas
were both singing songs
of praise and praying for
their captors there. An
earthquake shook the
prison, opened doors,
released the stocks. So,
when the gaoler saw the
earthquake's consequence,
he was about to kill himself
when Paul said, Put away
your sword, we are
all here. Don't be afraid.

The gaoler rushed right in,
his torch revealing all was
well. He fell down at the
feet of Paul and Silas: Sirs,
what must I do to find what
you reveal of faith?
Believe in *Yeshua*–Jesus,
the Christ: you and
your family will be saved.

When morning came, all
the authorities were told
the facts—that we, as
Roman citizens, had been
maltreated so appallingly.

Apologies were swiftly
made. The prisoners
were freed!

SILAS
Chapters 17 – 18

We travelled on to
Thessalonica via
Amphipolis and Apollonia.
Paul went
into the synagogue,
returning there each week
to preach Good News.
His messages concerning
the *Messiah* were well
received and mainly by
the Greeks. Some Jews, as
usual, stirred up a great
amount of strife. Because
they failed to find Paul, the
man who sheltered them—
Jason, a friend—was gaoled
and had to pay much money
before he was released. As
night fell, Paul and Silas
were aided so that they
escaped right to Berea.

The people here were open-
minded and quite keen to
hear the Gospel
message until the rabble
rousers from Thessalonica
created such a fuss that Paul

was sent down to the coast.
Upon arrival in Athens, he
sent word back into Berea
for his team
to come also.

While awaiting Timothy
and I, Paul was much
disturbed at seeing all
the idols 'idolised'
within Athens!
He spoke at length to those
who paused to listen to his
words. Those of the
Epicurean or Stoical intent
debated many issues that
intrigued them there.
Athenians were taken up
with the debates that raged
interminably about
the 'this and that' of life.

Then Paul was ushered in
to stand before the Council
that was convened to there
adjudicate the issues raised.
The things you preach
sound strange to us. What
do you mean? We're given
to inquire of you
about all that is new in
town. Paul took his chance
Paul took his chance. He
pointed out the many idols
on display throughout

Athens. This tells me that you are sincere in how you wish to worship here. I was surprised, however, to observe a statue dedicated to 'The Unknown God'! I now declare to you that this idol you worship here in ignorance does represent the One whom I'll disclose to you today! The LORD, Creator of the heavens and the Earth, does not live in temples made with hands!

He is the One who grants you life and breath. He dwells not far from any one of us: it is in Him we live and move and have our being. We are 'The Family of God'! His Being is self-existent—it is not composed of gold nor brick. He understands all those who have not heard of Him. In being introduced to you, He will require that all turn from their wickedness.

All proof you need, determining validity of what I say, is in the death and resurrection of *Yeshua*–Jesus Christ, known as *Messiah.* Accept this truth and live for Him!

AQUILA
Chapter 18

My wife, Priscilla, also I, heard much news on the 'grape-vine', so to speak. It was so meaningful to meet Paul face to face. We'd come from Rome quite recently for Emperor Claudius had ordered every Jew to leave. We now reside in Corinth with some ease.

Because we are tent-makers by trade, we met with Paul soon after his arrival for he also earns his living making tents. He met with us and decided to accept our hospitality. Some days after this, when Timothy and Silas both arrived, Paul gave his time to preaching the Good News. Some Jews thought ill of this so Paul decided, finally, to cut his ties, dust off his shoes and go towards the Greeks!

There were some Jews

that did believe Paul and
accepted *Yeshua* as Saviour
and were 'born again'.
Crispus, the ruler of the
synagogue, was one such
man! We praised the Lord
for this. Paul was
encouraged by a vision
where the Lord appeared
to strengthen him:

Don't be afraid, Paul, for
I'm with you. Speak up!
Speak on! Do not give up.
You won't be harmed for
many here are My own
people; they'll care for you!

There were so many 'ups
and downs' but, all in all,
the Gospel News was well
received much of the time.
Paul stayed for many
seasons here. But, finally,
he knew it was the time to
set sail once again for home
with his good friends.

As for Priscilla and myself,
we departed from the team
at Ephesus and Paul went in
to the Ephesian synagogue
to hold discussions with the
Jews—always a challenge
but the people pleaded for a
longer stay. He could not

comply but promised,
if possible, to return.

He came at last to Caesarea
and went on down into
Jerusalem to greet the
church (the people of the
Lord) and then return to
Syrian Antioch. After some
respite from all his mission
journeying, he set out once
more for Galatia and
Phrygia to encourage
the Community of Faith.

APOLLOS
Chapter 18

I am a man of Alexandria;
my name—Apollos,
meaning *a destroyer*—
does not sit happily with
me. I came to Ephesus and
found much opportunity to
be expounding Hebrew
Scripture. It is known I am
an orator, requested
frequently to share my in-
depth understanding of
God's written word and
all things spiritual.

I have been introduced to
the story of the Nazarene.

I teach with some insight, the facts concerning Him. In some ways, though, I realise my lack of what occurred after John the Baptist's time. I long to be informed. I must say that I'm well received within the Ephesian synagogue.

Now, something quite remarkable has taken place today. I met a couple— Aquila and Priscilla by name—who, when hearing the oration I presented at the synagogue, invited me into their home. They took the opportunity of enlarging all my knowledge of the ways of God in the light of *Yeshua*–Jesus, the Christ.

There is a 'HALLELUJAH' in my re-claimed heart! I'm going to Achaia with this new-found faith now ringing in my ears and soul.

Addendum:

I praise the Lord that I have been the means of giving hope and help to new believers here with all debating resounding in

the corridors of power!

PAUL
Chapter 19

I have come on to Ephesus where I have been disturbed to find a great lack of understanding in the fledgling Church. Have you received the Holy Spirit in your life since you believed in Christ? The Holy Spirit? Who, or What is He? We have not even heard of Him. How could He be received?

I found I needed to explain how John the Baptist had prepared the way for One much greater who had come to save all people from their sin. It gave much Joy, therefore, to find that all the followers of John embraced the Gospel News and, as I placed my hands on them with uttered prayer: O Holy Spirit, come, it seemed to me that Pentecost had now returned!

I remained within this dear Community of Faith one whole season, counselling, encouraging, admonishing, explaining all the Gospel News to them. During this time, the miracles occurring frequently were quite unusual but helpful to the ministry. The spirit of all evil did attack the company and great hardship was experienced. But how great is God's grace! Evil was put into its place! The sorcerers gave up their trade and burned their books.

Believers then confessed short-comings and within this unifying spirit evident throughout, God's word was spreading, and was strengthening, equipping all who believed in *Yeshua.*

DEMETRIUS
Chapter 19:21 – 41

I've been observing this absurd phenomenon—the coming of the man named Paul has set us all aghast. I am a silversmith and my so marvellous production of our goddess, Artemis, rejoices all the people (and the profit is

Immense—we do rejoice!)

I'll mobilise my men—my fellow artisans. They'll see how vital is the need to stop Paul in his tracks. How dare he rant and rave about our glorious silver Artemis! Only Metal? Not a god? This news will bring us to the dust. It must be stopped!

Now listen, all Ephesians, if this prattling does continue, our temple will mean nothing and our Artemis will be destroyed although she's worshipped round the world. Can you turn blind eyes, deaf ears to this atrocity? Oh, great is Artemis! The crowd took up the chant; they collared Aristarchus and Gaius but I hear that Paul was secreted away— a coward, not to show his so offensive face!

The City Clerk stepped up into the fray. And shame, he stemmed the riot! He did endeavour to talk

sense, reminding all that
Paul and his associates
had done no actual wrong.
But he had quelled my
argument, my just
outrage, my strong
defence of Artemis,
our silver god.

The clerk announced that,
if I had a grievance, the
courts should deal with it.
There's no excuse for this
uproar. The riot now must
cease at once. So much for
fighting for our rights;
we got *un*just desserts!

DR. LUKE
Chapter 20

The uproar had died down
but Paul then called together
all to give encouragement
but also to express his last
farewell. He travelled
through the regions of
Macedonia encouraging
the faithful with his
messages of hope, of trust,
of joy and need for
faithfulness. We sailed from
Philippi after Passover and
the other members of

our now expanding team
re-joined us in Troas.

EUTYCHUS
Chapter 20:7 – 12

I've waited all my life, it
seems, to meet with Paul.
But when he came to Troas,
there were so many who had
pushed into the room that I
could find no place to park
myself. There was the
window ledge, of course
and finally, I took the hint to
sit upon the windowsill.
Paul spoke with power but
he went on and on until well
past midnight. I must
confess a yawn or two.

And after that, I fell
asleep—that is, before I fell
out of the window, to
the street below. I did not
wake— I was unconscious
there—some said that I had
died. I do believe they're
right. But Paul, he threw
himself upon my lifeless
body on the ground. And
then he spoke, The boy's
alive! All went straight back
upstairs and shared a meal.

The meeting finally broke
up at dawn and I went home
alive and well!
How great is God!

PAUL
Chapter 20

I want so much to be back
in Jerusalem by Pentecost
so I'm arranging all my
team to synchronise their
journeying. I came to
Ephesus to meet Church
elders for it would mean
a last farewell. We sat
together and we reminisced
on all our past experience.

Please do keep watch
on all you do and over all
the flock entrusted to your
care. Do be on guard for
some will come with plans
of subterfuge. Remember all
the tears and fears of those
three years when I remained
to counsel you. I worked
with these own hands,
providing all the needs
of my own team. I do
commend you to the grace
and care of God. He's able
to keep you all from falling

and failing. We parted then
with copious tears.

DR. LUKE
Chapter 21

After all those sad
goodbyes, we took
a ship that was Phoenicia
bound. Our route was via
Cyprus then on to Syria.
At Tyre, we disembarked
and stayed a week together
with the local Church where
we were warned off going
to Jerusalem. We did,
however, then continue on
our way from Tyre to
Caesarea where we were
pleased to meet with
Philip, the evangelist.

While here, we also met
the prophet Agabus. His
message was profound,
deep felt! He took Paul's
belt to signify that he'd be
bound up in Jerusalem and
then handed over to
Gentiles. We remonstrated
with our Paul but he was
adamant: Why do you break
my heart? Do you not know
I'm ready now to die for the

sake of *Yeshua*–Jesus?
We all gave up and prayed,
God's will be done. We
journeyed then together
up to the city heights:
Jerusalem!

JAMES
Chapter 21

Paul and close associates
have come to visit me
today. He has been
welcomed warmly by the
Church. The elders were
all present. We received a
comprehensive coverage
of all that God had done
throughout the Gentile
world visited by Paul.

It is for me a solemn task
to now inform you that so
many, many Jews are now
believers. Some are sad that
you have done away with
key Mosaic Law. They'll
surely hear that you've
arrived. What can be done?
We do advise that you will
go, with these four men
who've taken vows, up to
the Temple to be involved
in the Purification

Ceremony being sure to pay
for all expenses there. This
will enable you to show
your faithfulness to Moses'
Law. They'll be convinced
there is no truth in the
entirely false news.

Paul accompanied the four
men next day, participated
(with shaved head) in the
ceremony as advised. Just
when its end was near, some
Asian Jews spied Paul,
seized him, shouting his
infidelity to God. Confusion
spread. Men dragged Paul
from the Temple. Then
the doors were closed.

The Roman Guard was
called. In seeing the
Commander there, the mob
ceased thrashing Paul but he
was then arrested though
the Commander could
determine nothing of the
fault. At last, to save
Paul's life, he was then
carried from the frenzied
mob into a safer place.

PAUL
Chapters 21 – 23

Commander, may I speak
with you? I am a Jew, born
in Tarsus in Cilicia. I am a
Roman citizen also. Do let
me speak now to the people
here. My fellow Jews,
please listen as I seek here
to defend myself.
Let me outline for you
my history …

I laid out all my life's
experience: my birth, the
student of Gamaliel, and
on… Cast your minds back
to the day of Stephen's
stoning. I was there,
approving of his death. And
following, I gained
permission to seek out all
believers for to persecute,
annihilate! But then, the
Lord called me to go into
the Gentile world to speak
for Him. That's when the
tide then turned. I heard,
Away with him. Kill him!

The Commander took
control, ordered his men to
take me to their Fort, to
whip me there in hope of
finding out the reason for
the riot. I'd had enough of
it! Sir, is it lawful that you

whip a Roman citizen who
has not yet been tried for
any crime, large or small?

The officer dispatched to
whip 'the prisoner' returned
in haste, explaining my
predicament
The Commander then was
horrified. He verified my
status. Listen to me,
he said, I am a Roman
citizen only because I paid
a vast amount for such a
privilege! I then replied,
But I am 'free-born' Sir.
The Commander showed
some fear then, at what
was done to me.

Next day, my chains were
off. The Commander
ordered the Chief Priests
and Council to deliberate
upon my fate. I was
required to testify. I was
straightforward, telling the
whole saga of my ministry.
The High Priest ordered I be
struck across the mouth for
blasphemy. When this was
'sorted out', I noticed that
there was disparity within
the Council ranks: there
were the Pharisees and

the Sadducees! I took
the reins, proclaimed:
My fellow citizens, I am on
trial simply because I do
believe the dead will rise
again! This set the factions
in a quarrel (my intent).
Some lawyers—Pharisees—
stood up and said
deliberately: We find no
fault at all with Paul.

Perhaps an angel spoke
to him to set him on the
Gentile path! I'm of the
opinion that, because of
the continuing violence, the
Commander thought that I'd
be torn apart! He ordered
that his men secure me in
the Fort. That night, the
Lord came, stood by me
to comfort me. I heard
Him say:

Take courage, Paul, don't be
afraid; you've witnessed well
within Jerusalem and you will
witness then in Rome.

I've been informed about a
group of some forty Jews
who've vowed to neither eat
nor drink until they have me
slain. They put a scheme in

place but my sister's son
came to let me know of this.
I then arranged that he
inform the Commander
of this treacherous plan.
My nephew outlined details
of the plot to him and he
was charged to keep his
silence on the scheme
before being sent away.

The Commander took
control. He gave
instructions for a troop, two
hundred strong, to make
ready their departure north
to Caesarea. Take Paul to
Governor Felix, provide
him with the details of the
plot to kill this noble man.

The Governor queried me
to find the crux of all the
issues that surrounded me.
He then decided to await
arrival of accusers who'd
stirred up the strife. I should
report that now I'm under
guard within the Governor's
T.H.Q. in town.

FELIX
Chapter 24

This really is perplexing!

I have a Jew—a Roman
citizen—incarcerated here
and now they come, the
High Priest and his
entourage, to state their case
for the penalty of death.

**Their lawyer, named
Tertullus, was so scathing in
accusations re the prisoner.
But first, those slinking
adulations of myself—I've
heard it all before; I'm tired
of it! The lawyer then
began his rant: This is
a dangerous man. He
instigates a riot every-
where he goes. He is,
I understand, the leader of
that sect, 'The Nazarenes'.
He tried to taint the
Temple in Jerusalem.
He was arrested, placed
within your hands. I rest
my case, he said.**

I then commanded Paul to
outline his defence. These
are his basic points:
* He'll stand before my court
* He went to worship
* He was not arguing
* He did not cause a riot
* There is no proof
* This is what he does admit:

I worship *YHVH*–LORD of
ancestors
I stand by all the Law of
Moses
I believe the prophets of
Israel
I hope in God
I trust in *Yeshua's* death,
resurrection
I strive to keep my
conscience clear
I ask: state my crime

I see no fault in Paul's
testimony. I'll ponder it,
await Commander Lysius
and then I will decide the
case. This court is now
adjourned! Make sure the
prisoner's friends are free to
visit and provide for him.

My wife, Drusilla (who, by
the way is Jewish) and I
requested that Paul come
to speak with us about
what has been dubbed,
'The Way'.
I understood what he
declared about the Christ
but, when he spoke about a
basic goodness and one's
need of self-control, then
Judgement Day, I must

confess I was unnerved.
So, thank you Paul; I'll call
for you another day when
time is more convenient.

**Well yes, I dillydallied
with Paul's case for I
thought to gain some
coinage from that Roman
citizen as an exchange for
freedom but no coins
arrived! Besides, it is
expedient to curry favour
with the Jews… Where
did those two years go?**

life, His death and
resurrection too, because
I came to faith years later,
steeped in Gentile attitudes.
It's Paul who gave the
reason and the opportunity
to take the quill to write the
Gospel and this 'Letter'
to you, Theophilus. You
see, I utilised some time
in Caesarea to share with
friends of *Yeshua*–Jesus and
thus I itemised the facts that
fell in place and now
contained, my friend, within
the Gospel and these 'Acts'!

DR. LUKE
Chapter 24:27

This is an aside for reasons
that become quite clear.
For two whole years we
waited for a verdict but it
never came. I stayed nearby.
It really was imperative that
I ensured continued health
for Paul. How else could he
sustain the inhumane
treatment meted out to him.

There were some doubts
that I could ever write that
first-hand record of
Yeshua's birth, His earthly

FESTUS
Chapter 25

Just three days following
induction as the Governor,
I went from Caesarea down
to Jerusalem. I had a time of
it for the Chief Priests and
all their retinue endeavoured
to entice me
to bring the prisoner, Paul,
with me. But they were
unaware I'd been informed
that they had hatched
a plot to have him slain. So,
I replied: I am returning
north to Caesarea soon.

Come back with me to
ascertain if he is in the
wrong. What do you say?

Just ten days later we
returned and, on the next
day, I called the court to
order. Paul was ushered in
and stood before all his
accusers with an innocence
none could disprove.
I realised that I must keep
right in with all these Jews
if I'll succeed in governing
this querulous crowd.

Will you be willing to return
down to Jerusalem to there
be tried? The man replied, If
I have broken any law, I do
not seek escape. If I deserve
the penalty of death, so be
it. But, as no charge is
proved, no one can hand me
over to that court.
Therefore: I will appeal
to Caesar now!
You have appealed
to Caesar, so to the
Emperor you will go!
This court is closed!

AGRIPPA
Chapters 25 – 26

My wife, Bernice, and I had
thought it a diplomatic
nicety to pay a visit to
Festus, purposing to
welcome him into this
jurisdiction. We had hoped
for pleasant company. Not
long after arriving there, we
were informed of this man,
Paul, and how he languished
in the gaol. I understand the
prisoner has now appealed
to Rome. It could be of
some passing interest to
interrogate the man and
Festus did agree.

How grand, you'd be
amazed: the auditorium was
crammed with military
personnel together with
some leading citizens. Amid
much pomp and undue
circumstance, proceedings
soon were underway. Paul
was brought forward as
Festus began his long
harangue of things
pertaining to captivity.

I said to Paul: You may now
speak on your behalf. He
then began by first
acknowledging that I would
understand all of the

circumstance because of Jewish heritage. I listened most attentively as he resorted to a history of Israel and how he'd followed studiously the Faith of ancestors through the years.

I stand before you for the hope I hold: the promise God had made has been fulfilled in raising people from the dead. I am a Pharisee by birth and those will testify to the validity of what I claim this day. I'd set about my purpose to destroy all evidence of sects believing in the 'Nazarene'. But God then intervened. I was transformed.

I came from **darkness** into *LIGHT*. I saw the Truth in *Yeshua*–Jesus. I've sought henceforth to speak the Truth lodged in my soul. I have been stoned, imprisoned, flogged, and left for dead, in danger all the while. Yet I've been faithful to the calling of the Lord. I stand before you innocent of any crimes!

I challenged Paul: Almost, almost, you've changed my mind and turned me to the Christian Way! We then stood up and made our exit from the crowded auditorium.

There is one thing that we've agreed: this man is innocent! If he'd not made appeal to Caesar, he could have been released.

DR. LUKE
Chapters 27 – 28

In setting sail for Rome, we were most fortunate that a Roman officer named Julius from the 'Emperor Regiment' had charge of Paul. He was most kind, allowing Paul to visit friends at various ports of call in the voyage.

The changing weather patterns in the Mediterranean made it most advisable to winter in a port and Paul advised the Captain thus. But he and crew disliked the thought of

whiling months away
in such a minor scene

The sails were set again as
a mild breeze had floated in
from azure skies. The
sailing was serenity itself
until a sudden storm gushed
in on us. All were afraid of
shipwreck then. The sails
were lowered, excess cargo
cast into the foaming waves.

The light became so dim
that it was nigh impossible
to sort the night from day!
We surrendered all our
hope. The wind would not
abate. The sails were furled,
the rudder of no use as we
were driven solely by the
gale. No one could tell
if we'd be saved.

Paul then stood tall among
us all. Most sadly, you had
failed to listen to advice I
gave before we sailed this
route. But I now beg of you:
take courage for I do declare
before you all: not one of us
will lose our life although
the ship will not be saved.
I've had this word from

YHVH–LORD. I know I'll
stand before the Emperor.
So, do take courage: prepare
to be cast up on land! The
drama lasted fourteen days
then, in the morning, Paul
advised that we eat some
food—we'd need much
strength for what's ahead.

Paul prayed for us...
Some land was seen,
a beach beckoned. The
prisoners were released;
we gave ourselves to waves
and found they carried us
up to a foreign land: Malta.
The people were so friendly
and they built a fire to keep
us warm and comforted.

There was a moment
fraught with fear when Paul
was bitten by a snake. The
natives thought he was,
therefore, an evil man—
saved by the waves though
would not live! Paul smiled:
there was no ill effect. They
were amazed! He is a god!
When Paul was able to
make well, through prayer,
the father of the Chief,

the islanders worked hard to
ease our hardship, tend our
needs. And then, at last,
we sailed for Rome.

The citizens of Rome were
kind to us and though a
soldier guarded him, Paul
was permitted to abide
alone. When three days
passed, he called the local
Jewish leaders so that he
could then explain his
current circumstance.

When all was said, their
answer came: We've heard
no word of this. We know
of no ill will concerning
you. We would be pleased
to hear this Gospel News.
They listened well. Some
did believe, others
declined… Paul then
continued on for two whole
years, to preach,
to teach with boldness as
he witnessed for the Lord.

….. oOo …..

THE TEACHING YEARS

MISSION LETTERS OF PAUL
SAUL—PAUL

Because you've already
met with me via Dr. Luke's
comprehensive coverage of
the birth and development of
the Early Church, I'll make
my introduction relatively
concise. So, to begin, a little
about myself.

Oh yes, I was a pharisaic
Pharisee! Though birthed far
from the Jewish hub of
things, Jerusalem, I donned
the 'colours' of a narrow-
minded bigot.

I was born in Tarsus in
Cilicia. I came from a
privileged family, being
'free-born' as a Roman
citizen. This brought a
freedom from the usual
restrictions placed upon a
subjugated race by Rome.
My greatest privilege, no
doubt, was acceptance into
the most elite of all Jewish

schools, that headed by Gamaliel (the name still has a ring to it—he was respected round the world).

There was no greater means of absorbing—in my narrow mind—the values of Mosaic law, the Torah (precious word of *YHVH*–LORD) and topped up by the many by-laws associated with Mishnah, the Midrash, Talmud and the like, accrued within the holy halls and Temple talk where one was pleased to live according to the Holy Law and traditional outlook and *in*-look, too!

Dear Dr. Luke has already provided you with all the details of my youth when, just about to try my fledgling wings, a young man by the name of Stephen was dragged outside the city walls and stoned to death while I stood by, approving of it all while minding the assassins' cloaks. I did approve of it!

My fury at this man for what he claimed to see while rocks were hurled at him determined my intent to annihilate them all, all those wicked Nazarenes! My anger was heightened by a niggling question-mark for I did believe the dead would rise again! Then, when I met Him in that *LIGHT* upon my vengeful route to Damascus, I think I knew before I asked: here was *Yeshua*–Jesus, the Christ! Though I was blinded by the *LIGHT,* I'd never 'seen' so well.

As I have testified in Luke's account of 'The Acts of the Apostles (and the Holy Spirit!') I was transformed—yes, 'born again', renewed within my soul. That encounter is the means whereby I am sustained to preach the word and give witness to the Lord. I live, and move, and have my being in the power of the Holy Spirit—my constant Guard and Guide. While I could waste away behind prison bars, currently I still have much opportunity to write to you, 'The Community of Faith'. I lift the quill now to communicate with the members of the Church that I hold most dear:

THE ROMAN CHURCH
Chapter 1

Paul, the Apostle
Circa A.D. 53 – 59

To the Roman Church,

I am so pleased to introduce myself and to share the Message I convey to all the fledgling churches of the Gentile world for it is my aim to visit you as soon as this can be arranged.
The news concerning the vitality of your Community of Faith delights my heart!

I learned of you through Aquila and Priscilla and, through them, I feel I know you very well. Since then, I've met with many travellers who are faithful to the cause of Christ and they've confirmed all that I've heard of you. Although you will have heard of me and of the triumphs and the tragedies—in prison, floggings, stoning, rioting as well—I do desire to place before you now a basic outline of all that it is I teach and preach. I will commence by setting out in bold outline, the Faith that I hold most dear:

MY APOSTOLIC MANDATE

I'm called by God to carry Gospel News to all the world. This News is really not new news! The prophets long ago proclaimed that, at a future time, *Messiah* (you know Him as the Christ) would come. It is my privilege to relate His birth, His life of perfect holiness, His death and resurrection too, which is the confirmation of Divinity! This is the reason why I write to you for you are also called to be His Family.

First and foremost, I do pray with thankful heart for all the world knows of your steadfastness. This prayer continues as I ask the Lord to help prepare the way for me to come to you so I'll become a blessing unto you as you will be to me. I'm eager to discuss

my faith with you
as I'm convinced of God's
almighty power to save all
peoples—Jews and Gentiles
too—for we are both put
right with God through faith
in Jesus Christ.

Reason for God's Distress:
Do let me share the major
themes I emphasise: I must
begin right at the starting
place: of human sin—the
guilt of suffering
humankind! All peoples
have a mind to clarify
what's right or wrong. It's
possible for humans to
control the will, determining
the good, refusing ill! When
evil is so knowingly flung in
the face of God, He turns
from them for they have
flung conscience away—
the means whereby He'd
speak to them advising
them. They have no mind to
change their ways,
preferring evil gains and
they condone wrongs
perpetrated in the world
at large. They have no care
for those in need.

....

ROMANS 2
GOD'S RIGHTEOUS
JUDGEMENT

You'll know of people
who'll pass judgement on
their neighbours, strangers
too. Evil people scorn
God's kindness,
righteousness!
The day will come when
judgement speaks to sinful
minds and sinful acts,
determining the
consequence.

The *YHVH*–LORD will
judge all people, granting
grace for goodness but
deliver retribution for
all wrongdoing then.
Jews have the Law and are
required to uphold all its
verities. The Gentiles also
have a Law: it's written on
their hearts. Our conscience
will dictate the rules by
which we choose to live.
The conscience will convict
but it confirms also the
actions that are of pure
worth.

**The Law according
to Judaism:**

Jews are so prone, because
of their penchant to uphold
Law (it is a boast) they're
sure they'll guide the blind,
become a light for those that
dwell in night; instructing
fools and teaching the naïve.
They focus on the 'other',
why not focus on
themselves?
They are no 'signpost' for
what's pure. Outward
appearance is of little worth
if all the inner life is stained
with sin. It's time to
circumcise the heart!

ROMANS 3
THE QUESTION OF
RIGHTEOUSNESS

The Jews are God's own
special people—He entrusted
them with Holy Law. But
what He needs is faithfulness.
Does God 'do wrong' by
punishment of evil and
recalcitrance? If He's not just,
He cannot be our Judge.
But what if purity is
shown up by impurity?
Let us be evil so that good
will come? No way!

Is anyone righteous?

Are Jews more holy than
Gentiles?
Preposterous! We stand as
one under The power of sin.
The Scripture says:

*There's no one righteous,
wise, for all have turned to
their own ways. No one
does good… They have not
learned the paths of peace
nor have they learned
to reverence God.*

One cannot be made right
by trusting in the Law!
Rather, it is because of law
that we become so
conscious of our sinfulness.

How things are made right
The LORD has now
revealed the way to make
things right. The Law could
not achieve what God has
done: We are made right
through faith in *Yeshua*–
the Christ. There's nothing
we can boast about, no
works can save, no good
intent. The Lord has paved
the way for change: step out
in faith believing in His
power to save. It's not
the Jews who gain

sole access into grace!
The Gentiles are full heirs
to grace through faith in
Christ. So, is the Law
redundant then? No way!
It's faith that will uphold
the righteous Law!

ROMANS 4
THE EXAMPLE OF
ABRAHAM

What can we say of
Abraham in light of this?
Was he made right with
God because of his good
deeds? If that's the case,
he'd have the right to boast
but not before the LORD!

The Scriptures say that
Abraham believed the
LORD. Because he did, the
LORD accounted him a
righteous man. It's as King
David said in Psalms:

How happy are all those
whose wrongs have been
forgiven, whose wrongs are
pardoned and whose sins
will never be accounted up
against their name.

Are David's words meant

just for Jews? No way! We
stand upon the word of God.
And Abraham believed in
God—this was the basis of
his righteousness. He is the
'father of the faithful'—of
the Jews and of the Gentiles
too! Let us, as children,
follow in his steps!

God's Promise is for all!
If all God's promises belong
to those who live within the
Law, then faith means
nothing and God's promises
are nullified. God chose that
we should live by faith so
that His promise is the
wondrous, gift of grace!

Our 'father Abraham'
had exercised
his hope without a reason
for a hope—how could he
cling to hope, believe a son
would come to birth after
his fertile years? Yet hope
was then fulfilled in Isaac,
Jacob–Israel. But what has
this to do with us? When
there's no reason for a hope
that we'd be saved, the
LORD stepped in—a Son
was birthed that, through
His death and resurrection,

we'd be saved!

ROMANS 5
PUT RIGHT WITH
GOD!

What may we now expect
when we're put right with
God through faith? Peace
flows into our lives through
Yeshua–Jesus, the Christ.
He ushers us into this new
experience where we may
share the hope of Glory
now. But what, you ask,
will life be like when
awful trouble comes?

Our troubles will produce
endurance which engenders
stable character. This gives
us hope that will not
disappoint because the love
of *Yeshua*–Jesus is poured
out in our hearts. This is the
Holy Spirit's work in us. He
died for us when we were
dead—without a hope.

What's the significance
of such a love? It's this:
though few would find it
possible to die for those
deemed righteous folk, God
commends His love to us in

that it was when we were
deep in sin that Jesus gave
His life for us. We do
rejoice because the LORD
has reconciled us to
Himself. Let's put
the wonder of it all like this:
just as by one man—
Adam—sin had entered in
the world, by one Man—
Yeshua—by grace, through
faith, all may be granted
Life! I launch into a hymn
I've found within my heart:

FAITH'S VISION
Tune: *Harton-Lea* L.M.

Faith brings the ample
evidence
Of boundless things not seen
nor heard
For, with the eyes and ears
of faith,
Our inner sense of truth
is stirred.

Faith brings ability to trust
Though clouds obscure the
path ahead;
Its vision sees, beyond
the night,
That light will dawn and doubt
be dead.

Faith brings assurances that all
The promises of God are real,
The promise known, the
promise claimed;
Such gifting will God's
grace reveal.

Faith brings the access into
grace
Wherein we stand and we
rejoice
In hope of all God's glory here;
His love outpoured
is matchless grace.

ROMANS 6
FROM DEATH TO LIFE

What can we say to this?
So, let's not worry if we sin,
for grace will cover us? No
way! Through *Yeshua*–
Jesus, our old self dies—it's
'crucified' with Him! That's
how He conquered sin. Why
should we think of raising it
again? We've been
transformed. Don't be a
slave to sin! So, if we died
with Christ, we also live
with Him. Do realise that
you are dead to sin, you are
alive to Christ. Do not allow
a sin to reign. Present
yourself to God in

righteousness that is the gift
of God through Jesus
Christ! Remember, you're
not under Law: you live
by grace through faith!

What is the difference here?
In being set free from sin to
be a servant of the Lord,
you will rejoice in righteous
ways by bearing fruits of
holiness. The difference is:
the wages earned through
sin is death! Now, contrast
that with this: the gift of
God is our eternal life in
Jesus Christ, our Lord!

ROMANS 7
RELEASED FROM
LIVING
BY THE LAW

What shall I say to this? Is
Law then sinful, stained by
evil deeds? No Way!
We would not know what
sin implies if Law had not
described those deeds.
The lesson to be learned is
this: the law reveals the
nature of a sin—it has no
power to cure that vice;
It does not help perform
the good. ('Thou shalt

not…' won't release;
'Thou shalt be free': this is
our hope! The good I
would, I cannot do! The evil
I abhor, that's what I do.
Oh, wretched soul, who can
deliver me? Thank God, it's
been achieved! He changed
my life around—I am alive
to Christ right now!

ROMANS 8
WE'RE FREE AT LAST!

We're free of every
condemnation now for we
rely on Jesus Christ
and His great power to set
us free. This is because
The Law—that of the Holy
Spirit—sets us free from all
the laws of sin and death!
For, what the Law could not
achieve, the LORD has
done! He set His miracle
in place so that the righteous
rules of Law could all be
satisfied in us because we
live according to the Holy
Spirit's guidance; we're no
longer bound by human
frailties.

No one will please the
LORD persisting in their
wilful ways. As Christ
indwells our human life,
His Holy Spirit IS our life!
Oh yes, our bodies die but,
if the Spirit lives in us, then
He who raised Christ from
the dead will also then
impart new life to us.
All those who are alive
in Christ are now the
children of our God.
The Spirit does not bind
us into slavery nor 'gift'
us with a fear, the Holy
Spirit will make us the
children of the LORD. It is
by Spirit Power that we
address the *YHVH*–LORD
as *Abba*, Father. As His
children, we are blessed and
if we share His suffering,
we'll also share the glory
of the Christ!

Great Expectations

I'm of the mind that what
we suffer in these present
days can't be compared
with what the Lord will
have prepared for us. Search
far horizons, you'll discern
that all of nature, every
clime, awaits a glorious
release from drought, from
flooding rain, from blazing

heat. All nature waits, it
longs in hope to be set free
from death. The groans
arising from the pains that
nature bears are quite akin
to birth pain agonies. It's
not the natural world alone
that groans, anticipating
'Spring'; we groan also
as we await God's
Masterpiece: Eternal Life
in Jesus Christ.

We hope! This hope does
not induce a sham. If we
now see all that for which
we hope, it is no
longer hope! Do hold to
hope; await the Glory Day
with patience, bear hope
well. You have a need? You
don't know how to pray?

You can't express the
deepest yearnings of your
heart? The LORD sees deep
into the soul; the Holy Spirit
prays for us! From all
experience we know that
everything pertaining to our
life will work together for
our utmost good for He has
called us each according to
His purpose and He sets
apart His own—the called.

And those He called, He
reconciled unto Himself and
those He reconciled, He
plans their glory too!

Love revealed in Christ
In view of all this wondrous
truth, what can be said? It's
this: if God is for us, who
can rise against us now?
God won't—He gave to us
His only Son: He'll freely
give us all! We cannot stand
accused for God declares
His own 'Not Guilty!' And
The Christ does not
condemn: He died to set us
free from sin! Indeed, who
could now separate us from
the love of Christ? Deep
trouble won't, nor
persecution, hunger,
poverty, nor danger, even
death, for as the psalmist's
often sings:

*For You, O Lord, we are in
danger all the while; we are
like sheep en route into the
slaughter house...*

No! we are not consumed!
We have the victory!
Because God loves us so,
in every danger: we are
more than conquerors!

I am convinced of this:
it's neither death nor life;
nor angels, demons; not the
present nor the future, any
power, nor height nor depth;
nor anything in all
creation can ever separate
us from God's love that we
have found in Jesus Christ,
our Lord! This truth rejoices
all my heart: these hymns
of praise are the result!

THERE IS NO CONDEMNATION

Tune: *Penlan* 7.6.7.6. D.

There is no condemnation
For those in Jesus Christ;
Through Him, God's Holy Spirit
Has set us free to trust!
We would not live the
world's way,
We are aligned to grace;
Our minds are on His motives,
Our hearts know life
and peace.

We're led by God's own Spirit,
We are His children dear;
We ask our Abba, Father,
To cast aside our fear!
The Holy Spirit counsels
That we are heirs with Christ,

For—if we share His
suffering—
Also, we'll share His rest.

All wait in expectation
To see God's glory rise;
For any present burdens
Cannot outweigh His grace.
And all creation waits still
To overcome decay,
While we await redemption
To the Eternal Day.

Our hope is without measure
And unconfined God's aid;
His Spirit helps our weakness,
He prays at God's own side!
What then are our responses?
If God is for us, none,
No, none can overcome us,
We praise what He has done.

WE KNOW!

Tune: *Rutherford* 7.6.7.6. D.

We know that all things
work now
Together for the good
Of those who truly love Him,
Our great, eternal God.
According to His purpose
Before all time began,
He moulds us in the likeness
Of Jesus Christ, His Son.

And who can separate us
From Christ, our living Lord?
Shall hardship, tribulation,
Shall peril, or the sword?
Jesus is interceding
Before the Throne of Grace
He stands at God's right
hand and
Through Him we find
our peace.

In all things, ours the victory!
We're more than conquerors
Through Jesus Christ who
loved us;
Our faith with courage soars!
I am convinced there's nothing,
No creature ever could
Detach us from God's loving
In Jesus Christ our Lord!

CHAPTER 9
GRIEF AND GLORY

I speak the truth!
There is a grief that clings
to me: my people are not
saved! God has revealed His
glory unto them; He
covenanted, gave His Law
to them. They did receive
His promises: they are
not saved!

God's promises don't fail!
But all descendants of our
Abraham are not the
children of the LORD. You
see, the children born by
natural means are not His
'family' until they take His
word, His promises. God's
will in this is based upon the
call He makes and not upon
the excellence of human
traits, or lack of them.

Can it be said,
therefore, that God
is quite unjust? No way!
Clay pots do not chastise the
potter who has formed them
on the wheel: Why did you
form me in this way? Some
pots hold precious things,
and others hold just
ordinary things.

The News I give to you
is this: the ways of God
are glorious! He pours His
grace and mercy out on us
though we deserve it not!
He's called us to Himself
from both the Jew and
Gentile stock. He said
as much through Hosea
so many years ago:

The people once not Mine
I will receive now as My
very own; They'll be my
true beloved family. Once
thought not as My people,
They'll be called the
'children of the living God'!

Isaiah speaks of God's own
people in this way: though
numerous as sand upon the
shores of seas, there are
but few that will be saved.
Without the grace of God,
there would be none that
bear the 'family name'.
And what of you, the
Gentiles who had never
thought to be His own?
You're saved by grace
through faith!

Was Israel's fault because
they did not hold to faith but
placed their trust
in Law? They stumbled o'er
the stumbling stone—the
Rock that made them fall
into the dark! This Rock has
challenged them: they don't
believe! But all who trust in
Him shall live!

CHAPTER 10

UNIVERSAL SALVATION

My friends, I pray for Israel.
My people are a nation
that's devoted to the Law
but they don't know the
Path to Life! They have set
up, for self, a pathway built
with feeble hands and
human frailty. They don't
submit to God Who would
put all things right. Moses
spoke of Law with due
reverence. He thought the
coming of those rules on
Sinai would cleanse the soul
of sin. The Law is Life!

He thought that
'climbing up the mount'
would make things right.
This was so very wrong.
That 'God came down to
man' is what has given hope
of Glory now!
God's message is the word
of grace; it's near you: take
it to your heart. If you
confess that *Yeshua* is Lord,
believing God has raised
Him from the dead, you will
be saved. It is by faith that
we're made right with God.
There is no difference

between you and myself!
He is the same Lord of us
both. He blesses all who
place their trust in Him.
How can a person call to
God for help if they don't
know of Him? How can
they know the Gospel News
if there's no one to preach
the precious word?

The messenger is sent
from God: how
beautiful the coming of
the one who speaks with
power the words of Life!
The message must be heard
in order that each can
decide if they will walk the
Way that God requires.
The Gospel News has gone
out to the world and Faith
has come through listening
and receiving it!

CHAPTER 11
THE PRECIOUS
REMNANT

Has God cast Israel away?
No way! The man, Elijah,
could mislay his hope by
thinking all was lost when
fleeing to the desert from

Queen Jezebel. Not so!
The LORD encouraged him:
Yet seven thousand men are
true! So, if salvation is by
grace our work does not
save us. If it's by what
we do, then faith is of
no true avail. This means
that eyes are gifted but they
fail to see the light; their
ears are open yet they fail
to hear the truth. The
Gentiles have received
the word of God with joy.

We hope that Jews will see
and hear also because they
recognise the Truth that
others hold! If their ignorant
state has brought, instead,
Truth to the Gentiles, how
wonderful the day when
they accept the Truth for,
in reality, it will be as life
arising from the dead!

Oh, may the olive bear its
fruit. The root, when well,
will grant its worth unto the
branch. Do not allow
yourself to be lopped off—
the branch must bear the
fruit. You are the grafted
branch that brings a purity
to trees behaving as

a bramble does before
the grafting is applied to it.
The day will come when
Israel will find it's grafted
in the tree God grew. Yes!
Israel will be saved. The
LORD has promised to
erase their sin.

A people disobedient to
Law have found God's
mercy now applied. He
wrought this miracle for you
that, through His mercy
shown to you, all Israel
will find that mercy too.
How deep the riches of
God's grace! His wisdom is
without a boundary!
Who could become God's
counsellor or who could
read His Mind? It is of Him,
it is through him, it is to
Him all things apply. So!
Let His glory shine!

CHAPTER 12
THE LIVING
SACRIFICE

What kind of sacrifice does
God require? It is the living
sacrifice—the sacrifice
acceptable to Him. It is

with reason He desires the
gift that will ensure the
service of the soul.

Be not conformed to
worldly ways but be
transformed. How so, you
ask? Allow your mind to be
renewed so you may prove
God's perfect will. Don't
think yourself to be so great:
you see, the body is
composed of many parts
and each of these have
purpose to fulfil. And so
do we: one body within
Christ but each of us,
a role to play in serving
Him, the Lord.

Let us now utilise the gifts
God gives that we may
serve Him well according to
the grace poured out into
our lives.
A prophet? Prophesy!
A minister? Use your gift!
A teacher? Expound Truth.
An encourager? Deal kindly
A philanthropist? Generous
A leader? Be most diligent.
An example? Show mercy

Christian Behaviour

Here is a list of hints
for you:

Love with sincerity
Cling to the good,
abhor all evil
Be affectionate
Be diligent, serve God
Rejoice in hope, be patient
Be steadfast in your prayers
Be hospitable, be generous
Bless the persecutor
Rejoice with the rejoicing
Be ready to shed tears for
another's grief
Show a warm united stance
Repay no evil for evil deeds
Show due regard for good
And live in *shalom* peace.

CHAPTER 13
RIGHTS OF
GOVERNMENT

You think because we do
belong to Christ there is no
need to give due deference
to governing authorities?
God is the One Authority,
let others stand aside? Do
what is good; you'll find no
angst for praise will come.
Should you pay tax? Indeed,
you should, so render all
that's due: your tax, your

customs and your honour
too—don't be in debt but
live in love *agape* style.
This will fulfil all the
requirements of the law—
love will never harm a
neighbour or a foe. Awake
from sleep; the night is
spent; the sun will rise so
cast off every form of
darkest night and don the
LIGHT! Above all else, put
on the Christ, you have no
need to live for all the
superficialities of life. it is
the soul that counts.

CHAPTER 14
THE LAW OF LIBERTY

Be kind unto the weak.
Some think that what we eat
or do not eat is what will
count with God. No way!
Don't set yourself to be a
judge despising those who
fail to think or act like you.

What's all the 'fuss' about
which days are best for
worshipping? One day suits
one, the other bows another
day. It's attitude that counts.
We do not live entirely for

ourselves and no one dies in
the same way. For, if we
live, we live for Christ and
if and when we die, we die
for Him. In both these
issues, we're the Lord's.

It was for this that Jesus
died for He is Lord of living
and the dead. Why do you
judge your brother
detrimentally? We all will
stand before God's
Judgement Throne and
there, all knees will bow,
all tongues confess He is
the LORD. We're all
accountable to God.

THE LAW OF LOVE

Let not the good in us be
judged as wrong. God's
Kingdom does not focus on
the rules and regulations
that concern our 'eats and
drinks'. God's Kingdom is
all righteousness: It's peace,
it's joy in Holy Spirit power
so do rejoice in this today.
The Community of Faith
always pursues the things
that make for peace, that
which will build each other

up. Do nothing that would
cause one's fall from grace.

CHAPTER 15
A BURDEN TO BEAR

Those that are strong among
our company should stand
by all the weak and think of
others, not ourselves. The
Scriptures give good
guidelines whereby we
will learn the gracious ways
of patience, comfort and
of hope in *YHVH*–LORD.

Receive each other just
as *Yeshua* has done.
Now may the God of Hope
infill your soul with joy and
peace that you'll abound in
hope in Holy Spirit power.
I am most confident that
goodness floods your soul,
that wisdom grants ability
to encourage one another in
The Faith. But you may
wonder why I write so
boldly to you all. It is
because God's grace
enables me to be a minister
of Jesus Christ, our *Yeshua,*
to share with you the Gospel
News in its entirety. I would

not dare to speak of things unknown to me. But, through the signs and wonders, through the Holy Spirit, I have shared this News around the world. It's not my plan to preach where others preach. I've trod new ground in introducing Christ to all the world, to Jews and Gentiles too. And now it is my aim to visit you. I plan to journey on to Spain but my desire is, first, to meet with you before too long. The route is comprehensive though: I plan to take the aid that Gentile churches have donated for the Faith Community in Judea and Jerusalem. Please pray for me for there are those who plan disruption of my ministry and also do me harm. My deliverance will mean that I can come to you with joy by virtue of God's precious will always. Now, may God's peace reign in your hearts... So be it, LORD: Amen.

CHAPTER 16
ADDENDUM

I commend my fellow travellers and those who carry on the work at home. Receive Phoebe, do greet Priscilla and Aquila, my good friends and fellow labourers. There are so many who have touched my life and yours (I've listed them within the 'first edition' of this scroll). Please greet them with the holy kiss. Be wise in all that's good; His grace and peace be yours. My friends—yes, Timothy and Luke, my secretary, Tertius, my host, Gaius, all greet you too.

To Him who's able to establish you by Gospel News, according to the revelation of the mystery— hidden in history but now made known through prophets: News that all may come to faith, believing and obeying *YHVH*–LORD: to Him be all the glory always through the Lord *Yeshua,* the Christ... So be it LORD. Amen.

..... oOo .....

PAUL
TO THE
CORINTHIAN
CHURCH

THE FIRST LETTER

This is a massive city! Probably, there are as many as half a million citizens with a large proportion consisting of slaves. Corinth has good reason to think itself to be the premier city of the Greeks. This is also a strategic centre. It is a major crossroad of the Greek world. The travellers are now flowing continually through its environs and traders have lucrative enterprises.

Though they not as intellectually minded as Athens, for example, Corinthians love to think of themselves as wise. They thrive on debating in philosophical terms.

I ascertain that there are as many as twelve temples in the metropolitan area (with as many gods no doubt.) Aphrodite is adored—this will give me cause to make some extensive comments on the nature of purest love. Apollo also holds a pride of place. There is also a Jewish synagogue.

It must be said that Corinth is much tainted by rampart immorality. Is it any wonder that I've been requested to address the flagrant disregard for decency, even within the fledgling Church? One cannot expect maturity in those still barely adolescent.

I will set about outlining the most appropriate instructions regarding quality living but also endeavour to increase an appreciation of personal holiness. And, there's been some false attitudes arising regarding the Faith due to some weak teachers who require themselves to be instructed in the Faith we hold. I now set myself to the task:

Paul, Apostle
Pastor, Teacher
Circa A.D. 55

To the Church at Corinth,

Those called to be holy
In the Name of Jesus Christ
Charis and *Shalom*
Grace and peace to you!
(I love to meld the Gentile
and the Jewish greetings
for those with whom I
correspond.) I am most
thankful to the LORD for all
the grace that He has given
you. Through Him you are
enriched in every way.

The LORD will keep you
safe until the very end so
that there'll be no fault
accrued to you on
Judgement Day. Trust God.
He called you to this place
where we enjoy rich
fellowship in *Yeshua*–Jesus.

I've been requested, though,
to bring some counsel to
your Faith Community. It is
the Lord who grants me this
authority. Please 'hear me
out': To cease divisions in
your Church, work well to
be united now. Let thinking
be akin to grace, in one
accord. The quarrels must
be put aside. The point is
not that Paul, Apollos, even

Peter carries a unique
aspect of Truth to share with
you. The Lord can't be
divided. Was it Paul
who died for you?
I'm thankful of my purpose
not to baptise but to preach!
The Truth about the Lord—
that is, the Christ—can't be
displaced by pointless
argument. The wisdom of
the world is bleak!

The Jews want miracles!
The Greeks? Wisdom! But
as for us: we speak of
Christ. He is the focus of
our thought, our faith.
Christ is the Power of God,
His Wisdom too! What
seems to be His
'foolishness' is wiser
than all human thought.

Remember what You were
and how you lived before
you knew the Lord. Yes!
God has made the Christ to
be our wisdom and, by Him,
we are made right with God.
If you must boast, do make
your boast in Him!

CHAPTER 2

POWER OF THE GOSPEL

You will recall that, when I came to you, I did not come with intellectual genius; I spoke of nothing but the Christ, His death upon the cross. I came in weakness but God gave the content of my words. It was the power of Gospel News that won't rely on wit but on His word!

The wisdom that I preach to the mature is not that of this world. It is God's word. The intellectuals know nought of it for, if they did, they would not have crucified our Saviour, Lord.

It is the Spirit of the Lord who grants the power to preach Good News. Those who do not know Him can't receive His gifts of grace. 'Our words are nonsense', they declare! You have the Holy Spirit? You will value scripture's authenticity: Who has known God's Mind? And who is able to advise the LORD? Don't fret: we share the Mind

of Jesus Christ!

CHAPTER 3
THE PEOPLE OF GOD

When I first came to you, I had to speak as to a little child for everything I said was all so new to you. Milk was the menu and no solid food was shared until the rudimentary facts became digestible. There are no 'three course meals' for you as yet because the world claims much of what you think and do. In many ways, you don't know what to think: 'Apollos? Paul? Who can we follow now?' My friends, I planted all the seeds; Apollos watered, nurtured them. But it was God who made it grow. We are His partners and each has his task to do in sharing God's own word!

Let's put it all another way: You are the building of the Lord. I laid foundations and another built on these. You have your tools as well. Be careful how you build 'the house'. The only true foundation is the Lord! Some use fine gold or precious stones when building up the Church— the 'body' of the Lord— but others use just grass or straw. The building's quality (or less) will finally show up for what it is on Judgement Day.

Fire will consume the lesser work yet you'll be saved (though as by fire). The point I make is this: You are God's Holy Temple now! His Spirit dwells in you! Don't think the world will make you wise—this is a foolish attitude. All things are yours: Paul, Peter and Apollos, too. The world, one's life or death, the present and the future—all are yours for you belong unto the LORD!

CHAPTER 4
SERVANTS OF GOD

Please think of us as servants of the Lord. The one thing that's required of us is faithfulness to God. I'm not concerned about a judgement made of me. My conscience is quite clear. Am I without a fault? God passes judgement there! So, don't fling judgements all about on neighbours for it's God who shines the *LIGHT* on good or ill. My illustration is, of course, Apollos and myself to help you see the points I make.

Who made just any one of us superior to others? So, how can you boast of powers that you possess? (What is your preference—a whip or gentle grace, *agape* love?) Do you possess all things? You're rich beyond your dreams? This does not mean you're further up the ladder of success by the Lord's judgement for, until you learn to serve, God's values are not known.

Though persecution is endured, we faint not in the task He's placed within our hands. Therefore, I counsel you, not for your shame, but to instruct you, begging you to follow the example you've been given. I will be sending Timothy— he's like a son to me— to guide you in the principles that lead to Everlasting Life (and I'll come too, if possible.) Remember that the Lord does not depend on words but Holy Spirit power!

CHAPTER 5
SCOURGE OF IMMORALITY

The news that is conveyed leaves me aghast! Not even honest heathen would engage in such gross immorality reported recently. Even though I'm far away, I stand beside you in my soul. It leaves me sad.

I say to you: discard the evil one from all your fellowship. It's like the leaven working in the dough. Take out the 'yeast' of sin so that you will be pure. Go, bake some bread that you'll be ready for 'Passover': 'bread' with no

'yeast': the 'bread' of Truth. By rooting out the sin, I do not mean pagans who've yet to learn of Christ. You can't divorce yourself from all the world. I do mean: have no association with the one who pats himself upon the back: I *do* believe, I *do* belong!" but really is immoral and a liar. It's such a one that lives in sin!

CHAPTER 6
THE STATUS OF THE LAW

How should a Christian solve disputes with fellow followers of Christ? How infamous, to bring a lawsuit, state your case before a pagan judge! You have the brains, the soul, to judge yourselves and come to a decision that's in harmony with Law.

Why should an unbeliever judge the case? Instead of upright character, you will provoke another to retaliate: surely you know that you will not inherit what the

Lord prepares for you.
Wake up! You were once
purified and justified and
sanctified, put right with
God by *Yehua*–Jesus.
It's not essential that every

CHAPTER 7
SANCTITY OF
MARRIAGE

man should wed but, while
some are so prone to
immorality, I do advise that
men and women share the
vows set forth by satisfying
the needs of each. I do
prefer celibacy but all can't
be as I. Each has a special
gift from God. With due
regard to marriages, I speak
now from the *YHVH*–
LORD:
Divorce is alien to the
LORD's decree. Each
partner should remain
faithful until a death
does separate.

Now, with regard to
Christian and a pagan
partnership, if they continue
to be true to one another,
they'll be blessed. The Lord

calls you to live in peace.
(Those who agree to cease
the partnership, so let it be.)
These are the rules I teach
in all the churches—
many matters cause
a quandary. I speak
this way so you will know
and do what's right before
the *YHVH*–LORD.

CHAPTER 8
CONTAMINATED
FOOD

You've asked what can be
done about the food that's
offered to idols. It's easy to
sound wise and there are
many who will pride
themselves with wisdom.
But it's love that builds each
other up. We know that
idols have no life so they
require no food at all!

There are so many so-called
gods, yet there is only one
true God. He is the
Father of us all. He has
created everything through
Yeshua–the Christ:
in Him we live! Not all can
place their trust in one they

do not know. No food will
introduce them to the Lord.
It makes no difference to
our faith. My strong advice
to you is this:
Do not allow the weak to
fall because of you—who
are so strong—being seen
partaking of such food.
You'll cause the weak to
perish so, you will have
sinned. Do not allow the
weak to sin because of
deeds you do!

CHAPTER 9
THE LIFE OF AN
APOSTLE

I trust you will receive my
words for you will surely be
aware that I was called by
God to do the work
required: to serve the people
in my care. You'll realise
that you, yourselves, are
proof of my apostleship. I'm
criticised, of course, for
many things. (I do have
answers for them each.)
Moses helps me here.

Don't muzzle oxen when
they're threshing grain.

This does apply to all
apostles too for we have
sown the seed; is it too
much if we now reap the
grain? Apostles bear much
grief but claim no rights—
I'd rather die than vilify
or undermine my Lord!

I am the servant of the Lord.
What is my recompense?
The utmost joy for me is
preaching Christ, the
crucified Saviour.
I am a free-man but I make
myself a slave that I may
win the lost to *Yeshua*.
To Jews, I am a Jew;
to Gentiles, I accord with
them. This does not mean
I'd cast away the Law:
I live the Law of Christ.

I'm willing to become all
things to all that I may save
those that believe. I do all
things I do for the bless'd
Gospel's sake. As runners in
a race, so run that you may
win the prize. It will require
strong discipline but, last
out to the end: you'll gain
the 'laurel wreath'.

....

CHAPTER 10
HERITAGE OF
FAITHFUL

Let me draw to your
attention here, the holy
word of God which gives
examples of the 'Faith of
fathers known of old'—

Observe the list:
* Baptism in the cloud
  through Exodus
* The desert diet: daily
  sustenance
* The stream that gushed
  from rock

These: the 'foreword'
to *Yeshua,* the Christ.

The failures of His chosen
people there are prime
examples that will guard
and guide us from the evil
ways that many dabbled in
throughout the years of
Exodus—complaining,
faithlessness. So, if you
stand, take heed lest you
should fall. There's no
temptation you have faced
that is not common to
us all. But God is faithful!
He will not allow you to be
tempted past capacity. He

will provide the path for
your escape so you may
bear the trial. The bread
and wine of worship is
an illustration of the life
we share in Christ:
His body broken and
His blood poured out
for us—the symbol is
no greater than
the sacrifice!

Let all your focus be
on Him and not
the elements of Earth.
We are made 'one' in Him.
You eat the bread, you drink
the wine? These are but
symbols pointing you to
Him who has accepted you
by grace. Are symbols
helpful to your faith? Then
utilize them well but those
who relegate the symbol for
the sacrifice are mindful of
the One who gives us *Life.*

As to the things we choose
to eat: Let not your diet be
the means of leading others
into gluttony, false attitudes
and faithlessness. Let all
you eat and drink and all the
things you do be honouring
unto the LORD.

CHAPTER 11
TRADITION CAN OFFEND

There are traditions that may cause another to offend. There are some old-world practices that elevate our learning from the past. We find that custom can't exonerate or cause a harm to others in their modes of worship. That we come together to give praise should not be cause to worsen your relationships.

I speak as prophet, pastor now: When you partake the Supper of the Lord, you should acknowledge there His 'cup' of suffering, His body broken for His love is paramount. Let it be known among you all that they who will participate within this sacred act, must first examine their intent. Let no unworthy hands or lips partake of it lest judgement falls upon you then.

CHAPTER 12
GIFTS OF THE HOLY SPIRIT

I must address the Spirit's gifts as granted severally to all that honour *Yeshua*– Jesus, the Christ. There's much diversity, for all do not receive a gift identical with all. There is a difference in each gift but all are gifted by the self-same Holy Spirit— He is the one gift given to the Church.

To one is wisdom given,
To another: faith, to
another, gifts of healing
And another: working
miracles To one: the gift of
prophecy another:
interpreting those 'tongues'.
It is the Holy Spirit who
imparts each gift according
to His will.
We've been considering the
unity and the diversity that's
evident within God's
family: we have one body
that consists of many parts.

Let there be none of this:
The foot—I'm not the hand,
I don't belong!
The ear—I'm not the eye, I
don't fit in! If all were feet,
where would we be? How

could we serve? What could
we see? The eye should not
deplore the hand: I have no
need of you. The head
would not announce to feet:
I don't depend on you!
This emphasises our great
need to care for each in
Christian love. If any
If any suffer, let us suffer
with them too; rejoice with
those enjoying happiness.
What am I saying here?

Not all will be apostles,
teachers, preachers and the
like. Not all display the
'front-line' gifts. Is
everyone a prophet? No!
Or teachers? No! Miracle
workers? No! Desire the
gifts that grace your work!
And now, consider the most
excellent of all:

CHAPTER 13
THE LAW OF LOVE

Let me begin by a reminder
of the four great facets of
what we call love: All are
indebted to the Greeks for
their portrayal of the faces
of the love we feel:
Storge: family love

Philia: love of friends
Eros: romantic love
Agape: wide open to all
the attitude of *agape*,
reborn in Christian
principles, enables me
to find a patience in
disturbances, a kindliness
to overcome ill-will.

All jealousy has skipped
away in an appreciation of
the aptitudes that others
hold. And as for me, I see
that God has granted me
some gifts that I may utilize
without conceit. When tired,
or less than well, I give my
irritation up to Him who
blesses me with peace.

He grants the gifts
of graciousness and
gratefulness to each.
I have no lists, in mind
or as a note to keep, that
tabulate a long record of
wrongs. I give no place to
hatefulness; instead I am
rejoicing in the Truth. I find
the strength each day to
keep this attitude of *agape*
for it will never fail: it holds
to faith, to hope. When I
was immature, I thought as

children do: I've put away my childish ways. Today our vision is through clouded glass but one day we will see Him face to Face. My knowledge is so limited but one day I will fully know as I am fully known. For now: these three great blessings will remain: Faith … Hope … and Love The greatest of them all is LOVE!

These qualities of *agape* pertain to what the Lord gifts us: Eternal Life. Such excellence of love should send us into song:

LORD OF LOVE
Tune: *St Margaret* 8.8.8.6.
(Repeat 3rd line)

O Lord of Love, today we pray,
Your blessing give: so rich
and free,
As we have come our vows
to pay
And, by Your love, to ask
that You
Will guide through all our way.

Lord, You have taught us love
is kind,

Patient, enduring, suffering
long;
No evil thought ensnares
the mind
When love does keep no score
of wrong;
Your love as 'one' will bind.

It's known that true love
never fails,
It bears all things, it's hope
is sure;
Though knowledge won't
always avail—
We know in part—we do
know when
the perfect will not fail!

We see today through clouded
glass,
But one day, face to Face
with You;
While life shall last Your
blessings prove
There now abides faith, hope
and love—the greatest, best,
is love!

CHAPTER 14
THE GIFTS OF SPEECH

Both forms of speech will
hold a gift: the one: so able
to enunciate an unknown
tongue, and he who

prophesies—that is,
proclaims God's word.
Sometimes, it's true also
to speak of future times,
events. But there is need for
Gospel News to be
proclaimed, made known!
It must be said that
unknown tongues give no
encouragement to seeking
souls unless interpreters can
share the news they speak.

So, let the Church be edified
by words that clarify the
Faith. It's wonderful to pray
in spirit speech, also to pray
in words that are quite
understood. It's beautiful to
sing God's praise in spirit
voice but better with an
understanding too.

And I would much prefer
just five words spoken
comprehensibly than all ten
thousand known by none. If
none can give interpretation
of a prayer or speech, how
will it edify the Church?
The uninformed can come
to Faith by hearing clearly
Gospel News.

And now, also, a word

about what order should
prevail. Let all proceedings
be well planned so that
the whole Community of
Faith will then be edified.
You'll realise, of course that
God is not the Author of
confusion but of peace.
Let all things be performed
with decency and tact.

CHAPTER 15
FAITH'S REALITY

I preach to you again the
Gospel you received from
me when first I came to you.
It is the Faith in which you
stand. Hold fast to Faith: the
Christ has died to set us free
from sin according to the
word of God. My faith came
from my interview with
Yeshua–Jesus. Although
born out of the due time and
being least of all apostles
for I persecuted the
Community of Faith. But,
by the grace of God, He
made me what I am. This
grace was not in vain for I
have laboured so abundantly
and yet, not I but by the One
enabling me! You've heard

the Gospel that I preach—
how can you say, therefore,
there is no resurrection from
the dead? If this is so, then
Christ did not arise:
all faith is vain—Just empty
words, invalid faith! Just
think of this: If in this life
alone we have a hope,
we are of all people most
pitied, forsaken and
deprived! My friends, I now
reiterate: Christ has risen
from the dead! He is alive!

Yes, through one man all
die but, by one Man: the
resurrection from the dead.
For, as in Adam all will die,
in Christ shall all be made
alive! He is the 'First Fruit'
that will guarantee the
harvest time: that is the time
when He'll deliver all
His Kingdom to the
Father's hands. His
Kingdom reigns until all
enemies (the last of which is
death) are crushed beneath
His feet. So! what
advantage would there be
if we can't rise again?
Let's eat and drink, be
merry now for there'll be no
tomorrow anymore!

You ask, instead, what is
the style of reclaimed life?
Look to the seed:
it looks so dead but it will
rise to beauteous flower
and fruit! Just so, the body
is once sown in a corrupted
state but it will rise up
incorruptible. No flesh and
blood inherits the
Eternity of God.

But now, I speak a mystery:
We won't all sleep but we
will all be changed—in the
twinkling of an eye, right
when the final trumpet
sounds! That's when the
dead will rise as
incorruptible and we'll be
changed: this mortal man
must put on immortality:

O death, where is your
sting? O grave, where is
your victory? The sting of
death? The sin! The strength
of sin? The Law!
Thanks be to *YHVH*–
LORD:
He gives the victory through
Yeshua–Jesus. Be steadfast
then, dear friends,
immovable, abounding in
good works for these will

never be in vain!
So! Let this be our
Victory Song:

THE VICTORY
Tune: *Spohr* 8.6.8.6.8.6.

Christ died because of
human sin,
According to God's word;
He died upon a cross
of shame.
For us He shed His blood.
The third day He was raised
to life:
He is the Son of God!

If Christ had not been raised
to life,
Our faith would be in vain;
How could we testify, or prove
The Lord now lives again?
If in this life alone is hope,
What solace could we gain?

But Jesus Christ has risen
indeed,
The Firstborn from the dead.
Since death had come by just
one man,
By one Man, death has fled!
Our Lord will reign forever
King:
The Victor over death!

How may the dead be raised
to life?
Just as a seed is sown
Into the waiting soil in death,
It is transformed: life won!
Though sown as weak we're
raised in power:
Christ's saving work is done!

This is a glorious mystery:
We'll all be changed, it's found!
Within the twinkling of an eye,
The trumpet call will sound;
Then, clothed with immortality,
We're, in Christ's likeness,
crowned!

So where, O death, is now
your sting?
And grave, your victory?
The power of sin has been
destroyed.
Christ's death is history:
Now unto God be all
the praise,
He gives us victory!

CHAPTER 16
PRACTICAL MATTERS

You are aware that I'm
receiving the donations for
the churches in Judea where
the need is great.

Each Sunday, be prepared to
set aside the amount most
appropriate to your simple
circumstance. Do choose
a courier to bear your gifts
down to Jerusalem.

I plan to come to you
when passing on from
Macedonia. I hope to
'winter' then with you. But
presently a most effective
door has opened up for me
in Ephesus (and many
hardships too.) When
Timothy arrives take care
of him. Respect his youth.
Apollos does intend to come
at a convenient time.
And, finally, I say to you:
Keep watch, stand fast, be
brave, hold to the Faith with
great tenacity.

As I sign off, I send the
greetings of the Church in
Asia. Also, Aquila and
Priscilla and the church that
meets together in their
home, do greet you heartily.
The grace of Jesus Christ be
with you... I send my love
to you—this salutation is
now written in my
own hand. Come Lord to us.

PAUL: TO THE CORINTHIAN CHURCH

THE SECOND LETTER

INTRODUCTION

Following the mailing of
my previous letter to
Corinth, I received some
very disquieting news to the
effect that some subversive
elements had infiltrated the
Faith Community there only
to cause much disruption by
challenging my authority as
an apostle of Christ. It had
been insinuated that I was
not to be trusted, I lacked
integrity and, what's more, I
was pocketing the proceeds
of the Church's collection on
behalf of the needy in
Jerusalem.

Things had become so
tenuous that I dispatched
Titus to Corinth to ascertain
the truth of this
disconcerting information.
I'm happy to report that
Titus has returned with
excellent news. On the
strength of this, I now set

out to communicate with all my friends in Corinth—and indeed, through Achaia (Southern Macedonia)—to re-establish my 'diplomatic relations' with them all. I feel the need to open up my heart as never before. Here is the Faith I hold expressed in deepest terms:

Paul, Apostle
Timothy Assisting
Circa (late) 55 A.D.

To the Community of Faith, Corinth and Achaia:

Dear friends,
Grace and peace to you!
the *YHVH*–LORD, the
Father of our Lord, Christ,
is the Bless'd, the Great
Encourager (He is the com-*fort*-er)! He comes to us
to bring His consolation in
the midst of all our strife
and You will find His
com**fort**—He consoles us in
our grief. When burdened
beyond measure, thinking
death was immanent,
the LORD delivered us once
more! We sensed your
prayers. They aided our

deliverance.

We continue to conduct
ourselves with all sincerity
in simple faith—it's not by
wisdom but through grace.
The LORD is faithful! All
His promises are 'Yes!
Amen!' So let it be!
The One who has anointed
me 'apostle' sealed His
promise with the
Holy Spirit in my heart.

I need to tell you that my
plans to come to you were
changed. This was to spare
you greater hurt. You do
not need a further sorrow
for, if I have caused you
pain, where is someone
who'd ease your grief?

**CHAPTER 2
GRACE OF
FORGIVENESS**

I have no wish to cause you
pain. It is my joy to know
that you are joyful too. The
first letter was penned
in anguish for I wanted you
to know my love for you.
The man who caused the
pain has hurt you much but

now's the time to find
forgiveness in your heart.
Thanks be to God who
grants the triumph over
woe, for He enables us to be
like fragrance wafting in the
souls of those who come
to faith in Christ.

CHAPTER 3
'LETTERS' FROM
THE LORD

Who needs the written letter
now? You are the letters
printed on our heart.
The 'letter' Timothy and I
received was not penned in
an ink but by the Holy
Spirit's hand; nor carved
upon a stone but deep
within our hearts.

We find an all-sufficiency
for strength is all from God.
He made us ministers of the
New Covenant. And,
speaking of the first, the
Moses Covenant was truly
glorious whereby he'd need
to veil his face for glory
shining brightly there.
But how much more the
glory that suffuses the New

Covenant now ratified in
Christ: by grace, we are
redeemed through faith.
With unveiled face we do
behold, as in a mirror, all
the glory of the Lord. Yes,
we–the Faith Community–
are being transformed into
the likeness of the Christ
by Holy Spirit power!

CHAPTER 4
GOSPEL
ILLUMINATION

Now, since we have this
ministry through God's own
grace, we'll stand firm in
good heart. We've left the
past behind. So, if the Truth
we teach is veiled, it's only
veiled to those that perish
for they lack the Living
Faith. Their eyes are blinded
lest the glory of the Christ
should shine on them. We
don't stand for ourselves.
We preach the Gospel
News. You see, my friends,
it is the *YHVH*–LORD who
caused the *LIGHT* to shine
upon the darkest void.
He shone within our hearts
to give to us the *LIGHT* of

His own glory in the Face
of Christ. How wonderful!
We hold this precious gift in
rough 'clay pots' so that
the glory shines where it
belongs: In Jesus' Face!

We are hard pressed, not
crushed. We are perplexed,
there's no despair. We're
persecuted, not destroyed!
Our bodies show deep
marks of Christ's own
suffering. It is our will,
through this, to illustrate His
claims on us. We know that
God, who raised up Jesus
Christ, will raise us up also.

The things we suffer now
will serve to spread the
Gospel News so that His
glory may abound each day.
Therefore, we don't lose
heart. While physically we
waste away, within our soul
we are renewed. Our focus
isn't on the visible, our eyes
are fixed on Christ for what
is seen is temporary. The
things pertaining unto Him:
these place Eternity within
responding hearts.

CHAPTER 5

FAITH THAT ENDURES

We know that, if this earthly
'tent'—the body—is
destroyed, we have a
'house' not built with
hands: the Home prepared
for us in Heaven. While in
the earthly 'tent' we groan
with burdens difficult to
bear; our Heavenly Home
awaits us there and, one
day, mortal frames will be
engulfed by immortality.
The Holy Spirit is God's
guarantee of this eternal
bliss. While draped still in
our human garb, we wait
the Glorious Day. We walk
by faith and not by sight.
We'll all appear before
the Judgement Seat.
Choose Life!

It is the love of Christ that
yet compels us day by day
to live for Him. It's our
desire that all be reconciled
to God for, if anyone is IN
Christ Jesus, he is born
anew, created once again.
Old things, old values, have
all gone, all things are new
for God has reconciled us to
Himself through *Yeshua*—

Jesus. For this great Truth
we have become
ambassadors: we stand
for Christ!

My friends, be reconciled to
God. This is the glorious
news: The *YHVH*–LORD
made *Yeshua*–Jesus to be as
sin for us although He knew
no sin within Himself. His
sacrifice has made it
possible for us to be the
righteousness of God
through Him!

CHAPTER 6
THE MARKS OF
MINSTRY

Do not receive God's grace
in vain. Today is the
accepted time to stand
for Christ. We do commend
the ministry though we
experience distress, yes;
tribulation, yes; the
whiplash, gaol, riots,
hunger, yes! But balance
these with purity, with
patience, kindness, *agape*
love, God's righteousness,
His power, much honour,
God's righteousness, His
power, much honour, good

report. Dying? Yet alive!
Sorrow? Yet there's joy!
Poor? Possessing all!

My dear Corinthians,
we've opened up our hearts
to you and now we ask that
you stay clean: be
sanctified, made holy. Do
not try the merging of the
LIGHT with **darkness** for
you are the temple of the
LORD. There is no place
for idols in our heart. It is
the LORD who said:

*I'll dwell with them, I'll
walk
with them, I'll be their God
and they will be My own.
Therefore: Come out from
them; be separate; don't
dally with what is unclean:
I will welcome you.*

CHAPTER 7
PERFECTING
HOLINESS

You hold such precious
promises! Let all remain in
holiness. I'm sure you know
the joy that's in our hearts:
we are much comforted.
You know that we'd been

troubled but the news that
Titus brought consoles us
for your zeal, your keen
desire to stand firm in the
Faith. Repentance is a
wondrous gift—your godly
sorrow brought a clearing
of the problems that had
marred your life IN Christ.
We joy in God for this.
We've confidence in you!

Chapter 8
THE GIFT OF
GENEROSITY

It's wonderful to see the
generosity of those who
give beyond capacity. In
poverty, they prove how
rich they are in gifts of
grace—to bear with other
needy folk that they
might ease the burden of
the penury of purse yet
wealth in *agape*—love.

O, may you yet abound just
so. You know the grace of
Yeshua—though He was
rich, for your sakes He
became so poor that,
through His gift, you would
be rich. Allow your

readiness to give now be
actual; the willing mind
now balanced by the ready
hand. We'll take your gift
with us into Judea,
and then, Jerusalem.

CHAPTER 9
ADMINISTRATIVE
MATTERS

I know your willingness to
give, I've boasted of your
readiness. I trust the boast is
not in vain. I've sent some
envoys to assist. So! In
regard to cheerfulness in
sharing with those far afield
I say: the man who sows
just sparingly will reap
a sparing harvest too.

Be bountiful in what you
sow, the reaping will be
bountiful! You purpose to
do well in this? Then give
as well without regret.
The LORD so loves your
cheerfulness and He will
make all grace abound
to you. He is the One who
does supply the seed that
you may eat your bread,
increase your faith. You'll

be enriched in every way
and all the while you'll
thank the LORD for His
Gift indescribable.

CHAPTER 9
SPIRITUAL WARFARE

I plead with you with
gentleness though boldly
state my case with you.
You see, we don't rely on
worldly ways, we do not
fight for worldly claims.
Do not rely on outward
signs of Life. You have
concerns about the boldness
of the mail I sent to you?

I cast my speech upon the
page solely to edify. I mean
no harm; it's my desire to
strengthen you. My letters
are so bold, so powerful, yet
I am weak. What do I say?
I speak for Christ alone.
This means that I can't
boast because of powerful
words. In Christ alone I
boast. The words I speak,
the deeds, are all because
of hopes I hold for you. If I
should glory, I will glory in
the Lord whom I boldly

commend to you.

CHAPTER 11
FAITHFULNESS

Do bear with me; I do
have some concerns
for days that lie ahead
for there are some
that turn aside so very
easily. The 'evil serpent'
can deflect by his great
subtlety, the simple faith
that keeps one strong.
The words I speak are not
inferior to others that you
know I'm not untrained in
oratory! Yet I have humbled
my achievements so that
Christ alone be glorified.

I've asked no funds for what
I do. I have endeavoured not
to throw a burden on your
backs. I've warned of those
who falsely come
pretending their apostleship,
credentials too. I am no
fool. I urge you not to
entertain those prattlers
wearing 'wisdom' cloaks.
Perhaps I've been too weak
to boldly state their flaws!
So, I'll make bold for once:
Are they the Hebrew seers,

the seed of Abraham? Well,
so am I! Are they the
Ministers of Christ? Here
is my foolishness: Well so
am I, and more so for the
scars I bear! I'm beaten by
their 'best'; stoned by the
'righteous' rioters!
Shipwrecked; imperilled in
the city, country, desert too;
endangered by my own, the
Jews, and wearied by the
toil, the violence, the hunger
and the thirst. These are the
things for which I boast.
The LORD knows that
I speak the truth!

CHAPTER 12
VISIONS OF PARADISE

I turn from what I have
achieved, what I have
suffered in the past.
I'd tell of one who was
'caught up' to Paradise
some years ago—I do
not speak his name, you'd
know him well. This man
was given visions of God's
Paradise, to see and hear of
things quite inexpressible.
I could well boast of him,
but won't. This is no foolish

talk, it's Truth! I will refrain
from telling all lest any put
me on a pedestal. To keep
me from an exaltation here,
I did receive a 'thorn' that
cut deep in my flesh. I asked
the LORD to be. relieved.
He said:

My grace is all you need.
The strength I give
will be perfected in your
weakness now.

And so I make my boast in
these infirmities so that the
power of Christ remains
with me. When I am weak,
that's when I'm truly strong.
Forgive that foolish
paragraph; it is to re-enforce
the worth of what
you learned throughout my
ministry. I'm making ready
now to come again and vow
that I'll not burden you.
I'll gladly spend and to be
spent for you no matter
what you think of me.
We look for no advantages
from you, intending just to
share with you and edify the
Faith Community.
Let there be peace
among you all.

CHAPTER 13
APOSTOLIC
AUTHORITY

In coming twice before
to you, I will return upon
this third occasion solely
speaking out the Gospel
News and clarifying what
you've yet to learn. You
seek the proof that *Yeshua*
does speak through me? The
Lord is mighty to save and
keep all those that do
believe. Look deep within:
do you now hold to Faith?

Examine where you stand.
Is Christ IN you? Don't be
disqualified! We're happy if
our weakness means that
you are strong! We pray that
you will be complete
IN Him. As I sign off I urge
you all to be of God's good
comfort, unified, and
dwelling in His peace:
complete! The grace of
Yeshua, the love of God
and Holy Spirit power,
be with you all.

....

PAUL
MY TESTIMONY TO
THE GALATIANS

My ministry in Galatia has
enabled me to gain some
understanding of a people
who engage in intriguing
concepts for their fertile
minds to contemplate. They
crave wisdom but do appear
to be somewhat unstable,
being inconsistent with their
fluctuating points of view.
An argument must be
digested, but there is no
certainty that they will take
such 'food' into the diet
offered them. They love to
quarrel if there's contention
in their fellowship.

I realise the need to
enthuse, encourage them in
order to ensure that they will
make the effort to re-engage
with Gospel Truth. Because
Galatians are so passionate, I
will endeavour to utilize this
trait in hope that they'll
regain the wonder of grace
so that they'll be lifted from
their wretched narrow-
minded religiosity.

How does one change the

attitudes that superstitious souls will venerate? Their traditional beliefs cloud the verities that offer Eternal Life. But how great the grace of God! I now set out to emphasise that all are saved by grace through faith! God grants this grace to all who open their mind to Him. This is the Faith I now present to Galatia as I take up my quill to speak my faith:

Paul, Apostle
Circa A.D. mid 50s

Dear brothers and sisters:

Greetings! May the LORD grant you His Grace and Peace. My first thought of you as I lift my quill, must be this News: our blessed Lord, *Yeshua*–Jesus Christ, has gifted up His life for us that we may gain true life, being saved from sin. God planned that we'd be rescued from this sin-stained world in which we live. For this I give Him glory now! I speak Good News to you as I have done when visiting your Church.

I am surprised that you have wilted badly from your first intent.
The LORD has called you to Himself and you received His grace into your life. But now, so soon, you have decided on a different course, the course of falsity. It's not Good News. Your mind is now enamoured with the latest fad in terms of what you will believe.

I ask you now to think again. You've heard the Gospel; you took hold, then dropped the Truth that led you into Life! May I remind you that the Gospel News is not composed by any man no matter how so charismatic he may be. It came through Christ!

You know that I was steeped in Judaism and, so furious, I had set out to persecute the Church— the Faith Community— I was endeavouring to destroy all those who did believe that Jesus is alive.

But then He stopped me in my murderous intent. The *LIGHT* had dawned: I was reborn! Christ challenged me to live for Him, to tell the world they could be free by trusting in the LORD.

The Gospel News has not been altered, suiting whims of each and all.
The news was spread that I—the one who persecuted all who trusted Christ—had been reformed. He now was serving God by introducing folk like you to Christ. This News had been received with utmost joy.

CHAPTER 2
PROCLAMATION OF
THE GOSPEL

When fourteen years had passed, I went up to Jerusalem to share my mode of ministry. This was acceptable to those who'd held some doubts about what I believed concerning liberty in word and deed, as granted by the *YHVH*– LORD. The questions that

arose about procedures which ensured the right of membership were solved. The 'Pillars of the Church', that is: James, John and Peter, had perceived that I was *bone fide* in the faith that I proclaimed. They offered then the hand of fellowship, enabling both Barnabas and I to be, for Gentiles, teacher–preachers.

Just one specific rule was now required: to help the poor! Then Peter had some qualms when he arrived in Antioch. He felt, I think, quite 'out-of-depth' and found it difficult to 'fellowship' with foreigners, those integral to all the faithful there. I challenged him to see the point and act on it: a person is not justified by rules set down by man but by the faith they hold in Jesus Christ.

No law will justify, make pure, the one accepting *Yeshua* as Lord! this is the Gospel that I preach: I am quite dead to Law

I am alive to God: I have been crucified with Christ. It is no longer Paul that lives, it's Christ who lives in me! The life that I now live, I live by faith in *Yeshua* who loved and gave Himself for me. I cannot set aside the grace of God. If law could bring Eternal Life, then Jesus Christ has died in vain!

CHAPTER 3
JUSTIFIED BY FAITH

You've been bewitched! You know the choicest of all news. Did you discover this through Law? You had commenced your walk along the path of Faith. You did so well in learning how to 'hike'! But you're now of the mind that your physique will lead you into Life.

Remember Abraham! He trusted in the *YHVH*– LORD: this was his righteousness. God gave to him the promise that, through his descendants, all the nations would be blessed through Faith!

By trusting Christ, you live no more according to the 'curse' of Law as it is much inferior. Take note: the just shall live by Faith. Don't take the shackles of the Law–this is constraint from which we have been freed.

This blessing Abraham endowed: the Law cannot annul the Covenant of Christ. There is no promise in the Law. God's promise is in Christ. What is the power of Law? God gave 'The Ten' at Sinai that Israel would stop transgressing what was good within God's sight.

What is the power of His own promises? We're free, redeemed to live by grace through faith in Him. Would you prefer to live in chains, restricted by the guardianship of Law or be released to live for Christ, discovering daily grace enabling you to live IN Holy Spirit power. The Law was given to tutor but, through faith, the tutoring is past, long gone!

All those that live by Law
are students, adolescents

yet. You can be whole
through faith in Christ for
we are counted 'one' in
Him. It is not Jew, nor
Greek, not slave, nor free
and neither is it male or
female: ALL ARE 'ONE'!

CHAPTER 4
HEIRS OF GOD'S
KINGDOM

Although an heir, a child
does not enjoy the fulness of
his heritage. He goes to
school, he learns a trade,
he's tied to study books till
time to 'try his wings'. Just
so, as children, we are
'bonded' to the world. But
in the fulness of the time
arranged, God sent
His Son, born 'under Law',
to be Redeemer setting free
the slave to be adopted into
God's own family.

My friends, you are no
longer slaves! You're free!
You are adopted in God's
family; you are an heir to
Life! The question that

I ask is this:

**If once you were set free,
how come you've let
those 'gaolers' clamp the
shackles on your life once
more? I am afraid for you.
It seems I've worked in
vain for you.**

You know it was with great
infirmity I brought the
Gospel to your view. You
had received the Gospel
News with joy; you loved
and cared for me. Have I,
who once was loved by you,
become rejected, cast aside?
I'll hold concerns until the
Lord will be re-formed in
you. Take stock!

Now seek in wisdom what
you'll choose: which
Covenant for you? Think of
the lessons to be learned
through Abraham's two
wives: Hagar: bond slave,
Sarah: chosen by love.

CHAPTER 5
THE LIBERTY OF
FAITH

Take hold of liberty—
a freedom that is gained
through Jesus Christ.
You think, as Gentiles, that
you must become like Jews?
You wish to now be
justified by Law? Or, if IN
Christ, to eagerly await the
hope of righteousness that's
gained by faith? This is the
way to Life: it's faith
at work through love. You
ran so well! What tripped
you up? Don't let the
'leaven' spoil the 'loaf'!

I do have confidence that
you'll remove the 'leaven'
that has soured your life.
You have been called to
liberty. But do not use that
liberty to disregard your
faith. You plan to live by
Law? Then let it be this
Law: the Law of Love for
Love will cover all the Law!

Now, how would you
propose to so fulfil the Law
of Love? Walk in the Spirit:
He's the secret of true
sanctity. There are great
lists of laws that will
prescribe the dos and don'ts.
I give a better list:

These are the fruits of
Holy Spirit Life:
God's gifts: Love, Joy,
Peace
Others: gentle, kind good
Personal: faithful, gentle,
self-controlled.

CHAPTER 6
BEAR, SHARE
BURDENS

It's all too often that we see
someone who's fallen by
the Path of Life. Be ready,
hearts engaged and hands
involved to lend the aid
required. If you can bear
with one another, sharing,
caring, you'll fulfil the Law
of Love. There is no room
for one's self-praise. Don't
be deceived: the Lord is
wide awake to all you do or
fail to do. So, don't be late
to lift a load to aid another.
Don't lose heart: be good,
do good: a plan for Life!
You sow the seed? The
harvest will be reaped in
time allowed.

To finalise these thoughts
with you, I say: God forbid

that I should glory in my
work: I glory in the cross
of Christ alone. It is by Him
the world is crucified to me
and I unto the world!
Please, do not further
trouble me: the marks
of God are on my life.
I hope to bear them well.
Now, may His grace
bless you. Amen.

....

PAUL
MY TESTIMONY

TO THE
WORSHIPPING
COMMUNITY

EPHESUS

I set my sights on Asia
Minor now and write, in
particular, to Ephesus. The
harbour is superb. Sailors
search the Aegean horizon in
the hope of an early entry to
enjoy respite from their
weary toil. This city is an
industrious metropolis,
being a major trade route to
the wider world.

The focus for most
citizens is the pagan temple
dedicated to the worship
of—for the Romans: Diana,
for the Greeks: Artemis. I
worked each day among the
bourgeoning Community of
Faith for about three years as
I introduced the citizens to
the one Living God who
gifts Eternal Life through
His Son *Yeshua*–Jesus,
Messiah (to Greeks: the
Christ.)

My reason for presenting
to you this testimony edition
is to emphasise the power of
God and His purpose
revealed to us through His
amazing grace. It is my hope
that this mail will also travel
on from Ephesus so that it
may encourage and edify
believers in the churches
throughout the regions
where I've ministered. It is,
therefore, in truest sense, an
open letter. I want the whole
world to know the wisdom
that is sourced in God, that
we are saved by grace
through faith in Christ.

I'll sing the glory of the
LORD today and invite you,
my readers, to join with me

in worship, rejoicing in His will to draw all things together to Himself through Christ. I desire that all the Church may know the part you play in sharing this wonder, worship, witness, wisdom and work that has a world-wide span! By this means we are all involved in the LORD's ultimate goal for the Church: Eternal Life—via Redemption, Reconciliation, Renewal and Righteousness which is of Christ.

I trust that these themes will resonate with you as I deem this Testimony to The Faith to be a peon of praise. I therefore invite the Church to give a corporate witness to the Faith we hold in these hymns of praise. Affirm your Faith in worship now:

and wide;
Blessings in abundance
flooding:
Love unfathomed is this tide.

Praise is offered to the Saviour
Who is all our heart's delight;
He has chosen us to be now
Holy, blameless in His sight.

Chosen from before creation,
He predestined us to be
Members of His own dear
Family,
Holy, cleansed by grace
so free.

We will praise His glorious
grace now:
Gifted through the Son
He loves;
This is now the Lord's good
pleasure,
Heavenly peace now flows
to us.

CHAPTER 1
GRACE AND PEACE

Overture
Tune: *Sardis* 8.7.8.7.
Trochaic

Hallelujah! Grace of God and
Peace is streaming deep

WE HAVE
REDEMPTION
Tune: *Silchester* S.M.

We have redemption found
In Jesus Christ our Lord;
In Him forgiveness comes to us
According to His word.

We have been chosen, bless'd
In Jesus Christ our friend;
We praise and glorify the Lord:
Our hope will know no end.

We have been sealed by Him:
The Holy Spirit came!
We have redemption through
His blood;
To live in Christ, our aim.

CHAPTER 2
WE ARE ALIVE!
Tune: *Sagina*   S.M.

Now made alive, though we
were dead,
Walking sin's way, friend of
the world;
But God is rich in mercy free,
In love, He has His Son
involved!
When we were dead, He raised
us up
To glorious honours yet untold.
We are alive in Jesus Christ!
From death to life, how truly
blessed.

Exceeding rich, God's grace
to us,
His kindness shown in Christ,
His Son.
It is by grace that we are saved

Through faith in Jesus Christ
alone!
Created new, we trust in Him,
Not famous works that we
have done!
We are made free in Jesus
Christ!
Of all God's creatures, we
are blessed.

Strangers we were and alien
souls,
Having no life, no hope in God;
But now, in Christ, we are
made whole,
We're washed in Jesus'
precious blood.
He is our peace, we rest
in Him;
We're unified through Christ
our Lord.
We are made new in Jesus
Christ;
We have new hope and we
are blessed.

No more as strangers, far
from home,
No more alone, we live in Him!
Our fellowship His Spirit seals
As citizens of God's own
Heaven!
We're living as His temple
here,

Our gracious Lord to dwell
within.
*We are made whole in Jesus
Christ;
We are His own, how truly
blessed.*

CHAPTER 3
BEHOLD THE
MYSTERY

Tune: *Beethoven* L.M.

Behold! The mystery of Christ,
The 'open secret' is made plain!
The Holy Spirit has disclosed
This is the glorious truth
we gain:
We are the kin of Jesus Christ!
And, as 'one body', we
each day
Are sharing in God's promises
As heirs of His Eternity!

The gift of grace He gives
to us,
Through His almighty power
within.
Although we are unworthy now,
This grace is given, freely
given.

That which was hidden in
the past
By shrouding mists of time
unknown,

Has now become God News
for all;
The Church displays the victory
won!

We are the family of God!
We have derived our name
from Christ;
His name is written on
our heart
And in His riches we are
bless'd.

The Spirit comes empowering
us;
Within our inner life is peace
For Christ now dwells within
our heart;
By faith, He nurtures us
in grace.

Lord, we are finding, by Your
grace,
How deep and high, how wide
and long
The love of Christ: this love
we know
And all God's fullness is
our song.

CHAPTER 4
THESE ARE THE
MARKS

Tune: *Rockingham* L.M.

The marks of holiness
are these:
Humility with gentleness
And patience borne with each
in love;
These are the marks of
Christlikeness.

Baptised with Fire! He has,
in might,
Set all our hearts aflame
in Him.
The 'Fire', His Holy Spirit,
comes
To energise and victory win.

We have been cleansed by
Holy Fire,
Refined within His furnaces.
By faith made bold and free
from sin,
The Lord has sanctified
our days.

Christ calls us to a servant path
So that God's people may be
blessed
And reach a unity of faith
Mature and made complete
in Christ.

No longer infants in the Faith,
Tossed to and fro by every
quest;
Instead, the speech of love

declares
That we will grow up into
Christ.

We are made new in Jesus
Christ
Within our attitude of mind;
Created to become like Him,
His righteousness and peace
we find!

Our one true hope is Jesus
Christ!
One Lord, one faith one
cleansing: His!
One God and Father of us all;
He's over all, He's all in all!

CHAPTER 5
ABIDING IN CHRIST
Tune: *Warrington* L.M.
(with Proclamation)

We have received the word
of God,
The Gospel of His grace in
Christ;
His truth has taught us to abide
In Christ who is our heavenly
Guest.

He calls us to become like Him,
To live in love as He has loved;
We give our all into His hands

That, by our witness, love
is proved.

We find our strength in Christ
our Lord
And Truth is on our banners
here;
Evil will find no foothold where
The speech is pure and heart
sincere.

Once darkness closed us off
from God,
But day has dawned: we walk
in Light!
Within this Light God's
goodness shines,
His truth now makes the
pathway bright.

We would not grieve God's
Spirit for
We have been sealed:
Redemption's Plan!
As Christ forgave, so we
forgive,
We live in the eternal span!

Proclamation (Chorus):
Put off the ragged 'clothes'
of sin:
Deceitful styles, corrupted
dress;
Put on the new: the purest life,
Declare allegiance: Christ
confess!

Now sing with psalms and
songs within
Your heart; make music to
the Lord;
With thankfulness displayed
in love,
Give witness to the One
adored.

CHAPTER 6
PUT ON THE ARMOUR
Tune: *Maryland* D.L.M.
(with Proclamation)

Put on the Armour of our God
So you may stand firm in
the Lord;
Our struggle's not in Earth's
vain wars,
We fight the Saviour's worthy
cause.

Proclamation:
*Be strong in Christ and in
His power,
Be ready for the soul's
great fight!
Be firm: He is your Captain
now,
He'll lead you to Eternal Light!*

Stand firm in Christ and
buckle on
The Belt of Truth: it will secure

The whole so you will win
the fight;
Truth stands the test, you will
endure!

Let Righteousness secure
your heart,
On this, your life will now
depend!
The Gospel of His Peace
proclaim:
Prepare to march through
every land.

Take up the Shield of Faith,
be strong!
No matter where the arrow
flies,
All evil will be thwarted by
A Faith that is alive and wise!

Let every thought of Jesus'
blood
And His great grace now be
your guard;
The Helmet of Salvation wear
And take the Spirit's Sword:
God's word!

Now be at prayer, stand watch
each day;
Request the Lord to power
your best.
To share Good News, proclaim
God's word:

The mystery now known in
Christ.

....

PAUL
MY TESTIMONY
TO THE
PHILIPPIANS

You will deduce, I'm sure,
that I've arrived at last in
Rome though not according
to plan. I had been intending
to journey westward to Spain
via Rome, entering the great
city as a 'free-man' citizen
from birth although
thoroughly Jewish (and a
Pharisee at that!).

My plans were foiled by
that ghastly confrontation in
Jerusalem which saw me
then then transferred to
Caesarea where, as a last
resort, I appealed to the
Emperor. So to Rome I
came, via shipwreck, perils
on the sea and land.
Although incarcerated here,
I am afforded some liberties
as I am well housed with
friends and associates able to

visit, attending to my needs.

Here I am then, yearning for the opportunity of visiting once more the many churches that arose from my preaching and my teaching ministry.

Today, I think of Philippi. What wonderful memories I hold of you. From that first day, meeting your good friend and mine, Lydia, I have known the grace of many who continue to enrich my life. What a wonderful heritage is held by Philippi. As the name suggests, this city is indebted to Philip, father of none less than Alexander the Great! Of surprise to all, perhaps, is the fact that the mighty Roman Empire was birthed on these shores over forty years before the birth of Christ— the outcome of that decisive battle between Brutus and Octavian—Augustus.

The premier city of the region, Philippi marks the crossroad between Europe and Asia. You'll realise, therefore, that, as the Community of Faith arose from the dust of paganism there were representatives from Rome, Greece and Asia in our midst. Because of this there was an intermingling of divergent philosophy, superstition and religion—a fertile ground in which to plant the seed of faith in Christ!

When I first arrived in the city of Philippi, there was no synagogue in which I could introduce myself and my faith. Silas and I made our way down to the riverside where we met with Lydia. The rest is history! How rich indeed the fellowship within Philippi! Do allow me to share my testimony once more with you. I address you most affectionately:

Paul, prisoner of Christ
Timothy assisting
Circa A.D. 60

To the saints–the holy–in Christ Jesus, leaders and congregation:

Grace: *charis* and peace: *shalom*!
My prayers are always emphasised with joy whenever thoughts

of you come to my mind.
I do rejoice for you
partnered me
In sharing Gospel News.
As I address myself to you,
I find a hymn of
thankfulness
for all these special friends
have meant to me along
the way.

REJOICING IN THE FAITH

Tune: *Chalvey*   D.S.M.

The Faith that claims
our hearts
Has called us to this place;
We come today with
joyful hearts
Secured by Heaven's peace.
The drawing power of friends
Who've served with us
each year,
Reminds us that our
mighty God
Has made them all so dear.

We come to voice our joy
For all the years where grace
Has saved us, peace
enfolding us.
We'll sing in heartfelt praise
For all the memories held

Of His great blessings here.
We render now our gratitude
For all His loving care.

O may God's love abound,
Enriching heart and mind.
Relying on the Lord, we stand
Redeemed, renewed, refined.
We offer once again
Our hearts, our will, our hands.
As we give witness for
our Lord,
We joy in love's demands!

And as for me? To live is
Christ, to die is gain but,
for the sake of those who'd
missed 'The Way' because
I had not witnessed to
God's love, I see the need
to preach His word. Always
ensure that you'll be true
and worthy of the Gospel
News that, if I come or am
delayed, yet still you'll
prove your worth. I
emphasise the heritage
we share in Christ.

OUR HERITAGE

Tune: *He Wipes the Tear*
DLM

Ours is the heritage of Faith—

The mighty Gospel we
proclaim!
The blood of Jesus cleanses
us,
We gladly bless His holy
Name.

Chorus:
We lift our hearts in joy to Him
Eternal peace He did ordain;
As soldiers of the cross
of Christ,
We now would claim His
coming reign.

Ours is the heritage of grace—
Yes, God's eternal, wondrous
aim
Has manifested Life for us:
To save our souls He came!

Ours is the heritage of Fire—
The Holy Spirit's inner flame;
Now energised by power
Divine,
We'll serve in Jesus'
matchless Name.

CHAPTER 2
FAITHFULNESS

You ask a reason for our
faithfulness? How is it
possible to stay the course?
Where may we find the
guidelines that will keep us

on the track mapped out by
matchless grace, the gift of
God? If there's a strength to
be observed, It is that unity
pervades the whole!
These verses will express
this need:

THE EXAMPLE OF
JESUS
Tune: *Arizona* L.M.

The Lord has challenged us
today
To be united now with Christ;
This is the comfort of His love:
The fellowship of lives so
blessed.

So that all joy should be
complete,
Unite your mind with Jesus
now;
Reflect His own exampled love,
Be one in purpose, pure
and whole.

Have no ambition trained
on self
No vain conceit, no false
renown;
Consider others more the
blessed;
Look on their interests, not
your own.

So, let your attitude be like
The attitude of Christ our Lord;
In nature, He's unique with
God,
He came to us to live the word.

He knew the path of
servanthood,
He came to be like us so that,
In life, we could become
like Him;
He went to Calvary for that.

Therefore, He is exalted now
That, at His name, His
holy Name,
We all should bow and praise
the Lord
Confessing His transcendent
fame.

CHAPTER 3
WHAT GAIN A LOSS?

You know my shameful
past; I persecuted those of
Faith—My thinking was
that of a Jew steeped in the
attitude of Pharisees. There
was no one as 'good' as I!
But now I see the gain
was loss, I count all things
a deficit against that proved
most excellent. I've

suffered 'loss' of
everything—it's in the
rubbish basket now for my
desire is to be found in
Jesus Christ my Lord;
to have no righteousness
accounted as the good so
'rightfully' in me! The
righteousness in which
I live is that which is
of God through faith.
This truth now rises in
my trusting soul:

THE UTMOST GOAL
Tune: *Rest* 8.6.8.8.6.
(Repeat 3rd line)

My goal in life is to be whole
And testify to peace;
I will press on confirming
grace:
The Lord now guides my ways.

The past is well behind
me now,
The Call of God is heard;
I press towards the goal
He marks.
He walks along my road.

Take up the challenge:
walk with God,
Be an example too;

Now be conformed to
Jesus Christ
In everything you do.

CHAPTER 4
BE UNIFIED

I speak now to my friends:
You are my joy, my crown!
Keep unified, in deepest
peace, Rejoice in God
always. Rejoice! Be gentle
with your friends and foes.
No fretting should erode
your faith. You'll find that
prayer will help. Petitions
should be 'spiced' with
thanks. All your requests
are known to God. He
grants His peace to guard
your heart, your mind.
How could we ever plumb
such depths of grace?
And finally, my friends,
an extended benediction:

LET PEACE PREVAIL
Tune: *Who is He?*
7.7.7.7.7.7.

Saviour, Lord, we bow
the knee;
Ever blessed, we voice
our thanks
For Your goodness and

Your grace.
Guard our hearts, Lord, from
all wrong:
We would stand firm in
the Faith
As we celebrate Your peace.

Everything is possible,
Placing all our hope in God.
Every need is met in Christ,
All the riches of His grace
Are available to those
Who in Jesus place their trust.

Whatsoever things are true,
What is noble, what is right,
Whatsoever things are pure,
What is lovely, most admired,
Whatsoever is of worth,
Think on these and peace
be yours.

....

PAUL
MY TESTIMONY
TO
THE COLOSSIANS

Epaphras is my envoy in
Colosse as my work in
Ephesus had precluded any

lengthy stay in this city, once so predominant in Asia Minor. Situated on the trade route from Ephesus to the mighty Euphrates, it's now a poorly rated market town—the neighbouring Laodicea and Hierapolis are much the mightier now. I must introduce Epaphras.

During my ministry in Ephesus, Epaphras was converted and I found him to be so erudite, wise and energetic for Christ and the Gospel that he became the ideal missionary to Colosse.

The Good News had also spread to the grander cities already mentioned. The house churches in these cities flourished effectively. Epaphras has encountered a variety of contentious issues and asks me to send counsel regarding some very confronting problems–what to eat or not to eat; how to worship during the many local festivals he has encountered there for much superstition is rife.

The Grecian philosophic divides will raise many quandaries and traditional values impinge upon an acceptance of the Gospel Truth for those Gnostic attitudes—it is a formidable form of reasoning—are emerging and gaining strength. The proponents of this heresy assume that God can only be reached via a plethora of spirit beings bent on their own agendas.

As I set myself to the task of responding to the request of Epaphras I will need to emphasise that the faithful must allow no such false teaching to encroach upon their salvation, their life in Christ.

Of greatest concern to me is the apparent refusal of some Colossians to give *Yeshua*–Jesus, the Christ, His rightful place as Son of God. These problems will be faced as I take up the quill and with it, my prayers, my hopes, my challenges that the Church will be true to the Faith.

My advice to Colosse is: Be wise: allow the word to dwell in you richly as you encourage one another in all the psalms and hymns and spiritual songs, singing with grace in your hearts to the Lord. Also recall my words: It is Christ IN you that is the hope of Glory!

Paul, Prisoner for the Gospel,
Courier: Tychicus.
Circa A.D. 60.

To the holy and faithful at Colosse:

Grace: *charis* and peace: *shalom*. I am so thankful, praising God as I remember you before His Throne of Grace. We've heard of your own faithfulness to Christ and love for all the Church at Colosse.
I offer you the opportunity to voice with me these hymns of grace, of peace, of power:

GRACE AND PEACE TO YOU
Tune: *Holy Spirit, Faithful Guide* 7.7.7.7.D.

Grace and Peace to you, dear friends,
Holy, faithful to God's word;
Faith will spring from living hope,
Love will flow on from the Lord.
All your faith has come from God!
Gospel truth reveals the hope
That is stored for you in Heaven:
Word of God has wondrous scope!

Round the world the Gospel sounds,
Bearing fruit in every land.
Since the day we heard it first,
Growth has come from fertile ground.
In the secret room of prayer
Thank the Lord for living faith;
Ask Him for continued grace.
Pleasing Him, you are of worth.

Live your life in praise of God,
Drawing on His matchless grace,
Pleasing Him in every way,
Bearing fruit that lasts always.
God will grant you daily strength
So that you may walk upright.
Trust His mighty power alone,
Live within the Kingdom Light.

CHAPTER 2
LET GRACE BE YOURS

Tune: *Maryland*   D.L.M.

Now be encouraged in
your heart,
United, blessed within
God's love,
Enriched as you are called
apart;
Abundant treasure flows
from Him.
You know the mystery
of God:
This is the Lord. Yes! Jesus
Christ;
He is the source of every good;
Your faith is nurtured well
in Him.

In Christ, the fulness of
our God
Has lived within the human
frame;
In Him you're given all
things good,
You share all fullness now,
in Him!
He is the Head, His power
is shown,
Authority is His alone!
And you've been marked out
as His own,
Virtue has flowed to you
from Him.

You're made alive in Jesus
Christ,

Forgiven now are all your sins!
No longer should you live
with guilt;
Sin's stains were all removed
by Him!
When they were conquered on
the cross,
The shadows of the past
were lost!
O live within the light of grace,
For you are now complete
in Him.

Prayer:
O may you now walk worthily
And pleasing God in every way;
Each bearing fruit in how you live
While learning more of Him
each day.

CHAPTER 3
SET YOUR HEART ON
HEAVEN
Tune: *Martyrdom* C.M.

Since you are raised to life
in Christ,
Now set your heart on Heaven;
As Christ is seated at
God's side,
Now set your mind on Him.

So put to death the sins
of Earth,

Throw off the garb of dross;
Put on the new to be like Christ
And live in holiness.

We are at one in Jesus Christ,
For He is all in all!
So let the peace of God
now rule;
His peace will make us whole.

Be thankful! May the words
of Christ
Dwell deep within your soul.
And sing with gratitude to God
For He will keep you whole.

New life is ours in Jesus Christ,
The old has passed away!
When Christ appears, we'll
stand with Him
In the most glorious Day!

CHAPTER 4
SEIZE THE DAY
Tune: *Ramsgate* 7.7.7.7. D.

Let your life be bathed
in prayer,
Watchful for the needs of all;
Thankful for God's loving care,
Be devoted to His will.

Chorus:
Seize the day and live
for Christ!
Speak for Him: He is The Life;

Share your faith and make
it clear,
Christ is able, peace He'll give!

Take the time each day to pray
For the serving Church of God;
God will open doors
through faith
For the Gospel to be heard.

Pray for those who face
fierce trials,
Pray for any grieved or
maimed;
Pray most earnestly for grace,
Trust the Truth that is
proclaimed.

Wisdom counts when serving
Christ,
Make the most of every day;
May your converse honour
Him,
Gracious, kind in every way.

Wrestle through the night
of doubt,
God will bring the morning light
So that you'll stand firm
by faith;
Let His will be your delight.

..... oOo .....

PAUL
MY TWO TESTIMONIES TO THE THESSALONIANS

Thessalonica is a major city of strategic importance in terms of Grecian philosophy. Also, it is the proud owner of Rome's stamp of approval—it possesses the much-coveted status of 'Free City'. Upon our initial arrival, we discovered a city steeped in the culture and commerce that bred great success. Thankfully, the Church also had begun with gusto and is developing into a thriving Community of Faith. You can appreciate, I'm sure, my desire to ensure the continuing development of this Church. Consider, if you will, the city as a centre for world trade, Greek culture, Roman government and the Jewish community.

The cause of Christ would be of great value here. We rolled up our sleeves and began the work for we had been much grieved by the continuing onslaught on the Community of Faith by Jews zealous in their aim to disrupt and destroy what we had begun (so effectively.) In the face of rampant opposition, a bourgeoning Church had prospered.

Currently, I am in Corinth and, because we had received news of grave concern, we needed to ascertain the health of the Church.

Opposing Jews have slandered my character viciously; there were indications of sexual immorality. Adding to these distressing issues, the whole Thessalonian church was perplexed by the non-arrival of *Yeshua*–Jesus once more to Earth. Also, there was need to encourage the Church in matters of heart-holiness. You can appreciate my desire to ensure the continuing development of the Church.

THE FIRST LETTER

My valued assistant, yes:

Timothy, has become my envoy to ascertain the situation in Thessalonica and to return with news about the matters of concern. Timothy has returned to give me the heart-warming details of his assessment.

I know a great relief and will commence at once to respond to the Church's faithfulness in the face of grave circumstance. Here is a Church of inner fortitude and faith, made so in the face of the most appalling persecution.

Paul, with Silas
and Timothy
Circa A.D. 50

To the Church in
Thessalonica,

Charis, Shalom, to you!
I am so thankful for you all;
you are often in our prayers.
We do recall your faithful
work of love, your patience
and your hope in Christ.
You realise, beloved of the
Lord, that you are integral
to the fellowship of the
believers—you received
God's word with joy but
also, in the Holy Spirit's
power, you then became
the followers of Him who is
the Lord. You stood firm in
the Faith though threatened
with much harm. Your joy
is such that all in Macedonia
now emulate the fine
example you display.
You turned from idols,
bowed to God!

CHAPTER 2
THE TRUTH
PROCLAIMED

Our coming to your shores
was not in vain! We do
rejoice as we recall, though
treated roughly by all the
antagonists, you did observe
our honesty and recognised
the truth about the Lord as
you received the Gospel
News. We sought no glory
for ourselves but shared the
Gospel and our very lives
for all your sakes. You will
remember how we toiled to
bring to you the knowledge
of the Lord and His great
love for you! We laboured
in your cause to verify the

Gospel News in daily life.
We sought to comfort,
strengthen, introduce you to
the Lord so that you
would walk worthy of the
One who calls you to
His Kingdom now.
We thank the Lord for you
received the word of Life;
you knew the Gospel is
from God, you took it to
your heart though suffering
from those tyrants who had
killed their prophets and
The Lord—but He then rose
again! What is our hope, our
joy? It is to see you all
rejoicing when the Lord
returns to Earth!

CHAPTER 3
WE SHARE CONCERNS

Our deep concern for you
was such that Timothy was
sent to see how well you
have maintained the faith
you hold. I knew that he
would be the means of
comforting, encouraging,
your life in Christ. He has
returned to speak with joy
of your great steadfastness.
We have desired so much

the perfecting of your own
faith. O may you now
abound in love to all.

CHAPTER 4
GROW UP

So, finally, my friends, we
urge that you will grow up
in your faith, walk daily in
the sight of God to please
Him, whole. God calls us all
to holiness. So, live in
peace, serene, with care
with care to help all others:
they will recognise you live
for Christ. You wonder why
the long delay in Christ's
return? Don't be disturbed:
you do believe He died for
all, He rose again, He'll
come again and those who
'sleep' won't be passed by.
The dead in Christ shall rise
to Life Eternal when He
comes. Those yet alive will
be 'caught up' with them.

CHAPTER 5
WHAT TO EXPECT

We do not know the day or
night: The Lord will come
back unannounced. Don't

be afraid of night: you're of the day. The Lord has given *LIGHT* to you. Don't fall asleep on faith and hope. Take care to help all those who work to see the Kingdom grow. And comfort all who mourn. In everything be thankful as God blesses you with peace.

....

THE SECOND LETTER

I am pleased to confirm that my first letter has been very effective. However, the Church at Thessalonica is still burdened by the continuing controversy as to when *Yeshua*–Jesus will return. I had been misquoted and would need to set matters right.

I need to counsel the Church concerning matters pertaining to discipline. Also, you will ascertain from this letter now, my further correspondence, that I have a great desire to encourage those yet feeble in their faith,

to advise about ways to face persecution and to exhort my friends to faithfulness and courage as they face the future as one.

Paul, Pastor
Circa A.D. 50 – 51

To the Church in Thessalonica:

Charis and *shalom* to you all.

How fitting it is that I voice my testimony of praise today! I emphasise my thankfulness because you are much strengthened in the faith you hold and utilise: you act in loving kindness to all those in need. I speak of you at length among the Faith Communities throughout all Macedonia: although enduring much affliction, you retain your patience and your faith. I do rejoice!

The Lord cares for your health of soul: the persecutors find a retribution in their time. And you? You'll find the

rest that's gifted by the Lord
when He appears. When
Jesus comes, He will
be glorified in you because
you have received our
testimony to faith with joy.
We pray you'll be
accounted worthy of His
calling as you serve
so that He's glorified, and
you in Him.

CHAPTER 2
BE ON GUARD

My friends, do not be
shaken in your mind
regarding a set time and
circumstance of Christ's
return. Don't be deceived.
You are afraid it is delayed
for far too long? Let me
enlighten you:

**First comes the time when
the vile son of sin will be
revealed. He will exalt
himself; he will pretend he
is the LORD! He'll make
a show of the miraculous.
(I've warned you of these
things.) The mystery of
lawlessness is even now at
work and will be till the
YHWH–LORD destroys**

**him by His awesome
'Breath'. It's all to do
with the satanic wiles:
deception and
unrighteousness.
All those who find a
pleasure in his ways
Will be condemned.**

But you are called
according to God's grace:
you have God's grace;
you have believed and you
are saved. There is
a holiness revealed in you.
Stand fast, therefore, hold to
your faith and the Lord
will bless you all, always!

CHAPTER 3
EXHORTATIONS

Please, pray for us that
God's own word will carry
far afield— indeed it has
with you. Do pray for our
deliverance for there are
those that cloak themselves
in goodness but whose
hearts are far from God.
The Lord is faithful: He will
guard you from the evil one,
He will establish you in
faith, good works.

Withdraw from any who are
tainted by the evil one—
disorderly and lazy,
busybodies too. And be
prepared to live according
to God's word. Do not grow
weary in good works. Now,
may the God of peace
grant peace to you.
The Lord be with you all
in grace. Amen.

..... oOo .....

THE TEACHABLE YEARS

PAUL'S PASTORAL LETTERS

TIMOTHY'S TESTIMONIES

In this edition, Paul allows
me to testify to what I've
learned from him. Greetings!
I can most assuredly present
to you the double greeting—
that of the East: *charis*:
(grace) and that of the West:
shalom: (peace) for both
have met within my family.

My Mother Eunice and
Grandmother, Lois, are
Jewish and my Father is
Greek. I knew the
differences but absorbed the
qualities of each so I am
doubly blessed.
Let me explain a little about
myself. I could be titled
'Timid Timothy' for such I
was and remain so to some
extent for my mentor, Paul
(Saul of Tarsus,) has sought
all through the years of our

association to place some stronger 'metal' in my soul.

I grew up in Lystra so I carried both cultures 'in my genes', so to speak. The day of Paul's arrival in Lystra changed my life! I was 'captivated' by the freedom offered in accepting Christ as personal Saviour of my soul. Paul saw potential in this timid lad! I was, quite soon, to join the Team. Paul and Silas welcomed me and I was keen to accompany them.

My mentor counsels me in all that *Yeshua*–Jesus requires of me. As I've matured somewhat, I must admit that I am still at times in fear of my life for there is much to challenge us. I have endeavoured always to be supportive of the ministry. I've journeyed with Paul to various cities and climes and this 'Timid Timothy' had always stayed at his side before being commissioned to take responsibility for the Church at Ephesus.

In prison, as things became increasingly difficult for him, Paul took up his quill to counsel me and I will give testimony now to what I have read and how I do respond in witness, work, and will:

CHAPTER 1
THE FAITH WE HOLD

How wonderful! In dear
Paul's greeting, there's a
bridge: between the *charis*
and *shalom* there's *eleos*,
mercy! (For peace, there is
grace—the gift we don't
deserve, and mercy—
release from what we do
deserve!) There's mercy
yet for me!

Now, let me see, what can
I share with you of the
advice Paul gives?
I am to remain at Ephesus,
to love with a pure heart,
good conscience and a faith
sincere—we know that
some can act the part but
sadly lack the will to live
the law they idolise. (The
Law is good, handled
lawfully!)
Paul speaks of grace with
joy—it is the reason we
hold faith: we're saved by

grace through faith. This is
the platform of our creed:
Christ came into the world
to save us from our sin.
Though 'chief of sinners'
mercy flows to me from
Him, the One immortal and
invisible, uniquely wise. All
glory, honour be to *YHVH,
El Shaddai*—THE LORD,
ALMIGHTY GOD!

CHAPTER 2
THE INTERCESSOR

I am exhorted to speak often
with the Lord in giving
thanks while interceding for
the kings and presidents, all
those who wield authority,
that peace may reign. The
Lord is pleased when we
affirm His will that all may
know the Truth, be saved.
Paul's emphasis is on these
words: 'There is one
Mediator 'twixt
the *YHVH*–LORD
and humankind':
The Man Christ Jesus,
Lord; He gave Himself to be
a ransom so all people
could, through Him,
be saved eternally.

And he explains the mode
of witness men and women
ought to give. He longs to
see that all continue in the
faith in love and holiness.

CHAPTER 3
LEADER
QUALIFICATIONS

The faithful need to live a
blameless life. Aspiring to
become a leader is a noble
aim. A leader should control
his home and family for, if
he can't, how can he lead
the Faith Community?
A leader should be well
respected in the wider world
lest Faith fall down.
All leaders and assistants
too, should hold the mystery
of faith with purity, with
boldness speak and act the
Faith. Paul likes to
emphasise the mystery of
godliness. The 'mystery' is,
for faithful souls, an 'open
secret': hidden in God,
known through Christ!

CHAPTER 4
BEWARE APOSTACY

Paul gives me warning here:
in latter days some souls
will fall from faith; lies and
hypocrisy will then be rife,
distorting Christian qualities
of life. I'll be required to
give instruction to the
Church about those issues
that would stain all
godliness. Though hardship
will cut deep, my trust in
God ensures all will be well.

God knows I hold some
doubts on my ability to lead.
Paul says: Let no one
denigrate your youth! I am
to be a good example to
the 'flock'; I am to give
attention to all that I teach
and not neglect the gifts he
sees in me. He says: Take
heed to all the doctrine, so
that my teaching ministry
will be effective, saving
many—and myself!

CHAPTER 5
CARING FOR THE
CHURCH

Treat older men as fathers,
younger lads as brothers
(such wise words for me.)

Paul follows up this sound
advice with many other
matters too regarding
women of the 'flock'.
Widows—blameless:
idle gossipers don't aid the
Church! Encourage them or
else the Faith Community
may suffer from a careless
speech or foolish action
here. I'm given guidance,
too, concerning how to
utilise the worthy elders
well in roles conducive to
enhance the whole. I'm not
to make decisions hastily.
It's wise to wait upon the
Lord for good works are
soon evident and those not
good aren't hidden long!

CHAPTER 6
THE GOOD
CONFESSION

Paul has helped me greatly
in the matter of the
treatment of bond-servants,
masters too.
Let there be honour for the
master; let no servant be
despised. I like the way
that Paul has emphasised
true godliness with our

contentment. It's a blessing to us all. If we are reaching for great wealth, we must remember that we carried nought into the world nor will we lift ought out! The love of money is the seed of greed, of evil too, for many fall from faith desiring worldly wealth. I hear Paul's words—they ring so very true to me.

And now, his great encouragement: Pursue the good—heart holiness, faith, love, patience, gentleness. Fight the good fight of faith, take hold of Life; be pure in thought, in word, in deed. And finally, he challenged me to guard all that is committed to my trust!

·········

2nd TIMOTHY

The situation's changed! The news is dire. I have received a further letter from my mentor, Paul—this man is like a father to me: he helped me to grow up to be a man of faith. I'm made very much aware that his present imprisonment is now more iron-clad. He's clamped in chains behind prison bars with a death-sentence looming large.

Paul does not have much time as his life is all but at its end. Yet he has thought of me! The letter I am holding in my hand spells out much grief, it's true but, emanating from the whole, I read—in deeper measure now—his passion for the Faith, his love for all the Church as it continues its expansion to many centres round our world.

Paul's hand is feeble now, but not his heart—I sense its beating: strong for Christ, warm for his many friends and colleagues, and still firm for me! Oh, let me share with you the words of wisdom, comfort, counsel, courage too, that Paul has sent on in this mail.

CHAPTER 1
THE FAITH WE HOLD

Paul's first words are of *LIFE!* He speaks of this as

death is closing in. I find,
also, that he reminds me of
the mercy that gives balance
to the grace and peace.
He cheers my heart!
I see that Paul is given now
to much reflection for, what
else is there to do behind
those prison bars? His
prayers hold thankfulness—
especially for my family: he
knows their faith is genuine.

And then, of all things on
the page, he says: 'The Lord
has not bequeathed to us the
gift of fear—He's granted
us His power, His love, His
wisdom that
will conquer all by faith.'
He does remind me that
there is no shame in Christ,
nor in His prisoner. Though
suffering for the Gospel's
sake, God's power will see
us through: He saved us,
called us, keeps us by His
grace: that given before all
time IN Christ! Just think on
that! And then rejoice: His
grace has been revealed as
Christ brought Life—
Eternal Life—to light:
abolishing the power of
death! Paul states he's not

ashamed to suffer for the
sake of Gospel News. I
quote: 'I know Whom I've
believed and I'm persuaded
He can keep what I've
committed unto Him until
He comes again.'
My son, Paul writes, hold
fast to what you learned,
keep to the Faith by
Holy Spirit power.

CHAPTER 2
THE STRENGTH OF
GRACE

Be strong in Jesus' grace,
my son. I know that you'll
encounter hardship:
be a soldier in the Lord's
Army! Be an athlete,
keeping to the rules;
be a farmer, tending 'crops'!
Timothy: my chains do not
hold me! The word of God
is never chained.
It's free! Just think on this:
If we die with Him, we'll
live with Him. If we endure,
If we endure, then we shall
reign. If we deny Him, He'll
deny us too. If we are
faithless, He remains
faithful: He can't deny

Himself! Remind your
people of these things.
Be diligent, be confident!
Shun all that is profane—
the Lord knows who are
His! Be a 'vessel' fit to hold
the precious things of life;
flee all that harms, avoid all
foolishness. Be a servant of
the Lord! What sound
advice my teacher gives.

CHAPTER 3
PERILOUS TIMES

Paul followed this advice by
warning me of times most
perilous about to come,
describing vividly the traits,
the characteristics of
unholiness where men can
hold a form of godliness yet
live afar from God.
I am reminded of the ways
Paul dealt with persecution
and that I have the ability to
follow in his steps. He's
challenged me to carry on,
reminding me that, from my
childhood, I have known the
Scripture and it's made me
wise. It is God's word in
teaching and reproving,
correcting, instructing and
preparing us to be complete,

equipped to serve the Lord.

CHAPTER 4
THE CLIMACTIC
ADVICE

I read from Paul's own
hand: O Timothy, my son,
do preach the word—be
ready at all times to teach,
to preach, convince, rebuke,
exhort. The time will come
when even all the listeners
will turn away for many will
prefer the fables to the faith.
But, Timothy,
you are the Lord's
evangelist:
fulfil your ministry.

My son, he said, I'm ready
to depart—I've fought the
fight of faith, I've reached
the 'finish tape'. The race is
run and won! But, Timothy,
there is awaiting me the
Crown of Righteousness.
The LORD will grant it
to me then for I will
be *ALIVE!*

Do try to come in time—
only Dr. Luke is with me
now. Please, call on Mark,
ask him to come—I find

him helpful to the ministry.
Do bring the cloak (I'm
very cold). Though all
forsake, the Lord stands by
to strengthen me—to Him
be glory, now and ever!
Also, may the Lord be
now with you!

..... oOo .....

TITUS

I've little need to
introduce myself as Paul has
occasionally mentioned me
in dispatches from the early
days of ministry. I remember
that he made mention of me
when writing to the Church
in Galatia.

I was assisting when he
and Barnabas journeyed to
Jerusalem to discuss the
vexing question of how to
merge the Jewish and
Gentile streams of The Faith.
(Back those years ago, the
brethren in Jerusalem had
accepted me, a Gentile,
without the need to
circumcise—a breakthrough
in diplomatic relations!

Following on from the
Third Mission, Paul
appointed me to pastor the
Church at Corinth. Then,
following his release from
that first imprisonment, I
was commissioned as
overseer to the work in
Crete.

This is a challenging task,
though I am encouraged
greatly by the obvious trust
Paul has placed in me. This
is confirmed in the receipt of
his letter addressed to me in
Crete. I'll share Paul's
cherished advice as I set
down my testimony for you
all to read:

CHAPTER 1
A CHALLENGING
TASK

Paul first speaks of himself
as 'servant'—I had
imagined I was servant to
my mentor from the start.
But Paul serves Jesus
Christ. His platform is the
Faith he speaks and lives:
his hope of Life Eternal.
God, who planned it all
before Creation Day, has

brought the Truth to light now through the preaching of His word, revealing Christ.

Paul addressed me as 'son in the Faith we hold: may grace and peace remain with you.' I do rejoice, I am encouraged now! Paul then outlines his reason for requiring me to stay in Crete—there is some straightening out to do and also leaders must be sought and trained. I will do well to keep in mind the qualities required of them: No blame attached—each with one wife. Good tempered, patient too; sober men not given to a selfish gain; hospitable and self-controlled; upright and holy, disciplined through life. It's vital that they know the message to be taught and speak it well. Rebellious men should be refused their mastery. To all the pure, all things are pure; to the corrupt, all is corrupt. The claim to know God must be matched by proof in daily life.

CHAPTER 2
THE CURRICULUM

This is the teaching schedule:

1. Sound doctrine
Temperance, respect, self-control, faithful, loving, enduring well.

2. Family life
All disown slander, addiction. Love of husband, wife, children. Kind to all Well organised at home.

3. Youth work
Self-control (set example). Integrity, clean speech. Claim the Truth.

4. Master–Servant ties
Slaves be obedient/masters kind. Endeavour to please. Be true to quality living. God's word will attract.

5. Quality living
Salvation: revealed to all Ability to say NO to ungodliness.
Be examples to the flock

CHAPTER 3

TRANSLATING WORDS TO DEEDS

Paul gives some sound advice:
As I example quality living in the sight of God and fellow man, I am reminded of our own past life— it's not a pretty sight. Since we received the kindness, love, of God through Jesus Christ, we have been saved, not by our merit but God's mercy, we are made clean, renewed, by His own Spirit in our lives. We have therefore become His heirs.

The points that Paul has made are trustworthy and I'm to stress these qualities in all I say and do for they are excellent for Christian growth in faith.
Paul's final words are sent that I will help his Team to be in readiness for what eventuates. The Team have sent their greetings and I am to send these on to all. His heart-felt prayer is:
Grace be with you all.

….. oOo …..

PHILEMON

I've just received a most heart-warming letter from our leader, Paul. I'll need to introduce myself but there is not so very much to tell. I trust this will suffice: my name is Philemon.   I do endeavour to aspire to its meaning—that is, my name means *affectionate*!

I live in Colosse. You've come to know my hometown well. I find that life is pleasant here, especially as I am the owner of some slaves for   whom   I   have endeavoured to retain as mine through kindness and consideration and not too much by way of expectations or demands.

This is the reason why the disappearance of Onesimus has raised my ire! I did extend my care to him but he forsook the warm security of my estate and took with him some valued treasures, too.

You   can   imagine   my surprise when Paul—whom I had come to know and to appreciate—writes in such support of my own offending

slave! I'll have to think on it!
I find that I must now
respond—to give my
testimony regarding the
events and the quandary that
I now face:

Paul's indicated that he's
now incarcerated for his
faith in Christ. And he
reminds me that he thinks of
me as friend. He also notes
assistance I have given him
when visiting my home.
You see, the local Faith
Community meets in our
home; most pleasing
too! Paul does assure me
of his earnest prayers.

Someone informed him of
my aid to the Colossian
Church. He prays for me.
How kind. He says that I've
encouraged him and all the
team. Then he, quite
suddenly, has launched into
the purpose for this mail. He
is appealing as an aged man
now in imprisonment.
So! Here's the thing that has
surprised—no, shocked me
to the core! It seems that my
own thieving slave,
Onesimus, has had a change

of heart! He's been of great
assistance to my friend,
since he's been chained.
He's 'like a son' to Paul.
That's news indeed! Paul
has admitted that the boy
was useless at the first;
but since his new-found
faith took hold, he's highly
valued now! Here's the
amazing thing: Onesimus is
being sent home by Paul
who would prefer to keep
him still at hand.

However, Philemon, Paul
says, I do not want to act
without your true consent.
Perhaps the boy's return
could be a new beginning
for you both—no more a
slave but a dear brother you
can cherish as I do. If you
still think now somewhat
well of me,
do welcome him as you
would me. If he has done
you any wrong, please
charge it up to me.

I need not mention that you
owe to me your life. I'm
confident—in knowing
you—that you'll do more
than I could ask. Oh, and

one thing more, prepare
a guest room for I do intend
to come as soon as I'm
released. God answers
prayer always!

That is the gist of it:
Paul's plea that I'll receive
Onesimus…
As I have said: I need to
think on it…
Yes, Paul, the grace of God
in Jesus Christ is with my
spirit still today!

..... oOo .....

THE THEOLOGICAL YEARS

A LETTER TO THE HEBREWS

Greetings! I are pleased to be given the privilege of testifying to the validity of this document—precious, paramount and profound, though it stands devoid of a signature.

No doubt there will be questions, possibilities, probabilities, but no certainties as to authorship. Conjecture will outweigh any attempt at confirmation. 1, who testify in this edition, therefore, must also remain anonymous There's much within the document that cries out for Paul. The language nuances, however, do not align themselves with him. Yet the content shouts out for Paul. Because of this, I will allow myself some hints for you to scrutinize. That godly, priestly man we know so well—Barnabas, early missionary with Paul, could well have wielded his quill to produce the in-depth theology (so akin to Pauline teaching). You'll note also, in your reading of the First Edition, the hints given by reference to imprisonment and also strong evidence by virtue of Timothy's inclusion!

There is another thought that should be considered fully before reaching for yet another quill. Why is this magnificent treatise devoid of a signature? It may just be to secure the longevity of the work! To whom was the letter addressed? To Jews! And who was he, despised of Jews? Why, Saul of Tarsus—Paul, of course! (he was tutored by none other than the great Gamaliel, foremost professor of his day). Yet the vocabulary is not Pauline. You ask for my response on this? If indeed one can settle on St Paul: he sets himself to write to fellow Jews. What language does he choose? Hebrew, without a doubt.

But, you say, the letter is written in Greek. Here is a man who knows that a letter headed: *"From Paul, Missionary to the Gentiles, to Hebrews"* could be directed to the waste basket!

The writer puts a cloak about the work. He scrawls his treatise in Hebrew and then hands the document over to a trusted, wise and erudite Greek to translate into his own 'tongue'. And who, you ask, would be the ideal candidate for the project? Apollos—a close associate of Paul could raise his hand, if pressed.

There is, however, none better for the task than Paul's doctor—the ever-ready aide, Luke! His Gospel is renowned as being near the very best document of all first century literature.

I leave my suggestion for you to contemplate as I now set out to emphasise, by my own personal testimony, the depth of truth expressed by one who, though unnamed, has complete precedence in his knowledge of Hebrew history and how it is fulfilled in Christ.

My task is to present this

work in a quite personalised form for all to contemplate. These words of life will exemplify all Gospel truth:

HEBREWS 1
God's supreme revelation

Creator God has spoken
many times: He spoke
through patriarchs and
prophets. In these latter days
He speaks to us through
Christ who is appointed
Heir Supreme: The Son,
Christ Jesus, has revealed to
us the nature of the *YHVH*–
LORD. He's now at God's
right hand, superior to all,
including every angel there.
The *YHVH*–LORD has
testified:

You are My Son,
You have been born a
human Child! I'll be Your
Father and You'll be My
Son: The angels are My
ministers but You, My Son,
are King! Your throne's
eternal for You are
Messiah–Christ, anointed
One. You laid foundations
for the Earth, the heavens
were wrought by You:

though they grow old, yet
You remain: Your years
will never end.

No angel will be seated at
God's right hand; they are
His ministers.

HEBREWS 2
Salvation's work

It's vital that we all give
heed to Gospel News. In
past times, disobedience had
blighted Truth, but how
shall we escape if we
neglect salvation offered us?
The Gospel is confirmed by
signs, by wonders and by
miracles, also the Holy
Spirit's gifts of grace.
How did the Gospel reach
our ears and heart? It is
Because the son
was born to be a man.

But what is man that he'd
be blessed? The *YHVH*–
LORD made Him to be,
once, lower than the angels
but, through sacrifice for
sin, He reigns on High
above all beings. He tasted
death for us and, by this

means, so many come
to Eternal Glory.
Christ shared in our
humanity that we may share
His Glory. He is our great
High Priest—He brings
propitiation for our sins!
Because He knew
temptation, He will help
us as we face the tempter's
wily ways each day.

HEBREWS 3
Jesus' faithfulness

Consider Jesus, if you will,
the High Priest who is
faithful—as was Moses,
leader of Israel. The Man,
Christ Jesus, is accounted
worthier than Moses was
(this is explosive news; I'd
best be circumspect). Moses
was faithful in his
father's house as is a servant
now. But Christ is Lord of
all the 'house'.
We are that 'house' if we
hold fast our hope with
confidence. Take note of
what the Holy Spirit says:

*If you will hear My voice
today, don't harden hearts
as did your fathers in the
wilderness—they tested Me
for forty years! They would
not enter My rest.*

Exhort each other while it is
today. The man that holds
his confidence unto the
end partakes the joys
of Heaven!

HEBREWS 4
God's promises are sure

You know the promise of
God's rest, Why would you
come up short of it? I urge
you: if you'd hear God's
voice today, don't block
your ears! God's loyal
people will find rest!
Can you believe? The word
of God is powerful! It's
sharper than a two-edged
sword—it cuts between the
good and bad, the truth and
falsity. All stand each day
within the scrutiny of God.

Seeing we have the great
High Priest, *Yeshua*–Jesus,
let us hold a true confession
of our faith. He knows
our weaknesses. He was a
man and He was tempted,
yet He lived in perfect

purity. Let us come boldly
now before Him so that
we'll find His mercy
and His grace applied to us.

HEBREWS 5
The great High Priest

We know the obligations of
high priests: They're chosen
from the priesthood to then
intercede for all! Only the
one appointed to the task
(as Aaron was), may
undertake this call. Christ is
the One appointed by the
YHVH–LORD to act as did
Melchizedek for, as a Son,
He learned obedience by
which He qualified as
Author of salvation to those
obedient. You'll find this
hard to understand for you
are yet so immature. You
are not weaned from milk!
The time has come to
upgrade diets now. Receive
the solid food that does
belong to those who can
discern the differences
between the **shadows**
and the *LIGHT*!

HEBREWS 6

Spiritual stagnation.

The time has come to move
on from the elementary
teaching of the past: step on
towards perfection—set
your sights on Life for why
do nothing more than lay
foundations all the while!
We've known about
repentance for long years.

Move on to matters that
pertain to resurrection and
the judgement to Eternal
Life—or death! How foolish
To have heard, received
The Gospel News, then
let it drop! Discard the
Truth, you'll crucify the
Lord again. There is
no other certain way
by which we can be saved.
Reflect upon the soil
receiving seed: What is your
crop? The herb or brier?
You know the end of all
the briers! We hold a
confidence in you. The Lord
does not forget your worthy
enterprise—your diligence
is much approved. Do not
grow lax in this.

Remember Abraham: he is

accounted 'Father of the Faithful'. Is he now your 'father' too? Then emulate his faithfulness. God does not lie: He will receive you as His own. The hope we hold is like an anchor to the soul!

HEBREWS 7
Salem's priestly king, Melchizedek

You will recall Melchizedek: the King of Righteousness. He was the regal personage who came to meet the pilgrim, Abraham, near Salem's Gate. A tithe was offered to the king. Who was this priestly king? There is no genealogy! With no beginning and no end, he is a symbol of the Christ!

He had the right to bless the 'Father of the Faithful' and, by right, receive the tithe! Therefore, if a perfection comes through Levite priests, what reason could there be to choose another priest according to the order of Melchizedek? If Aaron's line sufficed, why change that priestly line? (Our Lord is of the Judah Clan!) This High Priest has reason, not of fulfilling Law, but to ensure an endless life for those who do believe! The Moses law made nothing whole!

But this High Priest, our *Yeshua*–Jesus, is the Guarantee of a greater Covenant. He saves unto the uttermost all those who come to God through Him. He is the One who intercedes for us today. He is the One who has no need for daily cleansing, daily sacrifice. He is Eternal, perfect now!

HEBREWS 8
Priestly service relating to the new Covenant

Here is the main point of this Treatise... The High Priest chosen by the *YHVH*–LORD, seated at His side in Heaven. This High Priest is the Minister in the

Sanctuary—the 'tabernacle' that's not built with human hands! The priests that serve within the Temple in Jerusalem are symbolic of the One High Priest selected by the *YHVH*–LORD. He is the Mediator of the better Covenant! You'll realise that, if the former Covenant was faultless, there's no need for what is New! You'll know of these profound words:

This is the covenant that I will make with you: I'll place My Laws within the human
mind and write them on their heart. I'll be their God; they'll be My people. Then there'll be no need for prophets anymore! There'll be no need to say, "Know God!" for all will know, from least to great: I will be merciful, I will forgive their sins!

Then: with the coming of the New, the older Covenant is obsolete!
It's growing old, it will decay, be gone!

HEBREWS 9
The Sanctuaries:

You know the earthly Sanctuary so well: the Holy Place and there, beyond the veil, the Holiest of all Holies. Do have the furnishings in mind: they are indicative of how to worship in the former Sanctuary—just once a year the high priest enters in to intercede for all. That plan has failed to bring about an inner purity!

So, then Christ came—the Great High Priest whose 'tabernacle' is not made by human hands. He now makes clear salvation can't be found in blood of bulls or goats. It's by His precious blood, once shed on Calvary, that Jesus purchased our release! The truth is now made plain: where there's a testament, the testator must die! The desert sacrifice required the blood—much more, the new: without the shedding of our Saviour's blood, there's no redeeming grace!

Today's high priest will
enter in the inmost
Sanctuary but once each
year to seek atonement
there. The risen Christ, the
great High Priest, has
entered in the heavenly
Holiest Place. There is no
need for a repeat! *Yeshua*—
Christ— was offered once
to bear our sins. It is
enough: in Him we find
eternal grace!

HEBREWS 10
The difference in the
sacrifices:

This matter has to do with
Law: the shadow of reality.
The symbol can't outweigh
the actual sacrifice where
Christ fulfils the Law and
actuates salvation through
His blood! How could a bull
or goat atone for sin?
You've sung with us, the
Psalmist's song:

*I have no pleasure in burnt
offerings; I don't desire
your sacrifices multiplied!*

Christ said:

*I've come to do Your will
O YHVH Elohim.*

Herein: the sacrifice of Life
for life—a life that is now
sanctified. Christ's death
perfects all those made
holy through His holy,
cleansing blood.

Therefore, hold fast your
faith. Be bold to enter in the
'Holiest Place' by merit of
Christ's blood. This is
the New and Living Way!
Let us draw near to Him for
we are sprinkled with His
blood. Hold fast to faith, to
hope! He who is faithful
grants you hope. If you
forsake this faith, this hope,
there is no other way
whereby you can be saved.
Don't cast away your
confidence in Christ

THE JUST SHALL LIVE
BY FAITH!

HEBREWS 11
Salvation through Faith

So! What is faith?
There is substance in our
faith: it is the source of

hope, the evidence of what
is yet invisible. How may
we utilise our faith? Use
inner sight. These are the
issues: so now ponder well
your Hebrew history:

Of Creation: by God's Word
Of Cain he failed, Abel won
Of Enoch , no death: he won
Of Noah: warned, acted: won
Of Abraham called: won
Of Sarah: old age birth: won

These knew a righteousness
that's born of faith. Without
your faith, it is impossible
to please the LORD.
One can't approach the
LORD unless he does
believe that God exists. The
patriarchs and followers
have died in faith, the
promise not fulfilled. They
held to faith. They were on
pilgrimage. God has
prepared their 'Home'.

True faith is seen in
Abraham, in Isaac, Jacob,
Joseph too. By faith, Moses
obeyed the LORD. How can
we find the space to tell of
Gideon, Barak, Samuel,
David and the prophets too?

They conquered in the
strength of faith: This dark
world is not worthy of
such faithful souls as they!

HEBREWS 12
The Race of Life:

We stand together now,
surrounded by a host of
witnesses. They give to us
a confidence to lay aside
those things which weigh
us down: the snares, the
obstacles, so that the race is
run with confidence that's
born of faith. Look to the
One who starts the race,
who also finishes—
perfects—our faith.

It was the joy He knew
that led Him on: for this
our Lord endured the cross,
despised the shame,
conquered the tomb and
now resides in Heaven!

Therefore, take heed if you
would run this race: you
have not faced the cross but
hardship looms—this will
increase your strength to
win. No trial fills one with

joy yet it will prove your own ability to run and win the race! So: activate those halting hands; those knees need strengthening. Go, *RUN*! Since we receive the Heavenly Kingdom, now receive His grace applied and serve Him well!

HEBREWS 13
The need for Love

How do we exercise our familial love? An 'open house' would help (who knows, an angel may come in!) Give aid to prisoners: remember that you're part of Christ's own 'body' too. Give honour to all marriages and be content with what you have.

Indeed, you 'have' the Lord, His grace always, all ways: enough for all! The Lord, *Yeshua* is the same today as yesterday, the same tomorrow too. Hold to sound doctrine and be well established by His grace. Be ready to move out, beyond the 'camp' (inner security). Our 'city' is the one to come. And let our sacrifice be one of praise; obey the rulers, all. And pray for us that we will be restored to you. Now may the God of Peace who raised the Christ from death—the Shepherd of our souls—lead you to perfection: be complete!

..... oOo .....

THE
THANKFUL
YEARS

THE LOVE LETTERS

JAMES TO JUDE

JAMES

I've known Him since my earliest days. You see, He is my Brother! Yes! I know, He is your Brother too. But I mean my kin by natural birth. Our Mother is Mary! At the time that I am writing this letter to the 'diaspora' scattered wide across the Earth, I will be known as the leader of the Jerusalem Council. You'll also know of James bar Zebedee.

Let there be no confusion: the dear disciple James was assassinated for his faith quite soon following on from Pentecost. My story is a chequered one. I challenged *Yeshua* (you'll know Him also as Jesus Christ) in the midst of His earthly ministry.

I misunderstood Him from the start and all the way to Calvary. Yet still I dug in my heels! But then…

He came to me! He was, and is, *ALIVE*!

All the antagonistic walls were then broken down. The memories of my early joys in playing with my eldest Brother among the wooden shavings of Father's carpentry business came flooding back. From that early Resurrection Morning, He had my devoted obedience. It was by *Yeshua's* direction that I took the reins of the Church and, as leader now, I take my quill to write to you as pastor in order to bring encouragement and some instruction to all my brothers and sisters in The Faith in the midst of your hardship, peril and threat of death.

As your pastor, then, it is my hope to be more like my Big Brother: I'll be a good shepherd, too, keeping watch over the 'flock' now scattered over the rugged hills of the world. Please do remember that sheep need also to be shorn for both rod and staff will have their use today!

CHAPTER 1
THE TRIALS OF FAITH

Though other matters will
arise, this is the Document
of Faith! Where once I
found no faith in *Yeshua,*
today He claims my all!

I do encourage you to
follow in the path of faith.
Take heed: in face of trials
that surely come, when faith
is tested you will find a
patience that's perfected in
your soul. If you lack
wisdom, ask
in faith: you'll find a deeper
understanding that will
flood into your life to
strengthen you.

**A doubting man is like a
wave upon a churning sea,
wind tossed, unstable,
lacking trust in God.
I send a warning to
the rich who find it easy
to forget that, like a daisy
in the field, they'll surely
wilt and die. Riches first,
you'll be last!**

Remember that temptation
is no sin unless you do

succumb. You are my
beloved brothers now.
Please know that every
perfect gift comes from
the LORD of *LIGHT,* there
is no **shadow** of a change
in Him, the LORD!
These are the qualities that
bear the unmistakeable
marks of grace: Be swift to
hear but slow to speak.
Be slow to anger, lay aside
all filth. Be doers of His
will: both hear and act.
Look to the perfect Law of
Liberty—pursue this aim by
deeds of love and kindness
to all those in need.

CHAPTER 2
FAVOURITISM

My brothers, sisters, all:
don't fall into the trap of
finding favourites,
neglecting those who are
alone. Remember, outward
finery is not a guide to inner
qualities! By looking for the
most important pride of
place, you'll overlook
a kindness born of grace.

Herein lies sin:

transgression of The Law:
for just one minor point:
guilty! Judgement has no
mercy for the unmerciful.

One cannot brag of faith
if there's no kindness in
his works. You speak
a word of grace yet show
no care? If faith remains
unbalanced by a lack of
kindness, it is dead! You
do believe in God. Good—
but so do demons too!

Take the example of old
Abraham: his faith was
balanced by his willingness
to 'gift' his son. One's faith
will be perfected in the
work beside the will.
What do I mean by this?
You have no spirit?
You'd be dead.
You've faith, no works?
The faith is dead.

CHAPTER 3
TAME THAT TONGUE!

All teachers of the word
hold great responsibility.
We're prone to stumble but
stability reveals a perfect
stance. A horse has need
of bridle like a ship requires
its rudder to remain
on course despite strong
gales. The tongue? So
small, so big its boast!

Consider that a spark
can fire forests just like
tongues —a fire of
iniquity. Though nature
can be tamed, no one can
tame unruly tongues.
We bless the LORD
but curse all else?

Can one spring yield
both sour and sweet
water? A fig tree grows
no grapes! You would be
wise? Reveal what's in
your heart by conduct that
is pure, astute. If there's
an envy in your heart,
don't act the blatant lie
of kindness by your
ever ready hands!

The wisdom that originates
'Above' is pure and
peaceable. Wisdom reveals
a gentleness and mercy too.
You would display a
righteousness that's born of
God? Go, live in peace.

CHAPTER 4
PRIDE VERSUS HUMILITY

Submit your will to God,
resist Satan—he'll flee from
you so fast! Draw near to
God, He'll come to you.
Make clean your hands
and hearts. Your life is not
a 'laugh'—be serious!
Speak well of others; do not
stomp on them. judge others
and you will also
be judged. You have
no claim on what you'll do
tomorrow for you do not
know the future yet!

What is your life? It's like
a mist that's here just now
but gone so soon.
Acknowledge all the will of
God for you. Know what is
right and then proceed lest
sin takes hold!

CHAPTER 5
GUIDELINES OF GRACE

**You're rich? You may
know misery! Both gold
and silver do corrode,
the dust will then deride
your lack of generosity.
Do you not hear the cries
of all who slave in fields
afar? The weeping of the
reapers will be heard by
God. Listen: act to bless!**

Take heed to counselling:
Be patient, as a farmer
watching crops.
Engage your hearts in
patient hope. Don't be a
grumbler: know grace,
your Judge is standing at the
door! You seek examples
yet? Take heed
of prophets speaking
through a woe: Job
persevered, so persevere
with patience as you seek to
emulate the good!

Be circumspect: stand by
your word without the need
for oaths. Are you
suffering? Then be at
prayer. And you're joyful?
Sing your Psalms. You're
ill? Call Elders, they will
pray for you—the faithful
prayers bring health. Share
griefs, short-comings,
sins—much healing comes
through openness.
Remember this:

the fervent prayers of
righteous folk bring peace
upon the suffering. You'd
save a soul from death?
Then work to turn him from
his sins. And finally,
test faith by works!

..... oOo .....

PETER
THE FIRST
LETTER

So much has happened
since I shared with you the
extraordinary ways in which
Yeshua–Jesus changed my
attitudes. You will recall that
my early apostolic exploits
were so blessed as the Holy
Spirit gave me power to
preach, to take the early lead
in guiding the Faith
Community, also finding it
possible to work miracles by
taking hold of faith that's
born of God. But it required
that amazing vision of
'unclean' beasts made
'clean' by the Lord and His

command to arise and eat,
for me to really see the
LIGHT!

Since that attitude-
changing event in Joppa, I
have endeavoured to fulfil
the Lord's Calling each step
of His chosen way for me.
As I write, I am very aware
of your present suffering
under extreme persecution.
My dear Jewish believers:
friends, you are really
endeavouring to remain true
to your commitment to
Yeshua Christ—our Saviour,
Messiah. You have been
transformed, born again to
live for Him. Yours is a
living hope but you need to
emulate the Lord you love.

The Holy Spirit is forming
Christian character in you as
you strive to emulate the
character of Christ. I write
today to you in order to bring
some encouragement that
you may stand firm in the
faith as you are confronted
with the fiery trials God's
enemies inflict on you.

Don't think on such trials
as some strange affliction—
remember *Yeshua*... Calvary:

His sacrifice for you. In this we do rejoice for we will share not only in His suffering but also the victory of faith over failure and of hope over despair.

CHAPTER 1
THE INCORRUPTIBLE INHERITANCE

Peter, Apostle and Pastor
Circa A.D. 60–65

To Pilgrims of the Diaspora,

You of the 'Dispersion' are truly the Elect of God! How so? This is a trinity of reasoning: Elect of *YHVH*– LORD's Omniscience, by the Holy Spirit's matchless Omnipotence and by *Yeshua's* Own Blood! Yes! you are reborn into a Hope—a living hope—birthed by the resurrection to an inheritance that's undefiled and incorruptible. This living hope will never fade—it's held in Heaven for you. How so? The power of God ensures that you are kept

by faith in *Yeshua's* saving grace. Oh boundless Joy! In midst of trials, you hold a living hope!

Your faith is precious— much more so than gold that perishes at last in dust. Your worth is tested in the flames and comes forth pure to praise, to honour and to glorify. You've never seen the Lord and yet, today, you love Him and rejoice with joy abundant that is inexpressible—where are the words most adequate to speak of it? The prophets preached on grace that is outpoured on you. They knew they would not see this time eventuate, but you know grace today that even angels would desire. So then, stand firm and rest your hope upon this grace outpoured on you!

You are the children of the LORD: conform yourselves to His utmost desires for you: be holy for He's holy. So conduct yourselves according to His will for you. You know you were redeemed by virtue of the precious blood of *Yeshua*– Jesus, the Lamb that had no blemish and no blame. Love one another most sincerely for you are God's children for Eternity according to the word of God—all flesh is grass that will disintegrate but God's own word endures always. This is the Gospel that you hold!

CHAPTER 2
THE LIVING STONES

You've laid aside all worldly claims. Being born again, you'll need pure milk: the word of God is 'food for growth'. Make sure of diet's gain. Let us now look to *Yeshua*—He is 'The Rock of Ages, cleft for us': He is the Living Stone rejected by this world but chosen, precious, and the Stone by which we find our strength. You also are the 'living stones' that are now utilised to build the 'house' of God. Recall: you are God's temple now!

You are a 'house' that's spiritual. You are, indeed, the holy priesthood that will offer up the sacrifice that is acceptable to God. The LORD has duly lain the 'Cornerstone' on which is built the holy 'house'. So, learn from this: You are the chosen family, a royal priesthood and a holy people that you may proclaim with praise the word of God—remember that you came from **shadows** into *LIGHT!*

Once not a people, now God's own; once knowing not a mercy, now: a mercy great and grace that's free! As pilgrims, now abstain from worldly worth—reveal instead, the worth of God that, by your life, all may at last give praise to God. The LORD requires your upright lives: obey the laws of lands in which you dwell.

By living godly lives, you'll silence fools. You're free but don't take liberties! Honour all and love the

Faith Family. Fear God;
treat leaders well.
Servants, work well,
behave—remember that
Yeshua has suffered for
your sake so follow in His
steps: He bore our sins in
His own body on the cross
that we could truly live
in righteousness—it's by
His death you live: you
were like straying lambs;
He searched for you, found
you and took you to His
'fold'. He is your Shepherd
and He watches over you!

CHAPTER 3
SUBMITTING,
SERVING, SUFFERING

My friends, allow me now
to emphasise the Christian
mode for a behaviour that is
pleasing to the LORD. As
family is axiomatic to
community, I have
reminded you of how the
Lord submitted His own life
to save us from all sin.
He wills that we live well:
the wives: it's wise if you'll
submit to your own
husbands—even if they

don't give heed to *Yeshua*.
Your chaste behaviour is
sure to have a good effect:
they may accept The Faith!
The husband should give
honour to his wife and
recognise that both are heirs
of that God bequeaths.
In speaking to the Faith
Community: do exercise
compassion with
a unity expressed in
kindness and in courtesy.

Seek peace, pursue it and
the Lord will bless you if
you will apply yourself
to goodness, grace and
helpfulness: who'd harm
you then? So you're your
opportunities to testify:
defend your faith, speak of
your hope and back it up
with conduct that's a
witness in itself!

Unbelievers recognise good
works. Take for example,
Yeshua: the Just upon a
cross to save all the unjust.
The disobedient can
recognise obedience and
grace that is applied to
them. The sinner may be

saved by realising that the
Living Christ died for the
wrong and wronged: He
loves each one!

Commit yourself to God.
The Lord committed His
own life to save your life
for all Eternity!

CHAPTER 4
JESUS—OUR EXAMPLE

I urge you now to be at one
with Christ, that—as He
suffered for us all—so let us
always be prepared to stand
the test. Already you had
spent much time in
following your own
footsteps—they led to sinful
ways. But now you're
suffering for Christ:
you live to do the will of
God. Some will take stock
of you and wonder why they
find no sinful ways in you.

One day, they'll need to
give account for their own
sins. The End Times are at
hand. I ask of you: be
watchful, serious, with love
in action so the LORD is
glorified in you. It is not
strange that you should
suffer for your faith. When
Christ returns, you'll know
exceeding joyfulness.

CHAPTER 5
SHEPHERDING GOD'S
FLOCK

I now exhort the Elders in
their task of shepherding the
flock of God. You know
me as a witness to Christ's
suffering and a fellow Elder
now. Therefore, take heed
to shoulder well the task
God asks of you. Be good
shepherds to all those who
need your faithful
leadership. Feel no
compulsion in this role—
be willing shepherds, ready
both to guard and guide
the flock, exampled by the
Good Shepherd who gave
Himself for all the sheep.
When He appears, He'll
give to you the Crown
of everlasting Life!

A word now for the "lambs"
and "sheep": Obey the
Elders, follow the example
they portray. Allow God's
hand to guard and guide

you on your way. You need to be aware that Satan sets himself to be 'a roaring lion' in search of a most tasty meal! Cast all your care upon the Lord: He cares for you. Be steadfast, vigilant and reassured that He, the God of grace, will strengthen you, establish, settle and perfect your soul. Give Him the glory and dominion now and evermore. Amen!

Silas is my secretary and young Mark, who's like a son, is my able aide. Greet everyone with love from me.

..... oOo .....

PETER
THE SECOND
LETTER

My greetings to you all, beloved friends. I write by my own hand today. You'll notice the contrasting data in this present epistle because the first, with which you'll be familiar now, was written by Silas from my dictation: a letter to the Diaspora—Jews of the Dispersion scattered abroad in flight from persecution, peril and the sword. That was a letter to 'sheep' fleeing from 'roaring lions', sheep in need of holding firmly to the faith we hold—our precious faith.

Today I will address matters that concern internal issues. I feel the need to highlight the dangers of false doctrine that could seep right through the Community of Faith if not confronted by the strength of argument that counts with God.

I'll emphasise those qualities that mark one out as a true follower of *Yeshua*— Messiah, Christ.

Allow me to remind you of the gifts of grace: moral purity, enlightenment, self-discipline, retain a stick-ability, godliness, familial kindness, and selfless love. What a contrast to that of the many false doctrinaires: arrogance, and sensuality, greed, envy, superficiality. In this letter also, three great issues of our times will be

addressed: 1. Grow up,
2. Be wise,
3. Be alert!
The balance between faith
and practice will be seen.

CHAPTER 1
GROWING IN GRACE

Simon Peter, Bond Servant
Babylon (Rome)
Circa A.D. 66 –68

To those of precious faith,

May grace and peace be
multiplied to you as you
learn still more of *Yeshua.*
Through Him, we have
received all things
pertaining to the
transformed life.
How great the promises
of God: of precious worth,
exceeding all of Earth. By
these great gifts, you may
rejoice in Christ's own
nature through whom
you've escaped corruption
of the world.

It's for this reason that I
write: Be energised by The
Spirit's power that you'll be
diligent, investing all of life
in grace by these additions

to be made:

* To your faith, add virtue
* To your virtue, add
  knowledge
* To your knowledge, add
  self-control
* To your self-control, add
  perseverance
* To your perseverance,
  add godliness
* To your godliness, add
  kindness
* To your kindness, add
  agape love

These gifts are yours.
If they abound, you'll bear
much fruit through *Yeshua.*
If one is lacking in these
gifts, there is short-
sightedness regarding
Christ. Do not be blind,
forgetful of what grace has
done for you. Be diligent in
exercise of all these things.

If so, you'll never fall: the
Everlasting Kingdom's door
has opened wide to you. I
have good reason to remind
you of these things: as long
as I am dwelling in my
'earthly tent' I will
encourage you for soon

I must discard this body for
the soul's true Home. My
words will then continue on
to stir you up in faith after
I will depart this life. I've
spoken not in fables or in
parables to you. I was eye-
witness to the life, death,
rising of *Yeshua*. I saw
humanity and majesty
stamped on the life of
Christ. I testify to His
great grace, His sacrifice,
His very *LIFE!*
I heard the *YHVH*–LORD
speak on the mount.

He said to us:

This is My beloved Son,
I am so very pleased
with Yeshua, My Son!

This is the confirmation that
the Lord is He of whom the
prophets spoke: the holy
men prepared our hearts
for Him who brought His
earnest followers
from **shadows** into *LIGHT!*

CHAPTER 2
FALSITY, FALLACY
v. FAITH

I spoke of prophets but
not all were true—
there was a falsity within
their speech that rang
not true. Indeed,
they infiltrate the Faith
Community today!
Destructive heresies,
compounded by denial
of the Lord and many
flock to them,
blaspheming Truth.

They wish to stand up
high within the Church,
exploiting you. They
would remain within—
they must be rooted out,
have done with them!
Recall our history:
the LORD has spoken,
acted in the past.
Remember Noah's day!
Recall Gomorrah, Sodom
too, though God delivered
Lot who had kept whole
amid their lawlessness.

Know that the Lord delivers
those who trust in Him—
All, saved by grace!

Such persons vilify that
which they do not
understand—they will
receive the wages of their

**sinfulness. Unrighteous-
ness has no reward but
death (dumb donkeys—
Balaam's ass— can draw
a man to truthfulness
if there's a will for
righteousness). Know the
alternative is like an
empty well or tempest-
driven clouds: dim
darkness manifest.
Alluring words must
be examined in
the** *LIGHT of Truth!*

Take care! Don't be
entangled by such snares
after you find true liberty!
Far better not to have once
known the True and Living
Way than be like swine
when cleansed returning
to a wallowing in the mire.

CHAPTER 3
HOLD TO GOD'S
PROMISES

I write with earnestness,
that you will take to heart
the prophecies that warned
of those who'd come in the
End Times and strutting on
the platforms of the proud.
We have been warned!

they'd fling their questions:
how, and when, and where
is He who's bound to come?
Such soothsayers forget that
by the Word of God the
Earth and heavens were
made; how then destruction
came with floodtides that
did overcome the ancient
world. Remember this: a
whole millennium is but a
day with God! He is not
slack; He's patient and
longsuffering. He does not
will that you should die.

Rather, repentance is His
aim. But know: the great
Day of the LORD will come
just like a thief at night—
when least expected, He
will come. Because the
elements of Earth
will be dissolved how
should we act?: with holy
conduct and in godly
expectation of the coming
of the Lord. Expect, look for
the New World where all
righteousness pervades
the whole. Be firm now in
your faith and let Him find
you, on that Day, in peace,
and blameless in His sight.
I should remind you of how

Paul, beloved Apostle,
counselled you. Seek deeper
understanding of
his words as you now grow
in grace and in the
knowledge of our Lord
and Saviour: *Yeshua,
Messiah*: Christ.

….. oOo …..

JOHN
THE FIRST LETTER

If you are wondering at
the omission of any personal
identification in this letter,
you will not require my
signature—there's   proof
enough in the themes of
LIGHT and Darkness, Life
and Death, Love and Hate, to
seal it mine. *LIGHT,* LIFE
and LOVE: that's what I
found in following *Yeshua*–
Jesus.

I am John, son of Zebedee
and Salome—sister to Mary
of Nazareth, Mother of
Yeshua who was, and *IS*, my
cousin. Much more than

earthly ties, our link is
spiritual.

You met me first where
Jordan meets with the Dead
Sea; then as a fisherman on
Galilee with James, my
brother. We left the fish to
fish for folk! When *Yeshua*
called me to the ministry, we
shared a close affinity. He
taught me the value of *agape*
love. You'll find that I write
much of it and I have
endeavoured to live that love
for all humanity.

You have already caught
up with me via my rendition
of the Gospel News though,
in that edition, I chose to
provide you with a new
Book of Psalms so that you
may sing the Gospel too.

I feel the need to write
again for many years have
passed since my early life on
Galilee   and   on   into
discipleship. My quill is
eager to shed *LIGHT* on the
darkness that overshadows
the falsity of bourgeoning
Gnostic beliefs.

My purpose is to expose
such falsity and to contrast it
with the assurance of all our

salvation that is by faith in Christ. I will encourage you to trust the Lord's Divinity—there's proof enough!

Because of it, there'll be a focus, too, on how we live in light of *LIGHT*! There are no shades of grey with sin. We all must choose between the **shadows** and the *LIGHT*. With the coming of this *LIGHT* all darkness is displaced!

My letter will reveal the Great Divide so that there will be no mistake regarding sin. From the moment I took up my quill to be a torchbearer for *Yeshua*, I have endeavoured to bring *LIGHT* into the dark places of the world. As I begin this epistle, I ask you first to reflect on the Prologue to my Gospel for it has its place right here:

CHAPTER 1
LIGHT

In the beginning was the *logos* (Word.) He dwelt with God and was, indeed, the *YHVH*–LORD. All things were made by Him: the 'Word' whom we now know as *Yeshua.* In Him was Life. This Life gives *LIGHT* to all! The *LIGHT* o'er darkness shines: no darkness overcomes the Eternal *LIGHT.*

The *logos*–Word—existed from before all time began. God loved our world so much, He sent the *logos*–Word, who was His own beloved Son, so that we would not perish—we'd enjoy Eternal Life! This, then, is our starting place: the Truth expressed first in my Gospel News of Him who is the *LIGHT, THE LIFE AND LOVE* Personified!

We saw this Man, we lived and worked with Him. Here was Humanity—Divinity in flesh! I now declare this word to you again that you may also know the fellowship experienced in knowing *Yeshua*, the Christ, for God is *LIGHT*—no darkness dwells in Him.

Observe the Great Divide:

**To testify to *LIGHT* yet
walk in night: this is a
lie—there is no truth
in such a lie as this!**

If we will walk in *LIGHT*
as He is in the *LIGHT*, we
share a fellowship born of
His saving power.

**If we give testimony
that there's no sin in us,
we live the lie!**

If we confess our sins, the
LORD is faithful to forgive
and cleanse us from
unrighteousness.

**If we would claim we have
no sin, we make the LORD
to be a liar. There is no
place for His own Word
in us at all!**

CHAPTER 2
LIFE

It's for this reason that I
write: If any find they're
guilty of a sin, there is an
Advocate who'll stand
for us, who'll plead our
cause and give Himself to

take our place, propitiate,
to make us free from sin
and from the world! You
know the Lord?
So, follow Him, keep
His commands!

**To testify that He is
known but yet not follow
Him: this is a lie—Truth is
not known by you!**

If we will keep our faith,
His Love will be perfected
in our souls.

**That one who testifies
that he abides in God
should walk with Him!**

You're looking for a new
commandment now?
There's nothing new in the
command to follow all the
Laws of God! A new
command you ask?

Do work this out: the
darkness of the night is
passing for the *LIGHT*
already shines on you!

**You say you walk in
LIGHT but hate your
brother? This is but
darkness yet, I know!**

You love your brother? So,
  You do abide in *LIGHT*.
  You'll walk upright; you
will not stumble in the dark.

**The one who hates abides
in darkness still and
cannot find the way for he
is blind within his soul.**

I write now to the Family:
To children: For His sake,
know your sins forgiven for
  you believe in *Yeshua*.
To fathers: You've known
  Him from the start.
To youth: in overcoming
wickedness, you're strong!

**To those who love the
world: love of the Father
is not known.**

This lusting world will pass
  away: accept God's will,
    you will abide.

**The Anti-christ, an evil
one, is here: Some of the
Family left the 'fold',
so now they don't belong.**

You are anointed of the
LORD; you know the Truth,
  you do not lie. You share
His promise of Eternal Life.

Abide in God for, on the
Day that he appears, you
Will not be ashamed: you're
reborn to God's Family!

CHAPTER 3
LOVE

How great the love of God!
This love He showered on
us: we are His family now.
We do not know what we
will be but this we know:
when He appears, we'll see
Him as He is for we shall be
like Him! You have this
  hope? Keep pure!

**Whoever sins partakes in
lawlessness for that is what
sin is–acknowledge it!**

Those who abide in God
do not commit a sin: their
  life is upright, pure.

**Whoever sins belongs to
Satan—he's the one that
sinned right from the
start—the reason why
Yeshua has come! He will
destroy all Satan's work.**

Those who are born of God
don't sin for they belong

to Him.

**This is the Great Divide:
it's lack of righteousness
that marks one out as
Satan's own—he knows
a hate in place of love.**

This is the News I bring:
love one another for it's
love that binds us to
the LORD!

**You've proof of this in
Cain who is the architype
of hate and envy of the
righteous son.**

You have no need to
wonder If the world hates
you—you've passed already
into LIFE! You wish to
know how love will really
work? Just look to Christ:
He gave His life for us,
He loves us so! Now we
should follow His example
too and be prepared to
'place our lives upon the
line' for all the Faith
Community.

**If one who's rich in worldly
goods will shut his heart
against another's need
where's love for God?**

My children, let us not rely
upon a statement that we
love but, rather, let the deed
express that love.

What is the will of God for
us? He wills that we believe
in Christ and love each
other well. This is the
testimony unto Truth:
keep His commandments
and believe the precious
Name: *Yeshua*—Jesus and
love each other well!

CHAPTER 4
TRUTH v. ERROR

It's time for testing now!
What is the Truth and what
is false? How do we choose
the right? Here is the Truth:

**There are false prophets
who declare they hold the
truth but speak the lie!**

If you confess the Lordship
of the Christ: that God the
Son was born in human
flesh, you're of the *LIGHT!*

**All liars are of the world
where darkness dwells.
They can't see the Truth
but lies are heard! The**

world will know its own!

My little children, you have
overcome for He who is
within is greater than the
worldly one.

**All those that find
no place with us don't
hear or recognise what is
of Truth: they live in
darkness yet.**

Let us then love each other:
love is of the LORD. You
find love for each other?
You belong to Him! I've
said before and say again
that God so loved the world
He gave His own beloved
Son that all who will believe
in Him will live eternally;
already you have passed
from death to LIFE! If God
loves us this much, we
ought to love each other too.

Though we've not seen the
Lord, if we have love
for others, God—the God of
Love— lives in our heart.
By this we know God's love
for He *IS* Love and he that
does abide in love, abides
in God and God abides in
him. Love is perfected so

we'll stand firm on the
Judgement Day
There is no fear in love for
love that is perfected will
cast out our fear. Because
God first loved us, we now
respond in love!

**CHAPTER 5
WITNESSING TO
LIGHT, LIFE AND
LOVE**

If we can testify that we
love God and show it by our
deeds of love, we truly
know that we belong—
we're members of His
Family. This is the very
thing that overcomes the
world and that by which we
have the victory: it is our
faith! It is the Holy Spirit
who will bear the witness
for He *IS* The Truth!

In actuality, there are Three
Persons who bear witness to
our faith in Heaven: the
YHVH–LORD, our
heavenly Father, *Yeshua*–
the *logos* Word, also the
Paraclete, the One who's by
our side: the Holy Spirit.

Know that these Three are all ONE! This is the testimony to The Faith: The *YHVH*–LORD has given to us eternal Life. How do we know? This Life is in the Son. All who declare allegiance to the Son have Life. Without the Son there's no real Life!

These things are written so you'll be assured that you partake of Life that's granted by your faith in Christ: this *IS* Eternal Life to all of faith! What is the outcome of continued trust? You'll activate your confidence that, if a prayer is in accordance with God's will, He hears. We know that, if He hears, He'll answer too and the petition will be granted then! I urge you all that, if you see a brother fall, pray for that one; encourage him to trust in God. And, before I place my last full stop, just one thing: Shun all idols now!

….. oOo …..

THE LETTERS OF JOHN

THE SECOND LETTER

This follow-up epistle is directed to a local Church. Again, there is no need for signatures. The 'elect lady' knows the identity of the author as I know her—the name of the 'lady' to whom I write is but a pseudonym.

This letter is addressed to a specific church to address some pressing problems experienced locally. You'll see that I express my deep affection for the Faith Community at this undisclosed address. The Church, you see, does not consist of floors and doors, nor walls and roof: the Church is composed of the 'bricks and mortar' of human flesh and fortitude in living out The Faith in terms of worship, witness and will.

The Church is the Family of God! My purpose in sending this letter is to give encouragement and also counsel for quality living. We must take heed lest we fall. I'm concerned for the welfare of this Family.

THE ELDER,

To the Elect Lady,
the Church and Family of
the LORD:

I love you all in Truth. All faithful souls do join with me because the Truth we hold is the 'Forever' Truth! My prayer for you is this: Grace, mercy, peace be with you all from *YHVH*–LORD and *Yeshua*, His well-beloved Son. I do rejoice in my awareness that, in meeting some of your family, I find them walking steadily in truth and following the guidelines of the LORD. But now, 'Elect Lady'—the Family of God, the *YHVH*-LORD— I plead with you: ensure that you are following not newly framed commands but that which we have known right from our rebirth IN the Lord. God asks His Family to love each other well. What kind of love does He require? *agape* love: the love that cares for all! To love like that is to be walking in the ways of *YHVH*–LORD.

I write to you to counteract the liars that have gone out into the world bent on deceit. Such people do declare that Christ has not come in the flesh. Such 'news' reveals the anti-christ! Look to yourselves, that you do not mislay the verities of faith. That one who cannot hold to faith in Christ is not of God!

If someone visits you who cannot speak the Truth of Christ, do not receive him for his evil ways. There's much to say but I'd prefer to come and share our faith with you. Your sister church greets you in LOVE.

..... oOo .....

THE LETTERS OF JOHN

THE THIRD LETTER

A most distressing matter has come to my attention and I must give counsel to Gaius, my dear friend whom I love for his steadfast faith, his devotion to the Truth that is proclaimed IN Christ.
I take up my quill to hurry off some words of a warm encouragement to him:

THE ELDER,

To the beloved Gaius,

I am at prayer for you,
dear friend, that you
continue in good health
in body, mind and soul.
I was so thrilled to meet
with men who brought me
news of you. Each testified
of your adherence to the
Truth—that which you hold,
that which you preach.

I find no greater joy than
this: that those I love IN
Christ still hold to Truth.
Your faithfulness I do
commend for you show
kindness to both friends
and strangers too.
Well done, Gaius!
The strangers also know
of Christ through you and,
if they go on living worthy
lives, you've done so well.
We will receive such men
as brothers too, working
together and rejoicing in the
Lord! Gaius, there is a need
to warn you of that prideful
Diotrephes who loves to
have pre-eminence within
the Church so envies worthy
men. He spreads malicious
words and shuns those
sanctified. He cuts
them off from their
own rightful place.

Beloved Gaius,
I urge you not to be
enamoured of such
company. Continue to
regard all that is good and
emulate the Lord. You seek
good company? Demetrius
is such a man. All give good
testimony about his
character. We add to that
ourselves—we know him
well: such testimony does

hold Truth. There is so much that I could write about. I'd rather visit you to sit with you as friend with friend. Our friends now greet you too.
Speak well of them by name.

..... oOo .....

THE LETTER
OF JUDE

Apostacy is gaining ground within the Church. It's time to be on the attack—time to fight for the Faith we hold. I feel a compulsion upon me to speak out for Christ in no uncertain terms. I came late into The Faith. You see, I'm Jude—the brother of James, leader of the Faith Community.

As James is my brother, I am also brother to *Yeshua*. Is it any wonder, after meeting up with Him again so soon after the Calvary atrocity—cum sacrifice for sin—on the Resurrection Day, that I then

would be committed fully to *Yeshua*–Jesus, the Christ!

So, late I was to stand up at His side, but quick to speak for Him today! You could use the alternative name—Judas—but I prefer Jude (for obvious reasons!) I therefore introduce myself as Jude as I put my quill to the parchment. I now boldly state to you my battle with all those who seek to twist God's grace into a granting of the glitter and the glamour of living licentiously within the Church. I'll point to past paths where Israel strayed disastrously.

All Christians need to be on guard. I trust this correspondence can assist the local leaders in their ministry:

JUDE,
Bond Servant of *Yeshua*

To the Called, the Holy Family of God the Father and *Yeshua* the Son:

Grace, mercy, love in abundance, is my prayer for you! The purpose of this letter is quite plain:

THE BATTLE-LINES
OF FAITH

You've read the
correspondence where
I wrote to you about how
we are saved. I've found it
necessary to exhort you now
concerning drawing up
the battle-lines against the
wrongs that seem to
infiltrate so easily into the
Faith Community unless we
do contend with evil on all
fronts. Call out those men
for what they do to turn
God's grace into
unmitigated gore!

I do remind you how the
LORD, who led His people
through the Exodus,
declaimed the sin by which
they sank into the mire.
Even fallen angels aren't
immune—they'll meet a
sorry end! You'll be aware
of Sodom and Gomorrah
that, because of utter
immorality, met with an
early fate. Michael,
Archangel of the LORD,
contends against the evil
one and knows the LORD
has victory! The men of
whom I write speak of

that which they do not
understand thereby
corrupting all the heart.
Woe unto them—they're
relegated to the realm of
Cain. They'll perish there.
Look to your Love Feasts
and take care: these men
will feast with you to serve
themselves. They are just
empty clouds or autumn
trees devoid of fruit—
twice dead: do have regard
to this: dead in body—
autumn time, dead in soul—
devoid of 'fruit'.
They are like raging seas
with no stability, or
wandering stars upon
a dark domain—forever so!

Old Enoch spoke of their
demise. Oh yes, they will be
judged! How sad it is to see
an apostate who once
believed, stumble and fall
into a pit of shame. Such
men rely on flattering,
ingratiating self to please
their pride. Oh, let me now
remind you of the
prophecies that, in the End
Time, their mockery of holy
men would cause a Great
Divide. But you, beloved

friends, behave in light of how the Lord instructs: build up your inner life to stand firm in the Holy Faith to which you testify; seek all your strength through prayer. Keep close to God, experience His love and look unto the mercy of the Christ: here is Eternal Life! Stretch out your willing hands to help the needy, ease their pain.

Now, look to Him for He is Lord. He'll hold you steady, keep you from a stumbling fall; He will present you without fault before His glory with abundant joy. Look to the *YHVH*–LORD who is the only God. To Him be glory, majesty, all power and authority throughout all ages and forevermore!

..... oOo .....

THE 'TIMELESS' YEARS

THE APOCALYPSE (REVELATION)

Greetings! I'm John bar Zebedee. It is my supreme joy, and yet my awesome responsibility, to present to you the Cosmic Christ— more so, He is the One who created the cosmos! He is the Ultimate Being: Son of God, yet God the Son! He IS, before the Beginning and after the End: the WORD— the *logos*—the Articulation of Divinity for He, the Creator of the universe, once laid aside His divine glory to take on the flesh of Earth, cloaking Himself in the vulnerability of humanity. He became like us so that, ultimately, we may become like Him.

Such concepts are beyond all human comprehension though the *YHVH*–LORD determined that we should know Him and be prepared to shake off the shackles of sin so that one Glad Day, we can meet with Him in the Eternity of His Heaven. I have been privileged to know *Yeshua* in His human form and rejoiced with Him on the Resurrection Morn. I also saw Him depart His 'clay-clad' years! Is this the end of it all? It is but the beginning of the News I am to offer you today.

Are your ears and hearts open to what the Lord is saying to His Church today? This is my task: to relate to you what these eyes have seen, these ears have heard, this heart embraced. He came to me most recently!

Here I am, on the Isle of Patmos, exiled from all I hold dear by force of Rome's iron boot. It was on the Lord's Day: Sunday morning, as I sat looking out upon the sea that separates us now. Deep in meditation, I became aware of a depth of spiritual sensitivity that drew me to the actual presence of the Lord! He asked me to convey to you a message with a volume far surpassing cosmic realities.

What I convey on this parchment will relate to the Past, the Present and also open up for you just what the Future holds. In order to express this News of what *YHVH*–LORD holds in store for you (in terms that you'll sense by virtue of your own spirituality), there is need to employ concepts of apocalyptic significance: truth will be conveyed in symbolic language.

You'll discover the significance of numerals; you'll recognise who 'dragons' really are; you'll understand what 'colours' will convey and you will unravel the pseudonym of 'Babylon'; for you will understand the Greek word *mysterion* is not, actually, a mystery as most know it. The real 'Mystery' that *YHVH*–LORD conveys through *Yeshua* was once unknown but now, through Christ, becomes the 'Open Secret': God has declared His love for the world through His Son who is now in the Father's presence as He prepares your Heavenly

Home.

There is so much more: for there's News of Heaven and Hell, translated by my heavenly Guest. Via this parchment, you will become partners in hearing, knowing and understanding His Plans, His Preparations, His Purpose and His awesome Power.

Are you ready? In Genesis, you found the Beginning; in the Gospels you discovered Redemption and, in the Apocalypse— Revelation, you will find the completion of the Story where Time passes into Eternity.

You will be blessed as you take to heart the Message scripted from the words of the Lord and from the symbolic language and numerals abounding in the book. In the numerals, you'll discover:
1. Unity, 2. Diversity,
3. Trinity, 4. Earth,
5. Grace, 6. Humanity,
7. Perfection, 8. Jesus,
9. 3x3, 10. Completion,
11. Disorganisation,
12. Good Government.

The 0s offer a number emphasised in magnitude. Translate the numbers to their meanings and you will find more to bless you as you read on.

The Apocalypse carries 9 titles for the Lord: *Yeshua*– Jesus and I now introduce you to the first:

THE PROLOGUE: "JESUS IS LORD"
Chapter 1

This is the Apocalypse— the Revelation of the Christ. I, John, do testify to all I've seen and heard. How BLESSED* are those who read, hear and take to heart this News for the "End Time" is coming soon.

*The 1st of 7 'Unknown' BEATITUDES.
Those known are found in Matthew 5.

Charis (grace) and *shalom* (peace) from Him who WAS and IS and is TO BE and from the *SEVEN*-fold Spirit of the LORD:

This News is from
Yeshua—
the Faithful Word, The
Lord! I sense a Psalm upon
my soul Please, sing this
News with me:

TO HIM WHO LOVES
US

Tune: *Toplady, Who is He?*
7.7.7.7.7.7.
Now to Him who loves us so
And has freed us from our sins
By His blood; He makes
us whole,
All to be His Kingdom priests:
He has bid us serve Him here,
"Glory"* echoes from the soul.
(* The 1st of 7 DOXOLOGIES).

Look! *The Lord* is coming soon,
See the clouds disperse
at noon!
Every eye shall see the Lord,
Even those that pierced
Him through.
And all peoples of the earth
Then shall mourn because
of God.

Alpha and *Omega*, God:
He's the One who Is and Was,
Past and Present, Future:
ONE!
He is God, the *YHVH*–LORD,

He is God, the One to come,
El Shaddai, the Mighty God!

Love Divine, the Lord is God:
YHVH, El Shaddai, LORD God!
Glory* to Your Holy Name.
All things flow at Your
command,
Power supreme is in
Your hand;
All things will Your Love
proclaim!

Before I open up the pages
of The Apocalypse—
what is this event?

APOCALYPSE

What does the future hold
for us,
The world, and all there is
to be?
Impending doom, announced
today:
Is this what God would have
us see?

I ponder on the claims
His word
Allows in terms of truth
and grace;
How may discernment come?
And what
Will God reveal today

of peace?

What can it mean,
Apocalypse?
This is a mystery, a drape
Across the windows of
my mind;
What could I see, of
Heaven's scape?

It is revealed! Apocalypse:
The death of Death, the birth
of Life!
The curtain opens on His Day;
This scene portrays an end
to strife!

.

It is unveiled—the scope of life
That's in His plan: we're
Heaven bound!
God's Word speaks *LIGHT* and
Life and Love:
The Dawn has come:
redemption found.

. . . .

I'm your companion in
our tribulation—also in
the Kingdom of the Lord.
I'm on this Isle a prisoner
because I testified of
Yeshua. I was
at prayer on Patmos Isle,
alert: a 'Trumpet Voice',

that of the 'First and Last',
declared His true identity
(I'd known that Voice from
early days in Galilee). He
asked of me to take
dictation for He must
communicate His will to all
the Churches , 7 Churches
that had need to hear
His Apocalyptic Word.

I turned to see
the 'Trumpet Voice'
(so musical, so dominant).
What I observed were 7
Lampstands: 7
CHURCHES!

The Lord required that
every Church would take to
heart the News He would
disclose. What's more, I
was to recognise that
lampstands aren't the
LIGHT, they bear the
LIGHT! the Church must
stand for Him who IS The
LIGHT! And there, right in
the midst of all 'The 7',
stood One like 'The Son of
Man'!

Christ had identified
Himself to me! The

Heavenly form was now
so changed but still Christ
held the human frame, was
known by one He loved!
A good place to begin.

*Don't be afraid—I am the
One who lives, was dead, is
now alive eternally! I hold
the Keys of Life and Death.
Now, this is what I do
require: Take notes of what
you've seen, see now, also
preview the future time—
the Past, the Present and
the Prophecy. Here is My
clue for Stars and Lamps:
Each Star: the angel/leader
of a church. Each Lamp: the
churches to address.*

My heart is overwhelmed:
I gaze upon the One I know
as *Yeshua*: 'The Christ'!

PART ONE
"JESUS: THE SON
OF MAN"
Chapter 2

I take my quill. The SON
OF MAN directs:

1st LETTER:

THE LOVELESS
CHURCH

*To EPHESUS, please write:
"I am the One who holds
the 7 Stars—the Leaders of
your church—I know you
well: your work, your
patience and your purity.
And you, I see, are not all
weary yet. But I must say
this one sad thing:*

**You've lost the love
you shared at first and so
you've fallen far.**

*I ask of you: repent or else
your Lampstand is removed.
You have an ear to hear?
Hear what The Spirit says to
you. If you can rectify this
fault, you'll eat the
'fruit of Paradise'.*

2nd LETTER:
THE PERSECUTED
CHURCH

*Write to the Leader of the
SMYRNA church: I know you
well—you live in poverty,
but you are truly rich! Do
not have fear of those who
persecute: you will be tested
for 10 days—the trials*

are then complete.
Be faithful unto death and
you'll receive the Crown
of Life. You have an ear
to hear? You won't be
harmed by the impending
2ⁿᵈ death!"

(A thought from me—yes,
John—There is no darkness in
this church! A troubled church
will seek the Lord, the *LIGHT*!
This church has *LIGHT*).

3ʳᵈ LETTER:
THE COMPROMISED
CHURCH

Write to the Leader of the
church at PERGAMUM:
I hold the two-edged sword.
I know where you all
dwell—near Satan's throne!
Yet you hold fast; you don't
deny the Faith. But some
things are not right:

There's immorality within
and there's false doctrine
that is heard in the ranks.

Repent today or I will come
to fight such liars by My
own word! You have an ear
to hear? If you can
overcome you'll feast on

manna sweet and carry the
White Stone on which your
new name's written down.

(A thought from me: a white
stone proves identity! It's
recognised by family today).

4ᵗʰ LETTER:
THE CORRUPT
CHURCH

Write to the Leader of the
church in THYATIRA next:
I know your works: there's
love and faith, fine service,
patience, too.
But this is also true:

There is a 'Jezebel' within
your midst—a
prophetess? A schemer
and a liar! here'll be great
tribulation
that results from all her
wiles: she'll lie in pain!

But unto those who will
remain well clear of her, I'll
place no further burdens on
your back. Be strong!
Hold fast the Faith you have
and be an overcomer; you'll
wield power and you'll
receive the Morning Star.

CHAPTER 3
5th LETTER
THE DEAD CHURCH

*Write to the Leader of the
church at SARDIS now:
I know your work,*

**but you don't know
yourself: you think that
you're alive but you are
dead. Do be alert, keep
watch, renew your faith
for death creeps nearer
still. Repent of wayward-
ness. And those that are
asleep: wake up or I will
come, as thieves, at night.**

*But there are those still
undefiled and they will walk
with Me in unstained
garments and your names
will then be written in
the 'Book of Life'. You have
an ear to hear? Then listen
as The Spirit speaks!*
(Again, a thought from me:
there's not much *LIGHT* seen
in this church. I am reminded:
LIGHT brings Life!)

Again, he spoke to me:

*Write to the Leader of the
church at PHILADELPHIA:
The One that holds the Key
of David says, 'I know you
well; I have unlocked and
opened up a door for you
that none can shut! You're
fragile, but you've kept My
word and you have
not denied My Name.*

**But those of Satan's
synagogue (they think
they're Jews, so wrong)
will one day change
their alien minds.**

*Your perseverance keeps
you safe from the Last Trial!
Hold fast that which you
have, that no one steals
your crown. If you can
overcome, you'll be
a pillar in the Temple of the
LORD and His New Name
will then be written on your
heart eternally. Do listen to
God's Voice today!*

6th LETTER
THE FAITHFUL
CHURCH

7th LETTER
THE LUKEWARM
CHURCH

Write to the Leader of the church at LAODICEA: This is what the Faithful and True Witness from before creation says to you:

I recognise your works! You're not ice cold nor are you warm! Neither: lukewarm—unpalatable, I will spit you out! You roll in wealth, there's not one thing you need. But, in reality, you're wretched, poor and blind!

Be counselled now: refine your gold, choose only the pure robes for they will cloak your nakedness. Procure the eye-salve that will cure the blind. Repent today! Behold, I stand outside your door. Will you now open up and welcome Me that I may share Heaven's joys with you? You have an ear to hear? Hark to The Spirit's words! (My thoughts to ponder on: This church has lost its way! There is no inner *LIGHT* to guide their path. Yet see how great the promises! This is the 7th church. What does that say to you? At the commence-ment of dictation, *Yeshua* made clear: The End is near! I write of Past, of Present, and of Prophecy. The 7 churches will be found today and in the future days. The 7 says it all— it will disclose finality! Laodicea is the very last: The End is nigh!)

….. oOo …..

PART TWO "JESUS: THE LAMB OF GOD"

CHAPTER 4
THE THRONE ROOM

The door of Heaven opened then to me! The Voice addressed my trembling soul: Come up to Me, I'll show you scenes relating to Eternity! All time and space lost meaning now! I stood in Heaven—at least, my soul observed the Throne of God, the glorious Entity enthroned. Encircling all the Throne, an emerald rainbow glowed—green, symbolising Life!

Situated to the left:
12 thrones, and to the right,
12 thrones: the thrones
of Elders—Tribes:
12 Apostolic:
12—Old and New
I saw 7 Lamps of Fire—
The Heavenly Menorah
here, symbolic of the 7-fold
Spirit of the LORD!

I viewed 4 Living Creatures,
4: globally significant.
These 4 I recognised:
the Lion, the Calf,
the Man, the Eagle:
these fourfold Gospel
Witnesses are here in
Heaven! These four give
universal praise unto
'The Trinity of Holiness':
the One who IS, who WAS,
who IS to BE! Now, Glory,
Honour, Gratitude:
The 2nd DOXOLOGY
is here expressed.

The Elders fall before the
Lord to worship Him. Their
hymn becomes the
3rd DOXOLOGY
directed to the Lord:
You're worthy, Lord:
receive all Glory, Honour,
Power—Creator and

Preserver, Governor
of all things: Past and
Present and Projected too!

CHAPTER 5
THE WORTHY LAMB

The One who sat upon the
Throne held out a Scroll.
Attached were 7 SEALS.
A loud enquiry came:
An angel asked, Who is the
Worthy One who may take
up this Scroll and open it?
No one stepped forth!
Then tears fell from my
eyes—is there no one who
is appropriate for such
a task as this in Heaven?
Not one who's worthy to
unroll this Scroll? An Elder
then spoke kindly, Do
not weep. Behold: here is
the Lion—of Judah's
Tribe—the Root of David:
He's prevailed! I saw the
Lamb, once slain, who took
the Scroll. Just then the
Elders and Four Creatures
fell upon their knees to
worship Him. They sang
this new song unto Him:

You're worthy, Lord,
You are the One to open it

for You were slain,
redeeming us!
From every nation, every
tribe, all peoples of the
Earth:
You make us kings and
priests
to rule with worth!

The Angels, Elders,
Creatures, all
10,000 times 10,000,
then bowed down before
The Lamb to sing
unprecedented words of
praise: the 4th
DOXOLOGY.
Then all in Heaven, all on
Earth, all under Earth joined
in the Chorus with
the 5th DOXOLOGY:

WORTHY IS THE LAMB
Tune: *Hendon* 7.7.7.7.

Worthy is the Lamb of God
Slain for us on Calvary;
Worthy to receive acclaim:
Worthy through Eternity!

Worthy our Redeemer, Lord,
With Your blood You bought
reprieve!
Out of every nation, tribe,

There will come those who
believe.

Worthy Christ, our living Lord,
You have made us to become
Citizens of Heaven and now
God's own Kingdom is our
Home!

Worthy Jesus, Son of God,
You have chosen us from birth,
Priests to serve You and obey;
We will reign with You
on Earth.

Worthy is the Lamb of God,
We proclaim, All worth and
praise, Wisdom, strength and
honour, power,
Glory to the Lord always!

You are worthy, Lord, our God,
Glory, honour, power are
Yours;
You created all things well,
Now receive our grateful
praise.

CHAPTER 6
6 BROKEN SEALS

(1st: 'The Conqueror')
The Lamb removed a Seal
I was invited to observe

a man upon a stallion of
pure white. He held a bow
and crown and rode out in
the world to conquer it.

(2nd : 'World conflict')
Come and see the 2nd Seal:

It's now removed: Behold,
a stallion: red—the
symbol of world conflict:
War!

(3rd: 'Famine')
See now: another seal

is broken and a rider on a
large black horse strode
out upon a ravaged world:
no fodder now.

(4th: 'Death')
Look! as the 4th Seal reveals

'Death' on a mangy horse
descending, Hades
following so close behind.
A quarter of all life is
taken from the Earth.
(The '4' will now be known as
'The 4 Horsemen of The
Apocalypse':
see Zechariah 1:8-11, 6:1-8.)

(5th: 'Martyrdom')
Observe the breaking of the
5th Seal

where all the souls of

martyrs are now sheltering
beneath the Altar there.

How long, O Lord, how
long before our blood will
be avenged?'

White robes were then
produced and, with the
robes, the answer came:
'Until the slaughter is
complete!

(6th: 'Cosmic Catastrophe')
I saw then, at the 6th Seal

An earthquake, darkened
sun, the moon like blood.
The stars fell out of place,
the mountains, islands
were displaced. The
mighty men of Earth
cowered in caves with
hope they would be
crushed to save them
from the wrath of God.
That Day has come!

CHAPTER 7
SALVATION OF ALL
ISRAEL

4 angels stood on Earth—
North, East, West, South
(N.E.W.S.)
They stood to wholly stay

the wind from devastating land and sea. Another angel came. He held the Seal of God. He said, Don't harm the Earth for it contains, until God's servants all receive His Seal upon their heads." I heard the number of the sealed: 144, 000 (12x12,000— a multitude of 12: precise— 12,000 from each Clan of Israel).

(A thought occurs to me:
$12 \times 12,000 = 144,000$
Is this the total of humanity that is reserved a Home in Heaven? The answer came).

I heard a Choir in great proportions far surpassing power to estimate: out from all nations, clans and peoples, nationalities— standing at the Throne, before the Lamb and clothed in pure white robes, palm branches held up high, proclaiming with delight:

Salvation is of God!
Amen…Blessing…Honour
Power…and…Might
Be given to the LORD
Forever…and…Forever…
Amen.

An Elder asked of me:
Who are these people draped in white? (the colour of all purity) and from whence did they all come?
What could I say?
Sir, you're the one who knows! These are they who've come from greatest tribulation and have washed their robes and made them pure by Blood of *Yeshua*, The Lamb!
They dwell with God.
They'll know no further agonies: The Lamb is at their side. He shepherds them,
He leads them to the fountains clear as crystal and the Lord will wipe all tears from their sad eyes.

…………

PART THREE

"JESUS: PRINCE OF GLORY"

CHAPTER 8
THE TRUMPETS
SOUND
(7[th Seal]: 'Culmination')

My eyes are clear once
more but, with the opening
of the 7th Seal,
all Heaven was calm; there
was no sound (I think, near
½ hour elapsed).
The 7 Angels standing near
the LORD received a
Trumpet and another Angel
with a golden bowl went to
the Altar and incense was
poured to represent the
prayers of saints.

The perfumed smoke rose
up to God. The bowl was
filled with fire and thrown
down to the Earth.
Great thunders, lightning,
earthquakes then erupted as
the 7 Angels each prepared
to sound their instruments.
These are the Trumpet
messages, meant to be
understood:

One:
Earth's foliage is on fire—
1/3 of vegetation: gone!

Two:
A burning mountain-like
monstrosity was cast into
the fuming sea.
1/3 of all marine life: gone!

Three:
A great 'Star',
Wormwood fell to Earth
and turned a third of
drinking water sour:
undrinkable!

Four:
1/3 of sunlight then grew
dim. Also 1/3 of moon
and starlight darkened as
1/3 of day and night then
failed to shine upon
the Earth.
WOE … WOE … WOE
to the Earth: Three great
WOES will ravage Earth.

CHAPTER 9
THE LOCUST PLAGUE

Five:
A 'Star' had fallen to the
Earth; he held the key into
the baseless pit. When
opened, smoke arose that
further darkened Earthly
light and from the smoke
came lethal locusts. Only
men without the Seal were
harmed. Their torment
was intense. They sought
to die—death would not
come. These locusts were

indicative of Earth's worst enemies: their king was named Apollyon. One WOE passed, yet two to come.

Six:

A Voice spoke to the Angel: Now release the 4 Angels held near Euphrates waiting for their 'time'. These 4 were then set free.

Alas! 1/3 of humankind was slain by lion-like horsemen with breast-plates of red, of blue and yellow hues symbolic, all, of war! The 1ˢᵗ of Fire, the 2ⁿᵈ of Smoke, the 3ʳᵈ was of Brimstone. These are each indicative of 3 World Wars where 1/3 of all humanity is slain. The power of the bold warriors was like 'ships of the air' with lethal weaponry both fore and aft. Beware, the whole wide world!

The residue of men not slaughtcrcd failcd to change their ways—they were not sorry for their sins, did not repent!

CHAPTER 10
THE LITTLE BOOK

I saw a mighty Angel coming on the clouds; there was a haloed rainbow round his head, his face: sunshine, and feet: of fire. A Little Book was in his hand. His right foot on the sea, his left on land— stupendous sight. (Sea and land: global significance).

All 7 Thunders then replied to his loud voice. Their News... I was forbidden to record the Thunders' News! An Angel did declare there'd be no more delay: The MYSTERY of God would be complete and it would be quite soon!

The Heavenly Voice then spoke to me: Go, take and eat the Little Book and it was given to me. Yes, here's the Book: it tastes as sweet as honey but it will be nauseous! What is the import of this Little Book? I have received instruction to proclaim the prophecies

that will concern the
peoples of the Earth—such
News of great import!

CHAPTER 11
THE TWO WITNESSES

A measuring rod was given
to me: Go now, the Angel
ordered, You're to measure
Temple, Altar, all who
worship in that Holy Place.
Don't utilise the rod across
the Outer Court—this now
belongs to Gentiles who
will trample it for 42
months.
(A thought, unbidden, comes:
7x6 = 42: the symbolic '7' =
'perfect'; and the '6' relates to
humankind, '1' short of '7':
take note of this!)

I'll give to My two
Witnesses the power to
preach for 180 weeks
(3x6x10!) in sackcloth,
marking grief. These
Witnesses, symbolic of
The 'Olive Tree': all Israel,
The 'Lampstand': it's the
Church, (the Old and New
Testaments). They'll wield
great power throughout their

time. The Pit will open:
unmitigated horror then.

**The Beast that dwells
therein will overcome and
kill the Witnesses. They'll
lie unburied in Jerusalem
for 3½ Days (½ of 7).
Humanity rejoices in
their death for all their
preaching has been mighty
powerful and guilt plagues
all the Earth!"**

A 'Resurrection Day' then
comes! Both Witnesses
revived; they stood,
renewed! Great fear fell on
all those who saw they were
alive. The Witnesses were
taken up to Heaven and
they ascended then.

**At that same hour
a massive quake:
catastrophe befell
the Earth; fear struck;
men turned to God.**
(an 'earthquake' is indicative
of political unrest, world
conflict, nations in turmoil).

**The 2ⁿᵈ WOE has passed:
(1 WOE is yet to come).**

Seven:

The 7th Trumpet blasted
forth. I heard adoring
voices chant:

The kingdoms of this world
are now the Kingdoms of
the LORD
and of His Christ. And He
shall reign forever more;
The Elders in accord:

With thanks we worship
now:
Oh *YHVH*–LORD, the *El
Shaddai,*
The One who IS, who
WAS, will BE—The time
has come, we cry with one
accord:

The Day of Judgement
is at hand; You will reward
Your servants: both the
Prophets and Apostles
in accord.

Then Heaven's Temple
opened and the Ark of
Covenant was seen amongst
the Cosmic Thundering!

....

PART FOUR

"JESUS: CHILD– ARTICULATION OF DIVINITY"

CHAPTER 12
THE MOTHER AND THE CHILD

A woman now appears
who brings bright hope.
Clothed in sunlight, moon
Supporting her, the woman
wore a garland on her head
composed of stars: twelve
stars. The woman cried in
pain, the child-birth near.
A Son was born. Just then,
another sign most sinister!

**A dragon that had 7
heads, 10 horns and
diadems upon each head.
1/3 of all the stars were
caught within his tail and
cast to Earth. He stood
with arrogance before the
woman as the Child was
born—he did intend
devouring Him at once.
The Son was born. He is
the One who'd rule the
nations powerfully.**

The Son ascended to His
Father: God. The mother
fled into the wilderness

where God prepared a place
of safety and ensured
that she was nourished there
for 1,260 days—180 weeks!
(180 weeks: 3x6x10. Take
note! It seems appropriate that
I should make some comments
on the symbolism
that you will encounter here:
The mother: Mary The Son:
Yeshua–Jesus. Twelve stars:
Israel. The wilderness: the
world. 'Off-spring': the
Church
The Dragon: counterfeit of
God: 7: Perfection, 10:
Completion).

**Then war broke out
in Heaven! Michael's
great Army fought the
Dragon—Serpent—
known as 'Satan' and
'the Devil'. He did not
prevail. He and his angels
were cast out. There was
no place for them in
Heaven. Where did they
go? He and his angels
were all cast unto Earth!**

The Voice of Heaven then
proclaimed: Salvation,
strength, the Kingdom of
our God and Christ's own
power, have cast old
Satan down.

The Faith Community can
overcome him by the Blood
of *Yeshua,* the Lamb, and by
their testimony. They stood
the test—they were
prepared for martyrdom.

**A WOE falls on the sea
and land for Satan wields
his wrath—he knows his
time is short. He sets
about a persecution of
the Child.**

The woman 'flew on eagle's
wings' into the wilderness,
remaining there for time and
times and half a time.
Note: 1+2 + ½ = 3½ — ½ of 7.

**Then Satan spewed a flood
upon the woman but the
Earth came to her aid!
Old Satan was enraged.
He then made war on all
her 'off-spring'—those
with faith in Christ.
Here is Earth's 3ʳᵈ WOE.**

CHAPTER 13
THE GLOBAL 'BEASTS'

**I saw a Beast arising from
the Sea—this Beast had 7
heads, 10 horns, 10 crowns**

each advertising blasphemy.
A fearsome Beast: part
leopard, bear and lion: fast,
powerful, and fierce!

> (I do recall he first emerged
> in Daniel's Day).

One head was wounded
mortally but the deadly
wound was healed. The
world was utterly amazed
and praised the Beast.

> (I, John, suggest another
> observation for the Beast is not
> the Devil, he's the Devil's
> man! This is a 'beast' who
> represents the Gentile world—
> a 'Sea' of every nationality.
> We're well aware that Nero is
> now dead but rumour has it
> here that he is alive again).

The Beast's authority
extended to all of 42
long months.

> (6x7 = 42 — 7x7 would have
> been 'perfect' in God's time!)

His words were
blasphemous, his actions:
utter blasphemy!
The beast waged war
against all those whose
names are there recorded
all those whose names are
there recorded in the Book

of Life belonging to the
Lamb of God. In turning
from this Beast, I saw
another fearsome Beast
emerging from the Land.

> (I could say that, as the Land,
> symbolically, will represent
> Israel: the 2nd Beast will
> come from there).

This Beast had 2 horns—
appearing like a lamb but,
when he spoke, he had a
dragon's tongue. This
beast will exercise great
power directing worship
to the 1st Beast whose
wound (presumably)
was healed.

Great signs and wonders
he performed, deceiving
all that hearkened to his
words and deeds.
A huge idol was raised and
all must worship it. He
caused the 'god' to speak.
All were required to wear
his mark, giving the power
to buy and sell. Without
the mark none could
participate in trade.

> (Here is some wisdom I'll
> relate: You are aware of what
> the numbers can convey when

symbolism is employed. Know this: the number of a man is 6! **666**: man at his worst— a 'trinity' of humankind! It would appear he is the leader of a mighty empire that will wield a two-fold power— political, religious too).

CHAPTER 14
THE LAMB WITH
12 x 12 x 1,000

I saw the Lamb! He stood upon Mount Zion and, with Him, stood 144,000 with our Heavenly Father's Name—*YHVH*— emblazoned on all foreheads there. I heard the Voice of Heaven—so dominant—like waterfalls and thunder claps, together with melodious harps. A mighty Choir then sang a Song quite new. No one could learn to sing this song except the 12x12,000! These are the Redeemed of all the Earth. They are the 'First Fruits', faultless too. Another Angel, holding all the universal Gospel News, began to speak. He said:

Respect the LORD, the Hour of Judgement comes. Worship the Creator, *YHVH*–LORD! An angel followed on; his News was staggering! Babylon (the symbol of a later City–Empire), Babylon has fallen and her fornication has reduced the 'City–State' to rabble and to ruin. I heard the Voice of Heaven say to me: Write: BLESSED are the dead who die IN Christ; they'll find their rest! (This is the 2nd 'Unknown' BEATITUDE).

Then, as I looked, I saw One like The Son of Man holding a sickle in His hand. He wore a golden crown. An angel from Heaven's Temple then cried: "Take Your sickle for the Time of Reaping has now come." The sickle swung, the Earth was reaped! Another Angel joined the throng. He also held a sickle. And another came who had instructions to impart: Go! thrust your sickle in the 'vines'; the 'grapes' are ripe." These grapes were cast into the winepress of God's wrath. The grapes were trampled—blood was drawn, so deep and wide for 4x4x1,000 stadia.

(The '4': the world—N.E.W.S! Also, a thought occurs to me: Why the two harvests at the End? The grain: the Gentile world The grapes: all Israel.)

....

PART FIVE

"JESUS: SOVEREIGN LORD"

CHAPTER 15
THE GRAND ACKNOWLEDGEMENT

SEVEN mighty Angels were
a sign for me: each held a Plague. Via these the wrath of God would then be finalised. What did appear to be a Sea of Glass mingled with Fire held those who gained the victory over Image, Mark, and Number that related to the vile

Beast's Name. They sang the 'Moses' and 'The Lamb' songs with Heaven's Harps:

YHVH–EL SHADDAI

How great, how marvellous:
Your works evoke our praise
O *YHVH–El Shaddai:*
LORD,
Almighty God. Your ways,
How just and true!
O LORD,
You are The King.
Our voice we raise
In awe of Your great Name.
On Perfect Holiness
we gaze.
Your judgements are made known.
We worship You for all our days!

I looked and saw the Tabernacle of the Testament in Heaven open. Through this door, the 7 Angels came, each dressed in purest white, and holding Plagues. One of the 4 Living Creatures gave to each a Golden BOWL

that held the wrath of the
Almighty God. the Temple
filled with smoke—the
Glory of the LORD o'er-
powered the whole and
none could enter in until the
7 BOWLS were bare and
7 Plagues from 7 BOWLS:
all done!

CHAPTER 16
THE BOWLS OF
WRATH

First:
**The Angel poured his
BOWL of wrath and
loathsome sores erupted
on the skin of those
adoring of the Image.**

Second:
**This BOWL was poured
out on the sea which
turned to blood; marine
creatures then died.**

Third:
**The 3rd Angel attacked
Earth's springs and
waterways. They also
ran with blood.
This angel said:**

You are righteous, Lord:

Who IS, who WAS, will BE:
Your judgements are against
all those who shed the blood
of saints and prophets.
this blood all will see.

Fourth:
**The sun received this
BOWL outpoured,
resulting in scorched skins
of many men. Great heat
caused blatant blasphemy.
No one repented of a sin.**

Fifth:
**This BOWL was poured
out on the Beast's own
throne. The land became
a darkened mass. His men
all screamed with pain!**

Sixth:
**This angel flew due east to
pour his BOWL on
Euphrates. The mighty
river course was drained.
The eastern kings are able
now to cross. Three frog-
like creatures sprang out
from the Dragon, Beast,
and the False Prophet,
manipulating signs to
wonder at. The leaders of
the world were called to
battle on the Day of**

El Shaddai. The place
prepared was
ARMAGEDDON!

I hear the word of *Yeshua*!
*Behold! I'll come as thieves
at night. How BLESSED is
he who is awake, alert and
wears the garment of the
pure to save from
nakedness and shame.*
(This is the 3rd 'Unknown'
BEATITUDE).

        Seventh:
The 7th angel poured
his BOWL upon the air.
A voice spoke from the
Throne:

        IT'S FINISHED NOW!

Thunder, lightning,
earthquake—the largest
ever known—rolled on.
Jerusalem was split
into three parts!
        (3 modes of Faith???)

The world's great Capitals
all fell and 'Babylon'
received her just desserts.
The islands, mountains,
disappeared; a great
hailstorm caused
blasphemy—this Plague
had great intensity.

CHAPTER 17
THE SCARLET
WOMAN

One of the 7 Angels came to
me: Come, I'll show what
happens to the 'harlot' who
now fornicates with kings.
All men are drunk with lust
for her. We found her in the
wilderness astride a Scarlet
Beast of Blasphemy (the
beast of 7 heads, 10 horns).
The woman was arrayed in
purple and adorned with
gold and precious stones
and pearls. She held a cup
brim-full of filthiness. Her
forehead held her name:

I'm 'Babylon'—the
mother of all harlots and
of all Earth's felonies.

I gazed upon the 'woman'
with amazement for I saw
her drunkenness was on the
blood of martyrs, saints.
The Angel counselled me:
        This is the mystery:
The Beast: was, is not, but
will ascend the Baseless Pit
        into Perdition then!
The 7 Heads: mountains in
the mist (for example:
count the Hills of Rome)

The Kings: 5 fallen, 1 is,
1 is yet to come.

The 10 Horns: 10 kings
whose power is brief. They
give their power unto
the Beast. They will make
war against The Lamb but
will be overcome for He is
Lord of lords and King of
kings and those who stand
with Him are Called and
Chosen and Faithful!
**The Waters where
the woman sits**
are Nations of the Earth.
The 10 Horns on the Beast
each hate the 'harlot',
conquer her. God's purpose
is to be fulfilled: World
Kingdoms are the Beast's
until the word of God
will be fulfilled.
The woman? She's the city
that still rules the kings
of Earth.

..... oOo .....

PART SIX
"JESUS: THE
WORD"

CHAPTER 18

THE FALL OF
'BABYLON'

An Angel with authority
shone on the Earth. His
proclamation was:
Hark! 'Babylon' the Great
has fallen; demons now
reside in her. All nations
were enamoured of her
wickedness.
Another Voice:
My People, now escape
from her lest you receive
her plagues. Repay her
double for her sins—
the so-called 'Queen of
Sleaze'. Her lot has come:
the fire consumes!

All kings that sat by
watching the demise of
'Babylon' will weep at
smoke arising from this City
of the World. Alas, Alas,
they cry. The merchants
grieve for loss of gold and
finery: their greed caught
up with them. They weep
and wail for loss of her: In
one short hour The End has
come! The sailors on all
seas bewail their loss:
Where is a City like to this?
But she is desolate today!
All Heaven rejoices now.

The Prophets and Apostles
are at last avenged—
no more, the great
atrocities of 'Babylon'!
A mighty Angel took
a rock, so like a millstone,
cast it to the sea:
This signifies the loss
of 'Babylon'. She will
be found no more!
No more cacophonies
of crime; no lamp
shall shine; no bride
will there rejoice again
for, in your streets,
the residue of Prophets
and the Saints is found
in clotted blood!
(A word from me; yes, John:
I sense this is a future time—
of judgements yet to come.
'Babylon' is a pseudonym for
Rome to ensure that empire
would not read of its demise.
That would be the end of me).

CHAPTER 19
THE HALLELUJAH
CHORUS

A Choir rejoiced in Heaven
as a multitude proclaimed:

Hallelujah! Salvation! Glory!
Honour! Power be given
to God!

His righteous judgements seal
the doom of sin
The blood of martyrs
is repaid.
Praise to the LORD!

The four Creatures chimed
right in:

Amen! ... Amen ... Amen!
(This is the 7th DOXOLOGY!)

The Voice replied:
Praise to the LORD!
Hallelujah–all peoples small
and great.

A multitude with voice like
waterfalls and thundering
replied:
Hallelujah, for *YHVH*–LORD
does reign Omnipotent.

Let us be glad. Rejoice:
The Lamb becomes the
Groom of Heaven; His
'Wife' (the Faith
Community) is ready now!
So, let the Service start! The
Voice then said to me,
Write down:
How BLESSED are they,
the Called into the Wedding
Feast!
(This is the 4th 'Unknown'
BEATITUDE!)

I fell before his feet
to worship him but he
rejected this: I am your
fellow servant, of the
brethren who hold
to faith in Christ! So!
Worship God—the Spirit
of all Prophecy is *Yeshua*!
All Heaven opened then.
Behold: a White Stallion—
the steed of Victors—He
that sat upon the horse
is named 'Faithful and
True'; in righteousness He
conquers all. His eyes like
fire, His Diadems displayed
an Unknown Name! His
robes were dipped in
blood—His Name? 'THE
WORD': The Spoken
Thought of God!

I saw Heaven's Armies—
robed in white and clean,
aligned with Him. His Word
is powerful as a two-edged
sword. With this, He'll
conquer all the world.
It's He who treads the
Winepress of the wrath
of *YHVH–El Shaddai*!
A title is inscribed on Gown
and Hip: 'King of kings
and Lord of lords'!
An angel standing in the sun

proclaimed unto the birds:
Come, gather: feast upon
the Supper now prepared.
This is a Day of Judgement
and it falls on all Earth's
wickedness. The Lake of
Fire consumes the Beast
and all his followers. Gone!

CHAPTER 20
THE MILLENNIUM OF
PEACE

Satan has been bound! An
angel with the keys into the
Baseless Pit took hold of
Satan, bound him up in
chains to last 1,000 years!
He was cast down into the
Pit, imprisoned there: the
nations would be free of
him until he is released for
a short while. Thrones were
put in place where judges
sat. The souls of saints
who had withstood the
Beast, his Idol and all
wickedness, reigned there
with Christ. (This is the
1st RESURRECTION).
BLESSED, holy, those
participating now for the
2nd Death will have no
power. They will be priests

of God and Christ to reign
1,000 Years. (This is the 5th
'Unknown' BEATITUDE).

When 1,000 years will have
elapsed, Satan will go to
Gog and to Magog to gather
troops for the Last Battle.
(Gog is the king, Magog:
his realm). The army—
numerous as sands
of seas—come to the most
Beloved City and they there
encamp. But Fire from
Heaven consumed them all.
Then Satan, who'd deceived
them all, was cast into the
Lake of Fire: the Beast, False
Prophet were both there to
keep him company! Their
torment will not cease!

ALL THE SHADOWS:
GONE!

I saw a Great White Throne
and Him that sat on it.
Humanity could not look on
Him—His Face is *LIGHT*!
Then all the dead, both
small and great, were
standing there, before their
Judge. The Book of Life
was opened then—
all judged according to
their works good or ill.

The sea churned out its
dead, Hades disgorged
victims and all were judged
according to their deeds.

Death and Hades are no
more—they're in the Lake
of Fire. If names are not
included in the Book of
Life, these souls go to
Eternal Fire!
(This is the 2nd Death).

….. oOo …..

PART SEVEN

"JESUS: THE ALPHA AND OMEGA"

He is the First and Last!
This Name appeared at first
and now, at last,
this NAME is fully known!

CHAPTER 21
THE NEW JERUSALEM

My eyes are not yet dim!
I see a New Heaven and
a New Earth—the first
of each has passed away.
There was no sea—that is,
it seems to say I'll know no

further isolation on the
Patmos Isle, no exile now!
Yes, it is I—John, son
of Zebedee, the man
who sailed on Galilee.

I saw, with my own eyes,
the Holy City coming down
from God, dressed as a
Bride! I heard the Voice
proclaim: Behold, the
Dwelling Place of God
is with humanity. He will
abide with them, they'll live
for Him. The LORD will
wipe the tears—all
sorrow—from their lives
for there will be no death,
no tears, no grief.
There'll be no pain—
the former life has gone.
The One enthroned said:

*Behold, I'm making all
things new. Write this: The
True and Faithful statement
of the LORD, 'I AM the
Alpha and Omega: The
Beginning and the End!'
I give the Water of Eternal
Life to all who thirst. And
those that overcome will
then inherit all: I'll be their
God and they will be My
Family! All sin has gone!*

CHAPTER 22
THE RIVER OF LIFE

He showed to me a River:
pure, the Waters of the
Stream of Life. As clear
as crystal, this deep River
flows out from the Throne
of God and of The Lamb!
Along the Street and on the
River banks, the Tree of
Life that bears 12 Fruits
and yielding Fruit each
month. The Leaves were
medicine to heal humanity.

There'll be no further curse:
the Throne of God and of
The Lamb is in the midst.
All serve Him well. They'll
see His Face. His Name is
on their foreheads: *YHVH–
YESHUA*! The sun, the
moon, are not required, for
He is *LIGHT*! They'll reign
forever more. He said to
me: These words are True
and Faithful for the *YHVH–
LORD* has sent His
Messengers—the Angels—
to reveal these prophecies:
The past, Present, Future.

EPILOGUE

"JESUS: THE BRIGHT MORNING STAR"

Behold, I'll come quite soon. BLESSED are they who keep these words of prophecy.
(This is the 6th 'Unknown' BEATITUDE).

He said to me:
Don't seal this News: the time is now at hand! The unjust will be unjust still... He who is holy will be holy still! But, bear in mind, I will be coming soon. I'll hold the gifts of Heaven for those whose deeds are pure. I am the Alpha and Omega, the Beginning and the End, I am the First and Last. How BLESSED are they who do the will of God for they will there partake the Tree of Life and enter in the Eternal City Gates!
(This is the 7th 'Unknown' BEATITUDE).

All that is immoral and adrift from God will have no right to enter in. I send My Messengers to tell this News about Eternity to that great Faith Community. To verify Identity: I am the Root and Off-spring of King David; I'm the Bright and Morning Star
(This is the 9th TITLE of our Lord *Yeshua.*)

Come now, to hear the invitation for The Spirit and the Bride say, Come: Let all that thirst now come, drink freely from the Water of Eternal Life! Take nothing from this Prophecy, nor add a word to it. Make sure your name remains within the Book of Life. Behold! I'll come without delay.

Amen! Oh, come Lord *Yeshua*!

The Grace of *Yeshua* remain with you:
Amen ... Amen ... Amen.

..... oOo .....

THE TITLES OF CHRIST

In Revelation

(Selected verses may be sung
as a hymn)
Tune: *Rimington*   L.M.

JESUS IS LORD!
From cradled hay
In Bethlehem to the 'Last Page'!
The wonder of His Life brings joy;
There's Truth and Grace for
every Age.

Jesus, Eternal Son of God,
Speaks of Himself as
'SON OF MAN'.
Here is Divinity in clay:
The LORD of Heaven's
Eternal Plan!

Jesus, the precious
LAMB OF GOD,
Became, Himself, a sacrifice;
His blood can cleanse the
sin-stained life,
His love is here expressed
in grace.

The *PRINCE OF GLORY,*
Jesus Christ,
But had nowhere to lay His head;
He laid aside the Crown of
Heaven
To show God's love by word
and deed.

The *CHILD*—Divinity in Flesh—
Once took the form of humankind
That we could then become
like Him:
Such love as this our hearts
will bind.

King Jesus is the
SOVEREIGN LORD!
The lowly Man of Nazareth
Declined the accolades of Heaven
To bear a cross, save us from
death!

In the beginning was *THE WORD*:
And He was with the *YHVH–*
LORD.
He was, and is, the Lord!
He speaks
The Mind of God who is adored!

ALPHA, OMEGA, Jesus: LORD!
He is 'Beginning and the End';
The 'First and Last'—before
all time,
After the End: forever kind!

Jesus, *THE BRIGHT AND
MORNING STAR!*
His radiance outshines the sun;
He overcame the world's dark
night:
His *LIGHT* the victory has won!

Christ came into our
circumstance,
Redeeming blood has cleansed
the soul!
He leads us to the Perfect Day:
LORD JESUS CHRIST
will make us whole!

Gospel Window by LLT: The Salvation Army, Camberwell, Victoria.

CPSIA information can be obtained
at www.ICGtesting.com
Printed in the USA
BVHW031211140121
597842BV00011B/81/J